T0180906

Communications
in Computer and Information Science   270

P. Venkata Krishna   M. Rajasekhara Babu
Ezendu Ariwa (Eds.)

Global Trends
in Information Systems
and Software Applications

4th International Conference, ObCom 2011
Vellore, TN, India, December 9-11, 2011
Proceedings, Part II

 Springer

Volume Editors

P. Venkata Krishna
VIT University
School of Computing Science and Engineering
Vellore 632014, TN, India
E-mail: pvekatakrishna@vit.ac.in

M. Rajasekhara Babu
VIT University
School of Computing and Engineering
Vellore 632014, TN, India
E-mail: mrajasekharababu@vit.ac.in

Ezendu Ariwa
London Metropolitan University, UK
E-mail: e.ariwa@londonmet.ac.uk

ISSN 1865-0929   e-ISSN 1865-0937
ISBN 978-3-642-29215-6   e-ISBN 978-3-642-29216-3
DOI 10.1007/978-3-642-29216-3
Springer Heidelberg Dordrecht London New York

Library of Congress Control Number: 2012934198

CR Subject Classification (1998): I.2, H.3, H.4, C.2, I.4, I.5

Typesetting: Camera-ready by author, data conversion by Scientific Publishing Services, Chennai, India

Printed on acid-free paper

Springer is part of Springer Science+Business Media (www.springer.com)

Preface

Welcome to the fourth edition of the International Conference ObCom 2011—Recent Trends in Computing, Communication and Information Technology. Computing, communication and information technology are hand-in-glove responsible for the majority of innovations and novel transformations that occur around the world. Starting from how data are stored, processed and consumed, there have been several optimizations taking place in different geographical locations. In order to tap the cutting-edge solutions from different streams of computing, ObCom was launched in the year 2003. The Conference ObCom 2004 was eventually made available to the computing community in the year 2004 and it promoted the exploitation of parallelism and distribution in order to achieve better functionalities and performance in certain classes of computer applications. The next version of ObCom was in 2006 and it was focused on the theme "Mobile, Ubiquitous and Pervasive Computing." The theme was chosen to script the challenges and issues while designing and building the new spectrum of human–computer interfaces prevalent in mobile, ubiquitous and pervasive computing.

The ObCom 2011 conference addressed issues associated with computing, communication and information. Its aim was to increase exponentially the participants' awareness of the current and future direction in the domains and to create a platform for researchers, leading industry developers and end users to interrelate. The conference began with keynote address on the first day and continued on the second and third day with invited lectures by leading researchers in academia and industry.

We have grown into an international conference of high influence by catering to independent technical communities—the research/academic body and the industry/practices body. The academic–industry synergy will eventually make technologies available at large. A glance at the participants' record reveals an equal mix of high-caliber research academics and dominant industry engineers and managers in the software industry. ObCom 2011 was fortunate to attract people who are experts in their area of interest.

ObCom's research paper selection process is unique and is praised for its thoroughness and fairness in representation of the best practices in the research community. ObCom had a large Program Committee, both form the host country and other developed countries, with a cross-section of skills and talents across computing and engineering disciplines. The Program and Advisory Committee increased gradually to fulfill the needs of the conference. The received papers were reviewed by several expert critics (about two or more reviews per paper), while the Organizing Chair kept a close watch on review quality and reviewer thoroughness. Conflicts of interest were made transparent and handled to avoid disputes. Thus, every research paper accepted at ObCom 2011 was carefully examined and discussed among a body of world-class researchers. The conference accepted 173 papers from 842 submissions, which includes keynote and invited papers.

Research papers are just one element of ObCom 2011. We had several tracks making up the conference and catering to different segments of the community. In conjunction, we had an international ObCom student conference, OSIC 2011, dealing with research papers of UG, PG and PhD students, a PhD Forum exclusively for doctoral students to present their research challenge and find out its feasibility with a huge research panel of ObCom participants. Poster presentations, workshops, and keynotes completed the event. Each of these had its own committee and processes for review and selection of papers.

The principal objective of this proceedings volume is to collect the cutting-edge results in the field of computing, communication and information technology. Accordingly, we selected papers representing such works.

The proceedings consist of invited paper dealing with the review of performance models of computer and communication systems and contributed papers dealing with the issues of networking, cloud computing, fuzzy logic, mobile communication, image processing, navigation systems, biometrics and Web services covering literally all the vital areas of the computing domains.

The conference as a whole was pulled off with an extremely engaged and committed team, and we thank those people involved in addressing the various needs of the conference. Recognition is given on our website with their respective roles and titles. The list might not cover many whose work was valuable for the conference.

Thanks to Alfred Hofmann, Leonie Kunz and other members of the editorial team of Springer CCIS for their kind cooperation during the publication process.

Sincere thanks to our VIT University Chancellor G. Viswanathan, Vice President (Administration), Sankar Viswanathan, Vice President (Operations) G.V. Sampath, Vice President (University Affairs), Sekar Viswanathan, Vice President (Chennai campus), G.V. Selvam, Vice Chancellor V. Raju, Pro-Vice Chancellor (Vellore campus), S. Narayanan, and Pro-Vice Chancellor (Chennai campus), Anand A. Samuel for their valuable suggestions and encouragement.

Lastly, thanks to everyone who attended this conference making it bigger in all respects.

P. Venkata Krishna
M. Rajasekhara Babu
Ezendu Ariwa

Organization

Chief Patron

G. Viswanathan   Chancellor, VIT University

Patrons

Sankar Viswanathan   Vice President, Administration
G.V. Sampath   Vice President, Operations
Sekar Viswanathan   Vice President, University Affairs
G.V. Selvam   Vice President, Chennai campus

Co-Patrons

V. Raju   Vice Chancellor
S. Narayanan   Pro-Vice Chancellor (Vellore campus)
Anand A. Samuel   Pro-Vice Chancellor (Chennai campus)

Convenor(s)

M. Khalid   VIT University, Vellore
Margret Anouncia S.   SCSE, VIT University, Vellore

Conference Chair

P. Venkata Krishna   VIT University, Vellore

Technical Chair

Ezendu Ariwa   London Metropolitan University, UK

Technical Co-chair(s)

Sumanth Yenduri   University of Southern Mississippi, USA
H.R. Vishwakarma   VIT University, Vellore, India

Honorary Chair

Rajkumar Buyya   The University of Melbourne, Australia

Publicity Chair

Ezendu Ariwa   London Metropolitan University, UK

Sponsorship Co-chairs

S.R. Pullobhotla   PAT, VIT University, India
Samuel Rajkumar V.   PAT, VIT University, India
Singaravelan M.   CTS, VIT University, India

International Advisory Board

Bettina
  Harriehausen-Mühlbauer   Fachbereich Informatik, Germany
Kam-Hoi Cheng   University of Houston, USA
Phil Prins   Seattle Pacific University, USA
Suiping Zhou   NTU, Singapore
Pramod Kumar Meher   NTU, Singapore
Pururav Thoutireddy   California Institute of Technology, USA
Jaspal Subhlok   University of Houston, USA
Boleslaw K. Szymanski   Rensselaer Polytechnic Institute, USA
Hans Martin Gündner   UAS Esslingen, Germany
Eberhard Kienzle   UAS Esslingen, Germany
Gareth J. Monkman   UAS Regensburg, Germany
Wolfgang Köster   UAS Darmstadt, Germany
Arno G. Kostka   Technical University of Darmstadt, Germany
Hermann Hartig   Technische Universität Dresden, Germany
Uwe Wloka   UAS Dresden, Germany
Axel Toll   UAS Dresden, Germany
H.-W. Philippsen   UAS Bremen, Germany
Richard Aubele   UAS Esslingen, Germany
Lothar Issler   UAS Esslingen, Germany
Albrecht Eßlinger   UAS Esslingen, Germany
Bertold Deppisch   University of Technology, UAS Karlsruhe,
                                        Germany
Frieder Keller   University of Technology, UAS Karlsruhe,
                                        Germany
Christine Roueche   Esigelec, France
Robin Pollard   Monash University, Australia
Mike Mannion   Glasgow Caledonian University, UK
John MacIntyre   David Goldman Informatics Centre, UK
T. Radhakrishnan   Concordia University, Canada
Dheeraj Sanghi   IIT, Kanpur, India
Phalguni Gupta   IIT, Kanpur, India

D. Janakiram	IIT-M, Chennai, India
Sudip Misra	IIT, Kharagpur, India
S.C. Misra	IIT, Kharagpur, India
Manfred Goetze	University of Applied Sciences, Germany
B. Srinivasan	Monash University, Australia
Sumanth Yenduri	University of Southern Mississippi, USA
Ram Chakka	Research & Development, MIET, Meerut, India
Lim Chee Peng	Universiti sains Malaysia (Science University of Malaysia), Penang, Malaysia
Palaniappan Ramaswamy	University of Essex,UK
Loo Chu Kiong	University of Malaya, Kuala Lumpur, Malaysia
Vijanth Sagayan a/l Asirvadam	University Technology Petronas, Malaysia
Vijay Devabhaktuni	The University of Toledo, USA
Shonali Krishnaswamy	Monash University, Australia
Asai Asaithambi	University of North Florida, USA
K. Baskaran	Deakin University, Australia
Wanlei Zhou	Deakin University, Australia
Lynn Batten	Deakin University, Australia
Sita Ramakrishnan	Monash University, Australia
Sita Venkatraman	University of Ballarat, Victoria, Australia

Local Advisory Board

B.V.A. Rao	
M. Khalid	SCSE, India
D. Subhakar	VIT University, India
K. Chidambaram	VIT Community Radio and Proctoring Scheme, VIT University, India
M. Adithan	Academic Staff College, VIT University, India
S.R. Pullobhotla	PAT, VIT, India
K. Kannabiran	Students' Welfare, VIT University, India
Margret Anouncia S.	SCSE, VIT University, Vellore, India
Ayee Goundan	Aethros, India
Asoke K. Talukeder	IIIT-B
Deependra Moitra	Infosys, Bangalore, India
P.C.P. Bhat	Philips Innovations Center, Bangalore, India
Pethuru Raj	Project Manager, India
Sundaresan Krishnan	Infosys, Mysore, India
K. Chandrasekharan	NIT, Suratkal, India
H.R. Vishwakarma	VIT University, Vellore, India
E. Bhaskaran	Dy. Director of Industries and Commerce, India

Technical Program Committee

Abdul Gaffar H.	SCSE, VIT University, Vellore, India
Anthoniraj A.	SCSE, VIT University, Vellore, India
Arunachalam V.	SENCE, VIT University, Vellore, India
Balamurugan B.	SITE, VIT University, Vellore, India
Bhagyavathi M.	SCSE, VIT University, Vellore, India
Bhulakshmi Bonthu	SCSE, VIT University, Vellore, India
Chandra Mouli P.V.S.	SCSE, VIT University, Vellore, India
Dhinesh Babu L.D.	SITE, VIT University, Vellore, India
Ganapathy G.P.	CDMM, VIT University, Vellore, India
Ganesh Gopal D.	SCSE, VIT University, Vellore, India
Ilango P.	SCSE, VIT University, Vellore, India
Jaisankar N.	SCSE, VIT University, Vellore, India
Kalaivani D.	SCSE, VIT University, Vellore, India
Kamalakannan J.	SITE, VIT University, Vellore, India
Kannadasan R.	SCSE, VIT University, Vellore, India
Kauser Ahmed P.	SCSE, VIT University, Vellore, India
Kumar K.	SCSE, VIT University, Vellore, India
Lakshmanan K.	SCSE, VIT University, Vellore, India
Madhu Viswanatham V	SCSE, VIT University, Vellore, India
Manjula R.	SCSE, VIT University, Vellore, India
Suresh Thanga Krishnan	SCSE, VIT University, Vellore, India
Muhammad Rukunuddin Ghalib	SCSE, VIT University, Vellore, India
Rajasekhara Babu M.	SCSE, VIT University, Vellore, India
Ramesh Babu K.	SCSE, VIT University, Vellore, India
Ravikanth A.S.V.	SAS, VIT University, Vellore, India
Saleem Durai M.A.	SCSE, VIT University, Vellore, India
Samuel Rajkumar V.	PAT, VIT University, Vellore, India
Sendhil Kumar K.S.	SCSE, VIT University, Vellore, India
Singaravelan M.	CTS, VIT University, Vellore, India
Sivanesan S.	SCSE, VIT University, Vellore, India
Swarnalatha P.	SCSE, VIT University, Vellore, India
Thirunavukkarasu A.	SMBS, VIT University, Vellore, India
Tripathy B.K.	SCSE, VIT University, Vellore, India
Vijaya Rajan V.	SCSE, VIT University, Vellore, India
Vijayasherly V.	SCSE, VIT University, Vellore, India
Viswanathan P.	SITE, VIT University, Vellore, India
Vivekanandashanmuganathan P.	SMBS, VIT University, Vellore, India
Andrews Samraj P.	SCSE, VIT University, Chennai, India
B. Sarojini	Avinashilingam University, India
A. Srinivasan	MNM Jain Engineering College, Chennai, India
Maragatham Natraj	Avinashilingam University for Women, India
S.N. Sivanandam	Karpagam College of Engineering, India

K. Sankaranarayanan	Easa College of Engineering and Technology, India
R.M. Somasundaram	SNS College of Engineering, India
G. Thokappia Arusu	Jayam College of Engineering and Technology, India
R. Pugazendi	KSR Arts College, India
Kannan Ramakrishnan	Multimedia University, Malaysia
Shohel Sayeed	Multimedia University, Malaysia
Lim Chee Peng	Universiti Sains Malaysia, Malaysia
Zubeir Izaruku Daffala	Colleges of Applied Sciences, Oman
G. Prakash	Intel Engineering College, India
B. Baskara Rao	RGMCE, India
S.S. Gantayat	GIET, India
H.K. Tripathy	CSIR-IMMT, India
D. Mohanthy	NII, India
Mohanakrihsna Varma	Kukman University, Korea
Shoba Bindhu	JNTUA, India
K. Komathy	Eswary Engineering College, India
T.S. Pradeep Kumar	VIT University, Chennai, India
V. Saritha	VIT University, Vellore, India
Ch. Pradeep Reddy	VIT University, Vellore, India

Organized by

School of Computing Science and Engineering

UNIVERSITY
(Estd. u/s 3 of UGC Act 1956)

Vellore-632 014, Tamil Nadu, India.
www.vit.ac.in

Table of Contents – Part II

Errata

Table of Contents – Part I

An Examination of Word Stemming in Latent Semantic Index Searches

Louise Perkins, David E. Sallis, and Sumanth Yenduri

The University of Southern Mississippi,
730 East Beach Blvd.,
Long Beach, MS 39560

Abstract. In this paper we describe an application with large geographic data sets that was improved using Latent Semantic Analysis (LSA) in combination with word stemming. The results are consistent with other published works, and demonstrate value added skill.

1 Problem Domain

In this paper, our data sets are described by standardized metadata records. We utilize the Federal Geographic Data Committee (FGDC) and the Federal Content Standard for Digital Geospatial Metadata (FGDC-STD) standards. These metarecords included 147 compound elements and 217 individual data elements. Our metadata records comprise the United State's National Oceanographic and Atmospheric Administration's (NOAA) Coastal Data Development Center (NCDDC). They are searchable via keyword on automatic and manually tagged fields. However, they have limited available search terms, which restricts the flexibility of search functionality. In addition, users perceive the search function as insufficient. For this reason we wish to augment their search options with LSA.

Our documents are viewed as word frequency vectors over a dictionary of words that comprise a typically sparse matrix. An entire corpus of documents may be defined to represent an entire collection of similar (or dissimilar) documents with each documents vector packaged into a large matrix (c.f. [Rishel et al., 2006]).

During a search, a query is projected onto the vector space spanned by the corpus matrix, and similarity can then be measured directly albeit approximately. Raw term frequencies can be given local and global weighting to focus the search if desired. For example, to minimize the effects of document length, each vector may have unit length. Other weightings are possible, of course, to emphasize different aspects of the context.

The resulting matrices, over a large dictionary, may be sparse, and can be very large as well. Their use and storage may prove impractical. Historically, different methods have been utilized to minimize their size, and/or construct smaller related matrices. For example, the Semi-Discrete Matrix Decomposition [c.f. Kolda and O'Leary, 1999], or SDD, approximates a matrix as a weighted sum of the outer products of vectors whose values are constrained to $\{-1, 0, 1\}$.

P.V. Krishna, M.R. Babu, and E. Ariwa (Eds.): ObCom 2011, Part II, CCIS 270, pp. 1–4, 2012.

Similarity can be measured via queries that are represented in a similar vector format, over the same ordering of the dictionary. However, the dictionary can be modified in several ways to capture different types of relevance. [Perkins et al., 2007], for example, added Parts of Speech and demonstrated that the size of the documents was important to obtaining accurate results with that method. Here we compare unaltered words with stemming, which alters the space over which we perform our data mining.

The term-document matrix is sometimes referred to as the knowledge matrix. Queries against this knowledge matrix compute a cosine normalized projection, resulting in a scalar quantity that can be ordered to approximate importance. Measuring the angle between the query vectors and each column of the knowledge matrix is computationally prohibitive however. Typically LSA reduces the large sparse matrix to a manageable size (ex. 50 x 50) of the largest singular values resulting in an SVD of the original matrix. A small angle result indicates high similarity; while a large angle result indicates the concepts are less similar (perhaps we can even use the word semantically orthogonal here).

2   Comparision Study

We used existing software packages, SDDPACK and LSISDD, to compute our matrix decomposition. We utilize the MEDLINE data base, a collection of documents frequently utilized in information retrieval studies. It contains references to Life Science Journal Articles with an emphasis on biomedicine. Hence it defines a clear but non-trivial context that still contains significant diversity. The system has over a thousand document abstracts, a set of canned queries to use as tests, and a list of relevant documents per query to use as ground truth. We also included a list of 571 "stop words" used to filter out extraneous terms before we construct the original matrix. A list of terms that occur only once in the collection was also compiled, and those least frequently used words, which could never help us make a paradigmatic connection, were also discarded to reduce the size of the knowledge matrix. However, such an omission precludes syntagmatic connections from being recognized. In the LSA approach, however, no method for syntagmatic connections is present.

LSI requires preprocessing of each document before queries can be run. This can be divided into three phases, the lexicographical analysis phase, the preparation phase, and the decomposition phase.

The lexicographical analysis performed here utilizes 'flex' to generate a text parser. The document is parsed into collections of discrete terms to create a list of unique terms (we avoid calling them words from this point forward since they may have been reduced to their stem or root). The stem algorithm utilized represents terms as concatenations of consonants and vowels symbolically. Over 70 rules comprise the system to remove suffixes and prefixes to reveal the stem. In particular, there are two distinct components of this step:

- Plurals and past particples are returned to the simple present tense,
- Complex suffixes are removed iteratively.

An example of stemming a document is presented in Fig. 1.

...the crystalline lens in vertebrates, including humans...

    a) crystalline lens vertebrates including humans
    b) crystalline len vertebr include human

Fig. 1. (a) Without Stemming vs (b) with stemming. Stemming provides for matching several different forms with the same meaning.

We then utilize the parser output to create a term-document matrix. Lastly we decompose the term-document matrix.

3   Results

Against thirty system provided queries, we achieved the percentage improvements shown in Fig. 2. By improvement, we mean that more documents from the corpus produced a positive relevance value. As you can see, stemming was significantly more effective at locating more possibly related documents. Nearly all queries showed improvement in relevance values when stemming was used. The average improvement was just over 50%.

Q. 1	58.9%	Q. 11	78.7%	Q. 21	36.9%
Q. 2	74.4%	Q. 12	40.9%	Q. 22	47.9%
Q. 3	64.9%	Q. 13	73.7%	Q. 23	52.9%
Q. 4	64.9%	Q. 14	63.7%	Q. 24	89.0%
Q. 5	56.5%	Q. 15	23.5%	Q. 25	72.0%
Q. 6	83.3%	Q. 16	64.4%	Q. 26	4.6%
Q .7	48.6%	Q. 17	-52.9%	Q. 27	50.2%
Q. 8	74.6%	Q. 18	35.6%	Q. 28	85.2%
Q. 9	56.5%	Q. 19	28.9%	Q. 29	60.9%
Q. 10	0%	Q. 20	47.9%	Q. 30	26.3%

Fig. 2. Thirty optimized queries, and their respective improvements with stemming. Only one query, 17, was less effective. In addition query 10 showed no change. All other 28 queries showed improvements.

References

1. Kolda, T.G., O'Leary, D.P.: Computation and uses of the semidiscrete matrix decomposition. Technical Report Number ORNL-TM-13766, Oak Ridge National Laboratory, Oak Ridge, TN (April 1999),
   `http://csmr.ca.sandia.gov/~tgkolda/ref#ORNL-TM-13766`
2. Perkins, Rishel, Yenduri, Zand.: Determining the Context of Text Using Augmented Latent Semantic Indexing. Journal of the American Society for Information Science, JASIS (2007)
3. Rishel, Perkins, Yenduri, Zand, Iyengar.: Augmentation of a Term/Document Matrix with Part-of-Speech Tags to Improve Accuracy of Latent Semantic Analysis. WSEAS Transactions on Computers 5(6), 1361–1366 (2006)

Financial Sequences and the Hidden Markov Model

Shreeya Sengupta, Hui Wang, William Blackburn, and Piyush Ojha

School of Computing and Mathematics,
University of Ulster, Jordanstown, BT370QB, Northern Ireland, UK
sengupta-s@email.ulster.ac.uk, {h.wang,WT.Blackburn,pc.ojha}@ulster.ac.uk

Abstract. Our aim is to develop algorithms for learning noisy sequences of symbols taken from discrete, finite alphabets, i.e. predicting the next symbol from the preceding sequence. With this in mind, financial sequences of a five-letter alphabet representing sharp fall, slight fall, no change, slight rise and sharp rise in the stock prices of five technology companies were derived from the daily closing price between January 2008 and May 2011 on the NASDAQ exchange. Accuracy of baseline predictions from a probabilistic analysis was compared with the accuracy of a hidden Markov model. Probabilistic analysis shows clear evidence of non-stationarity of the underlying time series. The hidden Markov model accounts for some but not all non-stationarity. It is argued that an analysis based on contextual probability is expected to outperform the hidden Markov model.

Keywords: noisy sequences, probabilistic analysis, hidden Markov model.

1 Introduction

Predicting the next element in a sequence is one of the staples of intelligence testing. It is also a key task in machine learning [1] and has many applications: text messaging on modern phones is made tolerable by predictive texting; adaptable user interfaces adapt to the pattern of use by predicting the next action a user is likely to take; a stock trader would dearly love to be able to tell whether the market will rise or fall next. The difficulty of the task depends on the regularity of the statistics: regular sequences are easier to predict than noisy, irregular sequences.

We present preliminary work on prediction of financial sequences. Such sequences are intrinsically noisy and irregular and therefore hard to predict. We define the problem formally in Section 2 and discuss the data and the method of analysis. Results are presented and discussed in Section 3 and extension of this work in the contextual probability framework is discussed in Section 4.

P.V. Krishna, M.R. Babu, and E. Ariwa (Eds.): ObCom 2011, Part II, CCIS 270, pp. 5–12, 2012.
© Springer-Verlag Berlin Heidelberg 2012

2   Problem Definition, Data and Method

2.1   Problem Definition

Let Σ be an alphabet. Let $D = \{S_1, S_2, \cdots, S_n\}$ be a set of m-long sequences, where $S_i =< s_{i1}, s_{i2}, \cdots, s_{im} >$, and $s_{ij} \in \Sigma$. We write $S_i = S_i' \cdot s_{im}$, so S_i' is now an $(m-1)$-long sequence $S_i' =< s_{i1}, s_{i2}, \cdots, s_{i,m-1} >$.

Let S be an m-long sequence such that $S = S' \cdot s_m$. We ask the following question:

- Based on D and only D, what is the most likely symbol after S'? In other words, what is the most likely value of s_m?

This is the *sequence prediction* [1] problem. As the sequences considered here are derived from financial time series, this can be thought as a special case of the well known *time series prediction* problem.

2.2   Data

Daily closing price of Dell shares on NASDAQ covering the period from 2 January 2008 to 10 May 2011 was downloaded from Yahoo Finance (finance.yahoo.com). Daily fractional 'intrachange' was calculated from the daily closing price: $I_i = (C_i - C_{i-1})/C_i$. The WEKA suite was used to discretise the daily intrachange into five roughly equally populated categories: sharp fall (A), slight fall (B), no change (C), slight rise (D) and sharp rise (E). The DELL share price data set is now turned into a sequence of symbols. Other share price data sets were obtained and processed similarly.

2.3   Method

The discretised intrachange sequence was analysed with a probability-based method and the results were compared with a Hidden Markov Model.

Probabilistic Prediction. The dataset was divided into a training set comprising the first 506 data points covering the period from 2 January 2008 to 4 January 2010 and a test set comprising the remaining 340 data points covering the period from 5 January 2010 to 10 May 2011. Probabilities $p(S')$ of occurrence of sequences S' of length 1, 2 and 3 and conditional probabilities $p(s|S')$ were extracted from the training data. When a particular sequence, S', was encountered in the test data, the next symbol was predicted to be the one for which the conditional probability $p(s|S')$ is maximum. This gave prediction rules $S' \rightarrow \bar{s}$ – sequence S' is followed by the symbol $\bar{s}$ – for S' of length 1, 2 and 3. Ties were resolved in favour of the symbol which comes first in lexical order, i.e. A, B, C, D, E.

Hidden Markov Model. A Hidden Markov Model [2][3] is a stochastic model with the following characteristics (fig 1):

- Time is discrete and increases in unit steps.
- The state $x(t)$ of the system at time t is one of n possible states, $\sigma_1, \sigma_2, \ldots, \sigma_n$.
- The state at $t+1$ is determined entirely by the state at t (Markov property). If the system is in state σ_i at t, its state at $t+1$ is determined stochastically by the state transition probability, $p_T(\sigma_j|\sigma_i)$.
- At each time step, the system produces an output y from the set of p possible outputs, $\omega_1, \omega_2, \ldots, \omega_p$. The output is determined stochastically by the state via the emission probability $p_E(\omega_j|\sigma_i)$.

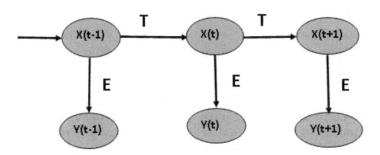

Fig. 1. Structure of an HMM. At each time step, the system is in one of n possible states. The state $x(t)$ at time t is determined by the state $x(t-1)$ at $t-1$ by the state transition matrix T. At each time step, the system produces one of p possible outputs which is determined by $x(t)$ and the emission matrix E.

If the initial probability distribution of states (at time 0) is represented by the vector $\boldsymbol{\pi}_0$, then the probability distribution at t is

$$\boldsymbol{\pi}_t = T^t \boldsymbol{\pi}_0 \qquad (1)$$

where T is the $n \times n$ state transition matrix, $T_{ji} = p_T(\sigma_j|\sigma_i)$.

The probability distribution of outputs at t is then given by

$$\boldsymbol{y}_t = E\boldsymbol{\pi}_t \qquad (2)$$

where E is the $p \times n$ emission matrix, $E_{ji} = p_E(\omega_j|\sigma_i)$. The most likely output is taken to be the predicted output.

The HMM training (estimation of transition and emission matrices) and prediction regime we have used is described next (fig 2) .

Consider a sequence of outputs of length L: $Y_0, Y_1, \ldots, Y_{L-1}$. We predict Y_i by training an HMM on the preceding W symbols in the sequence, i.e. we use the data in a W-wide window to predict the symbol which immediately follows

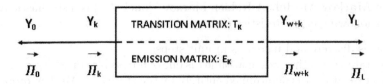

Fig. 2. Sliding window for HMM prediction. In order to predict the output at $t = W + k$, the HMM is trained on the preceding W datapoints, the probability distribution of states is propagated from $t = k$ to $t = W + k$ with the transition matrix and the probability distribution of the outputs is calculated by pre-multiplying the state distribution vector by the emission matrix. The most probable output is taken to be the prediction. Initially the window covers the data points from $t = 0$ to $t = W - 1$ and a prediction is made for $t = W$. After each prediction, the window is shifted one step to the right.

the window. The first step is to train the HMM on $Y_0, Y_1, \ldots, Y_{W-1}$ and determine the transition and emission matrices T_0 and E_0 respectively. At the $k - th$ training step, the HMM is trained on $Y_k, Y_{k+1}, \ldots, Y_{W+k-1}$ and the transition and emission matrices, denoted T_k and E_k, are estimated. The state distribution $\boldsymbol{\pi}_k$ at k, i.e. at the beginning of the window, is determined by propagating the (as yet unknown) initial state distribution $\boldsymbol{\pi}_0$ with the transition matrices determined in the previous training steps:

$$\boldsymbol{\pi}_k = T_{k-1} T_{k-2} \ldots T_1 T_0 \boldsymbol{\pi}_0. \tag{3}$$

The state distribution at $W + k$ – the end of the window – is then estimated by propagating $\boldsymbol{\pi}_k$ with the most recent transition matrix:

$$\boldsymbol{\pi}_{W+k} = T_k^W \boldsymbol{\pi}_k. \tag{4}$$

Let $r(Y_i)$ denote the index of the $i - th$ symbol in the output set, i.e. $Y_i = \omega_{r(Y_i)}$. The initial state distribution, $\boldsymbol{\pi}_0$, is chosen to maximise the average probability that the predicted symbol matches the data from W to L:

$$\sum_{k=W}^{L} \pi_{k\,r(Y_k)} / (L + 1 - W).$$

3   Results and Discussion

Table 1 illustrates the derivation of prediction rules from probability analysis, $S' \to \bar{s}$, for S' of length 1 for the Dell dataset. It lists $p(S')$ for sequences of length 1 in column 1 (i.e. frequencies of the five symbols listed in column 2). Conditional probabilities $p(s_m | S')$ are listed in columns 3-7 and give the following prediction rules:

$$A \to E, B \to E, C \to E, D \to B \text{ and } E \to A, \tag{5}$$

i.e. A is followed by E, B is followed by E etc. We have computed similar probability and conditional probability tables for sequences S' of length 1, 2 and 3 for all five datasets and derived corresponding prediction rules.

If the financial sequence was produced by a stationary process, we would expect the statistics of Table 1 to apply to the next 340 data points covering the period from 5th January 2010 to 10th May 2011. In that case, the expected prediction accuracy would be

$$p_0 = \sum_{S'} p(S')p(\bar{s}|S').$$

Table 1. Conditional probabilities $p(s_m|S')$ derived from the first 506 points of the Dell dataset covering the period 2 January 2008 to 4th January 2010. S' is a sequence of length 1. The probability $p(S')$ is given in the first column.

$p(S')$	$S'\backslash s_m$	A	B	C	D	E
0.234	A	0.271	0.102	0.203	0.127	0.297
0.194	B	0.214	0.194	0.173	0.184	0.235
0.172	C	0.207	0.253	0.115	0.149	0.276
0.158	D	0.188	0.263	0.150	0.188	0.213
0.242	E	0.254	0.197	0.197	0.156	0.197

In table 2, we present the accuracy of probabilistic prediction when sequences of length 1, 2 and 3 are used to predict the next symbol. The row labelled 'Exact Match' gives the fraction of cases where the predicted symbol is identical to the symbol in the test data whereas the row labelled 'Difference of 1' gives the fraction of cases where the predicted symbol is 'adjacent' to the actual symbol in the test data (e.g. when the actual symbol is B and the prediction is either A or C OR when the actual symbol is E and the prediction is D). The number in brackets in the third column of table 2 is the accuracy that would be expected if the statistics of the test data were consistent with the statistics of the training data (table 1 for Dell), i.e. if the time series was produced by a stationary process. The difference between the bracketed and unbracketed numbers in the third column is thus a measure of the degree of non-stationarity of the underlying process. Note that the exact match accuracy is always lower than the expected accuracy.

We illustrate this further by computing the probabilities $p(S')$ and conditional probabilities $p(s|S')$ for S' of length 1, 2 and 3 from the 340-point test data. Results for S' of length 1 for Dell are given in Table 3. Clearly, these are quite different from the statistics of the training data.

The accuracy reported in Table 2 can be obtained from the prediction rules and data statistics as follows:

$$p_0 = \sum_{S'} p(S')p(\bar{s}|S') \tag{6}$$

Table 2. Accuracy of probabilistic prediction for the 340-point test set for all five companies. 'Length of S'' is the number of symbols in the sequence used for predicting the next symbol; the row labelled 'Exact' gives the fraction of cases where the predicted symbol exactly matches the actual symbol in the data; the row labelled 'Difference of 1' gives the fraction of cases where the prediction is 'adjacent' to the actual data, e.g. the actual symbol is B (slight fall) whereas the prediction is A (sharp fall) or C (no change). The accuracy expected for a stationary process is given in brackets in the third column.

Stock	Type of Match	Length of S'		
		1	2	3
Dell	Exact	0.179 (0.266)	0.200	0.200
	Difference of 1	0.247 (0.192)	0.282	0.291
Sony	Exact	0.138 (0.250)	0.194	0.158
	Difference of 1	0.305 (0.219)	0.285	0.332
Toshiba	Exact	0.161 (0.252)	0.176	0.176
	Difference of 1	0.226 (0.237)	0.326	0.332
IBM	Exact	0.191 (0.262)	0.179	0.194
	Difference of 1	0.282 (0.206)	0.311	0.317
HP	Exact	0.194 (0.277)	0.211	0.220
	Difference of 1	0.305 (0.250)	0.326	0.352

$$p_1 = \sum_{S'} p(S')(p(\bar{s}_{-1}|S') + p(\bar{s}_1|S')) \qquad (7)$$

where p_0 is the probability of an exact match, p_1 the probability of a match with a 'difference of 1', $\bar{s}$ the symbol which follows S' according to the prediction rules, and $\bar{s}_{-1}$ and $\bar{s}_1$ are symbols 'below' and 'above' $\bar{s}$. The accuracy reported in table 2 (unbracketed numbers) is based on the statistics of the test data and the expected accuracy (bracketed numbers) is based on the statistics of training data.

We have also analysed the dataset with a Hidden Markov Model (HMM) comprising four states. The model has 28 free parameters altogether: 12 independent transition probabilities and 16 independent emission probabilities. For predicting

Table 3. Conditional probabilities $p(s_m|S')$ derived from the last 340 points of the Dell dataset covering the period 4th January 2010 to 10th May 2011. S' is a sequence of length 1. The probability $p(S')$ is given in the first column.

$p(S')$	$S'\backslash s_m$	A	B	C	D	E
0.150	A	0.216	0.137	0.255	0.235	0.157
0.209	B	0.141	0.268	0.268	0.225	0.096
0.242	C	0.134	0.183	0.256	0.256	0.171
0.265	D	0.111	0.256	0.200	0.300	0.133
0.133	E	0.178	0.156	0.244	0.311	0.111

a symbol, the HMM was trained on the preceding W symbols where W is 400, 300, 253 or 200. We did not consider $W < 200$ viable because then too little data would be used to estimate too many free parameters. The HMM was trained with the Baum-Welch algorithm. Results are given in table 4.

We note that with the exception of IBM, the 'Exact Match' accuracy of the HMM improves marginally as W decreases from 400 to 253. We attribute this to the fact that a wider window suffers more from non-stationarity and as W decreases, the HMM is having to cope with milder effects of non-stationarity. At $W = 200$, the accuracy drops significantly because too many parameters are being estimated from too little data.

We also note that in all five cases the best 'Exact Match' accuracy with the HMM is intermediate between the actual and the expected accuracy of the probability method – unbracketed and bracketed numbers in the 3rd column of table 2. We take this as an indication that the HMM is accounting for some but not all non-stationarity of the underlying process.

Table 4. Accuracy of Hidden Markov Model predictions for the datasets. 'Training Window Size' is the number of preceding symbols on which the HMM was trained. Please see the main text for definition of 'Exact Match' and 'Difference of 1'.

Stock	Type of Match	Training Window Size			
		400	300	253	200
Dell	Exact	0.211	0.218	0.226	0.150
	Difference of 1	0.306	0.294	0.365	0.209
Sony	Exact	0.179	0.182	0.223	0.132
	Difference of 1	0.294	0.341	0.341	0.241
Toshiba	Exact	0.226	0.220	0.238	0.135
	Difference of 1	0.364	0.305	0.338	0.200
IBM	Exact	0.202	0.200	0.194	0.126
	Difference of 1	0.367	0.364	0.391	0.244
HP	Exact	0.161	0.197	0.200	0.164
	Difference of 1	0.373	0.358	0.361	0.214

4 Future Work

In probability-based prediction, the conditional probabilities which are used to derive prediction rules encapsulate the statistics of the data. The longer the sequence S' for predicting the next symbol, the greater the data required for accurate estimation of conditional probabilities. Likewise, the transition and emission matrices of the HMM comprise a view, albeit different, of data statistics. The larger the number of hidden states, the greater the number of independent elements of the transition and emission matrices and the greater the data required for accurate estimate of these. In either case, greater prediction accuracy requires a richer model and greater amount of data for accurate estimation of statistics.

Our next step is to consider contextual probability [5] for the probabilistic model with the expectation that it would require less data for comparable accuracy. Contextual probability is probability (satisfying probability axioms) calculated by systematically examining the structures in a data space and counting the frequency of the structures occurring in a given data set. It is a probability that, under incomplete information, a rational person will assign to an option when required to make a decision. The choice of structure can be varied, depending on the purpose of the study. For example, in the case of multivariate data, the structure can be hypertuples [4] [6]. In the case of sequence data, the structure can be subsequences [7]; in the case of trees, the structure can be subtrees [8] [9]. In this paper we study time series, which are sequences of values, so the subsequence structure applies.

Given a sequence, a subsequence can be obtained by deleting 0 or more values (symbols). For example 'ac' is a subsequence of 'abbcd'. If we use contextual probability under the subsequence structure in our probabilistic model, the statistics table would be also big but there won't be so many zeros. For example, although 'abbcd' does not occur in the data set, 'ac' (or 'ab', 'ad', 'cd', 'bcd') may occur. A detailed discussion is out of the scope of this paper, but will be the subject of further study.

Acknowledgements. Shreeya Sengupta is supported by a Vice Chancellor's Research Scholarship of the University of Ulster.

References

1. Sun, R., Giles, C.L.: Sequence Learning: From Recognition and Prediction to Sequential Decision Making. IEEE Intelligent Systems 16(4), 67–70 (2001)
2. Rabiner L. R.: A tutorial on hidden Markov models and selected applications in speech recognition. Readings in Speech Recognition, 267–296 (1990)
3. Zhang Y: Prediction of Financial Time Series with Hidden Markov Models, Master thesis (2004)
4. Wang, H., Ivo, D., Guenther, G., Skowron, A.: Hyper relations in version space. International Journal of Approximate reasoning 36, 223–241 (2004)
5. Wang, H., Dubitzky, W.: A Flexible and robust similarity measure based on contextual probability. In: Proceedings of the 19th International Joint Conference on Artificial Intelligence, pp. 27–32 (2005)
6. Wang, H.: Nearest neighbors by neighborhood counting. IEEE Transactions on Pattern Analysis and Machine Intelligence 28(6), 942–953 (2006)
7. Wang, H.: All Common Subsequences. In: Proceedings of International Joint Conference in Artificial Intelligence (2007) (oral presentation)
8. Lin, Z., Wang, H., McClean, S., Wang, H.: All Common Embedded Subtrees for Clustering XML Documents by Structure. In: Proc. IEEE ICMLC 2009, pp. 13–18 (2009)
9. Lin, Z., Wang, H., McClean, S.: A multi-dimensional sequence approach to measuring tree similarity. IEEE Transactions on Knowledge and Data Engineering (in press, 2011)

A Dynamic Semantic Metadata Model in Cloud Computing

R. Anitha[*] and Saswati Mukherjee

Dept. of Information Science and Technology, College of Engineering, Anna University,
Guindy, Chennai-25, India
anitabalajim@yahoo.com

Abstract. With the advances in cloud computing technology it is now possible to store a huge number of images and raw data throughout the world. In order to access these distributed data with a reduced latency, this paper describes into the dynamic metadata model in cloud computing database. When designing a metadata, the storage location of metadata and the attributes inside the metadata is of importance for the efficient retrieval of data. We propose a new semantic metadata modeling architecture to reduce the overhead problem while retrieving the data from the data server. With theoretical analysis and experiments we show that our metadata modeling minimizes the latency time for fetching the data by reducing the search time to get the appropriate data.

Keywords: metadata, semantic metadata, data retrieval, cloud database.

1 Introduction

This Cloud computing has become the most attractive field in industries and in research. The requirement for cloud computing has increased due to the utilization of the software and the hardware with less investment[1]. Metadata File usage plays a major operation in searching files in Cloud storage systems[2][3]. Before a file is retrieved, the related metadata has to be found and permission to access it must be obtained. For efficiency, metadata is often stored physically close to the data it describes[4]. In some modern distributed file systems, data is stored on devices that can be directly accessed through the network, while metadata is managed separately by one or more specialized metadata servers[5]. Metadata can be static or dynamic, depending on its usage and the nature of the content domain. Static metadata remains unmodified from the creation to the last time it is used. An example of static metadata is author information. Dynamic metadata changes over time and requires periodic refreshing or recreation, such as updating the number of available stories in an online news portal[6]. Without adequate runtime information obtained from dynamic metadata, it is not possible to get the data appropriately, as the load in cloud storage gets fluctuating and hence metadata cannot be static. In this paper we propose a dynamic semantic metadata modeling for efficient retrieval of data stored across

---

[*] Corresponding author.

P.V. Krishna, M.R. Babu, and E. Ariwa (Eds.): ObCom 2011, Part II, CCIS 270, pp. 13–21, 2012.
© Springer-Verlag Berlin Heidelberg 2012

various data storage servers located in geographically dispersed locations. The metadata has been created automatically at the time of storage of file. Based on the type of the file the metadata schema is varied. In the Content based metadata type the metadata schema is created along with the keyword. The selection of keyword is done by using TFIDF. In content level metadata the metadata is represented by its respective ontology. The ontology is created by the domain expert based on the schema, keyword. The semantic metadata is represented in the form of RDF and the ontology is represented in OWL format using Protégé. The maintenance mechanisms in the proposed metadata model address three important objectives, viz. (i) Efficient retrieval of metadata file using ontology. (ii) overhead for maintaining the metadata file. (iii) Size of metadata file based on the metadata schema. Hence in order to overcome these issues, we propose a new metadata model which stores the metadata file independent of storage system and the size of metadata file is also limited. In this model, the creation, update and deletion of metadata schema plays a major role in reducing the time taken to fetch the data.

1.1   Types of Metadata

Metadata type depends on the type of the data storage. Depending on the type of metadata the attributes of metadata also gets varied. We distinguish between two basic classes of data storage: File level Metadata and Content level metadata (see Figure 1). Based on the type of metadata the schema inside the metadata file gets varied. The File level Metadata holds only the basic information whereas in the content level metadata type the schema keyword plays a major role. As the amount of raw content expands inside the metadata file, then the size of the metadata grows which has an impact on the efficient retrieval of metadata file.

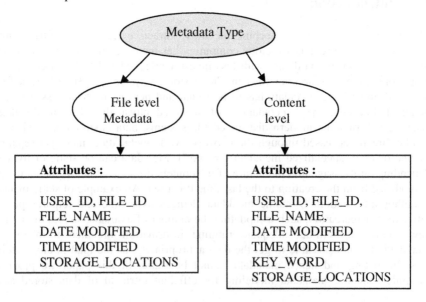

Fig. 1. Metadata Types

1.2   Architectural Design

In this section we present a dynamic semantic metadata modelling. The proposed architectural design is shown in the Figure 2.

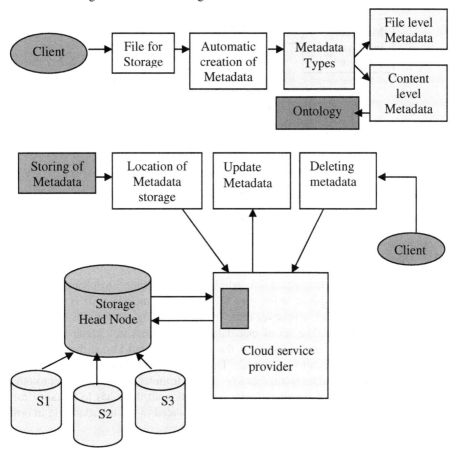

Fig. 2. Architectural Diagram

1.3   Creation of Metadata

The creation of metadata is done automatically. The elementary metadata captured at the time of file storage is used as a metadata schema. Based on GILS approach, which is an international standard profile of ISO 23950, there exists different characteristics of metadata schema and only a few have been routinely used for information discovery[11]. Figure 2 depicts metadata schema for different types of metadata. In this model, when the client stores the file, then the metadata information collector collects the information's and based on the template the metadata file is created. Our newly proposed metadata model, as shown in Figure 3 stores the metadata file at the cloud service provider location, which is independent of file storage system for efficient and easy retrieval of the metadata file.

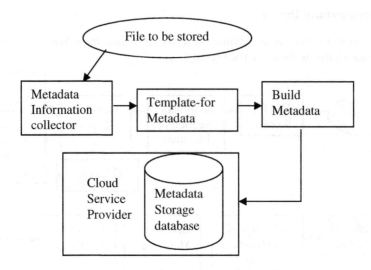

Fig. 3. Metadata Creation

1.4   Update of Metadata

The metadata schema gets updated only when the user commits any changes in file. In our proposed model as shown in Figure 4 the Updates in metadata file is triggered by the cloud service provider, whenever there exists any change in the metadata schema and its respective value. The set of metadata schema values in a cloud environment may vary at the time of modification of the existing file and also if there exists any changes in the storage location of the file. Due to the load balancing [8] reason some of the files in the cloud data storage can be moved from its original location to other. In this case the update of metadata under the location attribute has to be taken care. Whatever the changes may be, these have to be updated in the metadata file in order

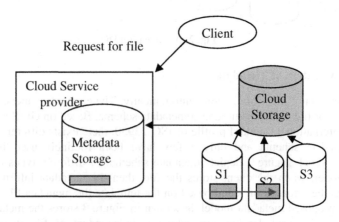

Fig. 4. Metadata Update

to fetch a correct data. Updating the metadata file continuously at runtime is expensive. Hence in our newly proposed metadata model, the update of the metadata file is done on triggered basis.

1.5   Deletion of Metadata

In a cloud environment, when a file is stored it has to be stored in multiple location for easy accessibility and also to avoid the failure rate of the server, i.e, if there is a server failure, the mirror location is able to satisfy the request of the client. The proposed model for deletion of metadata schema is as shown in the Figure 5. In order to make the proposed metadata model work more efficient, the time taken to find out the metadata file along with the exact schema plays a major role. In order to collect the exact metadata schema, the unused information from the metadata file has to be deleted which also reduces the overhead for maintaining the unused information inside the metadata file. Thus by deleting the unused information's inside the metadata file the size of the metadata file is reduced which leads to efficient and easy retrieval of the metadata file.

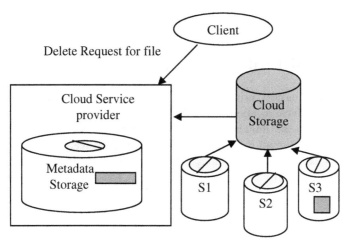

Fig. 5. Metadata Deletion

2   Mathematical Model

In this section, we provide the calculation that compares the efficiency of a metadata based retrieval with that of a direct method. We calculate the time taken to retrieve data when there exists no metadata and compare it with the time taken to retrieve the data when there exists metadata. Let us consider

T_{wm} - Total Time taken for retrieving the file without using metadata

T_{om} - Total Time taken for retrieving the file using metadata.

T_{ms} - Time taken to search metadata file using FILE_ID and USER_ID.

T_s - Time taken to search original file with all its attributes.
T_d - Time taken to fetch the data from the server.
$T_{(BWn)}$ - Time Taken due to receive the file with the corresponding
                  bandwidth of the nth server
N   - Total No of data servers.
n   - Total Number of locations of file storage.

$$T_{wm} = \sum_{N=1 \, to \, n} (T_s * N) + T_d + T_{BW_n} \qquad (1)$$

Time taken for finding the file using metadata

$$T_{om} = T_{ms} + T_d + T_{BW_n} \qquad (2)$$

Observation 1 : From Eq. 1 the value of T_{wm} has the factor "N" which ranges from to n and "n" may take more than 2 values.

Observation 2 : From Eq. 2 the value of Tom does not have the factor "N", hence T_{om} definitely will be a least value. Hence from observation (1) and (2)

$$T_{wm} > T_{ow}$$

Thus the model is proved for its efficiency mathematically.

3   Dynamic Metadata Modeling Algorithm

According to local access principle, when the user need a data the file will be searched in the available locations and will be given back to the user with an increase in latency time. So the thinking of the Metadata model algorithm is: Instead of traversing the request to all the storage servers the request reaches the cloud service provider which uses the metadata along with and gives back the file to the user with reduced latency time from the respective server. The Dynamic metadata model algorithm is illustrated as follows:

Algorithm :

```
void Clientrequest(string userid, filename)
{
//Authenticate the Userid
If ( Userid  = TRUE)
set=Query(Access_for_ file);
Switch ( )
{
Case 1:
Create Metadata( )
{
if (Filetype = File-level)
{
```

```
Metadataset = getattr(filedetails);
new[i]. ptr-> metadataset;
}
else
if (Filetype = content-level)
{
Metadataset = getattr(filedetails);
Processkeyword(keywordattr);
new[i]. ptr-> metadataset;
}
}
//Using Metadataset go the respective location fetch
the file.
Case 2 :
Update Metadata( )
{
If (Metdataexists = True)
{
Metadataset = getattr(filedetails);
new[i]. ptr-> metadataset;
}
//Check the existence of file in respective location
void response(Atributes,File)
{
User_request=output(file);
receive(file);
}
//Due to load imbalance file moved from one location to
another
if(temp don't exist in oldest)
{
releaselocation(newset, oldset)
metadataset=getattr(temp);
new[i]. ptr-> metadataset;
}
}


Case 3 :

Delete Metadata( )
{
If (Metdataexists = True)
{
Metadataset = getattr(filedetails);
```

```
new[i]. ptr-> metadataset;

//Check the existence of file in respective location

          void response(Atributes,File)
{
User_request=output(file);
receive(file);
}
//If any user deletes the file from one location
if(file don't exist in current location)
          {
          releaselocation(oldset);
          metadataset=getattr(temp); // Attribute gives
another location
          new[i]. ptr-> metadataset;
          }
if(file don't exist in all locations)
          {
          releaselocation(all);
          metadataset=delete(attributes);
          delete(metadataset);
          }
     }
void releasemetadata(Queue new, array oldset)
     {
     for(int i=0;oldset. size-1; i++)
     if(oldset[i] don't exist in newest)
     }
}
}
```

4   Implementation and Results

The experiments have been carried out in a cloud setup using eucalyptus [9] which contains one cloud controller which stores the metadata files. In our experiment, the system contains 4 image files, raw data and for each file there exists metadata file. The test model gets the metadata from cloud service provider. When the user gives the query, the model first finds out the metadata from the service provider which verifies the ontology which is built for each domain and then retrieves the file from its original location. The performance results shows the latency time for getting a file using metadata is less than that without using metadata. For evaluation purpose, the performance of file retrieval is tested using eucalyptus.

5   Conclusion and Future Works

We have proposed a new Dynamic Metadata modeling architecture for file retrieving in cloud computing. The paper focuses on how to create the metadata automatically, update the metadata and delete the unused metadata schema inside the file so that the overhead for maintaining the unused information is reduced and also reduces the size of the file which makes the proposed model to work more efficient. This approach proposes a dynamic model so that the maximum time taken for traversal towards the database servers is minimized. In addition, we propose a runtime update of metadata attributes based on the update and the deletion of the files which further reduces the complexity of metadata consistency. We show that our dynamic metadata modeling method also gives the detail about where the file is stored and from which near by server the file has to be downloaded, which performs much better than a static metadata approach. What does the future hold? Many further research are ongoing in some aspects. Firstly, the creation of metadata for content level metadata is extremely complex. In this paper the ontology is built manually but to make it more automation, this requires the content essence to be enhanced with explicit descriptions of semantics, for particular domain automatically. So Domain expert has to be built. Secondly, our current implementation is weak in security considerations of metadata. Finally, with all these feature the future work tends to give MaaS - Metadata as a Service.

References

1. Armbrust, M., Fox, A., Griffith, R.: Above the Clouds: A Berkeley View of Cloud Computing. edited by Technical Report, University of California at Berkeley (2009)
2. Powering Cloud Storage.: Parascale cloud storage (2009)
3. Amazon S3.: Simple storage service (2010)
4. Wu, J.-J., Liu, P., Chung, Y.-C.: Metadata Partitioning for Large-scale Distributed Storage Systems. In: Proceedings of the 2010 IEEE 3rd International Conference on Cloud Computing (2010)
5. Brandt, S.A., Xue, L., Miller, E.L.: Efficient Metadata Management in Large Distributed File System. In: Proc. of IEEE/11th NASA Goddard Conf. on Mass Storage Systems and Technologies, pp. 290–298 (April 2003)
6. Jokela.: Metadata Enhanced Content Management in Media Companies, Mathematics and Computing Series No. 114, Espoo, Published by the Finnish Academies of Technology, p. 155 (2001) ISBN 951-666-585-3, ISSN 1456-9418
7. Cammert, M., Kramer, J., Seeger, B.: Dynamic Metadata Management for Scalable Stream Processing Systems. In: ICDE Workshops 2007, pp. 644–653 (2007)
8. Liu, H., Liu, S., Meng, X., Yang, C., Zhang, Y.: LBVS: A Load Balancing Strategy for Virtual Storage. In: ICSS 2010 Proceedings of the 2010 International Conference on Service Sciences. IEEE Computer Society, Washington, DC, USA (2010)
9. Eucalyptus Public Cloud (EPC), http://eucalyptus.cs.ucsb.edu/wiki/EucalyptusPublicCloud/
10. Information on, http://www.dublincore.org/documents/dcmiterms/
11. Information on The GILS-standard – GILS, http://www.gils.net/technical/
12. OWL, http://www.w3.org/2001/sw/WebOnt/

A Novel Approach to Classify High Dimensional Datasets Using Supervised Manifold Learning

Binod Kumar Mishra, Praneet Saurabh, and Bhupendra Verma

TIT Bhopal (M.P., India)
{bkmishra21,praneetsaurabh,bk_verma3}@gmail.com

Abstract. Classifying high-dimensional datasets is a very challenging task. In high dimensional spaces, the performance of supervised learning methods suffer due to the huge difference between number of columns and number of rows, which degrades both accuracy and efficiency performance of classification. In this paper we propose a two phase approach to the given datasets to address the present scenario. Dimension Reduction Method Supervised Locally Linear Embedding (SLLE) is applied in the first phase to reduce dimension of the datasets and in next phase classification through K-NN and SVM is done. Experiments are carried on different high dimensional datasets and then we compared of different dimension reduction and classification methods.

Keywords: Supervised Locally linear Embedding, High Dimensional datasets, Intrinsic Dimensionality, KNN, SVM.

1   Introduction

High Dimension datasets is very emerging datasets. These type of data comes from any e-business transaction, DNA microarray or sensor devices. Classification is an effective technique for analyzing the patterns of high dimensional numerical data. It is a very challenging problem to classify high dimensional datasets, because, in high-dimensional feature spaces, the performance of supervised learning methods [1,2] suffer due to the curse of dimensionality [2]. In other words, in high-dimensional feature space, supervised learning methods (such as support vector machine and tree classifiers) often face the following problems. First, they need large volume of training data to achieve high generalization accuracy [1,2] and also in the full feature space, the time complexity of training the supervised learning methods may become the bottleneck of the system. Second problem is the specificity of similarities between points in a high dimensional space diminishes. It was proven in [3] that, for any point in a high dimensional space, the expected gap between the Euclidean distance to the closest neighbor and that to the farthest point shrinks as the dimensionality grows. This phenomenon may render many data mining tasks (e.g., clustering) ineffective and fragile because the model becomes vulnerable to the presence of noise.

P.V. Krishna, M.R. Babu, and E. Ariwa (Eds.): ObCom 2011, Part II, CCIS 270, pp. 22–30, 2012.

The high dimensional datasets having no. of columns is much more than no. of rows, for example in DNA microarray datasets, no. of variable or column is probably 10,000 and no. of sample or row is not more than 50 [4]. Classification of these type of datasets is very time consuming, complexity and erroneous. So, before classification we apply Dimension reduction method to remove irrelevant information and reduce dimension of the datasets. When we reducing dimension of datasets, we must take care of the impact of datasets could not be changed with the help of Intrinsic Dimensionality Method. We apply different dimension reduction and classification method on datasets. And find out which one is good for particular datasets.

With the help of Intrinsic Dimensionality we can find out how much dimension is require to classify the datasets, so that impact of the datasets is not change. And from Dimension Reduction method, we can reduce the dimension of the datasets. Principal Component Analysis (PCA), Locally Linear Embedding (LLE), Supervised Locally Linear Embedding (SLLE), Partially Supervised Locally Linear Embedding (αSLLE), these are the different Dimension reduction method.

In Main-Processing, we apply classification method, i.e K-Nearest Neighbor (KNN), Support Vector machine (SVM).

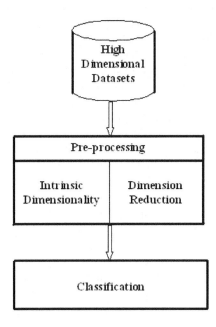

Fig. 1. Steps of Classification of High Dimensional Datasets

Above fig.1 shows that how High Dimensional Datasets is classified using dimension reduction method. The performance of the classification method may be improved by applying above technique.

2   Intrinsic Dimensionality

With the help of Intrinsic Dimensionality, we can find out the minimum number of
feature or dimension is required so that the information of data could not be vanished.
It is the minimum number of parameters needed to account for the observed properties of the data [2]. Techniques for intrinsic dimensionality estimation can be used in
order to circumvent the problem of selecting a proper target dimensionality to reduce
the dataset. Several techniques have been proposed in order to estimate the intrinsic
dimensionality of datasets.

Techniques for intrinsic dimensionality estimation can be subdivided into two main
groups:

1. Estimators based on the analysis of local properties of the data
2. Estimators based on the analysis of global properties of the data.

3   Dimension Reduction

Dimension Reduction is the transformation of high-dimensional data into a meaningful representation of reduced dimensionality. Ideally, the reduced representation has a
dimensionality that corresponds to the intrinsic dimensionality of the data. Dimensionality reduction is important in many domains, since it facilitates classification, visualization, and compression of high-dimensional data, by mitigating the curse of dimensionality [6] and other undesired properties of high-dimensional spaces.

Suppose we have $n \times D$ dimension of data matrix X, consisting of n data vectors x_i
with dimensionality D, and this dataset has intrinsic dimensionality d (where $d < D$, or
often $d \ll D$). In geometric terms, intrinsic dimensionality means that the points in
dataset X are lying on or near a manifold with dimensionality d that is embedded in
the D-dimensional space. A dimensionality reduction technique transforms dataset X
into a new dataset Y with dimensionality d, while retaining the geometry of the data
as much as possible.

The main distinction between techniques of dimensionality reduction is the distinction between linear and nonlinear techniques. Linear techniques assume that the data
lie on or near a linear subspace of the high-dimensional space, Nonlinear techniques
for dimensionality reduction do not rely on the linearity assumption as a result of
which more complex embeddings of the data in the high-dimensional space can be
identified.

3.1   Linear Technique

Linear techniques perform dimensionality reduction by embedding the data into a linear
subspace of lower dimensionality. Although there exist a lot of various techniques to do
so, PCA is the most popular and classical linear technique. Therefore, in our comparison, we only include PCA as a benchmark. We briefly discuss PCA below.

Principal Component Analysis (PCA)
PCA constructs a low-dimensional representation of the data that describes as much of the variance in the data as possible [7]. This is done by finding a linear basis of reduced dimensionality for the data, in which the amount of variance in the data is maximal.

PCA try to find a linear transformation T that maximizes T^T cov $x - \bar{x}$ T, where cov $x - \bar{x}$ is the covariance matrix of the zero mean data X. It can be shown that linear mapping is formed by the d principal eigenvectors of the covariance matrix of the zero-mean data. Therefore, PCA solves the eigenproblem

$$\underset{X - \bar{X}}{\text{cov}}\, v = \lambda v \tag{1}$$

The eigenproblem is solved for the d principal eigenvalues. The low-dimensional data representations y_i of the datapoints x_i are computed by mapping them onto the linear basis M, i.e., $Y = (X - \bar{X})T$.

PCA has been successfully applied in a large number of domains such as face recognition [8], coin classification [9], mean-square error sense and seismic series analysis [10]. The main drawback of PCA is that the size of the covariance matrix is proportional to the dimensionality of the datapoints. As a result, the computation of the eigenvectors might be infeasible for very high-dimensional data. In datasets in which n < D, this drawback may be overcome by computing the eigenvectors of the squared Euclidean distance matrix, instead of the eigenvectors of the covariance matrix. Alternatively, iterative techniques such as Simple PCA or probabilistic PCA [11] may be employed.

3.2   Non-linear Techniques

Non-Linear technique are, capable of constructing nonlinear transformation between the high dimensional data representation X to low dimensional counterpart Y, whereas it preserve the local or global properties of data. It can be shown that local techniques for dimensionality reduction can be viewed upon as definitions of specific local kernel functions [12, 13].

Locally Linear Embedding (LLE)
The locally linear embedding (LLE) algorithm developed by Roweis and Saul [14]. It consist of three steps. In the first step select a number of nearest neighbors of each data point based on the Euclidean distance. In second step compute the optimal reconstruction weight for each point by its nearest neighbors. And in last step performs the embedding by preserving the local geometry representation by the reconstruction weights [15, 16]. The overview of three steps is shown in fig. 2.

As mentioned previously that manifold learning is a promising nonlinear dimension reduction method. Here, we will give a outline of LLE and will introduce its Supervised and Partial Supervised (SLLE & α-SLLE) version.

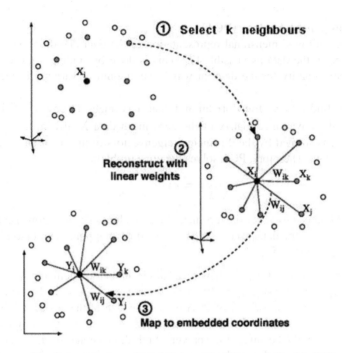

Fig. 2. An overview of local linear embedding as defined in [17]

Let us consider matrix $X = \{ x_1, x_2, ... x_N\}$ be a sets of N points in a high dimensional data space R^D. The data points are assumed to lie on or near a nonlinear manifold of intrinsic dimensionality $d < D$. The goal of LLE is to find a low a low dimension embedding of X by mapping the D dimensional data into a single coordinate system in R^d by $Y = \{y_1, y_2, ..., y_N\}$.

$$\phi(Y) = \sum_{i=1}^{n} \left| y_i - \sum_{j=1}^{n} w_{ij} y_j \right|^2 \tag{2}$$

$$\sum_{i=1}^{n} y_i = 0 \tag{3}$$

We construct a sparse matrix M representing the matrix of weights W and calculate low dimensional projection of the original inputs by performing eigen decomposition on the matrix M as given in equation.

$$\lambda v = M v \tag{4}$$

Supervised Locally Linear Embedding (SLLE)
Supervised LLE (SLLE, [18, 19]) is extension of LLE, to deal with data sets containing multiple manifolds, corresponding to classes. For fully disjoint manifolds, the

local neighbourhood of a sample x_i from class c ($1 \leq c \leq C$) should be composed of samples belonging to the same class only. This can be achieved by increasing the pre-calculated distances between samples belonging to different classes, but leaving them unchanged if samples are from the same class:

$$\Delta' = \Delta + \alpha \max(\Delta)\Lambda, \alpha \in [0,1] \tag{5}$$

where max (Δ) is the maximum entry of Δ and $\Lambda_{ij} = 1$ if x_i and x_j belong to the same class, and 0 otherwise. When $\alpha = 0$, it is treated like unsupervised LLE (called LLE), when $\alpha = 1$, the result is the fully supervised LLE [41] (called 1-SLLE). The value of α is between 0 and 1 gives a partially supervised LLE (α-SLLE) [18].

For 1-SLLE, distances between samples in different classes will be as large as the maximum distance in the entire data set. This means neighbours of a sample in class c will always be picked from that same class. In practice, one therefore does not have to compute (2), but instead one can just select nearest neighbours for a certain sample from its class only. 1-SLLE is thereby a nonparameterised supervised LLE. In contrast, α-SLLE introduces an additional parameter α which controls the amount of supervision. For $0 < \alpha < 1$, a mapping is found which preserves some of the manifold structure but introduces separation between classes. This allows supervised data analysis, but may also lead to better generalisation than 1-SLLE on previously unseen samples.

4   Classification

Classification performance can be improves if (a) more precise class parameter values are used, (b) class separability increases, (c) the ratio of the training sample size to dimensionality increases or (d) a more appropriate classifier is chosen. Considering the factors listed above helps to understand the roles of the methods recently proposed for the preprocessing stage.

4.1   K-Nearest Neighbor (K-NN) Classifier

The KNN classifier is a well-known nonparametric classifier. It is based on a simple and effective supervised classification technique [20]. K-NN is a most common and nonpa-rametric method. To classify an unknown sample x, K-NN extracts k closest vectors from the training set using similarity measures, and makes decision for the label of the unknown sample x using the majority class label of the k nearest neighbors. We adopt Euclidean distance to measure the similarity of samples. Pearson's coefficient correlation and Euclidean distance have been used as the similarity measure.

4.2   Support Vector Machines (SVM)

Support Vector Machines (SVM), originally developed by Vapnik [23], is one of the most powerful techniques for classification. It is a part of Supervised Learning, a branch of statistical learning which part from a series of examples that create a "decision-maker" system which tries to predict new values. This technique can be subdivided into two distinct parts:

- Learning: consists of training SVM with examples at its disposition
- Prediction: where new samples are inserted in which the result is not known.

The SVM classifier aims to separate data into different classes by a hyperplane with largest margin. Often we do not only require a prediction rule but also need to identify relevant components of the classifier. Thus, it would be useful to combine feature selection methods with SVM classification. Feature selection methods aim at finding the features most relevant for prediction. In this context, the objective of feature selection is three-fold: (i) improving the prediction performance of the predictors, (ii) providing faster and more cost-effective predictors, and (iii) gaining a deeper insight into the underlying processes that generated the data.

5   Experimental Result

Here we are using different High Dimensional Datasets to test our proposed method. They are Leukemia data [24], Colon data [25], Prostate data [26]. Others[1] are created through MATLAB function. The overview of above datasets is summarized in Table 1.

Table 1. Summary of the High Dimensional Datasets

Sr. No	Datasets	Dimension	Number of sample	Description
1.	Leukemia	7129	72	47 sample of class "ALL" and 25 sample with class "AML"
2.	Colon	2000	62	40 sample with tumor class and 22 sample with normal class
3.	Prostate	12600	102	62 sample with tumor class and 40 sample with normal class

---

[1] Others are like Swiss-Roll & Twin-Peaks.

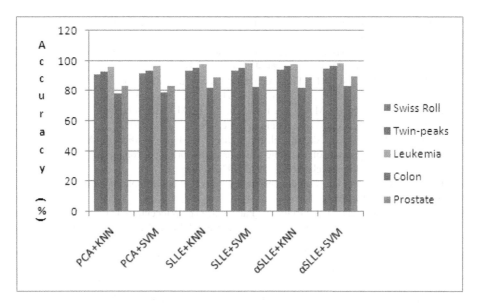

Fig. 3. Accuracy of given datasets (%)

Here we see in fig.3 that α SLLE+SVM method is giving good performance.

6   Conclusion and Remarks

This paper propose a novel approach for classify High Dimesional Datasets using SVM based upon α SLLE. This new technique adopted for its has good performance. The experiment result indicate that our algorithm is workable with a higher performance rate on different types of datasets. Compare with other method, this algorithm is easy in implementation and efficient in result. Future work is under consideration to improve it through following way (1) Apply this method into some low dimensional datasets. (2) For classification, speed can be improved by modifying Support Vector Machines. (3) The proposed method can be extended to handle distortion problem for DNA microarray.

References

1. Mitchell, T.M.: Machine Learning. McGraw-Hill (1997)
2. Fukunaga, K.: Introduction to Statistical Pattern Recognition. Academic Press, Inc., San Deigo (1990)
3. Levina, E., Bickel, P.J.: Maximum likelihood estimation of intrinsic dimension. In: Advances in Neural Information Processing Systems, vol. 17. The MIT Press, Cambridge (2004)
4. Young, R.A.: Biomedical discovery with DNA arrays. Cell, 9–15 (2000)
5. Fukunaga, K., Olsen, D.R.: An algorithm for finding intrinsic dimensionality of data. IEEE Transactions on Computers C-20, 176–183 (1971)

6. Fukunaga, K.: Introduction to Statistical Pattern Recognition. Academic Press Professional, Inc., San Diego (1990)
7. Hotelling, H.: Analysis of a complex of statistical variables into principal components. Journal of Educational Psychology 24, 417–441 (1933)
8. Turk, M.A., Pentland, A.P.: Face recognition using eigenfaces. In: Proceedings of the Computer Vision and Pattern Recognition 1991, pp. 586–591 (1991)
9. Huber, R., Ramoser, H., Mayer, K., Penz, H., Rubik, M.: Classification of coins using an eigenspace approach. Pattern Recognition Letters 26(1), 61–75 (2005)
10. Posadas, A.M., Vidal, F., de Miguel, F., Alguacil, G., Pena, J., Ibanez, J.M., Morales, J.: Spatial-temporal analysis of a seismic series using the principal components method. Journal of Geophysical Research 98(B2), 1923–1932 (1993)
11. Partridge, M., Calvo, R.: 'Fast dimensionality reduction and Simple PCA. Intelligent Data Analysis 2(3), 292–298 (1997)
12. Bengio, Y., Delalleau, O., Le Roux, N., Paiement, J.-F., Vincent, P., Ouimet, M.: Learning eigenfunctions links spectral embedding and Kernel PCA. Neural Computation 16(10), 2197–2219 (2004)
13. Ham, J., Lee, D., Mika, S., Schölkopf, B.: A kernel view of the dimensionality reduction of manifolds. Technical Report TR-110, Max Planck Institute for Biological Cybernetics, Germany (2003)
14. Roweis, S.T., Saul, L.K.: Nonlinear dimensionality reduction by local linear embedding. Science 290, 2323–2326 (2000)
15. Friedrich, T.: Nonlinear dimensionality reduction with locally linear embedding and Isomap. Master's thesis, Department of Computer Science, The University of Sheffield (2002)
16. Roweis, S.T., Saul, L.K.: Pseudocode for LLE algorithm
17. Weinberger, K., Saul, L.K.: Unsupervised learning of image manifolds by semidefinite programming. In: Computer Vision and Pattern Recognition (2004)
18. Eisen, M.B., Brown, P.O.: DNA arrays for analysis of gene expression. Method Enzymbol. 303, 179–205 (1999)
19. Kouropteva, O., Okun, O., Hadid, A., Soriano, M., Marcos, S., Pietikäinen, M.: Beyond locally linear embedding algorithm. Technical Report MVG-01-2002, Machine Vision Group, University of Oulu, Finland (2002)
20. Huang, H., Li, J.W., Feng, H.L.: Face Recognition on Semi-supervised Manifold Learning. Computer Science 35(12), 220–222 (2008)
21. Raudys, S., Pikelis, V.: On dimensionality, sample size, classification error, and complexity of classification algorithm in pattern recognition. IEEE Trans. Pattern Anal. Machine Intell. PAMI-2(3), 242–252 (1980)
22. Jimenez, L.O., Landgrebe, D.A.: Supervised classification in high-dimensional space: geometrical,statistical,and asymptotical properties of multivariate data. IEEE Transactions on Systems, Man and Cybernetics 28(1), 39–54 (1997)
23. Vapnik, V.: The Nature of Statistical Learning Theory. Springer, New York (1995)
24. Golub, T.R., Slonim, D.K., Tamaya, P., Huard, C.: Molecular classification of cancer: class discovery and class prediction by gene expression monitoring. Science 286, 531–537 (1999)
25. Alon, U., Barkai, N., Notterman, D.A., Gish, K.: Broad pattern of gene expression revealed by clustering analysis of tumer and normal colon tissues probed by oli- gonucleotide arrays. Proc. Natl. Acad. Sci. USA 96, 6745–6750 (1999)
26. Singh, D., Febbo, P.G., Ross, K.: Gene Expression Correlates of Clinical Prostate Cancer Behavior. Cancer Cell 1, 203–206 (2002)

Term-Frequency Inverse-Document Frequency Definition Semantic (TIDS) Based Focused Web Crawler

Mukesh Kumar and Renu Vig

University Institute of Engineering and Technology, Panjab University, Chandigarh, India
mukesh_rai9@yahoo.com, mukesh_rai9@pu.ac.in,
renuvig@hotmail.com

Abstract. Rapidly growing size of the World-Wide-Web poses unprecedented challenges for general purpose crawlers and Search Engines. It is impossible for any search engine to index the complete Web. Focused crawler cope with the growing size by selectively seeking out pages that are relevant to a predefined set of topics and avoiding irrelevant regions of the Web. Rather than collecting all accessible Web documents, focused crawler analyses its crawl boundary to find the links likely to be the most relevant for the crawl. This paper presents a focused crawler that makes use of TIDS (Term-frequency Inverse-Document frequency Definition Semantic) score, derived from the set of documents marked as highly relevant to the domain by the Web users while browsing the Web, to decide upon the set of link to be included for future crawl that can lead to the pages most relevant to the domain.

Keywords: Focused Web crawler, information retrieval, Tf-Idf, semantics, search engine, indexing.

1   Introduction

Currently World Wide Web contains billions of publicly available documents. Besides its huge size the Web is characterized by its huge growth and change rates. It grows rapidly in terms of new servers, sites and documents. The addresses of documents and their contents are changed, and documents are removed from the web. As more information becomes available on the Web it is more difficult to find relevant information from it. Web search engines such as Goggle, Atla Vista provides access to the Web documents. A search engine's crawler[14] collects Web documents and periodically revisits the pages to update the index of the search engine. Due to the Web's immense size and dynamic nature no crawler is able to cover the entire Web and to keep up all the changes. This fact has motivated the development of focused crawlers [8, 10, 11, 12]. Focused crawlers are designed to download Web documents that are relevant to a predefined domain, and to avoid irrelevant areas of the Web. The benefit of the focused crawling approach is that it is able to find a large proportion of relevant documents on that particular domain and is able to effectively discard irrelevant documents and hence leading to significant savings in both computation

P.V. Krishna, M.R. Babu, and E. Ariwa (Eds.): ObCom 2011, Part II, CCIS 270, pp. 31–36, 2012.
© Springer-Verlag Berlin Heidelberg 2012

and communication resources, and high quality retrieval results. In this paper a focused crawler architecture that retrieves the documents based upon TIDS score is proposed.

2   Related Work

In some early works on the subject of focused collection of data from the Web, Web crawling was simulated by a group of fish migrating on the Web [9]. In the so called fish search, each URL corresponds to a fish whose survivability is dependent on visited page relevance and remote server speed. Page relevance is estimated using a binary classification by using a simple keyword or regular expression match. Only when fish traverse a specified amount of irrelevant pages they die off. The fish consequently migrate in the general direction of relevant pages which are then presented as results. J. Cho, H. Gracia-Molina and L. Page [4] proposed calculating the PageRank [6] score on the graph induced by pages downloaded so far and then using this score as a priority of URLs extracted from a page. They show some improvement over the standard breadth-first algorithm. The improvement however is not large. This may be due to the fact that the PageRank score is calculated on a very small, non-random subset of the web and also that the PageRank algorithm is too general for use in topic-driven tasks. M. Ehrig and A. Meadche [7] considered an ontology-based algorithm for page relevance computation. After pre-processing, entities (words occurring in the ontology) are extracted from the page and counted. Relevance of the page with regard to user selected entities of interest is then computed by using several measures on ontology graph (e.g. direct match, taxonomic and more complex relationships). Most of the existing focused crawlers [1, 2, 3] are based on simple keyword matching or some very complex machine learning techniques for guiding the future crawls.

3   Proposed Work

Tf-Idf [13] (Term frequency–Inverse document frequency) weight is a statistical measure used to evaluate how important a word is to a document in a collection or corpus. The importance increases proportionally to the number of times a word appears in the document but is offset by the frequency of the word in the corpus or in turn to the domain. If we are having a corpus of documents which are all highly related with a specific domain then the Tf-Idf score of a term in a document gives the importance of that term for that document with respect to the whole corpus. Now if we add Tf-Idf score obtained by a term for all documents in the corpus, then the resulting score can be seen as a meaningful, semantic, score for that term with respect to the whole corpus. Based upon this thought a TIDS Score Table is constructed, whose entries are supposed to help the crawler for deciding the future crawls. The TIDS Score Table is adaptive is nature, means that for each crawler's complete run the Web page having highest relevancy to the domain, if the page is not present in the Relevant Page Set, is added to the Relevant Page Set and TIDS Score Table is regenerated and used for the future crawl. The TIDS Score Table generation algorithm is given below:

Algorithm 1:   TIDS Score Table Generation

1. User browses the Web for domain related pages.
2. If the page is not highly relevant to the domain then GOTO 1.
3. Remove Stop Words from the page.
4. Apply Stemmer to the page.
5. Add the page to the Relevant_Page_Set.
6. If Relevant Page Set limit is not reached then GOTO 1.
7. Generate Tf-Idf Score Inverted Index Table for all the documents in the Relevant_Page_Set.
8. For each term t in the Tf-Idf Score Inverted Index Table Do
   - 8.1. Calculate sum of the Tf-Idf score obtained by t in all documents from Tf-Idf Score Inverted Index Table, let it be TIDS_Score.
   - 8.2. Insert entry <t, TIDS_Score> into TIDS Score Table.
   - 8.3. Normalize the TIDS_Score values in TIDS Score Table.

According to the TIDS Score Table Generation Algorithm user, while browsing the Web, marks the pages which seems to be most relevant to the specific domain. Before adding a page to the Relevant_Page_Set stemming, which is the process for reducing inflected (or sometimes derived) words to their stem, base or root form—generally a written word form, stop words removal is performed upon the page. After construction of a healthy Relevant_Page_Set, Tf-Idf score of the collection is calculated. The term frequency $\mathrm{tf}_{t,d}$ of term t in document d is defined as the number of times that t occurs in d, df_t is the document frequency of t, means the number of documents that contain t. The df_t is an inverse measure of the informativeness of t also $\mathrm{df}_t \leq N$ where N is the total number of documents in the Relevant Page Set. Then the idf (inverse document frequency) of t is given by

$$\mathrm{idf}_t = \log \ (N/\mathrm{df}_t) \tag{1}$$

The Tf-Idf weight of a term t in the document d ($w_{t,d}$) is the product of its tf weight and its idf weight and will be given by

$$w_{t,d} = \log(1 + \mathrm{tf}_{t,d}) \times \log \ (N / \mathrm{df}_t) \tag{2}$$

The TIDS_Score of a term t is given by

$$\mathrm{TIDS\_Score}(t) = \sum\nolimits_{d \in Relevant\_Page\_Set} \mathrm{tf.idf}_{t,d} \tag{3}$$

TIDS Score Table is used by the crawler which works as according to the Algorithm 2. According to the TIDS Crawler Algorithm, SeedUrls, which is the set of preferred urls which can act as starting point for the crawler, is initialized to the set of urls returned by various existing popular search engines for the particular domain. Similarity score for the Seed Urls is calculated and all the SeedUrls are inserted into a priority queue, CrawlQueue, along with their description text similarity score.

Now the highest sore url is dequeued from the CrawlQueue, the url page is downloaded and its text similarity score is calculated. Anchor similarity score for each link present in url is calculated and text similarity score of the parent is added to it to obtain the final score for the link of the url. If the calculated score is greater than some Relevancy_Threshold then the url is enqueued to the CrawlQueue.

Algorithm 2:   TIDS Crawler

1. Initialize SeedUrls.
2. Create TIDS Score Table from the users browsing patterns.
3. While SeedURls is not empty
   3.1 URL=SeedUrls.Next();
   3.2 URL_Score= Similarity score of URL.discription terms from TIDS Score Table.
   3.3 Enqueue(CrawlQueue, URL, URL_Score);
4. While CrawlQueue is not empty
   4.1 URL=Dequeue(URL_with_maximum_score, CrawlQueue);
   4.2 Doc= Download(URL) .
   4.3 If Doc is not present in the Crawler Repository then add Doc to the Crawler Repository else GOTO 4.
   4.4 Doc_Score= Similarity score of URL.text terms from TIDS Score Table.
   4.5 If Doc_Score is greater than or equal to the text Similarity score of Relevant Page Set pages and the Doc is not present in the Relevant Page Set
      4.5.1 Add Doc to Relevant Page Set and regenerate TIDS Score Table.
   4.6 For all Link in Doc.links
      4.6.1 Linkscore= Similarity score of Link.anchor terms from TIDS Score Table.
      4.6.2 Score= Doc_Score + Linkscore;
      4.6.3 If Score > Relevancy_Threshold
            4.5.3.1 Enqueue(CrawlQueue, Link, Score);

4   Experimental Results

The proposed TIDS crawler is implemented in Java using MySql Server as backend on a machine having Windows 7(64-bit) operating system, 3.0 GB of RAM, Intel Core 2 Duo 3.0 GHz processor. The experiment is conducted on Industry domain i.e. we want to retrieve the pages belonging to the Industry. SeedUrls is initialized with 20 top links resulted by Google with respect to the domain specific quires. Initially TIDS Score Table is generated for 300 highly domain relevant pages, in the Relevant Page Set, as marked by the users while browsing the Web and looking for Industry. *Discard Ratio* and precision is calculated for various time durations for the proposed crawler.

Let *Discarded* denotes the total number of Web pages discarded by the TIDS crawler (Step 4.6.3 of TIDS Crawler Algorithm) up to a certain time.

Selected denotes the total number of pages present in the Crawler Repository at a certain time.

Related denotes the number of pages which are relevant to the domain, from the Crawler Repository.

Then *Discard Ratio* is given by

$$Discard\ Ratio = \frac{Discarded}{Discarded + Selected} \times 100 \tag{4}$$

Precision is given by

$$Precision\ Value = \frac{Related}{Selected} \times 100 \tag{5}$$

The results for the mentioned setup are plotted as a graph as shown in Fig. 1.

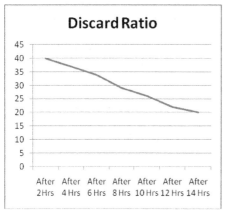 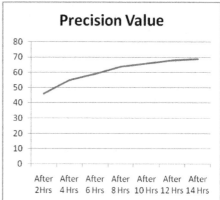

Fig. 1. Precision and Discard Ratio Graph

The graph shows that with passage of time the *Discard Ratio* tends to decrease while *Precision Value* tend to increase this is because with the passage of time Relevant Score Set goes on enriching and the future crawl links tends to be more relevant to the domain.

5   Conclusion

A focused crawler that makes use of TIDS (Term-frequency Inverse-Document frequency Definition Semantic) score, derived from the set of documents marked as highly relevant to the domain by the Web users while browsing the Web, to guide the future crawl is proposed. Results shows that the proposed crawler tends to increase the relevant quotient of the relevant pages with time and also the discarded pages going out of the more relevant pages tend to decrease indicating the quality of the pages being retrieved.

References

[1] Aggarwal, C., Al-Garawi, F., Yu, P.: Intelligent Crawling on the World Wide Web with Arbitrary Predicates. In: 10th International WWW Conference, Hong Kong (2001)

[2] Bergmark, D., Lagoze, C., Sbityakov, A.: Focused Crawls, Tunneling, and Digital Libraries. In: 6th European Conference on Research and Advanced Technology for Digital Libraries, pp. 91–106 (2002)

[3] Ester, M., Gro, M., Kriegel, H.P.: Focused Web crawling: A generic framework for specifying the user interest and for adaptive crawling strategies: Technical report, Institute for Computer Science, University of Munich (2001)

[4] Cho, J., Garcia-Molina, H., Page, L.: Efficient Crawling Through URL Ordering. In: 7th International WWW Conference, Brisbane, Australia (1998)

[5] Cho, J., Gasrcia-Molina, H.: Parallel Crawlers. In: WWW (2002)

[6] Page, L., Brin, S., Motwani, R., Winograd, T.: The PageRank Citation Ranking: Bringing Order to the Web. Stanford Digital Library Technologies Project

[7] Ehrig, M., Maedche, A.: Ontology-focused Crawling of Web Documents. In: ACM Symposium on Applied computing (2003)

[8] Cho, J., Garcia-Molina, H.: The evolution of the web and implications for an incremental crawler. In: VLDB, Cairo, Egypt (2000)

[9] De Bra, P.M.E., Post, R.D.J.: Information retrieval in the World-Wide Web: Makingclient-based searching feasible. Computer Networks and ISDN Systems 27(2), 183–192

[10] Chakrabarti, S., van den Berg, M., Domc, B.: Focused crawling: a new approach to topic specific Web resource discovery. In: 8th International World Wild Web Conference, Toronto, Canada (1999)

[11] Brin, S., Page, L.: The Anatomy of a Large-Scale Hypertextual Web Search Engine. Computer Networks and ISDN Systems 30(1), 107–117 (1998)

[12] http://www.google.co.in

[13] http://www.wikipedia.org

[14] Boldi, P., Codenotti, B., Santini, M., Vigna, S.: UbiCrawler: a scalable fully distributed web crawler. Software Pract. Exper. 34(8), 711–726 (2004)

Multiple 3D Chaotic Systems Based Approach for Visual Multimedia Content Protection

Musheer Ahmad, Tanvir Ahmad, and Chirag Gupta

Department of Computer Engineering, Faculty of Engineering and Technology,
Jamia Millia Islamia, New Delhi-110025, India

Abstract. The sharing, distribution and transmission of proliferated digital multimedia contents over the insecure worldwide available Internet and wired/wireless networks has encouraged the copyright fraud, unauthorized access and illegal usage. This brings new technical challenges to provide the end-to-end security to multimedia contents for establishing ownership rights, ensuring authorized access, preventing illegal replication etc. To address the above mentioned requirements, a visual multimedia content protection technique is proposed. The technique is based on the high dynamic responses of multiple high-dimensional chaotic systems. The multimedia encryption is achieved by randomly picking the actual encryption keys out of numbers of hybridized keys that are extracted from complex sequences of three high dimensional chaotic systems. Accordingly, a high encryption effect is turned up in the encrypted content. The proposed technique is experimented on the multimedia color imagery. The decomposed R, G, B components of color plain-image are initially diffused with their self, before diffusing with encryption keys. It is experimentally verified that the proposed technique has great encryption performance and achieves high confidential security. Eventually, the statistical results confirm the practicability and suitability of the approach for visual multimedia content protection.

Keywords: Multimedia protection, multiple chaotic systems, diffusion, security, color image encryption.

1   Introduction

With the recent advancements in multimedia technologies and explosive growth of Internet, the multimedia-based communication has become essential in everyone's life. It includes voice over IP, video/voice conferencing, e-learning, mobile-TV, news telecasting, video on demand, e-passport etc. The proliferation of multimedia contents over the worldwide available Internet and shared networks has also encouraged the copyright frauds, unauthorized access, illegal usage and uncontrollable distribution of multimedia content [1]. Consequently, multimedia picture industry in particular loses billions of dollars every year. The efforts have been done by researchers, academicians and practitioners for enforcing security, providing protection, establishing ownership rights, ensuring authorized access, preventing illegal replication, facilitating content authentication of multimedia content [2]. In order to

P.V. Krishna, M.R. Babu, and E. Ariwa (Eds.): ObCom 2011, Part II, CCIS 270, pp. 37–46, 2012.

deal with the technical challenges pertinent to multimedia content, two major multimedia techniques are applied: (i) multimedia watermarking and (ii) multimedia encryption [3]. Multimedia watermarking techniques are applied to achieve copyright protection, ownership trace and authentication. However, multimedia encryption techniques are applied to provide end-to-end security when distributing digital content. Multimedia encryption techniques transform the visual content of multimedia into an unintelligible form that can be recovered with the correct secret key. The authorized customer who owns the key can successfully recover the content [4]. Thus, the strength of such techniques lies in the secret key. The key space of the technique should be large enough to resist the brute-force attack. At the same time, the encryption technique should be cryptographically strong enough to withstand the conventional and other types of cryptographic attacks [5]. Hence, secure multimedia communication demands new encryption techniques that may efficiently and efficiently handle the multimedia data. Due to the intrinsic features of multimedia contents like: their bulk data capacity, high spatial and temporal redundancy, etc., the conventional cryptographic techniques such as DES, triple-DES, RSA, IDEA, AES are inefficient in dealing with the huge multimedia data. Therefore, it requires such techniques that are credential, efficient and effective while processing large amount of multimedia data. In the past decade, the chaos-based encryption techniques have suggested some new and efficient ways to fulfill the need of secure multimedia communication [6-16]. This is because, the chaotic signals are blessed with characteristics such as high sensitivity to initial conditions/parameters, long periodicity, high randomness and mixing, which can be exploited to employ in a cryptographic process. These characteristics make chaos-based multimedia protection schemes excellent and robust against statistical attacks.

In this paper, a visual multimedia content protection technique has been proposed. The technique exploits the complex dynamic responses of the high dimensional chaotic systems. The complex orbits of each chaotic system are recorded as real valued chaotic sequences. The keys are extracted from these random sequences after preprocessing and quantization operations. To strengthen the diffusion process of the proposed technique, the keys are hybridized using XOR operation to generate a number of encryption keys. However, the actual encryption of plaintext data is performed with their random selection. The approach is applied on multimedia color images to report the simulation results. The organization of the paper is as follows: the proposed technique is discussed in Section 2, followed by the simulation analysis of the technique is presented in Section 3. Finally, the work is concluded in Section 4.

2   Proposed Multimedia Protection Approach

In this section, the details of proposed multimedia protection approach are presented. The proposed technique is based on the use of multiple high-dimensional chaotic systems. The one-dimensional chaotic system provides: low key space, their iteration operations generate single sequence and they are weak against adaptive parameter synchronous attack [6]. Likewise, the usage of single chaotic system in an encryption process also fails in providing the sufficient security and large key space. To overcome the limitations of low-dimensional and single chaotic systems, multiple three-dimensional Chen, Rossler and Chua chaotic systems are employed in the design. The dynamics of these systems are more complex and generate more unpredictable, distinct and stochastic chaotic sequences as compared to low-dimensional systems. Eventually, high security, extremely large key space and high statistical properties are achieved.

2.1   Multiple 3D Chaotic Systems

Following three-dimensional chaotic systems are employed in the proposed design:
  (1) Chen Chaotic System:

$$
\begin{aligned}
\dot{x}_1 &= a_1(x_2 - x_1) \\
\dot{x}_2 &= (c_1 - a_1)x_1 - x_1 x_3 - x_2 \\
\dot{x}_3 &= x_1 x_2 - b_1 x_3
\end{aligned}
\tag{1}
$$

  (2) Rossler Chaotic System:

$$
\begin{aligned}
\dot{y}_1 &= -(y_2 + y_3) \\
\dot{y}_2 &= y_1 + a_2 y_2 \\
\dot{y}_3 &= b_2 + y_3(y_1 - c_2)
\end{aligned}
\tag{2}
$$

  (3) Chua Chaotic System:

$$
\begin{aligned}
\dot{z}_1 &= \alpha(z_2 - z_1 - h(z_1)) \\
\dot{z}_2 &= z_1 - z_2 + z_3 \\
\dot{z}_3 &= -\beta z_2 - \gamma z_3 \\
h(z_1) &= m_1 z_1 + 0.5(m_0 - m_1)(|z_1 + 1| - |z_1 - 1|)
\end{aligned}
\tag{3}
$$

Where $a_1 = 35$, $b_1 = 3$, $c_1 = 27.7$, $a_2 = 0.15$, $b_2 = 0.20$, $c_2 = 9.0$, $\alpha = 10$, $\beta = 14.78$, $\gamma = 0.0385$, $m_0 = -1.27$ and $m_1 = -0.68$. These 3D differential equations are solved using RungeKutta-4 method with step size of $h=0.001$. The ideal cryptographic sequence should have good statistical properties. The pre-processing done in Eq. 4 enhances the statistical properties of the chaotic sequences generated by the above systems [6].

$$
\hat{\theta}(i) = \theta(i) \times 10^5 - floor(\theta(i) \times 10^5)
\tag{4}
$$

Where $\theta(i) = x_1(i)$, $x_2(i)$, $x_3(i)$, $y_1(i)$, $y_2(i)$, $y_3(i)$, $z_1(i)$, $z_2(i)$ and $z_3(i)$ are real-valued chaotic sequence generated by systems of Eq. (1), (2), (3) respectively in the ith iteration and $0 < \hat{\theta}(i) < 1$.

2.2   Multimedia Color Image Encryption

The schematic diagram of the proposed technique is shown in Figure 1. The algorithmic steps of the approach are as follows:

1. Let P_R, P_G and P_B be the R, G and B components of the color plain-image P to be encrypted. Perform initial diffusion of each components with their self as:

$$for\ \tau = N{\times}M\ to\ 2$$
$$P_R(\tau - 1) = P_R(\tau - 1) \oplus P_R(\tau)$$
$$P_G(\tau - 1) = P_G(\tau - 1) \oplus P_G(\tau)$$
$$P_B(\tau - 1) = P_B(\tau - 1) \oplus P_B(\tau)$$
$$end$$

2. Take proper initial conditions for Chen, Rossler and Chua chaotic systems.
3. Iterate Eq. (1), (2) and (3) for n_0 times to discard their transient effects.
4. Iterate Eq. (1), (2) and (3) to obtained chaotic variables $\theta(t+n_0)$ $(t > 0)$ and preprocess them according to Eq. (4).
5. Perform 8-bit quantization $(G = 2^8)$ of the preprocessed chaotic variables as:

$$\left.\begin{aligned}
\pi_{1,2,3}(t) &= (\ floor\ (\hat{x}_{1,2,3}(t + n_0) \times 10^{14}\ )) \bmod(\ G\ ) \\
\omega_{1,2,3}(t) &= (\ floor\ (\hat{y}_{1,2,3}(t + n_0) \times 3^{29}\ )) \bmod(\ G\ ) \\
\psi_{1,2,3}(t) &= (\ floor\ (\hat{z}_{1,2,3}(t + n_0) \times 7^{16}\ )) \bmod(\ G\ )
\end{aligned}\right\} \tag{5}$$

6. Generate hybridized keys from the quantized 8-bit variables obtained in previous step according to the rules given in Eq. (6) below:

$$\left.\begin{aligned}
\phi_1(t) &= \pi_1(t) \oplus \omega_2(t) \oplus \psi_3(t) \\
\phi_2(t) &= \pi_2(t) \oplus \omega_3(t) \oplus \psi_1(t) \\
\phi_3(t) &= \pi_3(t) \oplus \omega_1(t) \oplus \psi_2(t) \\
\phi_4(t) &= \pi_2(t) \oplus \omega_1(t) \oplus \psi_3(t) \\
\phi_5(t) &= \pi_3(t) \oplus \omega_2(t) \oplus \psi_1(t) \\
\phi_6(t) &= \pi_1(t) \oplus \omega_3(t) \oplus \psi_2(t) \\
\phi_7(t) &= \pi_1(t) \oplus \omega_1(t) \oplus \psi_1(t) \\
\phi_8(t) &= \pi_2(t) \oplus \omega_2(t) \oplus \psi_2(t) \\
\phi_9(t) &= \pi_3(t) \oplus \omega_3(t) \oplus \psi_3(t)
\end{aligned}\right\} \tag{6}$$

7. Evaluate the indices i, j, k, l, m and n of hybridized keys to randomly decide the inputs for $2{\times}1$ multiplexers from the preprocessed chaotic variables obtained in step 4.

$$i = (floor(x_1{\times}10^8){\times}floor(y_2{\times}10^4))mod(9) + 1$$
$$j = (floor(x_3{\times}10^6){\times}floor(z_2{\times}10^7))mod(9) + 1$$
$$k = (floor(y_3{\times}10^7){\times}floor(z_1{\times}10^5))mod(9) + 1$$
$$l = (floor(z_3{\times}10^5){\times}floor(x_2{\times}10^7))mod(9) + 1$$
$$m = (floor(y_1{\times}10^7){\times}floor(z_2{\times}10^6))mod(9) + 1$$
$$n = (floor(x_3{\times}10^5){\times}floor(y_3{\times}10^6))mod(9) + 1$$

8. Select lines s_0, s_1 and s_2 decide the actual encryption keys K_R, K_G and K_B for the components of multimedia color image.

$$s_0 = lsb\,(\pi_1(t)) \oplus lsb\,(\pi_2(t)) \oplus lsb\,(\pi_3(t))$$
$$s_1 = lsb\,(\omega_1(t)) \oplus lsb\,(\omega_2(t)) \oplus lsb\,(\omega_3(t))$$
$$s_2 = lsb\,(\psi_1(t)) \oplus lsb\,(\psi_2(t)) \oplus lsb\,(\psi_3(t))$$

9. Encrypt the R, G and B components of color image C as:

$$C_R(t) = P_R(t) \oplus K_R(t) \oplus C_B(t-1)$$
$$C_G(t) = P_G(t) \oplus K_G(t) \oplus C_R(t-1) \qquad (7)$$
$$C_B(t) = P_B(t) \oplus K_B(t) \oplus C_G(t-1)$$

10. Repeat steps 4 to step 9 for $N \times M$ times to encrypt all pixels of the plain-image.

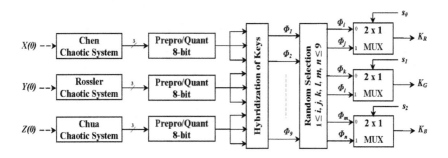

Fig. 1. Schematic diagram of proposed multimedia protection scheme for color images

The decryption of encrypted image is performed by applying the above steps of encryption process in reverse order.

3   Simulation Analysis and Results

The simulation results and analyses of the proposed approach are illustrated in this section. The secret key of the encryption process are initialized with values as: $x_1(0)$ =-10.058, $x_2(0)$=0.368, $x_3(0)$=37.368, $y_1(0)$=-3.491, $y_2(0)$=7.523, $y_3(0)$=17.039, $z_1(0)$=10, $z_2(0)$=0.6, $z_3(0)$=0.1, n_0=500 and $C_R(0)$=$C_G(0)$=$C_B(0)$=127. To report the effectiveness, the proposed design is experimented with three color plain-images *Peppers*, *Baboon* and *Parrots* of size 512×512×3, which are shown in Figure 2. The encrypted color images obtained with proposed encryption approach are depicted in Figure 3. As can be seen, the encrypted images are indistinguishable and visually meaningless for a casual observer as they look like noise-images. The images are successfully recovered with correct secret key. To check the statistical encryption performances of the encrypted images, the images are examined under the following analyses to report the high security provided by the proposed approach.

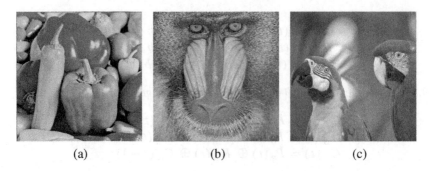

(a)   (b)   (c)

Fig. 2. Color plain-images of (a) *Peppers* (b) *Baboon* and (c) *Parrots*

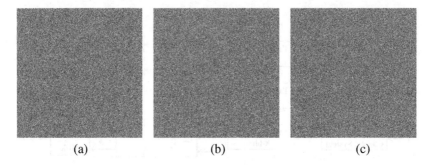

(a)   (b)   (c)

Fig. 3. Encrypted Color images of (a) *Peppers* (b) *Baboon* and (c) *Parrots*

3.1   Histogram Analysis

As seen in Figure 5 that the distributions of gray values in R, G and B components of encrypted *Peppers* image are fairly uniform and much different from the histograms of R, G and B components of plain-image shown in Figure 4. The statistical properties of Color plain-images are changed absolutely in encrypted images in such a manner that encrypted images have good balance property. To quantify the balance property of the ciphered images, the mean gray values of plain-images and encrypted images are evaluated and listed in Table 1. It is evident from the mean gray values that no matter how gray values of plain-images are distributed, the mean gray values of encrypted images come out to about 127. The mean gray values obtained in our case are close to the ideal value = 127.5 (for an 8-bits gray-scale perfect white noise image). This shows that the encrypted images don't provide any information regarding the distribution of gray values to the attacker. Moreover, the standard deviation in frequencies of pixel intensities determines the flatness/uniformity of the histogram of images. Lower the value of this deviation, more flat/uniform would be the histogram, means it will be more close to the histogram of perfect white noise-image. The value of this standard deviation in two sets of color images are found and listed in Table 2. The values of deviation indicate that the histograms shown in Figure 5 are almost flat and the pixels are uniformly distributed in encrypted images shown in Figure 3.

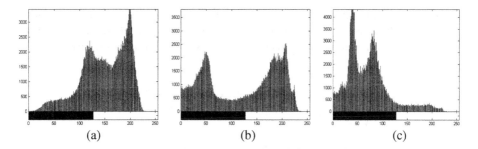

Fig. 4. Histograms of (a) Red (b) Green and (c) Blue components of *Peppers* plain-image

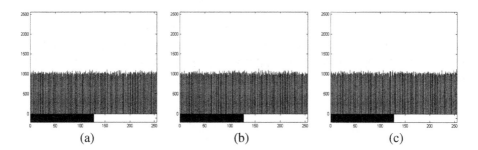

Fig. 5. Histograms of (a) Red (b) Green and (c) Blue components of Encrypted *Peppers* Color image

Table 1. Mean Gray values in Color images

Color image	Original			Encrypted		
	R	G	B	R	G	B
Peppers	149.82	115.56	66.53	127.54	127.46	127.40
Baboon	137.39	128.86	113.12	127.64	127.59	127.56
Parrots	130.79	120.60	81.94	127.57	127.45	127.76

Table 2. Standard deviation in frequencies of pixels intensities in Color images

Color image	Original			Encrypted		
	R	G	B	R	G	B
Peppers	925.25	1130.71	1404.82	30.56	32.31	31.34
Baboon	576.77	756.33	566.55	31.87	30.24	28.95
Parrots	1006.03	770.64	1187.04	31.30	31.87	30.96

3.2   Correlation Analysis

In multimedia images, there exists high correlation among adjacent pixels. It is mainstream task of an efficient encryption technique to eliminate the correlation of pixels. Two highly uncorrelated sequences have approximately zero correlation coefficient; where as, two exactly similar sequences have correlation coefficient of ±1. The correlation coefficient between adjacent pixels in an image is determined as:

$$\rho = \frac{N \sum_{i=1}^{N} (x_i \times y_i) - \sum_{i=1}^{N} x_i \times \sum_{i=1}^{N} y_i}{\sqrt{(N \sum_{i=1}^{N} x_i^2 - (\sum_{i=1}^{N} x_i)^2) \times (N \sum_{i=1}^{N} y_i^2 - (\sum_{i=1}^{N} y_i)^2)}} \qquad (8)$$

Where x, y are gray values of two adjacent pixels in the image and $-1 \leq \rho \leq 1$. In the proposed algorithm, the correlation coefficient of 5000 randomly selected pairs of adjacent pixels in R, G and B components of plain-images/encrypted images are determined and presented in Table 3. The values of correlation coefficients show that the adjacent pixels in the plain-images are correlated to each other, whereas the values obtained for encrypted images are close to zero. Plots given in Figures 6 and 7 also justify that the proposed encryption approach highly de-correlates the adjacent pixels in encrypted images.

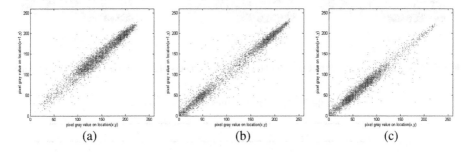

(a)   (b)   (c)

Fig. 6. Correlation of 5000 pairs of adjacent pixels in (a) Red (b) Green and (c) Blue components of *Peppers* plain-image

Table 3. Correlation coefficients of adjacent pixels in Color images

Color image	Original			Encrypted		
	R	G	B	R	G	B
Peppers	0.97098	0.99046	0.97558	-0.00241	0.00568	0.00061
Baboon	0.88657	0.78571	0.89516	0.00069	-0.00200	-0.00051
Parrots	0.98433	0.97524	0.97651	-0.00014	0.00446	0.00294

3.3   Entropy Analysis

Shannon entropy is the minimum message length requires to communicate information. It measures the uncertainty associated with a random variable [17]. Entropy H of a message source S can be calculated as:

$$H(S) = -\sum_{i=0}^{255} p(s_i) \log_2(p(s_i)) \tag{9}$$

Where $p(s_i)$ represents the probability of symbol s_i and the entropy is expressed in bits. If the information entropy of an encrypted image is significantly less than the ideal value 8 (for an 8-bits gray-scale perfect white noise image), then, there would be a possibility of predictability which threatens the image security. The values of information entropy obtained for plain and encrypted images are listed in Table 4. The values obtained for encrypted images are close to the ideal value. This implies that the information leakage in the proposed design is negligible and is secure against the entropy-based attack.

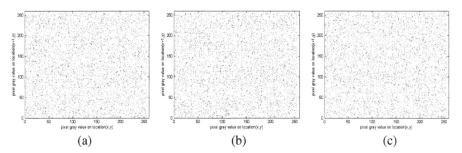

Fig. 7. Correlation of 5000 pairs of adjacent pixels in (a) Red (b) Green and (c) Blue components of Encrypted *Peppers* image

3.4   Key Space Analysis

A good encryption scheme should have sufficiently large key space to controvert the brute-force attack. Thus prevents attacker to decode plaintext data even after using large amounts of time and resources. In the proposed design, all the variables are declared as type *double,* which has a 15-digit precision, therefore the key space comes out to be $(10^{14})^9$ i.e. $10^{126} \approx 2^{418}$. Inclusion of system parameters of Eq. (1), (2), (3) and $C_R(0)$, n_0 etc further increases the size of the key space. Thus, the key space of the scheme is extensively large enough and capable to withstand the above attack.

Table 4. Shannon entropies in Color images

Color image	Original			Encrypted		
	R	G	B	R	G	B
Peppers	7.33883	7.49625	7.05831	7.99936	7.99927	7.99933
Baboon	7.70673	7.45727	7.75224	7.99930	7.99937	7.99943
Parrots	7.42326	7.53812	7.29288	7.99933	7.99931	7.99934

4   Conclusion

In this paper, multiple high-dimensional chaotic systems based multimedia protection scheme is presented. The complex dynamic responses of multiple third-order chaotic systems are exploited to generate hybridized keys. The encryption keys are randomly generated out of numbers of hybridized keys to strengthen the encryption performance of the design. As a result, high security and large key space is achieved. The proposed approach is experimented on standard color images to report the encryption performance. The statistical analyses results confirm the effectiveness of the proposed approach for visual multimedia content protection.

References

1. Izquierdo, E., Hyoung, J.K., Macq, B.: Introduction to the Special issue on Authentication, Copyright Protection, and Information Hiding. Special Issue IEEE Transactions on Circuits and Systems for Video Technology 13(8), 729–731 (2003)
2. Kundur, D., Karthik, K.: Video Fingerprinting and Encryption Principles for Digital Rights Management. Proceedings of the IEEE 92(6), 918–932 (2004)
3. Furht, B., Kirovski, D.: Multimedia Security Handbook. CRC Press, Boca Raton (2005)
4. Lin, E.I., Eskicioglu, A.M., Lagendijk, R.L., Delp, E.J.: Advances in Digital Video Content Protection. Proceedings of the IEEE 93(1), 171–183 (2005)
5. Schneier, B.: Applied Cryptography: Protocols Algorithms and Source Code in C. Wiley, New York (1996)
6. Fu, C., Zhang, Z., Cao, Y.: An Improved Image Encryption Algorithm Based on Chaotic Maps. In: International Conference on Natural Computation, pp. 189–193 (2007)
7. Dang, P.P., Chau, P.M.: Image Encryption for Secure Internet Multimedia Applications. IEEE Transactions on Consumer Electronics 46(3), 395–403 (2000)
8. Zhou, Y., Panetta, K., Aagaian, S.: Partial Multimedia Encryption with Different Security Levels. In: IEEE Conference on Technologies for Homeland Security, pp. 513–518 (2008)
9. Hasimoto-Beltrán, R.: High Performance Multimedia Encryption System based on Chaos. CHAOS 18, 023110:1-8 (2008)
10. Hamdi, M., Boudriga, N.: Secret-Image Sharing for Multimedia Chaotic Encryption. In: 3rd International Conference on Information and Communication Technologies: From Theory to Applications, pp. 1–6 (2008)
11. Francia, G.A., Yang, M., Trifas, M.: Applied Image Processing to Multimedia Information Security. In: International Conference on Image Analysis and Signal Processing, pp. 104–107 (2009)
12. Corron, N.J., Reed, B.R., Blakely, J.N., Myneni, K., Pethel, S.D.: Chaotic Scrambling for Wireless Analog Video. Communication in Nonlinear Science and Numerical Simulation 15(9), 2504–2513 (2010)
13. Ahmad, M., Farooq, O.: A Multi-Level Blocks Scrambling Based Chaotic Image Cipher. In: Ranka, S., Banerjee, A., Biswas, K.K., Dua, S., Mishra, P., Moona, R., Poon, S.-H., Wang, C.-L. (eds.) IC3 2010. CCIS, vol. 94, pp. 171–182. Springer, Heidelberg (2010)
14. Chen, Z., Ip, W.H., Cha, C.Y., Yung, K.: Two-level Chaos based Video Cryptosystem on H. 263 Codec. Nonlinear Dynamics 62(3), 647–664 (2010)
15. Lian, S.: Efficient Image or Video Encryption based on Spatiotemporal Chaos System. Chaos, Solitons & Fractals 40(5), 2509–2519 (2009)
16. Ahmad, M., Farooq, O.: Secure Satellite Images Transmission Scheme Based on Chaos and Discrete Wavelet Transform. In: Mantri, A., Nandi, S., Kumar, G., Kumar, S. (eds.) HPAGC 2011. CCIS, vol. 169, pp. 257–264. Springer, Heidelberg (2011)
17. Shannon, C.E.: A Mathematical Theory of Communication. Bell Systems Technical Journal 27(3), 379–423 (Part I), 623–856 (Part II) (1948)

Kannada Word Sense Disambiguation
Using Association Rules

S. Parameswarappa and V.N. Narayana

Department of Computer Science & Engineering,
Malnad College of Engineering, Hassan, Karnataka, India
Affiliated to Visvesvaraya Technological University, Belgaum
`param.phd@gmail.com`, `vnnarayana@yahoo.com`

Abstract. Disambiguating the polysemous word is one of the major issues in the process of Machine Translation. The word may have many senses, selecting the most appropriate sense for an ambiguous word in a sentence is a central problem in Machine Translation. Because, each sense of a word in a source language sentence may generate different target language sentences. Knowledge and corpus based methods are usually applied for disambiguation task. In the present paper, we propose an algorithm to disambiguate Kannada polysemous words using association rules. We built Kannada corpora using web resources. The corpora are divided in to training and testing corpora. The association rules required for disambiguation tasks are extracted from training corpora. The example sentences needs to be disambiguated are stored in testing corpora. The proposed algorithm attempts to disambiguate all the content words such as nouns, verbs, adverbs, adjectives in an unrestricted text using association rules.

Keywords: Association rules, Machine Translation, Kannada Word Sense Disambiguation, web corpora, Computational Lexicon.

1 Introduction

Word Sense Disambiguation (WSD) is the problem of determining in which sense a word having a number of distinct senses is used in a given sentence. The word may have more than one sense, the sense in which the word is used can be determined in most of the times, by the context in which the word occurs.

Consider a word ನೆರೆ [nere], it has several senses out of which ನೆರೆ [nere] as flood and ನೆರೆ [nere] as biologically matured can be easily disambiguated from the context. Look at the following sentences

ಪಾಕಿಸ್ತಾನ ನೆರೆ ಸಂತ್ರಸ್ತರಿಗೆ ನೆರವು. [paakistaana nere santrastarige neravu].
'Help for Pakisthan flood victims'
ರಮಾಬಾಯಿ ಮೈ ನೆರೆದರು. [rammabaayi mai neredaru].
'Ramaabaayi matured biologically'.

P.V. Krishna, M.R. Babu, and E. Ariwa (Eds.): ObCom 2011, Part II, CCIS 270, pp. 47–56, 2012.
© Springer-Verlag Berlin Heidelberg 2012

In the present example sentences, the context in which the word ನೆರೆ [nere] appears is enough to deduce its meaning. But disambiguating the word ನೆರೆ [nere] as flood and ನೆರೆ [nere] as neighbor is more difficult. It is illustrated with the help of the following example.

ನೆರೆಯಲ್ಲಿ ಸಿಲುಕಿ ಜನ ಜಾನುವಾರುಗಳೆಲ್ಲಾ ಸಂಕಷ್ಟಕೀಡಾದವು.

[nereyalli siluki jana jaanuvaarugaLellaa sankstakiiDaadavu].
'Due to flood, the people and animals are end up with critical problem'.
ನೆರೆಯಲ್ಲಿ ಗಲಾಟೆ.

[nereyalli galaaTe].
'violence or quarrel in the neighbor'.

The process of identifying the correct sense of the words in a given context is called Word Sense Disambiguation (WSD). WSD contributes significantly to many natural language processing tasks such as Machine Translation and Information retrieval. Disambiguation of words having different part-of-speech (POS), for example, the sense of the word ನೆರೆ [nere] as a noun (flood) or as a verb (biologically matured) can be determined, if we are able to find the correct part-of-speech for the word in the given context. POS taggers are currently more effective compare to WSD techniques, where the sense distinctions are due to varying POS tags. So the focus of research in WSD is on distinguishing between senses of words within given syntactic categories (same POS).

Lexical features are shown to be reliable indicators for a target word sense. But not all words in the context are helpful for determining the sense of a target word. Syntax can help in identifying relevant parts of the context there by eliminating noise. Using syntactic features for WSD is not new. Ng, Yarowsky, Agirre et al [1-3] used syntactic features along with lexical features for sense disambiguation.

Initial research on WSD focused on disambiguating a few selected target words in a given sentence. Until recently, research in WSD did not focus on disambiguating all the content words in a text in one go. Disambiguating all the content words is called unrestricted WSD [4, 5].

In the present work, we propose a machine learning algorithm based on Association rules for unrestricted Kannada text WSD. The motivation behind the current work is, the lack of basic resources for computer processing of Kannada language. Kannada is one of the technologically least developed language in India today. The proposed system acts as pre-requisite tool for achieving good accuracy in Kannada Machine Translation tasks.

The rest of the paper is organized as follows. Section 2 explores previous work done in word sense disambiguation and presents the current state of the word sense disambiguation. Section 3 introduces linguistic preliminaries of the Kannada language and association rules basics. Section 4 discusses the basic infrastructure requirement of the present work. Section 5 describes the methodology and the proposed algorithm used for disambiguation task. Section 6 provides the detailed information required to implement the proposed algorithm. Section 7 discuses the algorithm testing and evaluation. Section 8 concludes the paper.

2   Related Work

WSD methods can be categorized as Knowledge based, Corpus based and hybrid methods. Knowledge based methods uses some form of external knowledge about the senses of a word and the context in which it occurs. The external resources typically used in knowledge based WSD are machine readable dictionaries, thesauri, computational lexicons etc. Lesk's algorithm [6], walker algorithm [7], Conceptual density [8] and random walk algorithm [9] are some of the Knowledge based methods used for WSD task. All these methods do machine readable dictionary look up for disambiguation. These are fundamentally overlap based algorithms, which suffer from overlap sparsity.

Corpus based methods can be further classified into two types, they are supervised and unsupervised methods.

Supervised methods require a sense tagged corpora for training. They use machine learning techniques to build a model from the training data and then disambiguate test data using the model. Some of the machine learning techniques used for WSD is decision lists [10], Naive bay's classifier [11] and association rules [12].

Unsupervised methods disambiguate word senses with out any supporting tools such as dictionaries, thesauri and labeled training text. It is based on unlabeled corpora. Firth [13], Schutze [14], Miller and Chorles [15] are some of the unsupervised methods for WSD task.

Hybrid approaches [16] uses combination of more than one knowledge sources (Wordnet as well as Small amount of tagged corpora). This allows them to capture important information encoded in Wordnet [17] as well as draw syntactic generalization from minimally tagged corpora.

The ultimate aim of WSD is to disambiguate all the content words in a given sentence. This is known as unrestricted WSD. Rada Mihalcea [4] proposed a method based on semantic density to do unrestricted WSD. This method attempts to disambiguate all the nouns, verbs, adjectives and adverbs in text, using the senses provided in Wordnet.

3   Linguistic Preliminaries

This section describes the brief overview of the Kannada language and the Association rules used for word sense disambiguation.

3.1   Kannada Language

Indian languages can be classified into four language families. They are The Indo-Aryan, The Tibeto Burmun, The austro-asiatic and Dravidian. Kannada belongs to Dravidian family. It is spoken by over 60 million people, mainly in the state of Karnataka, south India, where it is the official language. It is one of the twenty two languages recognized by the Indian constitution. It has a rich literary tradition going back to the ninth century and exhibits a complex pattern of sociolinguistic and stylistic variations, marked in part by a thorough assimilation of Indo-Aryan (Sanskrit, Prakrit, Hindi, Urdu etc) and more recently, English elements [18].

Kannada is an agglutinating language of the suffixing type. Nouns are marked for numbers and case and verbs are marked in most cases for agreement with the subject in number, gender and person. This makes the Kannada relatively free word order language. Kannada exhibits a very rich system of morphology, morphology includes inflection, derivation, conflations (sandhi) and compounding [19].

Even though, Kannada has a very old and rich literary tradition, when it comes to technology, Kannada is one of the technologically least developed language in India today. As of today, the publicly available resources for Kannada are 3 million word corpora developed by Central Institute of Indian Languages (CIIL) Mysore [20] and a Shallow parser developed by International Institute of Information Technology (IIIT), Hyderabad. Compare to what needs to be done, what is already done and what is currently being done is very small. To address the issue, as a contributory work, we designed an algorithm and implemented it using Program Extraction and Reporting Language (Perl) under Linux environment to construct web corpora automatically. We used the same corpora for training the machine learning algorithm and as a test bed for Kannada WSD task. We constructed a Kannada machine readable dictionary using semi automatic approach.

3.2   Association Rules

Association Rules [21] are rules extracted from a data and have two parts called antecedent and consequent and are usually represented as "antecedent => Consequent" and each rule has Confidence and Support associated with it. A rule A => B with Confidence C and Support S means that "if antecedent is true then the consequent is true" in C% of cases and there are S instances in the data which have both A and B.

The formal statement of the problem is, Let $I = \{i_1, i_2... i_m\}$ be the set of literals called items. Let D be the set of transactions, where each transaction T is a set of items such that T is a subset of I. Associated with each transaction is a unique identifier, called its TID. We say that a transaction T contains X, a set of some items in I, if X is a subset of T. An association rule is a implication of the form X => Y, where X belongs to I and Y belongs to I and $X \cap Y = \Phi$. The rule   X => Y holds in the transaction set D with confidence C, if C% of transaction in D that contains X also contains Y. The rule X => Y has a support S in the transaction set D if S transactions in D contain X U Y.

Given a set of transaction D, the problem of mining association rules is to generate all association rules that have Support and Confidence greater than the user specified minimum Support (minsup) and minimum Confidence (minconf) respectively.

In the above formal definition, we took the transactions as a set of items with no order. But for our purpose, we think a transaction as a tuple in a relational table. i.e.

The association rules will be of the form

$$\{(A_1, a_1), (A_2, a_2)... (A_m, a_m)\} => \{(B_1, b_1),(B_2, b_2),.........,(B_n, b_n)\}$$

Here A_i is an attribute and a_i is its value. Similarly, B_i is an attribute and b_i is its value.

4   Experimental Setup

The details of the corpora and parser used for our experimentation are as follows.

4.1   Corpora

A Corpora is a large and representative collection of language material stored in a computer processable form [22]. It provides realistic, interesting and insightful examples of language use for theory building and for verifying hypothesis [23]. Corpora provide the basic language data from which lexical resources, such as dictionaries, thesauri, Wordnet etc can be generated [24]. Language technologies and applications are greatly benefited from language corpora.

For the proposed algorithm testing, we have used randomly selected set of sentences from the Kannada web corpora developed by us for experimentation. We automated complete corpora collection process by writing Perl script. The corpora include wide variety of subjects such as, Kannada news papers, Wikipedia articles, blogs, books, novels etc. The selected set of sentences from the Kannada web corpora are grouped into two categories, namely training and testing corpora. Both the categories are parsed with Kannada Shallow Parser. Given a sentence, the parser assigns to it a syntactic structure. This information is used for extracting association rules.

4.2   Parser

The Lexical and syntactic structure of the sentence in training and testing corpora are extracted by the Kannada Shallow Parser. It is developed by IIIT Hyderabad [25]. For each parsed sentence, the shallow parser produces eight intermediate stage outputs. Namely, Tokenization, Morphological analysis, POS tagger, chunker, pruning, pick one Morph, Head computation and Vibakti computation. These outputs help us to extract Lexical and Syntactic structure of the sentence for further processing.

5   Experimentation

This section describes the methodology used to do unrestricted WSD and proposes an algorithm to disambiguate all the content words in a given sentence.

5.1   Methodology

Our proposed algorithm uses association rules extracted from training corpora to disambiguate all the content words in the testing corpora. All ambiguous content words in a sentence are disambiguated using the following two steps. a) In the first step, we will mine all possible combination of an Association rules from training corpora. b) In the second step, the algorithm will assign correct meaning for ambiguous content words in a sentence using the association rules.

5.2   Algorithm Unrestricted Kannada WSD

1. Extract sentence from the testing corpora.
2. Assign sense no1 and a Confidence of 1.0 for all monosemous words in a Sentence.
3. Assign sense no1 and a Confidence minconf for all polysemous words in a Sentence.
4. For each word W in the sentence
5. Find all the links in which W participates.
6. Find all the association rules which are applicable to the links found in step 5.
7. Let S and C be the sense and confidence for the rule having maximum Confidence, if the Confidence for the previously assigned sense (in previous Iteration) is less than C then the Sense S is assigned for the word W.
8. Exit if the sense for the word did not change from previous iteration else go to Step 4 for next iteration.

6   Implementation

This section describes the files and the modules required for the implementation of an algorithm. The algorithm is implemented using Perl.

6.1   Files

The following files are used during program execution.

a) Training corpora: This file contains a sense tagged randomly selected set of sentences from Kannada web corpora. The association rules required for content word sense disambiguation are extracted from this file.

b) Testing Corpora: This file contains a sense tagged randomly selected set of sentences from a Kannada Web Corpora. These are different from the set of sentences present in training Corpora. This file acts as input file. The sentences in the file are given as an input for an algorithm. The algorithm disambiguates all the content words in a given sentence.

6.2   Implementation Modules

The program uses two modules for disambiguation task. Namely, word classifier and Sense disambiguator.

a) Word classifier: This module identifies all the monosemous and polysemous words in a input sentence.

b) Sense disambiguator: This module disambiguates all the polysemous content words in an input sentence.

7   Evaluation

We used the sentences from testing corpora as a test bed for testing the program.

7.1   Test Document

Table 1 shows the partial list of sentences used to test the program.

Table 1. Partial list of sentences extracted from test Corpora

Example Sentences
ಪಾಕಿಸ್ತಾನ ನೆರೆ ಸಂತ್ರಸ್ಥರಿಗೆ ನೆರವು. [paakistaana nere santhrastharige neravu]   'Help for Pakisthan flood victims'
ಬಟ್ಟೆಗಳು ಒಣಗಿವೆ. [baTTegaLu oNagive] 'Cloths are dried'.
ರಮಾಬಾಯಿ ಮೈ ನೆರೆದರು. [rammabaayi mai neredaru]   'Ramaabaayi matured biologically'
ರಾಮನಿಗೆ ಅನ್ನ ಇಡು. [raamanige anna iDu] 'serve rice to rama'
ನೆರೆಯಲ್ಲಿ ಸಿಲುಕಿ ಜನ ಜಾನುವಾರುಗಳೆಲ್ಲಾ ಸಂಕಷ್ಟಕೀಡಾದವು.   [nereyalli siluki jana jaanuvaarugaLellaa sankstakiiDaadavu]   'Due to flood, the people and animals are end up with critical problem'
ನೆರೆಯಲ್ಲಿ ಗಲಾಟೆ [nereyalli galaaTe] 'violence or quarrel in the neighbor'.
ವ್ಯವಸ್ಥೆಯ ಎದುರು ಈಜುವ ಹೆಣ್ಣುಮಕ್ಕಳಿಂದ ನಾನು ಆತ್ಮವಿಶ್ವಾಸದ ಪಾಠ ಕಲಿತಿದ್ದೇನೆ   [vyavastheya eduru iijuva heNNumakkaLinda naanu aatmavishvaasada paaTha kalitiddeene]. 'I learnt a lesson of confidence from females who swim against the system'
ರಾಜಬಾಗ್ ಸವಾರನ ಉರುಸು ಖ್ಯಾತವಾಗಿದೆ. [raajabaag savaarana urusu khyaatavaagide]. 'raajabaag savaara's fair is popular'
ಸೀತೆ ನೆರೆದರು [siite neredaru] 'Seethe matured biologically'
ರಾಮನು ಪಂಡಿತರ ಬಳಿ ಹೋಗಿ ಯಂತ್ರ ಹಾಕಿಸಿಕೊಂಡು ಬಂದನು. [raamanu panDitara baLi hoogi yantra haakisikonDu bandanu]   'Rama received an astrological device from a astrologer'

7.2   Result

The results obtained for the test sentences are shown in Table 2.

Table 2. The program execution result

Example Sentences	Comment
ಪಾಕಿಸ್ತಾನ ನೆರೆ ಸಂತ್ರಸ್ಥರಿಗೆ ನೆರವು	Correct
ಬಟ್ಟೆಗಳು ಒಣಗಿವೆ.	Correct
ರಮಾಬಾಯಿ ಮ್ಶೆ ನೆರೆದರು.	Correct
ರಾಮನಿಗೆ ಅನ್ನ ಇಡು.	Correct
ನೆರೆಯಲ್ಲಿ ಸಿಲುಕಿ ಜನ ಜಾನುವಾರುಗಳೆಲ್ಲಾ ಸಂಕಷ್ಟಕೀಢಾದವು.	Correct
ನೆರೆಯಲ್ಲಿ ಗಲಾಟೆ	Correct
ವ್ಯವಸ್ಥೆಯ ಎದುರು ಈಜುವ ಹೆಣ್ಣುಮಕ್ಕಳಿಂದ ನಾನು ಆತ್ಮವಿಶ್ವಾಸದ ಪಾಠ ಕಲಿತ್ತಿದ್ದೇನೆ	Partially correct
ರಾಜಾಬಾಗ್ ಸವಾರನ ಉರುಸು ಖ್ಯಾತವಾಗಿದೆ.	Incorrect
ಸೀತೆ ನೆರೆದರು	Incorrect
ರಾಮನು ಪಂಡಿತರ ಬಳಿ ಹೋಗಿ ಯಂತ್ರ ಹಾಕಿಸಿಕೊಂಡು ಬಂದನು.	Correct

7.3 Discussion

During the disambiguation process, the following observations are made.

a) The accuracy of the algorithm is entirely depends on the training examples present in the training   corpora. If the size of the training corpora is high then the accuracy of the disambiguation system is   also high. But manually creating large size sense tagged training corpora is difficult, labor intensive   and time consuming. Hence it needs automation.

b) The system assigns incorrect sense 'gather' for a sentence ಸೀತೆ ನೆರೆದರು [siite neredaru] instead of 'biologically matured' sense. This is because of the insufficient context information. This kind of problems can be   easily addressed at discourse level analysis but it is behind the scope of the present work.

c) In a sentence ರಾಜಾಬಾಗ್ ಸವಾರನ ಉರುಸು ಖ್ಯಾತವಾಗಿದೆ [raajaabaag savaarana urusu khyaatavaagide], ರಾಜಾಬಾಗ್ ಸವಾರನ [raajaabaag savaarana] is a proper noun and also, it is a multiword expression. But, during the disambiguation process, the system interpret it, as a two separate words and assigns the senses separately, it leads to incorrect disambiguation. Hence, handling multiword expression is a critical issue in the disambiguation task.

d) In a sentence ವ್ಯವಸ್ಥೆಯ ಎದುರು ಈಜುವ ಹೆಣ್ಣುಮಕ್ಕಳಿಂದ ನಾನು ಆತ್ಮವಿಶ್ವಾಸದ ಪಾಠ ಕಲಿತ್ತಿದ್ದೇನೆ [vyavastheya eduru iijuva heNNumakkaLinda naanu aatmavishvaasada paaTha kalitiddeene], ಹೆಣ್ಣುಮಕ್ಕಳಿಂದ [heNNumakkaLinda] and ಆತ್ಮವಿಶ್ವಾಸದ [aatmavishvaasada] are compound words, because both the words are formed using two word combination, according to linguistic principles the meaning of the compound words must be deduced using the constituent words in it. But these words are not available in lexical database, hence our system interprets the constituent parts of the compound word as a separate words, it leads to wrong result during the disambiguation process.

8   Conclusion and Future Work

In this paper, we proposed a Kannada Word Sense Disambiguation system. It is a valuable resource for resource poor Kannada Language. As an experimental setup, we constructed reasonable size Kannada web corpora using a tool developed by us. A part of the constructed corpora is sense tagged and then it is divided in to training and testing corpora. A set of Association rules are extracted from the training corpora and then used them for disambiguating the sentences in the testing corpora. Experiments are conducted and the results obtained are described. The performance of the system with respect to applicability and precision are encouraging.

In future, we are planning to build a robust Kannada Word Sense Disambiguation system by addressing the multiword expression and discourse level issues. We are also planning to build an automatic sense tagging system to construct sense tagged corpora automatically for Kannada Language.

References

1. Ng, H.T., Lee, H.B.: Integrating multiple knowledge sources to disambiguate word sense: An exemplar-based approach. In: 34th Annual Meeting of the ACL, pp. 40–47. Morgan Kaufmann Publication, San Francisco (1996)
2. Yarowsky, D.: Hierarchical decision lists for word sense disambiguation. Computers and the Humanities 34(1-2), 179–186 (2000)
3. Martinez, D., Agirre, E., Marquez, L.: Syntactic features for high precision word sense disambiguation. In: COLING (2002)
4. Mihalcea, R., Moldovan, D.: A method for word sense disambiguation of unrestricted text. In: 37th Annual Meeting of the ACL, Maryland, pp. 152–158 (1999)
5. Wilks, Y., Stevenson, M.: Word Sense Disambiguation using optimized combination of knowledge sources. In: 36th Annual Meeting of the ACL, Canada, pp. 1398–1402 (1998)
6. Lesk, M.: Automatic sense disambiguation using machine readable dictionaries: How to tell a pine cone from a ice cream cone. In: SIGDOC Conference, Toronto Canada, pp. 24–26 (1986)
7. Walker, D., Amsler, R.: The Use of Machine Readable Dictionaries in Sublanguage Analysis. In: Analyzing Language in Restricted Domains, pp. 69–83. LEA Press (1986)
8. Eneko, A., Rigau, G.: Word sense disambiguation using conceptual density. In: 16th International Conference on Computational Linguistics (COLING), Copenhagen, Denmark (1996)
9. Rada, M.: Large vocabulary unsupervised word sense disambiguation with graph based algorithms for sequence data labeling. In: Joint Human Language Technology and Empirical Methods in Natural Language Processing Conference (HLT/EMNLP), Vancouver, Canada, pp. 411–418 (2005)
10. David, Y.: Decision lists for lexical ambiguity resolution: Application to accent restoration in Spanish and French. In: 32nd Annual Meeting of the Association for Computational Linguistics (ACL), Las Cruces, USA, pp. 88–95 (1994)
11. Gale, W.A., Church, K.W., Yarowsky, D.: Estimating upper and lower bounds on the performance of word sense disambiguation programs. In: 30th Annual Meeting of the Association for Computational Linguistics, pp. 249–256. University of Delaware, Newark (1992)

12. Fakhrahmad, S.M., Rezapour, A.R., Zolghadri Jahromi, M., Sadreddini, M.H.: A New Word Sense Disambiguation System Based on Deduction. In: World Congress on Engineering, London, U.K, vol. II (2011)
13. Firth, R.: Man and Culture, An evaluation of the work of bronislaw malinowski, pp. 167–169. The Humanities Press (1957)
14. Schutze, H.: Dimensions of meaning. In: Supercomputing 1992, Minneapolis, pp. 787–796 (1992)
15. Miller, G., Charles, W.: Contextual correlates of semantic similarity. Language and Cognitive Proceesses 6, 1–28 (1991)
16. Navigli, R., Velardi, P.: Structural Semantic Interconnections: A Knowledge- Based Approach to Word Sense Disambiguation. IEEE Transaction on Pattern Analysis and Machine Intelligence (2005)
17. Fellbaum, C.: WordNet: An Electronic Lexical Database. The MIT Press (1998)
18. Sridhar, S.N.: Modern Kannada Grammar. Manohar Publishers & Distributors, New Delhi (2007)
19. Kushaalappa Gowda, K.: Kannada Bhashe & VyakaranagaLa Ondu samiikshe (Kannada Language and its Grammar). Karthik enterprises, Bangalore, India (2008)
20. Narayana Murthy, K.: Computer Processing of Kannada Language. In: Workshop at Kannada University, Hampi, University of Hyderabad, Hyderabad (2001)
21. Agrawal, R., Imielinski, T., Swami, A.N.: Mining Association rules between sets of items in large databases. In: ACM SIGMOD International Conference on Management of Data, Washington D.C, pp. 207–216 (1993)
22. Sinclair, J.: Corpus, Concordance, Collocation. Oxford University Press, Oxford (1991)
23. Barlow, M.: Corpora for theory and Practice. J. Corpus Linguistics 1(1), 1–38 (1996)
24. Dash, N.S., Chaudhuri, B.B.: Relevance of Corpus in Language research and applications. J. Dravidian Linguistics 32(2), 101–122 (2002)
25. Kannada Shallow Parser. IIIT, Hyderabad, http://ltrc.iiit.ac.in/analyzer/Kannada

K-Means Clustering of Use-Cases Using MDL

Sunil Kumar[1], Rajesh Kumar Bhatia[2], and Rajesh Kumar[3]

[1] Department of Computer Science & Engineering,
Thapar University,
Patiala
sunilgautam82@gmail.com
[2] Department of Computer Science & Engineering
Deenbandhu Chhotu Ram University of
Science & Technology Murthal (Sonepat)
rbhatiapatiala@gmail.com
[3] School of Mathematics & Computer Application,
Thapar University,
Patiala
rakumar@thapar.edu

Abstract. Software architecture plays an important role during the design stage. It is one of the responsible factors for software quality. Functionalities of the software components have been distributed among the constituents of software architecture. In this paper partitional clustering of the use cases has been proposed. The components to be clustered have been extracted from the mdl file formed by default in Rational Rose. Rational Rose has been taken as the modeling tool to model the software during the design stage. MDL is the model description language describing the facts about the model components in Rational Rose. It is a textual representation of the various aspects about the design of the software. The QUID (qualified unique identifier) has been extracted from the MDL file on which k means clustering algorithm has been applied which results into non overlapping clusters. Euclidean distance measure has been used to measure the distance between the components. In order to represent the partitional clustering, graphs have been drawn.

Keywords: MDL, QUID, Use- Case, Clustering.

1   Introduction

Component based development (CBD) is now a day's comes out to be an effective field in the development and maintenance of information system [1]. A component is a block of software that can be designed and if necessary can be integrated with the other components [2]. During the design phase the software components have been determined by use case model, object model and dynamic or collaboration diagrams [3]. To enhance the reusability one approach is to cluster the software components. Our approach will cluster the use cases extracted in the form of numerical or coded values from the mdl file [6]. Clustering has to be performed by evaluating the distance between the software components. The aim of clustering is to improve the technical

P.V. Krishna, M.R. Babu, and E. Ariwa (Eds.): ObCom 2011, Part II, CCIS 270, pp. 57–67, 2012.
© Springer-Verlag Berlin Heidelberg 2012

assessment criteria proposed by [4]. There are many clustering methods like hierarchical and partitional. Hierarchical clustering algorithms can be further categorized into two types [5], Agglomerative and Divisive. Agglomerative clustering initializes with N clusters and each of them includes only one object. A series of merge operations then follow which finally had all objects to the same group. Based upon the distance between the clusters agglomerative clustering can be further categorized. But we are concerned only with the partitional clustering only. In this method of clustering data has to be partitioned into different clusters. One such technique is the K- means [18] algorithm. k- means clustering is a partitional clustering technique to find the k non-overlapping clusters. The clusters are the representation of cluster centers i.e centroids. A centroid is the mean of the data points in a cluster. In this technique initially k initial centroids are selected randomly and clusters are evaluated. In this evaluation every data point in the data is assigned to the closest cluster center. Thus collection of the data points assigned to a cluster center forms a cluster. There may be several iterations done in order to find the non overlapping clusters. This process is repeated until there is no change in the cluster data points. The data to be clustered has been extracted from the mdl file. An instance of the mdl file is shown below in figure 1. Quid refers to the qualified unique identifier contains 12 hexadecimal digits. Name of the stereotype has been mentioned after the name of the object that is either the object is an actor or a use case.

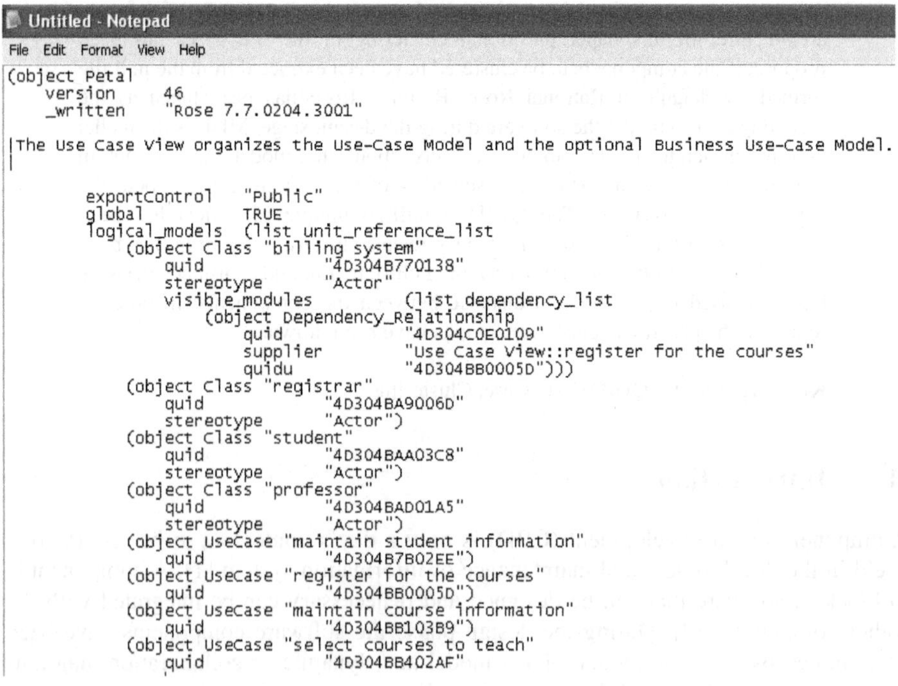


```
(object Petal
    version     46
    _written    "Rose 7.7.0204.3001"

|The Use Case View organizes the Use-Case Model and the optional Business Use-Case Model.
|

        exportControl   "Public"
        global          TRUE
        logical_models  (list unit_reference_list
            (object Class "billing system"
                quid                "4D304B770138"
                stereotype          "Actor"
                visible_modules         (list dependency_list
                    (object Dependency_Relationship
                        quid                "4D304C0E0109"
                        supplier            "Use Case View::register for the courses"
                        quidu               "4D304BB0005D")))
            (object Class "registrar"
                quid                "4D304BA9006D"
                stereotype          "Actor")
            (object Class "student"
                quid                "4D304BAA03C8"
                stereotype          "Actor")
            (object Class "professor"
                quid                "4D304BAD01A5"
                stereotype          "Actor")
            (object UseCase "maintain student information"
                quid                "4D304B7B02EE")
            (object UseCase "register for the courses"
                quid                "4D304BB0005D")
            (object UseCase "maintain course information"
                quid                "4D304BB103B9")
            (object UseCase "select courses to teach"
                quid                "4D304BB402AF"
```

Fig. 1. MDL File

Distance measure is an important decision for clustering. This will evaluate the similarities or dissimilarities between two components. Also the shape of the clusters is to be decided by the distance measure. Distance measures are available for different dimensions. There are so many distance measures available. In our approach we are using Euclidean distance measure.

A distance between the components is to be measured by using Euclidean Formulae. This formula can be applied from one to N dimension datasets.

For one dimension: $\sqrt{(x-y)^2} = |x - y|$

For two dimensions: $d(p, q) = \sqrt{(p_1 - q_1)^2 + (p_2 - q_2)^2}$

For three dimensions: $d(p, q) = \sqrt{(p_1 - q_1)^2 + (p_2 - q_2)^2 + (p_3 - q_3)^2}$

For n dimensions: $d(p,q) = \sqrt{(p_1 - q_1)^2 + (p_2 - q_2)^2 + (p_3 - q_3)^2 \ldots\ldots + (p_i - q_i)^2 + \ldots\ldots + (p_n - q_n)^2}$

2   Literature Survey

In [7], the static and dynamic relationships between the classes have been analyzed. Static relationship measures the relationship strength and dynamic measures the frequency of messages exchange at run time. To evaluate the overall strength of the relationship between the classes, the static and dynamic results have been combined.

In [8], a decomposition method of requirements has been proposed. Hierarchical clustering has been performed to partition the system.

In [9], a tool called as UML analyzer has been proposed. Tool will abstract the class diagrams and object diagrams in UML at higher level. It can extract the classifiers, relations and semantics. It is an automated abstraction technique and had in built abstraction rules for class and object diagrams. Rational Corporation has also adopted this tool and has implemented it on the Rational Rose [17].

In [10], a systematic UML based method to identify the components has been discussed. It is based upon the assumption that the object oriented model for the target domain is available. This includes the use case model, object model and dynamic model. The method utilises these artifacts and transforms them into components [9].

In [11] a method to measure the interclass relationships in terms of create, retrieve update, and delete CRUD has been proposed. Clustering   algorithm   for   shifting rows   and   columns   was implemented to make appropriate clusters. Based upon the data dependency   and   interclass   relationships   among   the   classes, clusters were formed [10].

In [12], an assessment system for UML class diagram called as UML class diagram assessor UCDA has been proposed. The tool gets an input in the form of Rational Rose petal files. The tool will evaluate the class diagram on the basis of three aspects: structure, correctness and language used. The output of the tool is a list of comments on the diagram that are to be used in understanding the requirements. The naming convention for the class and its attributes were based upon the Malay language. The author had also proposed an extraction technique that extracted the notation information from the Rational Rose Petal files and were kept in the tables for further assessment.

In [13], OMG has clearly specified the representation of a software asset. An asset comprises of profile name, description, classification, solution, usage, and related asset. These are the reusable asset specification of an asset. Profile describes the particular type of asset being described. Description provides the summary of the asset. Classification contains the description which classifies the characteristics and behavior of the asset. Solution contains the location of the specific artifact that comprises the asset. Usage defines how to use the asset. Related asset describes the relationship between the assets.

[14] has developed a tool to check the syntax, rules and notations imposed by the UML specifications similar to the [9] called as UMLST, unified modeling language specification tool. Many tools are available to develop the UML specification like Visio [15], Cadifra [16], and Rational Rose [17]. [9] uses the java programming and deals with the architecture and design mismatches in the UML models, where as this tool uses C++ programming and deals with the UML diagram abstract syntax, its well formed, semantics and notations used in the UML specifications. UMLST first checks the diagrams against each other for any mismatch word and then check the diagram abstract syntax, its well formed, semantics and notations. It has been implemented to check the compliance between the class diagrams, activity diagram, interaction and use case diagram.

3   Proposed Approach

Extraction of design components from the mdl file followed by clustering has been used. The approach can be better understood by the following block diagram in fig 2. The starting point of the process is the requirement analysis. On this basis the use case view has to be modeled. The requirements of the software have been mapped to use case diagram. The model has been saved by some name e.g abc in the same directory in which the rational files have been saved. The file is then reopened in the notepad. It will appear as an unstructured text file containing all the information contained in the model drawn. From this file the quid of the components of use case view has been extracted and converted to their decimal equivalent. Prime factorization theorem has been applied on these decimal numbers and a graph has been formed. The graph visualizes the clusters.

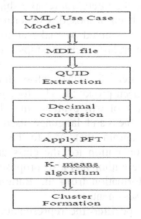

Fig. 2. Process

The above process has been implemented on the use case view. Microsoft visual studio .net and SQL server 2005 has been used. The screenshots of the extracted information has been shown below in fig 3.

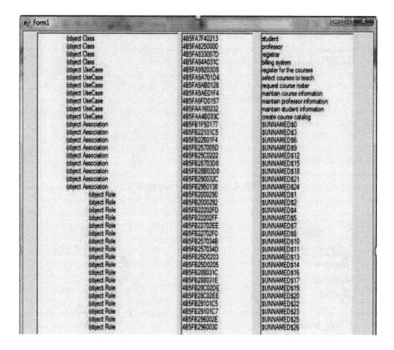

Fig. 3. Extracted Information

The quids extracted from the mdl file are converted to their decimal equivalents. Analysis of the hexadecimal quid and the decimal equivalent of the actor and use cases have been done that resulted into the observations listed in section 3.

3.1   Hexadecimal to Decimal Conversion

Mathematically, let

$$X = h_1h_2h_3h_4h_5h_6h_7h_8h_9h_{10}h_{11}h_{12}$$

be the quid of any actor or use case.
Convert this no to its decimal equivalent and add. Let it be D.

$$D = d_1+d_2+d_3+d_4+d_5+d_6+d_7+d_8+d_9+d_{10}+d_{11}+d_{12}$$

Where d_1.......d_{12} is the decimal equivalent of h_1.........h_{12}.
The use case and class diagram of online marks analysis system is shown in fig 4 and fig 5 below:

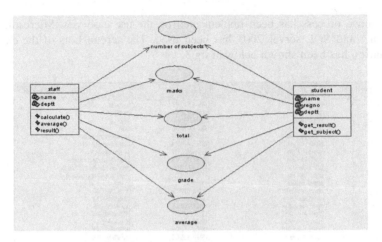

Fig. 4. Use- Case Diagram

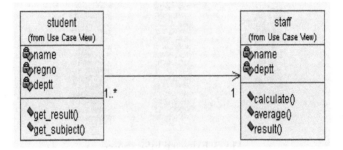

Fig. 5. Class Diagram

Consider the use case diagram only:

Now look at the MDL file of the above diagrams. The components in the above model can be clustered by using the following process:

1. Analyse the MDL file of the above model.
2. Extract the quids of the components contained in the above model.
3. Convert the hexadecimal quid into decimal no.
4. Now calculate the difference between the decimal equivalents of the actor and use cases in which a relationship exists like the actor staff and use case no. of subjects.
5. Now implement prime factorization theorem on the differences obtained from the quids and draw a graph. From t h e above facts the differences obtained are as under:

    1, 5, 3, 21, 10, 15, 21, 13, 5, 26. Obtain the factors of the above numbers:

    No = factor1 x factor2
    1= 1x1
    5=1x5

3=1x3
21=3x7
10=2x5
15=3x5
21=3x7
13=1x13
5=1x5
26=2x13

Now factor 1 will be on the x axis and factor 2 will be on the y axis. This form a table as below:

Table 1.

A	(1, 1)
B	(1, 5)
C	(1, 3)
D	(3, 7)
E	(2, 5)
F	(3, 5)
G	(3, 7)
H	(1, 13)
I	(2, 13)
J	(1, 5)

3.2   K Means Clustering

k means clustering is a method of data mining whose aim is to partition n data items into k clusers. In this every data item belongs to the nearest mean or the cluster center. The algorithm is composed of following steps:

1. Place K points into the space represented by the data points which are to be clustered.
2. Initially assume the value of k i.e no of clusters.
3. Assign each data item to the group that has the closest centroid.
4. When all data items have been assigned, recalculate the position of the K centroids.
5. Repeat Steps 2 and 3 until the centroids no longer move. This produces a separation of the objects into groups.

Let us apply k means clustering on the data set in Table 1. The duplicate values in the above table must be omitted. Therefore the new data set will be shown in table below. There are eight data items in the data set.

Table 2.

1	A	(1, 5)
2	B	(1, 3)
3	C	(3, 7)
4	D	(2, 5)
5	E	(3, 5)
6	F	(1, 13)
7	G	(2, 13)

Assume K= 2 and the initial cluster centers as B and D i.e (1, 5) and (3, 7).

First we list all points in the first column in the table drawn below. The initial cluster centers means are (1, 5) and (3, 7) chosen randomly. Next we will calculate the distance from the first point (1, 5) to each of the two means by using the distance measure.

Table 3.

		(1, 5)	(3, 7)	
	Point	Mean 1	Mean 2	Cluster
A	(1, 5)	0	4	CC1
B	(1, 3)	4	6	CC1
C	(3, 7)	4	0	CC2
D	(2, 5)	1	3	CC1
E	(3, 5)	2	2	CC1 & CC2
F	(1, 13)	8	8	CC1 & CC2
G	(2, 13)	9	7	CC2

By carefully analyzing the above table it is clear that points F and G belongs to both the cluster centers. It means that the cluster centers should be re-calculated. This can be clearly visualized from the graph in fig 6 that both the clusters are overlapping.

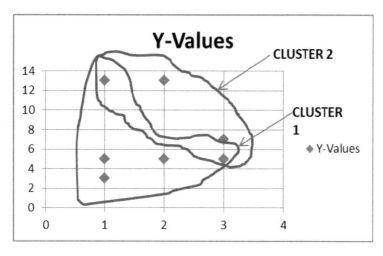

Fig. 6. Graph showing Overlapping of Clusters

As shown in the graph cluster1 and cluster 2 are overlapping. So let us re-calculate the cluster centers. For this calculate the mean for both the above clusters.

For cluster 1
NCC= (1.5, 5.3)
For cluster 2
NCC= (2.2, 9.5)

Now calculate the mean for new cluster centers as in the table 4 below:

Table 4.

		(1.5, 5.3)	(2.2, 9.5)	
	Point	Mean 1	Mean 2	Cluster
A	(1, 5)	0.8	5.7	CC 1
B	(1, 3)	2.8	7.7	CC 1
C	(3, 7)	3.2	3.3	CC 1
D	(2, 5)	0.8	4.7	CC 1
E	(3, 5)	1.8	5.3	CC 1
F	(1, 13)	8.2	4.7	CC 2
G	(2, 13)	8.2	3.7	CC 2

Two separate clusters are shown in the graph (fig 7) below on the basis of above table.

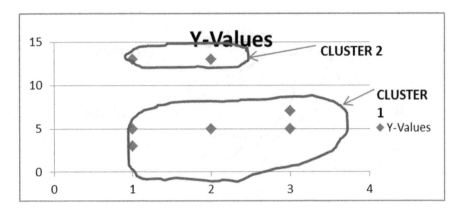

Fig. 7. Graph Showing Cluster Formation

4   Results

The graph shown above indicates two clusters, which are located at far distances from each other. Now let us map the clustered points to actual components.

Cluster 1includes the data points 5, 3, 21, 10, 15. These are the difference values obtained from the decimal equivalents of the quids in the use case diagram. This includes the components staff (actor), marks (use case), total (use case), no of subjects (use case), marks (use case), average (use case), grade (use case).

Cluster 2 includes the data points 13, 26. This includes the components student (actor), no of subjects (use case), average (use case). Our approach deals with the clustering of use- cases. The novelty in our method is the extraction of components from the mdl file in the form of quids. We applied clustering on the values obtained from quids. We consider only the use- case diagram. Clustering can be applied for other UML components also. Since each diagram or view in a model comprises of various components.

References

1. Peng, L., Tong, Z., Zhang, Y.: Design of Business Component Identification method with graph segmentation. In: 3rd Int. Conf. on Intelligent System and Knowledge Engineering, pp. 296–301 (2008)
2. Wu, R.: Componentization and semantic mediation. In: 33th Annual Conference of the IEEE Industrial Electronic Society, Taiwan, pp. 111–116 (2007)
3. Kim, S., Chang, S.: A Systematic method to identify Software Components. In: Proc. of 11th Software Engineering Conference, pp. 538–545 (2004)
4. Mili, A., Mili, R., Mitterweir, R.T.: A survey of Software Reuse Libraries. Annals of Software Engineering 5, 349–414 (1998)
5. Xu, R., Wunsch, D.: Survey of Clustering Algorithms. IEEE Transactions on Neural Networks 16(3), 645–678 (2005)
6. Dahm, M.: Grammar and API for Rational Rose petal files (July 2001)

7. Jain, H., Chalimeda, N.: Business Component Identification- A Formal Approach. In: Proc. of the 5th IEEE Int. Conf. on Enterprise Distributed Object Computing, p. 183 (2001)

8. Lung, C.H., Zaman, M., Nandi, A.: Application of Clustering Technique to Software Partitioning, Recovery and Restructuring. Journal of System and Software, 227–244 (2004)

9. Egyed, A.: Semantic abstraction rules for class diagrams. In: Proceedings of 15th International Conference on Automated Software Engineering, ASE 2000 (2000)

10. Kim, S.D., Chang, S.H.: A systematic method to identify software components. In: Proceedings of 11th Asia Pacific Software Engineering Conference, APSEC 2004 (2004)

11. Lee, S., Yang, Y., Cho, E., Kim, S., Rhew, S.: COMO: A UML based component based methodology. In: Proceedings of the IEEE Sixth Asia Pacific Software Engineering Conference (December 1999)

12. Ali, N.H., Shukur, Z., Idris, S.: A Design of an Assessment System for UML Class Diagram. In: Fifth International Conference on Computational Science and Applications (2007)

13. OMG. OMG unified modeling language, UML (2004), http://www.omg.org/

14. Ibrahim, R., Ibrahim, N.: A tool for checking the conformance of UML specification, http://www.waset.org/journals/waset/v51/v51-45.pdf

15. Microsoft Visio Toolbox (2008), http://www.visiotoolbox.com

16. Cadifra UML Editor (2008), http://www.cadifra.com/

17. Rational Rose (2008), http://www.rational.com

18. MacQueen, J.: Some methods for classification and analysis of multivariate observations. In: Cam, L.M.L., Neyman, J. (eds.) Proc. 5th Berkeley Symp. Math. Stat. Probab., vol. I, Univ. California Press, Berkeley (1967)

Topological Characterization of Rough Set on Two Universal Sets and Knowledge Representation

B.K. Tripathy, D.P. Acharjya[*], and L. Ezhilarasi

School of Computing Science and Engineering, VIT University, Vellore 632014,
Tamil Nadu, India
tripathybk@rediffmail.com,
{dpacharjya,ezhilvijayanand}@gmail.com

Abstract. The notion of rough set captures indiscernibility of elements in a set. But, in many real life situations, an information system establishes the relation between different universes. This gave the extension of rough set on single universal set to rough set on two universal sets. In this paper, we introduce an interesting topological characterization of rough set on two universal sets employing the notion of the lower and upper approximation. Also, we study some basic set theoretic operations on the types of rough sets formed by the topological characterization. In addition to that, we provide a real life example for the depth classification of the concept.

Keywords: Rough set, lower and upper approximation, solitary set, Boolean matrix, roughly definable, internally undefinable, externally undefinable, totally undefinable.

1 Introduction

In modern era of computing, there is a need of development in data analysis and knowledge representation. Many new mathematical modeling tools are emerging to the thrust of the real world task. Fuzzy set by Zadeh [29], rough set by Pawlak [21, 22], soft set by Molodtsov [17] are such mathematical models gained its popularity in past few decades. Development of these techniques and tools are studied under different domains like knowledge discovery in database, computational intelligence, knowledge engineering, granular computing etc. [9, 10, 11, 16, 20, 30].

The rough set [21, 22] philosophy specifies about the depth understanding of the object and its attributes influencing the object with a depicted value. So, there is a need to classify objects of the universe based on the indiscernibility relation between them. The basic idea of rough set is based upon the approximation of sets by pair of sets known as lower approximation and upper approximation. Here, the lower and upper approximation operators are based on equivalence relation. However, the requirement of equivalence relation is a restrictive condition that may limit the application of rough set model. Therefore, rough set is generalized to some extent.

---

[*] Corresponding author.

P.V. Krishna, M.R. Babu, and E. Ariwa (Eds.): ObCom 2011, Part II, CCIS 270, pp. 68–81, 2012.
© Springer-Verlag Berlin Heidelberg 2012

For instance, the equivalence relation is generalized to binary relations [4, 7, 8, 18, 27, 32], neighborhood systems [12], coverings [31, 33, 34, 35], Boolean algebras [15, 19], fuzzy lattices [13], and completely distributive lattices [5].

On the other hand, rough set is generalized to fuzzy environment such as fuzzy rough set [6], and rough fuzzy set [28]. Further, the indiscernibility relation is generalized to almost indiscernibility relation to study many real life problems. The concept of rough set on fuzzy approximation spaces based on fuzzy proximity relation is studied by Tripathy and Acharjya [2, 24]. Further it is generalized to intuitionistic fuzzy proximity relation, and the concept of rough set on intuitionistic fuzzy approximation space is studied by Tripathy [25]. The different applications are also studied by Tripathy and Acharjya [1, 3, 23]. Further rough set of Pawlak is generalized to rough set on two universal sets with generalized approximation spaces and interval structure [26]. We continue a further study in the same direction.

The rest of the paper is organized as follows: Section 2 presents the foundations of rough set based on two universal sets. In Section 3, we study the topological characterization of rough sets on two universal sets. Basic set theoretic operations on topological characterization of rough sets on two universal sets are studied in Section 4. In Section 5, we discuss a real life problem and verify the results obtained due to set theoretic operations in Section 4. This is further followed by a conclusion in Section 6.

2   Rough Set Based on Two Universal Sets

An information system is a table that provides a convenient way to describe a finite set of objects called the universe by a finite set of attributes thereby representing all available information and knowledge. But, in many real life situations, an information system establishes the relation between different universes. This gave the extension of rough set on single universal set to rough set on two universal sets. Wong et al. [26] generalized the rough set models using two distinct but related universal sets. Let U and V be two universal sets and $R \subseteq (U \times V)$ be a binary relation. By a knowledge base, we understand the relational system (U, V, R) an approximation space. For an element $x \in U$, we define the right neighborhood or the R-relative set of x in U, $r(x)$ as $r(x) = \cup\{y \in V : (x, y) \in R\}$. Similarly for an element $y \in V$, we define the left neighborhood or the R-relative set of y in V, $l(y)$ as $l(y) = \cup\{x \in U : (x, y) \in R\}$.

For any two elements $x_1, x_2 \in U$, we say x_1 and x_2 are equivalent if $r(x_1) = r(x_2)$. Therefore, $(x_1, x_2) \in E_U$ if and only if $r(x_1) = r(x_2)$, where E_U denote the equivalence relation on U. Hence, E_U partitions the universal set U into disjoint subsets. Similarly for any two elements $y_1, y_2 \in V$, we say y_1 and y_2 are equivalent if $l(y_1) = l(y_2)$. Thus, $(y_1, y_2) \in E_V$ if and only if $l(y_1) = l(y_2)$, where E_V denote the equivalence relation on V and partitions the universal set V into disjoint subsets. Therefore for the approximation space (U, V, R), it is clear that $E_V \circ R = R = R \circ E_U$, where $E_V \circ R$ is the composition of R and E_V.

For any $Y \subseteq V$ and the binary relation R, we associate two subsets $\underline{R}Y$ and $\overline{R}Y$ called the R-lower and R-upper approximations of Y respectively, which are given by:

$$\underline{R}Y = \bigcup \{x \in U : r(x) \subseteq Y\} \tag{1}$$

$$\overline{R}Y = \bigcup \{x \in U : r(x) \cap Y \neq \phi\} \tag{2}$$

The R-boundary of Y is denoted as $BN_R(Y)$ and is given as $BN_R(Y) = \overline{R}Y - \underline{R}Y$. The pair $(\underline{R}Y, \overline{R}Y)$ is called as the rough set of $Y \subseteq V$ if $\underline{R}Y \neq \overline{R}Y$ or equivalently $BN_R(Y) \neq \phi$.

Further, if U and V are finite sets, then the binary relation R from U to V can be represented as $R(x, y)$, where

$$R(x,\ y) = \begin{cases} 1 & \text{if } (x, y) \in R \\ 0 & \text{if } (x, y) \notin R \end{cases}$$

The characteristic function of $X \subseteq U$ is defined for each $x \in U$ as follows:

$$X(x) = \begin{cases} 1 & \text{if } x \in X \\ 0 & \text{if } x \notin X \end{cases}$$

Therefore, the R - lower and R - upper approximations can be also presented in an equivalent form as shown below, where $\wedge$ and $\vee$ denotes minimum and maximum operators respectively.

$$(\underline{R}Y)x = \bigwedge_{y \in V} ((1 - R(x, y)) \vee Y(y)) \tag{3}$$

$$(\overline{R}Y)x = \bigvee_{y \in V} (R(x, y) \wedge Y(y)) \tag{4}$$

Example 1. Let $U = \{x_1, x_2, x_3, x_4, x_5\}$ and $V = \{y_1, y_2, y_3, y_4, y_5, y_6\}$. Consider the relation R given by its Boolean matrix:

$$R = \begin{pmatrix} 1 & 1 & 0 & 0 & 1 & 0 \\ 0 & 0 & 1 & 0 & 0 & 1 \\ 0 & 1 & 0 & 1 & 0 & 0 \\ 1 & 0 & 1 & 1 & 1 & 1 \\ 1 & 1 & 0 & 0 & 1 & 0 \end{pmatrix}$$

From the above relation R it is clear that, $r(x_1) = \{y_1, y_2, y_5\}$; $r(x_2) = \{y_3, y_6\}$; $r(x_3) = \{y_2, y_4\}$; $r(x_4) = \{y_1, y_3, y_4, y_5, y_6\}$ and $r(x_5) = \{y_1, y_2, y_5\}$. Therefore, we get $U / E_U = \{\{x_1, x_5\}, \{x_2\}, \{x_3\}, \{x_4\}\}$. Similarly, $V / E_V = \{\{y_1, y_5\}, \{y_3, y_6\}, \{y_2\}, \{y_4\}\}$.

Let us consider the target set $Y = \{y_1, y_2, y_4, y_5\}$. Therefore, the R-lower approximation, $\underline{R}Y$ is given as $\underline{R}Y = \{x_1, x_3, x_5\}$ whereas the R-upper approximation,

$\overline{R}Y$ is given as $\overline{R}Y = \{x_1, x_3, x_4, x_5\}$. The R-boundary of Y is given as $BN_R(Y) = \{x_4\}$.

Definition 1. Let U and V be two universal sets. Let R be a binary relation from U to V. If $x \in U$ and $r(x) = \phi$, then we call x is a solitary element with respect to R. The set of all solitary elements with respect to the relation R is called as solitary set and is denoted as S. Mathematically,

$$S = \{x \in U : r(x) = \phi\} \tag{5}$$

2.1   Algebraic Properties of Rough Set Based on Two Universal Sets

In this section, we list the algebraic properties as established by Guilong Liu [14] that are interesting and valuable in the theory of rough sets as below. Let R be an arbitrary binary relation from U to V. Let S be a solitary set with respect to the relation R. For subsets X, Y, in V

(i) $\overline{R}Y = \underset{y \in Y}{\cup} l(y)$ (6)

(ii) $\underline{R}\phi = S$, $\overline{R}\phi = \phi$, $\underline{R}V = U$ and $\overline{R}V = S'$, where S' denotes the complement of S in U.   (7)

(iii) $S \subseteq \underline{R}X$ and $\overline{R}X \subseteq S'$ (8)

(iv) $\underline{R}X - S \subseteq \overline{R}X$ (9)

(v) $\underline{R}X = U$ if and only if $\underset{x \in U}{\cup} r(x) \subseteq X$; $\overline{R}X = \phi$ if and only if $X \subseteq (\underset{x \in U}{\cup} r(x))'$ (10)

(vi)   If $S \neq \phi$, then $\underline{R}X \neq \overline{R}X$ for all $X \in P(V)$, where $P(V)$ denotes the power set of V.   (11)

(vii)   For any given index set I, $X_i \in P(V)$, $\underline{R}(\underset{i \in I}{\cap} X_i) = \underset{i \in I}{\cap} \underline{R}X_i$ and $\overline{R}(\underset{i \in I}{\cup} X_i) = \underset{i \in I}{\cup} \overline{R}X_i$.   (12)

(viii) If $X \subseteq Y$, then $\underline{R}X \subseteq \underline{R}Y$ and $\overline{R}X \subseteq \overline{R}Y$ (13)

(ix) $\underline{R}X \cup \underline{R}Y \subseteq \underline{R}(X \cup Y)$, and $\overline{R}(X \cap Y) \subseteq \overline{R}X \cap \overline{R}Y$ (14)

(x) $(\underline{R}X)' = \overline{R}X'$, and $(\overline{R}X)' = \underline{R}X'$;   (15)

(xi)   There exists some $X \in P(U)$ such that $\underline{R}X = \overline{R}X$ iff R is serial.   (16)

(xii)   If G is another binary relation from U to V and $\overline{R}X = \overline{G}X$ for all $x \in P(V)$, then $R = G$.   (17)

(xiii) If G is another binary relation from U to V and $\underline{R}X = \underline{G}X$ for all $x \in P(V)$, then $R = G$.   (18)

3   Characterization of Rough Set Based on Two Universal Sets

In this section, we introduce an interesting topological characterization of rough set on two universal sets employing the notion of the lower and upper approximation. It results four important and different types of rough sets on two universal sets as shown below:

Type 1:   If $\underline{R}Y \neq \phi$ and $\overline{R}Y \neq U$, then we say that Y is *roughly R-definable* on two universal sets.

Type 2:   If $\underline{R}Y = \phi$ and $\overline{R}Y \neq U$, then we say that Y is *internally R-undefinable* on two universal sets.

Type 3:   If $\underline{R}Y \neq \phi$ and $\overline{R}Y = U$, then we say that Y is *externally R-undefinable* on two universal sets.

Type 4:   If $\underline{R}Y = \phi$ and $\overline{R}Y = U$, then we say that Y is *totally R-undefinable* on two universal sets.

Example 2. Let us consider two universes U and V as $U = \{x_1, x_2, x_3, x_4, x_5\}$ and $V = \{y_1, y_2, y_3, y_4, y_5, y_6\}$. Consider the binary relation R from $U \rightarrow V$ as $R = \{(x_1, y_1), (x_1, y_2), (x_1, y_5), (x_2, y_1), (x_2, y_2), (x_2, y_3), (x_3, y_4), (x_3, y_5), (x_4, y_1), (x_4, y_2), (x_4, y_3), (x_5, y_4), (x_5, y_6)\}$. Therefore, the relational system $K = (U, V, R)$ is an approximation space. The above relation can be represented by its Boolean matrix as:

$$R = \begin{pmatrix} 1 & 1 & 0 & 0 & 1 & 0 \\ 1 & 1 & 1 & 0 & 0 & 0 \\ 0 & 0 & 0 & 1 & 1 & 0 \\ 1 & 1 & 1 & 0 & 0 & 0 \\ 0 & 0 & 0 & 1 & 0 & 1 \end{pmatrix}$$

From the above relation R we get, $r(x_1) = \{y_1, y_2, y_5\}$; $r(x_2) = \{y_1, y_2, y_3\}$; $r(x_3) = \{y_4, y_5\}$; $r(x_4) = \{y_1, y_2, y_3\}$; $r(x_5) = \{y_4, y_6\}$. Thus, $U / E_U = \{\{x_1\}, \{x_3\}, \{x_2, x_4\}, \{x_5\}\}$. Similarly, $V / E_V = \{\{y_1, y_2\}, \{y_3\}, \{y_4\}, \{y_5\}, \{y_6\}\}$. The sets Y_1, Y_2, Y_3, Y_4 are examples of different types of rough sets on two universal sets, where $Y_1 = \{y_1, y_2, y_5\}$, $Y_2 = \{y_1, y_2\}$, $Y_3 = \{y_1, y_2, y_4, y_5\}$ and $Y_4 = \{y_3, y_5, y_6\}$. The corresponding lower and upper approximations are given below:

$\underline{R}Y_1 = \{x_1\} \neq \phi$;	$\overline{R}Y_1 = \{x_1, x_2, x_3, x_4\} \neq U$	(Type 1)
$\underline{R}Y_2 = \phi$;	$\overline{R}Y_2 = \{x_1, x_2, x_4\} \neq U$	(Type 2)
$\underline{R}Y_3 = \{x_1, x_3\} \neq \phi$;	$\overline{R}Y_3 = \{x_1, x_2, x_3, x_4, x_5\} = U$	(Type 3)
$\underline{R}Y_4 = \phi$;	$\overline{R}Y_4 = \{x_1, x_2, x_3, x_4, x_5\} = U$	(Type 4)

4   Set Theoretic Operations on Types of Rough Set Based on Two Universal Sets

In this section, we discuss the set theoretic operations such as union and intersection on types of rough sets on two universal sets. We state the corresponding tables for union and intersection operations and provide proofs of ambiguity cases, wherever necessary in support of the results obtained.

4.1   Table of Union

In the case of union as shown in Table 1, out of sixteen cases as many as nine cases are unambiguous whereas seven cases consist of ambiguity. In one case it can be any one of the four types. These ambiguities are due to inclusion $\underline{R}X \cup \underline{R}Y \subseteq \underline{R}(X \cup Y)$ of equation 14. We denote the entry in i^{th} row and j^{th} column of the table by (i, j). In the following proof, we use equation 12 and 14 to deduce the different possible cases.

Table 1. Table of union

$\bigcup$	Type 1	Type 2	Type 3	Type 4
Type 1	Type 1 / Type 3	Type 1 / Type 3	Type 3	Type 3
Type 2	Type 1 / Type 3	Type 1 / Type 2 / Type 3 / Type 4	Type 3	Type 3 / Type 4
Type 3	Type 3	Type 3	Type 3	Type 3
Type 4	Type 3	Type 3 / Type 4	Type 3	Type 3 / Type 4

Proof of $(1, 1)$. Let us consider $Y_1 \subseteq V$ and $Y_2 \subseteq V$ both are of Type 1. Then

(i) $\underline{R}(Y_1 \cup Y_2) \neq \phi, \ \overline{R}(Y_1 \cup Y_2) \neq U$ or

(ii) $\underline{R}(Y_1 \cup Y_2) \neq \phi, \ \overline{R}(Y_1 \cup Y_2) = U$

Case (i) is of Type 1 whereas case (ii) is of Type 3.

Proof of $(1, 2)$. Let us consider $Y_1 \subseteq V$ be of Type 1 and $Y_2 \subseteq V$ be of Type 2. Then

(i) $\underline{R}(Y_1 \cup Y_2) \neq \phi, \ \overline{R}(Y_1 \cup Y_2) \neq U$ or

(ii) $\underline{R}(Y_1 \cup Y_2) \neq \phi, \ \overline{R}(Y_1 \cup Y_2) = U$

Case (i) is of Type 1 whereas case (ii) is of Type 3.

Proof of $(2, 2)$. Let us consider $Y_1 \subseteq V$ and $Y_2 \subseteq V$ both are of Type 2. Then

(i) $\underline{R}(Y_1 \cup Y_2) \neq \phi, \ \overline{R}(Y_1 \cup Y_2) \neq U$ or

(ii) $\underline{R}(Y_1 \cup Y_2) = \phi, \ \overline{R}(Y_1 \cup Y_2) \neq U$ or

(iii) $\underline{R}(Y_1 \cup Y_2) \neq \phi, \ \overline{R}(Y_1 \cup Y_2) = U$ or

(iv) $\underline{R}(Y_1 \cup Y_2) = \phi, \ \overline{R}(Y_1 \cup Y_2) = U$

Case (i) is of Type 1, case (ii) is of Type 2, case (iii) is of Type 3 whereas case (iv) is of Type 4.

Proof of (2, 4). Let us consider $Y_1 \subseteq V$ be of Type 2 and $Y_2 \subseteq V$ be of Type 4. Then

$$\underline{R}(Y_1 \cup Y_2) \supseteq \phi, \quad \overline{R}(Y_1 \cup Y_2) = U .$$

Hence, there exists two cases $i.e.,$ $\underline{R}(Y_1 \cup Y_2) = \phi, \quad \overline{R}(Y_1 \cup Y_2) = U$ and $\underline{R}(Y_1 \cup Y_2) \neq \phi, \quad \overline{R}(Y_1 \cup Y_2) = U$. Therefore, $(Y_1 \bigcup Y_2)$ is of Type 3 or Type 4.

Proof of $(4, 4)$. Let us consider $Y_1 \subseteq V$ and $Y_2 \subseteq V$ are of Type 4. Then

(i) $\underline{R}(Y_1 \cup Y_2) \neq \phi, \quad \overline{R}(Y_1 \cup Y_2) = U$ or

(ii) $\underline{R}(Y_1 \cup Y_2) = \phi, \quad \overline{R}(Y_1 \cup Y_2) = U$

Case (i) is of Type 3 whereas case (ii) is of Type 4.

4.2   Table of Intersection

It is interesting to see from the given Table 2 that, out of sixteen cases for intersection, seven cases are ambiguous whereas nine cases are unambiguous. Also it is observed that, in one case it can be any one of the four types. Now, we provide proof for the ambiguity cases. We denote the entry in i^{th} row and j^{th} column of the table by the notation (i, j). In the following proof, we use equation 12 and 14, to deduce the possible cases.

Table 2. Table of intersection

$\cap$	Type 1	Type 2	Type 3	Type 4
Type 1	Type 1 / Type 2	Type 2	Type 1 / Type 2	Type 2
Type 2	Type 2	Type 2	Type 2	Type 2
Type 3	Type 1 / Type 2	Type 2	Type 1 / Type 2/ Type 3 / Type 4	Type 2 / Type 4
Type 4	Type 2	Type 2	Type 2 / Type 4	Type 2 / Type 4

Proof of (1, 1). Let us consider $Y_1 \subseteq V$ and $Y_2 \subseteq V$ both are of Type 1. Then

(i) $\underline{R}(Y_1 \cap Y_2) = \phi, \quad \overline{R}(Y_1 \cap Y_2) \neq U$ or

(ii) $\underline{R}(Y_1 \cap Y_2) \neq \phi, \quad \overline{R}(Y_1 \cap Y_2) \neq U$

Case (i) is of Type 2 whereas case (ii) is of Type 1.

Proof of (1, 3). Let us consider $Y_1 \subseteq V$ be of Type 1 and $Y_2 \subseteq V$ be of Type 3. Then

(i) $\underline{R}(Y_1 \cap Y_2) = \phi, \quad \overline{R}(Y_1 \cap Y_2) \neq U$ or

(ii) $\underline{R}(Y_1 \cap Y_2) \neq \phi, \quad \overline{R}(Y_1 \cap Y_2) \neq U$

Case (i) is of Type 2 whereas case (ii) is of Type 1.

Proof of (3, 3). Let us consider $Y_1 \subseteq V$ be of Type 3 and $Y_2 \subseteq V$ be of Type 3. Then

(i) $\underline{R}(Y_1 \cap Y_2) \neq \phi, \quad \overline{R}(Y_1 \cap Y_2) \neq U$ or

(ii) $\underline{R}(Y_1 \cap Y_2) = \phi, \quad \overline{R}(Y_1 \cap Y_2) \neq U$ or

(iii) $\underline{R}(Y_1 \cap Y_2) \neq \phi, \quad \overline{R}(Y_1 \cap Y_2) = U$ or

(iv) $\underline{R}(Y_1 \cap Y_2) = \phi, \quad \overline{R}(Y_1 \cap Y_2) = U$

Case (i) is of Type 1, case (ii) is of Type 2, case (iii) is of Type 3 whereas case (iv) is of Type 4.

Proof of (3, 4). Let us consider $Y_1 \subseteq V$ be of Type 3 and $Y_2 \subseteq V$ be of Type 4. Then $\underline{R}(Y_1 \cap Y_2) = \phi, \quad \overline{R}(Y_1 \cap Y_2) \subseteq U$. Therefore, we get

(i) $\underline{R}(Y_1 \cap Y_2) = \phi, \quad \overline{R}(Y_1 \cap Y_2) = U$ or (ii) $\underline{R}(Y_1 \cap Y_2) = \phi, \quad \overline{R}(Y_1 \cap Y_2) \neq U$

So, $(Y_1 \cap Y_2)$ is of Type 4 or Type 2.

Proof of (4, 4). Let us consider $Y_1 \subseteq V$ and $Y_2 \subseteq V$ both are of Type 4. Then

(i) $\underline{R}(Y_1 \cap Y_2) = \phi, \quad \overline{R}(Y_1 \cap Y_2) = U$ or

(ii) $\underline{R}(Y_1 \cap Y_2) = \phi, \quad \overline{R}(Y_1 \cap Y_2) \neq U$

Case (i) gives us Type 4 whereas case (ii) gives us Type 2.

5   Rough Sets on Two Universal Sets and Knowledge Representation

In this section, we demonstrate how the above concepts can be applied to real life problems. We consider an example in which we study the relation between customers and the supermarkets in a particular metropolitan city. In general, supermarket takes care of customer's everyday household needs and more. Therefore, it spread across a wide range of products of food and non food items, ranging from basic necessities such as, fruits and vegetables, staples, personal care, home care, household care products, general merchandise, and dairy products. Hence it is a one stop solution for the customers to fulfill daily shopping needs at a convenient location close to the customer. Apart from this the best possible value for customer's money, quality of the product, style and the behaviour of supporting staff play a vital role in choosing a supermarket. However, there exist many other factors to choose a supermarket. For this reason, in general, customer has to depend on more than one supermarket in a city. Therefore, it is essential to establish the relation between the customers and the supermarkets in a city. To make our analysis simple and for clear understanding, we consider a small universe U of 10 customers and another small universe V of 7 supermarkets in a particular city. We define the relation R between U and V by the following Boolean matrix.

$$R = \begin{pmatrix} 1 & 1 & 0 & 0 & 1 & 1 & 0 & 1 & 1 & 0 \\ 1 & 1 & 1 & 0 & 0 & 1 & 1 & 1 & 0 & 0 \\ 0 & 0 & 0 & 1 & 0 & 0 & 1 & 0 & 0 & 1 \\ 1 & 1 & 1 & 0 & 0 & 1 & 1 & 1 & 0 & 0 \\ 1 & 0 & 0 & 1 & 1 & 0 & 1 & 1 & 1 & 1 \\ 1 & 1 & 0 & 0 & 1 & 1 & 0 & 1 & 1 & 0 \\ 1 & 1 & 1 & 0 & 0 & 0 & 1 & 1 & 0 & 0 \end{pmatrix}$$

Therefore, we get $r(x_1) = \{y_1, y_2, y_5, y_6, y_8, y_9\}$; $r(x_2) = \{y_1, y_2, y_3, y_6, y_7, y_8\}$; $r(x_3) = \{y_4, y_7, y_{10}\}$; $r(x_4) = \{y_1, y_2, y_3, y_6, y_7, y_8\}$; $r(x_5) = \{y_1, y_4, y_5, y_7, y_8, y_9, y_{10}\}$; $r(x_6) = \{y_1, y_2, y_5, y_6, y_8, y_9\}$; $r(x_7) = \{y_1, y_2, y_3, y_7, y_8\}$; $U / E_U = \{\{x_1, x_6\}, \{x_2, x_4\}, \{x_3\}, \{x_5\}, \{x_7\}\}$ and $V / E_V = \{\{y_1, y_8\}, \{y_2\}, \{y_3\}, \{y_4, y_{10}\}, \{y_5, y_9\}, \{y_6\}, \{y_7\}\}$.

5.1   Ambiguity Cases in Union

Here, we provide examples to show the ambiguous cases in the above Table 1 actually arise. We continue with the example stated above in section 5. This is as follows:

Example for (1, 1). Let $Y_1 = \{y_4, y_7, y_{10}\}$ and $Y_2 = \{y_3, y_4, y_7, y_{10}\}$. Therefore, we get $\underline{R}Y_1 = \underline{R}Y_2 = \{x_3\} \neq \phi$, and $\overline{R}Y_1 = \overline{R}Y_2 = \{x_2, x_3, x_4, x_5, x_7\} \neq U$. It implies that both Y_1 and Y_2 are of type 1. Now, $(Y_1 \cup Y_2) = \{y_3, y_4, y_7, y_{10}\}$ and thus $\underline{R}(Y_1 \cup Y_2) = \{x_3\} \neq \phi$, $\overline{R}(Y_1 \cup Y_2) = \{x_2, x_3, x_4, x_5, x_7\} \neq U$. It indicates that $(Y_1 \cup Y_2)$ is of type 1.

However, taking $Y_1 = \{y_1, y_2, y_5, y_6, y_8, y_9\}$, and $Y_2 = \{y_4, y_7, y_{10}\}$ we have $\underline{R}Y_1 = \{x_1, x_6\} \neq \phi$, $\overline{R}Y_1 = \{x_1, x_2, x_4, x_5, x_6, x_7\} \neq U$, $\underline{R}Y_2 = \{x_3\} \neq \phi$, and $\overline{R}Y_2 = \{x_2, x_3, x_4, x_5, x_7\} \neq U$. This specifies Y_1 and Y_2 is of type 1. Now, $\underline{R}(Y_1 \cup Y_2) = \{x_1, x_3, x_5, x_6\} \neq \phi$ and $\overline{R}(Y_1 \cup Y_2) = \{x_1, x_2, x_3, x_4, x_5, x_6, x_7\} = U$. Therefore, $(Y_1 \cup Y_2)$ is of type 3.

Example for (1, 2). Let $Y_1 = \{y_4, y_7, y_{10}\}$ and $Y_2 = \{y_3, y_4\}$. Therefore, we get $\underline{R}Y_1 = \{x_3\} \neq \phi$, $\underline{R}Y_2 = \phi$, and $\overline{R}Y_1 = \overline{R}Y_2 = \{x_2, x_3, x_4, x_5, x_7\} \neq U$. This depicts that Y_1 and Y_2 is of type 1 and type 2 respectively. Now, $\underline{R}(Y_1 \cup Y_2) = \{x_3\} \neq \phi$, and $\overline{R}(Y_1 \cup Y_2) = \{x_2, x_3, x_4, x_5, x_7\} \neq U$. It indicates that $(Y_1 \cup Y_2)$ is of type 1.

Similarly, on taking $Y_1 = \{y_1, y_2, y_3, y_5, y_6, y_8, y_9\}$, and $Y_2 = \{y_3, y_4, y_{10}\}$ we get $\underline{R}Y_1 = \{x_1, x_6\} \neq \phi$, $\overline{R}Y_1 = \{x_1, x_2, x_4, x_5, x_6, x_7\} \neq U$, $\underline{R}Y_2 = \phi$, and $\overline{R}Y_2 = \{x_2, x_3, x_4, x_5, x_7\} \neq U$. This states that Y_1 and Y_2 is of type 1 and type 2 respectively. Now, $\underline{R}(Y_1 \cup Y_2) = \{x_1, x_6\} \neq \phi$, and $\overline{R}(Y_1 \cup Y_2) = \{x_1, x_2, x_3, x_4, x_5, x_6, x_7\} = U$. Thus, $(Y_1 \cup Y_2)$ is of type 3.

Example for (2, 2). Let $Y_1 = \{y_3, y_4\}$ and $Y_2 = \{y_3, y_7, y_{10}\}$. Therefore, we get $\underline{R}Y_1 = \underline{R}Y_2 = \phi$, and $\overline{R}Y_1 = \overline{R}Y_2 = \{x_2, x_3, x_4, x_5, x_7\} \neq U$. This depicts that Y_1 and Y_2 both are of type 2. Now, $\underline{R}(Y_1 \cup Y_2) = \{x_3\} \neq \phi$, and $\overline{R}(Y_1 \cup Y_2) = \{x_2, x_3, x_4, x_5, x_7\} \neq U$. Therefore, $(Y_1 \cup Y_2)$ is of type 1.

Again on taking, $Y_1 = \{y_3, y_{10}\}$ and $Y_2 = \{y_3, y_4\}$ we get $\underline{R}Y_1 = \underline{R}Y_2 = \phi$, and $\overline{R}Y_1 = \overline{R}Y_2 = \{x_2, x_3, x_4, x_5, x_7\} \neq U$. This depicts that Y_1 and Y_2 both are of type 2. Now, $\underline{R}(Y_1 \cup Y_2) = \phi$, and $\overline{R}(Y_1 \cup Y_2) = \{x_2, x_3, x_4, x_5, x_7\} \neq U$. Thus, $(Y_1 \cup Y_2)$ is of type 2.

Again on taking $Y_1 = \{y_3, y_7, y_{10}\}$ and $Y_2 = \{y_4, y_5, y_6\}$ we get $\underline{R}Y_1 = \underline{R}Y_2 = \phi$, $\overline{R}Y_1 = \{x_2, x_3, x_4, x_5, x_7\} \neq U$, and $\overline{R}Y_2 = \{x_1, x_2, x_3, x_4, x_5, x_6\} \neq U$. It states that Y_1 and Y_2 both are of type 2. Now, $\underline{R}(Y_1 \cup Y_2) = \{x_3\} \neq \phi$, and $\overline{R}(Y_1 \cup Y_2) = \{x_1, x_2, x_3, x_4, x_5, x_6, x_7\} = U$. Thus, $(Y_1 \cup Y_2)$ is of type 3.

Further on taking $Y_1 = \{y_3, y_{10}\}$ and $Y_2 = \{y_5\}$ we have $\underline{R}Y_1 = \underline{R}Y_2 = \phi$, $\overline{R}Y_1 = \{x_2, x_3, x_4, x_5, x_7\} \neq U$, and $\overline{R}Y_2 = \{x_1, x_5, x_6\} \neq U$. This depicts that both Y_1 and Y_2 are of type 2. Now, $\underline{R}(Y_1 \cup Y_2) = \phi$, and $\overline{R}(Y_1 \cup Y_2) = \{x_1, x_2, x_3, x_4, x_5, x_6, x_7\} = U$. Thus, $(Y_1 \cup Y_2)$ is of type 4.

Example for (2, 4). Let $Y_1 = \{y_3, y_4, y_{10}\}$ and $Y_2 = \{y_3, y_5, y_7\}$. Therefore, $\underline{R}Y_1 = \underline{R}Y_2 = \phi$, $\overline{R}Y_1 = \{x_2, x_3, x_4, x_5, x_7\} \neq U$, and $\overline{R}Y_2 = U$. This specifies that Y_1 and Y_2 is of type 2 and type 4 respectively. Now, $\underline{R}(Y_1 \cup Y_2) = \{x_3\} \neq \phi$ and $\overline{R}(Y_1 \cup Y_2) = U$. Therefore, $(Y_1 \cup Y_2)$ is of type 3.

Further on taking $Y_1 = \{y_3, y_4\}$ and $Y_2 = \{y_3, y_5, y_{10}\}$ we get $\underline{R}Y_1 = \underline{R}Y_2 = \phi$, $\overline{R}Y_1 = \{x_2, x_3, x_4, x_5, x_7\} \neq U$, and $\overline{R}Y_2 = U$. It specifies that Y_1 and Y_2 is of type 2 and type 4 respectively. But, $\underline{R}(Y_1 \cup Y_2) = \phi$ and $\overline{R}(Y_1 \cup Y_2) = U$. It indicates that $(Y_1 \cup Y_2)$ is of type 4.

Example for (4, 4). Let $Y_1 = \{y_3, y_5, y_7\}$ and $Y_2 = \{y_2, y_4, y_{10}\}$. Therefore, $\underline{R}Y_1 = \underline{R}Y_2 = \phi$, $\overline{R}Y_1 = \{x_1, x_2, x_3, x_4, x_5, x_6, x_7\} = U$, and $\overline{R}Y_2 = U$. This specifies that Y_1 and Y_2 both are of type 4. Now, $\underline{R}(Y_1 \cup Y_2) = \{x_3\} \neq \phi$ and $\overline{R}(Y_1 \cup Y_2) = U$. Therefore, $(Y_1 \cup Y_2)$ is of type 3.

Further on taking $Y_1 = \{y_3, y_5, y_7\}$ and $Y_2 = \{y_2, y_{10}\}$ we get $\underline{R}Y_1 = \underline{R}Y_2 = \phi$, $\overline{R}Y_1 = U$, and $\overline{R}Y_2 = U$. It specifies that Y_1 and Y_2 both are of type 4 respectively. But, $\underline{R}(Y_1 \cup Y_2) = \phi$ and $\overline{R}(Y_1 \cup Y_2) = U$. It indicates that $(Y_1 \cup Y_2)$ is of type 4.

5.2   Ambiguity Cases in Intersection

Here, we provide examples to show the ambiguous cases in the above Table 2 actually arise. We continue with the example stated above in section 5. This is as follows:

Example for (1, 1). Let $Y_1 = \{y_3, y_4, y_7, y_{10}\}$ and $Y_2 = \{y_4, y_7, y_{10}\}$. Therefore, we get $\underline{R}Y_1 = \underline{R}Y_2 = \{x_3\} \neq \phi$, and $\overline{R}Y_1 = \overline{R}Y_2 = \{x_2, x_3, x_4, x_5, x_7\} \neq U$. It implies that both Y_1 and Y_2 are of type 1. Now, $(Y_1 \cap Y_2) = \{y_4, y_7, y_{10}\}$ and thus $\underline{R}(Y_1 \cap Y_2) = \{x_3\} \neq \phi$, $\overline{R}(Y_1 \cap Y_2) = \{x_2, x_3, x_4, x_5, x_7\} \neq U$. It indicates that $(Y_1 \cap Y_2)$ is of type 1.

However, taking $Y_1 = \{y_3, y_4, y_7, y_{10}\}$, and $Y_2 = \{y_1, y_2, y_3, y_5, y_6, y_8, y_9\}$ we have $\underline{R}Y_1 = \{x_3\} \neq \phi$, $\overline{R}Y_1 = \{x_2, x_3, x_4, x_5, x_7\} \neq U$, $\underline{R}Y_2 = \{x_1, x_6\} \neq \phi$, and $\overline{R}Y_2 = \{x_1, x_2, x_4, x_5, x_6, x_7\} \neq U$. It indicates that both Y_1 and Y_2 are of type 1. Now, $(Y_1 \cap Y_2) = \{y_3\}$ and hence $\underline{R}(Y_1 \cap Y_2) = \phi$ and $\overline{R}(Y_1 \cap Y_2) = \{x_2, x_4, x_7\} \neq U$. Therefore, $(Y_1 \cap Y_2)$ is of type 2.

Example for (1, 3). Let $Y_1 = \{y_3, y_4, y_7, y_{10}\}$ and $Y_2 = \{y_3, y_4, y_5, y_7, y_{10}\}$. Therefore, we get $\underline{R}Y_1 = \underline{R}Y_2 = \{x_3\} \neq \phi$, $\overline{R}Y_1 = \{x_2, x_3, x_4, x_5, x_7\} \neq U$, and $\overline{R}Y_2 = U$. This depicts that Y_1 and Y_2 is of type 1 and type 3 respectively. Now, $\underline{R}(Y_1 \cap Y_2) = \{x_3\} \neq \phi$, and $\overline{R}(Y_1 \cap Y_2) = \{x_2, x_3, x_4, x_5, x_7\} \neq U$. It indicates that $(Y_1 \cap Y_2)$ is of type 1.

Similarly, on taking $Y_1 = \{y_4, y_7, y_{10}\}$, and $Y_2 = \{y_1, y_2, y_3, y_4, y_7, y_8\}$ we get $\underline{R}Y_1 = \{x_3\} \neq \phi$, $\overline{R}Y_1 = \{x_2, x_3, x_4, x_5, x_7\} \neq U$, $\underline{R}Y_2 = \{x_7\} \neq \phi$, and $\overline{R}Y_2 = U$. This states that Y_1 and Y_2 is of type 1 and type 3 respectively. Now, $\underline{R}(Y_1 \cap Y_2) = \phi$, and $\overline{R}(Y_1 \cap Y_2) = \{x_2, x_3, x_4, x_5, x_7\} \neq U$. Thus, $(Y_1 \cup Y_2)$ is of type 2.

Example for (3, 3). On taking $Y_1 = \{y_1, y_2, y_3, y_4, y_6, y_7, y_8, y_{10}\}$ and $Y_2 = \{y_4, y_5, y_7, y_{10}\}$ we get $\underline{R}Y_1 = \{x_2, x_3, x_4, x_7\} \neq \phi$, $\underline{R}Y_2 = \{x_3\} \neq \phi$ and $\overline{R}Y_1 = \overline{R}Y_2 = U$. This states that Y_1 and Y_2 both are of type 3. Now, $\underline{R}(Y_1 \cap Y_2) = \{x_3\} \neq \phi$, and $\overline{R}(Y_1 \cap Y_2) = \{x_2, x_3, x_4, x_5, x_7\} \neq U$. Therefore, $(Y_1 \cap Y_2)$ is of type 1.

Again on taking $Y_1 = \{y_1, y_2, y_3, y_7, y_8\}$ and $Y_2 = \{y_3, y_4, y_5, y_7, y_{10}\}$ we get $\underline{R}Y_1 = \{x_7\} \neq \phi$, $\underline{R}Y_2 = \{x_3\} \neq \phi$, and $\overline{R}Y_1 = \overline{R}Y_2 = U$. It states that Y_1 and Y_2 both are of type 3. Now, $\underline{R}(Y_1 \cap Y_2) = \phi$, and $\overline{R}(Y_1 \cap Y_2) = \{x_2, x_3, x_4, x_5, x_7\} \neq U$. Hence, $(Y_1 \cap Y_2)$ is of type 2.

Again on taking $Y_1 = \{y_2, y_4, y_7, y_{10}\}$ and $Y_2 = \{y_2, y_4, y_6, y_7, y_{10}\}$ we have $\underline{R}Y_1 = \underline{R}Y_2 = \{x_3\} \neq \phi$, and $\overline{R}Y_1 = \overline{R}Y_2 = U$. It depicts that both Y_1 and Y_2 are of type 3. Now, $\underline{R}(Y_1 \cap Y_2) = \{x_3\} \neq \phi$, and $\overline{R}(Y_1 \cap Y_2) = U$. Thus, $(Y_1 \cup Y_2)$ is of type 3.

Further on taking $Y_1 = \{y_4, y_7, y_8, y_{10}\}$ and $Y_2 = \{y_1, y_2, y_3, y_4, y_7, y_8\}$. Therefore, we get $\underline{R}Y_1 = \{x_3\} \neq \phi$, $\underline{R}Y_2 = \{x_7\} \neq \phi$ and $\overline{R}Y_1 = \overline{R}Y_2 = U$. This depicts that Y_1 and Y_2 both are of type 3. Now, $\underline{R}(Y_1 \cap Y_2) = \phi$, and $\overline{R}(Y_1 \cap Y_2) = U$. Thus, $(Y_1 \cap Y_2)$ is of type 4.

Example for (3, 4). On taking $Y_1 = \{y_1, y_2, y_3, y_7, y_8\}$ and $Y_2 = \{y_3, y_5, y_7\}$ we get $\underline{R}Y_1 = \{x_7\} \neq \phi$, $\underline{R}Y_2 = \phi$, $\overline{R}Y_1 = U$ and $\overline{R}Y_2 = U$. This specifies that Y_1 and Y_2 is of type 3 and type 4 respectively. Now, $\underline{R}(Y_1 \cap Y_2) = \phi$ and $\overline{R}(Y_1 \cap Y_2) = \{x_2, x_3, x_4, x_5, x_7\} \neq U$. Therefore, $(Y_1 \cap Y_2)$ is of type 2.

Further on taking $Y_1 = \{y_1, y_2, y_3, y_7, y_8\}$ and $Y_2 = \{y_2, y_4, y_7\}$ we get $\underline{R}Y_1 = \{x_7\} \neq \phi$, $\underline{R}Y_2 = \phi$, $\overline{R}Y_1 = U$ and $\overline{R}Y_2 = U$. It specifies that Y_1 and Y_2 is of type 3 and type 4 respectively. But, $\underline{R}(Y_1 \cap Y_2) = \phi$ and $\overline{R}(Y_1 \cap Y_2) = U$. It indicates that $(Y_1 \cap Y_2)$ is of type 4.

Example for (4, 4). On taking $Y_1 = \{y_2, y_4, y_5\}$ and $Y_2 = \{y_1, y_4, y_5\}$ we get $\underline{R}Y_1 = \underline{R}Y_2 = \phi$, $\overline{R}Y_1 = U$ and $\overline{R}Y_2 = U$. This specifies that Y_1 and Y_2 both are of type 4. Now, $\underline{R}(Y_1 \cap Y_2) = \phi$ and $\overline{R}(Y_1 \cap Y_2) = \{x_1, x_3, x_5, x_6\} \neq U$. Therefore, $(Y_1 \cap Y_2)$ is of type 2.

Further on taking $Y_1 = \{y_1, y_2, y_4\}$ and $Y_2 = \{y_2, y_4\}$ we get $\underline{R}Y_1 = \underline{R}Y_2 = \phi$ and $\overline{R}Y_1 = \overline{R}Y_2 = U$. It specifies that both Y_1 and Y_2 are of type 4. But, $\underline{R}(Y_1 \cap Y_2) = \phi$ and $\overline{R}(Y_1 \cap Y_2) = U$. It indicates that $(Y_1 \cap Y_2)$ is of type 4.

6   Conclusion

In this paper we extended the study of rough sets on two universal sets further by defining their topological characterization and establishing results on intersection or union of any two elements of any topological characterization. We have also provided a real life example to verify the ambiguity cases raised due to union and intersection. These results are important for their application in knowledge extraction and design of knowledge bases.

References

1. Acharjya, D.P., Ezhilarasi, L.: A Knowledge Mining Model for Ranking Institutions using Rough Computing with Ordering Rules and Formal Concept Analysis. International Journal of Computer Science Issues 8(2), 417–425 (2011)
2. Acharjya, D.P., Tripathy, B.K.: Rough Sets on Fuzzy Approximation Space and Application to Distributed Knowledge Systems. International Journal of Artificial Intelligence and Soft Computing 1(1), 1–14 (2008)

3. Acharjya, D.P., Tripathy, B.K.: Rough Sets on Intuitionistic Fuzzy Approximation Spaces and Knowledge Representation. International Journal of Artificial Intelligence and Computational Research 1(1), 29–36 (2009)
4. Bonikowski, Z.: Algebraic structure of rough sets. In: Ziarko, W.P. (ed.) Rough Sets, Fuzzy sets and Knowledge Discovery, pp. 242–247. Springer, London (1994)
5. Chen, D., Zhang, W., Yeung, D., Tsang, E.C.C.: Rough approximations on a complete completely distributive lattice with applications to generalized rough sets. Information Sciences 176, 1829–1848 (2006)
6. Dubois, D., Prade, H.: Rough fuzzy sets and fuzzy rough sets. International Journal of General System 17, 191–208 (1990)
7. Kondo, M.: Algebraic Approach to Generalized Rough Sets. In: Ślęzak, D., Wang, G., Szczuka, M.S., Düntsch, I., Yao, Y. (eds.) RSFDGrC 2005. LNCS (LNAI), vol. 3641, pp. 132–140. Springer, Heidelberg (2005)
8. Kondo, M.: On the structure of generalized rough sets. Information Sciences 176, 589–600 (2006)
9. Kryszkiewlcz, M.: Rough set approach to incomplete information systems. Information Sciences 112, 39–49 (1998)
10. Lin, T.Y.: Granular Computing on Binary Relations I: Data Mining and Neighborhood Systems. In: Skoworn, A., Polkowski, L. (eds.) Rough Sets In Knowledge Discovery, pp. 107–121. Springer, Heidelberg (1998)
11. Lin, T.Y.: Granular Computing: Examples, Intuitions and Modeling. In: Proceeding of the IEEE International Conference on Granular Computing, Beijing, China, pp. 40–44 (2005)
12. Lin, T.Y.: Neighborhood systems and approximation in database and knowledge base systems. In: Proceedings of the Fourth International Symposium on Methodologies of Intelligent Systems, pp. 75–86 (1989)
13. Liu, G.L.: Generalized rough sets over fuzzy lattices. Information Sciences 178, 1651–1662 (2008)
14. Liu, G.: Rough set theory based on two universal sets and its applications. Knowledge Based Systems 23, 110–115 (2010)
15. Liu, G.L.: Rough Sets over the Boolean Algebras. In: Ślęzak, D., Wang, G., Szczuka, M.S., Düntsch, I., Yao, Y. (eds.) RSFDGrC 2005. LNCS (LNAI), vol. 3641, pp. 124–131. Springer, Heidelberg (2005)
16. Maji, P.K., Roy, A.R.: An Application of Soft Sets in A Decision Making Problem. Computers and Mathematics with Applications 44, 1077–1083 (2002)
17. Molodtsov, D.: Soft Set Theory-First Results. Computers and Mathematics with Applications 37, 19–31 (1999)
18. Pawlak, Z., Skowron, A.: Rough sets and boolean reasoning. Information Sciences 177(1), 41–73 (2007)
19. Pawlak, Z., Skowron, A.: Rough sets: some extensions. Information Sciences 177(1), 28–40 (2007)
20. Pawlak, Z.: Decision rules and flow networks. European Journal of Operational Research 154(1), 184–190 (2004)
21. Pawlak, Z.: Rough Sets. International Journal of Computer Information Science 11, 341–356 (1982)
22. Pawlak, Z.: Rough Sets: Theoretical Aspects of Reasoning about Data. Kluwer Academic Publishers (1991)
23. Tripathy, B.K., Acharjya, D.P.: Association Rule Granulation using Rough Sets on Intuitionistic Fuzzy Approximation Spaces and Granular Computing. Annals. Computer Science Series, 9th Tome, 1st Fasc, pp. 125–144 (2011)

24. Tripathy, B.K., Acharjya, D.P.: Knowledge Mining using Ordering Rules and Rough Sets on Fuzzy Approximation Spaces. International Journal of Advances in Science and Technology 1(3), 41–50 (2010)
25. Tripathy, B.K.: Rough Sets on Intuitionistic Fuzzy Approximation Spaces. In: Proceedings of 3rd International IEEE Conference on Intelligent Systems (IS 2006), London, September 4-6, pp. 776–779 (2006)
26. Wong, S.K.M., Wang, L.S., Yao, Y.Y.: Interval structure: a framework for representing uncertain information. In: Proceedings of the 8th Conference on Uncertainty in Artificial Intelligence, pp. 336–343 (1993)
27. Yao, Y.Y.: Constructive and algebraic methods of the theory of rough sets. Information Sciences 109, 21–47 (1998)
28. Yao, Y.Y.: Two views of the theory of rough sets in finite universes. International Journal of Approximation Reasoning 15, 291–317 (1996)
29. Zadeh, L.A.: Fuzzy sets. Information and Control 8, 338–353 (1965)
30. Zhong, N., Skowron, A.: A Rough Set-Based Knowledge Discovery Process. International Journal of Applied Mathematics Computer Science 11(3), 603–619 (2001)
31. Zhu, W., Wang, F.Y.: On three types of covering rough sets. IEEE Transactions on Knowledge and Data Engineering 19(8), 1131–1144 (2007)
32. Zhu, W.: Generalized rough sets based on relations. Information Sciences 177(22), 4997–5011 (2007)
33. Zhu, W.: Properties of the First Type of Covering Based Rough Sets. In: Proceedings of the Sixth IEEE International Conference on Data Mining (IEEE Xplore), pp. 407–411 (2006)
34. Zhu, W.: Properties of the Fourth Type of Covering Based Rough Sets. In: Proceedings of the Sixth International Conference on Hybrid Intelligent Systems (IEEE Xplore), p. 43 (2006)
35. Zhu, W.: Properties of the Second Type of Covering Based Rough Sets. In: Proceedings of the International Conference on Web Intelligence and Intelligent Agent Technology (IEEE Xplore), pp. 494–497 (2006)

A Novice Approach for Lossless Visible Watermarking Approach by Pioneering the Best Block (LVW-PBB)

R. Sinduja, I. Rachel Rupala, and R.D. Sathiya

School of Computing, SASTRA University, Thanjavur
{sinduja99,rchlrubi}@gmail.com,
sathya@it.sastra.edu

Abstract. Watermarking techniques have been proposed to solve the problem of copyright protection and authentication. Using the idea from [1] in this paper [LVW-PBB], the best block for embedding the watermark is identified, that is based on similarity between DCT coefficients of original image and the watermark image. The embedding method is based on [2] which use the deterministic one-to-one compound mappings of image pixel values. The compound mappings are proved to be reversible, which allows for lossless recovery of original images from watermarked images. Different types of visible watermarks, including opaque monochrome and translucent color ones, are embedded by using the proposed approach. For Security protection, parameter and mapping randomizations have also been proposed. In case of various attacks such as JPEG compression, filtering, cropping, and additive Noise, the quality of cover image is acceptable even after the watermark extraction. Thus the proposed method is robust.

Keywords: Lossless Visible Watermarking by Pioneering the Best Block (LVW-PBB), Discrete Cosine Transform (DCT), Mapping Randomization, Parameter Randomization.

1 Introduction

Copyright protection of intellectual properties has, therefore, become an important topic. Therefore *Watermarking* is a best technique to avoid the copyright. *Digital watermarking* [3]–[7], which means embedding of certain specific information about the copyright holder (company logos, ownership descriptions, etc.) into the media to be protected.

The watermarking approaches are classified by several manners. For example, there are three types they are non-blind, semi blind, blind[1].

Digital Watermarking methods are classified into two groups. The watermarking can be done in a spatial [3, 4] or transform domain [5,6,7].Both the approaches has some conflicts regarding to robustness, transparency and security. Therefore, finding a proper place (block) to embed the watermark is very important.

P.V. Krishna, M.R. Babu, and E. Ariwa (Eds.): ObCom 2011, Part II, CCIS 270, pp. 82–91, 2012.
© Springer-Verlag Berlin Heidelberg 2012

Cox in [9] advises that the watermark should be embedded in the low frequency coefficients in the DCT domain to ensure the robustness. Bami and Hsu [10, 11] recommend that the watermark should be embedded in the middle frequency coefficients to reduce the distortion. But Huang in [12] points out that the DC coefficient is more proper to be used for watermark embedding. In [13] the proposed DCT IDWT methods embed a binary visual watermark by modulating the middle-frequency components. These two methods are robust to common image attacks; but geometric attacks are still challenges

Digital watermarking methods for images are usually categorized into two types: *invisible* and *visible*. *Invisible* means the image that is embedded cannot be viewed by human perception and *visible* means the image embedded can be viewed by human perception. A group of techniques, named *reversible* watermarking [15]–[19], allow legitimate users to remove the embedded watermark and restore the original content as needed. In [18],[19] two different watermarking approaches have been proposed. But disadvantage of these methods is ,they are more complex approach.

The Watermarking technique should be a reversing technique. *Lossless image recovery*, which means that the recovered image is identical to the original, pixel by pixel.

In [19],[20],[21] a common approach for monochrome watermarking is introduced. In [21] the disadvantage is that it can embed only binary image as watermark.

To overcome this problem in this LVW-PBB a new method is proposed for embedding different types of visible watermarks into cover image by using one to one compound mapping. The mappings are proved to be *reversible* for lossless recovery of the original image. Both opaque monochrome watermarks and no uniformly translucent full-color ones can be embedded into color images.

Based on these ideas, the proposed method consists of following two major parts.

1 Best Block Extraction
In this method by using[1] , DCT is applied to original image and watermark image for finding the best matching block of original image , based on the similarity between one block of watermark and all blocks of original image. Indices of the best match blocks are stored as secret key.

2 One to One Compound Mapping
LVW-PBB is a reversible mapping technique [2]. The pixel values are chosen and they are replaced by the new pixel values by using the mod functions. After embedding the watermark image the original image is got back by using the reverse mapping.

2   Proposed Approach

2.1   Finding the Best Block

In the LVW-PBB as [1] the original image and the watermark image is represented as I and W respectively with the size MxN and LxK.

2.1.1 Procedure to Find the Best Block for Watermark Insertion

The original image and watermark images are divided into 8x8 and 4x4 blocks respectively. Then DCT is applied to the blocks.

Then for each (L/4xK/4) blocks of watermark image, all the (M/8xN/8) blocks of original image is evaluated to find the best block in the original image, and corresponding block number is taken as the secret key. To evaluate each block of watermark image with the original image, the first sixteen DCT coefficients of the original image and all the DCT coefficients of the watermark image is subtracted. The first sixteen coefficients of the original image are got through the zig-zag transformation. Figure 1 represents the zig- zag transformation.

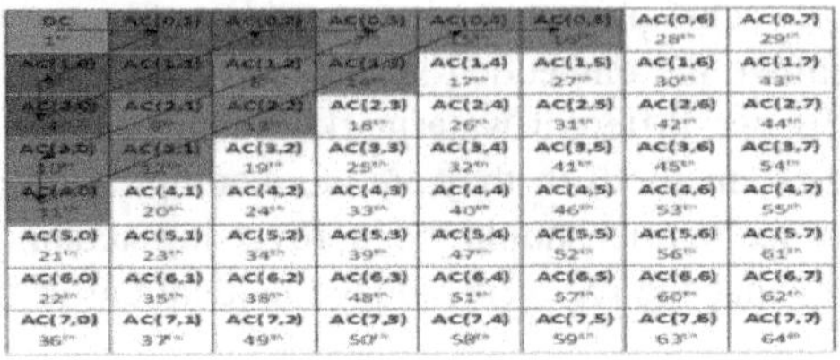

Fig. 1.

Algorithm 1(Best Block for watermark insertion and key generation)
Input: watermark image W and original image I
Output: Best Block and public key.

Step1: The original and the watermark image are divided into 8X8 and 4X4 non-overlapping blocks respectively. Then DCT is applied to each block and DCT coefficients are obtained.

Step2: For each block of watermark image process all the blocks in the original image find the best block in the original image for watermark insertion. The best block is obtained by using the following relation:

$$T_{i,j} = \alpha_1 \times (|DC_1 - DC_w| \ )^3 + \sum_{x=2}^{6} \alpha_x \times (DCT_{1,x} - DCT_{w,x})^2 + \sum_{x=7}^{16} \alpha_x \times (|DCT_{1,x} - DCT_{w,x}|)$$

$$\alpha_x = \begin{cases} Coefficient\ for\ DC\ value, & if\ x = 1; \\ Coefficient\ for\ AC(0,1)value, if x = 2; \\ Coefficient\ for\ AC(1,0)value, if\ x = 3; \\ Coefficient\ for\ AC(2,0)value, if\ x = 4; \\ Coefficient\ for\ AC(1,1)value, if\ x = 5; \end{cases}$$

$$best - block = \min\{T_{i,j}\}, 1 \leq i \leq \frac{M}{8,1} \leq j \leq \frac{N}{8}$$

Were $DCT_{1,\ x}$ and $DCT_{w,\ x}$ are the DCT coefficients of element in (i, j) block of the original and watermark image respectively.

Step3: Generate the secret key with the size of (L/4 X K/4) bytes from block numbers with corresponds the best block value for each watermark block. The owner marks the secret key using the digital signature methods and given to Secret certification authority (CA). Then CA timestamp the key by using the time and the date it is received and returns as a public key. This will protect the secret key from attacks and modification[23].With the public key value the watermark is embedded into the original image and the watermarked image is called as the test image (Γ).

2.2   Proposed Approach for Watermarking

Watermark Insertion is done by using One-to-one compound mapping of pixels values[2].

2.2.1   Properties of Compound Mapping

Compound mapping means it coverts a set of values into another set of values. Example P= {p1, p2.....pm} if mapping is done on these values then it will be converted into another set of values Q= {q1, q2........qm} and the values are reversible. p_i and q_i deals with image pixels values. Mapping is denoted by a function F_x and x=a or b. They are expressed in the following way(1). The (1) is reversible.

$$q = f(p) = F_b^{-1}(F_a(p)) \quad (1) \qquad p = f^{-1}(q) = F_a^{-1}(F_b(q)) \qquad (2)$$

Where $F^{-1}{}_x$ is the inverse of F_x, according to compound mapping. It means that $F_a(p)=p'$ and $F^{-1}{}_a(p')=p$ for all values of a and p. $F_a(p)$ and $F_b(p)$ will give produce different set of values and unequal. Equation (1) is reversible and it proved by the following:

Lemma 1 (Proof for reversible compound mapping) :
    If q=$F^{-1}{}_b(F_a(p))$ for any one to one function F_x with a parameter x, then p=$F^{-1}{}_a(F^{-1}{}_b(q))$ for any values of a,b,p and q.(proved in [2])

2.2.2   Watermarking Approach

It is possible to use the compound mapping $q = F_b^{-1}(F_a(p))$ to convert a numerical value p to another value close to a prefferred value l.(proved from lemma2 in[2]).
    With this simple compound mapping, p->q.This makes the extraction process easy.

Theorem 1. (Lossless Reversible Visible Watermarking) There exist one-to-one compound mapping for use to embed into given image I a visible watermark Q whose pixel values are close to those of a given watermark L, such that the original image I can be recovered from Q lossley.(proved in [2])
    The above ideas are valid for embedding a watermark in a gray scale image, but if both the watermark and the cover image is color then mapping should be applied for each and every color channel to get multiple independent results.

2.2.3   Watermark Insertion

Using Therom1 [2] the algorithm for watermark embedding is proposed and given in algorithm 2.

Algorithm 2:Generic Visible Watermark Embedding
Input: An image I and a watermark L.
Output: watermarked image W.
Steps:

1)Select a set P of pixels from I where L is to be embedded,and call P a watermarking area.

2)Denote the set of pixels corresponding to P in W by Q.

3)For each pixel X with value p in P,denote the corresponding pixel in Q as Z and the value of corresponding pixel Y in L as l,and conduct the following steps.

(a) Apply an estimation technique to derive a to be a value close to p,using the values of the neighboring pixels of X(excluding X itself). (b)Set b to be the value l (c) Map p to be a new value $q=F_b^{-1}(F_a(p))$.(d)Set the value of Z to be q.

4)Set the value of each remaining pixel in W, which is outside the region P,to be equal to that of the corresponding pixel in I.

2.2.4   Watermarking Extraction

Thus the watermark is embedded successfully and the extraction on that watermark is achieved by using reverse compound mapping[2].Algorithm 3 is used for extraction.

Algorithm 3:Generic Watermark Removal for Lossless Image Recovery
Input:a watermarked image W and a watermark L.
Output:the original image R recovered from W.
Steps:

1) Select the same watermarking area Q in W as that selected in Algorithm 1.

2) Set the value of each pixel in R, which is outside the region Q,to be equal to that of the corresponding pixel in W.

3) For each pixel Z with values q in Q, denote corresponding pixel in the recovered image R as X and the value of the corresponding pixel Y in L as l,and conduct the following steps.

(a)Obtain the same value a as that derived in Step 3a of Algorithm 1 by applying the same estimation technique used there. (b)Set b to be the value l. (c)Restore p form q by setting $p=F_a^{-1}(F_b(q))$.(d)Set the value of X to be p.

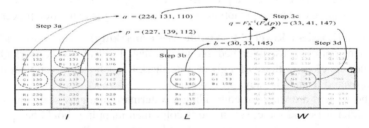

Fig. 2. Illustration of mapping the center pixel of a 3 X 3 image using Algorithm 1. Only the mapping of the center pixel is shown for clarity; the east and south pixels are depicted as TBD (to be determined) in W.

2.3   Security Aspect

In watermarking technique only the user owner should know how the insertion is done to protect from attackers. In the proposed method by using[2] there are two ways in which security is given. They are parameter randomization and mapping randomization. [2]. All these are a general idea for a new lossless watermarking approach. Now this approach is applicable for a opaque monochrome watermark and translucent watermark.

3   Procedure for Opaque Monochrome Watermark and Translucent Color Watermark

3.1   Approach for Opaque Monochrome Watermark

It describes how to embed a lossless-removable opaque monochrome watermark L into a color image I, using[2]. We represent the pixel in I which corresponds to black and white in L as P and P'. W in watermarked image as Q and Q'. The mapping is done by using F_a (p)=p-a. Also we apply modulo 256 in order to make the pixel values to fall into the range. Here a=p-$\sum$ and b=l+a+128. So with the mapping q=F^{-1}_b (F_a (p)) = b+$\sum$=a+128+$\sum$, means that the pixel values of Q are also distinctive with respect to those of the surrounding pixels in Q' as desired. P' and Q'are same.

Fig. 3. Illustration of pixels in watermark a)monochrome ,(b,c) area of P and P'(yellow)

To demonstrate the effectiveness of the proposed method, in one of our experiments we embedded the watermark of Fig. 2(a) into the images Lena and Sailboat, respectively, and the results are shown in Fig. 3 . The images recovered by using correct keys for the parameter and mapping randomization processes are shown in Fig. 3(c) and (g), and those recovered with incorrect keys are shown in Fig. 3(d) and (h). When the key was incorrect, the inserted watermark cannot be removed cleanly, with noise remaining in the watermarking area. Fig. 3. Experimental results of monochrome watermark embedding and removal. (a) Image Lena. (e) Image Sailboat. (b), (f) Watermarked images of (a) and (e), respectively. (c), (g) Images lossless recovered from (b) and (f), respectively, with correct keys. (d), (h) Images recovered from (b) and (f) with incorrect key. Thus a procedure for opaque monochrome watermark is discussed.

3.2   Approach for Translucent Color Watermark

Here we describe how to embed the translucent color watermark into an image. Translucent color means arbitrary RGB image with each pixel value is having an alpha component value. This value defines the opacity. Range of the alpha value is 0(transparent) to 255(opaque).

Fig. 4. Watermarked image of Lena with a translucent image of "Globe" superimpose using alpha blending

In this a process called Alpha Blending is used. Example showed in figure 4.
Algorithm for embedding a translucent color watermark is given below.

Algorithm 4 : Watermark Embedding of a Translucent Color Watermark
Input : an image I and a translucent Watermark L.
Output : a Watermarked image W.
Steps:

1)Select the watermark area P in I to be the set of pixels corresponding spatially to those in L which are nontransparent (with alpha values larger than zero).
2)Denote the set of pixel corresponding to P in W as Q.
3)For each pixel X with values p in P, denote the corresponding pixel in Q as Z and the values of the corresponding pixel Y in L   as l ,and conduct the following steps:
(a) Set the parameter α to be a neighbor-based color estimate value that is close to p by using the colors of the neighboring pixels of X that have already been processed
(b) Perform alpha blending with l over α to get the parameter b according to the formula $b = l \times \alpha + a(255 - \alpha)$ where α is the opacity of Y. (c)Map p to a new value $q = F_b^{-1}(F_a(p))$, (d)Set the Values of Z to be q
4)Set the values of each remaining pixels in W, which is outside the region P, to be equal to that of corresponding pixel in I.

4   Experimental Results

The LVW-PBB for finding the Best block for embedding is very robust. Based on experiments on different images, the values of a_x coefficients were selected as follows:

$$\alpha_x = \begin{cases} 5.6, & \text{if } x = 1; \\ 2.8, & \text{if } x = 2,3; \\ 1.3, & \text{if } x = 4,5,6; \\ 0.6, & \text{if } x = 7,8,9,10; \\ 0.2, & \text{if } x = 11,12,13; \\ 0.06, & \text{if } x = 14,15; \\ 0.03, & \text{if } x = 16; \end{cases}$$

The proposed method is implemented using JAVA. To measure the quantitatively we use some performance metrics. They are PSNR ratio. The quality of a watermarked image W is measured by the peak signal to noise ratio (PSNR) of W with respect to the no recoverable watermarked image B in the following way:

$$PSNR_W = 20 \times \log_{10}\left(\frac{255}{\sqrt{\frac{1}{m \times h} \sum_{y=1}^{h} \sum_{x=1}^{w} (w(x,y) - B(x,y)^2)}}\right)$$

Also, the quality of a image recovered image R is measured by sthe PSNR of R with respect to the original image in a similar way

$$PSNR_R = 20Xlog_{10}\left(\frac{255}{\sqrt{\frac{1}{w \times h}\sum_{y=1}^{b}\sum_{x=1}^{w}[R(x,y) - I(x,y)]^2}}\right)$$

It is desired to have the value of the PSNRw to be as high as possible, so that the watermarked image can be visually as close to the benchmark image as possible. For illicit recoveries, the $PSNR_w$ should be as low as possible to make the recovered image visually intolerable (e.g., very noisy). In particular, we want the region obscured by the watermark to be as noisy as possible in an illicitly recovered image. For this purpose, we introduce an additional quality metric for an illicitly recovered image that only takes into account the region Q recovered by the watermark. Specifically, we measure the quality of the recovered image by the following PSNR measure

$$PSNR_Q = 20Xlog_{10}\left(\frac{255}{\sqrt{\frac{1}{Q}\sum_{y=1}^{b}\sum_{x=1}^{w}SE_Q(x,y)}}\right)$$

5   Comparison

In all existing method for watermarking, only the embedding procedure will be stated, and no information about the location for insertion will be given. But the location for embedding is a major issue. Because while embedding the watermark should not hide the original information. So the location plays a major role. Thus in the proposed method, at first it will find the best block for embedding and in that block the watermark is embedded using a simple mapping technique. The proposed method is compared with the other four recently published techniques. Comparison is shown in

Table 1.

Method	Legitimate Recovery	Illegitimate Recovery	Watermark size	Binary Transparent Watermark	Binary Opaque Watermark	Color Translucent Watermark
Hu[24]	43-44dB	37-39dB	Unlimited	Yes	-	-
Hu[16]	Lossless	Not Reported	Limited	Yes	-	-
Tsai[20]	Lossless	Not Reported	Limited	Yes	-	-
Yip[21]	Lossless	Not Reported	Unlimited	Yes	Yes	-
Proposed	Lossless	12-14dB	Unlimited	Yes	Yes	Yes

table1. More importantly, the proposed approach allows embedding of arbitrary- sized watermark and has wider applicability than all four methods.

6   Conclusion

Thus in this LVW-PBB paper at first, the best block for watermark embedding is found based on the similarity of the DCT coefficients. Then a new method for reversible lossless visible watermarking is proposed. Watermarking is done by using a simple one to one compound mapping .With this method any arbitrary size of image can be embedded and different types of images can be inserted. The procedure for embedding a opaque monochrome watermark and translucent full color image watermark is also stated. The method also provides security by using parameter and mapping randomization, which prevent illicit recoveries of original image without correct input keys. Thus the experimental results show that the proposed method has low computational complexity and an effective security protection measures.

References

[1] Rahmani, R., Mortezaei, R., Moghaddam, M.E.: A New Lossless Watermarking Scheme Based on DCT Coefficients. Electrical and Computer Engineering Department. Shahid Beheshti University,G.C Tehran, Iran
[2] Liu, T.-Y., Tsai, W.-H.: Generic Lossless Visible Watermarking—A New Approach. IEEE Transactions on Image Processing 19(5) (May 2010)
[3] Martin, V., Chabert, M., Lacaze, B.: An interpolation-based watermarking scheme. Signal Processing 88(3), 539–557 (2008)
[4] Bender, W., Gruhl, D., Morimoto, N., Lu, A.: Techniques for data hiding. IBM Systems Journal 35(3), 313–336 (1996)
[5] Saxena, V., Gupta, J.P.: A Novel Watermarking Scheme for JPEG Images. WSEAS Transactions on Signal Processing 5(2), 74–84 (2009)
[6] Kang, X., Zeng, W., Huang, J.: A Multi-band Wavelet Watermarking Scheme. International Journal of Network Security 6(2), 121–126 (2008)
[7] Wang, X.Y., Hou, L.M., Wu, J.: A feature-based robust digital image watermarking against geometric attacks. Image and Vision Computing 26(7), 980–989 (2008)
[8] Lee, Z., Lin, S.W., Su, S.F., Lin, C.Y.: A hybrid watermarking technique applied to digital images. Applied Soft Computing 8, 798–808 (2008)
[9] Cox, I.J., Kilian, J., Leighton, T., Shamoon, T.: Secure spread spectrum watermarking for multimedia. IEEE Transaction 12(6), 1673–1687 (1997)
[10] Lu, C.S., Liao, H.Y.M., Huang, S.K., Sze, C.: Cocktail watermarking on images. In: Proceedings of the 3rd International Workshop on Information Hiding, pp. 333–347 (1999)
[11] Hsu, C.T., Wu, J.L.: Hidden Signature in Images. IEEE Transaction on Image Processing 8(I), 58–68 (1999)
[12] Wu, H.J., Shi, Y.Q., Dong, C.W.: Image Watermarking in DCT: an Embedding Strategy and algorithm. Acta Electronica Sinica 28(4), 57–60 (2000)
[13] Hsu, C.T., Wu, J.L.: Hidden Digital Watermarks in Images. IEEE Transactions on Image Processing 8(I), 58–68 (1999)

[14] Cheng, Y.J., Tsai, W.H.: A new method for copyright and integrity protection for bitmap images by removable visible watermarks and irremovable invisible watermarks. Presented at the Int. Computer Symp.—Workshop on Cryptology and Information Security, Hualien, Taiwan, R.O.C (December 2002)

[15] Huang, P.M., Tsai, W.H.: Copyright protection and authentication of grayscale images by removable visible watermarking and invisible signal embedding techniques: A new approach. Presented at the Conf. Computer Vision, Graphics and Image Processing, Kinmen, Taiwan, R.O.C (August 2003)

[16] Hu, Y., Jeon, B.: Reversible visible watermarking and lossless recovery of original images. IEEE Trans. Circuits Syst. Video Technol. 16(11), 1423–1429 (2006)

[17] Awrangjeb, M., Kankanhalli, M.S.: Reversible watermarking using a perceptual model. J. Electron. Imag. 14(013014) (March 2005)

[18] Tian, J.: Reversible data embedding using a difference expansion. IEEE Trans. Circuits Syst. Video Technol. 13(8), 890–896 (2003)

[19] Mohanty, S.P., Ramakrishnan, K.R., Kankanhalli, M.S.: A DCT domain visible watermarking technique for images. In: Proc. IEEE Int. Conf. Multimedia and Expo., vol. 2, pp. 1029–1032 (July 2000)

[20] Tsai, H.M., Chang, L.W.: A high secure reversible visible watermarking scheme. In: Proc. IEEE Int. Conf. Multimedia and Expo., Beijing, China, pp. 2106–2109 (July 2007)

[21] Yip, S.K., Au, O.C., Ho, C.W., Wong, H.M.: Lossless visible watermarking. In: Proc. IEEE Int. Conf. Multimedia and Expo., pp. 853–856 (July 2006)

[22] de Vleeschouwer, C., Delaigle, J.F., Macq, B.: Circular interpretation of bijective transformations in lossless watermarking for media asset management. IEEE Trans. Multimedia 5(1), 97–105 (2003)

[23] Li, X., Orchard, M.T.: Edge-directed prediction for lossless compression of natural simages. IEEE Trans. Image Process 10(6), 813–817 (2001)

[24] Hu, Y., Kwong, S., Huang, J.: An algorithm for removable visible watermarking. IEEE Trans. Circuits Syst. Video Technol. 16(1), 129–133 (2006)

Topological Properties of Incomplete Multigranulation Based on Rough Fuzzy Sets

B.K. Tripathy and M. Nagaraju

SCSE, VIT University, Vellore- 632 014, India
{tripathybk,mnagaraju}@vit.ac.in

Abstract. The definition of basic rough sets [3] depends upon either a single equivalence relation defined on a universe or several equivalence relations defined over the universe, taken one each taken at a time. In the view of granular computing, classical rough set theory is based upon single granulation. Extending this notion, a rough set model based on multi-granulations (MGRS) was introduced in [5]. In this approach, approximations of sets were defined through multiple equivalence relations on the universe and their properties were investigated. Using hybridization of fuzzy set [13] with rough set the concept of rough fuzzy set was introduced by Dubois and Prade [1]. Recently, a Rough Fuzzy Set Model was introduced and studied by Wu and Kou [12], which is based on Multiple Granulation. Topological properties of rough sets introduced by Pawlak in terms of their types were recently studied by Tripathy and Mitra [10]. These were extended to the context of incomplete multi granulation by Tripathy and Raghavan [11]. In this paper we introduce incomplete multigranulation on rough fuzzy sets, study their basic properties and extend the topological properties in [11] to this context. Our findings are true for both complete and incomplete fuzzy rough set models based upon multi granulation.

Keywords: Rough Sets, Fuzzy rough sets, equivalence relations, tolerance relations, type of rough sets, multi granular fuzzy rough sets.

1   Introduction

Two of the most successful models to capture impreciseness in real life data are the notion of fuzzy sets introduced by Zadeh [13] and the notion of rough sets introduced by Pawlak [3, 4].Two crisp sets, called the lower approximation and the upper approximation of a set X are used to define a rough set associated with X.. The modeling power of rough sets has been improved through the introduction of several extensions. Replacing the equivalence relations by tolerance relations is one such approach. These rough sets are sometimes called incomplete rough set models. The use of multiple equivalence relations to define a rough set led to the introduction of rough set model based on multi-granulations (MGRS) [5]. Incomplete rough set model based on multi-granulations was introduced and their properties were studied in [5, 6, 7]. The concept in [5] has been extended to rough fuzzy set model based on multi-granulations by Wu and Kou [12] (the authors call it fuzzy rough set model by

P.V. Krishna, M.R. Babu, and E. Ariwa (Eds.): ObCom 2011, Part II, CCIS 270, pp. 92–102, 2012.

mistake). In this paper, we extend the model further by introducing incomplete rough fuzzy set model based on multi-granulations (MGRFS) and study their properties.

To define topological characterization of rough sets Pawlak [4] categorised rough sets into four kinds (which we shall call as types in this paper). In this article, we shall obtain types of union, intersection and complementation of MGRFS in parallel to those results obtained in [10] and extended in [11].

2   Definitions and Notations

In this section we introduce the notations and definitions to be used by in presenting our work. In the next subsection we introduce the basic rough sets [3].

2.1   Basic Rough Sets

Let U/R denote the equivalence classes generated by an equivalence relation defined over a universe U. For every $x \in U$, we denote its equivalence class by $[x]_R$. A universal set U along with a set of equivalence relations defined on it is called a knowledge base S and we write $S = (U, P)$. Given a subset T ($\neq \phi$)$\subseteq$P,IND(T) represents the intersection of all the equivalence relations in T. IND(T) is called the indiscernibility relation over T.

Given any $Y \subseteq U$ and $R \in$ IND (T), the R-lower and R-upper approximations of Y, are denoted by $\underline{RY}$ and $\overline{RY}$ respectively and are defined as

$$\underline{RY} = \bigcup\{Z \in U / R : Z \subseteq Y\} \text{ and } \overline{RY} = \bigcup\{Z \in U / R : Y \cap Z \neq \phi\}.$$

The set $BN_R(Y) = \overline{RY} - \underline{RY}$ is called the boundary of Y with respect to R.

The set Y is said to be rough with respect to R if $\underline{R}Y \neq \overline{R}Y$ and R-definable otherwise. We see that Y is rough with respect to R is equivalent to $BN_R (Y) \neq \phi$. Similarly Y R-definable is equivalent to $BN_R (Y) = \phi$.

2.2   Multigranular Rough Sets

Using multiple equivalence relations the notion of MGRS was introduced by Qian and Liang [5]. A rough set based upon multi-granulation is defined as follows [5]:

Definition 2.1: Let $S = (U, \mathbf{R})$ be a knowledge base, $Y \subseteq U$ and $A, B \in \mathbf{R}.$ The lower approximation and upper approximation of Y in U are defined as

(2.1) $\underline{A+B}(Y) = \{x \in U / [x]_A \subseteq Y \text{ or } [x]_B \subseteq Y\}$ and

(2.2) $\overline{A+B}(Y) = (\underline{A+B}(Y^C))^C$

Several properties of such type of rough sets were established in [5]. However, some of these proofs were found to be faulty by Wu and Kou [12].

2.3   Rough Fuzzy Sets

Let us denote the set of all functions from U to the unit interval [0, 1], is called the fuzzy power set of U and is denoted by F(U). It follows that $P(U) \subseteq F(U)$.

It was established by Dubois and Prade [1] that the two theories of fuzzy set and rough set complement each other and they developed the hybrid models, called fuzzy rough sets and rough fuzzy sets. Rough fuzzy sets are defined as follows.

Let (U, R) be an approximation space. Then for any $Y \in F(U)$, the lower and upper approximations of Y with respect to R are given by

(2.3.2.1) $(\underline{R}Y)(y) = \inf_{x \in [y]_R} Y(x)$, for all $y \in U$ and

(2.3.2.2) $(\overline{R}Y)(y) = \sup_{x \in [y]_R} Y(x)$, for all $y \in U$.

2.4   Multi-granular Rough Fuzzy Sets Model

The concept of multi-granular rough sets was extended to define rough fuzzy sets based on multi-granulation by Wu and Kou [12] as follows:

Definition 2.4.1: Let K = (U, R) be a knowledge base, R be a set of equivalence relations on U and A, B $\in$ R. Then $\forall Y \in F(U)$, the lower approximation $\underline{A+B}(Y)$ and upper approximation $\overline{A+B}(Y)$ of Y based equivalence relations A, B are defined as follows:

(2.4.1) $\forall y \in U, (\underline{A+B})(Y)(y) = \inf_{x \in [y]_P} Y(x) \vee \inf_{x \in [y]_Q} Y(x)$,

(2.4.2) $\forall y \in U, (\overline{A+B})(Y)(y) = ((\underline{A+B})(Y^C))^C(y)$.

If $(\underline{A+B})(Y) = (\overline{A+B})(Y)$ then Y is called definable, otherwise Y is called a fuzzy rough set with respect to multi-granulations A and B. The pair $((\underline{A+B})(Y),(\overline{A+B})(Y))$ is called a MG-fuzzy rough set on multi-granulations A and B. It has been illustrated in [12] that fuzzy rough sets based on multi-granulations and fuzzy rough sets based on single granulations are different. The following properties of MG-fuzzy rough sets on multi-granulations were established in [12].

Property 2.4.1: Let K= (U, **R**) be a knowledge base, **R** be a set of equivalence relations. For every $V, W \in$ F(U) and $A, B \in R$, the following properties hold true.

(2.4.3) $\underline{A+B}(V) \subseteq V \subseteq \overline{A+B}(V)$

(2.4.4) $\underline{A+B}(\phi) = \overline{A+B}(\phi) = \phi$

(2.4.5) $\underline{A+B}(U) = \overline{A+B}(U) = U$

(2.4.6) $\underline{A+B}(V^C) = (\overline{A+B}(V))^C$

(2.4.7) $\underline{A+B}(V) = \underline{A}(V) \cup \underline{B}(V)$

(2.4.8) $\overline{A+B}(V) = \overline{A}(V) \cap \overline{B}(V)$

(2.4.9) $(\underline{A+B})((\underline{A+B})(V) = (\underline{A+B})(V) \subseteq \overline{(A+B)}(\underline{A+B})(V)$

(2.4.10) $(\underline{A+B})(\overline{(A+B)}(V) \subseteq (\underline{A+B})(V) = \overline{(A+B)}(\underline{A+B})(V)$

(2.4.11) $(\underline{A+B})(V) = (\underline{A+B})(V), \quad \overline{(A+B)}(V) = \overline{(A+B)}(V)$

(2.4.12) $\underline{A+B}(V \cap W) \subseteq \underline{A+B}(V) \cap \underline{A+B}(W)$

(2.4.13) $\underline{A+B}(V \cup W) \supseteq \underline{A+B}(V) \cup \underline{A+B}(W)$

(2.4.14) $\overline{A+B}(V \cap W) \subseteq \overline{A+B}(V) \cap \overline{A+B}(W)$

(2.4.15) $\overline{A+B}(V \cup W) \supseteq \overline{A+B}(V) \cup \overline{A+B}(W)$

3   MGRS in Incomplete Information Systems

A target information system (TIS) is a five-tuple (U, ATT, I, Dec, J), where A is a nonempty, finite set of attributes, I: $U \rightarrow Dom_a$, for any $a \in ATT$ Dec is a nonempty finite set of attributes called the decision attributes, J: Dec $\rightarrow Dom_d$ for any $a \in ATT$. Here, Dom_a and Dom_d are the domains of any attribute 'a' and a decision attribute 'd' respectively.

If the value of any attribute in a TIS is unknown then such a value is represented by '*'. Regular attributes are those attributes which do not have '*' as any domain value. Otherwise, it is called incomplete.

Definition 3.1: A system in which values of all attributes for all objects from U are regular (known) is called complete and is called incomplete otherwise.

An information system is a pair S = (U, ATT, I, Dec, J) is called an incomplete target IS if values of some attributes in ATT are missing and those of all attributes in D are regular (known), where ATT is called the set of conditional attributes and D is the set of decision attributes.

Definition 3.2: For an incomplete information system (U, ATT, I) and B $\subseteq$ ATT, we define a binary relation S(B) on U as

(3.1) $S(B) = \{(x, y) \in U \times U \mid \forall p \in B, p(x) = p(y) \text{ or } p(x) = * \text{ or } p(y) = *\}$.

If the attributes B $\subseteq$ ATT are numerical attributes, the relation S(B) is defined as:

(3.2) $S(B) = \{(x, y) \in U \times U \mid \forall p \in B, |p(x) - p(y)| \leq \alpha_p \text{ or } p(x) = * \text{ or } p(y) = *\}$.

It is easy to verify that S(B) is a tolerance relation and that

(3.3) $S(B) = \bigcap_{p \in B} S(\{p\})$.

We denote the set $\{y \in U \mid (x, y) \in S(B)\}$ by $S_B(x)$ and it consists of the objects which are possibly indistinguishable from x with respect to B.

Let $U/S(B) = \{S_B(x) \mid x \in U\}$, the set of tolerance classes induced by B, which is also called the set of information granules. This set forms a cover of U. A cover is a set of nonempty subsets of U such that their union is U.

The incomplete MGRS on Two Granulation Spaces is defined as follows.

Definition 3.3: Let (U, ATT, I) be an incomplete information system and A, B $\subseteq$ ATT be two attribute subsets. Then for any $V \subseteq U$, the lower and upper approximations of V with respect to the two granulations A and B are defined as:

(3.4) $\underline{(A+B)}(V) = \bigcup \{x \mid S_A(x) \subseteq V \text{ or } S_B(x) \subseteq V \}$ and

(3.5) $\overline{(A+B)}(V) = ((\underline{A+B})(V^C))^C$.

The rough set of V with respect to A+B is given by the pair $((\underline{A+B})(V),(\overline{A+B})(V))$ and its boundary region or the uncertainty region, denoted by $B_{(A+B)}(V)$ is defined as

(3.6) $B_{(A+B)}(V) = \overline{(A+B)}(V) \setminus \underline{(A+B)}(V)$

Property 3.1: Let (U, ATT, I) be an incomplete information system, $V \subseteq U$ and A, B $\subseteq$ ATT be two-attribute subsets. Then the properties (2.4.3) to (2.4.11) hold true.

Property 3.2: Let (U, ATT, I) be an incomplete information system, $V \subseteq U$ and A, B $\subseteq$ ATT be two-attribute subsets. Then the properties (2.4.12) to (2.4.15) hold true. In addition, we have the following properties:

(3.7) $\underline{(A+B)}(V \cap W) = (\underline{AV} \cap \underline{AW}) \cup (\underline{BV} \cap \underline{BW})$

(3.8) $\overline{(A+B)}(V \cup W) = (\overline{AV} \cup \overline{AW}) \cap (\overline{BV} \cup \overline{BW})$

(3.9) $V \subseteq W \Rightarrow \underline{(A+B)}V \subseteq \underline{(A+B)}W$

(3.10) $V \subseteq W \Rightarrow \overline{(A+B)}V \subseteq \overline{(A+B)}W$

4   MGRFS in Incomplete Information Systems

In this section we generalise both the MGRFS and MGRS on incomplete information systems to introduce the concept of MGRFS in incomplete information systems.

Let (U, ATT, I) be an incomplete information system and A, B $\subseteq$ ATT be two attribute subsets. Then for any $V \subseteq U$, the lower and upper approximations of V with respect to the two granulations A and B are defined as:

(4.1) $\underline{(A+B)}(V)(x) = \inf_{y \in S_A(x)} V(y) \vee \inf_{y \in S_B(x)} V(y), \forall x \in U;$

(4.2) $\overline{(A+B)}(V)(x) = ((A+B)(V^C))^C(x), \forall x \in U.$

Definition 4.1: The rough set of V with respect to A+B is given by the pair $((\underline{A+B})(V),(\overline{A+B})(V))$ and its boundary region or the uncertainty region, denoted by $B_{(A+B)}(V)$ is defined as

(4.3) $B_{(A+B)}(V) = \overline{(A+B)}(V) \setminus \underline{(A+B)}(V)$

Example 4.1: Let us consider the following incomplete target IS about an emporium investment project.

Project	Locus	Investment	Population density	Decision
a_1	common	high	0.88	Yes
a_2	bad	high	*	Yes
a_3	bad	*	0.33	No
a_4	bad	low	0.40	No
a_5	bad	low	0.37	No
a_6	bad	*	0.60	Yes
a_7	common	high	0.65	No
a_8	good	*	0.62	Yes

Let K = (U, AT, f, D), where $U = \{a_1, a_2, a_3, a_4, a_5, a_6, a_7, a_8\}$ and AT = {L, I, P}.

U/SIM (L) = $\{\{a_1, a_7\}, \{a_2, a_3, a_4, a_5, a_6\}, \{a_8\}\}$

U/SIM (P) = $\{\{a_1, a_2\}, \{a_1, a_2, a_3, a_4, a_5, a_6, a_7, a_8\}, \{a_2, a_6, a_7, a_8\}\{a_2, a_3, a_4, a_5\}\}$.

Suppose, $V = \{(a_1, 0.5), (a_2, 0.3), (a_3, 0.3), (a_4, 0.6), (a_5, 0.5), (a_6, 0.8), (a_7, 1), (a_8, 0.8)\}$.

$\underline{(L+P)}(V) = \{(a_1, 0.5), (a_2, 0.3), (a_3, 0.3), (a_4, 0.3), (a_5, 0.3), (a_6, 0.3), (a_7, 0.5), (a_8, 0.8)\}$

$\overline{(L+P)}(V) = \{(a_1, 1), (a_2, 0.8), (a_3, 0.8), (a_4, 0.8), (a_5, 0.8), (a_6, 0.8), (a_7, 1), (a_8, 0.9)\}$

Proposition 4.1: Let S = (U, ATT, I) be an incomplete target IS and A, B $\subseteq$ ATT two-attribute subsets, and V, W $\in$ F(U). Then the following properties hold true:

(4.4) $\underline{(A+B)}(V) = \underline{AV} \cup \underline{BV}$

(4.5) $\overline{(A+B)}(V) = \overline{AV} \cap \overline{BV}$

(4.6) $\underline{A+B}(U) = \overline{A+B}(U) = U$

(4.7) $\underline{A+B}(\phi) = \overline{A+B}(\phi) = \phi$

(4.8) $\underline{A+B}(V) \subseteq V \subseteq \overline{A+B}(V)$

(4.9) $\underline{A+B}(V^C) = (\overline{A+B}(V))^C$

(4.10) $\underline{(A+B)}(\underline{(A+B)}(V) = \underline{(A+B)}(V) \subseteq \overline{(A+B)}\underline{(A+B)}(V)$

(4.11) $\underline{(A+B)}(\overline{(A+B)}(V) \subseteq \overline{(A+B)}(V) = \overline{(A+B)}\overline{(A+B)}(V)$

(4.12) $\underline{(A+B)}(V) = \underline{(B+A)}(V), \quad \overline{(A+B)}(V) = \overline{(B+A)}(V)$

(4.13) $\underline{(A+B)}(V \cap W) \subseteq \underline{(A+B)}(V) \cap \underline{(A+B)}(W)$

(4.14) $\overline{(A+B)}(V \cup W) \supseteq \overline{(A+B)}(V) \cup \overline{(A+B)}(W)$

(4.15) $\underline{(A+B)}(V \cup W) \supseteq \underline{(A+B)}(V) \cup \underline{(A+B)}(W)$

(4.16) $\overline{(A+B)}(V \cap W) \subseteq \overline{(A+B)}(V) \cap \overline{(A+B)}(W)$

We shall use these properties to establish some topological properties of MGFRS in incomplete information systems.

5   Topological Properties of MGFRS in an Incomplete Information System

It has been noted by Pawlak that in the practical applications of rough sets two characteristics are very important. These are the accuracy measure and the topological characterization. The topological characterisation of rough sets depends upon the four types of rough sets. Following this approach, we define below four types of MGFRS in an incomplete information system. Here, we denote by the strict zero cut of a fuzzy set A by $A_{>0}$ and it contains all the elements of U which have positive membership value.

Definition 5.1: A MGRFS in an incomplete information space can be classified into following four types

(5.1) If $(\underline{A+B}(V))_{>0} \neq \phi$ and $(\overline{A+B}(V))_{>0} \neq U$, then we say that V is roughly A+B-definable (Type-1/T-1).

(5.2) If $(\underline{A+B}(V))_{>0} = \phi$ and $(\overline{A+B}(V))_{>0} \neq U$, then we say that V is internally A+B-undefinable (Type-2/T-2).

(5.3) If $(\underline{A+B}(V))_{>0} \neq \phi$ and $(\overline{A+B}(V))_{>0} = U$, then we say that V is externally A+B-undefinable (Type-3/T-3).

(5.4) If $(\underline{A+B}(V))_{>0} = \phi$ and $(\overline{A+B}(V))_{>0} = U$, then we say that V is totally A+B-undefinable (Type-4/T-4).

When we consider X as a crisp set instead of a fuzzy set then the above definitions reduce to their counterpart in the crisp rough set concept.

5.1   Results

In this section we shall find out the types of MGRFS in incomplete information systems. There are four sets of results accumulated in four tables. The first provides the type of A+B MGRFS from the types of A and B. The second table provides the types of the complement of a MGRFS. In the third table we obtain the types for the union of two MGFRSs of all possible types. Similarly we establish the types of the intersection of two MGRFSs of all possible types. These results will be useful for further studies in approximation of classifications and rule generation.

5.2   Table for Type of V with Respect to A+B

Here, the column headings represent the types of V with respect to A and the row headings represent those for B. We use T-1, T-2, T-3 and T-4 represent type-1, type-2, type-3 and type-4 respectively

	T-1	T-2	T-3	T-4
T-1	T-1	T-1	T-1	T-1
T-2	T-1	T-2	T-1	T-2
T-3	T-1	T-1	T-3	T-3
T-4	T-1	T-2	T-3	T-4

5.3   Table for Type of V^c with Respect to A+B

V	V^c		V	V^c
T-1	T-1		T-3	T-2
T-2	T-3		T-4	T-4

5.4   Table for Type of $V \cup W$ with Respect to A+B

In this table the column heads represent types W with respect to A+B and the row heads represent those for V.

	T-1	T-2	T-3	T-4
T-1	T-1 or T-3	T-1 or T-3	T-3	T-3
T-2	T-1 or T-3	T-1 or T-2 or T-3 or T-4	T-3	T-3 or T-4
T-3	T-3	T-3	T-3	T-3
T-4	T-3	T-3 or T-4	T-3	T-3 or T-4

We shall provide an example to show that for two multigranular rough sets of Type 1, the union can be of Type 1 or Type 3. The other cases can be justified in a similar manner.

Example 5.1

Let us consider the example 4.1 above.

Suppose, $V = \{(a_1,0),\ (a_2,0.3),(a_3,0),(a_4,0),(a_5,0),(a_6,0.8),(a_7,0),(a_8,0.8)\}$ and

$W = \{(a_1,0),\ (a_2,0.3),(a_3,0),(a_4,0),(a_5,0),(a_6,0),(a_7,1),(a_8,0)\}$. Then X and Y are both of Type 1 as

$\underline{(L+P)}(V) = \{(a_1,0),\ (a_2,0),(a_3,0),(a_4,0),(a_5,0),(a_6,0),(a_7,0),(a_8,0.8)\}.$

$\overline{(L+P)}(V) = \{(a_1,0),\ (a_2,0.8),(a_3,0.8),(a_4,0.8),(a_5,0.8),(a_6,0.8),(a_7,0),(a_8,0.8)\}.$

So that $((\underline{(L+P)}(V))_{>0} \neq \phi$ and $((\overline{L+P})(V))_{>0} \neq U.$

$\underline{(L+P)}(W) = \{(a_1,0),\ (a_2,0),(a_3,0),\ (a_4,0),(a_5,0),(a_6,0),(a_7,0.5),(a_8,0.8)\}.$

$\overline{(L+P)}(W) = \{(a_1,1),\ (a_2,0.3),(a_3,0.3),(a_4,0.3),(a_5,0.3),(a_6,0.3),(a_7,0.5),(a_8,0)\}.$

So that $((\underline{L+P})(W))_{>0} \neq \phi$ and $((\overline{L+P})(W))_{>0} \neq U$. Now, we have

$\underline{(L+P)}(V \cup W) = \{(a_1,0),\ (a_2,0),(a_3,0),(a_4,0),(a_5,0),(a_6,0),(a_7,0),(a_8,0.8)\}.$

$\overline{(L+P)}(V \cup W) = \{(a_1,0),\ (a_2,0.8),(a_3,0.8),(a_4,0.8),(a_5,0.8),(a_6,0.8),(a_7,0.8),(a_8,1)\}.$

So that $((\underline{(L+P)}(V \cup W))_{>0} \neq \phi$ and $((\overline{L+P})(V \cup W))_{>0} \neq U.$ So, V∪W is of Type 1.

Next, we take $V = \{(a_1,0),\ (a_2,0),(a_3,0),(a_4,0),(a_5,0),(a_6,0.8),(a_7,0),(a_8,0.8)\}$ and

$W = \{(a_1,1),\ (a_2,0),(a_3,0),(a_4,0),(a_5,0),(a_6,0),(a_7,0),(a_8,0.8)\}$. Both V and W are of Type 1 as $\underline{(L+P)}(V) = \{(a_1,0),\ (a_2,0),(a_3,0),(a_4,0),(a_5,0),(a_6,0),(a_7,0),(a_8,0.8)\}.$

$\overline{(L+P)}(V) = \{(a_1,0), (a_2,0.8),(a_3,0.8),(a_4,0.8),(a_5,0.8),(a_6,0.8),(a_7,0),(a_8,0.8)\}.$

So that $((\underline{L+P})(V))_{>0} \neq \phi$ and $((\overline{L+P})(V))_{>0} \neq U$.

$\underline{(L+P)}(W) = \{(a_1,0), (a_2,0),(a_3,0),(a_4,0),(a_5,0),(a_6,0),(a_7,0),(a_8,0.8)\}.$

$\overline{(L+P)}(W) = \{(a_1,1), (a_2,0),(a_3,0),(a_4,0),(a_5,0),(a_6,0),(a_7,1),(a_8,0.8)\}.$

So that $((\underline{L+P})(W))_{>0} \neq \phi$ and $((\overline{L+P})(W))_{>0} \neq U$ .Now,

$\underline{(L+P)}(V \cup W) = \{(a_1,0), (a_2,0),(a_3,0),(a_4,0),(a_5,0),(a_6,0),(a_7,0),(a_8,0.8)\}.$

$\overline{(L+P)}(V \cup W) = \{(a_1,1), (a_2,0.8),(a_3,0.8),(a_4,0.8),(a_5,0.8),(a_6,0.8),(a_7,1),(a_8,0.8)\}.$

So that $((\underline{L+P})(V \cup W))_{>0} \neq \phi$ and $((\overline{L+P})(V \cup W))_{>0} = U$ .So VUW is of Type 3.

Hence both the cases in the table position (1, 1) are possibilities.

Proof of Entry (1, 3)
Let V and W be of Type 1 and Type 3 respectively. Then from the properties of Type 1 and Type 3 of MGRFS, we have

$((\underline{A+B})(V))_{>0} \neq \phi$, $((\underline{A+B})(W))_{>0} \neq \phi$, $((\overline{A+B})(V))_{>0} \neq U$ and $((\overline{A+B})(W))_{>0} = U$.

So, using (4.14) and (4.15) we get

$((\underline{A+B})(V \cup W))_{>0} \neq \phi$ and $((\overline{A+B})(V \cup W))_{>0} = U$. Hence $V \cup W$ is of type 3 only.

5.5   Table for Type of $V \cap W$ with Respect to A+B

In this table the column heads represent types of W with respect to A+B and the row heads represent those for V

	T-1	T-2	T-3	T-4
T-1	T-1 or T-2	T-2	T-1 or T-2	T-2
T-2	T-2	T-2	T-2	T-2
T-3	T-1 or T-2	T-2	T-1 or T-2 or T-3 or T-4	T-2 or T-4
T-4	T-2	T-2	T-2 or T-4	T-2 or T-4

We shall provide an example to show that for two multigranular rough sets such that one is of Type 1 and the other one is of Type 3.The intersection can be of Type 1 or Type 2. The other cases can be justified in a similar manner.

Example 5.2
Let us consider the example 4.1 above. We take V = $\{(a_1,0), (a_2,0.3), (a_3,0), (a_4,0),$ $(a_5,0),(a_6,0.8),(a_7,0),(a_8,0.8)\}$ and W = $\{(a_1,1), (a_2,0),(a_3,0),(a_4,0),(a_5,0), (a_6,0),$ $(a_7,0),(a_8,0.8)\}$. Then V and W are of Type 3 and Type 1 respectively as

$\underline{(L+P)}(V) = \{(a_1,0), (a_2,0),(a_3,0),(a_4,0),(a_5,0),(a_6,0),(a_7,0),(a_8,0.8)\}.$

$\overline{(L+P)}(V) = \{(a_1,0.8), (a_2,0.8),(a_3,0.8),(a_4,0.8),(a_5,0.8),(a_6,0.8),(a_7,0.8),(a_8,0.8)\}.$

So that $((\underline{L+P})(V))_{>0} \neq \phi$ and $((\overline{L+P})(V))_{>0} = U$.

$\underline{(L+P)}(W) = \{(a_1,0),\ (a_2,0),(a_3,0),(a_4,0),(a_5,0),(a_6,0),(a_7,1),(a_8,0.8)\}.$

$\overline{(L+P)}(W) = \{(a_1,1),\ (a_2,0),(a_3,0),(a_4,0),(a_5,0),(a_6,0),(a_7,1),(a_8,0.8)\}.$

So that $\underline{((L+P)(W))}_{>0} \neq \phi$ So that $(\overline{(L+P)}(W))_{>0} \neq U.$ We have

$V \cap W = \{(a_1,0),(a_2,0),(a_3,0),(a_4,0),(a_5,0),(a_6,0),(a_7,0),(a_8,0.8)\}.$ Hence,

$\underline{(L+P)}(V \cap W) = \{(a_1,0),\ (a_2,0),(a_3,0),(a_4,0),(a_5,0),(a_6,0),(a_7,0),(a_8,0.8)\}.$

$\overline{(L+P)}(V \cap W) = \{(a_1,0),\ (a_2,0),(a_3,0),(a_4,0),(a_5,0),(a_6,1),(a_7,0),(a_8,0.8)\}.$

So that $((\underline{L+P})(V \cap W))_{>0} \neq \phi$ and $((\overline{L+P})(V \cap W))_{>0} \neq U.$ Hence $V \cap W$ is of Type 1.

Next we modify SIM(L) and SIM(P) slightly and define as

U/SIM(L) = $\{\{a_1,a_2\},\ \{a_3,a_4,a_5\},\{a_6,a_7,a_8\}\}$

U/SIM(P) = $\{\{a_1,a_2\},\ \{a_1,a_2,a_3,a_4,a_5,a_6,a_7,a_8\},\{a_6,a_7,a_8\}\}.$

Now, taking V = $\{(a_1,0.3),\ (a_2,1),(a_3,0.7),(a_4,0),(a_5,0.5),(a_6,0),(a_7,0.3),(a_8,0)\}$ and

W = $\{(a_1,0.3),\ (a_2,0),(a_3,0),(a_4,0.6),(a_5,0.5),(a_6,0),(a_7,0.4),(a_8,0.8)\}$, we find that V and W are of Type 3 and Type 1 respectively as detailed below.

$\underline{(L+P)}(V) = \{(a_1,0.8),\ (a_2,0.8),(a_3,0),(a_4,0),(a_5,0),(a_6,0),(a_7,0),(a_8,0)\}.$

$\underline{(L+P)}(W) = \{(a_1,0),\ (a_2,0),(a_3,1),(a_4,1),(a_5,1),(a_6,0),(a_7,0),(a_8,0)\}.$

So that $\underline{((L+P)(V))}_{>0} \neq \phi$ and $\underline{((L+P)(W))}_{>0} \neq \phi.$

$\overline{(L+P)}(V) = \{(a_1,1),\ (a_2,1),(a_3,0.7),(a_4,0.7),(a_5,0.7),(a_6,0),(a_7,0),(a_8,0)\}.$

$\overline{(L+P)}(W) = \{(a_1,1),\ (a_2,1),(a_3,1),(a_4,1),(a_5,1),(a_6,1),(a_7,1),(a_8,1)\}.$

So that $((\overline{L+P})(V))_{>0} \neq U$ and $((\overline{L+P})(W))_{>0} = U.$ Now,

$\underline{(L+P)}(V \cap W) = \{(a_1,0),\ (a_2,0),(a_3,0),(a_4,0),(a_5,0),(a_6,0),(a_7,0),(a_8,0)\}.$

$\overline{(L+P)}(V \cap W) = \{(a_1,0.3),\ (a_2,0.3),(a_3,0.5),(a_4,0.5),(a_5,0.5),(a_6,0),(a_7,0),(a_8,0)\}.$

So that $\underline{((L+P)(V \cap W))}_{>0} = \phi$ and $((\overline{L+P})(V \cap W))_{>0} \neq U.$ So, $V \cap W$ is of Type 2.

Hence both the cases for intersection operation in position $(3, 1)$ can occur.

Proof of Entry (2, 1)

Let V and W be of Type 2 and Type 1 respectively. Then from the properties of Type 2 and Type 1 MGRRFSs we get $((\underline{A+B})(V))_{>0} = \phi$, $((\underline{A+B})(W))_{>0} = \phi$, $((\overline{A+B})(V))_{>0} \neq U$ and $((\overline{A+B})(W))_{>0} \neq U.$ So using properties (4.13) and (4.16) we get $((\underline{A+B})(V \cap W))_{>0} = \phi$ and $((\overline{A+B})(V \cap W))_{>0} \neq U.$ So, $V \cap W$ is of Type 2. This completes the proof. The other cases can be established similarly.

6   Conclusions

In this paper we introduced the concept of multigranular rough fuzzy sets in incomplete information systems and established many properties of these sets. Also, we studied the topological properties of MGRFSs with respect to the three set theoretic operations of union, intersection and complementation. The tables show that there are multiple answers to some of the cases as like as the case of basic rough sets. Also, we provided examples in some cases to illustrate the fact that the multiple answers can actually occur. These results can be used in approximation of classifications and rule induction

References

[1] Dubois, D., Prade, H.: Rough fuzzy sets model. International Journal of General Systems 46(1), 191–208 (1990)
[2] Kryszkiewicz, K.: Rough set approach to incomplete information systems. Information Sciences 112, 39–49 (1998)
[3] Pawlak, Z.: Rough sets. Int. Jour. of Computer and Information Sciences 11, 341–356 (1982)
[4] Pawlak, Z.: Rough sets: Theoretical aspects of reasoning about data. Kluwer Academic Publishers, London (1991)
[5] Qian, Y.H., Liang, J.Y.: Rough set method based on Multi-granulations. In: Proceedings of the 5th IEEE Conference on Cognitive Informatics, vol. 1, pp. 297–304 (2006)
[6] Qian, Y.H., Liang, J.Y., Dang, C.Y.: MGRS in Incomplete Information Systems. In: IEEE Conference on Granular Computing, pp. 163–168 (2007)
[7] Qian, Y.H., Liang, J.Y., Dang, C.Y.: Incomplete Multigranulation Rough set. IEEE Transactions on Systems, Man and Cybernetics-Part A: Systems and Humans 40(2), 420–431 (2010)
[8] Tripathy, B.K.: On Approximation of classifications, rough equalities and rough equivalences. In: Rough Set Theory: A True Landmark in Data Analysis. SCI, vol. 174, pp. 85–136. Springer, Heidelberg (2009)
[9] Tripathy, B.K.: Rough Sets on Fuzzy Approximation Spaces and Intuitionistic Fuzzy Approximation Spaces. In: Rough Set Theory: A True Landmark in Data Analysis. SCI, vol. 174, pp. 3–44. Springer, Heidelberg (2009)
[10] Tripathy, B.K., Mitra, A.: Topological Properties of Rough Sets and their Applications. International Journal of Granular Computing, Rough Sets and Intelligent Systems (IJGCRSIS) 1(4), 355–369 (2010)
[11] Tripathy, B.K., Raghavan, R.: On Some Topological Properties of Multigranular Rough Sets. Journal of Advances in Applied science Research 2(3), 536–543 (2011)
[12] Wu, M., Kou, G.: Fuzzy Rough Set Model on Multi-Granulations. In: Proceedings of the 2nd International Conference on Computer Engineering and Technology, vol. 2, pp. V2-72 –V2-75 (2010)
[13] Zadeh, L.: Fuzzy Sets. Information and Control 8(11), 338–353 (1965)

Automated Heart Sound Diagnosis Using Feature Extraction Model for Bio-signals

P.S. Rajakumar[1,*], S. Ravi[2], and R.M. Suresh[3]

[1] Research Scholar, JNT University, Hyderabad
suraarus@yahoo.com
[2] Prof. and Head / ECE, Dr. MGR Educational and Research Institute, Chennai
ravi_mls@yahoo.com
[3] Prof. and Head/ CSE, RMD Engineering College, Chennai
rmsuresh@hotmail.com

Abstract. In this paper a model that can quantitatively predict human performance in typical spectral and temporal masking situations and be immediately applicable in the field of Automatic heart sound classifier (AHSC) is presented. The various features extracted in the experiments were studied in the presence and absence of noise and for various biomedical signals and the system reported to be robust. The developed model shall be used as front end for AHSC.

Keywords: AHSC, Murmur, Feature Extraction, Mel Frequency Cepstral Coefficient (MFCC), Continuous wavelet Coefficient (CWTC).

1   Introduction

Before any audio signal (heart sounds) can be classified under a given class, the features in that signal are to be extracted. The specific sound signal studied in this work is the signals produced by the heart. The heart signal visualized as a sound signal contains much useful information and can assist the clinician in diagnoses. Specifically, it is proposed that much information is derived by sound processing techniques. [1].

Procedure in performing Continuous Wavelet Transform on Signal

1. Select a wavelet and compare it to a segment at the beginning of the signal
2. Compute the CWT coefficient for that segment of the signal.
3. Move the wavelet to the right by the factor 'b', then repeat step2, covering the entire signal.
4. Scale the wavelet, then repeat steps 1 to 3 for the new scale factor 'a'. [6].
5. Repeat steps 1 to 4 for all other scale factors 'a'.

---

* Asst Prof, Department of Information Technology in Dr MGR Educational and Research Institute, Chennai.

P.V. Krishna, M.R. Babu, and E. Ariwa (Eds.): ObCom 2011, Part II, CCIS 270, pp. 103–109, 2012.
© Springer-Verlag Berlin Heidelberg 2012

Generally, the CWT coefficient is dependent on scale factor 'a'. In this paper, the coefficients are to be normalized by a suitable factor so as to remove the effects of different scales on the coefficients at the different frequencies. [5].

Murmurs and its types

Murmurs are caused by turbulent blood flow and there are a number of different murmurs which may be detected by cardiac auscultation. The important types of murmurs and their characteristics are listed in Table 1.

Table 1. Murmurs and its characteristics

Murmur Type	Characteristics
Systolic ejection	Occurs temporally between S1 and S2. Causes interference to the flow of blood, manifested as turbulence
Innocent Murmurs	Common in young age group and always occur during the systole.[7].
Diastolic murmurs	This murmur occurs at the middle to the end of the diastole and does not allow the laminar passage of blood.

Spectral Components

Heart sounds are caused by turbulence in blood flow and vibration of cardiac and vascular structures. In this paper, from the heart (sound) signal the following features are extracted. The block diagram of the proposed system is show in figure1. The dimension of the feature space is set equal to the number of extracted features.[2].

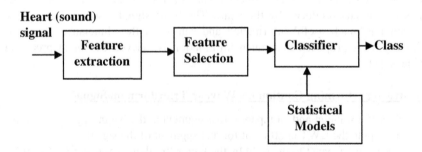

Fig. 1. Block diagram of proposed heart sound classifier

The following features are generally extracted from the spectral information : (i) Peak-finding (ii) Format-finding (iii) Peak-tracking (iv) f_o analysis (v) MFCC coefficients (vi) Thresholding (vii) Frequency shifting and (viii) Additive cross-synthesis.

Mel-Freq Cepstral Coefficients

The spectrum of a sound signal (heart) can be considered in terms of signal correlation terms with harmonic tones at regularly spaced spectral peaks.

MFCCs are a way of representing the spectral information in a sound (heart) signal. Each coefficient has a value for each frame of the sound. The sequence of steps in obtaining MFCC is

(1) Partition the signal into frames
(2) Get the amplitude spectrum of each frame
(3) Compute the log of these spectrums
(4) Convert to the Mel Scale (a perceptual scale based on human hearing)
(5) Apply the DCT

The purpose of DCT is to reduce the data ortho-normally and thereby leaving a series of uncorrelated values (the coefficients) for each frame of the heart sound [3] signal. This is illustrated in figure 2.

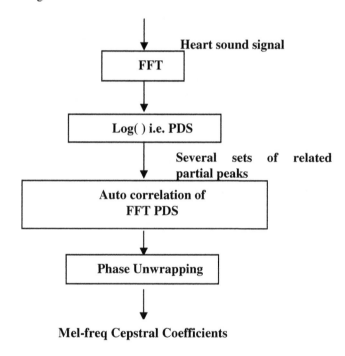

Fig. 2. Evaluation of MFCC

Feature extraction from heart sound signal

In this work, from the input heart sounds, different features are extracted. Normal and various types of abnormal heart sound signals were studied and the features (Magnitude and power spectrum, FFT, Zero Crossing, MFCC etc..,) were extracted from each case. For brevity, the heart sound signal corresponding to diastolic rumble alone is presented along with its extracted features (figure 3 to figure 7). The extracted features for the rumble heart murmur are listed in table 2.

Table 2. Extracted features for diastolic rumble

Feature	Remarks
1	Spectrogram (Time Vs Frequency plot)
2	FFT of Signal (Gives magnitude Vs Frequency)
3	Heart sound signal and its emphasis value
4	Fourier Transform (Energy Spectrum)
5	MFCC (Mel Frequency Cepstral Coefficient)

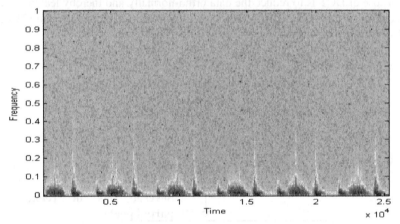

Fig. 3. Spectrogram (Time-Frequency) plot of the heart sound signal

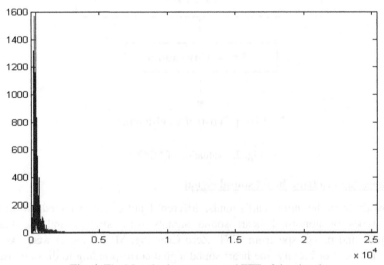

Fig. 4. The Magnitude response and FFT of the signal

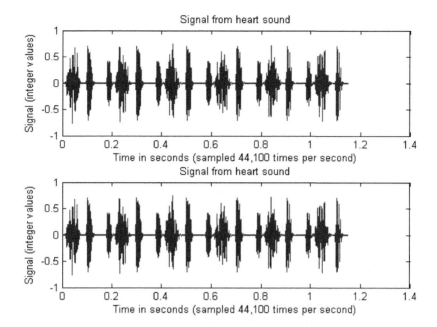

Fig. 5. Heart sound signal and its emphasis value

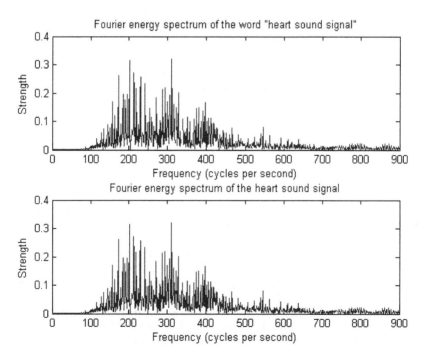

Fig. 6. The Energy spectrum of the signal

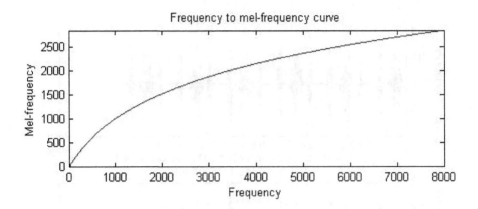

Fig. 7. Mel Frequencies of the heart sound signal

2 Conclusion

In this work the proposed robust model that quantitatively predicts human Cardio status and facilitates the field of Automatic Heart signal analysis is simulated and tested. The developed model shall be used as front end for ASR .The sharpness is measured using the ratio of arithmetic mean to the geometric mean of medium-duration power. [6]. When subtracting this bias level, power flooring is applied to enhance robustness. Future direction of study shall focus on the design of classifiers to process the extracted Features.

Acknowledgement. The authors would like to acknowledge Dr. M.G.R. Educational and Research Institute, Chennai-95 and M/s Micro Logic Systems, Chennai-17 for their coordination provided towards the conduct of experimental studies related to speech waveforms.

References

1. Ohnuki, K., Takahashi, W., Yoshizawa, S., Miyanaga, Y.: Noise Robust Speech Features for Automatic Continuous Speech Recognition using Running Spectrum Analysis. In: Proceedings of 2008 International Symposium on Communications and Information Technologies (ISCIT), pp. 150–153 (October 2008)
2. Chaiwongsai, J., Chiracharit, W., Chamnongthai, K., Miyanaga, Y.: An Architecture of HMM-Based Isolated-Word Speech Recognition with Tone Detection Function. In: Proceedings of 2008 International Symposium on Intelligent Signal Processing and Communication Systems (ISPACS) (December 2008)
3. Suktangman, N., Khanthavivone, K., Songwatana, K., Miyanaga, Y.: Robust Speech Recognition Based on Speech Spectrum on Bark Scale. In: EURASIP Proceedings of 2007 International Workshop on Nonlinear Signal and Image Processing (NSIP), pp. 135–138 (September 2007)

4. Yoshizawa, S., Wada, N., Hayasaka, N., Miyanaga, Y.: Scalable Architecture for Word HMM-Based Speech Recognition and VLSI Implementation in Complete System. IEEE Transactions on Circuits and Systems I 53(1), 70–77 (2006)
5. Hayasaka, N., Miyanaga, Y.: Spectrum Filtering with FRM for Robust Speech Recognition. In: IEEE Proceedings of International Symposium on Circuits and Systems (ISCAS), vol. (2), pp. 3285–3288 (May 2006)
6. Wada, N., Hayasaka, N., Yoshizawa, S., Miyanaga, Y.: Direct Control on Modulation Spectrum for Noise-Robust Speech Recognition and Spectral Subtraction. In: IEEE International Symposium on Circuits and Systems (ISCAS), pp. 2533–2536 (May 2006)
7. Kim, C., Stern, R.M.: Power function-based power distribution normalization algorithm for robust speech recognition. In: IEEE Automatic Speech Recognition and Understanding Workshop, pp. 188–193 (December 2009)
8. Raj, B., Parikh, V.N., Stern, R.M.: The effects of background music on speech recognition accuracy. In: Proc. IEEE Int. Conf. Acoust., Speech and Signal Processing, vol. 2, pp. 851–854 (April 1997)
9. Raj, B., Stern, R.M.: Missing-Feature Methods for Robust Automatic Speech Recognition. IEEE Signal Processing Magazine 22(5), 101–116 (2005)
10. Hirsch, H.G.: Aurora-5 Experimental Framework for the Performance Evaluation of Speech Recognitionin Case of a Hands-free Speech Input in Noisy Environments, http://aurora.hsnr.de/aurora-5/reports.html
11. Chen, C., Bilmes, J.A.: MVA Processing of Speech Features. IEEE Trans. on Speech and Audio Proc. 15(1), 257–270 (2007)
12. Thomas, S., Ganapathy, S., Hermansky, H.: Hilbert Envelope Based features for Far-field Speech recognition. In: Machine Learning for Multimodal Interaction (MLMI), Utrecht, The Netherlands (September 2008)
13. Hermansky, H.: Perceptual linear prediction analysis of speech. J. Acoust. Soc. Am. 87(4), 1738–1752 (1990)

Improved Intelligent Dynamic Swarm PSO Algorithm and Rough Set for Feature Selection

J. Anuradha and B.K. Tripathy

School of Computing Science and Engineering, VIT University, Vellore
{januradha,bktripathy}@vit.ac.in

Abstract. Feature Selection is one of the most important preprocessing steps in the field of Data Mining in handling dimensionality problems. It produces a smallest set of rules from the training data set with predetermined targets. Various techniques like Genetic Algorithm, Rough set, Swarm based approaches have been applied for Feature Selection (FS). Particle swarm Optimization was proved to be a competitive technique for FS. However it has certain limitations like premature convergence which is resolved by Intelligent Dynamic Swarm (IDS) algorithm. IDS could produce the reduct set in a smaller time complexity but lacks the accuracy. In this paper we propose an improvised algorithm of IDS for feature selection.

Keywords: Feature Selection, Data Mining, Particle Swarm Optimization.

1 Introduction

Dimensionality of the data is the major concern in data analysis. Higher dimensionality increases the complexity and accuracy of the algorithms. Dimensionality reduction is the interesting area of research which can contribute to various domains like pattern matching, image processing, classification, clustering, signal processing, Networks, optimization problems etc., Briefly higher dimensions leads to poor estimate of probability distribution and hence less accuracy. Feature selection algorithms provide solution to this problem by finding the best possible subset (reduct) from the training samples to address the predetermined targets. The selected subset should be necessary and sufficient in representing the patterns of the original samples to determine the targets. Feature Selection algorithms reduce the problem size, hence the solution space is reduced and thus improves the accuracy.

Evolutionary algorithms which evolved after biological inspiration of evolution are most popular in FS. Evolutionary algorithms like Genetic Algorithm (GA), Ant Colony, Particle Swarm Optimization (PSO), Simulated Annealing has been successfully used to handle this problem. Other techniques like rough set, statistical methods are also being used. Out of these PSO is proved to be competitive with other algorithms [2]. The conventional PSO algorithm can handle continuous variables but not well defined for discrete problems. The aim of the proposed algorithm is to

P.V. Krishna, M.R. Babu, and E. Ariwa (Eds.): ObCom 2011, Part II, CCIS 270, pp. 110–119, 2012.

- Reduce the dimension
- Increase the speed
- Increase the accuracy
- Applicability to handle both continuous and discrete data set

Intelligent Dynamic Swarm (IDS) address the discrete variables but uses only random number generation to decide on the position. It is successful in attaining its aim of reducing dimension and time complexity but does not guaranty the efficiency. The proposed algorithm works on the concept of both traditional PSO and IDS.

The following section gives the overview of literature review. Section 3 has the detailed explanation on the proposed algorithm and its flowchart. Section 5 gives the analysis of the IIDS algorithm. Section 4 gives the conclusion, Future Enhancement.

2   Literature Review

Particle swarm Optimization was derived from the flock of birds flying on the sky and their speed is controlled by the velocity and the position of each bird. The same concept is applied in PSO algorithm to solve optimization problems. It corresponds to the quality factors *pbest* and *gbest*. They are the best previous position and best global (best particle among all particle in the population) position respectively [3].

2.1   Particle Swarm Optimization Algorithm (PSO)

PSO is initialized with random solution and start its exploration for best particle among the population. The ith particle is represented as x_i, $y_j(t)$ and $y_j^\wedge(t)$ are the *pbest* and *gbest* of the particle i. The rate of the positional change (velocity) is represented as v_i. During the exploration, the particles are manipulated by updating the velocity and can be done by the following formulae [12]

$$v_i(t+1)=wv_{i(t)} + c_1\, r_1(t)(y_i(t) - x_i(t)) + c_2\, r_2(t)(y^\wedge(t) - x_j(t)) \qquad (2.1.1)$$
$$x_i(t+1) = x_i(t) + v_i(t+1) \qquad (2.1.2)$$

where w is the inertia weight. Suitable selection of inertia weight provides a balance between local and global exploration. $v_{ij}(t+1)$ is the velocity updated for jth dimension, j=1,2, ... d of ith particle. c_1 and c_2 are the acceleration coefficients that pull each particle towards pbest and gbest. Low values result in slow convergence where as higher value result in faster movement. $r_1(t)$ and $r_2(t)$ are the random variables with uniform distribution. x_i particle i is flying to new position $x_i(t+1)$ from $x_i(t)$. The following is the standard PSO algorithm [7]

set c_1, c2, t_{max} , t=0
initialize p
do while t ≠ t_{max} or *stopping condition is meet*
{
t=t+1

```
for i=1 to s
{
  if( f(xᵢ(t)) < f(yᵢ(t)) )
      yᵢ(t) = xᵢ(t)
  if( f(xᵢ(t)) < f(yᵢ^(t)) )
      yᵢ^(t) = xᵢ(t)
  Evaluate velocity updation using Eq.(2.1.1)
  Evaluate particle updation using Eq.(2.1.2)
}//end for
}//end while
```

PSO has been handled in different dimensions for feature selections. Research has been carried out in the directions of velocity updation, finding the *pbest* and *gbest* values, guaranteed convergence, fitness function, hybrid of PSO with other techniques etc,. An adaptive Feature selection algorithm resolves the complexity of finding the best particle in discrete variables. This algorithm uses binary vector x_{ij} as position of the particle and has the value 1 if the feature subset is included otherwise 0. Whereas in continuous variable, it uses the formula given in Eq.(2.1.2) for position updation. Discrete PSO transforms the velocity into probability vector through sigmoidal function.

$$S_{ij}^{t} = \frac{1}{1 + e^{-v_{ij}^{t}}}, \tag{2.1.3}$$

S_{ij}^{t} represent the probability that the jth bit included in x_i^{t} is 1. Hence, the position of the particle in discrete PSO can be updated as

$$x_{ij}^{t} = \begin{cases} 1 & if \ \delta < S_{ij}^{t} \\ 0 & otherwise \end{cases} \quad i, j = 1, 2, \dots k \tag{2.1.4}$$

Where δ is a uniform random number between 0 and 1. Inertia weight is updated at each iteration using Eq.(2.1.5)[10].

$$\omega^{t+1} = \omega_{max} - \frac{(\omega_{max} - \omega_{min})t}{T}, \tag{2.1.5}$$

Where ω_{max} and ω_{min} are the bounds of the inertia weights and T is the maximum number of PSO iterations. The velocity limitation v_{max} (maximum velocity) is the important constraint in controlling the global or local exploration of particle swarm, therefore one should be very conscious in fixing the maximum velocity. A larger v_{max} value facilitates global exploration and smaller v_{max} values support local exploration. When its value is too low, the particle will stuck in local optima and if it has too high value the particles may fly past good solutions. The limitation of PSO is the premature convergence. This was overcome by having an improved formula for velocity updation and simple rules to find the successive success and failures based on which the scaling factor is adjusted [3]. The following equation is for velocity updation

$$v_j(t+1)=wv_{j(t)} + y_j^\wedge(t)- x_j(t)+\rho(t)(1-2\ r_j(t))\qquad(2.1.6)$$

where $\rho(t)$ is the scaling factor causing PSO to generate the random values. This can be modified by

$$\rho(t+1) = \begin{cases} 2\rho(t) & if\ S_{num} > S_c \\ .5\rho(t) & if\ f_{num} > f_c \\ \rho(t) & otherwise \end{cases}\qquad(2.1.7)$$

where S_{num} and f_{num} indicate the number of successive success and failures respectively. S_c and f_c are the threshold values set to change $\rho(t)$. Simple rule for their updation is

$$\text{if } S_{num}(t+1) > S_{num}(t) \text{ then } f_{num}(t+1) = 0$$
$$\text{if } f_{num}(t+1) > f_{num}(t) \text{ then } s_{num}(t+1) = 0$$

this guarantees the convergence in exploring the best feature subset. An improved binary PSO algorithm (IBPSO) is the slight variant of binary PSO where this algorithm ensure that *pbest* will never struck in local optimum and therefore superior classification results can be obtained [2]. This method monitors the value of *gbest* and if it remains in the same position for more than the specified iteration, then it is considered to be trapped in local optimum. The IBPSO algorithm resets the trapped *gbest* value, there by exploring on a new space with new *gbest* value. This process achieves superior classification with reduced set.

2.2   Rough Set (RS)

Most of our traditional tools for formal modeling, reasoning and computing are deterministic and precise in character. Real situations are very often not deterministic and they cannot be described precisely. For a complete description of a real system often one would require by far more detailed data than a human being could ever recognize simultaneously, process and understand. This observation led to the extension of the basic concept of sets so as to model imprecise data which can enhance their modeling power. The fundamental concept of sets has been extended in many directions in the recent past. The notion of Fuzzy Sets, introduced by Zadeh [10] deals with the approximate membership and the notion of Rough Sets, introduced by Pawlak [9][10] captures indiscernibility of the elements in a set. These two theories have been found to complement each other instead of being rivals. The idea of rough set consists of approximation of a set by a pair of sets, called the lower and upper approximations of the set. The basic assumption in rough set is that, knowledge depends upon the classification capabilities of human beings. Since every classification (or partition) of a universe and the concept of equivalence relation are interchangeable notions, the definition of rough sets depends upon equivalence relations as its mathematical foundations.

Let U ($\neq \emptyset$) be a finite set of objects, called the universe and R be an equivalence relation over U. By U / R we denote the family of all equivalence classes of R (or classification of U) referred to as *categories* or *concepts* of R and $[x]_R$ denotes a category in R containing an element x∈U. By a Knowledge base, we understand a relation system k= (U, R), where U is as above and R is a family of equivalence relations over U.

For any subset P ($\neq \emptyset$) ⊆ R, the intersection of all equivalence relations in P is denoted by IND (P) and is called the *indiscernibility relation over* P. The equivalence classes of IND (P) are called P- *basic knowledge* about U in K. For any Q∈R, Q is called a Q-elementary knowledge about U in K and equivalence classes of Q are called Q-*elementary concepts of knowledge* R. The family of P-basic categories for all $\emptyset \neq P \subseteq R$ will be called the *family of basic categories* in knowledge base K. By IND (K), we denote the family of all equivalence relations defined in k. Symbolically, IND (K) = {IND (P): $\emptyset \neq P \subseteq R$}.

For any X ⊆ U and an equivalence relation R ∈ IND (K), we associate two subsets, $\underline{R}X = \bigcup\{Y \in U / R : Y \subseteq X\}$ and $\overline{R}X = \bigcup\{Y \in U / R : Y \cap X \neq \emptyset\}$, called the R-*lower* and R-*upper approximations* of X respectively. The R-*boundary* of X is denoted by $BN_R(X)$ and is given by $BN_R(X) = \overline{R}X - \underline{R}X$. The elements of $\underline{R}X$ are those elements of U which can be certainly classified as elements of X employing knowledge of R. The borderline region is the undecidable area of the universe. We say X is *rough* with respect to R if and only if $\underline{R}X \neq \overline{R}X$, equivalently $BN_R(X) \neq \emptyset$. X is said to be R- *definable* if and only if $\underline{R}X = \overline{R}X$, or $BN_R(X) = \emptyset$. So, a set is rough with respect to R if and only if it is not R-definable.

2.1.3 Definitions

Definition 2.1.3.1 (Indiscernibility relation (Ind (B))): Ind (B) is a relation on U. Given two objects x_i, $x_j \in$ U, they are indiscernible by the set of attributes B in A, if and only if a (x_i) = a (x_j) for every a∈B. That is, (x_i, $x_j \in$ Ind (B) if and only if $\forall$ a∈B where B⊆A, a (x_i) = a (x_j).

Definition 2.1.3.2 (Equivalence class ($[x_i]_{\text{Ind (B)}}$)): Given Ind (B), the set of objects x_i having the same values for the set of attributes in B consists of an equivalences classes, $[x_i]_{\text{Ind(B)}}$. It is also known as elementary set with respect to B.

Definition 2.1.3.3 (Lower approximation): Given the set of attributes B in A, set of objects X in U, the lower approximation of X is defined as the union of all the elementary sets which are contained in X. That is

$$\underline{X}_B = \cup \ x_i \mid [x_i]_{\text{Ind (B)}} \subseteq X\}.$$

Definition 2.1.3.4 (upper approximation): Given the set of attributes B in A, set of objects X in U, the upper approximation of X is defined as the union of the elementary sets which have a nonempty intersection with X. That is

$$\overline{X}_B = \cup \ \{x_i \mid [x_i]_{\text{Ind (B)}} \cap X \neq \emptyset \}.$$

Definition 2.1.3.5 (Roughness): The ratio of the cardinality of the lower approximation and the cardinality of the upper approximation is defined as the accuracy of estimation, which is a measure of roughness. It is presented as

$$R_B(X) = 1 - \frac{|\underline{X}_B|}{|\overline{X}_B|}$$

If $R_B(X) = 0$, X is crisp with respect to B, in other words, X is precise with respect to B. If $R_B(X) < 1$, X is rough with respect to B, That is, B is vague with respect to X.

Another attempt to capture impreciseness in data led to the development of the concept of rough sets, put forth by Z.Pawlak [10] in 1982. In rough set theory, with every set we associate two crisp sets called the lower approximation and the upper approximation of the set. If the lower and upper approximations coincide then we say that the set is crisp and otherwise it is called rough. Mathematically we define a rough set as follows:

Let U be a universal set and $X \subseteq U$. Let R be an equivalence relation defined over U. Then we define, $\underline{R}X = \{x \in U / [x]_R \subseteq X\}$ and $\overline{R}X = \{x \in U / [x]_R \cap X \neq \phi\}$, called the lower and upper approximation of X with respect R. X is rough with respect to R if and only if $\underline{R}X \neq \overline{R}X$ and crisp otherwise.

3   Improved Intelligent Dynamic Swarm Algorithm (IIDS)

Intelligent Dynamic Swarm (IDS) works on binary PSO for discrete variables. The IDS differs the standard PSO in finding the position of the particles for discrete values. The standard PSO uses the Eqs. (2.1.1) and (2.1.2) for finding the position of the particles. It works well for the continuous data, but not well defined for discrete data. The IDS does not use the above said equations for particle positioning. It rather uses random values for fixing the particle positions of *pbest* and *gbest* and discrete variables are handled by the following equation.

$$x_{ij}^t = \begin{cases} x_{ij}^{t-1} & if \ R_{ij}^{t-1} \in [0, C_w) \\ p_{ij}^{t-1} & if \ R_{ij}^{t-1} \in [C_w, C_p) \\ g_i & if \ R_{ij}^{t-1} \in [C_p, C_g) \\ x & if \ R_{ij}^{t-1} \in [C_g, 1) \end{cases} \qquad (3.1)$$

This method overcomes the drawback of handling discrete variables by using random number R_{ij}^t to update the values of P_{ij}^t and g_i based on the values of current weight (c_w), current pbest (c_p) and current gbest (c_g).

3.1   Intelligent Dynamic Swarm Algorithm (IDS)

The IDS complexity is reduced by eliminating the computation involved in moving the particle to next position i.e velocity updation and particle updation formulae.

Thus, the complexity of O(6nm) in standard PSO is reduced to O(3nm) (obtained by having two multiplication and one comparison)[1]. The flowchart of the individual update of *pbest, gbest* for discrete variable is given in Figure 1.

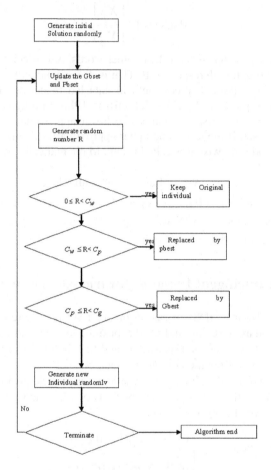

Fig. 1. Flowchart of the individual update

IDS though reduces the complexity of PSO, it still may not be efficient in finding the position of the individuals since it uses random positions rather exploring. Our proposed Improved IDS algorithm overcomes this problem and also has well defined model for discrete variable.

3.2   Improved Intelligent Dynamic Swarm Algorithm (IIDS)

IIDS works on discrete variables in addressing PSO feature selection problem. It uses the concept from both standard PSO and IDS. The positioning of particle can be found and updates using the *pbest* (P_i) and *gbest* (G) by the following formulae.

$$V_i(t+1) = \omega V_i(t) + C_1 R_1(t)(P_i(t) - X_i(t)) + C_2 R_2(G(t) - X_i(t)) \qquad (3.2.1)$$
$$X_i(t+1) = X_i(t) + V_i(t+1) \qquad (3.2.2)$$

The inertia weight can be updated using the Eq. (2.1.5). The fitness function helps in finding the best position based on the accuracy of the classification. This can be computed using rough set approach and is given by equation (3.2.3)

$$\text{Fitness}(i) = \alpha * \gamma_R(D) + \beta * \frac{|C| + |R|}{|C|} \qquad (3.2.3)$$

$\gamma_R(D)$ - Classification quality of condition attribute set R relative to decision
    attribute D

α, β -   Parameters corresponds to importance of classification quality and sub set
    length respectively where $\alpha \in [0,1], \beta = 1 - \alpha$

Swarm particles local best and global best can be generated for discrete variables based on the weight ω, pbest P_i, gbest G. If $0 \le V_i < \omega$ then the original individual will be kept , else if $\omega \le V_i < P_i$ then the original dimension will be replaced by *pbest* P_i else if $P_i \le V_i < G$ then the original dimension will be replaced by *gbest* G or else if $G \le V_i < 1$ then the original dimension will be replaced by new value X_i which is generated by Eq.(3.2.2). The improved IDS algorithm is given below.

1.   set the parameters c1,c2, $\omega_{max}, \omega_{min}$, v_{max} , v_{min}

2.   initialize $v_i^1 = 0$ $\omega = \omega_{max}$

3.   initialize particles x_i^1 for i= 1 to n randomly

4.   set $p_i^1 = x_i^1$ and G to index i

5.   while (the number of iteration or stopping condition is not meet)

6.   for i=1 to number of particles.

7.   if fitness(x_i) > p_i then
        $p_i = x_i$

8.   if any particle x_i > gbest
        gbest = i (position of the *gbest* particle)

9.   for j = number of dimension of the particle

10. $V_{ij}(t+1) = \omega V_{ij}(t) + C_1 R_1(t)(P_{ij}(t) - X_{ij}(t)) + C_2 R_2(G_j(t) - X_{ij}(t))$

11. if($V_{ij} > V_{max}$) then
        $V_{ij} = V_{max}$

12. if($V_{ij} < -V_{max}$) then
        $V_{ij} = -V_{max}$

13. If ($0 \le V_i < \omega$) then
        $x_i^t = x_i^{t-1}$

14. else if ($\omega \le V_i < P_i$) then

$x_i^t = P_i$ (*pbest*)

15. else if ($P_i \le V_i < G$) then

$x_i^t = G$ (*gbest*)

16. or else if ($G \le V_i < 1$) then

$x_i^t = x_i^{t+1}$ (updated new value)

17. next j value
18. next i value
19. next generation until stopping criterion
20. terminate the algorithm

The proposed algorithm thus works on the discrete variables with exploration of best particle position. Hence it will produce efficient results for discrete variables.

4   Analysis of Improved Intelligent Dynamic Swarm Algorithm (IIDS)

IIDS algorithm is capable of producing the accurate results since it works on the principle of standard PSO in exploring the best particle. It overcomes the limitation of standard PSO and IDS by handling the discrete variables and efficient exploration. However the complexity of the code might be nearly equal to standard PSO which is higher than IDS, but the accuracy will be comparatively higher than IDS since the later uses random positioning of particles.

The IIDS algorithm can be applied only to discrete data. Therefore continuous data can be discretized before applying to this algorithm. Data discretization can done by applying standard discretization techniques like binning, histrogram analysis, entropy method etc.,[5].

5   Conclusions and Future Work

PSO are found to be competitive methods for feature selection. There has been a tremendous growth in PSO Feature Selection algorithms. This paper provides an overview of evolution in PSO algorithms and we also proposed an improved algorithm for feature selection.

The proposed algorithm called the Improved Intelligent Dynamic Swarm (IIDS) is an efficient model for feature selection having discrete variables. However, continuous data need to be discretized before applying this algorithm. The complexity of the IIDS code is very much equal to standard PSO but has better efficiency. On the other hand the time complexity and efficiency of IDS are lower than PSO. Here we have sacrificed complexity to have better efficiency. The future work in this direction can be to reduce the complexity of the algorithm without affecting the efficiency.

References

1. Bae, C., Yeh, W.C., Chung, Y., Liu, S.: Feature Selection with Intelligent Dynamic Swarm and Rough Set. Expert System with Application 37, 7026–7032 (2010)
2. Chuang, L.Y., Chang, H.W., Tu, C.J., Yang, C.H.: Improved binary PSO for feature selection using gene expression data. Computational Biology and Chemistry 32, 29–38 (2008)
3. Fripi, H.A., Goodman, E.: Swarmed Feature Selection. In: Proceedings of 33rd Applied Imagery Pattern Recognition Workshop (2004)
4. Huang, C.L., Dun, J.F.: A distributed PSO – SVM Hybrid System with Feature Selection and parameter Optimization. Applied Soft Computing 8, 1381–1391 (2008)
5. Han, J., Kamber, M.: Data Mining Concepts and Techniques, 2nd edn. Elsevier Publication
6. Hung, C.C., Purnawan, H., Kuo, B.C., Letkeman, S.: Multispectal Image Classification using Rough Set Theory and Particle Swarm Optimization. In: Advances in Geoscience and Remote Sensing, pp. 569–596 (2007)
7. Kennedy, J., Eberhart, R.: Particle Swarm Optimization. In: IEEE International Conference, pp. 1942–1948 (1995)
8. Özbakır, L., Delice, Y.: Exploring comprehensible classification rules from trained neural networks integrated with a time-varying binary particle swarm optimizer. Engineering Applications of Artificial Intelligence (2010), doi:10.1016 /j.engappai. 2010.11.008
9. Pawlak, Z.: Rough sets. International Journal Computer and Information Science 11, 341–356 (1982)
10. Pawlak, Z.: Rough Set Theory –Theoretical Aspects of Reasoning About Data. Kluwar Academic Publishers, Norwell (1992)
11. Unler, A., Murat, A.: A discrete particle Swarm Optimization method for feature selection in binary classification problems. European Journal of Operation Research 26, 528–539 (2010)
12. Wang, X., Yang, J., Xiaolong, T., Xia, W., Jensen, R.: Feature Selection based on Rough Set and Particle Swarm Optimization. Pattern Recognition Letters 28, 459–471 (2007)

Estimating Database Size and Its Development Effort at Conceptual Design Stage

Samaresh Mishra[1], Elina Aisuryalaxmi[1], and Rajib Mall[2]

[1] School of Computer Engineering, KIIT University, Bhubaneswar, India
[2] Department of Computer Science & Engineering, Indian Institute of Technology, Kharagpur, India
{samaresh2,aisurya.elina}@gmail.com, rajib@cse.iitkgp.ernet.in

Abstract. In recent years, the database size of information system software is increasing rapidly along with the development of the technology of software and its estimation techniques. Generally, any software product may consist of basic three components: data, functional, and document. The estimation of development effort for software depends on the effort required for the development of these components. The database development effort primarily depends on the database volume. In this paper, a set of metrics have been proposed and validated for estimating database size using ER and Enhanced ER diagram artifacts. The effort of database development based on the proposed size metrics have been validated using COCOMO model.

Keywords: database size, size estimation, effort estimation, ER diagram.

1   Introduction

Software cost estimation is crucial for project management team as it helps to develop a quality and successful software. The successful implementation of any data-intensive software product primarily depends on the organization of data in the database. The relational database system (RDBS) is popular among practitioners for designing and developing database of a software product in both function-oriented and object-oriented development environment. Identifying the structure of data and their relationship can be done using either entity relationship model or UML class diagram model or both. After this, the above graphical models are converted into a data model (RDBS-Relational Database System) for implementation. The effort of development of database may depend on the database size volume and on the data complexity exist in the data model. The structure of database basically depends on the types of attributes exist in individual tables and the relationships exist among them, and the relationship exist among different tables. The database size is primarily depends on the number of data structures (tables) in the database and the size of individual database tables. On the other hand the data complexity depends on the type relationship exist among data elements and the number of integrity constraints exist in the data model. The table size is a measure of number of attributes (data fields), their type,

P.V. Krishna, M.R. Babu, and E. Ariwa (Eds.): ObCom 2011, Part II, CCIS 270, pp. 120–127, 2012.

size and the total number of tuples in the table [7]. As most effort estimating techniques considers the size as their input and COCOMO is a popular effort estimation model among them [4], so the effort of back-end (database) development may be measured based on the predicted database size. Now the requirement of effort estimation has been shifted to database size estimation during early phase of database life cycle process using ER diagram and its extension (EER diagram). As relational database system is rich with various types of integrity constraints [7] and some of these can be specified in both ER (and its extension, EER) diagram, so the necessity is there for identifying and using integrity constraints present in ER (and its extension) diagram artifacts.

This paper has been organized as follows: In section-2, we have presented the related work, in section-3 and 4, we presented our metric suit for measuring database size and the model for effort estimation, in section-5, we discussed our experimental study. Finally, section-6 concludes our work.

2   Related Work

The ER diagram of Chen's method was introduced in 1976 in order to capture data requirements of any proposed data intensive software. Although UML is popular for modeling software developed using object oriented approach, the data modeling is still based on relational approach irrespective of object oriented or function oriented approach of software development. The literature has a good number of proposed metrics measuring database quality using ER diagram artifacts [5]. The metrics on cost estimation using ER diagram is very rarely found in the literature. The researchers like Geoffrey J. Kennedy [1], Yuan Zhao [2], and Hee Beng Kuan Tan [3] have proposed and validated metrics based on ER diagram artifacts, for measuring database complexity and database size in order to estimate development effort. These works has considered the different types of structures exist for understanding data models and identifying anomalies in ER diagram [10], the total number of entities, total number of relationships, and total number of attributes [9][10][11] exist in ER diagram. In addition to the above artifacts, the number of path complexity [9] existing in an ER diagram also considered for measuring software effort. There are metrics for estimating database size directly from relational database elements such as the number of tables, attributes, constraints, triggers, and views [7] [8]. These elements always contribute to the total size of database system. Some of the above elements are represented in the ER diagram through one-to-one, one-to-many and many-to-many relationships [8]. There are some metrics [1] used to predict structural complexity of ER diagram and are used for measuring quality of database system. The COCOMO and subsequently COCOCMO-II are becoming very popular among practitioners for estimating effort and development time of software [4]. They primarily use the Lines of Code or Function Point metrics for estimating software size rather the database size [6]. As design and development of data in a database plays very crucial role in data-intensive software and again, the early phase estimation are necessary for project managers, so the ER diagram (and its extension) may be used for estimating size.

3   DBSE: The Proposed Database Size Estimation Metric Suit

For measuring database size from ER diagram artifacts, we adopted Peter Chen's method [12] for constructing ER model. The extension of ER diagram (EER diagram) has also been considered in order to capture the concepts of generalization, specialization and aggregation relationships and the constraints of generalizations. The mapping cardinalities such as one-to-one, one-to-many, and many-to-many relationships that exist among entity sets also predict the increase in table size in terms of number of attributes as well as the number of tables. So, in this work, we have used the following important artifacts of ER/EER diagram for estimating database size.

- Number of simple attributes.
- Number of composite attributes.
- Number of multi-valued attributes.
- Number of derived attributes.
- The mapping cardinalities of relationships, i.e. one-to-one, one-to-many and many-to-many relationships.
- Depth of inheritance tree (DIT) in a generalization.

The lines of code (LOC) required for creating tables and implementing different constraints determined from ER (EER) diagram directly depends on the presence of number above artifacts.

The information of the different artifacts of ER (EER) diagram shown in table-1:

Table 1. Information of different artifacts of ER diagram

SA	Number of Simple Attributes
MVA	Number of Multivalued Attributes
M:1P	Number of Many-to-One participation constraints
PKS	Number of attributes representing primary key
DIT	Depth of Inheritance Tree. It is the number of ancestor entity sets that can affect an entity set.
DA	Number of Derived Attributes
DSA	Number of Descriptive Attributes

The artifacts presented in Table-1 (except PKS and DA) are used for estimating table size of the corresponding entity set. The PKS are already available in SA and each DA is represented as functionality and needs to be implemented separately. Based on above considerations, the entity size (ES) is estimated using the following equation:

$$ES = SA + MVA + M_i 1P + DIT \tag{1}$$

Once ES is estimated, then the entity set size (ESS) is measured by multiplying entity size with number of tuples of this entity type as given in equation-2.

$$ESS = ES \times M \tag{2}$$

Here M indicates total number of tuples to be generated for the entity set.

Finally the total entity set size (TESS) can be estimated by taking the sum of size of each entity set (SES) as follows:

$$TESS = \sum_{i=1}^{n} (ESS)_i \tag{3}$$

Where n indicates total number of entity sets in ER diagram.

All derived attributes are implemented using procedural language. So, the size of all derived attributes may be estimated by summing the lines of codes (LOC) required for implementation of each derived attributes. The size of all derived attributes (SDA) appearing in ER diagram is estimated by the following equation.

$$SDA = \sum_{k=1}^{p} (LOC)_k \tag{4}$$

Here p indicates total number of derived attributes in the ER diagram.

Again, each relationship sets with many-to-many mapping cardinality is represented as a relation. The attributes of such relations are taken from the relationship set, called descriptive attributes and the primary key attributes taken from participated entity sets, called foreign keys. The number of foreign keys is depended on the degree of relationship. We use the variable Degree, which stands for total number of entity sets participating in a relationship. That is if the Degree is 1 then the number of foreign keys will be 1, if the Degree is 2 then the number of foreign keys will be 2 and so on. So, the relationship size (RS) may be estimated as follow:

$$RS = DSA + Degree \tag{5}$$

Once RS is estimated, then the relationship set size (RSS) is measured by multiplying relationship size with number of tuples of this relationship type.

$$RSS = RS \times N \tag{6}$$

Here, N indicates total number of tuples to be generated for the relationship set.

The total relationship set size (TRSS) can be estimated by taking the sum of size of each relationship set (RS) with the following equation:

$$TRSS = \sum_{j=1}^{m} (RS)_j \tag{7}$$

Here m indicates total number of relationship sets in the ER diagram.

After estimating entity size and relationship size of ER diagram, the total ER size is measured as a sum of total entity size, total relationship size, and size of all derived attributes as shown equation-8.

$$TERS = TESS + TRSS + SDA \qquad (8)$$

4   Proposed Effort Estimation Model Based on DBSE Metric Suit

We proposed a model (depicted in Fig.1) for estimating effort of developing the database part of an information system (data intensive) using our proposed size estimation metrics suit, DBSE. Initially all the data requirements of the system is gathered. Then based on the requirements, the ER/EER diagram is constructed. Subsequently, a catalogue table is created for keeping the information about all entity sets, the relationship sets exist among entity sets as well as the information about their structural representation (Table-1). From this, the size of ER diagram is estimated using proposed size metrics. Finally, the effort of back-end development is estimated using the popular COCOMO method. Here we have considered database projects under semi-detached category and used the effort formula: **Effort = 3.0 × (Size)$^{1.12}$ PM** and **Development Time = 2.5 × (Effort)$^{0.35}$ Month**. We have considered the person hour (PH) and hour as the unit of effort and development time respectively instead of PM and month.

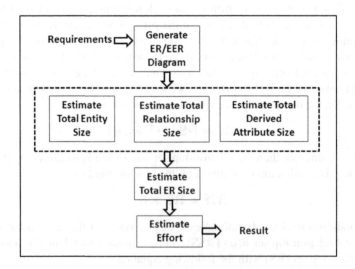

Fig. 1. Effort Estimation Model based on DBSE metric suit

5   Experimental Result and Comparison with Related Work

For empirical validation of our model, five number of student projects of KIIT University were taken as an experiment. All the projects considered here were information system based projects. We estimated size as per our proposed DBSE metrics. We used COCOMO model for effort estimation based on our proposed size estimation metric suit. We considered all five the projects are of semi-detached type. Here the front-end part of the system has not been considered for effort estimation rather only the back-end part has considered. In addition to the development effort, the development time also has been estimated using COCOMO method. The data of five projects and the associated result are depicted in Table-2.

Table 2. Effort Estimation Data

PROJECT No	No. of Entity Sets	No. of Relationship Sets	Number of DA	TESS	SDA	TRSS	TERS	ESTIMATED EFFORT (Using COCOMO in PH)	DEV TIME (in Hours)	ACTUAL EFFORT (in PH)	MMRE	Mean MRE
1	9	2	1	18265	5	4400	22670	15825.12	74	19200	0.18	
2	6	5	0	715	0	2260	2975	1627.6	33	2560	0.36	
3	3	1	1	1710	5	450	2165	1140.13	29	1760	0.35	0.29
4	3	1	1	2255	5	4800	7060	4284.52	47	5600	0.23	
5	5	1	0	2062	0	9	2071	1084.83	29	1600	0.32	

The observation from our experimental study indicates that, the effort of database development depends on the total database size. This database size has been greatly influenced by the existence of number of entities in the each entity set as well as the number of relationships in each relationship set. Although database size depends on the number of entity sets and relationship sets, but the number of such entities in the each entity set as well as the number of relationships in each relationship set has influence more on overall size estimation and subsequently on effort estimation. The Figure-2 has given a comparison between actual effort and estimated effort. The value of Mean MRE is 0.29, which is quite encouraging. The effect of derived attributes on effort estimation has found to have a limited role as their presence is very limited compared to other artifacts of ER diagram for modeling real world application system.

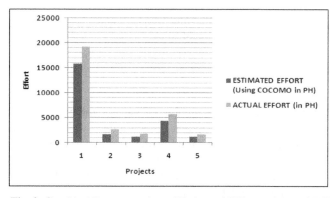

Fig. 2. Graphical Representation of Estimated Effort and Actual Effort

It has been observed from Figure-3 that, the main contribution to overall size of any database primarily depends on the total entity set size (TESS) as well as total relationship set size (TRRS). Some system may contribute more on relationships size compared to entity size in the total database size estimation process.

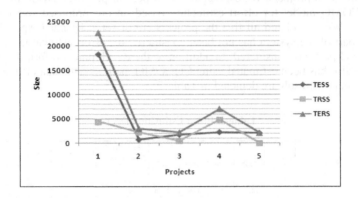

Fig. 3. Graphical comparison of TESS, TRSS and TERS

Our approach has considered the important artifacts of ER diagram such as many-to-one mapping cardinality, derived attributes, and depth of inheritances (DIT) for measuring database structure size in addition to the mostly used factors used by existing works such as number of entity sets, relationship sets and number of attributes. It has been found that the overall effort of database development depends on the database size and this size, again, depends on the number of entities and relationships exist in individual entity sets and relationship sets as well as the artifacts used for measuring database structure size.

Again, in order to check the effectiveness of our model, a multiple regression analysis approach was adopted to examine the relationship among effort and the artifacts such as TESS, TRSS and SDA. The following equation has been derived from regression analysis:

$$\text{Effort} = -202 + 0.99 * \text{TESS} + 0.72 * \text{TRSS} - 34.43 * \text{SDA}$$

The above equation indicates that the value of TESS and TRSS dominates the overall effort estimation as compared to value of SDA.

6   Conclusion

In this paper, we have identified a number of metrics for measuring database size from conceptual modeling of ER diagram. Based on this, we have estimated effort of development using the popular COCOMO model. Our experimental study results the mean MRE with a 0.29 value, which indeed favors a better accuracy. All these are applicable to small scale projects. So, the future work can be done on validation of this work by taking industry related projects.

References

1. Piattini, M., Genero, M., Calero, C.: Data Model Metrics. In: Handbook of Software Engineering and Knowledge Engineering (2001)
2. Tan, H.B.K., Zhao, Y.: Sizing Data-Intensive Systems from ER Model, The Institute of Electronics. Information and Communication Engineers, 1321–1326 (2006)
3. Elmasri, R., Navathe, S.B., Somayajulu, D.V.L.N., Gupta, S.K.: Fundamentals of Database Systems, 114,95,136. Pearson Education (2006)
4. Mall, R.: Fundamentals of Software Engineering, 2nd edn. PHI (2007)
5. Genero, M., Poels, G., Piattini, M.: Defining and Validating metrics For Assessing The Understandability of entity-relationship diagrams. Data and Knowledge Engineering, 534–557 (2008)
6. Ali, A., Qadri, S., Muhammad, S.S., Abbas, J., Tariqpervaiz, M., Awan, S.: Software Cost Estimation through Entity Relationship Model. Journal of American Science, 47–51 (2010)
7. Mishra, S., Tripathy, K.C., Mishra, M.K.: Effort Estimation Based on Complexity and Size of Relational Database System. International Journal of Computer Science & Communication, 419–422 (2010)
8. Jamil, B., Batool, A.: SMARtS-Software Metric Analyzer for Relational Database Systems. IEEE Transactions on Software Engineering, 978–983 (2010)
9. Zhao, Y., Tan, H.B.K., Zhang, W.: Software Cost Estimation through Conceptual Requirement. In: IEEE Third International Conference on Quality Software (QSIC 2003) (2003)
10. Kennedy, G.J.: Elementary structures in entity-relationship diagrams- a new metric for effort estimation. IEEE (1996)
11. Tan, H.B.K., Zhao, Y., Zhang, H.: Conceptual Data Model-Based Software Size Estimation for Information Systems. ACM Transactions on Software Engineering and Methodology 19(2), Article 4 (October 2009)
12. Chen, P.P.-S.: The Entity-Relationship Model-Toward a Unified View of Data. ACM Transactions on Database Systems 1(1), 9–36 (1976)

No Reference Image Quality Assessment Using Block Based Features and Artificial Neural Network

J.V. Bagade[1], Y.H. Dandawate[2], and Kulbir Singh[3]

[1] Department of Information Technology, VIIT, Pune-48, India
[2] Department of Electronics and Telecommunication, VIIT, Pune-48, India
[3] Department of Electronics and Telecommunication, Thapar University, Patiala, India
jayashrihedaoo@rediffmail.com, yhdandawate@gmail.com,
ksingh@thapar.edu

Abstract. In last decade, there has been explosive growth in multimedia technologies and its applications. For fast transmission, compression of image data is necessary. Due to this images are lead to distortion like blocking, ringing and blurring. The channel noise also gets introduced if transmitted over communication channel. Due to the distortion, image quality assessment plays an important role. In majority applications, original image is not available for reference. In such application, the metric which evaluates quality without reference is called "no reference quality" metric. Since human perception has limitation and in automated quality assessment application there is an immense need of developing no reference quality assessment framework. In this paper, we propose no reference image quality assessment scheme using the machine learning approach. Based on the degradation such as blocking, ringing artifacts, the related features such as average absolute difference between in-block image sample and zero-crossing rate, spatial frequency measure and spatial activity measures are computed for JPEG gray scale images. The earlier related work uses such parameters and mathematical predictors. Many time the correlation of extracted features, DMOS and output of predictor do not present correct assessment. In the proposed approach, properly trained back propagation artificial neural network with MOS as target is used. The result indicates that accuracy of quality assessment is better.

Keywords: Image Quality Assessment, Artificial Neural Networks, No Reference quality, Compression artifacts, blocking and ringing artifacts, block based features, quality score, machine learning approach, back propagation neural network, Mean Opinion Score.

1 Introduction

In last decade, there has been explosive growth in multimedia technologies and its applications. Representation of image data, transmission of the same over internet, security and retrieval are the real challenges. For multimedia applications like education, entertainment, business and telemedicine fast transmission of image data over internet is essential. For fast transmission, compression of image data is

P.V. Krishna, M.R. Babu, and E. Ariwa (Eds.): ObCom 2011, Part II, CCIS 270, pp. 128–138, 2012.
© Springer-Verlag Berlin Heidelberg 2012

necessary. There are two types of compression techniques viz Lossless and lossy compression. Since lossy compression offers large compression ratio, it is preferred over lossless compression in the application mentioned above. In lossy compression since there is loss of image data, this leads to distortions like blockiness, ringing, and blurring, which degrade the quality of compressed images. The channel noise also gets introduced if transmitted over communication channel. Images are also distorted during image acquisition, processing and reproduction. Due to the distortion, image quality assessment plays an important role.

The quality assessment of images is broadly classified into two categories 1) Subjective quality assessment and 2) Objective quality assessment. Subjective quality metric such as Mean Opinion Score (MOS) deals with average ranking given by different viewers [1,2]. This method is reliable but slow and expensive. Due to which, in last two decades efforts has been made to develop objective image quality metric. Objective quality measures are further classified as mathematically defined measures and Human Visual System (HVS) based measures. Though, mathematically defined measures like Mean Square Error (MSE) and Peak Signal to Noise Ratio (PSNR) are widely accepted, they are also criticised for not correlating with perceived quality of image [3]. To assess the perceived quality of image HVS based measures are developed and used to overcome drawback of mathematically defined measures quality assessment.

Objective quality measures are further classified into 1) Full Reference (FR) 2) Reduce Reference (RR) and 3) No Reference (NR) [4,5]. In majority applications, original image is not available for reference. For example output of digital camera, which are compressed images in JPEG format; images are transmitted over network. In such application, the metric which evaluates quality without reference is called "no reference quality" metric. Since human perception has limitation and in automated quality assessment application there is an immense need of developing no reference quality assessment framework.

In this paper, we propose no reference image quality assessment scheme using the machine learning approach. Based on the degradation such as blocking, ringing artifacts, the related features such as average absolute difference between in-block image sample and zero-crossing rate, spatial frequency measure and spatial activity measures are computed for JPEG gray scale images. The earlier related work uses such parameters and mathematical predictors. Many time the correlation of extracted features, DMOS and output of predictor do not present correct assessment. In the proposed approach, properly trained back propagation artificial neural network with MOS as target is used. The result indicates that accuracy of quality assessment is better. The proposed approach used parameters even though designed for JPEG compressed images, there are good quality image other than JPEG for no reference quality assessment. Thus it is necessary to make the quality assessment irrespective of only JPEG with blockiness.

The paper is organised as follows: Section 2 presents the related work on image quality assessment. Section 3 presents experimental methodology. In section 4 extracted features are discussed. Results are presented in section 5. Finally section 6 concludes this paper.

2   Related Work

S. Suresh *et al.* [6] proposed extreme machine learning based approach for image quality approach. The extracted features are edge amplitude, edge length, background activity, background luminance. This work is for JPEG compressed images and root means square error (RMSE) is 0.69 for training data set and 0.70 for testing data set. The score is calculated as posterior probability of features. Zhou Wang [7] used blockiness based features. Blockiness is estimated as average difference across block boundaries. The parameters are average absolute difference between in-block image sample and zero-crossing rate. For JPEG images he had given RMSE 0.75. Some other proposed parameters are pixel distortion, edge information, sharpness/blurriness by integrating just noticeable blur, statistical information on the gradient profile along strong edge [8, 9, 10]. The mathematical model is used to estimate the quality score. The score ranges from 0 to 10, where 10 is excellent.

Paolo Gastaldo *et al.* [11] proposed non-parametric features like first order histogram of image blocks, features derived from the co-occurrence matrix, features derived from frequency-based representation. The circular back propagation classifier is used to calculate quality score. This model gives 86% accuracy. In this paper pre-processing of original image is done using contrast enhancement filter. Michel Saad and A. C. Bovik [12] used probabilistic models to estimate quality score in which the DCT based features such as image structure and contrast are used and accuracy for this approach is 79%.

Some researchers reported NSS based features. A. K. Moorthy and A. C. Bovik [13] proposed an excellent framework for NR image quality assessment based on NSS model of images. A distortion specific signature is used to classify image in distortion category and evaluate the quality of images along each of this distortion. For classification multiclass support vector machine is used with 82% accuracy. Ming-Jung Chen *et al.* [14] used gradient histogram to calculate specific natural statistic. They proposed to evaluate the distance between the gradient statistics of an image and corresponding statistical model of natural scenes. For classification support vector machine is used. This model gives 96% accuracy.

From related work it has been noticed that most of the work used mathematical predictors; the model parameters were estimated using past data. These all predictors are mathematically calculated, but as mentioned earlier the human being is best evaluator for image assessment. Thus some research inclined towards machine learning approach for assessment.

3   Experimental Methodology

In the proposed framework, shown in fig 1 features are extracted from images and stored in database. This feature vector is used to train the back propagation artificial neural network [15]. The targets are given as Mean Opinion Score. This trained neural network computed quality score for test images. The architecture of the network that is most commonly used with the back propagation algorithm is the multilayer feedforward network. In proposed framework, feedforward network having one hidden layers of five logsig neurons followed by an output layer of one linear neuron is used. Multiple layers of neurons with nonlinear transfer functions allow the network to learn nonlinear and linear relationships between input and output vectors. The linear output layer lets the network produce values outside the range -1 to +1.

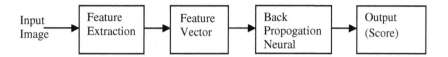

Fig. 1. Block diagram for methodology

To develop the model, we have selected two disjoint sets of images for training and testing. The training set images and its compression version are not used in testing set. 21 JPEG images and its compression version using quality factor 70, 50, 10 and blurred images with 50 quality factor are used for training; total 105 images are used for training. 10 JPEG images and its compression versions, total 50 images are used for testing. Feature vectors are extracted from training dataset to train back propagation neural network. This neural network has one hidden layer with three neurons and one output layer with one neuron. Non linear logsig function is used to lean non linear and linear relationship between input and output vector. This trained network is used to calculate the quality scores for test image dataset. We had done the following experiment: the MOS is given as target and extracted features as input to the neural network. This MOS had been taken from 20 objects, from which 10 are non experts and 10 are experts. The image quality scores for test image dataset are calculated.

4   Feature Extraction

JEPG is DCT-based lossy compression technique. Due to quantization operation applied to 8×8 DCT-block some of image details were lost. Effect of quantization created blocking and ringing artifacts. The blurring effect is due to loss of high frequency DCT coefficient and blocking effect is due to discontinuity at block boundaries. Discontinuity at block boundaries occurs due to block based quantization and blocks are quantized independently[7].

The effective way to examine both the blurring and blocking effects is to transform the signal into the frequency domain. The test image signal is denoted as $x(m, n) for\ m \in [1, M]$ and $n \in [1, N]$, and calculate a differencing signal along each horizontal line:

$$d_h(m, n) = x(m, n+1) - x(m, n), n \in [1, N-1] \ . \tag{1}$$

Let $f_m = |d_h(m,n)|$ be a 1-D horizontal signal for a fixed value of m. The features are calculated horizontally and vertically.

1. The blockiness is as the average difference across block boundaries

$$B_h = \frac{1}{M(\lfloor N/8 \rfloor - 1)} \sum_{i=1}^{M} \sum_{j=1}^{\lfloor N/8 \rfloor - 1} |d_h(i,8j)| . \tag{2}$$

It's values are ranges from 0.1 to 23for training dataset and 3.5 to 9 for testing dataset

2. Activity of image signal estimated using two factors. The first is the average absolute difference between in-block image samples:

$$A_h = \frac{1}{7} \left[\frac{8}{M(N-1)} \sum_{i=1}^{M} \sum_{j=1}^{N-1} |d_h(i,j)| - B_h \right] . \tag{3}$$

It's values are ranges from 0.1to 23for training dataset and 2 to 10 for testing dataset

3. The second activity measure is zero crossing rate(ZC)
   For $n \in [1, N-2]$,

$$Z_h(m,n) = \begin{cases} 1 \text{ horizontal } ZC \text{ at } d_h(m,n) \\ 0 \text{ otherwise} \end{cases} . \tag{4}$$

The horizontal ZC rate is estimated as

$$Z_h = \frac{1}{M(N-2)} \sum_{i=1}^{M} \sum_{j=1}^{N-2} Z_h(m,n) . \tag{5}$$

It's values are ranges from 0.005 to 0.54 for training dataset and 0.1to 0.5 for testing dataset

Similarly the vertical features are calculated. The overall features are calculated as

$$B = \frac{B_h + B_v}{2}, A = \frac{A_h + A_v}{2}, Z = \frac{Z_h + Z_v}{2} . \tag{6}$$

The score is calculated as

$$S = \alpha + \beta B^{\gamma 1} A^{\gamma 2} Z^{\gamma 3} . \tag{7}$$

Where α, β, $\gamma 1$, $\gamma 2$, and $\gamma 3$ are model parameters.

Such mathematical predictor used to calculate quality score. Researchers had reported good results [7,8,9,10]. Mathematical predictors are based on model parameters and these parameters are estimated using subjective data as training data. These estimated parameters were fixed for every test images. Thus, quality score for original image is less than proceed images.

As shown in fig. 2(a) computed score by mathematical predictor for original image is less than its 70 quality factor image. Same result is for fig 2(b). For both the original images the spatial activity measure (SAM) values are very high and spatial frequency measure (SFM) values are low. So it has high predictability and less detail. Due to compression artifacts there is remarkable change in these measures. Due to blocking artifacts SFM is decrease and as effect of ringing SFM is increase. SAM is decrease due to compression artifacts [16]. Thus these measures are also used as features.

Fig. 2. a) original image "Tiger.jpg" and its70 quality factor image with defined mathematical model score 2.7 and 7.5 and MOS 6.5 and 6.5 respectively. b) original image "Peppar.jpg" and its 70 quality factor image with defined mathematical model score 3.3 and 8.3 and MOS 6.7 and 5.3 respectively.

$$SFM = \sqrt{R^2 + C^2} \ . \tag{8}$$

$$R = \sqrt{\frac{1}{MN} \sum_{m=1}^{M} \sum_{n=2}^{N} (x(m,n) - x(m,n-1))^2} \ . \tag{9}$$

$$C = \sqrt{\frac{1}{MN} \sum_{m-1}^{M} \sum_{n=2}^{N} (x(m,n) - x(m-1,n))^2} \ . \tag{10}$$

$$SAM = \dfrac{\dfrac{1}{MN} \sum_{j=0}^{M-1}\sum_{k=0}^{N-1}|F(j,k)|^2}{\left[\prod_{j=0}^{M-1}\prod_{k=0}^{N-1}|F(j,k)|^2\right]^{\frac{1}{MN}}} \quad . \tag{11}$$

5   Results

In the experiment the MOS is compared with quality score computed by network. And this result is compared with the error between computed score by mathematical predictor and network output. This is shown in table 1. The proposed experiment is showing the edge on the mathematical predictor. The error between the MOS and network output ranges from ±0.5 to 1.9. The error between the score predicted by mathematical predictor and network output is vary from ±0.1 to 1.2. Sample original test images are shown in fig 3. Fig 4 shows the regression plot for experiment and Fig 5 shows performance of neural network. Regression coefficient for training of network is 0.96; for validating network it is 0.90 and for testing it is 0.96. Overall regression coefficient is 0.96. Table 2 shows the comparison for regression coefficients. Table 3 shows some sample results for test data set [17].

Table 1. Comparison for error

Experiment	Error
Defined Model Score	±0.5-1.9
MOS	±0.1-1.2

Table 2. Comparison for regression coefficient

Training data	Testing data	All
0.96	0.96	0.96

Fig. 3. Sample test images

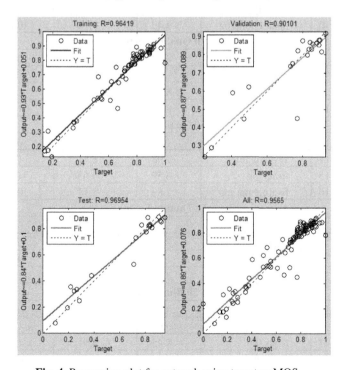

Fig. 4. Regression plot for network using target as MOS

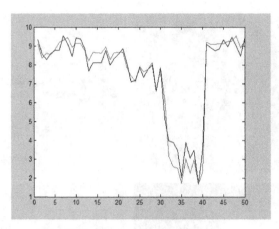

Fig. 5. Performance of neural network

Table 3. Sample result for test data set

Sr. No.	Image	Target	Output (score)	Error
Original Image				
1	tiffany.jpg	9.54	9.30	0.24
2	airplane.jpg	9.12	9.46	-0.34
3	fruits.jpg	8.45	8.92	-0.47
4	fishingboat.jpg	9.43	9.14	0.29
70 Quality Factor				
7	tiffany.jpg	8.77	8.63	0.14
8	airplane.jpg	8	8.28	-0.28
9	fruits.jpg	8.34	8.64	-0.30
10	fishingboat.jpg	8.57	8.66	-0.09
50 Quality Factor				
13	tiffany.jpg	7.76	7.75	0.01
14	airplane.jpg	7.98	8.11	-0.13
15	fruits.jpg	6.59	6.63	-0.04
16	fishingboat.jpg	7.83	7.77	0.06
10 Quality Factor				
19	tiffany.jpg	3.03	2.24	0.79
20	airplane.jpg	3.45	2.97	0.48
21	fruits.jpg	1.67	1.67	0.00
22	fishingboat.jpg	3.52	2.34	1.18
50 Blur Factor				
25	tiffany.jpg	9.45	9.25	0.20
26	airplane.jpg	9.01	9.54	-0.53
27	fruits.jpg	8.45	8.91	-0.46
28	fishingboat.jpg	9.46	9.27	0.19

6   Conclusion

Results demonstrated better result for machine learning approach in comparison with mathematically defined predictor. The observed shortcoming of uncompressed images having less score by predictor used is overcome by proposed machine learning approach. The accuracy of the quality assessment can be further increase by training the network using statistical parameters computed in frequency domain, textual parameter can also be used, since compressed images degrades the texture content. Other classifier such as fuzzy and support vector machine can be used for better accuracy.

Acknowledgements. The authors would like to thank Prof. (Dr.) A. S. Abhyankar for their support. We would also like to thank all people who support us for subjective analysis.

References

1. Wang, Z., Bovik, A.C.: Why is Image Quality Assessment so Difficult. IEEE Signal Processing Letters 4, 3313–3316 (2002)
2. Wang, Z., Bovik, A.C.: A universal image quality index. IEEE Signal Processing Letters 9(3), 81–84 (2002)
3. Avcibas, I., Sankur, B., Sayood, K.: Static evaluation of image quality measures. Journal of Electronic Imaging 11, 206–223 (2002)
4. Wang, Z., Bovik, A.C.: Modern Image quality assessment. Morgan & Claypool; ISBN: 1598290231
5. Lin, W., Jay Kuo, C.C.: Perceptual visual quality metrics: survey. Journal of Visual Communication and Image Representation 22(4), 297–312 (2011)
6. Suresh, S., Venkatesh Babu, R., Kim, H.J.: No-reference image quality assessment using modified extreme learning machine classifier. Applied Soft Computing 9(2), 541–552 (2009)
7. Wang, Z., Sheikh, H.R., Bovik, A.C.: No-reference perceptual quality assessment of JPEG compressed images. In: Proc. IEEE International Conference on Image Processing, vol. 1, pp. 477–480 (September 2002)
8. Sutharaharan, S.: No-reference visually significant blocking artifact metric for natural scene images. Signal Processing 89(8), 1647–1652 (2009)
9. Parvez Sazzad, Z.M., Kawayoke, Y., Horita, Y.: No reference image quality assessment for JPEG2000 based on spatial features. Signal Processing: Image Communication 23(4), 257–268 (2008)
10. Ferzil, R., Karam, L.J.: A No-reference objective image sharpness metric based on the notion of just noticable blur (JNB). IEEE Trans. Image Processing 18(4), 718–728 (2009)
11. Gastaldo, P., Zunino, R., Heynderickx, I., Vicario, E.: Objective quality assessment of displayed images by using neural networks. Signal Processing: Image Communication 20(7), 643–661 (2005)
12. Saad, M.A., Bovik, A., Charier, C.: A DCT statistics-based blind image quality index. IEEE Single Processing Letters 17(6), 583–586 (2010)
13. Moorthy, A.K., Bovik, A.C.: A Two-step framework for constructing blind image quality indices. IEEE Signal Processing Letter 17(5), 513–516 (2010)

14. Chen, M.J., Bovik, A.C.: No. reference image blur assessment using multiscale gradient. In: Proc. IEEE Quality of Multimedia Experience, pp. 70–74 (July 2009)
15. Hagan, M., Demuth, H., Beale, M.H.: Neural Network Design. Martine Hagan; ISBN:0971732108
16. Grgic, S., Mrak, M., Grgic, M.: Comparision of JPEG image coder. In: Proc. Of the 3rd International Symposium on Video Processing & Multimedia Communication, VIPromCom 2001, pp. 79–85 (2001)
17. Sheikh, H.R., Wang, Z., Cormack, L., Bovik, A.C.: Live image quality assessment database, http://www.live.ece.utexas.edu/research/quality

CAC Based Data Mining Workflow to Test and Re-engineer Software Agents

N. Sivakumar, K. Vivekanandan Kalimuthu, and A. Gunasekaran

Department of Computer Science and Engineering,
Pondicherry Engineering College, Puducherry - 605014, India
{sivakumar11,k.vivekanandan}@pec.edu, gunasekaran@email.com

Abstract. In the past couple of decades, agent-oriented technology has been arisen in order to assist in developing intelligent software that is able to solve challenging problems. Numerous methodologies for developing agent-based systems have been proposed in the literature. Though these methodologies are maturing rapidly, they emphasis only on analysis, design and implementation phase of development process. There is no complete and potential testing technique to build, verify and validate agent based system. Customer satisfaction and cost are the most important factors that a development methodology must emphasis on. So in this paper we present a re-engineering based agent oriented software development methodology to build a powerful agent based system. We also present here a Classification and Clustering (CAC) based data mining workflow to test and re-engineer an agent based system such that we achieve a customer satisfaction rating of 89% for meeting quality expectations and an average project budget variation of just 3%. Both figures are ranging far higher than industry standards.

Keywords: Agent-Oriented Testing, Re-engineering, Data mining workflow.

1   Introduction

Evolution of organizational architecture and the utilization of web-based application make the software system more and more complex. So, matching the evolution of organizations the software systems needed to continuously evolve in order to meet the demand and changes in business plus technologies. Under some situations these software systems must be autonomous and adaptive to take on different challenges. These autonomous systems are increasingly taking over all the steps and operations governing enterprise management and financing, the quality assurance needed to be given to their owners and their users that these complex systems operate properly. The agent oriented methodologies provide us a platform for making system abstract, generalize, dynamic and autonomous. This important factor calls for an investigation of suitable agent-oriented engineering frameworks, including requirements engineering and testing techniques, to provide high-quality software development processes and products.

P.V. Krishna, M.R. Babu, and E. Ariwa (Eds.): ObCom 2011, Part II, CCIS 270, pp. 139–148, 2012.
© Springer-Verlag Berlin Heidelberg 2012

The tight bonds between requirement engineering and testing have been commonly recognized [1]. Designing test cases early and in parallel with requirements helps discover problems early, thus avoiding implementing erroneous specification. The bond between requirement and testing is so relevant that considerable effort has been devoted to what is called test-first development. In such approach, tests are produced from requirements before implementing the requirements themselves [2].

Research in AOSE mainly addresses development issues in MAS. Several AOSE methodologies [2] have been proposed. Some of them offer specification-based formal verification, allowing software developers to detect errors at the beginning of the development process. Others borrow Object-Oriented (OO) testing techniques to be exploited later in the development process, upon a mapping of agent-oriented abstractions into OO constructs. However, a potential testing and development process for agent oriented systems is still missing.

Re-engineering [3] being the basic spine and a creative heart for modern day software development process, but on the contrary there is no any room for re-engineering process in agent oriented framework because of the complexity in testing and evaluating the quality of agent based software developed. Unless or otherwise there are necessary procedure and parameters to measure the quality of the agent based systems we cannot classify the different components that are effective to be re-engineered in future. Only when the components designed are classified under various quality criteria it can be selected for re-engineering process.

And one of the most important parts of testing an agent based systems are the size of their test suites. Since due to autonomous property and its ability to react in different forms for a given same input over a period of time the work of testing becomes complex and also the test suites grows in size over a period of time and even we can say infinity number of test cases that results in increased testing cost. So we propose a classification and clustering based methodology to reduce the size of the test suite and also to identify quality assured agent component for re-engineering and thereby making testing an effective process in agent-oriented software development lifecycle to verify and validate agent based systems.

2   Background and Related Works

There are many AOSE methodologies to develop agent based systems .Such methodologies include *TROPOS, Prometheus, MASE, MESSAGE, ROADMAP, GAIA, RAP/AOR, and PASSI*. Comparatively analyzing these methodologies each methodologies exhibit their own strength and weaknesses. *GAIA* [5] enables capturing and modeling the agent marketplace example in a more effective and flexible way but we aren't aware how the MAS are going to be implemented. *ROADMAP* [6] goes in that direction by proposing the use of use case model to capture functional requirements; this is not enough to continue to implementation phase. The *MESSAGE* [7] Design Model provides detailed agent interaction. It describes the relation between design, implementation and testing but actually doesn't have any specific implementation technique. Agent Tool implements all seven steps of *MASE* [8] as well as automated design support. It also provides the ability to semi-automatically derive the agent architecture directly from analysis phase. Hence it provides a direct mapping from analysis to design.

TROPOS [9] has only been applied so far to several modest-size case studies with encouraging results. Anyway, it still lacks tools that support the transition between different phases. In [10] the authors suggested the goal testing approach based on tropos methodology. *Prometheus* [11] can be extended with better support for early requirements as well as for implementation, testing and debugging. Two particular strengths of the *RAP/AOR* [12] methodology are its ontological Foundation and its use of simulation for achieving more agility. At present, it is difficult to evaluate the RAP/AOR methodology, mainly because some of its components in particular, certain model transformations and related tools have not yet been fully developed. *PASSI* strengths are ease of transition for designers, multiple views to analyze complex systems, support of specific design toolkit (PTK, Rational rose), the patterns reuse. The weakness is there is no standard testing procedure to test the system developed based on this methodology.

The above analytical studies reveals that there are no potential testing and development process for Agent oriented systems that provides complete, verified, validated agent based systems. Although there is a well-defined OO testing technique [1] [4] to test the agent based systems. But on contrary to it the testing techniques for the methodologies are very few and they do not outline a perfect testing procedure that caters a wide range of test case context in agent oriented framework.

3   The Proposed Methodology

3.1   A Process Model for Re-engineering Based Agent Development

The proposed re-engineering model described here is a representation of agent system development process, which extends the traditional software development life cycle process. The traditional lifecycle process and the methodologies available for the development of agent based systems guides the engineers in developing conceptual model, which is refined as a top down design incrementally from an early requirements model to system design artifacts and then to implementation. But we integrate here a re-engineering process to implement an efficient agent-based system. The proposed methodology is diagrammatically represented in Fig.1. This process starts off with *Requirement Engineering* where the requirements are gathered from various stakeholders. This phase is further subdivided into two categories, one is the *Early requirement engineering* phase constituting the user requirements and a model of the system-to-be where system requirements are modeled in terms of system goals, roles, and behaviors and the second one is the *Late Requirement engineering* phase specified in terms of a set of interacting software agents and requirements such as hardware and software needed to build an agent-based system.

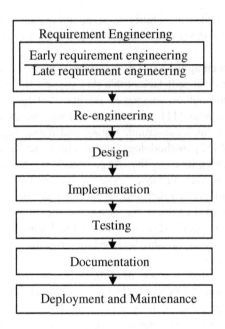

Fig. 1. Phases in re-engineering based development process

The next step is *Quality Assured components collection where* reputed projects are collected similar to the agent based system to be developed keeping the requirements in mind. The above step is followed by a *Datamining workflow* where test cases are extracted by knowledge mining and a clustering algorithm have been employed to reduce the size of the test suites thereby making testing cost efficient. This is followed by *Evaluation and Measuring* where test score is calculated for every components collected. Then the above process is followed by *Classification and selection* and this phase works on classifying the agent components collected based on their test score calculated and also the process of selecting the components for re-engineering, based on some criteria. The above phase is followed by an implementation phase where the entire coding process takes place. Then it is followed by *testing* phase where agents-based system implemented is tested. Then it's followed by *Documentation phase* where every detail is documented for future reuse. Finally the *Deployment and Maintenance* phase where the developed agent-based software is deployed to user and it's maintained.

3.1.1 Requirement Engineering
The primary measure of success of a software system is the degree to which it meets the purpose for which it was intended. Broadly speaking, *Requirements* Engineering (RE) [3] is the process of discovering that purpose, by identifying stakeholders and their needs, and documenting these in a form that is amenable to analysis, communication, and subsequent implementation. Zave provides one of the clearest definitions of RE: *"Requirements engineering is the branch of software engineering*

concerned with the real-world goals for, functions of, and constraints on software systems. It is also concerned with the relationship of these factors to precise specifications of software behavior, and to their evolution over time and across software families."

This definition is attractive for a two reasons. First, it highlights the importance of "real-world goals" that motivate the development of an agent-based software system. These represent the 'why' as well as the 'what' of a system. Second, it refers to "precise specifications". These provide the basis for *analyzing* requirements, *validating* that they are indeed what stakeholders want, *defining* what designers have to build, and *verifying* that they have done so correctly upon delivery. Here in our proposed work the requirements are gathered based on three criteria keeping in mind the agents goals, roles, behaviors, properties and those criteria's are first *User type*; (i.e., what type of users use the products) identifying the correct users and collecting the requirements, secondly *Stakeholders requirements*; gathering requirements from different levels of stakeholders who plays a part in the project, thirdly *System level requirements*; may be hardware, software or other requirements regarding system development.

3.1.2 Re-engineering Process

Reengineering is the fundamental rethinking and radical redesign of business processes to achieve dramatic improvements in critical, contemporary measures of performance such as cost, quality, service and speed. Re-engineering being the basic spine and a creative heart for modern day software development process, we can say *"Modern day's software development process is incomplete without Re-engineering process"*. The modeling artifacts produced along the development process are: *Quality Assured components collection*; here in this ten to fifteen reputed projects are collected similar to the agent based system to be developed, *Datamining Workflow*; this workflow includes a systematic knowledge mining process to derive test cases and clustering algorithm to reduce the test suites, *Evaluation and Measuring*; this process emphasis on evaluation (i.e., testing the components collected) of components and defining measures to each and every component, *Classification and selection*; this phase works on classifying the agent components collected based on their test score calculated and also the process of selecting the components for re-engineering based on some criteria, *Other sources*; after collecting necessary components to re-engineer

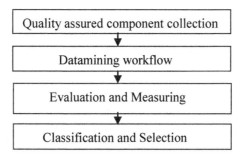

Fig. 2. Diagram representing entire re-engineering process

based on their quality score calculated specifications from other resources are collected if needed, *Implementation*; this is done based on three criteria the first is entire component re-engineering, second is re-engineering components with slight modifications, third is only by taking the specifications.

3.1.2.1 Quality Assured Components Collection

In this phase similar components related to the agent based system to be developed are collected. For example if the agent system under development is a multiagent system involving buyer agent and the seller agent, the components which are all similar to this agent which have been already developed are collected. The strict condition for selecting this project is that these components should be reputed and quality assured.

3.1.2.2 Datamining Workflow

This Datamining workflow [13] includes a systematic knowledge mining process to derive test cases and clustering algorithm to reduce the test suites. Test cases are derived or extracted clearly based on the requirements [16]. In this work, we show how to   incorporate clustering and classification mining. Since due to autonomous property and its ability to react in different forms for a given same input over a period of time the work of testing becomes complex and also the test suites grows in size over a period of time and even we can say infinity number of test cases that results in increased testing cost. So we employ a clustering algorithm to reduce the size of the test suite and make testing an effective process in agent-oriented software development lifecycle to verify and validate agent based systems. Using k-means clustering we reduced the test suite. The main advantages of this algorithm are its simplicity and speed which allows it to run on large datasets. Test suite reduction techniques try to remove redundant test cases of a test suite. The test suite minimization problem can be formally stated as follows. Given:

(1) A test suite T of test cases $\{t_1, t_2, t_3, \ldots, t_k\}$.
(2) A set of testing requirements $\{r_1, r_2, r_3, \ldots, r_n\}$ that must be satisfied to provide the desired testing coverage of the program.
(3) Subsets $\{T_1, T_2, T_3, \ldots, T_n\}$ of T, one associated with each of the r_i's, such that any one of the test cases tjs belonging to T_i satisfies r_i.

The test suite is given as the input to the knowledge mining module. This module mines the test cases by attribute selection and by applying the clustering techniques. The Output from this module is a reduced test suite.

3.1.2.3 Evaluation and Measuring

After extracting and reducing the test cases, the reduced test suites are taken and used for testing the collected components which will be further used for re-engineering. This testing process helps us in not only finding components to be re-engineered but also it provides the convenience for measuring their *Test Score*.

$$\text{Test score} = \frac{\text{No. of test cases successfully executed}}{\text{Total no. of test cases}} * 100$$

Test score is the ratio between the numbers of test cases executed successfully with respect to a particular requirement to the total number test cases derived for that particular requirement. This *Test score* is calculated for each and every agent component collected with respect to the requirements gathered. The test score calculation can be formally stated as follows. Given:

(1) Let components collected C be $\{c_1, c_2, c_3, \ldots, c_n\}$.
(2) A requirement suite R of requirements $\{r_1, r_2, r_3, \ldots, r_k\}$.
(3) For each requirement r1 the test suite T of test cases $\{t_1, t_2, t_3, \ldots, t_n\}$.
(4) And the test score for each component c1 is calculated as

$$\text{Test score } (c_1, r_1) = \frac{\text{No. of test cases successfully executed for } (c_1, r_1)}{\text{Total no. of test cases for } (c_1, r_1)} * 100$$

The above calculations are further done for $(c_1, r_2), (c_1, r_3), \ldots, (c_1, r_n)$ with respect to the requirements gathered initially. Finally test score for c1 is calculated as

Test score (c_1) = Test score (c_1, r_1) + Test score (c_1, r_2) + ... + Test score (c_1, r_n).

This test score is calculated for all the collected components $c_1, c_2, \ldots, c_n$. The above testing and measuring of test scores of each component collected for re-engineering is very important because, testing here is done with respect to requirement gathered .Since this testing is done at the beginning itself about 80 to 90 percentage of stakeholders requirements are met which encompasses to the implementation of effective, customer satisfied and cost effective agent-based software system.

3.1.2.4 Classification and Selection

The most important part of the process is the classification. Here the collected agent components are classified based on their *Test score* calculated. *Test score* calculation enables us to find and retrieve components which satisfies our requirements because entire test suites are derived only based on the requirements. With the help this classification the engineers can easily select the best component to be re-engineered. The component which has the highest Test score percentile carries the highest priority followed to down, to component which has the lowest priority.

The other most important part of this phase is the selection of component to be re-engineered. The selection can be done by three main categories.

(1) Selecting the entire component which meets the requirements based on the test score.
(2) Selecting a particular component in the way such that, some modifications are to be done to meet the stakeholder's requirements.
(3) Selecting a component and taking only their specifications which suit our stakeholder's requirements.

3.1.3 Design

Here in this phase the design functions and operations are described in detail, including screen layouts, business rules, process diagrams and other documentation. The output of this stage will describe the new system as a collection of modules or subsystems. The design stage takes as its initial input the requirements identified in the approved requirements document. For each requirement, a set of one or more design elements will be produced as a result of interviews, workshops, and/or proto- type efforts. Design elements describe the desired software features in detail, and generally include functional hierarchy diagrams, screen layout diagrams, tables of business rules, business process diagrams, pseudo code, and a complete entity- relationship diagram with a full data dictionary.

3.1.4 Implementation

In this phase, the actual application code is created using high level programming languages like JADE, ACL, JAVA eclipse etc. Java Agent Development Environment (JADE), it simplifies the development of multi-agent systems that compiles in accordance to "FIPA" [Foundation for Intelligent Physical Agent] and also provides some graphical tools that support debugging and deployment. Agent platforms are distributed across various systems or machines using "Remote GUI". Agent Communication Language (ACL) is used for communication between the agents and Knowledge Query and Manipulation Language (KQML) is used for feeding knowledge to the agents. The programming language is chosen according to the type of application, as well as the application requirements. The prime thing here is, implementation is done based on the selected components of re-engineering process.

3.1.5 Testing

In our re-engineering based methodology, two level of testing is accomplished. The first level is the requirement level testing and second one is the implementation level testing. At the requirement level, we test whether the component/agent to be re-engineered is matching with the requirements made in the analysis phase. Once the component/agent is identified for re-engineering, then at the implementation level the agent based software that has been developed is completely tested. At the implementation level, the main attributes to be tested are the functionalities of the component/agent, properties of agents that differs from objects such as social ability, autonomy, pro-activity, reactivity, adaptability, intelligence and mobility [14], [15], [17]. These testing are mainly done to emphasis on the quality of the agent-based system which will be further useful in selection of quality assured components for the purpose of re-engineering as mentioned in the first step of the re-engineering process.

3.1.6 Documentation, Deployment and Maintenance

This is the most important part of *"Re-engineering based agent development metho- dology"*. The entire process carried out to calculate test scores should be documented clearly. Because once the documentation is done clearly with all the above mentioned entities it will be very easy to carry the proposed methodology for upcoming projects. This makes this methodology a simple, effective and less time consuming one.

Deployment starts after the code is appropriately tested, is approved for release and sold or otherwise distributed into a production environment. People are often resistant to change and avoid venturing into an unfamiliar area, so as a part of the deployment phase, it is very important to have training classes for new clients of your software.

Maintaining and enhancing software to cope with newly discovered problems or new requirements can take far more time than the initial development of the software. It may be necessary to add code that does not fit the original design to correct an unforeseen problem or it may be that a customer is requesting more functionality and code can be added to accommodate their requests. If the labor cost of the maintenance phase exceeds 25% of the prior-phases labor cost, then it is likely that the overall quality of at least one prior phase is poor. In that case, management should consider the option of rebuilding the system (or portions) before maintenance cost is out of control.

4   Conclusion and Future Work

Due to agent based system's autonomous property and its ability to react in different format with same input over a period of time, the process of verification and validation of agent based systems is very complex. So in this project proposal, we had carried out clustering algorithm to reduce the test suites and sets of testing procedure to measure the *test score* for the agent components collected using different quality parameters and thereby classifying and re-engineering the agent components based on the calculated percentile which reduces time, cost and effort. Finally our proposed work makes testing more effective in agent based system development process. In the future work, we will also investigate certain testing process and quality measures for testing agent's properties such as autonomous, reactiveness, social ability and pro-activity by which we can ensure strong quality assurance for the agent-based systems we build.

References

1. Graham, D.R.: Requirements and testing: Seven missing-link myths. IEEE Software 19(5), 15–17 (2002)
2. Henderson-Sellers, B., Giorgini, P. (eds.): Agent-Oriented methodologies. Idea Group Inc. (2005)
3. Ricca, F.: Analysis, Testing and Re-structuring of Web Applications. PhD thesis, University of Genova, DISI (2003)
4. Srivastava, P.R., Karthik Anand, V., Rastogi, M., Yadav, V., Raghurama, G.: Extension of Object-oriented Software testing techniques to Agent Oriented software testing. Journal of Object Technology 7(8), 155–163 (2008)
5. Henderson, B., Giorgini, P.: The Gaia Methodology for Agent-Oriented Analysis and Design. Autonomous Agent and Multi-Agent Systems 3, 285–312 (2000)
6. Amato, N.: Roadmap Methods Randomized Motion Planning. Fall 2004. University of Padova (2004)

7. Caire, G., Leal, F., Chaino, L., Massonet, P.: Eurescom P907: MESSAGE–Methodology for Engineering systems of software agents
8. Wood, M.F.: Multiagent system engineering: A methodology for analysis and design of muti-agent systems. Master thesis, School of Engineering, Air Force institute of technology, USA (2000)
9. Giunchiglia, F., Mylopoulos, J., Perini, A.: The TROPOS software development methodology: Process, Models and diagrams. Department of information and Communication Technology, University of Trento via Somma rive, 14, I-38050 Povo, Italy
10. Nguyen, D.C., Perini, A., Tonella, P.: A Goal-Oriented Software Testing Methodology. In: Luck, M., Padgham, L. (eds.) AOSE 2007. LNCS, vol. 4951, pp. 58–72. Springer, Heidelberg (2008)
11. Padgham, L., Winikoff, M.: The Prometheus Methodology. RMIT University Melbourne, Australia (2004)
12. Wanger, G., Taveter, K.: Towards Radical Agent-Oriented Software Engineering Process Based on AOR modeling. In: Proceedings of EEE/WIC/ACM International Conference on Intelligent Agent Technology (IAT 2004), 0-7695-2101- 0/04 $ 20.00. IEEE (2004)
13. Raamesh, L., et al.: An efficient test case reduction method for test cases. International Journal of Engineering Science and Technology 2(11) (2010)
14. Dumke, R., Koeppe, R., Wille, C.: Software Agent Measurement and Self-Measuring Agent-Based Systems. Preprint No 11. Fakultatfur Informatik, Otto-von-Guericke-Universitat, Magdeburg (2000)
15. Wille, C., Dumke, R., Stojanov, S.: Quality Assurance in Agent-Based Systems Current State and Open Problems. Preprint No. 4. Fakultatfur Informatik, Otto-von-Guericke-Universitat, Magdeburg (2002)
16. Nwana, H.S.: Software Agents: An Overview. Knowledge Engineering Review 11(3), 1–40 (1996)
17. Alonso, F., Fuertes, J.L., Martinez, L., Soza, H.: Measuring the Social Ability of Software Agents. In: Proceedings of the Sixth International Conference on Software Engineering Research, Management and Applications, Prague, Czech Republic (2008)
18. Shoham, Y.: Agent oriented programming (Technical Report STAN-CS-90- 1335) Computer science department. Stanford University (1994)

An Ensembled Neural Network Classifier for Vehicle Classification Using ILD

K. Vijaya[1], Tessy Mathew[1], Kalyani Desikan[2], and L. Jeganathan[1]

[1] School of Computing Science and Engineering
[2] Department of Mathematics
VIT University, Chennai Campus
{vijaya.k,tessymathew}@vit.ac.in

Abstract. Vehicle classification is required to study various parameters related to traffic. It is impossible to estimate the density of vehicles, number of vehicle types etc. without vehicles classification. This paper reviews various neural network algorithms using single loop detector that can be used in real time traffic management system to classify vehicles. Since it is evident that neural network is a weak classifier, we propose a model which uses an ensembled neural network algorithm using ILD to achieve high speed and accuracy than the traditional method.

Keywords: Neural Networks, Inductive Loop Detector (ILD), Ensemble.

1   Introduction

The Traffic Department requires statistical information related to the flow of vehicles on roads for successful implementation of systems such as pervasive smart road security, surveillance systems, Transit Signal Priority, Emergency Vehicle Pre-emption etc. To implement these applications, various parameters of road traffic has to be measured directly which includes vehicle velocity, number of vehicles moving in the same direction, time-distance between the vehicles, length of the traffic jam, time of access to the traffic, noise level, pollution level, etc. The most important of all parameters are the class of the vehicles (i.e. motorcar, delivery van, lorry, trailer, etc.) and the number of moving vehicles belonging to the specific class. Classification of vehicles and statistics of the vehicle types is necessary for access control, weighing of vehicles in motion, traffic management and control [4].

Therefore, research in the area of vehicle classification aroused much interest among researchers, gaining much importance in intelligent transportation system. In recent years, surveillance systems have been widely used in traffic management. These surveillance systems need vehicles to be classified. Hence classification is one of the most frequently encountered decision making tasks of human activity. A classification problem occurs when an object needs to be assigned into a predefined group or class based on a number of observed attributes related to that object. For example, the criteria for the toll charge in the highway are based on the vehicle classification.

P.V. Krishna, M.R. Babu, and E. Ariwa (Eds.): ObCom 2011, Part II, CCIS 270, pp. 149–157, 2012.
© Springer-Verlag Berlin Heidelberg 2012

In this paper, we explore various neural network algorithms with ILD and make a comparison of their performance in classifying vehicles. The overall organization of the paper is as follows. After the Introduction, we present the technologies used for this work in Section2, Section 3 explains the different neural network algorithms in vehicle classification with their advantages and disadvantages, Section 4 compares the performance of the different algorithms and Section 5 proposes a new ensemble model for vehicle Classification.

2   Technology Description

Here we discuss about the basic technologies required for the vehicle classification using ILD and NN.

2.1   Inductive Loop Detector (ILD)

Inputs from piezoelectric equipment, surveillance video cameras, fibre optic cables and Inductive Loop detector can be used for vehicle classification. The greatest drawback of these technologies is that they are designed to operate in low and moderate volume rural settings. In congested conditions, where vehicles either accelerate or decelerate while crossing sensors, some sensors have accuracy problems related caused by the inability to distinguish between closely spaced vehicles[7]. At present, ILD are most popular form of detection system used in vehicle classification because of its better performance and minimum cost.

The detection system for inductive loop is formed by inductive sensors that are installed under road and an electronic circuit housed in an enclosure.

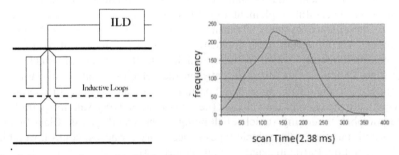

Fig. 1. Detector scheme with 4 inductive sensors   **Fig. 2.** Variation of Speed

The inductive sensor consists of a coil of wire installed under the road, excited by an alternating current. The electronic circuit that monitors the inductive loops can capture variations: increase in resonance frequency or decrease in signal amplitude on the loop, both proportional to the inductance variations of external links [1]. Fig 2 shows the variation of the speed in the output signal when a vehicle passes over the inductive coil.

2.2   Neural Network Architecture

Neural Network (NN)[10] is a set of connected input/output units in which each connection has a weight associated with it. During the learning phase, the network learns by adjusting the weights so that it can predict the correct class label of the input Fig (3).

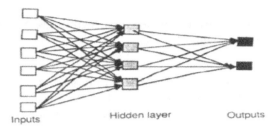

Fig. 3. Neural Network architecture

A typical neural network consists of an input layer, an output layer, and one or more hidden layers. These layers are connected by neurons to form a parallel distributed processing system. Each neuron is viewed as a processing element (PE) that receives inputs and generate outputs through an activation function. Each of the connections between the process elements has an associated weight. In the hidden layer, each neuron receives an activation signal (input), and generates a signal (output) through an activation function. The neuron (Process Element) produces an output through an activation function that can be either linear or non-linear, and one of the most commonly used activation function is the sigmoid function.

Advantages of neural network include their high tolerance of noisy data as well as their ability to classify pattern on which they have not been trained. Neural network algorithms are inherently using parallelization techniques to speed up the computation process. Several techniques have recently been developed for extraction of rules from trained neural networks. Due to its strong adaptive nature, ability to learn, nonlinear mapping capabilities, robustness and fault tolerance NN is used.[10].

3   Recent Approaches in Vehicle Classification Using Neural Network and ILD

3.1   Vehicle Classification Algorithm for Single Loop Detector NN

An algorithm [4] for vehicle classification using a Back Propagation Neural Network (BPNN), based on an ILD technique is reviewed. The magnetic profiles of the vehicles were gathered for 433 vehicles by the controller by sampling the ILD at intervals of every 2.38 ms. The magnetic profiles were classified according to the vehicle classes and the features of the magnetic profile were studied. The variation rate of frequency, waveform of magnetic profile, occupancy time, varied significantly according to the vehicle class. Single loop detector is used in place of dual ILD coil as dual ILD is expensive. The disadvantage of using BPNN[10] is that more number of computations are required to find the final weights. Since this methodology does not solve the problem of noise on frequency wave form, the extracted features from frequency wave form are not adequate to obtain all distinctive properties of the vehicles. The developed algorithm was evaluated at test sites and BPNN yielded a recognition rate of 91.5% in the experimental tests.

3.2   Artificial Neural Network Method for Length-Based Vehicle Classification Using Single-Loop Outputs

Based on 3 layers BPNN [5] the data frequency (features) obtained from single loop output is directly fed into the NN .This reduces hardware installations and also avoids the estimation of speed for vehicle length calculation as this reduces the classification accuracy. A specific neural network (Feed forward NN with the architecture of back Propagation) was designed and configured for each vehicle category. Vehicles were divided into four categories according to their lengths. Estimation of speed for vehicle classification is avoided as this degrades the efficiency of vehicle classification. Although this work has been tested for accuracy at a particular site, it has not been proven spatially transferrable.

3.3   Vehicle Classification Algorithm for Single Loop Detector with Neural Genetic Algorithm (GA)

Vehicle Classification [6] algorithm has been implemented using feed forward NN (FFNN) where the weights are obtained using genetic algorithm. Genetic algorithm is used for finding the weights of neural network .These weights are applied to the model. In this approach, the numbers of computations are reduced with minimum errors as compared to conventional algorithms of neural network. The NN model using GA works as follows: Step1Initialize the generation count and select the initial population (all possible solutions). Step 2.If current population has not converged then find the weights for each chromosomes (set of parameters which defines a proposed solution to the problem that GA is trying to solve); Step3 Apply input and target pattern to FFNN with the above obtained weight. Step 4 Else find Root Mean Square Error (RMSE).Step 5 Calculate the fitness function using RMSE. Repeat the same for finding fitness of each chromosome. Step6 The fitness function determines how well a program is able to solve a problem. Step 7 Replace least-fit chromosome with the best-fit. Also apply two-point crossover* by selecting parent pairs and their cross sites to generate a new population.Step8 Repeat till 95% of the chromosome in population converges to the best fitness value. Weights are optimized and local minima can be reduced using Genetic Algorithm. Only Slower improvements will be shown by Genetic Algorithms.

*Two-point cross over calls for two points to be selected on the parent organism strings. Everything between the two points is swapped between the parent organism, rendering two child organism

3.4   Vehicle Classification Algorithm Based on ILD Using NN

An algorithm [2] for vehicle classification based on neural network Multi Layer Perception (MLP) using Levenberg-Marquardt(LM) technique has been reviewed. The proposed algorithm yields a recognition rate of 92.43%.The MLP receives the input generated by the magnetic profile in the two inductive sensors. The ILD continuously measures the frequency at a given sampling rate. When the vehicle passes over the sensors, changes of signal from each channel are detected and stored. The signal generated is processed to obtain information that will serve as input to the MLP. The properly trained MLP performs the classification of vehicles.

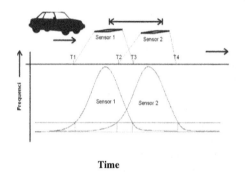

Fig. 5. Magnetic profile generated in 2 sensors   **Fig. 6.** Information's used in MLP

When a vehicle passes by the two sensors, variation of frequency is detected by the micro controller on the entrance of the vehicle at each sensor Fig.5. The information used as input to the network are the maximum variation in each sensor (Ma and Mb), area under the curve of changes in the periods of signals generated by the oscillators in the two sensors during the passage of vehicle (Aa and Ab), time of occupancy of the vehicle in each sensors (Ta and Tb), travel time (Td) and number of local maxima of the curve of the first sensor (Na) Fig. 6. NN/LM Algorithm speeds up convergence. For large size neural network LM is not practical as computation is very complex and it does not consider outliers in the data, what may lead to over-fitting noise.

3.5   Automatic Traffic Density Estimation and Vehicle Classification for Traffic Surveillance System Using Neural Networks

Real time vehicle classification and traffic density calculation methods [3] using neural networks are evaluated .Video processing techniques are used for extracting the features for classifying the vehicles. A Feed forward neural network algorithm is used with 14 input layers and 4 output layers. The input layers have 14 features extracted from the moving object detector and output layers are binary valued nodes and each representing a vehicle type.

The background of the video is subtracted from the current frame. Thus forming a difference matrix. To the difference matrix, a threshold is applied. The gray levels are compared with the threshold. If it is greater, difference matrix is updated as 1 else it is updated as 0, respectively. The binary matrix is used to show the difference between current frame and background. This matrix is analyzed in order to detect the moving object. Dynamic background calculation and pixel gray levels are stored as time series data methods. Performance is affected by many factors including fog, rain, snow, vehicle shadows and day to night transition.

3.6   Vehicle-Classification Algorithm Based on Component Analysis for Single-Loop Inductive Detector

In traditional approaches, raw magnetic profile with noise was fed into the algorithm. This approach [1] clears the noise from the magnetic profile using Discrete Fourier Transform (DFT). Feature extraction is accomplished with the Principal Component Analysis (PCA).The PCA is a way of identifying the patterns in the data and expressing the data in a way that highlights their similarities and differences. The patterns in a raw signal are difficult to be determined because of its large dimensions. Therefore PCA is a powerful tool for analyzing such signals.

In PCA, once these patterns in the data are identified, the data are compressed, i.e., by reducing the number of dimensions without much loss of information. Different statistical parameters can be extracted from the frequency waveform, e.g., median, mean, standard deviation, local maximum (Lmax), local minimum (Lmin), and frequency variation rate. Lmax is a useful parameter, which distinctively changes from one class to another due to the height variation of the vehicle. The features were given as input to BPNN to recognize the vehicle classes. BPNN classifies the vehicles into different groups and recognition rate is 94.21%.The new classification algorithm work as follows: Advantages: Noise less (Filtered) data are transferred to algorithm and PCA helps to get all the distinctive details about the input Data.

4   Comparison of Recent Vehicle Classification Algorithms Using Neural Network Algorithms with ILD

Table 1 summarizes the different algorithms and their recognition rates for vehicle classification. Gajda[7] measured the vehicle length and speed according to the patterns that represent the shape of measurement signals in the time domain with a single ILD. Xang[5] divided the vehicles into five groups and developed BPNN for each class. Ki[4] classified the vehicles into five groups according to their variation rate and the frequency waveform with BPNN. Sharma model[6] uses genetic algorithm for finding out the weights and applying those to the neural network and the number of computations for calculating the weights can be reduced. Celil and Camci [3]observed that through video processing and trained using NN can give accurate results in Vehicle Classification. Meta and Cinsdikici[1] proposed a model that filters the noises with DFT and passes to PCA where it is strengthened with a distinctive statistical parameter L $_{max}$. Further BPNN is used for pattern recognition. Oliveira[2] presents an algorithm for vehicle classification based on a NN MLP, with the information generated with the magnetic profile of the vehicle that can perform classification .

Table 1. Summarizes the different algorithms and their recognition rates for vehicle classification

Features Model	Parameters	Algorithm	Sensors	Classes	Rec .rate(%)
Gajda model (2001)	Signal Pattern	Signal Pattern Matching	1-loop coil	4	83
Zhang Model (2006)	Vehicle Length	BPNN	1-loop coil	4	Not given
Ki model(2006)	Frequency wave form and Variation rate	BPNN	1-loop coil	5	91.5
Bajaj and Sharma model (2007)	Frequency wave form and Variation rate	Genetic algorithm and BPNN	1-loop coil	5	Not given
Celil and Fatih Model (2009)	No of pixels,center of area..	FFNN	video camera	4	94
Meta and Cinsdikici Model (2010)	Local Max, Waveform frequency	DFT PCA BPNN	1-loop coil	5	94.21
Oliveria model (2010)	Frequency wave form	MLP	1-loop coil	4	92.43

5   Proposed Ensembled Model for Improving Accuracy of Neural Network Classifiers Using ILD

In all the above discussed techniques, for determining vehicle classification a single neural network classifier algorithm with ILD was used for classification. As neural network algorithms are weak classifiers, in order to boost its performance we propose a frame work, wherein we induce a collection of neural network algorithms which are both accurate as well as complementary so that the decisions of the learners are combined, and better accuracy on previously unseen data is obtained. This is a strategy of combining the prediction of several classifiers to supply single classification result. The predicted output of each classifier is combined and voted to produce the output of the ensemble. The ensembled classifier is a collection of classifiers representing a single hypothesis. This boosting algorithm, adaptively changes the distribution of the training set depending on how difficult each example is to classify.

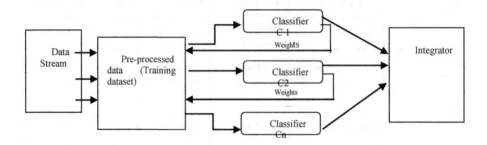

Fig. 7. Ensembled boosting for Vehicle Classification

Raw magnetic profile is cleaned from noise. This data is fed into the classifier C1. Boosting maintains a weight for each instance; higher the weight, more likely the instance will be selected for classifier training. Initially, the weights of the training examples are equal. After each iteration of the boosting process, the weights of the training data are updated Based on the correctness of the previous iteration, the weights of the correctly classified samples are decreased, and the weights of misclassified ones are increased.

A sample weight reflects the hardness of the classification higher the weight the more it has often been misclassified. These weights will be used to generate the training samples for the classifier of the next round. The basic idea is that when we build a classifier; focus more on the misclassified tuples of the previous round. In this way we build a series of classifiers that complement each other. Instead of sampling (as in bagging) re-weigh examples (Examples are given weights). At each iteration, a new hypothesis is learned (weak learner) and the examples are reweighted to focus the system on examples that the most recently learned classifier got wrong. Final classification is based on weighted vote of weak classifiers. After a series of classifier training under boosting approach, the final classifier aggregates the learned classifiers and the results should be better than single classifier method.

The magnetic profile is filtered for noise using DFT. Features considered in model is frequency wave form, occupancy time, vehicle length, height, size. Feature extraction is accomplished with Principal Component Analysis (PCA)[10].This ensembled model is trained using the training data set stored in PCA and tested for its performance and we have proposed a framework to achieve high computation speed both in training and testing phase.

6   Conclusions and Future Work

An Analysis and a comparison of recent neural network algorithms have been presented in this paper and our goal is to propose a framework for vehicle classification system using ensembled boosting methods. This model is faster than single classification algorithms. Besides they can achieve high computation speed both in training and testing phase. We believe that the exploration of new algorithms based on Ensembled Model for Vehicle classification will make online dynamic classification more practical. This work can be extended for implementing different classification algorithms that include concept drift and investigate the robustness of algorithms for large dataset and a rapid input rate.

References

1. Meta, S., Muhammed, G.C.: Vehicle-classification algorithm based on component analysis for single-loop inductive detector. IEEE Transactions on Vehicular Technology 59(6) (July 2010)
2. Oliveira, H.A., Barbosa, F.R., Otacílio, M.: A Vehicle Classification Based On Inductive Loop Detector Using Ann. In: 2010 9th IEEE/IAS International Conference on Industry Applications- Induscon (2010)
3. Ozkurt, C., Camci, F.: Automatic Traffic Density Estimation And Vehicle Classification For Traffic Surveillance Systems Using Neural Networks. Mathematical and Computational Applications 14(3), 187–196 (2009)
4. Ki, Y.-K., Baik, D.-K.: Vehicle-Classification Algorithm For Single-Loop Detectors Using Neural Networks. IEEE Transactions on Vehicular Technology 55(6) (November 2006)
5. Zhang, G.H., Wang, Y.H., Wei, H.: Artificial Neural Network Method For Length-Based Vehicle Classification Using Single-Loop Outputs. Traffic Urban Data, Transp. Res. Rec. 1945, 100–108 (2006)
6. Bajaj, P., Sharma, P., Deshmukh, A.: Vehicle Classification For Single Loop Detector With Neural Genetic Controller: A Design Approach. In: Proceedings of the 2007 IEEE Intelligent Transportation Systems Conference, Seattle, WA, USA, September 30- October 3 (2007)
7. Gajda, J., Sroka, R., Stencel, M., Wajda, A., Zeglen, T.: A Vehicle Classification Based On Inductive Loop Detectors. In: IEEE Instrumentation and Measurement Technology Conference Budapest, Hungary, May 21-23 (2001)
8. Opitz, D., Maclin, R.: Popular ensemble methods: an empirical study. Journal of Artificial Intelligence Research 11, 169–198 (1999)
9. Wang, Y.-R., Chen, Y.-J., Jeffrey Huang, C.F.: Applying Neural Network Ensemble Concepts For Modelling Project Success. In: 26th International Symposium on Automation and Robotics in Construction, ISARC 2009 (2009)
10. Han, J., Kamber, M.: Datamining Concepts and Technique, 2 edn. Elsevier
11. Martínez-Muñoz, G., Sánchez-Martínez, A., Hernández-Lobato, D., Suárez, A.: Class-Switching Neural Network Computer Science Department, Escuela Polit Ecnica Superior, Universidad Aut Onoma De Madrid, C Francisco Tom As Y Valiente (2007)

Climate Analysis Using Oceanic Data from Satellite Images – CAODSI

R.D. Sathiya[1], V. Vaithiyanathan[2], and G. VictorRajamanickam[3]

[1] Assisstant Professor, School of Computing, SASTRA University, Thanjavur,
Tamil Nadu – 613 402
sathya@it.sastra.edu
[2] Dean Research, School of Computing, SASTRA University, Tirumalaisamudram,
Thanjavur – 613 402
vvn@it.sastra.edu
[3] Director Research, Sai Ram Group of Institutions, Chennai
vrajamanickam@hotmail.com

Abstract. Image speaks thousands of information, Satellite image could show galaxy of rays to analyzed and derived with ocean parameters of Coastal observations to precede to future revelations. COADSI is a model, based on the observations of various satellites like IRS; INSAT captured image details were extracted and analyzed using the latest Soft computing techniques. These techniques play vital role in handling the satellite image derived data to further study, classify analyze and simulate a new model to bring our assumptions and predictions to prove to be happen in further observations of climatic conditions.

Keywords: weather forecasting, oceanography, feed forward neural network.

1 Introduction

There are so many systems such as prediction, logarithmic, sinusoidal and autoregressive methods in practice which will help in forecasting the weather. This paper deals with the stochastic simulation model and feed forward neural network in order to forecast the ocean parameters such as the temperature, salinity and so on, commonly known as physical oceanographic parameters or physical parameters that deals with the physical conditions of the ocean). So far the feed forward neural network is used in weather forecasting in continents. Here we are going to use that model in forecasting the ocean parameters.

Oceanography also called oceanology or marine science is a branch of Earth science that studies the ocean. It covers a wide range of topics, including marine organisms and ecosystem dynamics. The study of the oceans is linked to understanding global climate changes, potential global warming and related biosphere concerns. The atmosphere and ocean are linked because of evaporation and precipitation as well as thermal flux and solar insulation. Wind stress is a major driver of ocean currents while the ocean is a sink for atmospheric carbon dioxide.
Study Area: Nagapattinam Coastal Area.

P.V. Krishna, M.R. Babu, and E. Ariwa (Eds.): ObCom 2011, Part II, CCIS 270, pp. 158–164, 2012.
© Springer-Verlag Berlin Heidelberg 2012

Nagapattinam which is located in the eastern coast of south India is a big sea shore area and a dangerous one too because it is a low lying coast enabling the quick changes during cyclone and Tsunami. The process of calculating the oceanic parameters will be helpful to predict such dangerous disasters. We are going to use the feed forward neural network model for that process. **Nagapattinam** [Fig1] is a coastal city in Indian state of Tamil Nadu, it was carved out by bifurcating the composite Thanjavur district on October 18, 1991.. Nearby towns include Tiruvarur, Karaikal and Mayiladuthurai.

Fig. 1. Study area Nagapattinam

Surface topography varies on several scales of time and space. Satellite altimetry is capable of measuring these variations globally and almost instantaneously with centimeter accuracy, allowing scientists to:

- Enumerate the nature of deformations of the sea's surface in relation to global ocean circulation.
- Assess the major marine currents, such as the Gulf Stream and the Kuroshio, much as atmospheric pressure is measured by meteorologists.
- Monitor ocean changes (eddies, for example), tides and seasonal and climate events like El Nino,
- Estimate the topology of the ocean floor, little known, but of crucial importance.

The principal mission for altimetry today, however, is to provide accurate and continuous measurements of mean sea level. Since the launch of Topex-Poseidon in 1992, observations have revealed a mean increase in sea level of approximately 3 mm/year (with variations of ± 20 mm/year in some regions). This increase is an incontrovertible indicator of global warming.

Advance knowledge of mean wave heights and surface wind speeds helps navigators choose the best and safest routes. These data are processed and made available almost in real time by Meteo France. Marine navigation charts established with Jason aid the ships of both the French Navy and US Navy.

Jason data also help to develop tools for monitoring and modelling ocean drift resulting from the combined action of wind, currents and tides on ocean circulation. These tools have applications for tracking marine pollution or for search-and-rescue missions. Oceans play a decisive role in the evolution of climate, acting as both a regulating and disturbing influence. The oceans store considerable amounts of heat near the equator, are the range is gradually transferred toward the poles via ocean currents. Jason-1 is an element of the Mercator operational oceanography project launched in 1997, for which a public interest grouping was formed in 2002, under a partnership between CNES, CNRS/INSU, Ifremer, IRD, Meteo-France and SHOM. Mercator supports real-time monitoring of the oceans with weekly sea-state bulletins. One of its application is long-range forecasting —2 weeks.

These data are used to model the dynamic state of the oceans and to predict climatic trends for the months and years ahead, including the possible onset of drought, heavy rains, cold weather or heat waves. This information also contributes to a better understanding of large-scale climatic changes such as rising sea levels due to global warming, or El Niño events.

1.1   Materials and Methods

The process contains three phases. First phase is extracting the data from the satellite images using ferret. The second phase is to arrange the data in the excel sheet to feed as input for training. The third phase is to train the data and get the output.

Phase1- Ferret is an interactive computer visualization and analysis environment designed to meet the needs of oceanographers and meteorologists analyzing large and complex gridded data sets. It runs on most Unix systems, and on Windows XP/NT/9x using X windows for display.

The data obtained from ferret will be in the form of list with date. Table 1

Table 1.

```
24-DEC-2008 00 / 846:  19.21
31-DEC-2008 00 / 847:  15.84
07-JAN-2009 00 / 848:  12.12
14-JAN-2009 00 / 849:  14.36
21-JAN-2009 00 / 850:  13.23
28-JAN-2009 00 / 851:   9.46
04-FEB-2009 00 / 852:   6.26
11-FEB-2009 00 / 853:   4.21
```

*Phase2-*The extracted data will be arranged in an excel sheet as it has to feed as input to the neural network in order to train the data.

The excel sheet will have enormous data arranged in rows and columns Table2. When these data are fed for training they will relate those data and their outputs and then, the sample data for which we need output can be given and then the output will come.

The data arranged in the excel sheet will be of numerical format and therefore in order to train the data, the data should be in the range of 0 and 1, so that the data will be divided by a common value 1000 enabling to normalize them. These data are known as normalized data.

After the normalization process is over the phase 3 will come.

Phase3 - In phase 3 the data that is normalized will be given as input to the C program. The excel sheet will be saved in the format of .dat so that it can be directly given as input to the program.

The program uses the back propagation neural network algorithm, which is very useful in training. That is the back propagation network contains 3 layers. The input layer, Hidden layer, Output layer. There are number of nodes in these three layers which can be determined by the user. The input layer holds the data that is given. The hidden layer mostly containing nodes twice as the number of nodes in input layer to maps the input but the output that is given in the excel sheet. Next comes the output layer probably only one node that is for providing output that is mostly matching with the targeted output.

The process of taking BPN is that the error will be reduced to the maximum extent..

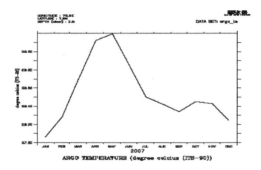

Fig. 2. Argo Temperature Analysis

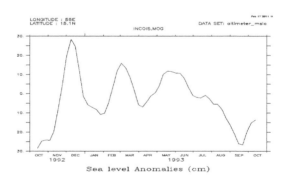

Fig. 3. Sea Level Anomalies – 1992-1993

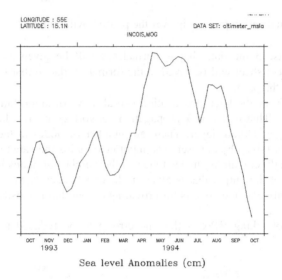

Fig. 4. Sea Level Anomalies – 1993-1994

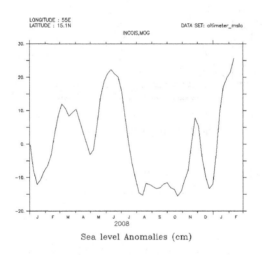

Fig. 5. Sea Level Anomalies - 2008

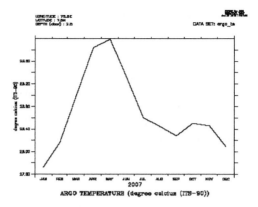

Fig. 6. Agro Temperature 2007

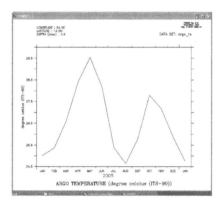

Fig. 7. Agro Temperature 2005

1.1.1 Spatial Mining

Spatial Mining has remained as the most prominent method to find the patterns in geographic data. Initially, it has focused on finding the patterns in textual and numerical electronic information. Spatial data mining is considered as the most complicated and challenging one than traditional mining because it deals with analyzing objects with corporeal existences in space and time. The reason is that the spatial data mining algorithms have to consider the neighbours objects in order to extract the useful knowledge. A spatial database contains objects which are characterized by a spatial location/ extension as well as by several non-spatial attributes.

Specific purposes of geographical data which forestall the use of general purpose of data mining algorithms are:

1. Variables and its spatial relationship.
2. Spatial structures of errors.
3. Observation those are not independent.
4. Non-linear interaction in future space.

Here the question arises whether we really need to forgo new algorithms or to just extent the existing algorithm for explicit model of spatial properties or not. Though it is difficult to work over a better option between them, as of now both approaches are gaining vitality.

A model for predicting the weather format using spatial attributes is generated by retrieving values from back end. We require the attributes namely humidity, pressure, ground temperature and wind speed respectively. The types of weather format were identified and the mean average of the temperature, humidity, pressure and wind speed was calculated using the given input data.

Output Result

Two conditions are set to identify the weather formats.

Condition I: The input humidity is lesser than the mean humidity and the input ground temperature is lesser than the mean ground temperature, and also if input pressure is greater than the mean pressure and input wind speed is greater than the mean speed.

Condition II: The input humidity is greater than the mean humidity and the input ground temperature is greater than the mean ground temperature, and also if input pressure is lesser than the mean pressure and input wind speed is lesser than the mean speed.

In general, the values are retrieved from the back end and hence, the average is calculated based on those values, from that weather conditions were diagnosed.

2   Conclusion

The results show that high rates of classification can be achieved on a large set of test data. It is interesting to note there is not much significant difference in classification rates between the two types of networks. This may imply the advantages that COADSI normally have over back propagation networks are invalidated since the feature vector naturally has good intra-class separation.

Having a good classification system is important since it opens up other areas of research. It is hoped that the system can be used to study the sequence of changes in climatic conditions. Since the methods used are covering a wide range of signal types, then the methods employed could be used for other marine signals.

Acknowledgements. The authors are thankful to Directors INCOIS for providing the necessary data.

References

1.   Rozovskii, B., Grimmett, G.: Stochastic modelling and applied probability
2.   Sanjaymathur, Kumar, A., Chandra, M.: A Feature Based Neural Network Model for Weather Forecasting Paras

Cloud Gaming with P2P Network Using XAML and Windows Azure

S. Prabu and Swarnalatha Purushotham

Professor / IT, PSNA College of Engineering and Technology,
Dindigul-624622, Tamil Nadu, India
drsprabu@psnacet.edu.in
AP [SG] / SCSE, VIT University Vellore - 632 014, Tamilnadu, India
pswarnalatha@vit.ac.in

Abstract. The next generation of Internet technology uses Windows Azure as a cloud for software as a service (Saas) and storage. In cloud gaming the responsibility for executing gaming engines(Saas) and graphics rendering is available in the cloud servers instead of mobile devices, PC's since mobile devices and PCs can not run the game beyond the random access Memory(RAM) available. The application in Cloud is developed using XAML so that it can be reused windows presentation framework desktop application and browser, multi-touch screen, mobile silver light applications are integrated as single application, depending upon the type of device, the game will run. Peer 2 peer network (P2P) allows the application running in one computer can be shared by another application so that single game can be shared and played by mobile user, PC user at a time eg., Foot Ball, Cricket. The article aims to present rich internet games to mobile and PC users irrespective of the available memory of device and capacity to share the single game across mobile and PC users. Cloud gaming with P2P Network based upon Windows Azure and XAML, using single application which will lead to integration of desktop, browser, multi-touch screen and mobile applications.

Keywords: Cloud Gaming, Peer 2 Peer Network, Windows Azure, XAML.

1 Introduction

Cloud Computing (CC) is widely accepted which gives large storage media and reusable services are deployed by once and shared by other users (Saas). With rapid evolution of mobile devices and their capabilities with rapid adoption to Internet access, there will be growing desire for enabling rich Internet games on mobile. As mobile device has constraints in terms of battery, memory available, they can not run the game beyond the memory available. Here the game is available in a cloud it is responsible for executing the gaming engines.

In Cloud Gaming, the game can be shared by mobile user, desktop user using P2P network from Cloud where Cloud is responsible for executing the gaming engines and rendering the Windows Azure which is a Microsoft cloud technology and can be used as a cloud. Here XAML is used for single application for mobile, desktop applications.

P.V. Krishna, M.R. Babu, and E. Ariwa (Eds.): ObCom 2011, Part II, CCIS 270, pp. 165–172, 2012.
© Springer-Verlag Berlin Heidelberg 2012

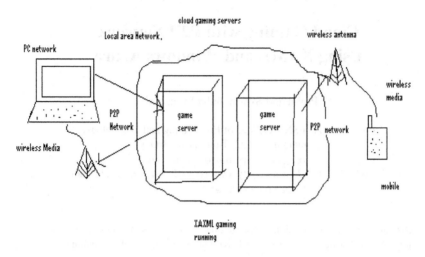

Fig. 1. Shows overview of Cloud gaming with P2P Network using XAML and Windows Azure

In the paper, as mobile devices are Context-aware running on the application in Mobile Internet Devices, which can be shared by many other games (eg: cricket).The windows azure cloud computing is mainly used for on-demand self-service, resource pooling and broad network access and windows azure provides shared resources, information and software and other devices on-demand. A number of cloud computing platforms already available for pervasively accessing of user data.

In proposed system, using Cloud gaming with P2P Network application will run beyond the device memory available and single application is shared by mobile, desktop users using XAML. The figure one shows general overview of P2P networking cloud mobile gaming in which game servers are available in cloud and can be accessed by wireless media, zigbee, local area network.

ZigBee is the name of a specification for a suite of high level communication protocols using small, low-power digital radios based on the IEEE 802.15.4-2006 standard for wireless personal area networks.

The rest of the paper is organized as follows: Section 2 presents related work, Section 3 deals with the cloud gaming for desktop and Mobile users and how Windows Azure used as a Cloud. Section 4 describes the Design of Cloud gaming with P2P network using XAML and Windows Azure. Section 5 focus on security issues that may arise. Section 6 gives the idea of implementation using WPF and finally, conclusions are presented in section 7.

2   Related Work

The mobile devices can access cloud games and graphics rendering will be done in cloud servers[10]. Accessing cloud video streaming using P2P Network instead of going for server at each time access from the nearest peer which will provide high bandwidth transfer rate[3]. Using mobile android application the patients health records can be updated and retrieved using Amazon's S3 cloud service[1]. While accessing the cloud application from Mobile to protect the data from unauthorized user and reducing mobile client energy while accessing [2]. As a mobile and desktop used as a terminal (remote display), the entire application is run by cloud, terminal display solutions i.e, battery life and context-aware is discussed[7]. Using computer-aided education platform using mobile application students can post the questions to the cloud.

The teacher can answer the question of accessing from cloud [2]. Cloud refers to access the computing resources that are typically owned and operated by a third-party provider on a consolidated basis in one, or usually more, data centre locations [2]. Offloading the computation related services from mobile devices to a cloud environment also save energy which is a key element for mobile devices [3]. Reduce the memory constraint of the mobile devices (Low Processing Units) such as cell phones and PDAs by providing the data on demand, so that there is no need of storing the data in limited memory contained by these devices [11].

3   Cloud Gaming for Mobile and Desktop Users

3.1   Principles of Windows Azure

The term cloud computing was given due to the fact that it uses internet for communication and generally internet is represented by the cloud symbols. Here using Windows Azure as a cloud, the devices used as a terminal and execution of game entirely maintained by the cloud. It is based on "Service-oriented" architecture. Hence, Windows Azure is responsible for running the instances for each group an instance and the single instance is shared by the group for playing the game.

Windows Azure provides results which can store the games in middle and execute the same instance again from the stage where it will be stopped. Cloud consists of gaming servers which is responsible for running the server based on the condition. Windows Azure used to build, host, scale manage, complete and compel the web-applications through microsoft data centers. Cloud computing incorporates infrastructure as a service (IaaS), platform as a service (PaaS) and software as a service (Saas). It provides on demand service game to both service providers and service consumers by reducing the operational cost.

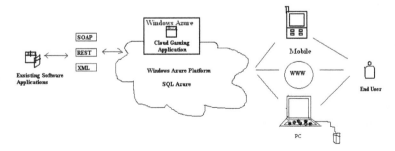

Fig. 2. Shows Windows Azure applicability with existing applications and invocation by end user

The windows azure is based on service oriented architecture in which service provider that provides service. The service provider will publish service in service broker from which a service requester can request a service. After finding the service, Service Requester binds to service provider using policy. And windows azure is used as a Saas (Software as a Service) and Storage purposes.

3.2   Windows Azure – Based Cloud Gaming Using Peer to Peer Network

A peer is an entity with capabilities similar to other entities. It allows the application running in one computer that can be shared by other computers. P2P network allows computers to directly connect to others rather than a central server. Each peer is heterogeneous in bandwidth contribution as the peer to peer relationship, many to one. And if more than one supplier we have to select the high bandwidth peer. To identify the disconnection while playing the game due to network failure it will send a message for every 30 seconds. P2P Network is advantageous due to more bandwidth, decentralization and more scalability. P2P network is robust network since address of broadcaster does not know to the peer.

The article conveys the usage of Peer to peer network application running on cloud that can be shared by all other users in same instance. From the cloud, the game will be accessed and ruined. PCs and Mobile devices are just used as end terminals.

4   Design of Cloud Gaming with Peer to Peer Network Using Windows Azure and XAML

XAML is a declarative markup language. It is used for creating rich interactive user interfaces at client side. XAML language is used by Windows Presentation Framework (WPF) and Silver light. Advantages of XAML are design/code (behavior) separation. At a time both designers and developers can share work and it will take hardware acceleration support to create new levels of visual complexity. For developing desktop applications Windows Presentation Framework will be used, for browser and PDA applications silver light is used. XAML language applications will run resolution independently and uses vector based rendering.

4.1   Invoking Cloud Gaming with XAML

The Cloud consists of different gaming servers and executing the games and sharing the game across the users done by peer 2 peer networks. Cloud creates an instance in a server for each group of a game.

Whenever a client (Mobile or PC) requests for a game cloud creates instance and the same instance can be shared by PC or other mobile user. Rendering the game in mobile phone and low running memory can overcome by using cloud. It will run the game beyond the available RAM Memory and storage capacity as Windows Azure cloud is taking care of storage and Software as a service (Saas). And the Peer 2 Peer networking gnutella protocol may be used for security request and response since application running in cloud can be shared by mobile, pc users which have to be authenticated.

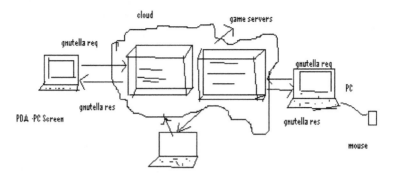

Fig. 3. Shows architecture of invoking Windows Azure Cloud Games with XAML application

The XAML is reused among Windows Presentation Framework and Silver light applications. So that single application can be used to control pda, touch screen and browser based applications. XAML uses vector based rendering and resolution independent. So XAML will provide rich internet client applications.

5   Security Issues

Windows Azure gives assurance that storage services are scalable, secure and easy access using BLOB(Binary Large Object Service), Windows Azure Drive, Queue Service and Table Service. BLOB service allows a simple way to store text and binary files to store results of game. Table service allows storing a huge amount of data and querying used when game is shared more than four people. Queue service used for persistence messaging between web and instances i.e., each instance is created for each group of gaming people. Windows Azure drive allows mount a page Blob which will be used for launching the game in mobile, desktop or web. Windows Azure also allows creating Virtual Networks. As peer to peer network allows application running in computer can be shared by another computer security has to be provided by using gnutella protocol.

6   Implementation of Gaming Using WPF

To have the gaming in the emulator, proceed for the following stages, we have to use the Windows Azure compute Emulator from the Microsoft visual studio as displayed in the figure four.

Fig. 4. Windows Azure Compute Emulator

As a whole, deploy the Windows Azure Project environment with sample screen shot of the gaming program for windows as provided in the figure five .

Fig. 5. Example of gaming source code

We have to further continue to the WPF Application which lead to the browser application includes a WPF user control library. And the library will direct to the WPF MVVM Application. After configuration for windows azure, lastly the WPF application for game development should be deployed for the gaming project as cited in the figure six.

Fig. 6. WPF Application for game development

7   Conclusion

From the past two decades rich Internet games are coming in market. These games can not run beyond the device memory available .For example mobile are constraint devices in terms of battery and memory available.

Technology is making so many things easier to us. Upto now, cloud computing used for software as a service and storage. Thus, in our proposed system the game will run on Cloud so that it will provide rich Internet games available to user and P2P network is used for sharing the same game across users mobile, desktop, browser users(Eg: Cricket) and can play the game from across the world .

XAML is next generation client slide application which can be used by PDA, Multi-touch screen Browser and desktop applications. So reusing XAML code among applications will save amount of time and will give high performance as it is vector based and resolution independent.

In the paper, we propose next generation Gaming using PDA, Touch Screen, Browser and desktop Applications. Using the cloud the single application will run across all applications.

References

[1] Doukas, C., Pilakas, T.: Mobile Healthcare Information Management utilizing Cloud Computing and Android OS. In: 32nd Annual International Conference of the IEEE EMBS (2010)
[2] http://en.citizendium.org/wiki/Cloud_computing
[3] Kumar, K., Lu, Y.-H.: Cloud Computing for Mobile Users: Can Offloading Computation Save Energy? pp. 51–56. IEEE Computer Society (2010)

[4] Klein, Mannweiler, A., Christian, S., Schotten, J., Hans, D.: Access Schemes for Mobile Cloud Computing. In: Eleventh International Conference on Mobile Data Management, pp. 387–392 (June 2010)
[5] Punithavathi, R., Duraiswamy, K.: An Optimized Solution for Mobile Computing Environment. In: International Conference on Computing, Communication and Networking (2008)
[6] Wang, S., Dey, S.: Rendering Adaption to Address Communication and Computation Constraints in Cloud Mobile Gaming. In: Proceddings of IEEE Globecom (2010)
[7] Wang, S., Dey, S.: Addressing Response Time and Video Quality in Remote Server Based Internet Mobile Gaming. Proc. of IEEE Transactions (2010)
[8] Itani, W., Kayssi, A., Chehab, A.: Energy- Efficient Incremental Integrity for Securing Storage in Mobile Cloud Computing. IEEE Transactions (2010)
[9] Zhao, W., Sun, Y., Dai, L.: Improving Computer Basis Teaching Through Mobile Communication and Cloud Computing Technology. In: 3rd International Conference on Advanced Computer Theory and Engineering (2010)
[10] Jin, X., Kwok, Y.-K.: Cloud Assisted P2P Media Streaming for Bandwidth Constrained Mobile Subscribers. In: 16th International Conference on Parallel and Distributed Systems (2010)
[11] Chen, Z., Zhao, Y., Miao, X., Chen, Y., Wang, Q.: Rapid Provisioning of Cloud Infrastructure Leveraging Peer-to-Peer Networks. In: 29th IEEE International Conference on Distributed Computing Systems Workshops (2009)

Active Contour Based Color Image Segmentation

G. Raghotham Reddy[1], M. Mahesh Chandra[1], Kama Ramudu[1],
and R. Rameshwar Rao[2]

[1] Department of ECE, KITS Warangal-15, India
[2] Department of ECE, OUCE, Hyderabad, India
grr_ece@yahoo.com, mamach@ieee.org,
ramudukama@gmail.com, rameshwarrao@hotmail.com

Abstract. In this framework we address color image segmentation using level set methods. We used Independent Component Analysis to work with independent components of color image. We also used Bhattacharyya Coefficient to find similarity between inside and outside contour and which besides helpful in redefining the new Level Set function. The experiments performed on real world color images, the final locking of images on features of interest is found to be satisfactory on real world color images. The proposed method avoids leakages and diffuses the contour towards the actual object boundaries.

Keywords: Image Segmentation, Level Set Method, Independent Components Analysis, Bhattacharya Coefficient.

1 Introduction

Image segmentation has been the subject of active research in computer vision and image processing. A large body of work on active contours implemented via level set methods has been proposed to address a wide range of image segmentation problems [16, 17, 18]. Level set methods were first introduced by Osher and Sethian [10] for capturing moving fronts. Kass et.al first to introduce the active contour snake model algorithm [1] which deforms a shape to lock onto features of interest within in an image. Snakes are the deformable contour methods (DCMs). These DCMs are now applied extensively in industrial and medical image applications. It is not easy to segment the medical images; various parameters will affect the final results such as complex procedures, multiple parameter selection, and location of initial contour.

The existing active contour models can be classified as either parametric active contour models or geometric active contour models according to their representation and implementation. In particular, the parametric active contours [15] are represented explicitly as parameterized curves in a Lagrangian framework, while the geometric active contours [4, 5, 13] are represented implicitly as level sets of a two-dimensional function that evolves in an Eulerian framework. Geometric active contours were introduced by Caselles et al. [16] and Malladi et al. [18], respectively. These models are based on curve evolution theory [20] and level set method [14]. The basic idea is

P.V. Krishna, M.R. Babu, and E. Ariwa (Eds.): ObCom 2011, Part II, CCIS 270, pp. 173–185, 2012.

to evolve a level set function representing the contours according to a partial differential equation (PDE). The main advantage of this approach over the traditional parametric active contours is that the contours represented by the level set function may break or merge naturally during the evolution, and the topological changes are thus automatically handled. Early geometric active contour models [1,2,3] utilize a Lagrangian formulation that leads to a certain evolution PDE of a parametrized curve. Then, a new evolution PDE for a level set function is obtained using the related Eulerian formulation from level set methods. More precisely, the new evolution PDE can be directly derived from the problem of minimizing certain energy functional defined on the level set function. These methods are known as variational level set methods [22, 23].

Active Contour or Snake can also be defined as is a thin elastic band on image that will update its position in every iteration to lock object boundaries of interest. The goal of basic snake model is to precisely capture the boundaries of object of interest. There are three main basic steps for any snake model, Snake Initialization, Snake evolution and stopping evolution after snake converged. Snake initialization can be done manually or automatically.

In Snake evolution active contour curves move under the influence of internal force and external forces. Internal forces coming from curves themselves, and Image data accounts for the external forces. In most of algorithms the snake evolution is stopped by specifying number of iterations in conjunction with distance parameter between old and new level set functions.

Active contour models categorized into two main families: Edge based model [3] and region based model. In edge based models gradients of image is used to distinguish object edges and also useful in halting the curve evolution. Each method has its own advantages for different applications. Chan and Vese latterly proposed a model [2] which is not based on gradient of image, the evolvement of curve is based on Mumford – Shah Formulation [4] of image segmentation and to model the region information by introducing the Heaviside function.

In this paper Level Set updates its position based on similarity score between intensity histograms. In the paper [8] by Dipti Prasad Mukherjee et. al the MR image skewness is adjusted by using Bhattacharyya Coefficient. It is a divergence-type measure[14], Useful in finding the similarity between two images or two sections of a image. This can be done by correlating the spatial information or by matching their spectral features. Bhattacharyya coefficient [14] is one of the criteria which gives a similarity measure between the densities (spectral information) of two images or sections of images.

$$Score(C_1, C_2) = \sum_{i=1}^{N} BC(h_i^1, h_i^2)$$

$$BC(h_i^1 h_i^2) = \int_{\mathbb{R}^N} \sqrt{h_i^1 h_i^2} \, dz$$

Similarity score ranges from 0 to 1, higher the similarity score higher the similarity. In our paper intensity histogram inside and outside the Level Set functions are calculated and incorporated in energy minimization in every iteration. If Active Contour separates image into two regions, the above specified coefficient tries to minimize the mutual information between the two region, i.e., maximizing distance between probability density functions (pdf) .

The rest of this paper is organized as follows. Section 2 describes previous work on segmenting an image using Active Contours and Section 3 discuss the proposed method section 4 details the experimental results and discussions, final section concludes summary.

2   Previous Work Done

Active contour is revolutionary snake model introduced by Kass [1] in the year 1988. An Active Contour or Snake is a thin elastic band on image that will update its position in every iteration to lock object boundaries of interest. The goal of basic snake model is to precisely capture the boundaries of object of interest. There are three main basic steps for any snake model, Snake Initialization, Snake evolution and stopping evolution after snake converged. The final result depends on Snake Initialization; the snake initialization can be done automatically or manually.

Active Contours or Snakes evolution is based on minimization of energy functional. This energy composed of internal and external energies. Snakes move under the influence of internal force and external forces. Internal forces coming from curves themselves, and Image data accounts for the external forces.

$$E_{ext}(X, Y) = -\int_0^1 f(X(s),Y(s))ds \qquad (1)$$

$f(x, y) = |\nabla I|^2$, $f(x, y)$ is gradient magnitude squared of image $I(x, y)$.

The external energy alone fails to find object boundaries in presence of noise. Addition of internal energy term to above energy functional can overcome the above problem. According to Kass[1] the internal energy is

$$E_{int}(X,Y) = \frac{1}{2}\int_0^1 \alpha\left[\left|\frac{dX}{ds}\right|^2 + \left|\frac{dY}{ds}\right|^2\right] + \beta\left[\left|\frac{d^2X}{ds^2}\right|^2 + \left|\frac{d^2Y}{ds^2}\right|^2\right]ds \qquad (2)$$

Where α, β are tunable parameters.

The final energy functional used for minimization is

$$E_{total}(X, Y) = E_{int}(X, Y) + E_{ext}(X, Y) \qquad (3)$$

For the minimization of above equation help of advanced mathematics such as Calculus of Variations is required. This method helps in taking derivative with respect to a function and then we equate it to zero to trace the minimum. Closed form solution for above obtained equations cannot be obtained, Gradient Descent method is one of the method used to solve above specified issues. In Gradient descent method the variable is updated in proportional to negative of derivative iteratively, when minimum value is reached the derivative gives zero value, this means at this value the energy functional has minimum or maximum value. One can also use Newton's method instead of gradient descent method for finding minimum but it is computationally expensive. From equation (3) the functional derivatives (Euler equations) using optimization tool Calculus of Variations is given by

$$\frac{\partial E}{\partial X} = -\alpha \frac{d^2 X}{ds^2} + \beta \frac{d^4 X}{ds^2} - \frac{\partial f}{\partial x} = 0 \tag{4}$$

$$\frac{\partial E}{\partial Y} = -\alpha \frac{d^2 Y}{ds^2} + \beta \frac{d^4 Y}{ds^2} - \frac{\partial f}{\partial y} = 0 \tag{5}$$

From the above mentioned gradient rules the new equations can be written as

$$\frac{\partial X}{\partial \tau} = \alpha \frac{\partial^2 X}{\partial s^2} - \beta \frac{\partial^4 X}{\partial s^2} + \frac{\partial f}{\partial x} = 0 \tag{6}$$

$$\frac{\partial Y}{\partial \tau} = \alpha \frac{\partial^2 Y}{\partial s^2} - \beta \frac{\partial^4 Y}{\partial s^2} + \frac{\partial f}{\partial y} = 0 \tag{7}$$

The following equations are discritized versions of (6) and (7)

$$\frac{X_i^{\tau+1} - X_i^{\tau}}{\zeta} = \alpha\left(X_{i+1}^{\tau} - 2X_i^{\tau} + X_{i-1}^{\tau}\right) - \beta(X_{i+2}^{\tau} - 4X_{i+1}^{\tau} + 6X_i^{\tau} - 4X_{i-1}^{\tau} + X_{i-2}^{\tau}) + f_x(X_i^{\tau}, Y_i^{\tau}) \tag{7}$$

$$\frac{Y_i^{\tau+1} - Y_i^{\tau}}{\zeta} = \alpha\left(Y_{i+1}^{\tau} - 2Y_i^{\tau} + Y_{i-1}^{\tau}\right) - \beta(Y_{i+2}^{\tau} - 4Y_{i+1}^{\tau} + 6Y_i^{\tau} - 4Y_{i-1}^{\tau} + Y_{i-2}^{\tau}) + f_y(X_i^{\tau}, Y_i^{\tau}) \tag{8}$$

τ and $\tau+1$ are successive time instants with step length ζ. All the additions and subtractions are modulo n additions and modulo n subtractions. There are also different approximations for second and fourth order derivatives mentioned in the above equation.

The equations (7) and (8) can also be written as

$$\frac{X^{\tau+1} - X^{\tau}}{\zeta} = -AX^{\tau} + f_x^{\tau} \tag{9}$$

$$\frac{Y^{\tau+1} - Y^{\tau}}{\zeta} = -Ay^{\tau} + f_y^{\tau} \tag{10}$$

A is matrix of size n X n.

$$A = \begin{bmatrix} c & b & a & & & & a & b \\ b & c & b & a & & & & a \\ a & b & c & b & a & & & \\ & \ddots & \ddots & \ddots & \ddots & \ddots & & \\ a & & a & b & c & b & a \\ b & a & & a & b & c & b \\ & & & & & & c \end{bmatrix}$$

Where $a = \beta,\ b = -(4\beta + \alpha),\ c = 6\beta + 2\alpha$.

The final iterative equations are

$$X^{\tau+1} = X^{\tau} - \zeta A X^{\tau} + \zeta f_x^{\tau} \tag{11}$$

$$Y^{\tau+1} = Y^{\tau} - \zeta A Y^{\tau} + \zeta f_y^{\tau} \tag{12}$$

The above two equations are called as explicit equation techniques, or snake evolution equations and stability of equations depends on time step ζ.

The equations (11) and (12) are used to update in every iteration and Level Set move towards object boundaries.

$$f_x^{\tau} \equiv [f_x(X_0^{\tau}, Y_0^{\tau}), \ldots, f_x(X_{n-1}^{\tau}, Y_{n-1}^{\tau})]^{T} \tag{13}$$

In the Kass snake model, the external force is simply the force due to the potential surface created by the image gradient magnitude. The image gradient force used in Kass snake may not be good enough in many applications. The limitation of the gradient external force becomes evident when we examine a homogeneous part of an image. The image gradient magnitude is essentially zero or close to zero in such portions of the image. Thus, if an active contour starts its journey here, there is little hope to guide it toward an edge.

Different forces were introduced by many authors like distance force, Balloon force, Gradient Vector flow [15] etc. To obtain distance potential force, we first build a distance surface (or distance map) D (x, y) from a binary image I(x, y):

$$D(x, y) = \min_{(p,q) \in \{(a,b): I(a,b)=1\}} [d(x, y; p, q)]$$

Where d(x, y; p, q) measures the distance between two locations (x, y) and (p, q). A familiar example distance metric is Euclidean distance:

$$d(x, y; p, q) = \sqrt{(x - p)^2 + (y - q)^2}$$

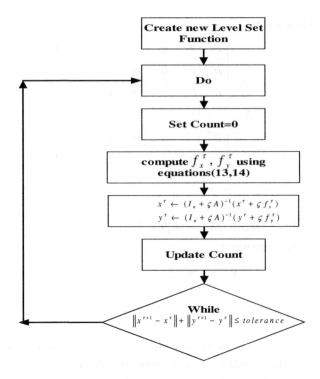

Fig. 1. Flow Chart of Kass Algorithm

Corresponding evolution equations are given by

$$\frac{\partial X}{\partial \tau} = \alpha \frac{\partial^2 X}{\partial s^2} - \beta \frac{\partial^4 X}{\partial s^2} - \alpha \frac{\partial D}{\partial x}$$

$$\frac{\partial Y}{\partial \tau} = \alpha \frac{\partial^2 Y}{\partial s^2} - \beta \frac{\partial^4 Y}{\partial s^2} - \alpha \frac{\partial D}{\partial y}$$

The above equations are almost same as Kass evolution equations.

3   Proposed Method

Independent Component Analysis is one of the signal separation techniques, widely known as cocktail problem. When there are two microphones in a room, each one captures other speaker's voice signal. ICA is used to separate this kind of signals. ICA outputs are not perfectly separated signals; human intervention is required to measure quality.

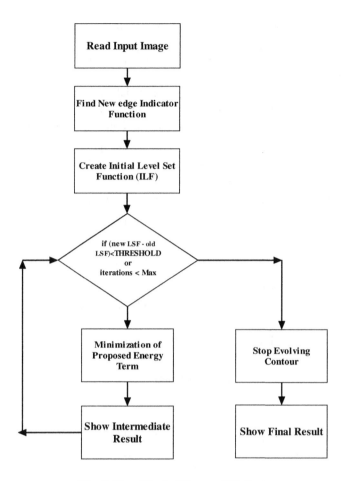

Fig. 2. Flow Chart of Proposed Method

If X=[X$_1$ X$_2$ .....X$_m$] is observed vector of input vector S= [S$_1$ S$_2$......... S$_m$] then

$$X= A.S \qquad (13)$$

A is called mixing matrix of size m x m. The goal is to find unmixing matrix 'W' that gives best approximation Y of S.

$$Y= WX \sim= S \qquad (14)$$

We can also separate the individual images from fusion of images [6] using fastica algorithm which is openly available on the internet [5]. We used this algorithm to define the new edge function that is gives accurate edges compared to canny edge detector; this can be clearly observed from the fig 2 and fig 3. Edges using proposed method enhanced the efficiency of contour evolution accurately. One more advantage of proposed edge is that there are minimum number of broken edges compared with canny edge output. Because this algorithm works on gray level images, the color images will be automatically converted to gray scale. For these calculated independent components gradient of image is calculated .The final results are shown in fig 2(a) and 3(a).

As shown in Fig 1 the next step is creating Initial Level Set function this can be done manually or automatically. Initial level set function or zero level set function is represented as $\phi_0(x) = \{x \mid \phi(x) \equiv 0, x \in \Omega\}$.Now this Level Set function updates its position iteratively from the data obtained from inside and outside the contour to minimize the energy. This evolution will be continued for a given number of iterations or until the difference between new level set function and old level set function is almost zero i.e., $\phi_\infty(x)$ locks to objects boundary. If there are two classes, the segmentation problem reduced to the problem of partitioning the domain of definition $\Omega \subset R^N$ of an image $I(x)$,*where* $x \in \Omega$ into two mutually exclusive and complementary subsets $\Omega_- and \Omega_+$.The color image is converted into its vector equivalent $J(x)$ by using ICA. Class conditional histograms are calculated inside and outside the initial level set function. This can be mathematically calculated as[7]

$$h_i^1 = \frac{\int_\Omega K_-(z - J(x))H(-\phi(x))dx}{\int_\Omega H(-\phi(x))dx} \qquad (15)$$

$$h_i^2 = \frac{\int_\Omega K_+(z - J(x))H(\phi(x))dx}{\int_\Omega H(\phi(x))dx} \qquad (16)$$

$H(\tau)$ is the heaviside function ,expressed in standard way as

$$H(\tau) = \begin{cases} 1, & \tau \geq 0 \\ 0, & \tau < 0 \end{cases}$$

$K_-(z), K_+(z)$ are two scalar valued kernels, $\phi(x)$ is levelset function.

The functions h_i^1, h_i^2 are kernel based estimates of probability density functions of inside (Ω_-) and outside (Ω_+) the Level Set function.

$$BC(\phi(x)) = \int_{\mathbb{R}^N} \sqrt{h_i^1 h_i^2} \, dz \qquad (A)$$

Taking first variation of $BC(\phi(x))$ w.r.t. $\phi(x)$

$$\frac{\partial BC(\phi(x))}{\partial \phi(x)} = \frac{1}{2} \int_{z \in \mathbb{R}^N} \left(\frac{\partial h_i^1}{\partial \phi(x)} \sqrt{\frac{h_i^1}{h_i^2}} + \frac{\partial h_i^2}{\partial \phi(x)} \sqrt{\frac{h_i^2}{h_i^1}} \right) \quad (B)$$

Differentiate equations (15) and (16) w.r.t. $\phi(x)$ and substituting in (B) we get,

$$\frac{\partial BC(\phi(x))}{\partial \phi(x)} = \delta(\phi(x))V(x)$$

$$V(x) = \frac{1}{2} BC(\phi(x))(A_-^{-1} - A_+^{-1})$$

$$+ \frac{1}{2} \int_{z \in \mathbb{R}^N} K_+(z - J(x)) \frac{1}{A_+} \sqrt{\frac{h_i^1}{h_i^2}} dz$$

$$+ \frac{1}{2} \int_{z \in \mathbb{R}^N} K_-(z - J(x)) \frac{1}{A_-} \sqrt{\frac{h_i^2}{h_i^1}} dz$$

The above equation minimizes to (18) if same kernel is used i.e., $K = K_-(z) = K_+(z)$.

The proposed gradient flow is

$$\phi_t(x) = \delta(\phi(x))(\alpha \kappa - V(x)) \tag{17}$$

Where κ is curvature of the snake, mathematically expressed as, $\kappa = -div\{(\nabla \phi(x))/\|\nabla \phi(x)\|\}$.

$$V(x) = \frac{1}{2} \tilde{B}(\phi(x))(A_-^{-1} - A_+^{-1}) +$$

$$\frac{1}{2} \int_{z \in \mathbb{R}^N} K(z - J(x))L(z \mid \phi(x))dz \tag{18}$$

$$L(z \mid \phi(x)) = \frac{1}{A_+} \sqrt{\frac{h_i^1}{h_i^2}} - \frac{1}{A_-} \sqrt{\frac{h_i^2}{h_i^1}} \tag{19}$$

The equation (17) converges to object boundaries by minimizing the energy, which increases the distance between h_i^1, h_i^2 .Probability distributions are updated in every iteration and new Level Set function derived from using equation (17).

4   Experimental Results and Discussions

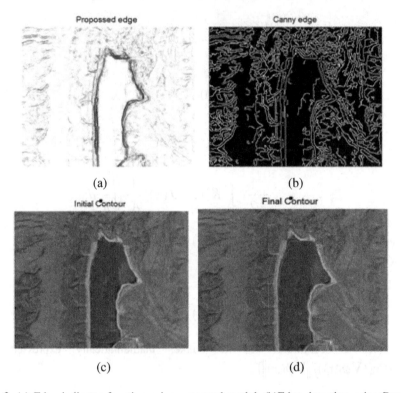

Fig. 3. (a) Edge indicator function using proposed methd, (b)Edge detection using Proposed method, (c) Initial Level Set function, (d)Final Contour using Proposed Method

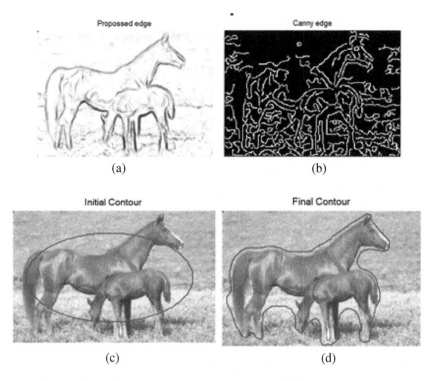

Fig. 4. (a) Edge indicator function using proposed method, (b)Edge detection using Proposed method, (c) Initial Level Set function, (d) Final Contour using Proposed Method

Table 1. Number of iterations and time taken using Our Method

IMAGE	PROPOSED		
	Time(Sec)	Iterations	size
Fig3	13.95	86	316 x 386
Fig4	5.77	67	144 x 216

5   Conclusion

In this paper, a novel Active contour snake model is modified and this algorithm is applied to real world images. In improved model instead of using image data directly, independent components of image with Kernel are used for image segmentation this will help in finding object boundaries accurately. The edge from proposed method compared with canny edge. By using new edge and energy functions the snake moves accurately towards object boundaries. The probability distributions inside and outside the Level Set functions are updated in every iteration to maximize Bhattacharyya coefficient. This method is giving satisfactory results on most of the real world images. In contrast to existing methods, the improved segmentation results were beneficial. However in some images time complexity is high, where our future work remains.

References

[1] Kass, M., Witkin, A., Terzopoulos, D.: Snakes: Active contour models. International Journal of Computer Vision, 321–331 (1988)
[2] Chan, T., Vese, L.: Active contour without edges. IEEE Transaction on Image Processing 10(2), 266–277 (2007)
[3] Xu, C.Y., Prince, J.L.: Snakes, Shapes, and Gradient Vector Flow. IEEE Transactions on Image Processing 7, 359–369 (1998)
[4] Mumford, D., Shan, J.: Optimal approximation, by piece-wise smoothes functions and associated variational problems. Communications on Pure and Applied Mathematics 42, 677–685 (1989)
[5] http://research.ics.tkk.fi/ica/fastica/
[6] Langlois, D., Chartier, S., Gosselin, D.: An Introduction to Independent Component Analysis: InfoMax and FastICA algorithms. Tutorials in Quantitative Methods for Psychology 6(1), 31–38 (2010)
[7] Michailovich, O., Rathi, Y., Tannenbaum, A.: Image Segmentation Using Active Contours Driven by the Bhattacharyya Gradient Flow. IEEE Transactions on Image Processing 16(11), 2787–2801 (2007)
[8] Mukherjee, D.P., Cheng, I., Ray, N., Mushahwar, V., Lebel, M., Basu, A.: Automatic Segmentation of Spinal Cord MRI Using Symmetric Boundary Tracing. IEEE Transactions on Information Technology in Biomedicine 14(5), 1275–1278 (2010)
[9] Osher, S., Sethian, J.A.: Fronts propagation with curvature dependent speed: Algorithms based on Hamilton–Jacobi formulations. Journal of Computational Physics 79, 12–49 (1988)
[10] Tsai, A., Yezzi, A., Willsky, A.: Curve evolution implementation of the Mumford-shah functional for image segmentation, denoising, interpolation, and magnification. IEEE Trans. Image Processing 10(8), 1169–1186 (2001)
[11] Vese, L., Chan, T.: A multiphase level set framework for image segmentation using the Mumford and shah model. Inter. J. Computer Vision 50(3), 271–293 (2002)
[12] Sattar, J.: Snakes, Shapes and Gradient Vector Flow. IEEE Transactions Image Processing 7(3), 359–369 (1998)
[13] Li, C.M., Xu, C.Y., Gui, C.F., Fox, M.D.: Level Set Evolution Without Re-initialization: A New Variational Formulation. In: IEEE Computer Society Conference on Computer Vision and Pattern Recognition, pp. 430–436 (2005)
[14] Lin, J.: Divergence measures based on the Shannon entropy. IEEE Trans. Information Theory 37, 145–151 (1991)
[15] Xu, C., Prince, J.L.: Gradient vector flow: a new external force for snakes. In: Proceedings of IEEE Computer Society Conference on Computer Vision and Pattern Recognition, pp. 66–71 (1997)
[16] Caselles, V., Catte, F., Coll, T., Dibos, F.: A geometricmodel for active contours in image processing. Numer. Math. 66, 1–31 (1993)
[17] Han, X., Xu, C., Prince, J.: A topology preserving level set method for geometric deformable models. IEEE Trans. Patt. Anal. Mach. Intell. 25, 755–768 (2003)

[18] Malladi, R., Sethian, J.A., Vemuri, B.C.: Shape modeling with front propagation: a level set approach. IEEE Trans. Patt. Anal. Mach. Intell. 17, 158–175 (1995)

[19] Osher, S., Sethian, J.A.: Fronts propagation with curvature dependent speed: Algorithms based on Hamilton–Jacobi formulations. Journal of Computational Physics 79, 12–49 (1988)

[20] Kimia, B.B., Tannenbaum, A., Zucker, S.: Shapes, shocks, and deformations i: the components of twodimensional shape and the reaction-diffusion space. Intl. J. Comp. Vis. 15, 189–224 (1995)

[21] Osher, S., Fedkiw, R.: Level set methods and dynamic implicit surfaces. Springer, New York (2002)

[22] Vemuri, B., Chen, Y.: Joint image registration and segmentation.Geometric Level Set Methods in Imaging. In: Vision and Graphics Geometric Level Set Methods in Imaging. Springer, New York (2003)

[23] Zhao, H., Chan, T., Merriman, B., Osher, S.: A variational level set approach to multiphase motion. J. Comp. Phys. 127, 179–195 (1996)

Inference of Naïve Baye's Technique
on Student Assessment Data

S. Anupama Kumar[1] and Vijayalakshmi M.N.[2]

[1] Research Scholar, PRIST University
[1,2] Dept of M.C.A
[1,2] R.V. College of Engineering, Bangalore, India
{kumaranu.0506,mnviju74}@gmail.com

Abstract. The main objective of any educational institute is to provide quality education to students and produce qualified students to the community. This can be achieved only when the institutions are capable of predicting the student's behavior, their attitude towards studies and also the outcome of their result in the forth coming examinations. This can be achieved through various data mining techniques like classification, clustering and rule based mining. Classification techniques like decision trees, Bayesian network and neural networks can be used to predict the student's outcome in the examination based on their attendance percentage, their marks in the internal examination, the historical data available in the form of their previously scored percentage etc. Bayesian classification technique is used to predict the student's outcome in the university examination based on the marks obtained by them in the internal examination. Bayes classification is used to predict the result of the student on an individual basis which has helped the tutor to identify the weak students in each subject. This result has helped the tutors to concentrate on those weak students and bring out better results. This prediction will also help the institution to reduce the drop out ratio and produce better results.

Keywords: Educational data mining, Classification, Bayesian network, Assessment, Predictive model.

1   Introduction

The advent of information technology in various fields has lead the large volumes of data storage in various formats like records, files, documents, images, sound, videos, scientific data and many new data formats. The data collected from different applications require proper method of extracting knowledge from large repositories for better decision making. Knowledge discovery in databases (KDD), often called data mining, aims at the discovery of useful information from large collections of data [1]. Data mining is an emerging methodology used in educational field to enhance the understanding of learning Process to focus on identifying, extracting and evaluating variables related to the learning process of students [2]. The Educational Data Mining community website, defines Educational data mining as "An emerging discipline, concerned with developing methods for exploring the unique types of data that come from educational settings, and using those methods to better understand students, and

P.V. Krishna, M.R. Babu, and E. Ariwa (Eds.): ObCom 2011, Part II, CCIS 270, pp. 186–191, 2012.
© Springer-Verlag Berlin Heidelberg 2012

the settings which they learn in."[15] .Data mining techniques like classification and clustering play a major role in extracting data from the education community and convert them into useful information. Classification techniques like decision trees, naïve bayes, and neural network can be used to behaviour of the student in the class, the result obtained by the student in the exam etc. The main objective of this paper is to predict the student's outcome in university examination using the marks obtained by them in the internal examination .This will also bring out betterment in the result by reducing the drop out ratio of the institution. The paper is divided into four sections namely, introduction, background investigation, Bayes classification technique, application using Bayesian network and conclusion.

2   Background and Related Work

There are many different methods used to perform data mining tasks. Classification is one of the most popular techniques used by data miners. Classification techniques are used in pattern recognition, medical diagnosis, loan approval, fault detection system etc. Prediction techniques can be used to predict the outcome of a student in the university examination. This requires many parameters to be considered. Data pertaining to the student's academic performance like the internal marks, the grades obtained due to assignment etc can be considered to predict his outcome in the examination. M.N. Quadri and Dr. N.V. Kalyankar [3] have predicted student's academic performance using the CGPA grade system where the data set comprised of the students gender, his parental education details, his financial background etc. The authors of [5] have considered only the internal marks obtained by the students to predict the performance of the students using decision trees. Pandey and Pal [4] conducted study on the student performance based by selecting 600 students from different colleges of Dr. R. M. L. Awadh University, Faizabad, India. They have used Bayes Classification to predict whether a student will be a good performer or underperformer using category, language and background qualification as parameters.

3   Bayesian Classification Techniques

Classification is the most commonly applied data mining technique, which employs a set of pre-classified examples to develop a model that can classify the population of records at large. This approach frequently employs decision tree or neural network-based classification algorithms. The data classification process involves learning and classification. In Learning, the training data are analyzed by classification algorithm. In classification, test data are used to estimate the accuracy of the classification rules. If the accuracy is acceptable the rules can be applied to the new data tuples. The classifier-training algorithm uses these pre-classified examples to determine the set of parameters required for proper discrimination. The algorithm then encodes these parameters into a model called a classifier. Classification maps data into predefined groups are classes. It is often referred to as supervised learning because the classes are determined before examining the data. They often describe these classes by looking at the characteristic of data already known to belong to the classes [6]. Bayes classification has been proposed on Bayes rule of conditional probability. Bayes rule is a technique to estimate the likelihood of a property given the set of data as evidence or input Bayes rule or Bayes theorem is,

$$P\left(\frac{x_i}{h_i}\right) = \frac{P(h_i)\, P(\frac{h_i}{x_i})}{P\left(\frac{x_i}{h_i}\right) + P\left(\frac{x_i}{h_2}\right) P(h_2)} \tag{1}$$

The approach is called "naïve" because it assumes the independence between the various attribute values. Naïve Bayes classification can be viewed as both a descriptive and a predictive type of algorithm. The probabilities are descriptive and are then used to predict the class membership for a target tuple. The naïve Bayes approach has several advantages: it is easy to use; unlike other classification approaches only one scan of the training data is required [6]. An advantage of the naive Bayes classifier is that it requires a small amount of training data to estimate the parameters necessary for classification. Because independent variables are assumed, only the variances of the variables for each class need to be determined and not the entire covariance matrix. In spite of their naive design and apparently over-simplified assumptions, naive Bayes classifiers have worked quite well in many complex realworld situations.

4   Application of Bayes Classification Technique

Predicting academic performance of students' result needs information about his academic performance in the class. Data pertaining to his performance in the internal exams can be used to predict his performance in the final examination. The following data mining steps are encountered while predicting the outcome of the students.

4.1   Data Set

Naïve Bayes works very well with a smaller set of training data. Therefore a sample data set of 120 students of First semester MCA has been taken. It consists of Roll No, Name, Internal marks obtained by the students in 8 subjects and result obtained by the student.

4.2   Data Preprocessing and Transformation

The raw data obtained from the college consists of numerical values and string values in an excel sheet. The file is converted into arff format so that it is easily accessible using WEKA software. Bayesian classifier needs numerical values to the converted into nominal values. For the purpose of mining, the marks of the students have been converted into nominal values using the following criteria.

Table 1. Nominal values of the internal marks

Criteria	Outcome of the student
Score between (0_45)	Fails
Score between (46_54)	Pass / Fail
Score between (55_100)	Pass

4.3   Implementation of Naïve Bayes Classifier

WEKA data mining software is used for the implementation of the naïve bayes algorithm. The algorithm generated the following output:

1. No. of instances considered for prediction   : 117
2. No. of correctly predicted instances   : 96
3. No. of. Incorrectly predicted instances   : 21

The algorithm also generated confusion matrix for all the attributes considering the result attribute as a target value.

Table 2. Confusion Matrix of MCA11

No. of Instances predicted Pass	No. of Instances predicted Pass/Fail	No. of Instances predicted Fail
64	23	19
1	8	2
3	3	3

From the table it is clear that out of the 96 correctly predicted instances, 63 are predicted as pass correctly by the miner and the algorithm, 23 instances were correctly predicted as pass/fail and 19 was predicted as fail. A similar kind of confusion matrix is generated for all the subjects specified. Graph 1 explains the confusion matrix of the overall result obtained.

Graph 1. Confusion matrix obtained for Overall result

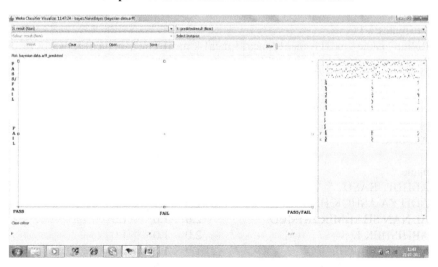

From the above graph, the confusion matrix generated by the system can be defined as:

Table 3. Confusion Matrix of Overall result

	No. of Instances predicted Pass	No. of Instances predicted pass/Fail	No. of Instances predicted Fail
No. of Instances predicted Pass	63	1	1
No. of Instances predicted Pass/Fail	5	21	5
No. of Instances predicted Fail	5	4	12

From the confusion matrix it is clear that 63 students are predicted pass out of 96 correct instances, 21 predicted pass/fail and 12 predicted as fail. Out of the 27 incorrect instances, 1 instance predicted as pass by the miner is predicted as pass/fail by the algorithm, 5 instances predicted as pass/fail by the miner is predicted pass by the algorithm and so on.

The system also generated the prediction of outcome of the result of the students on individual basis. Since the data set is small it has taken 0 secs to build the model.

The following detail shows the sample output from the system.

```
=== Run information ===
Scheme:      weka.classifiers.bayes.NaiveBayes
Relation:    bayesian data.arff
Instances:   117
Attributes:  11
Rollno , name , mca11, mca12,mca13,mca14, mca15,mca16, mca17, mca18,result
Test mode:   10-fold cross-validation

=== Classifier model (full training set) ===

Naive Bayes Classifier
```

	Class		
Attribute	P	F	P/F
	(0.55)	(0.27)	(0.18)
name			
ABHIJIT BASU	2.0	1.0	1.0
ADITYA ASHOK HEGDE	1.0	2.0	2.0
ADNAN SHAHMIR AHMED	2.0	1.0	1.0
ABHISHEK K S	2.0	1.0	1.0
AJAY TRIPATHI	1.0	1.0	2.0
ABHISHEK UNKAL	2.0	1.0	1.0
ANANDKUMAR MANTHATTI	1.0	2.0	1.0

5   Conclusions

Prediction of the student's outcome in the examination by applying the marks obtained by them in the internal marks is done using Naïve Bayes classification technique. From the results obtained from the algorithm, it is clear that students who fail in the internal examination tend to fail in the university exam also. The author in [10] has explained how decision tree can be used to predict the performance of the student using decision tree algorithm. The decision tree algorithm was able to predict the result of the student on a group basis and it was not able to show the confusion matrix for each subject individually. The tutors were analysing the subjects and the student result manually to identify the weak student. On the other hand, the Naïve bayes classification system gives the prediction for each subject on an individual basis. This technique has helped the tutor to identify the weak student's in each subject using their roll number easily and give them extra coaching so as to get better results. This will also help the educational institution to bring out quality results from the students. In future, various other attributes like attendance, the marks scored in the previous semester can also be incorporated to predict the student's outcome.

References

1. Mannila, H.: Data mining: machine learning. IEEE (1996)
2. El-Halees, A.: Mining Students Data to analyze e-learning Behavior: A Case Study (2009)
3. Quadri, M.N., Kalyankar, N.V.: Drop Out Feature of Student Data for Academic Performance Using Decision Tree. Global Journal of Computer Science and Technology 10(2) (April 2010)
4. Pandey, U.K., et al.: Data Mining: A prediction of performer or underperformer using classification (IJCSIT) International Journal of Computer Science and Information Technologies 2(2), 686–690 (2011)
5. Anupama Kumar, S., Vijayalakshmi, M.N.: Efficiency of Decision trees in predicting student academic performance. In: Proc. of CCSEA 2011, Computer Science and Information Technology, pp. 335–343 (2011)
6. Dunham, M.H.: Data Mining: Introductory and advance topic
7. Hijazi, S.T., Naqvi, R.S.M.M.: Factors affecting students performance: A Case of Private Colleges. Bangladesh e-Journal of Sociology 3(1) (2006)
8. Kumar, V.: An Empirical Study of the Applications of Data Mining Techniques in Higher Education. IJACSA - International Journal of Advanced Computer Science and Applications 2(3), 80–84, http://ijacsa.thesai.org
9. Ayesha, S., Mustafa, T., Sattar, A.R., Inayat Khan, M.: Data mining model for higher education system. European Journal of Scientific Research 43(1), 24–29 (2010)
10. Anupama Kumar, S., Vijayalakshmi, M.N.: Prediction of the students recital using classification Technique. IFRSA's International Journal of Computing (IIJC) 1(3), 305–309 (2011)
11. Deshpande, S.P., Thakare, V.M.: Data mining system and applications: a review. International Journal of Distributed and Parallel systems (IJDPS) 1(1), 32–44 (2010)
12. Goguadze, G., Sosnovsky, S., Isotani, S., McLaren, B.M.: Evaluating a bayesian student model of decimal misconceptions. In: The Proceedings of the 4th International Conference on Educational Data Mining (2011)
13. Flach, P.A., et al.: Naïve Bayesian Classification of structured data, pp. 1–37. Kluwer Academic Publishers, Boston

A Survey on Particle Swarm Optimization in Feature Selection

Vipul Kothari, J. Anuradha, Shreyak Shah, and Prerit Mittal

School of Computing Science and Engineering, VIT Vellore
januradha@vit.ac.in, vipul_here2003@yahoo.com,
shreyakshah19@gmail.com, preritmittal@ymail.com

Abstract. Particle swarm optimization is an evolutionary algorithm that depicts the movement of flock of birds in space in mathematical terms. In PSO we view each potential problem as a particle with certain velocity flying through a problem space just like a flock of bird. In the world of infinite data, the ability to handle imprecise and inconsistent information and to select important features from the data has become the important requirement of feature selection. PSO has come a long way since its beginning and has become an important tool for feature selection in numerous physical problems. In this paper we present a literary review of papers on PSO and chart its journey through inception and with implementing it in various physical problems. We will present a comparative table of implementation for PSO and review the success of PSO in various fields of science. This paper provides an incentive for the readers to join the PSO world.

Keywords: Particle swarm optimization (PSO), Feature Selection (FS), Support Vector Machine (SVM).

1   Introduction

1.1   Feature Selection (FS)

Computation of the result by using the entire features may not always give the best result because of unnecessary and irrelevant features, also referred as noisy feature. To remove these unnecessary features, we use **Feature selection** algorithm which selects a subset of important features from the parent set by removing the irrelevant features for simple and accurate data. By reducing the unwanted and irrelevant features we considerably reduce the size of the set. This is advantageous as it improves the computation speed and reduces the memory requirement and hence increasing the efficiency and accuracy of the selection.

1.1.1   Approaches in FS
There are two types of approaches of feature selection for unsupervised learning namely **filter approach and wrapper approach** [17]. Filter method does not use any clustering algorithm but only some intrinsic property of data to select the features.

P.V. Krishna, M.R. Babu, and E. Ariwa (Eds.): ObCom 2011, Part II, CCIS 270, pp. 192–201, 2012.
© Springer-Verlag Berlin Heidelberg 2012

Wrapper approach on the other hand uses a clustering algorithm on each feature subset and then evaluates the subsets based on specific function. For example in a set of random numbers the filter method will use any property of data like even/odd, prime/composite to select the data while the wrapper approach will apply a specific algorithm on each data entry to select the data entry.

1.1.2 Selection Process in FS

There are mainly three types of selection process in FS namely **forward selection, backward elimination and randomized selection** [17]. In forward selection Wrapper examines the effect of adding the feature not been selected and chooses the one with best accuracy from the feature set by adding them in an empty set. In backward elimination the feature which degrades the accuracy of classifier are deleted in backward elimination process from the feature set. And finally the randomized selections in which random set of features are selected and are evaluated by a fitness function. The best subset amongst them according to the evaluated result gets selected.

1.2   Filtering Methods in FS

There are mainly two types of filtering methods as follows:

i) Chi-Square Statistic (CHI):
This a statistical test in which the test statistic has a chi-squared distribution and it helps in measuring the convergence of the test and difference between calculated and observed frequency.

The CHI- square statistic   is defined as follows [3]:

$$\chi 2 \; = \; \sum_{i=1}^{R} \sum_{j=1}^{K} (O_{ij} - E_{ij})^2 / E_{ij} \qquad (1)$$

Where O_{ij} = observed frequency.

E_{ij} = expected (theoretical frequency).
R × K = number of possible outcomes of each events.

It can be used for two types of comparison: tests of goodness of fit and test of independence. The first test establishes whether or not an observed frequency distribution differ from theoretical distribution and the second test whether the paired observation on two variable are independent of each other.

ii) Document Frequency (DF):
Document Frequency measures the no. of time the word appeared in that document. Selecting frequent words may improve the chances that the features will be present in future test cases. Given a pair of terms, one way to use document frequency is to measure their frequency of occurrence in a collection and compare it with document frequency. The notion of document frequency varies with the specific uses.

2   Particle Swarm Optimization (PSO)

It is an evolutionary algorithm which was developed by Kennedy and Eberhart in 1995. The primitive model of PSO was to study and graphically simulate the choreography of flock of birds. These simulations were modified to standard PSO by introducing inertia weight by Shi and Eberhart in 1998. [16].

PSO gives better results compared to the other evolutionary algorithms such as genetic algorithm, rough set etc. [16]. The standard PSO algorithm is modified over the last decade and has experienced a long journey till date from just simulating the graphically the flock of birds to feature selection on various fields such as text selection, image processing, biomedical etc. The surprising better result from the PSO has revolutionized the feature selection process. In this paper we survey the evolution and implementation of PSO.

2.1   Standard PSO [16]

Particle swarm optimization uses a population where each particle represents a candidate solution. The system is initialized with a population of random solutions and searches for optima, according to some fitness function, by updating particles over generations; that is, particles "fly" through the N-dimensional problem search space by following the current better-performing particles. At each step of the optimization, each particle is allowed to evaluate its own fitness and the fitness of its neighbouring particles. Each particle can keep track of its own solution, which resulted in the best fitness, as well as see the candidate solution for the best performing particle in its neighbourhood.

ALGORITHM FOR STANDARD PSO [16]:

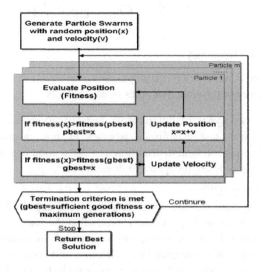

Fig. 1. Flowchart of Standard PSO

2.2   PSO Modifications

The world of PSO is not confined to the standard algorithm mention above. The PSO is modified according to the need of problem and thus makes it flexible to use in different application of different discipline. Today we deal with the issues of feature selection on daily basis. With so much data to handle and optimization needed to be done, we need to have efficient algorithms so that the necessary and wanted data can be separated. We first discuss how the PSO has been modified with the help of rough sets, support vector machines and intelligent dynamic swarm to make the selection process more efficient. Than in the latter parts of the paper we will discuss some real time examples of PSO based and modified algorithm on feature selection.

3   Surveys on Variations of PSO

The curse of dimensionality [6] states that as the dimension increases the estimate of probability distribution is less accurate if the number of labelled sample remains finite thus providing poor performance. PSO often represents global optimal search thus two extensions to PSO have been done namely guaranteed convergence particle swarm optimization (GCPSO) and Multi-Start PSO (MPSO). These are the two variations. The GCPSO is optimal for local search algorithm and MPSO is optimal for global search. Applying GCPSO on remote sensed images gives a better result of local convergence than the genetic algorithm. So the division of PSO into GCPSO yields better results for local optimisation problems.

The binary PSO uses only one and zero values as its velocity. The binary PSO in gene extraction results in greater feature selection and better optimization results. The fitness functions and the algorithm does not change much than the simple PSO, only velocity values are changed, but in the field of molecular biology this yields a far better results for areas such as gene abstraction, gene feature selections. Average classification accuracy for the proposed method will increase by 2.85% as compare to the previous study.

Intelligence dynamics Swarm is a modified version of PSO. IDS is an excellent algorithm to solve problems for feature selection. But the main issue with IDS is that it can only be used to solve discrete variables and continuous particles need to be converted to discrete variables before giving them as input. To remove this glitch we combine IDS with rough set for input values for the fitness function used in IDS

Experimental results performed on different data sets show that due to less computing used in IDS it is 30% faster than PSO. The IDS can successfully find optimal result in limited generation time.

Discrete particle swarm optimization takes only discrete values as its input. The discrete PSO differs from the original PSO in two aspects. First the feature subsets are coded in binary strings and the discrete PSO dynamically accounts for the relevance and dependence of the features to be added to the feature subset [15]. Feature subset selection problems where feature reduction is quite large, standard application of discrete PSO exhibits excessive diversification. As the study conducted in the paper

[14] shows that it is competitive in both the classification activity and computational performance. It yields 4% to 5% higher accuracy rates.

Two step swarm intelligence is yet another addition to family of PSO. In this approach the heuristic search performed by the agents is divided into two steps. First step the intermediate results are obtained which are then given as input to the next step. Some may argue that this can increase computational time and cost but studies on the other hand show that it actually obtains shorter reducts in minimum time [6].

4   Hybridization of PSO with SVM and Rough Set

Support vector machines (SVM) are learning machines that can perform binary classification and regression estimation tasks. They are becoming increasingly popular paradigm of classification and learning. They are designed to automatically trade off accuracy and complexity by minimising the generalization error, this concept was introduced 1998. The combination of PSO with support vector machines (SVM) effectively implements the feature selection process with better processing rate and accuracy. A SVM is used to evaluate the fitness values of the PSO's. The accuracy of the proposed method when applied on classification problems increases by four per cent; hence the PSO can be clubbed with SVMs to yield a better result for future selection problem.

The hybridization of PSO-SVM with continuous valued PSO when implemented in data mining system via web architecture also yields exceptional results too reduce computational time. The study conducted in [14] show that this hybrid method gives a test accuracy of more than 85 per cent.

Rough set theory is a tool for studying imprecision, vagueness and uncertainty in data analysis. It focuses on delivery pattern, rules and knowledge in data. We now consider PSO along with rough set as a study conducted in [16] explains. A large feature set can be divided into subsets using the rough set principle. Now applying PSO in this collection of subsets over many iterations result in a convergence. Each set eventually converge on good, possibly optimal solution.

5   Practical Implementations of PSO

Since its birth in 1995, PSO and its hybrids has been gradually implemented in various industries in solving their real time problems. We here by discuss few important real time problems were PSO has yielded a better result than their standard solutions

Face recognition is a global optimization problem and it needs to remove irrelevant noisy and redundant data from its data feature set. PSO when applied to images obtained by as shown in [12] discrete cosine transform and discrete wavelet transform achieves the best average recognition rate of 94.8% on DCT and 95.2% on DWT which is far better than the standard algorithms also the average recognition time is 0.05 second.

Product structure is used in mechanical industries for meeting their economic and production targets. The coal product structure, one of the subset of the industry, has multi factor influences. So we need a global convergence and need to avoid local optimization. As studies conducted in [7] shows that use of PSO gives fast convergence speed and better convergence result. The wide searching ability of optimizing product structure is far more complicated and the use of PSO can give a better convergence effect in less iterations.

Assembly line balancing problems (ALBP) are well-known NP hard problems. The need to maximize the production rate of the line and to distribute the work load as evenly as possible on the assembly line is one of the biggest challenges faced by many industries. The result obtained by using the PSO approach on standard ALBPs in [10] show that the results have a greater deviation to obtain the best ALBP solution. It consistently out performs the standard industry methods like MOGA. Although the application of PSO on ALBP is not straight forward, the difficulty can be overcome in the future.

Optimizing transportation network is very important for managing budget and total time travel. In the paper [1] PSO has been implemented on network of Sinoux fall. The inputs to the PSO are obtained from the arcs of the network and the parameters are given in hours and hours per thousand vehicles. While comparing PSO with ant colony optimization, study in [1] shows that the PSO has a better chance of performing and has been calibrated to suit the problem. The accuracy of PSO which stands at 0.96 is far better than that of ACO which stands at 0.82 and is comparable to hybrid ACO.

Control chart patterns are important statistical tools for determining whether a process is run in its intended mode or in the presence of unnatural patterns. A support vector machine based classifier is given as an input to the PSO to improve the generalisation performance of the recogniser. The experiment conducted by [13] shows that the PSO-SVM recognition system gives the accuracy between 99.5% to 98.3%. This proposed method helps the control chart patterns in improving the feature selection and parameter optimization.

The usage of PSO in the field of medical disease diagnosis is revolutionary. The time variant multi objective PSO [TVMO PSO] of radial basis function network (RBFN) is used for diagnosing medical diseases. The RBFN-TVMO PSO algorithm does a few basic changes on the objective function and introduces an assignment operator. The accuracy of this proposed algorithm in diagnosing diseases varies from 82% to 96% with respect to different data set. Never the less a good convergence is obtained. Power system security assessment deals with system's ability to continue to provide service in the event of an unforeseen contingency. The PSO algorithm used to minimise the error rate in classification. Although the CPU time used by the PSO is very high but high classification accuracy and minimal error rate is achieved. The performance evaluation of PSO on different data set varies from 94% to 98%.

6   Inferences

We surveyed the papers on variations and practical implementations of the PSO and their modified algorithms. PSO has been modified in various forms for the particular test cases and situations and it has generated great results as you can infer from the first table. Also when it's practically implemented in the industry for optimization it has shown that it can outperform the industry bench mark algorithms by significant margins as shown in the second paper.

Table 1. Variant of PSO Algorithms

Variations in PSO	Modification from the standard PSO	Field/Area	Accuracy and efficiency
Swarm intelligence	PSO divided in GCPSO and PNSO	Remotely sensed images	can divide local and global search
PSO SVM	Using SVM to find fitness values which is given input to PSO	--	Classification accuracy increases by 2% to 4% compare to other methods.
Binary PSO	Velocity value taken as 0 and 1	Gene extraction in molecular biology	Efficiency increased by 2.85% compared to best results of previously published data.
Discrete PSO	Feature subset coded in binary string	Tabu and scatter search	Results show excessive diversification
IDS	combined with rough set gives new fitness function	--	30% faster than PSO
Two step PSO	First step give intermediate output which is input for next step	--	Obtain shorter reducts than PSO so certainity of finding minimal reducts increases.

Table 2. Accuracy analysis of PSO in various Domains

Area in which PSO used	Modification in standard PSO	Accuracy and efficiency	Important note
Face recognition	PSO with discrete cosine transform and discrete wavelet transform	Recognition rate 96.2% higher than any other FR method Average recognition time 0.05 sec	Performs better than standard industry algorithm
Model of coal product structure	Input to PSO is a data set of coal product structure	Convergence effect come after 100 iteration	Solves the local convergence effect
Maximizing the production rate and work load smoothing	Input given are discrete	Consistently outperform the industry benchmark by 0.5 points	Hard to implement due to discrete nature
Optimizing transport networks	Input to the PSO are the arc of the network	Increases by 0.96 points	Hybrid ACO perform better than PSO
Control chart patterns	PSO-SVM is used	Recognition accuracy of 95.58%	Improves in chart patterns
Medical disease diagnosis	the time variant multi objective PSO [TVMO PSO]	Minimum training, validation and testing error	A good convergence is obtained
Static security assessment	Pattern recognition is used	Classification error rate minimum with 0% to 20% for 850 test samples	Cpu time used by the PSO is very high

7   Conclusion and Future Work

In this study, we surveyed the papers related to the modifications of standard PSO and its practical implementation in the real world problems. PSO has been here quite a while and rapid strides have been taken to make if more efficient and reliable in the feature selection. The two step PSO and the PSO SVM are the examples of how the PSO has been rapidly modified. The integration of the industry standard algorithm with the PSO and the practical implementation of PSO have also generated astonishing results. In the future, the authors would like to study more evolutionary algorithms and discuss how they are changing to suit the needs of the today's world.

References

1. Babazadeh, A., Poorzahedy, H., Nikoosokhan, S.: On Application of particle swarm optimization to transportation network design problem. Journal of King Saud University – Science 23, 293–300 (2011)
2. Bae, C., Yeh, W.-C., Chung, Y.Y., Liu, S.L.: Feature selection with intelligent dynamic swarm and rough set. Expert System with Application (2010)
3. Chitsaz, E., Taheri, M., Katebi, S.D., Jahromi, M.Z.: An Improved Fuzzy Feature Clustering and Selection based on Chi-Squared-Test. In: Proceedings of the International MultiConference of Engineers and Computer Scientists, IMECS 2009, Hong Kong, vol. I (2009)
4. Chung, L.– Y., Chang, H.– W., Tu, C.J., Yang, C.– H.: Improved binary PSO for feature selection using gene expression data. Computational Biology and Chemistry (2007)
5. Firpi, H.A., Goodman, E.: Swarmed Feature Selection. In: Proceedings of the 33rd Applied Imagery Pattern Recognition Workshop (AIPR 2004), pp. 1550–5219. IEEE (2004)
6. Gómez, Y., Bello, R., Puris, A., García, M.M.: Two Step Swarm Intelligence to Solve the Feature Selection Problem. Journal of Universal Computer Science 14(15), 2582–2596 (2008); submitted: 18/2/08, accepted: 30/6/08, appeared: 1/8/08
7. Zhang-Guoa, W., Ya-Lia, K., Zhea, L., Chang-Shengb, S.: Model of coal product structure based on particle swarm optimization algorithm. In: The 6th International Conference on Mining Science & Technology (2009)
8. Hang, C.-L., Dun, J.-F.: A distributed PSO-SVM hybrid system with feature selection and parameter optimization. Applied soft computing(2007)
9. Kalyani, S., Swarup, K.S.: Classifier design for static security assessment using particle swarm optimization (2009)
10. Nearchou, A.C.: On Maximizing production rate and workload smoothing in assembly lines using particle swarm optimization. Int. J. Production Economics 129, 242–250 (2011)
11. Qasem, S.N., Shamsuddin, S.M.: Radial basis function network based on time variant multi-objective particle swarm optimization for medical diseases diagnosis (2010)
12. Ramadan, R.M., Kader, R.F.A.: Face Recognition Using Particle Swarm Optimization-Based Selected Features. International Journal of Signal Processing, Image Processing and Pattern Recognition 2(2) (June 2009)
13. Ranaee, V., Ebrahimzadeh, A., Ghaderi, R.: Application of the PSO-SVM model for recognization of control chart patterns (2010)

14. Tu, C.-J., Chuang, L.-Y., Chang, J.-Y., Yang, C.-H., Iaeng.: Feature Selection using PSO-SVM. IAENG International Journal of Computer Science, IJCS 33(1), _33_1_18
15. Unler, A., Murad, A.: Discrete particle swarm optimization method for feature selection in binary classification problems. European Journal of Operational Research (February 2010)
16. Wang, X., Yang, J., Teng, X., Xia, W., Jensen, R.: Feature Selection based on Rough Sets and Particle Swarm Optimization
17. Zahran, B.M., Kanaan, G.: Text Feature Selection using Particle Swarm Optimization Algorithm. World Applied Sciences Journal 7 (special Issue of Computer & IT), 69–74 (2009)

Interaction Diagram Based Test Case Generation

Rohit Kumar[1] and Rajesh K. Bhatia[2]

[1] University Institute of Engineering and Technology, Chandigarh
rklachotra@gmail.com
[2] Deenbandhu Chhotu Ram University of Science & Technology
rbhatiapatiala@gmail.com

Abstract. Testing is defined as a process of validating and verifying the software system and artifacts so that they meet their business and technical requirements. It is a very important and time consuming part of software development life cycle. Most of the software fails because of not being tested properly and accurately. The reason behind failure mainly includes the error present in analysis and design phase which are more important than code.

In present work, design diagrams of the software are used for test cases generation. The test case generation using design helps to plan test case early. Generating test cases from design are more effective and efficient as design is closer to White Box testing. Sometimes during test cases generation, we come to know about any incompleteness and inconsistence in requirement, which can overcome by taking necessary measures taken in time.

In present work, design is used for test case generation. Using design is used for test case generation helps to plan test case early. If the software can be tested in the design phases then most of the errors in design and analysis phase can be eliminated and can be stopped from propagating to next phase. Thus there is a need to explore testing possibilities in earlier phases of software development.

Keywords: UML, Software, Testing, Test Cases, Petal file, SQL *Loader, Class, State diagram and Activity diagram.

1 Introduction

Software testing is a procedure, or a series of processes, intended to make sure that software system and its artifacts does what it was planned to do and that it does not do anything unintentional or undesirable. It is a dedicated discipline of evaluating the worth of the software system. [1], and one should test the system to find as many flaws as possible. [2]

Testing activities which are based on models are fetching popularity. UML models represent specification documents which present the perfect basis and ground for developing tests and developing testing situations [8]. A test requires various specification, or a explanation or documentation of what the tested unit should be and how it must act [3]. Even code based white box testing techniques that initially focus

P.V. Krishna, M.R. Babu, and E. Ariwa (Eds.): ObCom 2011, Part II, CCIS 270, pp. 202–211, 2012.

on the structure of the code, are based on specification [4]. The code is used only as a basis to describe input factor settings that guide to the coverage of different code artifacts. Models are very important if UML tools that support automatic test case generation are used. In general, one can discriminate between two ways of how to use the UML in tandem with testing activities [5]

2   Methodology

Following are the major steps in proposed techniques: -

1. **Input Petal File into the system:** The Petal file of Class diagram is given as input to the developed tool. Petal files [27] nothing but files which one gets by opening a Rational Rose file [7] in word pad or text file.

2. **Read mdl file:** The mdl file is read by the tool and with the concept of tokenized patterns like Class name, Class attributes, Class cardinality, Class operations, inheritance, dependency etc are found.

3. **Is pattern found:** If pattern is found then it is entered to the queue else next pattern is found.

4. **Store the patterns in a queue:** All pattern found is stored in a queue. There are different queues for every pattern like Class name queue; Class attributes queue, Class cardinality queue, Class operations queue, inheritance queue, dependency queue etc.

5. **Search for another pattern:** Tool searches for various pattern in petal for Class name if it is found then Class name is entered into Class name queue Else if it found Class attributes it enters it to the Class attributes queue similarly so on.

6. **Is EOF (End of File) is reached:** Tool keeps on searching the patterns until EOF is reached.

7. **Create text file from queue and store text file in database:** When end of file is reached, the tool generates the text file which contains all information about Class diagram in form of tuples which can be entered to the database easily using SQL *loader. SQL *loader loads all the data from the text file to the Oracle database.

8. **Are all Petal files input:** After Class diagram, Petal files of Activity diagram and State diagram are entered to the tool and loop back to second step in flow chart.

9. **Retrieving strings to generate test cases:** There are tables present in the Oracle database which contains the information from Class diagram, sequence diagram, State diagram. From Net beans IDE tool fires queries to generate test cases.

3   Proposed System and Implementation

Firstly Class diagram, sequence diagram and State diagram are drawn for a particular system using Rational Rose and corresponding mdl file of Class diagram, State diagram, Activity diagram [9] are saved. These diagram's petal files (mdl file) [7] are parsed by the tool. Firstly Class diagram petal file is parsed by the tool. The tool reads the petal file line by line. It tokenized the line into words and then matched the string with the pattern to find the Class name. When Class name is found it entered it to the queue and searched for another pattern, its attributes, its operations, its inheritance Classes, its dependency, its cardinality and all these are written on a text file. Similarly petal file of Activity diagram and State diagram are entered in the tool. Then the text files created are entered to the Oracle database using SQL *Loader [6]. Before loading text files to SQL *Loader it was necessary to create control file and a Dat file .The control file is a text file written in a language that SQL*Loader understands. The control file tells SQL*Loader where to find the data, how to parse and interpret the data, where to insert the data. Dat file was the file which contains the data i.e. the text file from the tool is saved with extension .dat and it served the purpose of dat file in SQL *Loader to load the data. Then is required to create a table in database and all the text files in the form of Dat file were loaded to Oracle database. Now Java and Oracle are connected and queries are fired from Java to extract the strings from database and use them to generate test cases.

Data from text file is entered to the tool with the help of SQL *Loader [6]. In order to enter the data from text file to Oracle database Dat and control files are created. Dat file is nothing but text file generated from tool with the extension of dat and control file is a text file written in a language that SQL*Loader understands. The control file tells SQL*Loader where to find the data, how to parse and interpret the data, and where to insert the data. The syntax of control file is given below:

The class test case information is entered into database. The below figure shows the data present in a class, which may extracted at later stage to generate the test case with the help of interface(Netbeans).

Table 1. The test case data from Class diagram in the database

CLASSNAME	OPERATION	ATTRIBUTE	DEPENDENCY	INHERITANCE
Admin	allow	ID	Room	null
Admin	deny	Passwrd	null	null
Admin	Validating_customer	null	null	null
Admin	Room_checking	null	null	null
Admin	Report_generation	null	null	null
Customer	Billing	Name	null	null
Customer	Signin	Contact	null	null
Customer	RoomCancel	Age	null	null
Customer	RoomSelectiobn	Gender	null	null
Customer	null	Address	null	null
More than 10 rows available. Increase rows selector to view more rows.				

The state diagram test case information is entered into database. The below figure shows the data present in a state diagram, which may extracted at later stage to generate the test case with the help of interface(Netbeans)

Table 2. The test case data from State diagram in the database

TRANSITION	INITIALSTATE	FINALSTATE
[bill_generation]	"RoomSelected"	"Credit_Card_Swapped"
[room_vacant>0]	"RoomSearched"	"RoomSelected"
[bal>=rent +1000]	"Credit_Card_Swapped"	"RoomConfirmed"
[bal<=1000+rent]	"Credit_Card_Swapped"	"quit"
[!valid_pin]	"Credit_Card_Swapped"	"Credit_Card_Swapped"
[report_ready]	"RoomConfirmed"	"ReportEmailedTocustomer"

Similarly Activity diagram test case information is entered into database. The below figure shows the data present in a state diagram, which may extracted at later stage to generate the test case with the help of interface(Netbeans)

Table 3. The test case data from activity diagram in the database

GUARDCONDITION	PRECONDITION	POSTCONDITION
[room_vacant==0]	pre_user_search_room	post_user_quit
[room_vacant>0]	pre_user_search_room	post_room_available
[bal<1000+rent]	pre_payments_details_provided	post_card_rejected
[!valid_pin]	pre_pin_required	post_swap_card_again
[bal>rent+1000]	pre_payment_details_ready	post_credit_card_accepted
[!ready_report]	pre_report_in_progress	post_user_wait
[report_ready]	pre_report_generated	post_report_sent_to_user

4   Case Study

4.1   Online Hotel Reservation System

This case study deals with automation of reservation of rooms of hotel and allows a person or an organization to book hotels online A person can search a hotel to find out accommodations with different rates, different place, and number of rooms available. In the system the testing is performed on three diagrams namely Class diagram Activity diagram and State diagram.

   With the help of Class diagram the following information is extracted which will serve the purpose of generating static test cases:-
a. Classes   b. Relationship between Classes   c. Dependency
d. Parent/child relationship   d. Associations

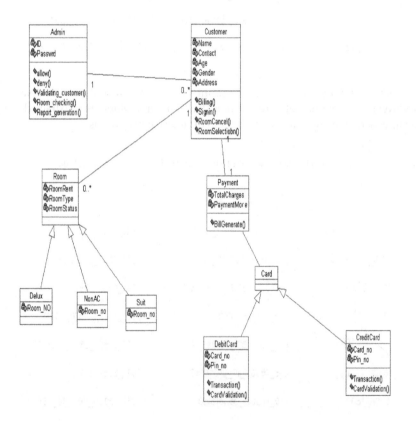

Fig. 1. Class Diagram of Hotel Reservation System

Table 4. Test Cases from Class diagram

CLASSNAME	OPREATION	ATTRIBUTE	DEPENDENCY	INHERITANCE
Admin	Deny	Passwrd	Null	Null
Admin	Validating_customer	Null	Null	Null
Admin	Room_checking	Null	Null	Null
Admin	Report_generation	Null	Null	Null
Customer	Billing	Name	Null	Null
Customer	Signin	Contact	Null	Null
Customer	RoomCancel	Age	Null	Null
Customer	RoomSelection	Gender	Null	Null
Customer	Null	Address	Null	Null

With the help of State diagram following information will be extracted:-
a. Initial state diagrams   b. Transitions   c. Final state diagrams

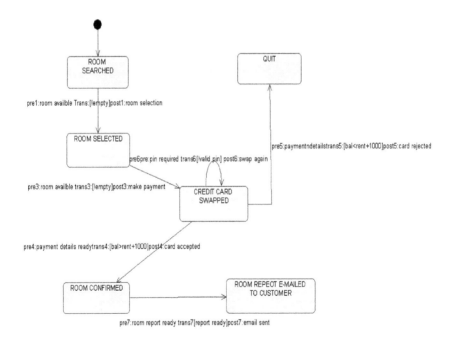

Fig. 2. State diagram of Hotel Reservation System

Table 5. Test Cases from State diagram

Transition	InitiaState diagram	FinalState diagram
[bill_generation]	"RoomSelected"	"Credit_Card_Swapped"
Room_vacant>0	"RoomSearched"	"RoomSelected"
[bal>=rent +1000]	"Credit_Card_Swapped"	"RoomConfirmed"
[bal<=1000+rent]	"Credit_Card_Swapped"	"quit"
[!valid_pin]	"Credit_Card_Swapped"	"Credit_Card_Swapped"
[report_ready]	"RoomConfirmed"	Report_Emailed

The information extracted from the Activity diagram includes, pre condition and post condition and guard condition between activities.

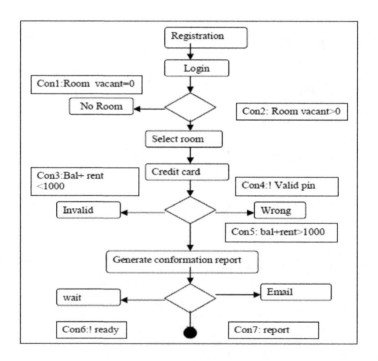

Fig. 3. Activity Diagram of Hotel Reservation System

Table 6. Test Cases from Activity diagram

Guard	PreCondition	PostCondition
[room vacant= =0]	pre_user_search_room	post_user_quit
[room_vacant> 0]	pre_user_search_room	post_room_available
[bal<1000+rent]	Pre_payments_details_prov ided	post_card_rejected
[!valid_pin]	pre_pin_required	Post_swap_card_again
[bal>rent+1000]	pre_payment_details_ready	Post_credit_card_acce pted
[!ready_report]	pre_report_in_progress	post_user_wait
[report_ready]	pre_report_generated	post report sent to u ser

4.2   Combine Test Cases from Activity and State Diagram of Hotel Reservation System

Both the information from Activity diagram and state diagram are clubbed together to form dynamic test cases. These test cases are the powerful form of test cases that are generated separately from individual state diagram and Activity diagram and are more accurate. These combined test cases cover broader aspect of dynamic testing

Table 7. Combined Test Cases from Activity and State diagram

Transition	InitiaState diagram	FinalState diagram	PreCondition	PostCondition
[bill_generation	RoomSelected	Credit Card Swapped	_____	_____
room_vacant>0	RoomSearched	RoomSelected	pre_user_search_ Room	post_room_available
[bal>=rent +1000]	Credit_Card_Swapped	RoomConfirmed	pre payment details _ready	post credit card Accepted
[bal<=1000 +rent]	Credit_Card_Swapped	Quit	pre payments details _provided	post_card_rejected
[!valid_pin]	Credit_Card_Swapped"	Credit_Card _Swapped	pre_pin_required	post_swap_card_agai n
[report_ready]	RoomConfirmed	ReportEmailed Tocustomer	pre_report_generated	post report sent to u ser

4.3   Snapshot of Tool

The following figure shows the snapshot of the tool that is developed for automatic static test case generation from Class diagram and dynamic test case generation from the combination of Activity and state diagram of Online Hotel Reservation System. The system has been developed with help of Java and Net beans.

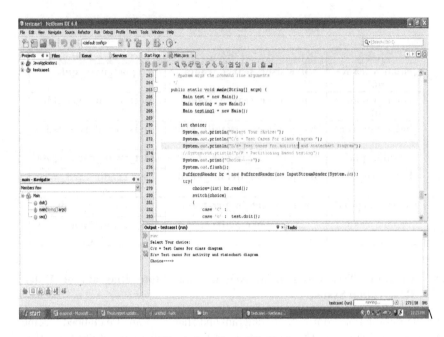

Fig. 4. Snapshot of the Tool

The following figure shows options provided to us after running the tool developed with Netbeans. Option C/c generates test cases of Class diagram which are static test cases and option S/s generates the dynamic test cases from Activity and State diagram diagram of system.

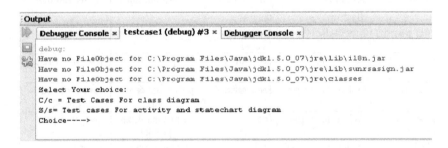

Fig. 5. Various output option in the tool

5   Conclusions

- A new algorithm has been proposed to extract information from petal file of Class, State diagram and Activity diagram.
- Proposed techniques generate test case information from combination of various UML diagrams.

- Generated test cases are more effective due to combination of three diagrams covers both static as well as dynamic aspect of software system.

6 Future Work

- Further work can be explored to use formal methods with UML diagrams.
- This technique further can be extended to include all types of software artifacts to predict changes for regression testing.
- Concept of overloading, polymorphism etc can be further used to generate automatic test cases.

References

[1] Herzl, C.W.: The Complete Guide to Software Testing, 2nd edn., p. 280. QED Information Science, Wesley (1988); ISBN: 0894352423.Physical description: IX
[2] Myers, J.G.: The Art of Software Testing, p. 177. Wiley, NewYork (1979); ISBN:0471043281 Physical description: xi
[3] Gross, H.-G.: Component-Based Software Testing with UML. Springer, Heidelberg (2005)
[4] Beizer, B.: Black-Box Testing Techniques for Functional Testing of Software and Systems. Wiley, New York (1995)
[5] Binder, R.: Testing Object-Oriented Systems: Models, Patterns and Tools. Addison-Wesley (2000)
[6] Gennick, J., Mishra, S.: Oracle SQL*Loader: The Definitive Guide, pp. 1–14. O'Reilly & Associates Inc. (2001)
[7] Dahm, M.: Grammar and API for Rational Rose Petal files (July 19, 2001)
[8] Component-Based Software Testing with UML Hans-Gerhard Gross, pp. 80–112. Springer, Heidelberg (2005)
[9] Wang, L., Yuan, J., Yu, X., Hu, J., Li, X., Zheng, G.: Generating test cases from UML activity diagram-based on Gray-Box method. In: Proc. 11th Asia-Pacific Software Engineering Conf (APSEC 2004), Busan, Korea, November 30–December 4, pp. 284–291. IEEE Computer Society, NJ (2004)

Wavelet Pave the Trio Travel for a Secret Mission – A Stego Vision

V. Thanikaiselvan[1], P. Arulmozhivarman[1], Rengarajan Amirtharajan[2], and John Bosco Balaguru Rayappan[2]

[1] School of Electronics Engineering
VIT University, Vellore-632014, Tamilnadu, India
[2] Department of Electronics & Communication Engineering
School of Electrical & Electronics Engineering
SASTRA University
Thanjavur, Tamil Nadu, India

Abstract. Image steganography is a rapidly developing field with immense applications to offer high data security. There are two types' or rather two domains in which image steganography has been achieved, spatial and frequency domain. Spatial domain steganography focuses on embedding of the payload on the LSB bits of the pixels on the image, while frequency domain steganography focuses on the transformation of the image pixels using various transform algorithms and then embedding data in the transformed pixels. The most commonly used transform mechanism is the IWT (Integer Wavelet Transform) because of the obvious reason that it yields integer coefficients which are very easy to work with. This paper elucidates the use of Haar Integer Wavelet Transform for Constant and Adaptive number of bit embedding method. Both types are analyzed and finally the method with the highest embedding capacity with high PSNR is adjudged best.

Keywords: IWT (Integer Wavelet Transform), LSB Embedding, Random Path.

1 Introduction

The advent of internet era has been a boon and a bane to the field of information security [1]. On one hand it has made the access and transfer of information so fast that people at two distant corners of the globe can exchange data in a fraction of a second. But one of the major drawbacks of the present internet age is its lack of privacy [1]. This is where the ingenious concept information hiding [1] comes in, it allows user to encrypt [2] data so that only the transmitter and the receiver know the content that or being sent or received. In the beginning cryptography [2] was used profusely used as an information hiding mechanism [2, 3]. But soon, its drawbacks became evident as, its seemingly impregnable algorithms started crumbling when they were beleaguered with an unending wave of attacks. This was because of the fact that cryptic messages consisted of an array of indiscernible symbols or recognizable symbols in a random order, which invited the attention of hackers [3]. Thus the need arose for a new method by which we can not only embed huge quantities of data but also remove any indication that data has been hidden.

P.V. Krishna, M.R. Babu, and E. Ariwa (Eds.): ObCom 2011, Part II, CCIS 270, pp. 212–221, 2012.

Steganography and watermarking [3-22] came as an answer to this question; they were able to hide information discreetly, so that an innocent onlooker may not suspect any tampering of the cover. Watermarking took advantage of the limitations of human vision to embed data into an image. Watermarking has many advantages like high security, robustness and importantly statistical undetectability. But steganography emerged as the clear winner in the information security race because, in addition to all the advantages of water marking, it allowed the usage of a variety of media (audio, video and images) for embedding information [4]. Of all the three types, Image steganography has been the most intriguing and versatile [5-22]. Image steganography is further bifurcated into two types, spatial [4-8, 18-22] and frequency domain [9-14] steganographic methods. Spatial domain deals with the embedding of information directly into the LSBs of the pixels in the cover image, while frequency domain uses various transformation mechanisms to transform the image into frequency domain in which embedding is done by a particular algorithm and then it converted back into the original spatial domain and transmitted.

Another simple classification is based on the modification on the cover images like substitution [4-8, 18-22], Transform [9-14], Distortion, Statistical, Spread spectrum [15-17] and cover generation based. The former two are extensively studied by more number of researchers because of ease of implementation [4-8, 18-22]. The former could be further classified as Least Signification Substitution (LSB) [5-7], Pixel Value differencing [18-20] and Pixel Indicator [20-21]. Another classification is simple raster scan based [4-7, 9, 11, 18-21] and random scan based embedding [8, 10, 22]. The later transform domain based further classified into DCT [10] based and DWT based [9, 11-14] methods.

In transform domain techniques [9-14], the spatial domain cover image pixel intensity values are transformed into transform domain coefficients and the secret data are inserted into the coefficients. The advantage in transform domain techniques is robustness i.e., withstanding abilities for intentional modification. Spatial domain image steganography is really good in payload [4-8] i.e., number of secret data to be embedded. Both these techniques expect good imperceptibility.

Along with imperceptibility, capacity and robustness image steganography always expects a helping hand from cryptography [2]. To offer good cryptic effect in image steganography random scan is a good choice [8, 10, and 22]. Another choice to introduce randomness is to adapt variable embedding [18-20] based on the surrounding pixels. Yet another way to introduce randomness while embedding the secret data is to go for pixel indicator based methods.

Considering all the aforementioned facts, this paper contains an in-depth analysis of various bit level embedding on IWT (Integer Wavelet Transform) Coefficients. Secret data is embedded into an image with random way of embedding in each method and the maximum embedding capacity for each method is found analyzed and tabulated.

2   Review on Literature

2.1   Haar Integer Wavelet Transforms

The Haar wavelet transform is the simplest of all the wavelet transforms present. It is mainly used to boost robustness and increase the capacity of embedding.

In this transform mechanism, the low frequency coefficients (L) are generated by averaging two pixel value and the high frequency coefficients (H) are generated by taking half of the difference of the same two pixels. Then this process is repeated again in the H and L portions of the image and four sub-bands namely LL LH HL HH is obtained. An Example is shown in Figure1. These 4 bands are classified into two types (based on the information contained in them) approximation band and the detail band. The approximation band is the LL band which contains sensitive information and the detail band consists of the high frequency components which contain the edge information of the original image. Here, the lifting scheme is used to find the IWT of the pixels.

Cover Image

After Wavelet Transform

Fig. 1. An Example of Wavelet transforms

Lifting Scheme:

Step 1: The odd and even column values are taken for column wise processing to get H and L values.

Apply the following formulae to get H and L values from the spatial domain image.

1. H = (Co-Ce)
2. L = (Ce- $|H/2|$)

Where Co and Ce is the odd column and even column wise pixel values

Step 2: Then we divide the H and L valued obtained from the previous step into further sub-bands to get HH HL LH LL. Here, row-wise processing is used instead of column wise processing to get 4 sub-bands. Firstly, separate the odd and even rows of H and L, then, apply the following formulae to get the sub-bands.

Hodd – odd row of H
Lodd- odd row of L
Heven- even row of H
Leven- even row of L
LH = Lodd-Leven
LL = Leven + $|LH/2|$
$HL = H_{odd} - H_{even}$
$HH = H_{even} + |HL/2|$

2.2   Least Significant Bit Embedding

Least significant bit (LSB) substitution is the most well known steganographic technique in data hiding field. In this method just the least significant bits of a pixel are altered to hide the data. By using this method we can embed fixed length of secret bits in fixed least significant bits of the pixels. This is a simple method for data hiding but if number of bits exceeds three then there will be a great distortion to the image quality. Several adaptive techniques have been proposed so as to reduce the distortion. This is done by varying the number of bits that are to be embedded in the LSB's by using various methods.

The mathematical representation for LSB insertion method is:
$$S = (CE - mod\ (CE, 2^K)) + m$$
S is the modified pixel value.
CE is the cover image pixel value.
K is the number of bits to be embedded.
m is the secret data in decimal form.
Mathematically, the equation for extracting the secret message is
$$m = mod(S, 2^K)$$
m= secret message
S= modified pixel value
K= number of bits that are embedded

2.3   Random Embedding

To escape from the blind steganalysis, it's better to go with Random path embedding for Image Steganography. This random path embedding could be carried out in many ways. This paper proposes a random path embedding for each frequency sub bands, which is shown in Figure 2.

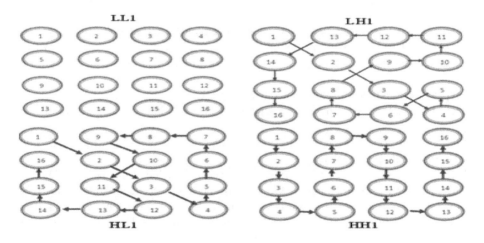

Fig. 2. Proposed Rand path traversing in various bands

3   Proposed Methodology

In this proposed methodology, initially the cover image has been preprocessed to fix the minimum intensity values as 15 and maximum value as 240, later split the cover image into 8×8 pixels which would be aiding the Integer Wavelet Transform(IWT). Then key1 is used for selecting the coefficients and Key2 is used for data embedding. As a final stage after embedding the secret data Inverse IWT is taken to form the final stego image.

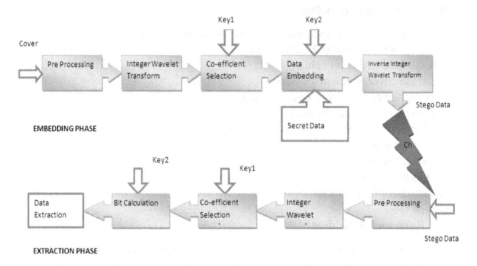

Fig. 3. Proposed Steganography system with Embedding and Extraction Phase

3.1   Embedding Algorithm

Step 1: Get a 256×256, 2D cover image and separate the RGB planes

Step 2: Do Histogram modification in all the planes, because when we apply IWT in all the planes the integer values returned will be greater than the required 255 to 0 range so by histogram modification, we change the pixel value range from 15 to 240.

Step 3: Random binary bits are generated as Secret data.

Step 4: Take the cover image and separate it into 8×8 blocks of pixels, in all the planes.

Step 5: Apply Haar wavelet transform to each 8×8 block to get LL1, LH1, HL1 and HH1 sub-bands in each block.

Step 7: It is also necessary to determine the pixels in which data can be embedded in. This is done by using Key-1. Key-1 is actually and 4×4 matrix consisting exclusively of numbers between 1 to 16 and it is shown in fig 1. The number 1 indicate that data has been embedded first in that particular pixel and the number 16 indicate that secret data has been embedded last in that particular pixel.

Step 8: Then we calculate the bit length to be embedded using an innovative algorithm. The Bit Length (BL) to be embedded is calculated by using Key-2 and the corresponding wavelet coefficient (CE) values of that particular pixel.

$$BL = \begin{cases} K+3 & if\ CE > 2^{K+3} \\ K+2 & if\ 2^{K+2} \le CE < 2^{K+3} \\ K+1 & if\ 2^{K+1} \le CE \le 2^{K+2} \\ K & if\ CE < 2^{K+1} \end{cases} \tag{1}$$

K=1, 2, 3 and 4

Here, data is embedded only in the HH, HL, LH planes and the LL plane which is extremely sensitive is left untouched.

Step 9: Inverse IWT is applied to all the planes to produce an image and then it is transmitted.

3.2   Extraction Algorithm

Step 1: Get the 256x256 stego image and separate the RGB planes.

Step 2: Separate each plane into a matrix of 8x8 pixels.

Step 3: Apply Haar wavelet transform to each 8x8 block and get the LL1, HH1, LH1, HL1 sub-bands.

Step 5: Using key-1 select the positions in which data is embedded

Step 4: Using key-2 calculate the Bit Length of each wavelet coefficient using the aforementioned equation.

Step 6: Using key-1 and key-2 the secret data is extracted from each pixel in each plane.

4   Results and Discussion

To evaluate the performance of our proposed method several experiments are performed. Three colour images are taken with size 256×256 and 512×512 as cover images. Our proposed method considers 8×8 blocks in each plane which do not overlap each other, more changes having less visual distortion. A large set of binary number is taken as secret data, and they are embedded into cover image.

Peak signal to noise ratio is used to evaluate the quality of the stego image, which is defined as given below, for an M × N grayscale image.

$$PSNR = 10 * \log_{10} \frac{255 \times 255 \times M \times N}{\sum_{i=1}^{M} \sum_{i=1}^{N} (C_{i,j} - S_{i,j})^2} \tag{2}$$

Where $C_{i,j}$ and $S_{i,j}$ denote the cover image pixels and stego image pixels, respectively. Using the proposed method the hiding capacity and PSNR for each image with various key-2 are tabulated in the table 1-4.

Table 1. Constant Bit Embedding on 256 × 256 RGB image

Image	KEY 2	Number of bits embedded	Channel 1 PSNR(dB) Red	Channel 2 PSNR(dB) Green	Channel 3 PSNR(dB) blue
Lena	1	147457	43.2837	43.4104	43.3449
	2	294913	42.4506	42.6337	42.5875
	3	442369	40.7166	40.8224	40.7286
	4	589825	37.3040	37.3829	37.4223
baboon	1	147457	40.8309	40.8313	40.8412
	2	294913	40.2731	40.3057	40.2890
	3	442369	39.0075	38.9874	38.9670
	4	589825	36.3581	36.3566	36.3031
Kaola	1	147457	42.2139	42.2652	42.2063
	2	294913	41.5913	41.5466	41.5720
	3	442369	39.8948	39.9215	39.9136
	4	589825	36.8289	36.8066	36.8088

Table 2. Constant bit Embedding on 5 1 2 × 5 1 2 RGB image

Image	KEY 2	Number of bits embedded	Channel 1 PSNR(dB) Red	Channel 2 PSNR(dB) Green	Channel 3 PSNR(dB) blue
Lena	1	589825	44.4768	44.6189	44.5394
	2	1179649	43.5513	43.6628	43.5648
	3	1769473	41.3597	41.4078	41.4157
	4	2359297	37.6375	37.6439	37.6843
baboon	1	589825	42.501	42.4553	42.5528
	2	1179649	41.7776	41.7212	41.792
	3	1769473	40.0579	40.0246	40.0809
	4	2359297	36.9056	36.8751	36.8911
Kaola	1	589825	43.3787	43.3746	43.5797
	2	1179649	42.493	42.4981	42.636
	3	1769473	40.5024	40.5154	40.6022
	4	2359297	37.1447	37.1652	37.1316

Table 3. Adaptive Embedding on 256 × 256 RGB image

Image	KEY 2	Number of bits embedded	Channel 1 PSNR(dB) Red	Channel 2 PSNR(dB) Green	Channel 3 PSNR(dB) blue
Lena	1	197211	42.4472	42.6898	42.6566
	2	321342	41.9706	42.1085	42.1577
	3	453815	40.9987	41.1321	41.1082
	4	593388	38.6518	38.8229	38.7472
Baboon	1	270777	39.6121	39.6183	39.6181
	2	371871	38.9228	38.9349	38.9164
	3	478526	38.2525	38.3488	38.3322
	4	600843	36.9129	36.8927	36.8797
Kaola	1	245129	40.9083	40.9615	40.9612
	2	351025	40.3782	40.3971	40.4332
	3	465654	39.6133	39.6545	39.6438
	4	595389	37.6887	37.7064	37.6963

Table 4. Adaptive Embedding on 512×512 RGB image

Image	KEY 2	Number of bits embedded	Channel 1 PSNR(dB) Red	Channel2 PSNR(dB) Green	Channel 3 PSNR(dB) blue
Lena	1	725479	43.838	44.008	43.913
	2	1240191	43.3696	43.5139	43.4315
	3	1790722	42.0959	42.2192	42.1698
	4	2364185	39.2752	39.4015	39.325
Baboon	1	971471	41.0078	40.9959	41.0179
	2	1468052	40.011	40.0016	40.0505
	3	1874908	39.1194	39.0985	39.1618
	4	2393230	37.4747	37.4588	37.5724
Kaola	1	930815	42.3757	42.3561	42.298
	2	1344717	41.8372	42.8263	41.7535
	3	1821703	40.7216	40.7355	40.6868
	4	2367405	38.3665	38.3857	38.3139

Random embedding is achieved by using key 1. Changes due to LSB embedding in these method are imperceptible to human vision i.e. the proposed method has overcome distortions resulted from embedding high capacity secret data. We have done the experiment with different values key-2 in constant and Adaptive embedding. For example, consider K=1, then only one bit will be embedded in selected co-efficient, For the adaptive case Equation (1) will be used to calculated the bit length to embedded the data. The results of proposed method are shown in Table 1-4 with embedding capacity and PSNR values for each method with different cover images.

Table 5. Comparative Analysis

Image	Method	No of Pixels used for Embedding	Total bits Embedded in one plane	PSNR (dB)
Lena (K=4)	**Proposed Method**	**75 %**	**788061**	**39**
	An Adaptive Steganographic Technique Based on IWT [12]	100%	986804	31.8
	A Steganographic method based on IWT and GA[11]	100%	1048576	35.17

4.1   Steganalysis

Steganalysis is the inspection of a secret data for steganography. In this proposed method minimum PSNR is 36dB, which says that this is highly robust against Human visual Attack.

Here embedding is done in the transform domain, so that secret data cannot be detected from the stego image directly. And the random path is adapted in each sub-band. Therefore this is highly robust against Blind steganalysis technique.

If any one of the hacker wants to hack the information from a 256 × 256 image, then he has to iterate these many times (3! * 3 * (32 *32) * 3!*16!).

First 3factorial inform as which plane to be selected first,
Then next 3 represent the RGB plan,
Furthermore 32*32 represents total no of 8×8 Matrices,
The 3! Represents sub-bands
Finally 16! Represents, 16 elements in a 4×4 matrix.

5   Conclusion

Steganography has two main objectives, they are High hiding capacity and the secret data must not be visible to others. Therefore the proposed method should be highly robust. It was found that the proposed method gives high capacity in the cover image with very less error. By referring the table-5, proposed method gives high hiding capacity and high PSNR. Above said method 75% of the co-efficient used to embed data with 788061 with 39dB. By changing the equation (1) to get high capacity for the various applications using wavelet transform, Key-1 and Key-2 provides enhanced double security to this method. The drawback of the proposed method is the computational time. This can be reduced by high speed computers and by optimized algorithms.

References

1. Cheddad, A., Condell, J., Curran, K., Kevitt, P.M.: Digital image steganography: Survey and analysis of current methods. Information Sciences 90, 727–752 (2010)

2. Schneier, B.: Applied Cryptography Protocols, Algorithm and Source Code in C, 2nd edn. Wiley, India (2007)
3. Katzenbeisser, S., Petitcolas, F.A.P.: Information Hiding Techniques for Steganography and Digital Watermarking. Artech House, Norwood (2000)
4. Bender, W., Gruhl, D., Morimoto, N., Lu, A.: Techniques for data hiding. IBM Syst. J. 35(3&4), 313–336 (1996)
5. Chan, C.K., Chen, L.M.: Hiding data in images by simple LSB substitution. Pattern Recognition 37(3), 469–474 (2004)
6. Thien, C.C., Lin, J.C.: A simple and high-hiding capacity method for hiding digit-by-digit data in images based on modulus function. Pattern Recognition 36(11), 2875–2881 (2003)
7. Lin, C., Lin, Y.B., Wang, C.M.: Hiding data in spatial domain images with distortion tolerance. Comput. Stand. Inter. 31(2), 458–464 (2009)
8. Amirtharajan, R., John Bosco Balaguru, R.: Tri-Layer Stego for Enhanced Security – A Keyless Random Approach. IEEE Xplore, doi:10.1109/IMSAA.2009.5439438
9. Thanikaiselvan, V., Arulmozhivarman, P., Amirtharajan, R., Rayappan, J.B.B.: Wave(Let) Decide Choosy Pixel Embedding for Stego. In: IEEE Conference on Computer, Communication and Electrical Technology ICCCET 2011, pp. 157–162 (2011)
10. Provos, N., Honeyman, P.: Hide and seek: An introduction to steganography. IEEE Security Privacy Mag. 1(3), 32–44 (2003)
11. Ghasemi, E., Shanbehzadeh, J., ZahirAzami, B.: A Steganographic method based on Integer Wavelet Transform and Genetic Algorithm. In: International Conference on Communications and Signal Processing (ICCSP), pp. 42–45 (2011)
12. El Safy, R.O., Zayed, H.H., El Dessouki, A.: An Adaptive Steganographic Technique Based on Integer Wavelet Transform. In: International Conference on Networking and Media Convergence ICNM, pp. 111–117 (2009)
13. Xuan, G., Chen, J., Zhu, J., Shi, Y.Q., Ni, Z., Su, W.: Lossless data hiding based on integer wavelet transform. In: IEEE Workshop on Multimedia Signal Processing, vol. 2, pp. 29–32 (2002)
14. Lai, B., Chang, L.: Adaptive Data Hiding for Images Based on Harr Discrete Wavelet Transform. In: Chang, L.-W., Lie, W.-N. (eds.) PSIVT 2006. LNCS, vol. 4319, pp. 1085–1093. Springer, Heidelberg (2006)
15. Amirtharajan, R., Rayappan, J.B.B.: Covered CDMA multi-user writing on spatially divided image. In: IEEE Wireless ViTAE Conference India (2011), doi:10.1109/WIRELESSVITAE.2011.5940912
16. Marvel, L.M., Boncelet Jr., C.G., Retter, C.T.: Spread spectrum image steganography. IEEE Trans. Image Process. 8(8), 1075–1083 (1999)
17. Kumar, P.P., Amirtharajan, R., Thenmozhi, K., Rayappan, J.B.B.: Steg-OFDM blend for highly secure multi-user communication. In: IEEE Wireless ViTAE Conference India (2011), doi:10.1109/WIRELESSVITAE.2011.5940918
18. Wang, C.M., Wu, N.I., Tsai, C.S., Hwang, M.S.: A high quality steganography method with pixel-value differencing and modulus function. J. Syst. Softw. 81, 150–158 (2008)
19. Wu, D.C., Tsai, W.H.: A steganographic method for images by pixel-value differencing. Pattern Recognit. Lett. 24(9-10), 1613–1626 (2003)
20. Padmaa, M., Venkataramani, Y., Amirtharajan, R.: Stego on 2^n:1 Platform for Users and Embedding. Information Technology Journal 10, 1896–1907 (2010)
21. Thanikaiselvan, V., Kumar, S., Neelima, N., Amirtharajan, R.: Data Battle on the Digital Field between Horse Cavalry and Interlopers. Journal of Theoretical and Applied Information Technology 29(2), 85–91 (2011)
22. Aura, T.: Practical Invisibility in Digital Communication. In: Anderson, R. (ed.) IH 1996. LNCS, vol. 1174, pp. 265–278. Springer, Heidelberg (1996)

Test Suite Amelioration Using Case Based Reasoning for an Agent-Based System

N. Sivakumar, K. Vivekanandan Kalimuthu, S. Hemanandh,
S. Praveen Kumar, and E. Sasidharan

Department of Computer Science and Engineering,
Pondicherry Engineering College, Puducherry - 605014, India
{sivakumar11,k.vivekanandan,hemanandh,spk295,
sasidharan1629}@pec.edu

Abstract. The paper elaborates on the principle of Test Case reuse by following the Case Based Reasoning Method and puts forward an automatic Test Case generation approach which minimizes the human burden in generating all the possible combinations of the test cases. Software test selects the input data to control the test program and observe the outcome after test execution. The Testing Engineers analyze the result and trace the bug after comparing the expected result and test result. In the software life cycle, testing is an important phase and takes up 30-50% cost. The main theme behind the paper is to reduce the cost and time by at least 10% of the overall cost which is present already. The designing of an agent environment is preferred for the constructing a software because they can work arbitrarily without any intervention, even if it has some obstacles it finds an alternate path for itself without human interference to reach the goal by using its intelligence. There are several methodologies available for the design, implementation and communication of multi agent environment. But the testing of the agents are not been dealt from time immemorial. We developed a Multi-Agent System (MAS) for e-learning application using MASE (Multi-Agent System Engineering) methodology for experimentation.

Keywords: Case Based Reasoning, Test Case Automation, Agent Oriented Software Engineering, Agent Oriented Methodologies.

1   Introduction

1.1   Agent Oriented Software Engineering

A software development methodology refers to the framework that is used to structure, plan, and control the process of developing a software system. A wide variety of such frameworks have evolved over the years, each with its own recognized strengths and weaknesses. Now an increasing number of problems in industrial, commercial, medical, networking and educational application domains are being solved by agent-based solutions[1]. The key abstraction in these solutions is the agent.

P.V. Krishna, M.R. Babu, and E. Ariwa (Eds.): ObCom 2011, Part II, CCIS 270, pp. 222–232, 2012.

An "agent" is an autonomous, flexible and social system that interacts with its environment in order to satisfy its design agenda. In some cases, many agents should interact with each other in MAS to solve single problem. In developing agent-based systems, developers will face new abstractions and concepts. Also they should handle main challenges that exist in the development of complex, open and distributed systems. For example, autonomy of agents, emergent behaviour and dynamic configuration are among the prominent features of multi-agent systems

Agent-Oriented Software Engineering (AOSE) is a new discipline that encompasses necessary methods, techniques and tools for developing agent-based systems. It is a powerful way of approaching complex and large scale software engineering problems and developing agent-based systems. Agent oriented software engineering is an extension to the object oriented software development where objects are replaced by agents.

1.2   Agent Oriented Methodologies

The agent oriented methodologies serves us the purpose of analyzing and designing the agent to the working environment. There are various methodologies in AOSE like Tropos, Prometheus, Gaia, Mase, Roadmap, Message etc. Each methodology differs from other in various aspects like analysis, design and implementation etc. Testing is an important activity in software development life cycle. However, testing is often disregarded in agent oriented atmosphere and the main focus is shifted to analysis, design and implementation activities alone. There is no specific testing technique developed for agent oriented approach. The existing testing fails to efficiently test the properties of agents such as heterogeneity, dynamism, autonomy, proactive and reactive behavior etc.

However, autonomy makes testing harder by their nature. Autonomous agents may react in different ways to the same inputs. Due to this fact, the number of test case derived for testing the autonomous property of an agent is very huge. The main objective of the paper is to reduce the number of test cases in the test suite by using Case Based Reasoning (CBR) without compromising the effectiveness of testing.

2   Literature

A. *AOSE Methodologies*
Designing software in agent oriented approach deals with new concepts such as: agent, goal, task, services, organization, interactions, environment, etc.[1] A number of methodologies have been proposed for implementing agent oriented software. Some of the agent oriented system development technologies and methodologies are

1) MASE (Multi-Agent System Engineering): MASE[3] is an iterative process. It deals the capturing the goals and refining the roles of an agent. It appears to have significant tool support. MASE treats the agents as simple software processes that interact with each other to meet the overall system goals. The development process consists of two main phases namely

1. Analysis
- Capturing goals: High-level goals are identified from requirements analysis. These goals are then decomposed into sub-goals and collected into a tree-like structure.
- Applying use cases: The second step generates use-cases and their corresponding sequence diagram.
- Refining roles: The last step of the analysis phase involves role refinement that maps goals into roles where every goal needs a delegated role.

2. Design
- Creating agent classes: Here, Agent classes are created with their interactive behavior .
- Constructing conversations: After each Agent class is recognized, constructing a conversation is the next step. In this step, designers construct conversation models used by Agent classes.
- Assembling agent classes: The assembling Agent class step creates Agent class internals.
- System design: The final step of design is system design, where the Agent classes are instantiated into actual Agents.

2) GAIA (Generic Architecture for Information Availability): GAIA[3] is role oriented, deals with less complexity management and it does not deal with the implementation issues. It is intended to allow an analyst to go systematically from a statement of requirements to a design that is sufficiently detailed and that can be implemented directly. The developing process consists of

Analysis Phase: Preliminary models are abstracted from requirements, which help to postulate implicit goals on divisions, environment, roles and interaction rules.

Architecture Design Phase: Explicit decisions about the desired structure are made at the architecture design stage to finalize role modeling.

Detailed Design: The detailed design stage takes roles and interactions to develop Agent classes and services.

3) PROMETHEUS METHODOLOGY: Prometheus[3] throws light on the agent interactions and outlines the capabilities of an agent. Prometheus methodology is composed of three phases:

System Specification phase, which involves two activities: determining the system's environment, and determining goals and functionality of the system.

Architectural Design phase, which defines agent types, the interaction between agents, and designs the system structure (System Overview diagram).

Detailed Design phase, which focuses on defining capabilities, internal events, plans and detailed data structures for each agent.

4) TROPOS METHODOLOGY: Tropos[3] is a requirements engineering approach. It is known for its rigorous requirements analysis. It offers a structured development process and supporting tools for developing complex, distributed systems. It is a goal oriented process and displays the flexible nature of the agent in adapting to the environment. The development stages in TROPOS are:

- Early requirements stage
- Late requirement stage
- Architectural design stage
- Detailed design stage
- Implementation phase

2.1 Testing in AOSE Methodologies

The agent-oriented paradigm can be considered a natural extension to the object-oriented (OO) paradigm[5]. Agents differ from objects in many issues which require special modeling elements but have some similarities. Agent-oriented methodologies, as they have been proposed so far, mainly focus on the analysis, design and implementation of Multi-Agent Systems (MAS). However, many of the tools that support each methodology include some features which are relevant to testing. These features are: interaction debugging, MAS behavior debugging, other debugging tool, unit testing framework, and other testing framework. Table given below compares the life cycle coverage and existing testing techniques in various AOSE methodologies.[4][6][7]

Table 1. Life cycle coverage, testing techniques in existing AOSE methodologies[6]

S. No	AOSE Methodologies	Life-Cycle coverage	Testing
1	Gaia	Analysis Design	-
2	Message	Analysis Design	Structured Refinement
3	Tropos	Early requirements analysis Late requirements analysis Architectural design Detailed design	eCAT tool with any test case generation technique
4	Prometheus	System specification phase Architectural design phase Detailed design phase	Prometheus Design Tool (PDT) supports interactive debugging
5	MaSE	Analysis Design	Interaction Debugging using model checking

3   Proposed Work

To test the agent properties such as autonomy, proactivity etc., maximum number of test cases should be generated to ensure complete testing[8]. The main objective of the paper is to reduce the number of test cases generated using Case Based Reasoning (CBR) without affecting the completeness of testing. To prove this, we took an e-learning system as an application where reduction of test case in a test suite can be done

3.1   E- Learning

The following are the agents involved in e-learning system,

- **Accumulator Agent:** It accumulates the areas of study of the   learners. When a test is conducted, it is evaluated. If the user performs well in a particular area, it will remove the particular area of study under the learner. If he/she scores well in an area and not in another, the area performed well is concentrated less and vice versa. It does by communicating with Evaluation agent.
- **Q-set Agent:** It analyses the priorities which was set as a result of the previous assessment. If the member is a fresher, the agent autonomously recognizes it and prepares a fresh set of questions. In test, if he/she performs well in an area and not in another, the next time the Q-set agent will set a question paper concentrating more on the area performed poorly and vice versa.
- **Evaluation Agent:** After the user submits the assessment script, the agent evaluates the script and stores the results which are used for the setting of next question paper. It gives suggestion to the user in the areas to improve based on the test results. After the evaluation of test, it stores the current status and sends it to accumulator agent and Q-set agent for future usage.
- **Query Cognizing Agent:** If a user has a doubt on particular topic, he/she posts the query. The Query cognizing agent sends the query to the experts(users who scores more) in the particular area. The agent will recognize the domain of the particular query and will post it under the corresponding domain using pattern matching algorithm. At the same time, it also intimates the user who is currently an expert in the particular domain.
- **Testing Agent:** This is an agent which autonomously logs a member in, generates the question paper set and evaluates. This process is recursively done. On each iteration, the question paper is set as well the results are recorded by the agent which in turn becomes the test suite for our Multi Agent System. For testing, the test case is generated using Case Based Reasoning (CBR) technique.

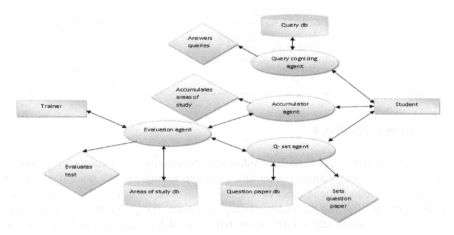

Fig. 1. E- learning Architecture

3.2   MASE

Here, we used MaSE methodology for designing our e-learning system. The Diagrammatic representation of all the following phases are given below,

A. Analysis Phase

In MaSE, analysis phase comprises of following diagrams
- a. Goal Hierarchy
- b. Use case and sequence diagram
- c. Task diagram

B. Design Phase

In design phase, the following diagrams are used
- a. Agent class diagram
- b. Agent architecture diagram
- c. Deployment diagram

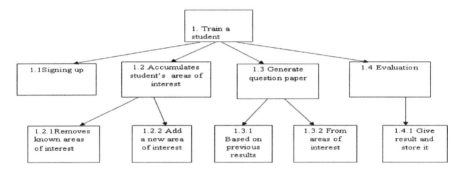

Fig. 2. Goal hierarchy

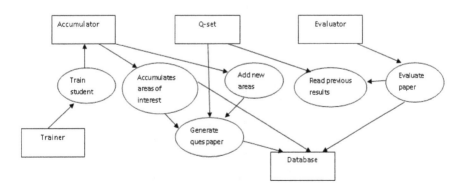

Fig. 3. Use case and sequence diagram

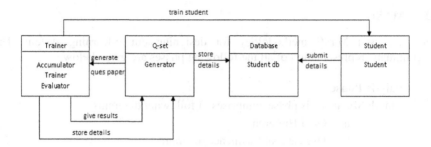

Fig. 4. Agent architecture diagram

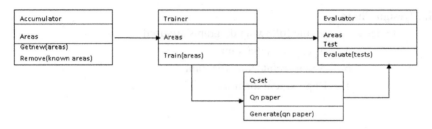

Fig. 5. Agent class diagram

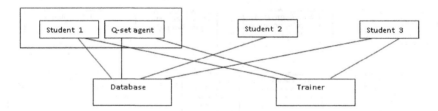

Fig. 6. Deployment diagram

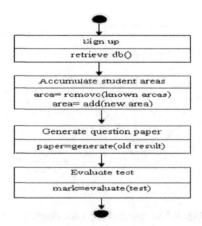

Fig. 7. Task diagram

3.3   Implementation

The agent based e-learning system was implemented using the Java Agent Development Environment (JADE)[9]. Agent Communication Language (ACL) is used for communication between the agents and Knowledge Query and Manipulation Language (KQML) is used for feeding knowledge to the agents. The e-learning system was developed for training the users in various areas of study. Let us consider the example of a user learning Data Structures and operating systems. The Accumulator agent stores the corresponding subjects under the user's areas of study. The Q-set agent generates the question paper and the user is made to write the test. After this, the Evaluation agent evaluates the test and gives the result. If the user scores well in Operating systems and less in Data Structures, then questions on   operating systems will be reduced in his question paper from the next time and   concentrates on the Data structures more. When a user has any doubt, he/she can post his/her query. The Query cognizing agent uses pattern matching to find the subject and forwards it to the users who are considered as experts (who score more) in the particular subject. The expert will answer the particular query and it will intimate the user who posted the query.

3.4   Testing

This phase of Agent Oriented Software Engineering is still in its infancy. The number of test cases required for testing AOSE is more than double the amount of test cases needed for testing an Object Oriented programming[10]. The main reason behind this is that, the agent does not behave the same at all time. Thus, testing in AOSE is still an area that demands research and enhancements[11]. The test cases can be automatically simulated by many means such as case mapping technique and random generation[12]. After the first run of test cases, the errors are identified and the program is debugged. This process of   debugging is followed by another run of all test cases inclusive of a few new test cases, for the errors that are corrected may result in new bugs springing up (regression testing)[9]. So above mentioned methods are less efficient since they do not follow any pattern and the test suite keeps on increasing in size from time and again. The number of test cases needed to test a software in the nth cycle is always constant and on the worst case are increasing drastically and thereby the cost of the testing shoots up.

Case Based Reasoning means using old experiences to understand and solve new problems. In Case-based Reasoning, a reasoner solves a problem based on the experience gained from solving a problem of the same kind. Case-based Reasoning

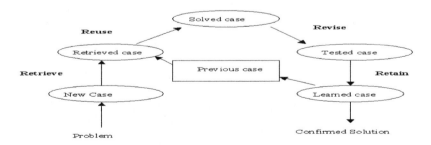

Fig. 8. Life Cycle in Case Based Reasoning

can mean adapting old solutions to meet more demands; using old cases to explain new situation; or reasoning from precedents to interpret a new situation. Case-based testing has it insight from the way a human solves a problem in the day-to-day life. And an agent is similar to a human since it acts upon the situation which has been given to it. Instead of relying solely on general knowledge of a problem domain, or making associations along generalized relationships between problem descriptors and conclusions, CBR is able to utilize the *specific* knowledge of previously experienced, concrete problem situations (cases). A new problem is solved by finding a similar case in the past, and reusing it to solve the new problem. A second important difference is that CBR is an approach towards incremental and sustained learning, for a new experience is retained each time a problem has been solved, and the experience gained is made use in solving problems in future. The CBR field has grown rapidly in the recent past, testified by a major share of papers at international conferences on the same topic, available commercial tools, and successful applications in daily use. There are four main phases in CBR namely Retain, Retrieve, Revise and Reuse.

$$T_{n+1} = \sum ((\log_x i) * (T_i)) \tag{1}$$

where $T_{(n+1)}$ – no of test cases in the $(n+1)^{th}$ Test suite
T_n - no of the test cases in the nth Test suite
x_i – the amount of failed cases in the ith Test Suite

The above given formula is an approximate value which is far less than the number of test cases in the preceding test suite. For testing our e-learning system, we use a testing agent which is a process oriented agent. It tests the system by automatically creating an account, starts its learning session and writes a test. It then checks whether every agents do their corresponding tasks. The test cases are generated using Case Based Reasoning (CBR) technique. Generally, CBR gains its efficiency only after

Table 2. Test suite Sample for the nth case

Test Case Id	Steps	Expected Output	Actual Output	Remarks
TS100	Registering without filling other details	Demand for the other details	Demand for the other details	Pass
TS101	Registering with a name which is already in existence and without filling other details	Error	Demand for the other details	Partially Failed
TS102	Registering with a name which is already in existence, without filling other details	Error	Demand for the other details	Partially Failed
TS103	Registering with a name which exist already	Error	Error	Pass
TS104	Register a user	Add to the Database	Added to Database	Pass
TS105	Register another user with unique name	Add to the Database	Added to Database	Pass
TS106	Register another user with unique name	Add to the Database	Added to Database	Pass
TS107	Register another user with unique name	Add to the Database	Added to Database	Pass
TS108	Register another user with unique name	Add to the Database	Added to Database	Pass

gaining experience. Hence, at first the test case generation seems to be like a Random test case generation technique. With the results of the test cases, the inputs that failed will be taken more care by CBR technique. Hence then onwards CBR technique's efficiency starts increasing since it has gained an experience from the previous set of test case generation. Likewise, the correctness of our e-learning system can be tested by automatically generating test cases using CBR technique.

The failed test cases are noted and when considering the inputs for the consequent test suites, the test cases that have more likelihood to have positive outcomes are neglected. These strategies are worked out only with the help of Case Based Reasoning. Among the issues to be dealt, the ones topping the list are prioritization among the test cases and selection of the best test suite. The above given test case is just a truncated view of the test suite. The next set of test cases are been listed below after the correction done in accordance to the failed test case.

Table 3. Test suite Sample for the $(n+1)^{th}$ case

Test Case Id	Steps	Expected Output	Actual Output	Remarks
TS200	Creating a name of the user and without filling other details	Demand for the other details	Demand for the other details	Pass
TS201	Creating a name which is already in existence and without filling other details	Error	Error	Pass
TS202	Creating a name which is already in existence and without filling other details	Error	Error	Pass
TS203	Creating a name which is already in existence and without filling other details	Error	Error	Pass
TS204	Create a name which is new	Add to the Database	Added to Database	Pass

Thus, clearly from the table the test suite has fewer numbers of test cases and is as we have predicted earlier in the formula.

4   Conclusion and Future Works

Generally, E-learning systems are designed to aid learners and provide them improved learning outcomes. In this developing world, it is very important to be outstanding in whatever we do such that it attracts the users. This paper describes the combination of computational intelligence of E-learning system and properties of intelligent agents. A set of E-learning agents that are capable of accumulating the student's areas of study, generating question paper based on the areas and previous performance, evaluating the student's performance in tests and reliable query-response system would improve the efficiency of e-learning environment. The cost of testing the environment is reduced to about 50-60% of the total of the actual cost of testing. Thus, we can deploy the algorithm or method to any software and not a specific e-learning system since it is just for justification that it has been brought in.

Future work can be directed towards the introduction of newly developed evolutionary algorithms and introduction of more agents within the e-learning environment in order to improve the training functionalities of the system. Efforts may be put in order to enhance the e-learning environment and introduce special features to the system

References

1. Ciancarini, P., Wooldridge, M.: Agent-Oriented Software Engineering. IEEE
2. Wadhwa, B., Jang, K.S., Nam, T.E.: Object and Agent Metrics Approach. IEEE
3. Dam, K.H., Winikoff, M.: Comparing Agent Oriented Methodologies. In: IEEE Conference
4. Yim, H., Cho, K., Kim, J., Park, S.: Architecture Centric Object-Oriented Design Method for Multi-Agent Systems. IEEE
5. Caire, G., Cossentino, M., Negri, A., Poggi, A., Turci, P.: Multi-Agent Systems Implementation and Testing. IEEE
6. Moreno, M., Pavón, J., Rosete, A.: Testing in Agent Oriented Methodologies. IEEE
7. Nguyen, D.C., Perini, A., Tonella, P.: A Goal-Oriented Software Testing Methodology. IEEE
8. Sterling, K.C.L.: Specifying Roles within Agent-Oriented Software Engineering. IEEE
9. Padgham, L., Winikoff, M.: Developing Intelligent Agent Systems. In: Conference held at the university of Melbourne
10. Srivastava, P.R., Karthik Anand, V., Rastogi, M., Yadav, V., Raghurama, G.: Extension of Object-Oriented Software Testing Techniques to Agent Oriented Software Testing. Journal of Object Technology published at Birla Institue of Technology and Science
11. Cabukovski, V.E.: An Agent-Based Testing Subsystem in an E-Learning Environment. IEEE
12. Yueh, T., Fei-Ching, C., Zhi, K., Zhou, Q.: Teaching Automated Test Case Generation. IEEE

Ocean Ambient Noise Classification Using Soft Techniques - OANCST

V. Vaithiyanathan[1], R.D. Sathiya[2], G. VictorRajamanickam[3], and G. Latha[4]

[1] School of Computing, SASTRA University, Tirumalaisamudram,
Thanjavur-613 402
vvn@it.sastra.edu
[2] School of Computing, SASTRA University, Thanjavur, Tamil Nadu
sathya@it.sastra.edu
[3] Sai Ram Group of Institutions, Chennai
gvictorajamanicam@hotmail.com
[4] Acoustics - NIOT

Abstract. Software applied in the device to filter the unwanted noise and pick up only the desired signal as information in any underwater acoustic signal processor is our aim

As the explosion of population is giving stress to the natural wealth, human beings have to look the 70% occupied ocean for help in meeting the food, shelter, etc. so, every nation is expanding the ocean exploration for protein rich food and energy including minerals. In such effort that deploy electronic devices with underwater towable sensors. In such case, while tuning the sensor is highly disturbed by the speed of the vessel the noise from the propeller waves, currents, tides, organic lives in the sea, other anthropogenic activities like sinking ships, speed boats, water sports, etc. Learning all these noises, an explorer prefers to have a sensor which is capable of filtering everything excepts the pulse noise generated from particular instrument. But for that, it is difficult to detect the targets and chosen feature. Many practical problems faced during the exploration, as strong motivation among the scientists have thought this part of studies.

Keywords: Ambient Noise, Blind Signal, acoustic signals processing.

1 Introduction

Blind signal separation techniques have been carried out for this problem, including the separation by second or higher order statistical criterion, separation by information-theoretic criteria, and separation by neural networks.

We are involving various soft computing techniques like Data mining for the purpose of identifying the various types of noises. Data mining is the principle of sorting through large amounts of data and picking out relevant information. It is usually used by business intelligence organizations, and financial analysts, but it is increasingly used in the sciences to extract information from the enormous data sets generated by modern experimental and observational methods. It has been described

P.V. Krishna, M.R. Babu, and E. Ariwa (Eds.): ObCom 2011, Part II, CCIS 270, pp. 233–242, 2012.
© Springer-Verlag Berlin Heidelberg 2012

as "the nontrivial extraction of implicit, previously unknown, and potentially useful information from data" and "the science of extracting useful information from large data sets or databases". An Ocean is a major body of saline water, and a principal component of the hydrosphere. Approximately 71% of the earth's surface is covered by ocean, a continuous body of water that is customarily divided into several principal oceans and smaller seas. More that half of this area is over 3000 meters deep. Average oceanic salinity is around 35 parts per thousand, and nearly all sea water has a salinity in the range of 30 to 38 %. Scientists estimate that 230000 marine species are currently known, but the total could be up to 10 times that number.

For many years, the principal means of probing the ocean using sound has been through the use of 'active' or 'passive' techniques. With an active system, an object is illuminated by a pulse of sound and its presence inferred from the echo it produces, whereas the passive approach involves simply listening for the sound that the object itself emits. Measurement of acoustic signals is possible if their amplitude exceeds a minimum threshold, determined partly by the signal processing used and partly by the level of background noise. Ambient noise is that part of the received noise that is independent of the source, receiver and platform characteristics. Ambient noise in the ocean spans at least five decades in the frequency domain and is the product of a plethora of sources, both natural and anthropological. It includes geological disturbances, non-linear wave-wave interaction, turbulent wind stress on the sea surface, shipping, distant storms, sonar and seismic prospecting, marine animals, breaking waves and spray, rain and hail impacts and turbulence. This ambient noise can be classified to study a variety of underwater characteristics and occurrences. It can be used to locate school of fishes, underwater volcanoes, etc.

Ambient noise can be recorded by means of hydrophone. This data can be classified in the specified ranges using **soft computing techniques**. After processing of data, output can be directly used for the intended purposes. The study aims at using the classified data:

- To calculate wind velocity over the region
- To make use of such technologies for civilian purposes

1.1   Scope

Analyzing of ocean parameters will be more beneficiary to the people of CMAR – CSIRO, IHB, FLIP, NOAA, NWS, NOS, NESDAS, NMFS, OAR Indian Scenario: The projects done on underwater acoustic and ambient noise classification are used mostly in Navy and Defence. But the finds are rarely used for civilian purpose. International Scenario: Internationally some of the projects have been going on for the American navy and various commercial usages but not yet for scientific and peace time development. Underwater acoustics is an important field of study and is still in an infant stage. A large volume of data classification is needed to be done but such expertises in such underwater acoustics are limited. Such expertise should have sufficient exposure in soft computing, being an inevitable tool for classification and processing of large amount of data in required format.

We have worked in the fields of Identification of Aerodynamic objects by the application of soft computing tools (AI) on the output of radar; removing noise from Images by designing 3D filters. These projects were successful. Similar identification techniques can be designed for the identifying the noise patterns in the data from acoustic sensors.

1.2   Methods

Neural Network- Neural network is the most extensive and most effective technique used so far in all the classification problems in the area of soft computing. We ourselves have made a good use of it in our previous classification based projects. It seems to be an effective technique.

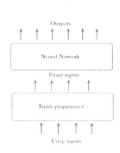

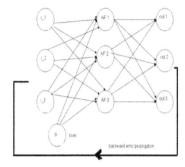

Fig. 1. Fuzzy logic as preprocessor to neural network

Fig. 2. Neural Network Backpropogation Method

Fuzzy Logic- Real life problems are not governed by computer based crisp logic. We have to think the problems on fuzzy logic. This technique will also be implemented in one of the solutions. We have used it also in our previous project successfully. It can be used both as pre-processor to [Fig 1] Neural network or post processor to it. [Fig 2] shows the backpropogation method of the Neural Network.

- **SOM-** A SOM is characterized by formation of topographic map of input patterns in which the spatial locations of the neurons in the lattice corresponds to the inherent feature of the input patterns. This is a better technique than the basic neural networks in theoretical basis. There are two methods in which we can train the SOM network:

  i) Supervised Training
  ii) Unsupervised training
     We can try either of them as per our requirements.

- **Neuro–fuzzy-** This is the method combining two important soft-computing techniques of neural networks and fuzzy logic. Results are normally better than fuzzy or neural alone but all depends finally on specific problem and data.

- **Data Mining –** This is the technique used to classify such a large amount of data that even we can't guess what range of data it corresponds to. This technique will be useful in our case as the noise ranges in infinite frequency domain and range of data cannot be defined. Several algorithms are available such as CERT, Decision tree classifier, dynamic pruning, Multi scale spatial data processing etc. Selection of algorithm depends on nature of problem data.

- Decision Tree (DT):
  (a) Tree where the root and each internal node is labeled with a question.
  (b) The arcs represent each possible answer to the associated question.
  (c) Each leaf node represents a prediction of a solution to the problem.

Decision Tree of Data Mining is the most popular technique for classification; Leanode indicates class to which the corresponding tuple belongs.

DATA:

The data recorded is 50KHZ in the interval of 5seconds with the sensitivity of -170db with reference to voltage per one micron unit. The voltage will be converted into frequency domain by FFT by using the data noise will be classified. We are going for a soft computing (data mining) based approach to detect the noise and process the data. Most of the data mining efforts are focused on developing highly detailed models of some large data set. Other researchers have described an alternate method that involves finding the minimal differences between elements in a data set, with the goal of developing simpler models that represent relevant data. When data sets contain a big set of variables, the level of statistical significance should be proportional to the patterns that were tested. For example, if we test 100 random patterns, it is expected that one of them will be "interesting" with a statistical significance at the 0.01 level. Cross validation is a common approach to evaluate the fitness of a model generated via data mining, where the data are divided into a training subset and a test subset to respectively build and then test the model.

In our approach we are going to select an initial structure of Neuro-fuzzy networks (NFNs) for the noise data with outlier regression. That is, the proposed soft computing technique is the fusion of neural network, fuzzy logic and support vector regression (SVR). Because the SVR approach is equivalent to solve a linear constrained quadratic programming problem under the fixed structure of SVR, the number of hidden nodes and adjustable parameters are easily obtained.

1.3   Explanation

For the classification of ambient noise, we have used advanced back propagation algorithm in neural network Fig [3]. All input vectors and output are normalized (between 0 and 1).

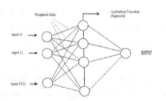   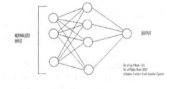

Fig. 3. ANN Architecture   **Fig. 4.** Training the data

Training: We use wind noise data for training purpose. These data represent voltage measured through hydrophone These data are in scientific form (like -1.72E-02). One sample data file is enclosed with this document (named "sample_data.txt"). These data have been converted into standard form (one sample data file is enclosed name as "modify_data.txt").

We calculated power spectrum of each file data (code for calculating power spectrum is enclosed with name "power spectrum") and put row wise in a file (one sample file is enclosed with this document named "training.dat"). Since we have used supervised learning algorithm, so training file must contain desired output. In this case, we know the class of data before training. Neural network has been trained for fixed number of loops.

Activation Function: We have tried with many activation functions like radial basis function, sigmoidal function, transcended function and linear function. We tried with unipolar and bipolar sigmoidal function but unipolar sigmoidal function gives more approximate result. Efficiency is calculated below.

Working of Neural Network: Working of neural network is common. So we are briefly explaining it here. Fig [6] First row data of training file is given input layer of neural network. In this case one row contains 513 data, and so number of input nodes in input layer is 513. These data values multiplied with hidden layer weights (initial random weight). Summation of all values goes as input to activation function associated with each node(here sigmoidal function is used). Same is done for output layer weight and output is calculated. Error is found by actual output and desired output (desired output present in training file in the last column). Then, error is back-propagated and weights have been updated. This process is continued for each row data of training file for a fixed number of loops. Now, the network has been trained to classify noise(wind, rain, mechanical noise, etc).

1.4   Testing and Efficiency of Network

Efficiency of neural network can be measured through testing. Data of unknown noise is fed to neural network. Based on the previous usage, neural network will identify the type of class this noise belongs. Efficiency of neural network depends upon various factors like amount of data used for training purpose, relation among data (nature of data), etc.

In this case, I have trained network for wind noise classification and ship noise classification. Neural network deals with numerical value, so far wind noise classification is concentrated I have taken 0.1 as desired output and for ship noise as 0.2 as desired outputs (i.e. approximately). During testing with other data (i.e. those which have not been used for training the network) when the output obtained has been accurate compared to the desired output data based on values I set threshold values which will decide whether given data is of wind noise or ship noise.

Wind Noise Classification: Desired Output = 0.1; Obtained Output Range=0.097 - 0.112; Average Output Obtained=0.105; Ship Noise Classification: Desired Output=0.2; Obtained Output Range=0.195 – 0.204; Average Output Obtained=0.197.

1.5   Advanced Back Propagation Algorithm

1. All the input vectors and output are in normalized form (between 0 and 1).

2. After every iteration we are checking whether the network is converging or diverging by checking weight value.

3. Weights are updated after the adopt phase cycle.

The detail and steps of the modified algorithm are as follows

- The normalized data has been fed to the network.

- The network reads the pattern and its corresponding Targeted output one by one from training data.

- The output is calculated by feed forwarding the network.

- The obtained output and targeted output are compared and error is calculated.

- Error is back propagated and weights are updated.

- After updating the weights, it checks

- Whether the network is converging or diverging. If diverging then, abort the training.

After error is reached to error tolerance or total no of cycles completed, updated weights will be saved and terminated. The following are the Data Configuration files for wind noise and ship noise respectively, used for training and testing the network.

Table 1. The Parameter vs. the Values

Parameter	Value
Sampling Frequency	500 kHz
Error Tolerance	0.01
Learning Parameter	0.016
No. of data sets	240
Activation Function	Unipolar Sigmoidal [f(x) =1/ (1+POW (e,-x))]
No. of iterations	2000
Wind noise Represented	0.1
Wind speed ranges	4.04m/s to 4.24m/s.

Wind Noise Data Configuration- 11.08.2005

Location	Chennai	
Latitude	N13°21.893′	
Longitude	E 080°27.438′	
Ocean Depth	58Mtrs	
Channel	Reson-3	
Hydrophone Depth	5mtr(* Varying Depth)	
Sampling Frequency	500KHz.	
Post Trigger	0.1sec	

s.no	Time	Wind Speed	Temperature		
1	10.30Hrs	4.24m/s	29.7°C	Ship Noise Goa-Data Configuration- 18.12.2003	
2	10.30Hrs	4.61m/s	29.9°C	Location	Goa
3	10.30Hrs	4.07m/s	29.1°C	Latitude	N15°24.486′
4	10.30Hrs	4.38m/s	29. 1°C	Longitude	E 073°45.6′
5	10.40Hrs	4.55m/s	29.3°C	Ocean Depth	12Mtrs
6	10.40Hrs	4.42m/s	29.1°C	Channel	B&k-5, Reson-2
7	10.40Hrs	4.02m/s	29.7°C	Hydrophone Depth	5Mtr B&K, 11Mtr Reson
8	10.40Hrs	4.84m/s	29.3°C	Hydrophone Distance	0.25Mtr Horizontal
9	10.50Hrs	4.84m/s	29.3°C	Sampling Frequency	200KHz
10.	10.50Hrs	4.51m/s	29.5°C	Nexus Amplifier Sensitivity	316µV/unit
11.	10.50Hrs	4.70m/s	29.3°C		
12.	10.50Hrs	4.15m/s	29.3°C		

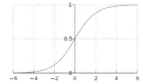

Unipolar Sigmoidal [f(x) =1/ (1+POW (e,-x))]

Fig. 5. It represents unipolar Sigmoidal Function where x-axis denotes domain (input value) and y-axis denotes range (output values)

Power spectral density for input data (signals) is calculated. Then 1sec data is fed to network for training to a specified number of input signals and iterations. While testing the following, outputs have been observed.

Each wind class must be represented by a number between 0 and 1. Here, wind class is represented by 0.1.Targeted output is 0.1. It represents Wind class. Obtained output is the actual output noted down while testing. A threshold value is set for wind class. If the obtained output lies between threshold values then given data belongs to this class.

Based on the output obtained, Threshold has been set for two classes of noises.

Threshold for class 1 wind noise data:[0.085,0.12] Threshold for class 2 wind noise data:[0.18,0.22].

Threshold for class 3 wind noise data:[0.28,0.33]. If output obtained is between 0.085 and 0.12 then, **class1.** If output obtained is between 0.18 and 0.22 then, **class2.** If output obtained is between 0.28 and 0.33 then, **class 3.**

Table 2. Success percentage

Result

Classification	Success in percentage
Wind noise in three classes	85%

1. In another attempt, network has been trained by calculating mean, median, mode, standard input deviation, maximum, minimum, range and variance of input signals. And obtained output is comparable with output obtained in previous cases.

2. Followings are the modifications done in Traditional Back propagation Algorithm.

    (a) At each iteration, network has been checked whether it is converging or diverging.

    (b)All input, and output, vectors are normalized.

3. Network is tested with various Activation Functions like Gaussian Radial Basis Function, linear function but network is giving comparable result only with Radial basis function.

4. The network has been trained and tested with seven classes of wind noises each with different wind speed ranges. But due to less difference in wind speed, network partially classifies different classes.

Table 3. Activation function and their description

S.no	Activation Function used	Description
1.	Unipolar sigmoidal function	It works fine with efficiency around 88%
2.	Gaussian Radial basis function	It is working but efficiency is less than unipolar sigmoidal function.
3.	Linear function	Network is not converging.
4.	Transcental function	Network is not converging.

The Wind noise is represented by 1 in case of traditional back propagation and 0.1 in case of proposed advanced back propagation. The obtained output is the average output taken by running the testing several times.

Training Data: We have been given wind noise data in several files. Each file contains 500000 data. We have created power spectrum of wind noise data of each file. Then, all these data (from all files) have been merged together. These data constitute data (in file Training.dat) for training of neural network.

Training: We have trained the neural network with these data. For wind noise data, we set range from 0.05 to 0.15   (in normalized form). After training got over, adjusted weights have been stored in weight.dat file.

Testing

Case1: (testing with wind noise data) we have taken wind noise data for testing. Output showed that it belongs to wind noise data.

Output: data belongs to wind noise data

Case 2:(testing with non wind noise data) we have taken randomly generated data for testing purpose. In this case output shows that it does not belong to wind noise data.

Output: Data does not belong to wind noise data.

Table 4. The comparison of the normal Back propagation vs. the advanced back propagation method

Comparison Table	Training Time	Targeted Output	Obtained Output	Difference	Efficiency
Traditional Back propagation.	100 %	1	1.5	0.50	50%
Proposed Advanced Back propagation.	60 %	0.1	0.117	0.017	83%

2   Conclusion

The result of the program of Neural Network brings out the feasibility of classifying the wind noise to the level of 83% success.

Acknowledgement. The authors are thankful to Earth Sciences of Ministry and to Directors NIOT for funding and provided the required clarification and Vice-Chancellor SASTRA for encouraging the research.

References

1. Chen, C.-H., Lee, J.-D., Lin, M.-C.: Classification of Underwater Signals Using Neural Networks Tamkang. Journal of Science and Engineering 3(1), 31–48 (2000)
2. Saran, A.K.: A Study of Marine Ambient Acoustic Noise in Relation to Marine Life in Antarctic Waters. During Austral Summer of Xviii Indian Eighteenth Indian Expedition to Antarctica, Scientific Report, Department of Ocean Development. Technical Publication No. 16, pp. 199–211 (2002)
3. Seekings, P., Potter, J.: Classification of marine acoustic signals using Wavelets & Neural Networks. Acoustic Research Laboratory, Tropical Marine Science Institute, National University of Singapore, 12a KentRidge Road, Singapore 119223
4. Bass, S.J., Alex, E.: HayAmbient Noise in the Natural Surf Zone:Wave-Breaking Frequencies. IEEE Journal of Oceanic Engineering 22(3) (July 1997)

Incident Management Process Capability:
A Simulation Study

Goutam Kumar Kundu[1], B. Murali Manohar[1], and Jayachandra Bairi[2]

[1] VIT Business School, VIT University, Vellore, TN, India
[2] Service delivery department, WIPRO, Bangalore 560008
{gkk,bmm}@vit.ac.in, bairij@rediffmail.com

Abstract. Business today depends heavily on the quality of IT support services. IT support organizations are required to restore normal service operation after a service disruption which is termed as an incident. Incident Management is the process through which IT support organizations manage to restore normal service operation after a service disruption.

This article presents the details on how Monte Carlo simulation was used for determination of incident management process capability. A Monte Carlo simulation spreadsheet model was used to model incident management parameters. It has used the simulation result of a case study to explain the various steps and the use of the results are also explained.

Keywords: IT support service, simulation, process capability.

1   Introduction

Today's Business depends heavily on the quality of IT services. For all the organizations whether they belong to any industry, IT support is very crucial for the smooth functioning of the business operations. Degradations in IT Service delivery can be costly for both the IT support service providers and their customers. Because of this, many organizations are implementing strict Service Level Agreements (SLA) to ensure high standards of IT service.

It is observed that many companies outsource even the provision of support services that are essential for its continuity, such as information technology and maintenance [6]. A Service Level Agreement (SLA) is used as a formal contract between service provider and consumer to ensure service quality [1]. It defines the boundaries of the project in terms of the functions and services that the service provider will give to its client, the volume of work that will be accepted and delivered, and acceptance criteria for responsiveness and the quality of deliverables. A well-defined and crafted SLA correctly sets expectations for both sides of the relationship and provides targets for accurately measuring performance to those objectives. As service level agreements (SLAs) are increasingly becoming a standard from subscribers, service providers must be able to offer agreed uptime guarantees, and in many cases it may be combined with money-back penalties in cases of failure or noncompliance.

P.V. Krishna, M.R. Babu, and E. Ariwa (Eds.): ObCom 2011, Part II, CCIS 270, pp. 243–255, 2012.

SLA is very important with respect to IT service delivery. Service Level Management (SLM) is an important process area – it has a set of processes which provide a framework by which services are defined, service levels required to support business processes are agreed upon, Service Level Agreements (SLAs) and Operational Level Agreements (OLAs) are developed to satisfy the agreements, and costs of services are developed.

The one of the objectives of Service Level Management processes is:

- To provide a practical approach for determining SLAs and help identify the right balance of service and associated costs to provision it

In order to effectively manage the service delivery and meet the expectation of its customers, IT support service providers need to first determine the current levels of service. This would help organization by providing a starting point in SLA negotiations with their customers. With performance data of the current levels of service, organization can make informed decisions regarding the SLAs. IT service organizations also need to experiment with multiple scenarios to determine resources needed to meet its business unit goals.

In order to determine the current level of service, IT support organizations require knowledge of the process capability of the incident management process. However, in many IT support organizations, appropriate baseline of the incident management process capability do not exist. IT support organizations are often forced to take decisions purely based on experience and subjective information in absence of any meaningful baseline process capability data of the incident management process.

The baseline metrics can be used for

- Evaluation of existing capability of the incident management process
- Identification of the areas for process improvement in an existing capability
- Reduction of variability in the incident resolution process

In this article, we have detailed the steps that were followed to develop the baseline of incident management process in an IT support service organization. While developing the baseline we had used simulation software.

The remainder of the article is structured as follows.

Section 2 describes the Methodology. In this section we have detailed the steps followed in the simulation. It describes the simulation methodology and at the end, the results of the simulation study. Section 3 contains discussion and conclusion of our study.

2   Methodology

Simulation is an exercise involving reality of function in an artificial environment [5]. According to Pristker [7], simulation can be defined as the process of designing a mathematical, logical model of the real world system on a computer. The simulated model can be used as a tool to analyze the responses of systems under various scenarios. Simulation has proved to be a useful tool to study resource-driven processes [8, 9]. The real power of simulation is fully realized when it is used to study complex systems [10].

We used Monte Carlo simulation for determining the capability of Incident Management Process. Monte Carlo simulation (using random sampling) is a well-established method for evaluation [3]. The essential element of Monte Carlo simulation is to replace constant estimated values within mathematical models with probability distributions, and replicate studies many times drawing instances of outcomes from these distributions for each replication. The results of a Monte Carlo simulation will be variable, reflecting the variety of data distributions. The Crystal Ball tool was used for the simulation. The Crystal Ball simulation model, an application of Monte Carlo simulation, is a spreadsheet of inputs and formulas.

This section covers the details of the model parameters, development of the simulation model and important baseline attributes. The process of building the simulation model and its execution comprised several steps-problem definition, scope definition, conceptual model design, data collection, model building, execution, validation and simulation results.

2.1   Problem Definition

A Service Level Agreement (SLA) serves as a formal contract between service provider and consumer to ensure service quality [1]. IT support organizations provide services within the framework of SLAs defined and agreed with the client. However, SLAs have to be monitored and assured properly [4]. A ticketing system is normally used for incident and problem management

Typically, incidents are categorized depending on the impact/potential impact on the business functions / operations of an organization and the number of users affected. Generally, the SLAs are defined by incident category. Sometimes the customer may decide to change the SLAs. There are cases, when the new customer may ask for different SLAs even though the service line may be same.

SLA definitions are customer specific and may vary from customer to customer. For a customer, SLAs may be same across service lines whereas for another customer the SLAs may vary across service lines.

It is important for IT support organizations to determine the capability of their incident management process. Developing baseline of the current capability of incident management process would help an organization to determine how their current processes are placed against the set SLAs and how the change in SLA would impact their service delivery. The baseline will provide an insight into the capability of the different service lines and will help identify the service lines where the incident management capability is required to be improved.

Objective of this study was to come up with a simulation based methodology for developing baselines of incident management process capability for different service lines.

2.2   Scope

The support service portfolio of this particular IT service organization included many service offerings such as handling of incidents, requests for change (RFC), service access requests, work requests, lights-on activities and other project and enhancement activities.

For our study, the scope was restricted to incident handling only. The other activities such as handling of requests for change (RFC), work requests, lights-on-checks were excluded from the scope.

2.3   Conceptual Model Design

A model is a broad concept containing many potential and employed explanations. Law and Kelton [2] defines a model as "a set of assumptions about how a system works, to try to gain some understanding of how the system behaves".

As part of the conceptual model design exercise, we studied the service delivery and support team structure of the service organization. We found the following:

- The service desk staff logged customer issues as incidents using an Incident Management tool. The incident management tool stored the details of all the incidents.
- Every incident had a life cycle and support engineers updated the work log details and the incident management tool captured the time stamps whenever there was change in incident status.
- Procedures and guidelines existed for the incident handling process
- All support engineers were familiar and followed the incident management process and guidelines.
- The roles and responsibilities of the support engineers were defined and support engineers were grouped according to the skills and technology.
- The SLA definition was by incident category and service line.
- All service lines selected for study were stable.

We decided to develop the baseline of the process capability by service lines and by incident category. We also studied the incident life cycle in detail. This was necessary for formulating inputs, assumptions and process definition required for development of the model. We found that the status of a particular incident changed many times during the life span of the incident.

Typically, for an incident status progressed as

'New' → 'Assigned' → 'In Progress' → 'Resolved' → 'Closed'.

However, sometimes the status of an incident status might be kept as 'Pending' when the support staff awaited information from users/other 3rd party vendors. In that case the incident status progression would take the path as

'New' → 'Assigned' → 'In Progress' → 'Pending' → 'Resolved' → 'Closed'

Sometimes an incident might take same status more that once. This would happen when an incident status changed either from 'Pending' to 'In progress' or from 'Pending' to 'Assigned'.

'Pending to In Progress' indicated that an incident was waiting for some action, and once that action was completed, there was still something remaining to be done.

'Resolved to Assigned' and 'Resolved to In Progress' indicated that the resolution provided was not satisfactory or did not resolve the problem, and that some more analysis and work was required to be performed.

'In Progress to Assigned' indicated a change in team, which could be due to incorrect assignment or due to work required to be performed by multiple teams.

Figure-1 below shows a schematic diagram of an incident through its life cycle. It shows the transition of an incident from one status to another.

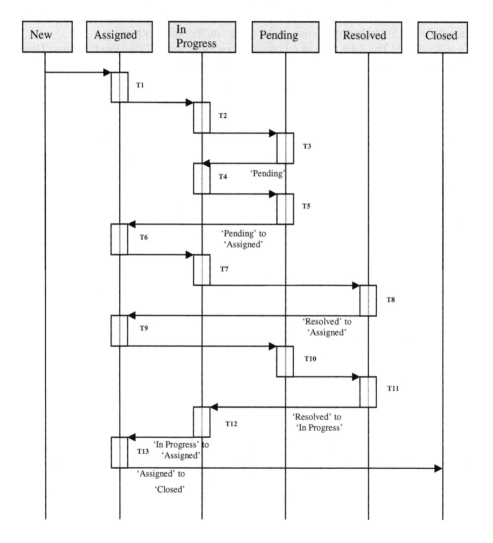

Fig. 1. Incident Life Cycle

An incident may spend time in a particular state the time spent in each state varies from one incident to another. The definition of time spent in each state is as follows:

TimeAssigned: The total time the incident was in "Assigned" status. This is the sum of all individual times this incident was in "Assigned" status.

TimeInProgress: The total time the incident was in "In Progress" status. This is the sum of all individual times this incident was in "In Progress" status.

TimePending: The total time in seconds this incident was in "Pending" Status. This is the sum of all individual times this incident was in "Pending" status.

TimeResolved: The total time in seconds this incident was in "Resolved" Status. This is the sum of all individual times this incident was in "Resolved" status.

With reference to Figure-1 , the time spent in different states can be calculated as follows.

TimeAssigned   : $T1 + T6 + T9 + T13$
TimeInProgress   : $T2 + T4 + T7 + T12$
TimePending   : $T3 + T5 + T10$
TimeResolved   : $T8 + T11$
The total time for the incident
     = TimeAssigned   + TimeInProgress   +
TimePending   + TimeResolved
     $= (T1 + T6 + T9 + T13)   + (T2 + T4 + T7 + T12)   + (T3 + T5 + T10) + (T8 + T11)$

Based on the study of the incident life cycle, we identified four variables as inputs to the simulation model. These variables were TimeAssigned, TimeInProgress,TimePending, and TimeResolved.

Resolution time and fix time are the two important SLA types. We need to forecast these two variables. The resolution and fix time can be simulated in two ways.

- Resolution and Fix Time without considering the TimePending
- Resolution and Fix Time taking into consideration the TimePending

2.4   Data Collection

We obtained the data for the model development from the Incident Management tool. Incident Management tool stored the attributes of every incident. The tool captured the time stamp when the status of a particular incident changed. However, the model required cumulative time spent in each status by an incident. It required some computation to obtain the status-wise cumulative time spent from the time stamp details available in Incident Management Tool.

Incident log data was extracted from the Incident Management tool. A program was developed to compute the status-wise time spent for the incidents by reading from the extracted data file.

This data was then segregated by service line and by incident category to serve as inputs to the simulation model. The unit of time was same for all the state times and it was in minute.

2.5   Model Building

It was observed that the input data on TimeAssigned, TimeInProgress, TimePending, and TimeResolved followed probability distribution.

To determine the probability distribution of the input variables, we carried out the distribution fitting. This mathematical fit was to determine the set of parameters for each distribution that best described the characteristic of the data. Highest rating fit was chosen to represent the data.

Thus, for each input (uncertain) variable, we defined the possible values with a probability distribution.

The outputs were Resolution time and fix time - the two important SLA types. The simulation would forecast these two variables.

2.6   Model Execution

The Crystal Ball simulation tool was used for Monte Carlo Technique of simulation. It used random numbers to measure the effects of uncertainty in the spreadsheet model. The simulation generated a set of values for the input variables that were defined.   These inputs fed into the formulas defined in the forecast cells. The process let us explore the ranges of outcome and we could view and use the forecasts to estimate the probability or certainty of a particular outcome.

A simulation would calculate numerous scenarios of the model by repeatedly picking values from the probability distribution for the uncertain input variables and keep track of the forecasts for each period.

After number of trials, we could view set of values and the statistics of the results (such as mean forecast values) and the certainty of any particular value.

The simulation results were obtained with 1000 trials.

The forecast results showed not only the different result values for each forecast, but also the probability of obtaining any value. The simulation tool normalized these probabilities to calculate another important number – the certainty. The chance of any forecast values falling between – infinity and + infinity is always 100%. However, the chance or certainly of the same forecast being at least a specific value might be some percentage. The tool calculated the resulting certainty.

2.7   Validation

Validation is required for ensuring the accuracy of the computer model with respect to the intended application of the model. Our validation results confirmed that the outputs from the simulation model were consistent with the real-world scenario. A comparison between the observed and simulated time spent statistics was conducted. The results, showed a good agreement between observed and simulated time statistics.

The simulation results were obtained with 1000 trials. Then, statistical tests, including the hypothesis test and paired t-tests, were conducted. The results of comparison of the statistics are summarized in Table 1. It was concluded that the simulation model was statistically identical to the historical incident data within a confidence level of 95%.

Table 1. Mean, Std dev and t-values of Simulation and Historical Sample

Type of Sample	Sample Size		Fix Service Level (with pending time)	Resolution Service Level (with pending time)	Fix Service Level (without pending time)	Resolution Service Level (without pending time)
Historical Incident Data	131	Mean	1058.52	1057.49	290.04	289.01
		Std Dev	1781.46	1781.47	676.20	676.21
Simulated result	1000	Mean	1,034.55	1,031.79	298.33	295.57
		Std Dev	1,486.94	1,487.08	607.34	607.46
Paired Hyp test	Calculated t-value		0.1693	0.1815	0.1449	0.1146
2-sided test (5%)	t-distribution		1.96	1.96	1.96	1.96

2.8   Simulation Results

The Crystal Ball simulation provided the results after the set number of trails. The simulation results given below are for one of the selected service line data of a particular incident category.

The simulation run used four variables as inputs-TimeAssigned, TimeInProgress, TimePending and TimeResolved.

The simulation model was run to forecast the four output variables:

Fix Capability (without considering Pending Time)
Fix Capability (including Pending Time)
Resolution capability (without considering Pending Time)
Resolution capability (including Pending Time)
Forecast of each of capability as percentile is also produced.

The parameters used for the simulation run are as follows:

Number of trials: 1000
Number of input variables (assumptions): 4
Number of output variables (forecasts)   : 4

Input Variables: The probability distribution statistics of the four input variables are presented in the tables below.

TimeAssigned
    Gamma distribution with parameters:
        Location   1.00
        Scale   1,342.56
        Shape   0.186518068

TimeInProgress
    Gamma distribution with parameters:
    Location   2.00
        Scale   73.53
        Shape   0.484216428

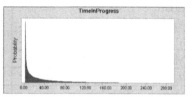

TimePending
    Weibull distribution with parameters:
        Location   0.00
        Scale   420.77
        Shape   0.524467713

TimeResolved
    Weibull distribution with parameters:
        Location   1.00
        Scale   0.05
        Shape   0.244043787

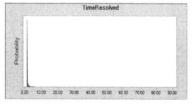

Output variables: The simulation run generated the forecast of the four output variables. The output variables follow probability distributions and the statistics of the output variables is presented in Table 2. The percentile forecast of incident management process capability is given in Table 3. Figures 2a, 2b, 2c and 2d depict histograms with distribution fitting.

Table 2. Statistics of the four forecast variables

Statistics	Forecast of Fix Service Level (with pending time)	Forecast of Resolution Service Level (with pending time)	Forecast of Fix Service Level (without pending time)	Forecast of Resolution Service Level (without pending time)
Trials	1000	1000	1000	1000
Mean	1,034.55	1,031.79	298.33	295.57
Median	469.42	468.37	88.89	84.90
Std. Deviation	1,486.94	1,487.08	607.34	607.46
Variance	2,210,980.25	2,211,413.34	368,866.19	369,011.93
Skewness	3.31	3.31	4.67	4.67
Kurtosis	18.60	18.60	32.90	32.92
Coeff. of Variability	1.44	1.44	2.04	2.06
Minimum	6.38	4.95	4.04	3.01
Maximum	12,964.97	12,963.97	6,612.19	6,611.19
Range Width	12,958.59	12,959.01	6,608.15	6,608.18
Mean Std. Error	47.02	47.03	19.21	19.21

Table 3. Percentile forecast of Incident Management process capability

Percentiles	Forecast of Fix Service Level (with pending time)	Forecast of Resolution Service Level (with pending time)	Forecast of Fix Service Level (without pending time)	Forecast of Resolution Service Level (without pending time)
0%	6.38	4.95	4.04	3.01
10%	66.09	62.41	9.60	7.40
20%	125.93	124.51	20.74	17.44
30%	201.87	199.64	35.73	33.09
40%	306.47	305.33	57.13	54.94
50%	467.98	466.98	88.78	84.01
60%	694.46	689.45	127.89	125.19
70%	1,082.08	1,080.98	203.48	200.69
80%	1,658.81	1,657.81	372.34	359.71
90%	2,617.59	2,616.10	782.06	778.45
100%	12,964.97	12,963.97	6,612.19	6,611.19

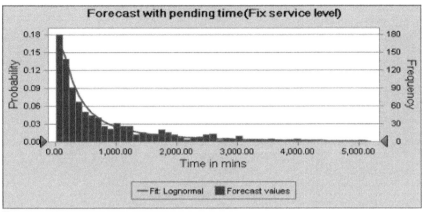

Summary :
Entire range is from 6.38 to 12,964.97
Base case is 1,064.86
After 1,000 trials, the std. error of the mean is 47.02

Fig. 2a. Forecast of Fix Service Level (with pending time)

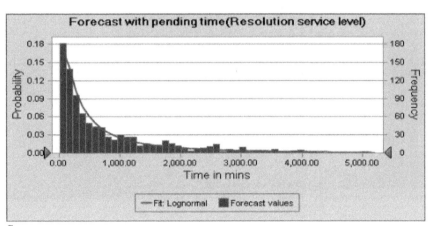

Summary :
Entire range is from 4.95 to 12,963.97
Base case is 1,062.47
After 1,000 trials, the std. error of the mean is 47.03

Fig. 2b. Forecast of Resolution Service Level (with pending time)

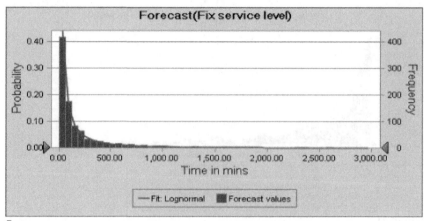

Summary :
Entire range is from 4.04 to 6,612.19
Base case is 291.41
After 1,000 trials, the std. error of the mean is 19.21

Fig. 2c. Forecast of Fix Service Level (without pending time)

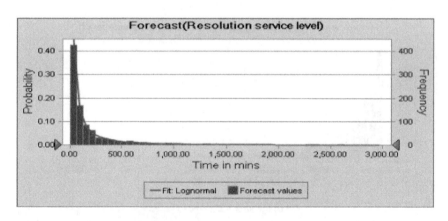

Summary :
Entire range is from 3.01 to 6,611.19
Base case is 289.02
After 1,000 trials, the std. error of the mean is 19.21

Fig. 2d. Forecast of Resolution Service Level (without pending time)

3   Discussion and Conclusion

In this article, we have demonstrated the significant role simulation can play in establishing baseline of incident management process. Simulation can also enhance the understanding and provide insight by revealing important characteristics and properties of the incident handling process. Establishment of baseline figures in terms of percentiles would provide useful insight.

This model can be extended to determine the baseline for other types of IT support activities such as Request for Change (RFC) and Service Access Request (SAR) by studying and indentifying the life cycle states and developing a mechanism to capture time spent data for these states.

This model can also be used to prepare baseline of capability by resource type (Senior, Mid-level, and Junior) for a service line by incident category.

If the timestamp data cannot be extracted from the incident management tool, then we would need to develop a mechanism to capture and record the cumulative time spent for each of the incident state. For collecting the data manually, we need to identify the service lines which are to be included in the time study. We can then conduct the time study to record the incident time spent in various states. This data can be used as input data for the model.

The model can be refined to include few more input variables such as the number of times incident status is kept as Pending, the number of different support groups involved in the analysis and resolution.

A simulation model can also be developed to find the optimum resource mix for a service line, considering the volume of incidents, the SLAs and cost of resources by resource type.

References

1. Buco, M.J., Chang, R.N., Luan, L.Z., Ward, C., Wolf, J.L., Yu, P.S.: Utility computing SLA management based upon business objectives. IBM Systems Journal 43(1), 159–178 (2004)
2. Law, A.M., Kelton, W.D.: Simulation Modeling and Analysis. McGraw-Hill, Singapore (2000)
3. Lorance, R.B., Wendling, R.V.: Basic techniques for analyzing and presentation of cost risk analysis. Cost Engineering 43, 25–31 (2001)
4. Sahai, A., Graupner, S., Machiraju, V., Van Moorsel, A.: Specifying and Monitoring Guarantees in Commercial Grids through SLA. In: Proceedings of the Third IEEE International Symposium on Cluster Computing and the Grid, Tokyo, Japan, p. 292 (2003)
5. Thavikulwat, P.: The architecture of computerized business gaming simulations. Simulation & Gaming 35(2), 242–269 (2009)
6. Van der Meer-Kooistra, J., Vosselman, E.: Management control of interfirm transactional relationship: the case of industrial renovation and maintenance. Accounting Organisations and Society 25, 51–77 (2000)
7. Pritsker, A.B.: Introduction to Simulation and SLAMM II. Systems Publishing Corporation, West LaFayette (1986)
8. Farrar, J.M., AbouRizk, S.M., Xiaoming, M.: Generic implementation of lean concepts in simulation models. Lean Construction Journal 1(1), 1–23 (2004)
9. Proctor, T.: Simulation in healthcare. Health Manpower Management 22(5), 40–44 (1996)
10. Kelton, D.W., Sadowski, P.R., Sadowski, A.D.: Simulation with Arena. WCB/McGraw-Hill, New York (1998)

An Efficient Numerical Method for the Prediction of Clusters Using K-Means Clustering Algorithm with Bisection Method

D. Napoleon, M. Praneesh, S. Sathya, and M. SivaSubramani

Department of Computer Science, School of Computer Science and Engineering,
Bharathiar University, India, Coimbatore-641046
mekaranapoleon@yahoo.co.in, {raja.praneesh,selvarajsathya72,
sivasu4all}@gamil.com

Abstract. The development of modern IT-based analysis methods, data mining, has been outstanding over the last decade. Using computers to analyze masses of information to discover trends and patterns. The current trend in business collaboration shares the data and mines results to gain mutual benefit. The main goal of the work is to introduce a bisection method which is capable of transforming a non-anonymous data set into adult data set. In this model, transform a table so that no one can make high probability association between records in the table and the corresponding entities. In order to achieve these goals we are implemented a bracket rule identifier for the prediction of the cluster. For this a suitable metric has been developed to estimate information loss by suppression which works well for both numeric and categorical data.

Keywords: Data Clustering, K-means, Cluster analysis, Bisection methods, Supression.

1   Introduction

Data mining involves the use of sophisticated data analysis tools for discover previously unknown, valid pattern and relationship is large data sets [1].Here clustering is alternatively refer to as unsupervised learning or segmentation. It can be thought of as participating or segmenting the data into groups that might or might not be disjointed. The main advantage of clustering is that interesting patterns and structures can be found directly from very large data sets with little or none of back ground knowledge. The K-means algorithm is successful in producing cluster for many practical applications. But the complexity of the K-means algorithm is very high especially for large data sets to predict the cluster [5]. Bisection method is a numerical method and at the same time gives a proof of the intermediate value theorem and provides a practical method to find the cluster of the corresponding intervals. In this approach the intervals are calculated by using bracket rule. The main consideration is sensitive knowledge which can be mined from a data base by using data mining algorithm should also be excluded, the main objective in privacy preserving data mining is to develop algorithms for modifying the original data in some way, so that private data and private data knowledge remain private even after the mining process. The implementation work was used in MATLAB programming software.

P.V. Krishna, M.R. Babu, and E. Ariwa (Eds.): ObCom 2011, Part II, CCIS 270, pp. 256–266, 2012.

2   Previous Work

The main objective of this previous work is hiding a data field using given data set. HAC algorithm and K-means clustering algorithm are applied to predict the optimal solution of cluster. But this approach is not effective, because of the anonymous data and it doesn't predict the suppression and performance factors. Such as accuracy for original and anonymized data set, time complexity and information loss. In order to overcome these problems we have introduced a new approach called Bisection method and suppression technique that works well for these factors.

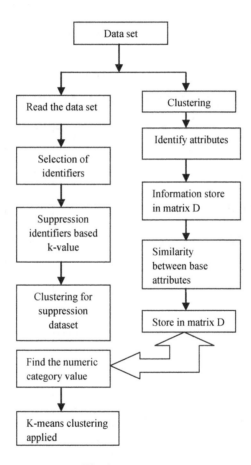

Fig. 1. Frame work

3   Proposed Work

The proposed methodology is used for analyzing the data using K-means clustering and Bisection method. The frame work of the proposed work is shows in Fig. 1.

In order to achieve we are applied a bracket rule identifier for predicting the cluster. This approach is a suitable metric that has been developed to Estimate information loss by suppression which works for numeric and categorical data.

3.1   Data Set

The Adult data set is downloaded from UC Irvine Machine Language Repository. The Donor of the data set contains the census data and has become a commonly used benchmark for K-anonymity. The Adult data set consist of fifteen fields with six continuous attributes and eight categorical attributes. The class attribute is income level with, two possible values <=50k, or >50k. The adult data contain about more than 30,000 records totally. Table. 1 shows the sample adult data set.

Table 1. Adult Dataset

Age	Work class	Flnwgt	Edu	Edu-num	Marital status	Occupation	Relation ship	Race	Sex	Salary
39	State-gov	77516	Bachelor	13	Never married	Clerk	Not in family	White	M	<=50 k
50	Self-not inc	83311	Bachelor	13	Married civ spouse	Manager	Husband	White	M	<=50 k
38	Private	21564	Hs grad	9	Divorced	Cleaner	Not in family	White	M	<=50 k
53	Private	234721	Hs grad	7	Married civ spouse	Cleaner	Husband	Black	M	<=50 k
28	Private	338409	Bachelor	13	Married civ spouse	Professor	wife	Black	F	<=50 k
37	Private	284582	Master	14	Married civ spouse	Manager	wife	White	F	<=50 k
49	Private	160187	9th	5	Married civ spouse	Other service	Not in family	Black	F	<=50 k
52	Self-not inc	209642	Hs grad	9	Married civ spouse	Professor	Husband	White	M	>50k
31	Private	45781	Master	14	Never married	Manager	Not in family	White	F	>50k
42	Private	159449	Bachelor	13	Married civ spouse	Manager	Husband	White	M	>50k

3.2   Bisection Method

Bisection method at the same time gives a Proof of the intermediate value theorem and provides a practical method to find the cluster of the corresponding intervals.[13,16] Here basically we are allocating the intervals in [1 - 15] for estimating the requirements. Let f(x) is the continuous function on the intervals [a, b]. let assume that f(a) < 0, while f(b) > 0 the other case being handled similarly, set a0=a, b0=b. Now consider the midpoint m0 = ($0 + b0)1/2$. Here the data is segmenting the initial node to end node. For classifying the data, we are following the basic properties are followed.

1. (a0) is increasing sequence; (bn) is a decreasing sequence.
2. an $\leq$ bn for all n.
3. f (an) < 0 for all n, f(bn) > 0 for all n.
4. bn-an = $2 -^n$ (b –a) for all n.

It follows from the first properties that the   sequence,(an) and (bn) coverage; set $\lim_{n \to \infty} an = a$ and $\lim_{n \to \infty} bn = b$. The third property and the continuity of the function f(x) imply that f (a) $\leq$ 0 and that f (b) $\geq$ 0. The crucial observation is the fact that the fourth properties implies that a = b. consequently. F (a) = f (b) = 0.

The length of initial condition interval is (b – a). After the first interval the length of the loop is (b – a) / 2, after the second interval the length of the loop is (b- a) /4, after n passes through the loop, the length of the remaining interval is (b – a) /2^n. In the fact we can solve this inequality for n as

$$\frac{(b - a)}{2^n} < \epsilon \tag{1}$$

Check the loop with 'n' times, whether the cluster in behind the centre or not, to check we are used the inequality condition as below.

$$2^n > \frac{b - a}{1} \epsilon \tag{2}$$

After Checking the inequality condition we are calculate the Length of the attributes with the help of the below condition

$$n > \frac{[\ln(a - b) - \ln(\epsilon)]}{\ln 2} \tag{3}$$

Fig. 2 represents bracket rule technique is used for entering the attributes of data clustering [14]. The main usage of bracket rule in applying data mining is to obtaining the data attributes to extract the cluster [15]. For an example the bracket rule attributes is [1 3 4 5 6 7 10]; so here first bisection algorithm finds the increasing sequence and decreasing sequence, then split the category into [1 3 4], [5], and [6 7 10]. Finally in order to classify the clusters we have applied the k-means algorithm.

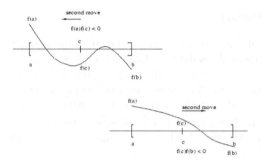

Fig. 2. Bracket Rule

3.3   K-Means Clustering Algorithm

K-means is an iterative clustering algorithm in which items are moved among sets of clusters until the desired set is reached. A cluster is a collection of data objects that similar to one another with in the same cluster and is dissimilar to the objects in the other clusters. It is the best suited for data mining because of its efficiency in processing large datasets. [1, 5] The cluster mean of Ki = {ti1, ti2,...tim} is definedas

$$= \frac{1}{m} \sum_{j=1}^{m} t_{ij} \tag{4}$$

> **Algorithm: The k-means clustering algorithm**
>
> **Input:**
>
>   D = {d1, d2,.......,dn} //set of *n* data items.
>
>   *k* // Number of desired clusters
>
> **Output:**
>
> A set of *k* clusters

Steps:

1. Arbitrarily choose *k* data-items from D as initial centroids;

2. Repeat Assign each item *di* to the cluster which has the closest centroid; Calculate new mean for each cluster.

Until convergence criteria is met. As a result of this loop, the k- centroids may change their position in step-by-step manner

4   Suppression Data Set

Suppression refers to removing a contain attribute value replacing occurrences of the value with a special value "?" Indicating that value k, suppress the corresponding of identifiers as k=25, 50, 75 and 100 suppression can be applied at the following levels.

Tuple
Suppression is performed at the level of row; a suppression operation removes a whole tuple.

Attribute
Suppression is performed at the level of column; a suppression operation obscures all the values of the column.

Cell
Suppression is performed at the level of single cells; as a result an anonymized table may wipe out only certain cells of a given tuple or attribute. The following table shows the corresponding suppression data set. The following Table. 2 refer the suppression anonymized data for hiding the data's in the given datasets. In this method we are hiding the data is used   either "*" or "0".

Table 2. Suppression Data Set

Age	Work class	Flnwgt	Edu	Edu-num	Marital status	Occupation	Relation ship	Sex	Salary
*	*	77516	Bachelor	13	Never married	*	Not in family	M	<=50 k
*	Self-not inc	83311	Bachelor	13	Married civ spouse	Manager	Husband	M	<=50 k
*	Private	21564	Hs grad	9	*	Cleaner	Not in family	M	<=50 k
*	Private	234721	Hs grad	7	Married civ spouse	Cleaner	Husband	M	<=50 k
*	Private	338409	Bachelor	13	Married civ spouse	Professor	wife	F	<=50 k
*	Private	284582	Master	14	Married civ spouse	Manager	wife	F	<=50 k

5   Categorical to Numerical Conversion

In order to explore the relationships among categorical items, the idea of co-occurrence is applied. The basic assumption of co-occurrence is that if two items always show up in one object together, there will be a strong similarity between them. When a pair of categorical items has a higher similarity, they shall be assigned closer numeric values. The proposed algorithm produces pure numeric attributes [17].

    The first step in the proposed approach is to read the input data and normalize the numeric attributes' value into the range of zero and one. The goal of this process is to avoid certain attributes with a large range of values will dominate the results of clustering. Additionally, a categorical attribute A with most number of items is selected to be the base attribute, and the items appearing in base attribute are defined as base items[18].

    This strategy is to ensure that a non-base item can map to multiple base items. If an attribute with fewer items is selected as the base attribute, the probability of mapping several non based items to the same based items will be higher. In such a case, it may make different categorical items get the same numeric value. After the based attributes defined, counting the frequency of co-occurrence among categorical items will be operated in this step. A matrix M with n columns and n rows is used to store this information, where n is the number of categorical items which represents the appearance of co-occurrence between the base items[17,18].

Table 3. Example of a sample dataset

Attribute W	Attribute X	Attribute Y	Attribute Z
A	C	0.1	0.1
A	C	0.3	0.9
A	D	0.8	0.8
B	D	0.9	0.2
B	C	0.2	0.8
B	E	0.6	0.9
A	D	0.7	0.1

$$M = \begin{pmatrix} 4 & 0 & 2 & 2 & 0 \\ 0 & 3 & 1 & 1 & 1 \\ 0 & 0 & 3 & 0 & 0 \\ 0 & 0 & 0 & 3 & 0 \\ 0 & 0 & 0 & 0 & 1 \end{pmatrix}$$

Since the frequencies of co-occurrence between base items and other categorical items is available by retrieving the elements in matrix M, and the similarity between them can be calculated by adopting following equation

$$D_{xy} = \frac{|\, m(X,Y)\,|}{|\, m(X)\,| + |\, m(Y)\,| - |\, m(X,Y)\,|} \tag{5}$$

Where X represents the event that item x appears in the set of objects; Y represents the event that item y appears in the set of objects; $m(X)$ is the set of objects containing item x; $m(X, Y)$ is the set of objects containing both item x and y. In the above equation, when two items always show up together in objects, the similarity between them will be one. If two items never appear together, it will get zero for the similarity measure. The higher value of D_{xy} means the more similar between item x and item y. However, only the values of D_{xy} larger than a threshold will be recorded, or zero will be assigned [23, 31].

6   Performance Measure

The transformation is aimed to achieve a predicate performance of a clustering algorithm trained on a transformed data set as similar as possible to the performance of a cluster trained on the original data set. In this method we are applied a k-means algorithm with bisection method for the prediction a clusters. After suppression of the data set we have analyzed the factors such as clustering accuracy for original and suppression data set, Time Complexity and Information loss. The accuracy is compared with after suppression and before suppression. The result shows that after suppression is efficient than before suppression.

7   Results

In this Work we have taken an adult dataset to computing the various techniques like clustering and bisection methods for predication of clusters. We have adopted the

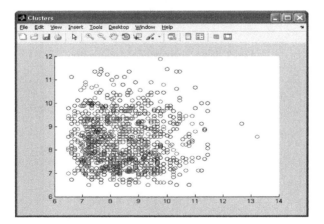

Fig. 3. Clustering Before suppression

suppression for given data set to find the cluster before suppression and after suppression (Fig. 3,4), time complexity(Fig. 5) and accuracy before suppression and after suppression (Fig. 6,7)and information loss(Fig. 8). Data points are better used to find out the different levels for the input.

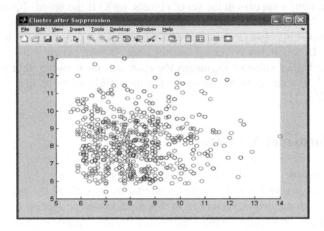

Fig. 4. clustering After suppression

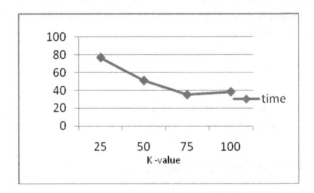

Fig. 5. Time complexity of Suppression

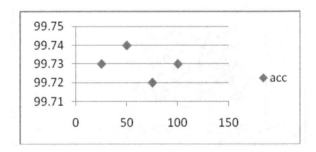

Fig. 6. Accuracy before Suppression

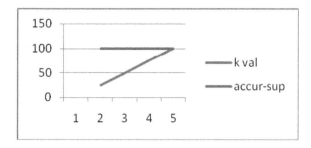

Fig. 7. Accuracy after Suppression

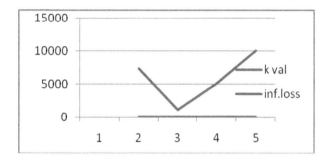

Fig. 8. Information loss

8   Conclusion

This work proposes a clustering algorithm for Analyze the data. Clustering algorithms has been widely applied to various domains to explore the hidden and useful patterns inside data. Because the most collected data in real world contain both categorical and numeric attributes, therefore, in this work we propose a new approach to explore the relationships among categorical items and convert them into numeric values. Moreover, in order to overcome the weaknesses of HAC clustering algorithm, a two-step method integrating Bisection method and k-means clustering algorithms is introduced. Data mining clustering algorithm k-means was implemented and tested on the Anonymized dataset. The proposed approach uses the idea of clustering to minimize information loss and thus ensure good data quality. As part of our approach we develop a suitable metric to estimate the information loss introduced by suppression, which works for both numeric and categorical data.

References

1. Dunham, M.H.: Data Mining- Introductory and Advanced Concepts. Pearson Education (2006)
2. Velmurugan, R., Santhanam, T.: Computational plexity between k-means and k-medoid clustering algorithm for normal and uniform distribution of data points. Journal of Computer Science 6(3), 363–368 (2010); ISSN 1549-3636

3. Borah, S., Ghose, M.K.: Performance analysis of AIM-K-Means and K-means inquality cluster generation. J. Comput. 1, 175–178 (2009)
4. Park, H.S., Lee, J.S., Jun, C.H.: A K-means like algorithm for K-medoids clustering and its performance (2006)
5. Rakhlin, A., Caponnetto, A.: Stability of k-Means clustering. Adv. Neural Inform. Process. Syst. 12, 216–222 (2007)
6. Xiong, H., Wu, J., Chen, J.: K-Means clustering versus validation measures: A data distribution perspective. IEEE Trans. Syst. Man Cybernet. Part B 39, 318–331 (2009)
7. Yuan, F., Meng, Z.H., Zhang, H.X., Dong, C.R.: A New Algorithm to Get the Initial Centroids. In: Proc. of the 3rd International Conference on Machine Learning and Cybernetics, pp. 26–29 (August 2004)
8. Almgren, A.S., Bell, J.B., Colella, P., Howell, L.H.: Adaptive projection method for the incompressible Euler equations. In: Proceedings of the Eleventh AIAA Computational Fluid Dynamics Conference, AIAA, p. 530 (June 1993)
9. Almgren, A.S., Bell, J.B., Crutchfield, W.Y.: Approximate projection methods. 1. Inviscid analysis. SIAM J. Sci. Comput. 22(4) (2000)
10. Almgren, A.S., Bell, J.B., Szymczak, W.G.: A numerical method for the incompressible Navier–Stokes equations based on an approximate projection. SIAM J. Sci. Comput. 17(2) (1996)
11. Baštinec, J., Diblík, J.: Asymptotic formulae for a particular solution of linear non homogeneous discrete equations. Advances in difference equations, IV., Comput. Math.Appl. 45(6-9), 1163–1169 (2003)
12. Baštinec, J., Diblík, J., Růžičková, M.: Initial data generating bounded solutions of linear discrete equations. Opuscula Math. 26(3), 395–406 (2006)
13. Diblík, J.: Discrete retract principle for systems of discrete equations. Comput. Math. Appl. 42(3-5), 515–528 (2001); Advances in Difference equations, III
14. Diblík, J.: Asymptotic behaviour of solutions of discrete equations. Funct. Differ. Equ. (11), 37–48 (2004)
15. Petersen, J., Bodson, M.: Control allocation for systems with coplanar controls. In: In AIAA Guidance, Navigation and Control Conference Proceedings. AIAA Paper 2000-4540 (2000)
16. Petersen, J., Bodson, M.: Fast implementation of direct allocation with extension to coplanar controls. Journal of Guidance, Control, and Dynamics 25(3), 464–473 (2002)
17. Friedman, A., Wolff, R., Schuster, A.: Providing k-Anonymity in Data Mining. Int'l J. Very Large Data Bases 17(4), 789–804 (2008)

A Primitive Solution of Video Super Resolution

A. Geetha Devi[1], T. Madhu[2], and K. Lal Kishore[3]

[1] Department of ECE, Shri Vishnu Engg., College for Women, Bhimavaram-534202, India
[2] Department of ECE, Swarnandhra Inst., of Engg., & Tech., Narasapuram, A.P., India
[3] Department of ECE, JNTUH, Hyderabad, A.P., India
geetha_agd@yahoo.co.in,
tennetimadhu@yahoo.com

Abstract. This paper proposes a primitive technique for improving the low quality video degraded by down sampling, compression and noise. To improve the perceptual quality and Resolution of the video simultaneously, a new algorithm which combines the adaptive regularization and interpolation super resolution is proposed. With the help of adaptive regularization process the quantization error due to compression is removed and the high frequency components like edges are preserved. Simultaneously the resolution is improved by interpolation process. Consequently, the combination of adaptive regularization and interpolation greatly eliminates the compression artifacts and compensates the missing high frequency components yielding better super resolution performance. Experimental results demonstrate that this method provide visually pleasing enlargements for various videos.

Keywords: Super resolution, adaptive regularization, interpolation based super resolution, compression artifacts.

1 Introduction

There is a great demand of band width and storage for the transmission of images/video. Due to these limitations most of the image /video exist in low quality version degraded from the source in many of the applications. The most common degradations include compression errors and down sampling The quality degradation lowers the requirement of storage and band width which makes the access of video practicable and convenient. But these advantages are obtained by degrading the perceptual experience of the viewers and the degradation also leads to information loss which results in blurring, blocking and ringing effects.

There is a very high demand for improving the perceptual quality of the video. Super resolution is one of the technique which improve the spatial resolution and perceptual quality of image /video.SR image video reconstruction algorithms find the relative motion information between the frames of a video sequence and increase the spatial resolution by fusing into a single frame. In doing so it removes the effect of blurring and noise in the Low Resolution Images. In this paper a practical solution for low resolution video is proposed, which includes adaptive regularization with interpolation, demand denoising of the frame.

P.V. Krishna, M.R. Babu, and E. Ariwa (Eds.): ObCom 2011, Part II, CCIS 270, pp. 267–276, 2012.
© Springer-Verlag Berlin Heidelberg 2012

Many single SR reconstruction technique are available in literature[2]-[5] into some categories such as interpolation, reconstruction based, classification based, learning based. In these methods the Low Resolution image taken into accounts are only degraded by down sampling which is not only sufficient in web environment and transmission of video but it also requires the addition of compression errors. Image compression reduce the perceptual quality of the image to a large extent. Hence, By using the methods in the literature compression artifacts will be exaggerated out and quality of the image will be poor.Multi image Super resolution[1] has been assumed a prior distribution of quantization noise and then utilized this knowledge into a Bayesian frame work ,whose performance mainly depends on the frame registration and motion estimation and these methods are not capable of reconstructing high frequency and fast complex objects and motion.

The various sections of this paper are organized as follows: Section 2 demonstrates the single image SR problem formulation. The adaptive regularization control is discussed in section 3. Section 4 is about the propose algorithm and Section 5 presents the experimental results. Section 6 concludes the paper.

2   Compressed Video Super Resolution

The overall implementation of single image Super Resolution algorithm is shown in Fig.1

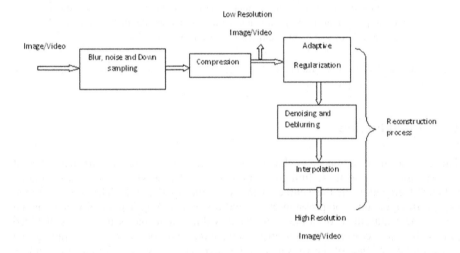

Fig. 1. Overview of the Super Resolution problem Formulation

Suppose X is the original image from which the low resolution observation Y is obtained. The original High Resolution (HR) image is first down sampled and passed through a low pass filter 'h' to form the Low Resolution (LR) observation Yo.

$$Yo=(h*X) \downarrow^{\lambda} \tag{1}$$

where$\downarrow^\lambda$is the decimation operator by a factor λ. Now Yo is compressed to get a LR compressed image

$$Y = Yo + N_Q \qquad (2)$$

where N_Q is the quantization error due to lossy compression like JPEG.

Now the actual input to the SR system is the LR compressed image Y. The first step to be applied on the LR image Y is regularization to obtain the artifact relieved LR image

$$Y^* = P^N(Y) \qquad (3)$$

P(.) denotes the PDE regularization function and the value N repreent the iteration number of regularization.

For each iteration the edge map of the image Y^* is added and then P(.) is again applied to preserve the high frequency edge components. The iteration number N represents the strength of the regularization. Then Y^* is up sampled with scaling factor α to get intermediate HR result X^*

$$X^* = (h \times Y^*) \uparrow \alpha \qquad (4)$$

h is the bicubic interpolation filter transfer function. The final image is $\tilde{X}$ obtained by applying denoising operator. This denoising operator used here is wiener filter.

$$\tilde{X} = (g \times X^*) \qquad (5)$$

2.1 Adaptive Regularization

Regularization is often applied to the ill-posed problem of surface reconstruction. Other methods depend strongly on assumptions of the viewing geometry statistics of the scene. Neither the viewing geometry nor the scene statistics are in general known for an active observer. In dynamic vision, the priori knowledge can be extracted from the reconstruction of the previous scenes. This leads to an adaptive regularization scheme capable of capturing the resulting scene statistics in the camera coordinate system. The knowledge required is the amount of noise in the data, and the statistics of the scene is only varying slowly. It is shown that the adaptive regularization yields results which are comparable to those of the weak string if the input is piecewise planar.

In this the prior distribution is stationary and the same distribution of the derivative at any position on the surface. This is not always an obvious assumption. In many applications, it might expected to find the ground plane in the lower part of image, while the upper part might be expected more or less vertical for the purpose of studying adaptive regularization. In future studies, the non stationary might be taken into account.

2.2 Interpolation

Interpolation is the process of defining a function that takes on specified values at specified points. We all know that two points determine a straight line. More precisely any two points in the plane (x1, y1) and (x2,y2), with x1 = x2, determine a unique

degree polynomial in x whose graph passes through the two points. Given n points in the plane,

$$(xk; yk); k = 1; : : : ; n, \tag{6}$$

with distinct xk's, there is a unique polynomial in x of degree less than n whose graph passes through the points. It is easiest to remember that n, the number of data points is also the number of coefficients, although some of the leading coefficients might be zero, so the degree might actually be less than n.. This polynomial is called the interpolating polynomial because it exactly reproduces the given data

$$P(xk) = yk; k = 1; : : : ; n \tag{7}$$

2.3   Image Deblurring and Image Denoising

In image deblurring, the original, sharp image should be recovered by using a mathematical model of the blurring process. The key issue is that some information on the lost details is indeed present in the blurred image but this information is "hidden" and can only be recovered if we know the details of the blurring process.

Image denoising is an important image processing task, both as a process itself, and as a component in other processes. There are many ways to denoise an image or a set of data exists. The main properties of a good image denoising model are that it will remove noise while preserving edges. Traditionally, linear models have been used. One big advantage of linear noise removal models is the speed. But a back draw of the linear models is that they are not able to preserve edges in a good manner: edges, which are recognized as discontinuities in the image, are smeared out. Nonlinear models on the other hand can handle edges in a much better way than linear models can.

3   The Proposed Video Super Resolution Algorithm

The proposed algorithm includes the following procedure.

  (i)   The first step is that to read the video.
  (ii)   Convert that video in to number of frames.
  (iii) Next step is to read the frames.
  (iv)   Remove the blur of each frame using deblurring techniques..
  (v)   After removing the blur then remove the noise of each frame.
  (vi)   Next step is to find out the edge of each frame and add this edge detected frame to the noise eliminated frame.
  (vii) This procedure continues until the convergence.
  (viii) The bicubic interpolation technique can be used to interpolate the frame.

The number of frame in the video is represented by N. If number of frames reaches N then stop the algorithm else go for the next frame.

3.1   PDE (Partial Differential Equation) Regularization

Among various available regularization techniques, anisotropic PDE's are considered to be one of the best, due to their ability to smooth data while preserving visually salient features in images. A brief restatement of PDE regularization is given below.

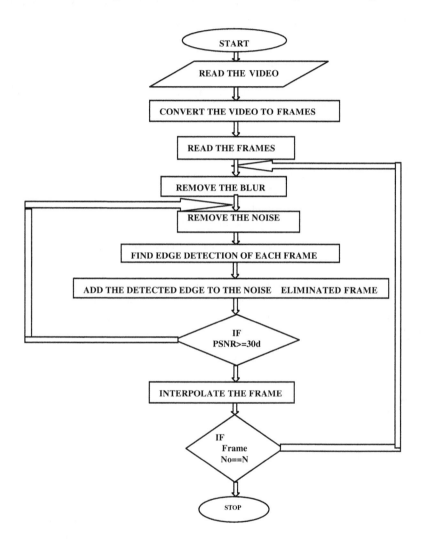

Fig. 2. Flow chart of the proposed video Super Resolution Algorithm

Suppose I is a 2D scalar image, PDE regularization can be formulated as the juxtaposition of two oriented ID heat flows along the gradient direction η and its orthogonal, named the isopoda direction   with corresponding weights cη and c.

$$\frac{\partial I}{\partial t} = c\xi \frac{\partial^2 I}{\partial \xi^2} + c\eta \frac{\partial^2 I}{\partial \eta^2}, \quad \eta = \frac{\nabla I}{\|\nabla I\|}, \quad \xi = \eta^{\perp} \tag{8}$$

Where $\|\nabla I\| = (I_x^2 + I_y^2)$ denotes the image gradient magnitude. The choice of $c\eta$ and c is not determinate only certain properties need to be satisfied.

$$c_\eta = \frac{1}{1 + \|\nabla I\|^2}, \quad c_\xi = \frac{1}{\sqrt{1 + \|\nabla I\|^2}} \tag{9}$$

This is one possible choice inspired from the hyper-surface formulation of the scalar case. In a numerical scheme, the input measurement is regularized iteratively in the nth iteration there is

$$f(I): I_n = I_{n-1} + \lambda \Delta I_n, I_0 = I, n = 1,2,3..., N \tag{10}$$

Where λ is a positive constant controlling the updating step N is the total iteration number, and the image intensity change velocity

The important step in the adaptive regularization is edge detection which is implemented by the canny edge detector algorithm. The steps to be followed.

Step 1: The first step is to filter out any noise in the original image before trying to locate and detect any edges.

Step 2: After smoothing the image and eliminating the noise, the next step is to find the edge strength by taking the gradient of the image. The Sobel operator performs a 2-D spatial gradient measurement on an image. The magnitude or EDGE STRENGTH, of the gradient is then approximated using

$$|G| = \sqrt{(G_x^2 + G_y^2)} \tag{11}$$

Step 3: Finding the edge direction is trivial, once the gradient in the x and y directions are known. The formula for finding the edge direction is

$$\theta = \tan^{-1}(G_y / G_x) \tag{12}$$

Step 4: Once the edge direction is known, the next step is to relate the edge direction to a direction that can be traced in an image.

Step 5: After the edge directions are known, Non-Maximum Suppression Algorithm (NMS Algorithm) now has to be applied.

Step 6: Finally, Hysteresis is used as a means of eliminating streaking. Streaking is the breaking up of an edge contour caused by the operator output fluctuating above and below the threshold.

3.2   Bicubic Interpolation

The interpolation method utilized in this algorithm is bicubic interpolation method.Bicubic interpolation is used for higher order for smoothness. Bicubic interpolation requires the user to specify at each grid point not just the function y(x1, x2), but also the gradients

$$\partial y/\partial x1 \equiv y1$$
$$\partial y/\partial x2 \equiv y2 \text{ and the cross derivative}$$
$$\partial 2y/\partial x1\partial x2 \equiv y12. \tag{13}$$

Then an interpolating function that is cubic in the scaled coordinates t and u can be found, with the following properties:

(i)   The values of the function and the specified derivatives are reproduced exactly on the grid points

(ii)   The values of the function and the specified derivatives change continuously as the interpolating point crosses from one grid square to another.

It is important to understand that nothing in the equations of bicubic interpolation requires you to specify the extra derivatives correctly. The smoothness properties are tautologically "forced," and have nothing to do with the "accuracy" of the specified derivatives.

3.3   Denoising and Deblurring

There are two powerful techniques to reduce the noise level in a signal: Wiener filtering and wavelet thresholding. Wiener filtering is a linear procedure. Wavelet thresholding is nonlinear. Classical versions of both methods tend to blur edges in images. We try to blend these two approaches in order to improve the performance.

Suppose a vector S is corrupted by Gaussian white noise with variance σ2 and mean 0,

$$X = S + \sigma Z \tag{14}$$

Wiener filtering is the following linear procedure:

$$\hat{X} = \sum_m \frac{\beta_m^2}{\beta_m^2 + \sigma^2} \langle X, g_m \rangle g_m \tag{15}$$

Here βm and gm are eigenvalues and eigenvectors of the covariance matrix of S. If S is Gaussian then X is the best mean square estimate of S In order to apply Wiener filter one needs to estimate the covariance matrix of the signal.

4   Results and Discussion

The low resolution video taken for the proposed algorithm contains 120 frames and the frame rate of the video is 15 frame/sec. The Fig.3.shows some selected frames of the video to be recovered. The frames shown here are the frame numbers 8,24,31,40,46,56,64,72,80,100. The Fig.4. shows the super resolved frames of the corresponding low resolution frames using the proposed algorithm.The Peak signal to Noise Ratio (PSNR) is taken as the parameter to converge the process.The iterations will be carried out till the PSNR value reaches 30 db.

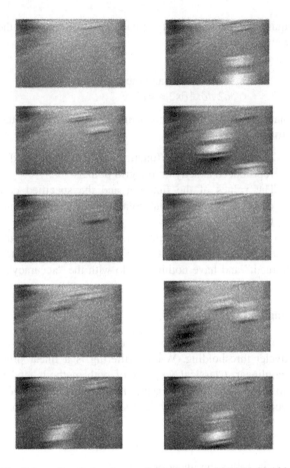

Fig. 3. Low Resolution frames 8,24,31,40,46,56,64,72,80,100

5   Conclusion and Future Work

A robust video SR method, which is competent for simultaneously increasing the resolution and perceptual quality of web image/video with different content and degradation levels. It has the Robust performance and low complexity, this provides a practical enlarge-preview for web images and video, especially those provided by image search engines. If the PSNR value is greater than 30db then the quality of the image is good. Hence the number of iterations can be stopped based on the peak signal to noise ratio video. The algorithm can be extended for the restoration of color video. The removal of compression artifacts and preservation of the edge and color information carries the future scope of the project.

Fig. 4. Super resolved frames 8,24,31,40,46,56,64,72,80,100

References

1. Xiong, Z., Sun, X., Wu, F.: Robust web image/video super resolution. IEEE Trans. Image Processing 19(8), 2017–2028 (2010)
2. Keys, R.G.: Cubic convolution interpolation for digital image processing. IEEE Trans. Acoust., Speech, Signal Process. 29(12), 1153–1160 (1981)

3. Allebach, J., Wong, P.W.: Edge-directed interpolation. In: Proc. IEEE Int. Conf. Image Processing, vol. 3, pp. 707–710 (1996)
4. Xin, L., Orchard, M.T.: New edge-directed interpolation. IEEE Trans. Image Processing 10(10), 1521–1527 (2001)
5. Xiong, Z., Sun, X., Wu, F.: Fast directional image interpolator with difference projection. In: Proc. IEEE Int. Conf. Multimedia & Expo., pp. 81–84 (2009)
6. Irani, M., Peleg, S.: Motion analysis for image enhancement: Resolution, Occlusion and transparency. J. Vis. Commun. Image Represent. 4, 324–335 (1993)
7. Morse, B.S., Schwartzwald, D.: Image magnification using level-set reconstruction. In: Proc. IEEE Conf. Computer Vision and Pattern Recognition, pp. 333–340 (2001)
8. Atkins, C.B., Bouman, C.A., Allebach, J.P.: Optimal image scaling using pixel classification. In: Proc. IEEE Int. Conf. Image Processing, p. 864 (2001)
9. Baker, S., Kanade, T.: Limits on super-resolution and how to break them. IEEE Trans. Pattern Anal. Mach. Intell. 2(9), 1167–1183 (2002)
10. Liu, C., Shum, H.Y., Zhang, C.S.: A two-step approach to hallucinating faces: Global parametric model and local non-parametric model. In: Proc. IEEE Conf. Computer Vision and Pattern Recognition, pp. 192–198 (2001)
11. http://www.youtube.com/
12. http://www.kodak.com/digitalImaging/samples/imageIntro.shtml

Designing of Power Optimized Bypassing Array Multiplier in Nanometer Technology

Ravi Nirlakalla[1,*], Bhaskara Rao Boothuru[1], Subba Rao Thota[2],
M. Rajasekhar Babu[3], Jayachandra Prasad Talari[1], and P. Venkata Krishna[3]

[1] RGM Engg College (Autonomous), JNT University Anantapur,
Nandyal, Andhra Pradesh-518501, India
[2] Sri Krishnadevaraya University, Anantapur, Andhra Pradesh 515003, India
[3] School of Computer Science & Engineering, VIT, Vellore 632014, India
{ravi2728,bhaskararaobrd}@gmail.com

Abstract. Multi-threshold CMOS is an increasingly popular circuit approach that enables high performance and low power operation. In this paper Reverse Body Bias (RBB) with high-Vth is used to reduce the leakage power in nanometer technology for the proposed array multiplier with CSA design. The results are carried out by H-Spice for 90nm and 65nm BSIM model files. MTCMOS circuits have shown good results than the conventional circuits.

Keywords: Bypassing Multiplier, MTCMOS, low power.

1 Introduction

The major emphases of the VLSI designers were performance and miniaturization. With the explosive growth in portable computing and wireless communication in the last few years, power has a critical issue among the issues of power, speed and area. Problems with heat removal and cooling are worsening because the magnitude of power dissipated per unit area is growing with scaling. Years ago, portable battery-powered applications were characterized by low computational requirement. Nowadays, these applications require the same computational performance as non-portable applications. It is important to prolong the battery life as much as possible. Need of more applications on a single processor will increase the number of transistors on a chip and cause to increase power consumption [1], [2].

To address these issues directly, it is essential to understand the different types and sources of power dissipation in digital Complementary Metal Oxide Semiconductor (CMOS) circuits. The reason for choosing the CMOS technology is that it is currently the most dominant digital IC implementation technology.

Multiplication is an essential arithmetic operation for common DSP (Digital Signal Processors) and Microprocessor applications. To achieve high execution speed, parallel array multipliers are widely used. These multipliers tend to consume most of

---

* Corresponding author.

P.V. Krishna, M.R. Babu, and E. Ariwa (Eds.): ObCom 2011, Part II, CCIS 270, pp. 277–284, 2012.

the power in DSP computations due to their circuit complexcity, and thus power-efficient multipliers are very important for the design of low-power DSP systems [1], [2].

The organization of the paper is as follows: Section 1 starts with introduction and the sources of power consumption in CMOS circuits. CSA, Bypassing multipliers with different designs are explained in Section 2. The leakage power sources and the reducing technique i.e MTCMOS with high Vth is discussed in Section 3. Results and discussions and Conclusion of the paper were given in Sections 4and 5 respectively.

1.1   Total Power Consumption in Digital CMOS Circuits

There are four sources of power dissipation in digital CMOS circuits[3], [4], [5], as describe in equation 1.1.

$$P = P_{\text{dynamic-switching}} + P_{\text{short-circuit}} + P_{\text{static-biasing}} + P_{\text{leakage}} \qquad (1.1)$$

where P is the total power dissipation, $P_{\text{dynamic-switching}}$ is the dynamic switching power, $P_{\text{short-circuit}}$ is the short-circuit power, $P_{\text{static-biasing}}$ is the static biasing power and P_{leakage} is the leakage power.

i. Dynamic switching power dissipation is caused by charging capacitances in the circuit.

ii. Short–circuit power is the second source of total power dissipation described in equation (1.1). During a transient on input signal, there will be a period in which both NMOS and PMOS transistor will conduct simultaneously, causing a current flow through the direct path existing between power supply and ground terminals. This effect usually happens for very small intervals.

iii.Ideally, in the steady state of CMOS circuits there is no static power dissipation. This is the most attractive characteristic of CMOS technology. However, the actual operation of CMOS circuits is slightly different. Degraded voltage levels feeding CMOS gates and pseudo-NMOS logic family, present a current flow from the power supply to ground nodes. This flow is known as static biasing current.

iv.Static current that flows from Vdd to ground nodes, without degraded inputs or in pseudo-NMOS logic family is known as leakage power. It is the main factor responsible for power dissipation during idle mode in standard CMOS gates. In past technologies the magnitude of leakage current was low and usually neglected. But as the devices have been being scaled to achieve higher density, performance, and lower dynamic power consumption, the leakage current in the nanometer regime is becoming a significant portion of power dissipation in CMOS circuits.

1.2   Multi Threshold CMOS Logic

Low-power design methodologies range from the device/process level to the algorithmic level. Of all these techniques, lowering the supply voltage (VDD) are the one that significantly reduces the power consumption because of the quadratic relationship between the supply voltage and the dynamic power consumption. To compensate for the performance loss due to a lower supply voltage, a transistor's threshold voltage (Vth) should also be reduced. However, this causes an exponential increase in the subthreshold leakage current [6], [7], [8]. Therefore, an important research area today is to develop circuit techniques to reduce the subthreshold leakage currents that are caused by the reduced Vth . Multi-Threshold Complementary Metal Oxide Semiconductor (MTCMOS) is an effective circuit-level technique that provides a high performance and low leakage power design strategy [9]. Multi-threshold CMOS was developed in order to reduce the leakage current during idle modes by providing a high threshold "gating" transistor in series with the low Vt circuit transistors.

2   Bypassing Technique

Dynamic power consumption can be reduced by bypassing method when the multiplier has more zeros in input data. To perform isolation, transmission gates can be used, as ideal switches with small power consumption, propagation delay similar to the inverter and small area [10]. To study the proposed design we have consider column bypassing multiplier in which columns of adders are bypassed. In this multiplier, the operations in a column can be disabled if the corresponding bit in the multiplicand is 0. The advantage of this multiplier is it eliminates the extra correcting circuit [11].

The column bypassing multiplier (CBM) only needs two tri-state gates and one multiplexer in a adder cell. When y_j is 0 then the corresponding diagonal cells are functioning unnecessarily. In all these cells the partial products $x_i \times y_j$ and the carry inputs are zero for $i = 0,1,\ldots,n-1$ and this chain does not contribute to the formation of the product. Consequently, the sum output of the above cell can bypass this unimportant diagonal with the use of transmission gates. To achieve all of the above we can replace the Full Adder with the cell called the Full Adder Bypassing (FAB) cell. The transmission gates in the FAB cell lock the inputs of the full adder to prevent any transitions when $y = 0$, and a multiplexer propagates the sum input to the sum output. When $y = 1$, the sum output of the full adder is passed [12].

In the proposed method, all the partial product rows of the multiplier are same as that of the conventional multiplier except the final addition to add carry bits. The final adder which is used to add carries and sums of the multiplier in the conventional is removed in this method. The carries of the multiplier at the final stage is carefully added to the inputs of next column of the multiplier as shown in the Figure 1. Here the carries of the multiplier are not neglected. The carry of the fourth column of the 4x4 multiplier is given to the input of the fifth column instead of zero. The full adder at the top of the fifth column have only two input data, so the third is considered as zero in conventional multiplier. But in the proposed the carry of the fourth column is given to the input of the fifth column first adder. The use of a full adder is to add given inputs. The full adder of Ripple Carry Adder (RCA) can do the same functionality at the final addition stage. That is why the carry of the fourth column is fed to the input of the first adder in the fifth column. In that adder the carry merges with the two inputs.

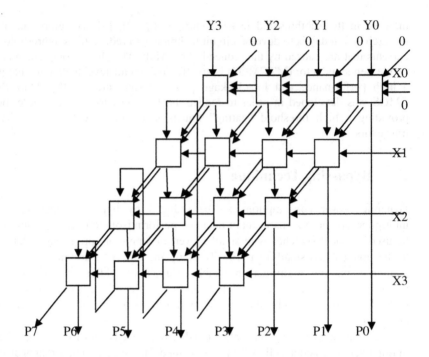

Fig. 1. Bypassing Multiplier with out RCA (white box represents FAB cells)

Then the carry of the fifth column is forwarded to the input of first adder of the sixth column so on. In this multiplier the carry of the seventh column of the adder is not neglected, it is considered as Most Significant Bit (MSB) of the multiplier. Due to elimination of four full adders at the final addition stage power and area can be trade off in the proposed design.

3   Leakage Current Mechanisms

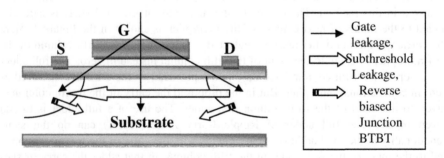

Fig. 2. Leakage current from different parts

For nanometer devices, leakage current is dominated by subthreshold leakage, gateoxide tunneling leakage, and reverse-bias pn-junction leakage. Those three major leakage current mechanisms are illustrated in Figure 2.1. There are other leakage components, like gate induced drain leakage (GIDL) and punch through current, but those can be neglected in normal mode of operation [14].

3.1.1 Subthreshold Current

Supply voltage has been scaled down to keep dynamic power consumption under control. To maintain a high drive current capability, the threshold voltage has to be scaled too. However, the threshold voltage scaling results in increasing subthreshold leakage currents. Subthreshold current occurs between drain and source when transistor is operating in weak inversion region, i.e., the gate voltage is below the threshold voltage.

3.1.2 Gate Tunneling Current

The aggressive device scaling in nanometer regime increases short channel effects such as DIBL and Vth roll-off. To control the short channel effects, oxide thickness must also become thinner in each technology generation. Aggressive scaling of the oxide thickness, in turn, gives rise to high electric field, resulting in a high direct-tunneling current through transistor gate insulator.

3.1.3 Band-to-Band Tunneling Current

The MOS transistor has two pn junctions – drain and source to well junctions. These two pn junctions are typically reverse biased, causing a pn junction leakage current. This current is a function of junction area and doping concentration. When n and p regions are heavily doped, band-to-band tunneling (BTBT) leakage dominates the reverse biased pn junction leakage mechanism.

3.2 Leakage Reduction Techniques

In CMOS circuit, the total power dissipation includes dynamic and static components during the active mode of operation. In the case of standby mode, the power dissipation is due to leakage currents. According to leakage mechanisms described in previous section, leakage power increases dramatically in the scaled devices. Particularly, with reduction of threshold voltage, to achieve high performance, leakage power becomes a significant component of total power consumption in both active and standby modes of operation.

The original propose of the substrate biasing was utilized to reduce sub-threshold leakage in standby mode for portable applications. Reverse body bias can reduce circuit leakage by three orders of magnitude in a 0.35µm CMOS technology [15], [16]. However, more recent data shows that the effectiveness of RBB to lower $Ioff$ decreases as technology scales due to the exponential increase in band-to-band tunneling leakage at the source/substrate and drain/substrate pn junctions . Moreover, smaller channel length with technology scaling and lower channel doping (to reduce *Vth*) worsen the short channel effect and diminish the body effect. This, in turns, weakens the *Vth* modulation capability of RBB.

4   Results and Discussions

The conventional and proposed array multipliers are designed with 14 –T full adders. The power, delay and energy delay product (EDP) of different adders are given in Table 1. Among four adders given in Table 1. 16-T shown good efficiency, the efficiency of 14-T full adder is little less than 16-T. Because of two less transistors 14-T has chosen to design the multipliers. The results were carried out by H-Spice at 2.0V of Vdd and 3.0V of RBB.

To reduce the leakage power in nanometer technology, substrates of pMOS devices are reverse biased (reverse body biasing) and maintained high Vth in 1-bit 14-T full adder cell. To study the power efficiency of Conventional full adder with MTCMOS technique, the circuits were synthesized with 90nm and 65nm BSIM technology files. The paper aims on power consumption, so high Vth is used to reduce the leakage power which decreases the performance of the design. That is why the methods slightly increased the performance of the design shown in Table 2. For 90nm 14-T full adder MTCMOS shown 5.37% of power saving. In 65nm the propagation delay slightly increased.

A new method was proposed [13] for bypassing multiplier in which the vector merging final adder has been removed and the carries were carefully added. The proposed method shown good efficiency than conventional bypassing array multiplier given in Table 3 which is synthesized with 90nm and 65nm technology files.

MTCMOS technique is applied for both Conventional Array with Carry Save Addition (CSA) and Array (CSA) with no Ripple Carry Adder (RCA). The results of these circuits are given in Table 4. MTCMOS Array multiplier and Array with No RCA has shown 34.27%, 135% power efficiency to 90nm technology respectively.

In order to decrease further the total power of Bypassing array multiplier with and with out RCA the MTCMOS is applied. For 90nm, conventional bypassing with MTCMOS has shown 200%, bypassing without RCA showed 233% power efficiency shown in Table 5. The Bypassing multiplier not only reduce the dynamic power due to switching activity also reduces leakage power by the MTCMOS technique.

Table 1. Performance comparison of different full adders

Adder Type	Power (watts)	Delay (Sec)	PDP	EDP (js)
TG-CMOS	5.07E-5	9.36E-10	4.74E-14	4.44E-23
TFA	3.05E-5	2.51E-09	7.65E-14	1.92E-22
14-T	2.33E-5	8.97E-10	2.09E-14	1.87E-23
16-T	1.36E-5	5.07E-10	6.89E-15	3.49E-24

Table 2. Performance of full adder with technologies

| Technology | 1-bit 14-T Full adder | | | |
| | Power(watts) | | Delay(sec) | |
	Conven	MTCMOS	Conven	MTCMOS
90nm	9.80E-8	9.30E-8	1.0062E-9	1.0062E-9
65nm	1.17E-7	1.12E-7	1.0075E-9	1.0071E-9

Table 3. Comparison of Bypassing Multiplier with Conventional

Technology	Bypassing Array Multiplier type	Total Power (Watts)	Prop- Delay (Sec)	Energy Delay Product (EDP) JS
90nm	Conventional	6.99E-4	2.70E-09	5.09E-21
	Proposed	6.13E-4	8.68E-10	4.61E-22
65nm	Conventional	2.57E-4	3.36E-09	2.90E-21
	Proposed	2.22E-4	2.41E-09	1.29E-21

Table 4. Power comparison of Conventional multiplier with MTCMOS

| Technology | 4x4 Array Multiplier | | | |
| | CSA | | CSA No RCA | |
	Conven	MTCMOS	Conven	MTCOMS
90nm	3.80E-4	2.83E-4	3.28E-4	1.39E-4
65nm	2.05E-4	1.43E-4	1.66E-4	5.77E-5

Table 5. Power comparison of Conventional Bypassing multiplier with MTCMOS

| Technology | 4x4 Bypassing Array Multiplier | | | |
| | CSA | | CSA No RCA | |
	Conven	MTCMOS	Conven	MTCMOS
90nm	6.99E-4	3.99E-4	6.13E-4	3.80E-4
65nm	2.05E-4	1.21E-4	1.66E-4	1.19E-4

5   Conclusion

Bypassing multiplier reduce the dynamic power due bypassing the blocks when the input of the block is zero. The removal of vector merging final adder also decrease the dynamic power of the bypassing multiplier. Still to reduce the total power of the circuit MTCOMS was used with Reverse Body biasing (RBB) technique. This technique is applied to Array with CSA and Bypassing with and without RCA is applied. The method had shown good power efficiency than the conventional circuits in nanometer technology. High Vth was used to obtain the good results in the designs.

References

1. Shiue, W.-T., Chakrabarti, C.: Memory Exploration for Low Power, Embedded Systems. In: 36th ACM/IEEE Design Automation Conference, New Orleans, pp. 140–145 (June 1999)
2. Shiue, W.-T., Chakrabarti, C.: Low Power Scheduling with Resources Operating at Multiple Voltages. IEEE Transactions on Circuit and Systems Part II: Analog and Digital Signal Processing 47(6), 536–543 (2000)
3. Chandrakasan, A.P., Sheng, S., Brodersen, R.W.: Low-power CMOS digital design. IEEE Journal of Solid-State Circuits 27(4), 473–484 (1992)
4. Devadas, S., Keutzer, K., White, J.: Estimation of power dissipation in CMOS combinational circuits using Boolean function manipulation. IEEE Transactions on Computer-Aided Design 11(3), 373–383 (1992)
5. Kao, J., Chandrakasan, A., Antoniadis, D.: Transistor Sizing Issues and Tool For Multi-Threshold CMOS Technology. In: ACM Proceedings, DAC 1997 (1997)
6. Douseki, T., Shigematsu, S., Yamada, J., Harada, M., Inokawa, H., Tsuchiya, T.: A 0.5-V MTCMOS/SIMOX Logic Gate. IEEE Journal of Solid-State Circuits 32(10) (1997)
7. Liu, W.: Techniques for Leakage Power Reduction in Nanoscale Circuits: A Survey. IMM Technical Report (4) (2007)
8. Gu, R.X., Elmasry, M.I.: Power Dissipation Analysis and Optimization of Deep Submicron CMOS Digital Circuits. IEEE Journal of Solid State Circuits 31(5), 707–713 (1996)
9. Mutoh, S., et al.: 1-V Power Supply High-speed Digital Circuit Technology with Multi-threshold Voltage CMOS. IEEE Journal of Solid State Circuits 30(8), 847–854 (1995)
10. Al Zahrani, A., Bailey, A., Fu, G., Di., J.: Glitch-Free Design for Multi-Threshold CMOS NCL Circuits. In: ACM Proceedings of GLIVLSI 2009, May 10-12 (2009)
11. Bekiaris, D., Economakos, G., Pekmestzi, K.: A Mixed Style Multiplier Architecture for Low Dynamic and Leakage Power Dissipation. In: IEEE Conference, pp. 258–261 (May 2010)
12. Wen, M.-C., Wang, S.-J., Lin, Y.-N.: Low-power parallel multiplier with column bypassing. Electronics Letters 41(10) (2005)
13. Kuo, K.-C., Chou, C.W.: Low Power and High Speed multiplier design with row bypassing and parallel architecture. Microelectronics Journal 41, 639–650 (2010)
14. Ravi, N., Subba Rao, T., Jayachandra Prasad, T.: Performance Evaluation of Bypassing Array Multiplier with Optimized Design. International Journal of Computer Applications (IJCA) 28(5), 1–5 (2011)
15. Agarwal, A., et al.: Leakage Power Analysis and Reduction: Models, Estimation and Tools. Proc. IEEE 152(3), 353–368 (2005)
16. Keshavarzil, A., et al.: Effectiveness of Reverse Body Bias for Leakage Control in Scaled Dual Vt CMOS ICs. In: Proceedings of Int. Symp. Low Power Electronics and Desining, ISLPED1998, SIGDA 2001, pp. 207–212. ACM, New York (1998)
17. Butzen, P.F.: Leakage Current Modeling in Submicrometer CMOS Complex Gates, Master thesis (September 2007)

Telecine Anti – Encoder: An Anti Piracy System in Movie Theatres

Arun Prashanth, Nazim Fazil, and Madhusudhanan

Department of Information Technology,
Sri Sairam Engineering College,
West Tambaram, Chennai-44, India
isaiarun@yahoo.com, {nazimfazil1,madhusudhanan.sairam}@gmail.com

Abstract. In recent scenario, piracy is ruling over the film industry. Screening movies are recorded with small cameras and pirated CDs are produced (TC Rip /TeleCine rip). To overcome this problem the concept of "Anti Piracy System in Cinema Theatres" is implemented. In this the piracy of movies is controlled by making the videos that is screened a non-recordable one. The Standard Frame rate (Frames per Second or FPS) of videos that is screened is 24frames/sec. Here the concept is that to *vary the frame rate* in such a way that no cameras can record it. The frame rate of video that is screened is changed with FPS converter software applications. It should lie in a range of values which is lesser or greater than the cameras recording Frame rate. Due to this difference between the frame rate of screening video and cameras recording, the video becomes non recordable by the cameras. Continuous waves or black frames will disturb the recording.

Keywords: FPS(FramePersecond), Distortion of frames, FRC(Frame Rate Converter), Frames, Video Splitter.

1   Introduction

The unauthorized use or reproduction of copyrighted material is known as piracy. Now-a-days, one of the biggest problems faced by cine industry is piracy of movies. Screening movies are recorded with small cameras and pirated CDs are produced (**TC Rip /TeleCine rip**) and sold soon after the release or even on the same day the movies are released. With lack of awareness, people also watch the movies in home rather moving out to theatres. This creates a huge loss for producers and theatre owners. To overcome the problem of piracy in movie theatres we are implementing our concept *"Anti Piracy System in Cinema Theatres"*.DVD can take several months to be sold in market. First it has to finish its run in the theater and then be transferred to DVD for sell to the public. But pirates are taking shortcuts and getting the movie early. Movie piracy is a serious crime and it is one that is affecting the movie industry and population tremendously. Movie piracy is very wide spread. Chances are if you live in a big metropolitan area you have seen people set up tables on the sidewalk selling movies. There is a high chance that many of them are pirated copies. Other people will go to share sites and download movies from the website. A person will

P.V. Krishna, M.R. Babu, and E. Ariwa (Eds.): ObCom 2011, Part II, CCIS 270, pp. 285–291, 2012.
© Springer-Verlag Berlin Heidelberg 2012

upload a movie and then others can share the file. Before long it has spread to too many different people.

Table 1. Types of RIP

Type	Label	Rarity
Cam	*CAMRip* *CAM*	Common; Quality issues make this an unpopular format
Telesync	*TS* *TELESYNC* *PDVD*	Very common
Telecine	*TC* *TELECINE*	Fairly rare; losing popularity due to R5 releases
Digital Distribution Copy	*DDC*	Extremely Rare
DVD-Rip	*DVDRip*	Very common
DVD-R	*DVDR, DVD-Full, Full-Rip, ISO rip,lossless rip, untouched rip, DVD-5/DVD-9*	Very common
HDTV or DS Rip	*TVRip* *DSR* *PDTV* *HDTV* *DVBRip* *DTHRip*	Very common
VODRip	*VODRip* *VODR*	Common, becoming more common

Movie piracy is against the law and is punishable with jail time and/or fines. It is illegal to make the pirated copies and it is illegal to buy them or download them from the computer. Even going to a website that does not require the people to download the movie butcamera's recording rate. Hence, they are recorded and pirated in CDs and DVDs.

2   Existing Technology

At present, the movies are projected by digital projectors with the playback and resolution of 4K (4096×2160) or **8.85 MP at 24 frames per second** .These screened movies are pirated by taking the cameras with them secretly or the movies are recorded in mobile phones cameras. The screening rate of projector in cinema theaters is 24 frames per second and this matches with the camera's recording rate. Hence, they are recorded and pirated in CDs and DVDs. Cam releases were the early attempts at movie piracy which are implemented by taping the on-screen projection of a movie in a cinema. This enabled groups to pirate movies which were in their theatrical period . But because these releases often suffered distinctly low quality and it is hard to do because people may notice, alternative methods were sought. Below is a table of pirated movie release types along with respective sources, ranging from the lowest quality to the highest. Scene rules define in which format and way each release type is to be packaged and distributed.

Fig. 1. Video Distortion

3   Objective and Copyright

The main objective is to **stop piracy** in movie theatres for the benefit of cine industry and mainly to safeguard our government laws. Besides protecting creative potential of the society, copyright contributes to a nation on economic-front as well . The copyright based industries together generate huge employment in the country of its origin. The national exchequer benefit from the contribution made by these industries in the form of excise duty, sales tax, income tax etc. from the production and sale of copyrighted products. Given the natural demand for such products from across the national boundaries exports help consolidate country's foreign exchange reserves position. there is a general consensus on the activities that come under copyright industries. It include printing and publishing of books, newspapers, journals & other periodicals, production and sale of audio products (Cassettes/CDs), production & distribution of cinemas, videos and cables, creation of computer softwares & databases and their distribution, radio and television broadcasting, advertising, photography, dramatic and musical performances etc. The total copyright industries taken together employed more than 5.7 million workers. India is the largest audio cassette market in the world in terms of number of units sold. In 1996, India sold more than 350 million audio cassettes & CDs and the industry's sales turnover stood at Rs.105,605 million.

4   Proposed System

The proposal here is to vary the frame rate of the video that is to be screened to a range that makes the recording of it impossible by the digital cameras. This is based on the phenomenon of *"Frame rate mismatch"* between projector and digital cameras. When the frame rate of the screening video is higher than the recording ability of the digital camera, the recording is affected through distortion. That is black waves jumps in video occurs making the recording video inviewable.

The proposal Anti-piracy system is composed of the following modules:

4.1   Video Splitter

Video splitter is a software aplication that is used to split the video files. The main purpose of splitting the video into multiple parts is that, each part can be converted with different FPS. This is done because if the pirate try to change and set the recording frame rate of his camera to match the screening video's frame rate, only the currentlty screening video part can be recorded without distortion. Such as trakAxPC Pro,Avs Video editor etc.

4.2   Frame Rate Converter

This piece of software that converts frame rates on progressive streams. It uses the mpeg tools which simply replicates or eliminates frames, It calculates intermediates frames by interpolating the motion between frames, using an MPEG-style motion compensation algorithm. This frame rate conversion can be processed using the hardware such as HD/SD UFM 30FRC.

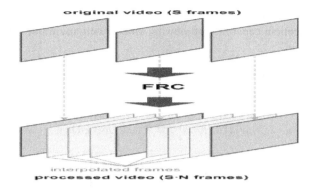

Fig. 2. The Process of **FrameRateConversion**

4.3   Video Queuer

Video Queuer arranges the videos that are with different frame rates according to the splitted order. Hence just like the **playlist in media players**, a queue of video files is created and they are sent to Projector in ordered fashion which appears in the screen. For video queuing the software applications such as Numark Cue Professional^{TM},PreScan^{TM} etc can be used for video queuing.

4.4   Movie Projector

Conventional movie projector is a device that continuously moves film along a path so that each **frame** of the film is stopped for a fraction of a second in front of a light source. The light source provides extremely bright illumination that casts the image on the film through a **lens** onto a **screen**. This has been evolved to digital projectors in which no films are implemented but digital video files are streamed directly on the screen. HDMI output with 1080p high quality videos with **24 frames per second** can be projected direct from a computer to the screen with higher clarity than the film roll technology. Since digital media is committed the frame rate of the video can be controlled and changed easily which is not possible in older film technology(fixed 24frames/second).

The key element in a projector is the light source. **Carbon arc** lamps have been used since the early 1900s but have a very short life. **Xenon** bulbs are the most commonly used lamps today. Xenon is a rare gas with certain properties that make it especially suited for use in projectors.

5   Methodology

The original source video is passed to the video splitter which extracts the audio and video separately. Then the video sources are splitted in different frame rate with the help of FRC(Frame Rate Converter) which can range high or low between the normal 24 frames per second. Then these splitted files are queued using the video queuer .The video queuer streams the video to the projector for appearing in the big screen with different frame rates. This variation does not affect the human viewing since human eyes have an excellent capability of viewing videos with any frame rate without any hindrance.

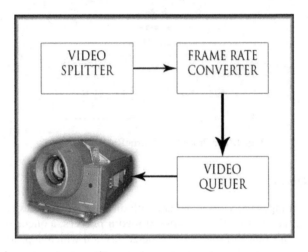

Fig. 3. Basic idea of anti piracy system

6   Workstation Specification

A Workstation system with minimum following specifications are required.

CPU speed : 2.66GHz processor
RAM   : 3GB of memory
Operating Systems: Win XP/ Win VISTA/Windows 7/Mac
Hard Disk: 160GB (minimum)
Softwares :Video splitter with queuer
Hardwares :Frame Rate Converter

NOTE: The access to the workstation system must be authenticated securely to avoid piracy from Hard Disk.

7   Conclusion

Thus the system provides reliable guiding information during the process of projection. A special type of projector must be developed by any authorized authorities which will support the various frame rate and projects the movie without any intensity variations in human eye viewing.Piracy is not a good thing for any content owner, but rather than the movie industry giving consumers what they want, convenience and choice, they choose to ignore the demands in the market. Rather than embrace digital distribution of the movies.

Acknowledgment. We would like to express our gratitude to all those who helped us complete this thesis. We want to thank the Dept of Information Technology, Sri SaiRam Engineering College and our HOD Prof **Dr.T.Sheela** M.S.,Ph.D., for giving us the permission to commence this thesis in the first instance, do the necessary research work and to use the departmental data.

References

1. Movie piracy. Houston Press
2. Film Piracy Issue! an issue from the 1970s on 16 mm Film Collectors being busted by the FBI, courtesy of Science Monster.Net
3. Strauss, B.: Film Piracy Heads North of Border. Daily News (April 7, 2009)
4. Piracy isn't just about price. O'Reilly Radar
5. Geist Canadian-backed report says music, movie, and software piracy is a market failure, not a legal one - thestar.com
6. Video CD: American Pie. Archived from the original. ISO News (February 11, 2005)
7. Wes Finley-Price – CNN.com Webmaster. Pirated copy of District 9 posted online (November 9, 2009) http://scitech.blogs.cnn.com (retrieved February 11, 2009)
8. The 2009 DVDR releasing standards. THE.2009.DVDR.RELEASING.STANDARDS-TDRS2K9 (2009)
9. The 2009 DVDR releasing standards. THE.2009.DVDR.RELEASING.STANDARDS-TDRS2K9 (2009)
10. AfterDawn.com – Guides - Introduction to video Media Splitter

A Novel FPGA Based Reconfigurable Architecture for Image Color Space Conversion

M.C. Hanumantharaju[1], G.R. Vishalakshi[1], Srinivas Halvi[2], and S.B. Satish[3]

[1] Department of Information Science & Engineering
[2] Department of Medical Electronics
[3] Department of Electronic & Communication Engineering,
Dayananda Sagar College of Engineering, Bangalore, India
(mchanumantharaju,vishala.gr2005,satishsbhai)@gmail.com

Abstract. In this paper, a novel Field Programmable Gate Array (FPGA) based reconfigurable architecture for image color space conversion is presented. The color space conversion plays an important role in preprocessing stage of digital image processing. Although it is possible to process an image in RGB color space the resulting image may not be processed optimally. The hardware implementation of algorithms like image enhancement, image compression, and communication techniques use color spaces such as Hue-Saturation-Value (HSV), Luminance-Chrominance blue-Chrominance red (YCbCr) and YUV etc. Therefore, it is desired to have an efficient and high speed architectures for color space conversion. The proposed scheme implements two novel architectures for color space conversion suitable for FPGA's and Application Specific Integrated Circuits (ASICs). The architectures developed exploits high degrees of pipelining and parallel processing in order to achieve real time performance. The hardware realization of color space conversion is based on Register Transfer Level (RTL) compliant Verilog code and is implemented using Xilinx XC2V2000-6bf957 FPGA device. The experimental results show that proposed approaches exhibit better performances when compared with the other existing implementations.

Keywords: Field Programmable Gate Arrays, Color Space Conversion, Hue-Saturation-Value, YCbCr.

1 Introduction

The color space [1] or color models or color systems provides a standard method of defining and representing colors. In the literature, there exist a many color space converters and most of them represent each color as a point in a three dimension (3D) coordinate system [2]. Further, color space selection and its optimization depends on specific application [3]. The three most popular color models are RGB (used in computer graphics); YIQ, YCbCr, and YUV (used in video systems); CMYK (used in color printing). All color spaces can be derived from the RGB information supplied by devices such as cameras and scanners. Jung et al. [4] proposed a visual tracking system based on adaptive color histograms.

P.V. Krishna, M.R. Babu, and E. Ariwa (Eds.): ObCom 2011, Part II, CCIS 270, pp. 292–301, 2012.

The RGB to HSV conversion architecture developed in this work is computationally complex. In addition, the latency achieved in the conversion process is not satisfactory. Ming et al. [5] has developed high performance architecture for enhancement of video stream captured under non-uniform lightning conditions. The RGB to HSV conversion adapted in this scheme use log-domain in order to avoid complex division process. However, this technique also increases the latency of the conversion process. Further, the HSV to RGB conversion adopted in this scheme is not an efficient from computation point of view. The RGB to YCbCr color space conversion proposed by Stefano Marsi et al. [6] had consumed a logic cells of 901 (0.75%). Iakovidou et al. [7] has been used YCbCr color space for image enhancement provides a satisfactory results. However, the algorithm is capable of processing 2.5 Mpixels at frame rate of 25 frames per sec. Although it is possible to enhance or compress a digital real color image by applying existing gray-level image processing algorithms to each red (R), green (G) and blue (B) channel, the resulting image may not be enhanced or compressed optimally . In addition, the algorithm is applied to individual channels without considering the correlation between R, G, and B component of the image. RGB color space has weakness in representing shading effects or rapid illumination changing [8]. In order to solve this problem, we consider converting an image from RGB space to other spaces [9].

This paper is organized as follows: Section 2 describes the review of color space conversion and its implementation issues. Section 3 gives brief details of hardware implementation. Section 4 provides experimental results and comparative study. Finally conclusion is presented in Section 5.

2   Color Space Conversion: A Review

Numerous researchers have proposed different color models, each oriented toward supporting a specific task or solving a particular problem [10]. Two popular color spaces widely used by many researchers are described below.

2.1   HSV Color Space

The HSV color space was defined by Smith (1978) and is based on cylindrical coordinates. The HSV [11] model defines a color space in terms of three constituent components. Hue represents type of color such as red, blue, or yellow that ranges from 0 to 360 degrees. Saturation is the vibrancy of color that ranges from 0 to 100 % . Value (intensity) is the brightness of the color that ranges from 0 to 100 % [4]. HSV color space, also known as hex cone color model; however, the human color space is a horseshoe-shaped cone [12]. In this work, hardware realization of RGB to HSV conversion[13] and vice-versa has been chosen since it offers satisfactory results for color image enhancement algorithms.

The digital hardware realization of RGB to HSV color space conversion is based on the Eqns. (1) to (3). The hue (H) component of HSV color space can be obtained from R, G and B channels using Eqn. (1)

$$H = \begin{cases} 0 + \frac{43 \times |G-B|}{Max(R,G,B)-Min(R,G,B)}, & \text{if } Max(R, G, B) = R \\ 85 + \frac{43 \times |B-R|}{Max(R,G,B)-Min(R,G,B)}, & \text{if } Max(R, G, B) = G \\ 171 + \frac{43 \times |R-G|}{Max(R,G,B)-Min(R,G,B)}, & \text{if } Max(R, G, B) = B \end{cases} \tag{1}$$

where $Max(R, G, B)$ is the maximum of three red, green, and blue pixel.

The saturation (S) component of HSV color space can be derived from R, G and B channels using Eqn. (2)

$$S = \left[\frac{Max(R, G, B) - Min(R, G, B)}{Max(R, G, B)} \right] \tag{2}$$

The value (V) component of HSV color space is given by Eqn. (3)

$$V = Max(R, G, B) \tag{3}$$

The flowchart for RGB to HSV conversion and HSV to RGB conversion is shown in Fig. 1. The RGB to HSV conversion process starts from computation of maximum and minimum element among R, G and B pixel values. The maximum value of RGB indicates the amount of white in the color image. The minimum value of RGB indicates the amount of black in the color image. The maximum of R, G and B represents the value or luminance or brightness of HSV. The difference component, which is computed by subtracting the minimum component from the maximum component of a gray image gives an indication of how much gray the color contains. The hue is computed by considering three cases. The hue represents type of color varying between 0 to 360 degrees and has fitted in the range 0 to 255. The digital value 85 is equivalent to 120 degree. The digital value 171 is equivalent to 240 degrees and finally the digital value 0 is equivalent to 360 or 0 degrees. The green color channel has been moved to 85 and blue is shifted to 171. The factor 60 degree has changed to a digital value of 43. Hue is no longer less than zero.

The HSV to RGB conversion is defined in Eqn. (4) and (5)

$$h_1 = \frac{h}{43} = \frac{3h}{128}$$
$$h_2 = floor(h_1)$$
$$f = \frac{255 \times h - 8192 \times h_2}{43}$$
$$p = v - vs$$
$$q = v - vfs$$
$$t = v - vs + vfs$$

$$\tag{4}$$

$$R'G'B' = \begin{cases} v,t,p: & \text{if } f = 0 \\ q,v,p: & \text{if } f = 1 \\ p,v,t: & \text{if } f = 2 \\ p,q,v: & \text{if } f = 3 \\ t,p,v: & \text{if } f = 4 \\ v,p,q: & \text{if } f = 5 \end{cases} \tag{5}$$

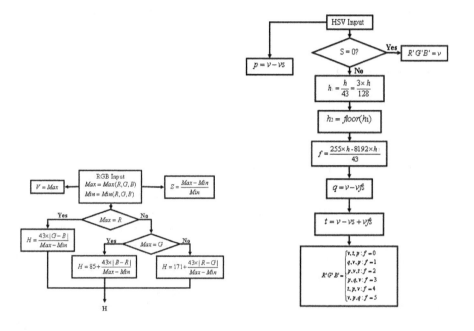

Fig. 1. Flow Chart for RGB to HSV and HSV to RGB conversion

2.2   YCbCr Color Space

In color image or video processing applications, a popular format is the YCbCr [14]. The RGB to YCbCr conversion and vice-versa is governed by the following expressions:

$$\begin{pmatrix} Y \\ Cb \\ Cr \end{pmatrix} = \begin{pmatrix} 0.299 & 0.587 & 0.114 \\ -0.169 & -0.331 & 0.500 \\ 0.500 & -0.419 & -0.081 \end{pmatrix} \begin{pmatrix} R \\ G \\ B \end{pmatrix} \tag{6}$$

$$\begin{pmatrix} R \\ G \\ B \end{pmatrix} = \begin{pmatrix} 1 & 0 & 1.406 \\ 1 & 0.352 & 0.711 \\ 1 & 1.781 & 0 \end{pmatrix} \begin{pmatrix} Y \\ Cb \\ Cr \end{pmatrix} \tag{7}$$

where R, G, and B are the picture element (pixel) values of three fundamental colors: red, green, and blue. Each of these color components is of size, 8 bits. An apt algorithm is developed without using multipliers for the computation of Y, Cb, Cr so that it may be efficiently mapped on to an FPGA/ASIC. The coefficients in the Eqn. (6) and (7) are scaled up by 128, and integers are retained, replacing multiplication operations by addition of relevant decimal weights of an multiplier or multiplicand. Finally, the results are scaled down to 128 in order to get back the correct results.

3   Hardware Implementation

In this section, hardware architectures designed for RGB-HSV and RGB-YCbCr color space conversion is described. The architecture has been designed in accordance with the color space conversion algorithm.

3.1   RGB-HSV Conversion Architectures

Hardware implementation of color space conversion starts with the Matlab verification followed by hardware architecture development, Verilog coding, logic synthesis, place and route and FPGA implementation [15]. First, we begin with realization RGB to HSV converter on FPGA. The RGB to HSV converter module design is based on Eqns. (1) to (3). The Hardware components used in RGB to HSV conversion are comparator, subtractor, divider, adder and hue selection. The Verilog codes developed for these modules are pipelined and processed parallel in order to speed up the conversion process [16]. The most complex module in this conversion process is the divider block. However, the divider employed in the conversion process is highly efficient. Finally, the hue selection block selects the individual hue values computed based on the maximum pixel value among R, G, and B.

The top level signal diagram for RGB-HSV color space conversion module is shown in Fig. 2. The detailed hardware architecture for RGB to HSV and HSV to RGB color space conversion is shown in Fig. 3.

3.2   RGB-YCbCr Conversion Architectures

The hardware realization of RGB to YCbCr conversion uses five pipeline stages. The format conversion scale-up the coefficients by 128, retaining integer and rearranging, we get the following expressions:

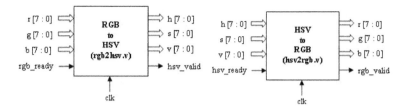

Fig. 2. Signal Diagram of RGB to HSV and HSV to RGB Converter Module

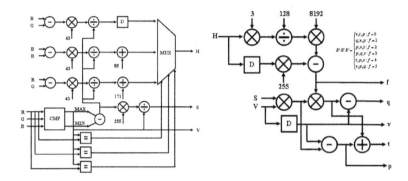

Fig. 3. Hardware Architecture for RGB to HSV and HSV to RGB Conversion

$$Y = 38R + 75G + 15B$$
$$Y = (32 + 4 + 2)R + (64 + 8 + 2 + 1)G + (8 + 4 + 2 + 1)B$$
$$Cb = -22R - 42G + 64B$$
$$Cb = -(16 + 4 + 2)R - (32 + 8 + 2)G + (64)B$$
$$Cr = 64R - 54G - 10B$$
$$Cr = (64)R + (32 + 16 + 4 + 2)G + (8 + 2)B$$

$$(8)$$

The above expressions may be easily realized by Verilog HDL since the multiplications involved are trivial, namely, multiplications by 64, 32, 16, 8, 4, 2 and 1. These multiplications are accomplished by left shifting by 6, 5, 4, 3, 2, 1 and nil bits respectively. The additions such as 32R + 4R + 2R ; 64 G + 8G + 2G + 1G, etc. are pipelined in such a way that only two terms are added at one time. The scaled coefficients are registered on the arrival of the rising edge of the clock. Finally, we scale down by 128 in the last clock cycle and thus accomplishing YCbCr conversion in about five pipeline stages.

$$R = 128Y + 180Cr = (128)Y + (128 + 32 + 16 + 4)Cr$$
$$G = 128Y + 45Cb + 91Cr$$
$$G = (128)Y + (32 + 8 + 4 + 1)Cb + (64 + 16 + 8 + 2 + 1)Cr$$
$$B = 128Y + 228Cb = (128)Y + (128 + 64 + 32 + 4)G$$

$$(9)$$

From the above expressions, multiplication can be easily replaced by left shift operation. The scaled coefficients are registered on the arrival of the rising edge of clock pulse. Finally, we scale down weights by 128 in the last clock cycle and thus accomplishing the RGB conversion from YCbCr conversion in about five pipeline stages. The top level signal diagram for RGB-YCbCr color space conversion module is shown in Fig. 4. The detailed hardware architecture for RGB to YCbCr and YCbCr to RGB color space conversion is shown in Fig. 5.

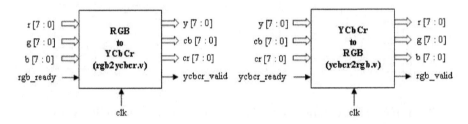

Fig. 4. Signal Diagram of RGB to YCbCr and YCbCr to RGB Converter Module

4   Experimental Results and Comparative Study

The proposed FPGA implementation of image color space conversion has been coded in Matlab (Ver. 8) and tested first in order to ensure the correct working of the color space conversion developed. The tests have provided satisfactory results. Subsequently, the entire design has been coded in Verilog HDL and has been simulated using Modelsim (Ver. SE 6.4). The Synthesis, Place & Route, and bit file generation is done using Xilinx 9.2i.

The ModelSim waveform results for RGB-HSV and RGB-YCbCr conversion is shown in Fig. 6. The Xilinx FPGA implementation of proposed RGB-HSV color space conversion is shown in Fig. 7. The proposed FPGA implementation of RGB to HSV conversion is compared with another implementation proposed by Jung et al. The data latency reported by Jung et al. method is 23 clock cycles. However, our method is capable of achieving conversion process within 16 clock cycles. The RGB to HSV and HSV to RGB color space conversion results using standard images with different environmental conditions are shown in Fig. 8.

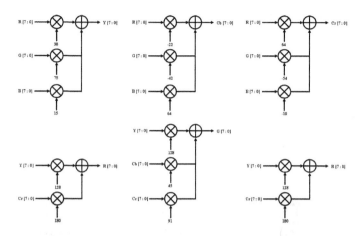

Fig. 5. First Row : RGB to Y, RGB to Cb, RGB to Cr, **Second Row** : YCbCr to R, YCbCr to G, YCbCr to B

Fig. 6. First Row: Simulation Waveforms for RGB to HSV, HSV to RGB Conversion, **Second Row:** RGB to YCbCr and YCbCr to RGB Conversion

RGBHSV Project Status			
Project File:	RGBHSV.ise	Current State:	Programming File Generated
Module Name:	rgb2hsv_new	• Errors:	No Errors
Target Device:	xc2v2000-6bf957	• Warnings:	351 Warnings (340 new, 0 filtered)
Product Version:	ISE 9.2i	• Updated:	Tue Jun 7 06:21:27 2011

Device Utilization Summary				
Logic Utilization	Used	Available	Utilization	Note(s)
Number of Slice Flip Flops	595	21,504	2%	
Number of 4 input LUTs	2,190	21,504	10%	
Logic Distribution				
Number of occupied Slices	1,366	10,752	12%	
Number of Slices containing only related logic	1,366	1,366	100%	
Number of Slices containing unrelated logic	0	1,366	0%	
Total Number of 4 input LUTs	2,501	21,504	11%	
Number used as logic	2,190			
Number used as a route-thru	95			
Number used as Shift registers	216			
Number of bonded IOBs	51	624	8%	
IOB Flip Flops	32			
Number of GCLKs	1	16	0%	
Total equivalent gate count for design	34,386			
Additional JTAG gate count for IOBs	2,448			

RGBHSV Project Status			
Project File:	RGBHSV.ise	Current State:	Programming File Generated
Module Name:	hsv2rgb_new	• Errors:	No Errors
Target Device:	xc2v2000-6bf957	• Warnings:	467 Warnings (463 new, 0 filtered)
Product Version:	ISE 9.2i	• Updated:	Tue Jun 7 08:17:07 2011

Device Utilization Summary				
Logic Utilization	Used	Available	Utilization	Note(s)
Number of Slice Flip Flops	430	21,504	1%	
Number of 4 input LUTs	382	21,504	1%	
Logic Distribution				
Number of occupied Slices	367	10,752	3%	
Number of Slices containing only related logic	367	367	100%	
Number of Slices containing unrelated logic	0	367	0%	
Total Number of 4 input LUTs	562	21,504	2%	
Number used as logic	382			
Number used as a route-thru	14			
Number used as Shift registers	166			
Number of bonded IOBs	51	624	8%	
IOB Flip Flops	24			
Number of MULT18X18s	1	56	1%	
Number of GCLKs	1	16	6%	
Total equivalent gate count for design	21,427			
Additional JTAG gate count for IOBs	2,448			

Fig. 7. RGB to HSV and HSV to RGB Color Space Conversion Implementation using XC2V2000-6bf957 Xilinx FPGA Device

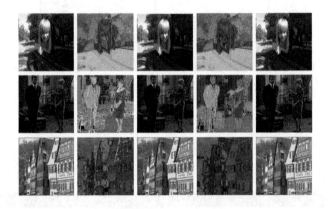

Fig. 8. RGB to HSV and HSV to RGB Conversion Results: **First Column** : Original 'Girl', 'Couple' and 'House' Images, **Second Column** : RGB to HSV Conversion using Matlab Software, **Third Column** : Restored RGB Images from HSV Color Space, **Fourth Column** :RGB to HSV Conversion using Proposed Hardware Technique, **Fifth Column** :Restored RGB Images from HSV Color Space using Proposed Hardware Technique

5   Conclusion

In this paper, efficient architectures suitable for FPGA/ASIC implementation of RGB-HSV and RGB-YCbCr color space conversion was presented. The potential applications of the proposed techniques includes image compression, image enhancement, and segmentation etc. Pipelining and parallel processing techniques are adopted in order to speed up the conversion process. The Verilog code developed for the complete system is RTL compliant and works for ASIC design. The implementation presented in this paper has been realized on an Xilinx XC2V2000-6bf957 FPGA device. The experimental results show that proposed color space conversion approaches exhibit better performances when compared with the other existing implementations.

References

1. Jain, A.K.: Fundamentals of Digital Image Processing. Prentice-Hall, Inc, Upper Saddle River (1989)
2. Bensaali, F., Amira, A.: Design and Implementation of Efficient Architectures for Color Space Conversion. ICGST International Journal on Graphics, Vision and Image Processing 5, 37–47 (2004)
3. Asmare, M.H., Asirvadam., V.S., Iznita, L.: Color Space Selection for Color Image Enhancement Applications. In: IEEE International Conference on Signal Acquisition and Processing (ICSAP), pp. 208–212 (2009)
4. Cho, J.U., Jin, S.H., Dai Pham, X., Kim, D., Jeon, J.W.: FPGA based Real Time Visual Tracking System Using Adaptive Color Histograms. In: IEEE International Conference on Robotics and Biomimetics (ROBIO 2007), pp, pp. 172–177 (2007)
5. Zhang, M., Seow, M., Tao, L., Asari, V.K.: Tunable High-Performance Architecture for Enhancement of Stream Video Captured Under Non-Uniform Lighting Conditions. Microprocessors and Microsystems 32(7), 386–393 (2008)
6. Marsi, S., Ramponi, G.: A Flexible FPGA Implementation for Illuminance-Reflectance Video Enhancement. Journal of Real-Time Image Processing, 1–13
7. Iakovidou, C., Vonikakis, V., Andreadis, I.: FPGA Implementation of a Real Time Biologically Inspired Image Enhancement Algorithm. Journal of Real-Time Image Processing 23(4), 269–287 (2008)
8. Pérez, P., Hue, C., Vermaak, J., Gangnet, M.: Color Based Probabilistic Tracking. In: Heyden, A., Sparr, G., Nielsen, M., Johansen, P. (eds.) ECCV 2002. LNCS, vol. 2350, pp. 661–675. Springer, Heidelberg (2002)
9. Hanumantharaju, M.C., Ravishankar, M., Rameshbabu, D.R., Ramachandran, S.: Adaptive Color Image Enhancement Based Geometric Mean Filter. In: Proceedings of International Conference on Communication, Computing & Security, pp. 403–408 (2011)
10. Tkalcic, M., Tasic, J.: Color Spaces: Perceptual. Historical and Applicational Background 1 (2003)
11. Zeng, D.: Future Intelligent Information Systems, vol. 1. Springer, Heidelberg (2011); ISBN: 3642197051
12. Siddiqui, A., Nazzal, S.: Measurement of Surface Color as an Expedient QC Method for the Detection of Deviations in Tablet Hardness. International Journal of Pharmaceutics 341(1-2), 173–180 (2007)
13. Bailey, D.: Design for Embedded Image Processing on FPGAs. Wiley (2011)
14. Bensaali, F., Amira, A.: Design and Efficient FPGA Implementation of an RGB to YCbCr Color Space Converter Using Distributed Arithmetic. In: Becker, J., Platzner, M., Vernalde, S. (eds.) FPL 2004. LNCS, vol. 3203, pp. 991–995. Springer, Heidelberg (2004)
15. Ramachandran, S.: Digital VLSI Systems design: A Design Manual for Implementation of Projects on FPGAs and ASICs using Verilog. Springer, Heidelberg (2007)
16. Bensaali, F., Amira, A.: Accelerating Color Space Conversion on Reconfigurable Hardware. Image and Vision Computing 23, 935–942 (2005)

Increasing Scalability through Affinity Measure in Clustering

A. Banumathi[1] and A. Pethalakshmi[2]

[1] Department of Computer Science,
Government Arts College, Karur – 3,
Tamilnadu, India
banukarthikeyan7811@gmail.com
[2] Department of Computer Science,
MVM Government Arts College for Women, Dindigul,
Tamilnadu, India
pethalakshmi@yahoo.com

Abstract. Clustering is a widely used technique in data mining application for discovering patterns in large dataset. In this paper the traditional K-Means algorithm is analyzed and found that quality of the resultant cluster is based on the initial seed where it is selected either sequentially or randomly. The K-Means algorithm should be initiated with the number of cluster k and initial seeds. For real time large database its difficult to predict the number of cluster and initial seeds accurately. In order to overcome this drawback the current paper focused on developing the UCAM (Unique Clustering with Affinity Measure) algorithm for clustering without giving initial seed and number of clusters. Unique clustering is obtained with the help of affinity measures.

Keywords: Cluster, K-Means, UCAM.

1   Introduction

Clustering has been used in a number of applications such as engineering, biology, medicine and data mining. The most popular clustering algorithm used in several field is K-Means since it is very simple and fast and efficient. K-means is developed by Mac Queen. The K-Means algorithm is effective in producing cluster for many practical applications. But the computational complexity of the original K-Means algorithm is very high, especially for large datasets. The K-Means algorithm is a partition clustering method that separates data into K groups. Main drawback of this algorithm is that of a priori fixation of number of clusters and seeds.

Unique Clustering with Affinity Measures (UCAM) algorithm which starts its computation without representing the number of clusters and the initial seeds. It divides the dataset into some number of clusters with the help of threshold value. The uniqueness of the cluster is based on the threshold value. More unique cluster is obtained when the threshold values is smaller.

P.V. Krishna, M.R. Babu, and E. Ariwa (Eds.): ObCom 2011, Part II, CCIS 270, pp. 302–310, 2012.

2   Data Mining and Clustering

Data mining is the process of autonomously extracting useful information or knowledge from large data stores or sets. It involves the use of sophisticated data analysis tools to discover previously unknown, valid patterns and relationships in large data sets. Data mining consists of more process than collecting and managing data, it also includes analysis and prediction. These tools can include statistical models, mathematical algorithms and machine learning methods such as neural networks or decision trees etc.

Data mining can be performed on a variety of data stores, including the world wide web, relational databases, transactional databases, internals legacy system, personal document format documents and data warehouses.

Data mining has been applied into many applications domains such as biomedical and DNA analysis, Retail industry and marketing, telecommunication, web mining, computer auditing, banking and insurance, fraud detection, financial industry, medicine and in education. Data mining is popularly known as knowledge discovery. Fig.1 shows the concept of data mining, which involves three steps:

1. Capturing and storing the data.
2. Converting the raw data into information.
3. Converting the information into knowledge.

Fig. 1. Data mining process

Data in this context comprises all the raw material an institution collects via normal operation. Capturing and storing the data is the first phase that is the process of applying mathematical and statistical formulas to mine the data warehouse. Mining the collected raw data from the entire institution may provide new information. Converting the raw information into information is the second step of data mining and from the information knowledge is discovered.

Clustering is a widely used technique in data mining application for discovering patterns in large dataset. The aim of cluster analysis is exploratory, to find if data naturally falls into meaningful groups with small within-group variations and large between-group variations. Often we may not have a hypothesis that we are trying to test. The aim is to find any interesting grouping of the data. It is possible to define cluster analysis as an optimization problem in which a given function consisting of within cluster similarity and between clusters dissimilarity needs to be optimized. This function can be difficult to define and the optimization of any such function is a challenging task.

In this paper the traditional K-Means algorithm is analyzed and found that quality of the resultant cluster is based on the initial seeds but it is difficult to predict the number of cluster and initial seeds accurately. In order to overcome this drawback the current paper focused on developing the UCAM (Unique Clustering with Affinity Measure) algorithm for clustering which works without giving initial seed and number of clusters. Unique clustering is obtained with the help of affinity measures.

3   K-Mean Clustering

The main objective in cluster analysis is to group object that are similar in one cluster and separate objects that are dissimilar by assigning them to different clusters. One of the most popular clustering methods is K-Means clusters algorithm. It is classifies objects to pre-defined number of clusters, which is given by the user (assume K clusters). The idea is to choose random cluster centers, one for each cluster. These centers are preferred to be as far as possible from each other. In this algorithm Euclidean distance measure is used between two multidimensional data points

$$X = (x_1, x_2, x_3, \ldots \ldots x_m) \tag{1}$$

$$Y = (y_1, y_2, y_3, \ldots \ldots y_m) \tag{2}$$

The Euclidean distance measure between the above points x and y are described as follows:

$$D(X, Y) = \left(\sum (x_i - y_i)^2 \right)^{1/2} \tag{3}$$

The K-Means method aims to minimize the sum of squared distances between all points and the cluster centre. This procedure consists of the following steps, as described below

Algorithm1: K-Means clustering algorithm

Input: $D = \{d_1, d_2, d_3, \ldots, d_n\}$ // Set of n data points.

          K - Number of desired clusters

Output: A set of K clusters.

Steps:

1.   Select the number of clusters. Let this number be k.

2.   Pick k seeds as centroids of the k clusters. The seeds may be picked randomly unless the user has some insight into the data.

3.   Compute the Euclidean distance of each object in the dataset from each of the centroids.

4.   Allocate each object to the cluster it is nearest to based on the distances computed in the previous step.

5. Compute the centroids of the clusters by computing the means of the attribute values if the objects in each cluster.

6. Check if the stopping criterion has been met (e.g. the cluster membership is unchanged). If yes, go to step 7. If not go to step 3.

7. [Optional] One may decide to stop at this stage or to split a cluster or combine two clusters heuristically until a stopping criterion is met.

Though the K-Means algorithm is simple, but it has some drawbacks in its quality of the final clustering, since it is highly depends on the initial centroids. Implementing K-Means algorithm in a very small sample data with ten students information, which gives clear view on its process.

Table 3.1. Students information

Stud-no	age	Mark1	Mark2	Mark3
S_1	18	73	75	57
S_2	18	79	85	75
S_3	23	70	70	52
S_4	20	55	55	55
S_5	22	85	86	87
S_6	19	91	90	89
S7	20	70	65	60
S_8	21	53	56	59
S_9	19	82	82	60
S_{10}	47	75	76	77

The process of K-Mean clustering is initiated with three initial seeds as represented in the below table 3.2

Table 3.2. The three seeds for table 3.1

Stud-no	age	Mark1	Mark2	Mark3
S_1	18	73	75	57
S_2	18	79	85	75
S_3	23	70	70	52

K-Means algorithm produces the following result by applying it on the sample data in table 3.1.

Table 3.3. Cluster C_1

Stud-no	age	Mark1	Mark2	Mark3
S_1	18	73	75	57
S_9	19	82	82	60

Table 3.4. Cluster C_2

Stud-no	age	Mark1	Mark2	Mark3
S_2	18	79	85	75
S_5	22	85	86	87
S_6	19	91	90	89
S_{10}	47	75	76	77

Table 3.5. Cluster C_3

Stud-no	age	Mark1	Mark2	Mark3
S_3	23	70	70	52
S_4	20	55	55	55
S_7	20	70	65	60
S_8	21	53	56	59

The K-Means execution results with three clusters as notated below

$$C_1 = \{ \ S_1, S_9 \ \} \tag{4}$$

$$C_2 = \{ S_2, S_5, S_6, S_{10} \} \tag{5}$$

$$C_3 = \{ S_3, S_4, S_7, S_8 \ \} \tag{6}$$

Where $S_1, S_2, \ldots S_{10}$ Student's details which considers only numeric attributes. In K-Means the initial seeds are randomly selected and hence result of two executions on the same data set will not get the same result unless the initial seeds are same. The main drawback in K-Means is that initial seeds and number of cluster should be defined though it is difficult predict in the early stage.

4   UCAM Clustering

In cluster analysis, one does not know what classes or clusters exist and the problem to be solved is to group the given data into meaningful clusters. Here on the same motive UCAM algorithm is developed. UCAM algorithm is a clustering algorithm basically for numeric data's. It mainly focuses on the drawback of K-Means clustering algorithm. In K-Means algorithm, the process is initiated with the initial seeds and number of cluster to be obtained. But the number of cluster that is to be obtained cannot be predicted on a single view of the dataset. The result may not unique if the number of cluster and the initial seed is not properly identified.

UCAM algorithm is implemented with the help of affinity measure for clustering. The process of clustering in UCAM initiated without any centorid and number of clusters that is to be produced. But it set the threshold value for making unique clusters. The step by step procedure for UCAM are given below

Algorithm 2: The **UCAM** algorithm

Input: $D = \{d_1, d_2, d_3... d_n \}$ // Set of n data points.

      S – Threshold value.

Output: Clusters. Number of cluster depends on affinity measure.

UCAM Algorithm Steps:
1. Set the threshold value T.
2. Create new cluster structure if it is the first tuple of the dataset.
3. If it is not first tuple compute similarity measure with existing clusters.
4. Get the minimum value of computed similarity S.
5. Get the cluster index of Ci which corresponds to S.
6. If S<=T, then add current tuple to Ci.
7. If S>T, create new cluster.
8. Continue the process until the last tuple of the dataset.

Implementing UCAM algorithm with the sample data given table 3.1. The process is initiated with threshold value T and results with following clusters as shown below

Table 4.1 Cluster C_1

Stud-no	age	Mark1	Mark2	Mark3
S_1	18	73	75	57
S_3	23	70	70	52
S_7	20	70	65	60

Table 4.2 Cluster C_2

Stud-no	age	Mark1	Mark2	Mark3
S_2	18	79	85	75
S_5	22	85	86	87
S_6	19	91	90	89

Table 4.3 Cluster C_3

Stud-no	age	Mark1	Mark2	Mark3
S_4	20	55	55	55
S_8	21	53	56	59

Table 4.4 Cluster C_4

Stud-no	age	Mark1	Mark2	Mark3
S_9	19	82	82	60

Table 4.5 Cluster C_5

Stud-no	age	Mark1	Mark2	Mark3
S_{10}	47	75	76	77

The UCAM execution results with five clusters   notated below

$$C_1 = \{ \ S_1, S_3, S_7 \ \} \tag{7}$$

$$C_2 = \{ S_2, S_5, S_6 \} \tag{8}$$

$$C_3 = \{ \ S_4, S_8 \ \} \tag{9}$$

$$C_4 = \{ \ S_9 \} \tag{10}$$

$$C_5 = \{ S_{10} \ \} \tag{11}$$

Uniqueness of the cluster is depends on the initial setting of the threshold value. If the threshold value increases number of cluster decreases. In UCAM there is no initial prediction on number of resultant cluster. Here, in this algorithm resultant cluster purely based on the affinity measure.

5   Comparative Analyses

UCAM algorithm produce unique clustering only on the bases of affinity measure, hence there is no possibility of error in clustering. One major advantage is that both rough clustering and accurate unique clustering is possible by adjusting the threshold value. But in K-Means clustering there is chance of getting error if the initial seeds are not identified properly. The comparative study of K-Means and UCAM clustering are shown in the following table.

Table 5.1 Comparative study on K-Means and UCAM Clustering algorithm

	Initial number of clusters	Centriod	Threshold value	Cluster result	Cluster Error
K-Means	K	Initial seeds	-	Depend on initial seeds	Yes, if wrong seeds
UCAM	-	-	T	Depend on threshold value	-

In the above study of K-Means clustering algorithm results with three clusters where low marks and high marks are found in all clusters, since the initial seeds do not have any seeds with the marks above 90. Hence if the initial seeds not defined properly then the result won't be unique and more over it has been constrained that it should have only three clusters.

In UCAM algorithm is initiated with the threshold alone which produces unique result with five clusters.

C_1 → Cluster with medium marks.

C_2 → Cluster with high marks.

C_3 → Cluster with low marks.

$$C_4 = \{ S_9 \} \tag{12}$$

$$C_5 = \{ S1_0 \} \tag{13}$$

S_9 is the student with good mark in two subjects and low mark in one subject. So, S_9 should be considered with more care in subject 3 so that it increases ranking of the institution. And s_{10} should be considered since his age is unique than other students. Both approximate clustering and unique cluster can be obtained by increasing and decreasing the threshold values.

6   Conclusions

In this paper, new UCAM algorithm is used for data clustering. This approach reduces the overheads of fixing the cluster size and initial seeds in K-Means. It fixes threshold value to obtain a unique clustering. The proposed method improves the scalability and reduces the clustering error. This approach ensures that the total mechanism of clustering is in time without loss in correctness of clusters.

References

1. Li, H., Nie, Z., Lee, W.: Scalable community Discovery on Textual Data with relations. University of California, Department of Information and Computer Science, Irvine, http://www.ics.uci.edu/~mlearn/MLRepository.html
2. Guha, S., Rastogi, R., Shim, K.: CURE.: An efficient clustering algorithm for large databases. In: Proc. 1998 ACM6SIGMOD Int. Conf. Management of Data (SIGMOD 1998), pp. 73–84 (1998)
3. Zhang, C., Xia, S.: K-Means Clustering Algorithm with Improved Initial center. In: Second International Workshop on Knowledge Discovery and Data Mining (WKDD), p. 7906792 (2009)
4. Yuan, F., Meng, Z.H., Zhangz, H.X., Don, C.R.: A New Algorithm to Get the Initial Centroids. In: Proceedings of the 3rd International Conference on Machine Learning and Cybernetics, p. 26629 (August 2004)
5. Chaturvedi, J.C.A., Green, P.: K - Modes clustering. Journals of Classification (18), 35–55 (2001)
6. Dembele, D., Kastner, P.: Fuzzy C means method for clustering microarray data. Bioinformatics 19(8), 9736 (2003)
7. Jiang, D., Pei, J., Zhang, A.: An Interactive Approach to mining Gene Expression Data. IEEE Transactions on Knowledge and Data Engineering 17(10), 13636 (2005)
8. Zhu, D., Hero, A.O., Cheng, H., Khanna, R., Swaroop, A.: Network constrained clustering for gene microarray Data 21(21), 4014–4020 (2005), doi:10.1093 bioinformatics / bti 655
9. Gupta, G.K.: Data mining with case studies

Efficient Use of Shares in Color Visual Cryptography

B. Dinesh Reddy[1], V. Valli Kumari[2], KVSVN. Raju[3], and Y. Jaya Lakshmi[4]

[1,4] Vignan Institute of Information Technology, Andhra Pradesh
[2] Andhra University, Andhra Pradesh
[3] Anil Neerukonda Institute of Technology and Sciences, Andhra Pradesh
{dinesh4net,vallikumari,kvsvn.raju,yarraguntla.jl}@gmail.com

Abstract. Visual cryptography is the concept of encrypting the secret image into n number of shares where each recipient gets one share. One share can't reveal any information. Sharing a Secret Gray Image in Multiple images allows gray image to be encrypted into two shares. In this paper, we propose Efficient use of Shares in Color Visual Cryptography, which encrypts three gray images, three cover images into three shares. The secret image is recovered by combining any two of the shares by applying some simple computations. In this paper Efficient use of Shares in Color Visual Cryptography the size of the shares is fixed; each share is used to reveal more than one color image. The recovered secret image is same contrast as original image.

Keywords: Visual Cryptography, Color Visual Cryptography, Secret Sharing Algorithm.

1 Introduction

Visual Cryptography (VC) is the concept of dividing a secret image into 'n' number of shares and revealing the secret image by stacking a qualified subset of 'n' shares. Visual Cryptography was first introduced by Naor and Shamir [5] in 1994, where original secret image is recovered by Human Visual System only. Hence there is no need to any cryptographic computations for decryption. Ateniese, Blundo, Stinson [6] extended this concept Visual Cryptography as General Access Structures in which only the qualified subsets of participants can recover the information, but other, forbidden, sets of participants can't recover the information. Up to the year 1999, the secret image is recovered by stacking the transparencies and recover secret images were black and white only.

In 1997 Verheul and Van Tilborg [7] proposed Visual Cryptography scheme for color images. In this scheme each pixel is divided into sub pixels and each sub pixel is sub divided into c-colored regions and there is exactly one color region colored and all other regions are black. Yang and Laih [2], [8] proposed a new colored visual cryptographic by using different structures. Chin-Chen Chang, Chwei-Shyong Tsai and Tung-Shou Chen [3] recently proposed a new scheme based on modified Visual Cryptography. In this scheme predefined Color Index Table (CIT) and small computations are required to recover the secret image. The disadvantage of this is, if the number of colors increases in the secret image the sub pixels also increased i.e. we

P.V. Krishna, M.R. Babu, and E. Ariwa (Eds.): ObCom 2011, Part II, CCIS 270, pp. 311–319, 2012.
© Springer-Verlag Berlin Heidelberg 2012

can get larger shares and additional space is required to store the Color index table. Chin-Chen Chang, Tai-Xing Yu [4] proposed a concept of sharing secret gray image (0-255 colors) in multiple images. The generated shares are camouflage image or cover images. Each share can be used to reveal more than on image [1]. This paper proposes efficient use of Shares in Color Visual Cryptography, which encrypts three secret color images into three shares and each secret image is obtained by combining any two of the shares. Each pixel is subdivided into 9 sub pixels. This scheme uses the basis matrices concept.

2   Visual Cryptography

Visual Cryptography (VC) is a new technique used for encrypting binary images into *n* shares. Decryption process is done by human visual system. In color visual cryptography each pixel is converted into sub pixels. The revealed secret images contrast is not same as the original image.

3   Proposed Scheme

This paper proposes a new scheme in multiple secret sharing with multiple cover images. In which three secret images are encrypted into three shares with the help of basis matrices concept. In this scheme one pixel is converted into 9 sub pixels.

3.1   Visual Cryptographic Encryption (Shares Generation)

Proposed scheme can generate three shares from three secret images and three cover images. The constraint is three secret images and cover images should be of same size.

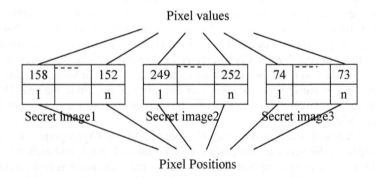

Fig. 3(a). Three secret images with pixel values and corresponding positions

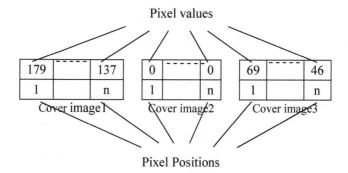

Fig. 3(b). Three cover images with pixel values and corresponding positions

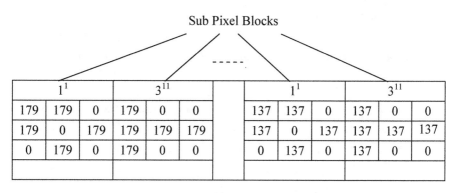

Fig. 3(c). Share1 with sub pixel block values and corresponding positions

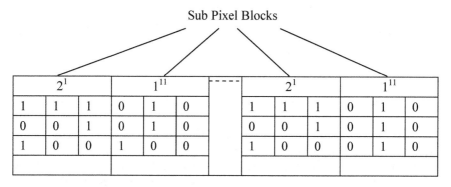

Fig. 3(d). Share2 with sub pixel block values and corresponding positions

Sub Pixel Blocks

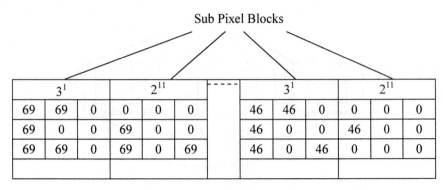

3^1			2^{11}			3^1			2^{11}		
69	69	0	0	0	0	46	46	0	0	0	0
69	0	0	69	0	0	46	0	0	46	0	0
69	69	0	69	0	69	46	0	46	0	0	0

Share3

Fig. 3(e). Share3with sub pixel block values and corresponding positions

3.2   Visual Cryptographic Decryption (Reconstruction of Original Image)

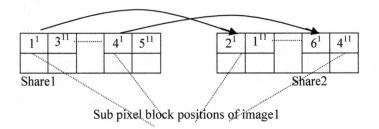

1^1	3^{11}	....	4^1	5^{11}		2^1	1^{11}	....	6^1	4^{11}

Share1   Share2

Sub pixel block positions of image1

Fig. 3(f). Block positions in Share1 and Share2

1^1+1^{11}		....		4^1+4^{11}

Revealed image 1

Fig. 3(g). Reconstructed image1

Figure 3(f) shows the procedure for obtaining the secret images. Let us consider two shares with the blocks positions as shown in figure 3(c) & 3(d). Each secret image could be obtained by converting first (3x3) blocks in first share and second (3x3) blocks in second share into (1x9) rows. The two (1x9) rows are converted into 1s and 0s (i.e. if the value is greater than or equal to '1' then convert it into 1). Then exclusive-OR of two rows except random bit and convert it into decimal value. The converted decimal value is equal to original secret image pixel value.

The resultant reconstructed image has the form as shown in above figure3(g). In the mathematical sense we can represent the decryption process as shown below:

$$SecretImage1 = Share1 + Share2$$
$$SecretImage2 = Share2 + Share3$$
$$SecretImage3 = Share3 + Share1$$

Consider a scenario where accessing a computer require high authentication (military). Let the scenario contain three people (X, Y, Z). To access the system we require two people (XY, YZ, ZX). Here this method will be the best for authentication. We use efficient use of shares in color visual cryptography to generate three shares which are distributed to each person (X, Y, Z). Any two members together with their shares can get the secret password and access the system. This method can easily authenticate the two persons.

3.3 *Algorithm* Encryption

Begin:

Input : Three secret images I1, I2 and I3, three cover images CI1, CI2, and CI3.
Output: Three shares

Step1:

```
p=row size of image;
q=column size of image;
random bit (r) =5;
```

Step2:

```
n=0;
for x = 1 to p do
for y = 1 to q do
   c=I1(x, y)
   c = (c₁,c₂,c₃,c₄,c₅,c₆,c₇,c₈)₂
for i=1 to 8 do
   if (cᵢ=1 and i<r) then
      n=n+1
      G1(i)=1, if(n%2=1)
      G1(i)=0, if(n%2=0)
   else if (cᵢ=1 and i>=r) then
      n=n+1
      j=j+1
      G1(j)=1, if(n%2=1)
      G1(j)=0, if(n%2=0)
   end // if
   if (n%2=1) then G1(r)=0
end // 'i' loop
```

Assign the rest null elements except random bit position
in G1 to 1 or 0 (total number of 1s must equal to 5).

```
j=0;

for i=1 to 9 do
    if (i≠r) then
        j=j+1;
        G2(i)=G1(i)⊕ cⱼ
    else
    if (n%2=1) then
        G2(i)=1
    else G2(i)=G1(i)⊕ 0
    end // if
end // for
```

Arrange G1, G2 into 3x3 blocks B_1& B_2 respectively.
```
end // 'x' loop
end //'y' loop
```

Repeat the **Step 2** for Secret image2 & Secret image3.

Step3:

Share1 is generated by placing the blocks B_1s of I1 &
blocks B_2s of I3 alternatively and fill the 1s with cover
image1 color (ck^1).

Share2 is generated by placing the blocks B_1s of I2 &
blocks B_2s of I1 alternatively and fill the 1s with cover
image2 color (ck^2).

Share3 is generated by placing the blocks B_1s of I3 &
blocks B_2s of I2 alternatively and fill the 1s with cover
image3 color (ck^3).

End algorithm.

3.4   *Algorithm* Decryption

Input: Two Shares sh1 & sh2 with size of 3m x 6n and
random bit.
Output: The hidden secret image I1 with size of m/3 x n/6

Step1:
Arrange the (3x3) blocks B_1, B_2 into 1 x 9 matrices i.e.
G1 & G2 respectively.

```
for i= 1 to 8 do
   j=i, if (i<r)
   j=i+1, if (i>=r)
   cᵢ=G1(j)⊕ 2(j)
end // for
```

Step2:

Convert 'c' into decimal value i.e. secret image pixel value. After determining all the pixels, the secret image hidden in two shares is recovered.

End algorithm.

4   Experimental Results

Experimental results of proposed scheme are shown in the below figures. For experimental results MATLAB R2009b tool is used. The three secret images are of size 125x125.

4.1   Input Images

Secret Image1

Secret Image2

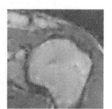
Secret Image3

Fig. 4(a). Secret image1, Secret image2, Secret image3 (125x125)

Cover Image1

Cover Image2

Cover Image3

Fig. 4(b). Cover image1, 2 & 3(125x125)

4.2   Generated Shares

Share1

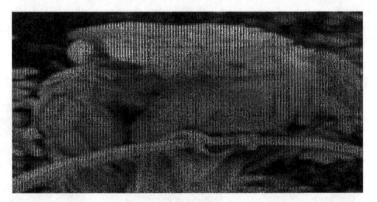

Share2

Share3

Fig. 4(c). Share 1, Share2, Share3 (375x750)

4.3   Reconstructed Images

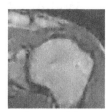

| Revealed | Revealed | Revealed |
| Original image1 | Original image2 | Original image3 |

Fig. 4(c). Reconstructed images 1, 2 & 3 (125x125)

5   Conclusion

The proposed scheme efficient use of Shares in Color Visual Cryptography is designed for encrypting three secret images into three shares using visual cryptography scheme. In this scheme one pixel is divided into 9 sub pixels only. The reconstruction of secret images could be done by Exclusive-OR of 1st block in one share with 2nd block in another share. In this scheme we have used the concept of basis matrices for generating the sub pixel values. The reconstructed image contrast is same as original image.

References

1. Dinesh Reddy, B., Valli Kumari, V., Kvsvn, R.: Rotation Visual Cryptography using basic (2, 2) scheme. TECHNIA – International Journal of Computing Science and Communication Technologies 3(2) (January 2011); ISSN 0974-3375
2. Revenkar, P.S., Anjum, A., Gandhare, W.Z.: Survey of Visual Cryptography Schemes. International Journal of Security and Its Applications 4(2) (April 2010)
3. Chang, C., Tsai, C., Chen, T.: A new scheme for sharing secret color images in computer network. In: Proceedings of International Conference on Parallel and Distributed Systems, pp. 21–27 (July 2000)
4. Chang, C.-C., Yu, T.-X.: Sharing a Secret Gray Image in Multiple Images. In: The Proceedings of the First International Symposium on Cyber Worlds: Theories and Practice, Tokyo, Japan, pp. 230–237 (November 2002)
5. Naor, M., Shamir, A.: Visual Cryptography. In: De Santis, A. (ed.) EUROCRYPT 1994. LNCS, vol. 950, pp. 1–12. Springer, Heidelberg (1995)
6. Ateniese, G., Blundo, C., de Santis, A., Stinson, D.: Visual Cryptography for general access structures. Information and Computation 129(2), 86–106 (1996)
7. Verheul, E., Tilborg, H.V.: Constructions and properties of k out of n visual secret sharing schemes. Designs, Codes and Cryptography 11(2), 179–196 (1997)
8. Yang, C., Laih, C.: New colored visual secret sharing schemes. Designs, Codes and Cryptography 20, 325–335 (2000)

Features Based Mammogram Image Classification Using Weighted Feature Support Vector Machine

S. Kavitha[1] and K.K. Thyagharajan[2]

[1] Department of Computer Science and Engineering,
SSN College of Engineering, Chennai – 603110, India
kavithas@ssn.edu.in
[2] Department of Information Technology,
RMK College of Engineering and Technology, Chennai – 601206, India
kkthyagharajan@yahoo.com

Abstract. In the existing research of mammogram image classification either clinical data or image features of specific type is considered along with the supervised classifiers such as Neural Network (NN) and Support Vector Machine (SVM). This paper considers automated classification of breast tissue type as benign or malignant using Weighted Feature Support Vector Machine (WFSVM) through constructing the precomputed kernel function by assigning more weight to relevant features using the principle of maximizing deviations. Initially, MIAS dataset of mammogram images is divided into training and test set, then the preprocessing techniques such as noise removal and background removal are applied to the input images and the Region of Interest (ROI) is identified. The statistical features and texture features are extracted from the ROI and the clinical features are obtained directly from the dataset. The extracted features of the training dataset are used to construct the weighted features and precomputed linear kernel for training the WFSVM, from which train model file is created. Using this model file the kernel matrix of test samples are classified as benign or malignant. These analysis shows that the texture features are resulted with better accuracy than the other features with WFSVM and SVM. However the number of support vectors created in WFSVM is less than the SVM classifier.

Keywords: Mammogram images, Texture features, Statistical features, Clinical features, Support Vector Machine, Weighted Feature Support Vector Machine.

1 Introduction

The Breast Cancer incidence rate is rising in every country of the world especially in developing countries such as India. India is one among the top ten countries in the world with high incidence and mortality rates according to a report by International Agency for Research [10] on Cancer. Breast Cancer is rapidly becoming one of the leading Cancers in females with one in 22 women likely to get affected during her lifetime. From the reports of Population Based Cancer Registry, the overall survival rate in India for 5 years is lesser than 60% indicates a high mortality rate [11]. Though

P.V. Krishna, M.R. Babu, and E. Ariwa (Eds.): ObCom 2011, Part II, CCIS 270, pp. 320–329, 2012.

the incidence rate in India is much lesser compared to the western countries, high mortality rate is due to the lack of instruments and techniques required for the early detection of breast Cancer. Early detection refers to tests and exams used to find breast Cancer, in people who do not have any symptoms.

One of the best methods used in the detection of breast Cancer is mammography. Mammography is the process of using low-dose amplitude X-rays to examine the human breast and is used as a diagnostic and a screening tool. Diagnostic mammogram is used to diagnose breast disease in women who have breast symptoms or an abnormal result on a screening mammogram. Screening mammograms are used to look for breast disease in women who are asymptomatic; that is, those who appear to have no breast problems. But both screening and diagnostic mammograms depends on the radiologist accuracy in reading the mammograms. On an average 21% of the breast cancers are missed by radiologists is reported in various articles [13].

In Computer Aided Diagnosis (CAD), feature extraction transforms the data from the high-dimensional space into lower dimensions and feature selection verifies the importance of selected features through classification techniques such as Neural Networks (NN) and SVM. NN is resulting with high computational complexity and slow learning where as SVM reduces computational complexity and has a faster learning rate. The data analysis performed by SVM can be classification or regression. In traditional SVM the existing kernel functions such as Linear, Polynomial and Radial Basis Function (RBF) are used widely for binary class and multi class classification. The recent WFSVM allows us to pre-compute the kernel matrix and function using the weighted features derived from the actual features of image or report [5].

In the research of breast cancer diagnosis with classification techniques, considers either the clinical features given by the radiologist report or the specific features extracted from the mammogram images [1], [2]. To resolve this issue, WFSVM classification is implemented with the feature set of statistical, texture and clinical data. From the extracted features the precomputed linear kernel is constructed and trained with weighted features. Then the test samples are validated with the kernel matrix of the test features [4].

This paper elaborates on the following sections. In Section 2, the system design of the proposed methodology is explained. The experimental results and performance of the SVM and WFSVM approaches based on the features from image and clinical data are analyzed and tabulated in Section 3. Conclusion and Future work are summarized at the end.

2   System Design

In this system the mammogram images of MIAS dataset are considered for analysis and evaluation in classification using SVM and WFSVM, as given in Fig. 1.

2.1   Dataset

The dataset of digital mammogram images are collected from the Mammographic Image Analysis Society (MIAS) database along with the clinical report [9]. It consists of totally 68 benign images and 51 malignant images. For WFSVM and SVM the images are divided equally for both training and testing in each class. In each set of train or test, 58 images are used in which 34 are benign and 24 are malignant.

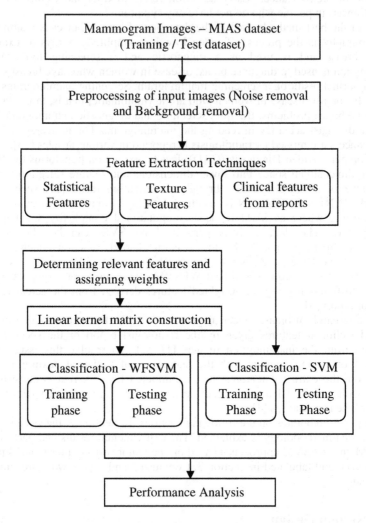

Fig. 1. An overall system design

2.2   Preprocessing

Noise Removal: Salt and pepper noise is added to the input image and removed using median filtering. The median filter is a nonlinear digital filtering technique, often used to remove noise. The main idea of the median filter is to run through the signal entry by entry, replacing each entry with the median of neighboring entries. The pattern of neighbors is called as "window", which slides, entry by entry, over the entire signal, resulted with a denoised image [15].

Background Removal: The purpose of cropping step is to focal point the process exclusively on the appropriate breast region, which reduces the possibility for erroneous classification. Hence, the regions of image which are not part of breast called as artifacts are cropped. On the denoised image, cropping was performed and cropped image is obtained [15].

2.3   Feature Extraction

The statistical image features such as mean, variance, skewness, uniformity, entropy, kurtosis, contrast, smoothness and the texture features using the average and variance of 6 Gabor filter responses aligned in 30 degree increments are extracted from the ROI of the mammogram images and the clinical features such as character of background tissue (fatty, fatty glandular, dense glandular) and class of abnormality present (asymmetry, miscellaneous, architectural distortion, calcification, circumscribed masses, spiculated masses) are obtained directly from the dataset.

Statistical Features: The eight statistical features of a mammogram image are computed using the parameters such as z_i is a random variable indicating the intensity, $p(z_i)$ is the histogram of the intensity levels in a region, L is the number of possible intensity levels and σ is the standard deviation [3] with the corresponding mathematical models.

Texture Features: Texture features are extracted using the 2-D Gabor filter, as given in Equation (1).

$$h(x, y) = \exp(-\alpha 2\omega(x^2 + y^2)/2)\exp(\omega\pi\alpha\omega(x\cos\theta + y\sin\theta)) \tag{1}$$

where $\alpha = 1/2^{1/2}$, $\omega = 0,1,2...$, $\theta = [0,2\Rightarrow]$

On a trial and error basis, it is found that the filter provides consistent and effective results for the values of $\omega =2$ and $\theta=5\pi/3$. Different choices of scale and orientation components can be used to construct a set of filters [6]. Here three scales and two orientations are used in the construction of 6 filters. A sample cell array of the Gabor filter bank in three scales and two orientations is 3 x 2 array, computed using the above formula {[1.2682 0.1991] [16.8892 2.6517] [288.7979 45.3932]}. To reduce the computational load, the filter-banks should be made as small as possible in evaluation.

Convolution: Once a series of Gabor filters have been chosen, image features at different locations, frequencies and orientations can be extracted by convolving the image $i(x,y)$ with the filters using the formula in Equation (2)

$$m(x, y) = L_h(i(x, y)) = i(x, y) \times h(x, y) \tag{2}$$

The filter bank is applied to the ROI of an input image and the mean and variance of the filtered image is obtained.

2.4   Relevant Features and Assigning Weights

After extracting the low level features, it is necessary to identify the relevant features so that the calculation of kernel function of the support vector machine is not dominated by the irrelevant features. The weights of the features are calculated using the technique of principle of maximizing deviations.

Principle of Maximizing Deviations: Consider two classes A and B. The feature vector of a sample that belongs to A and B are given as [7]:

$$A= (a_1, a_2,......a_n)$$

$$B= (b_1, b_2,......b_n)$$

If the difference between in the pth ($p=1,2,....n$) feature a_p and b_p of two samples that belongs to A and B is more, then that feature plays an important role in classification. Therefore, the feature with greater deviation should be given greater weight than the feature with smaller deviation. Each feature is a random variable. The deviation of random variables a_p and b_p is given in Equation (3)

$$d(a_p,b_p) = \int_{-\infty}^{+\infty} |a_p - b_p| f_p(a_p,b_p) da_p db_p \tag{3}$$

where $f_p(a_p,b_p)$ is the joint probability density function of random variables a_p and b_p. The same feature value of different samples are independent, thus we have

$$f_p(a_p,b_p) = f_p(a_p) f_p(b_p) \tag{4}$$

Now Equation (3) becomes

$$d(a_p,b_p) = \int\int_{-\infty}^{+\infty} |a_p - b_p| f_p(a_p) f_p(b_p) da_p db_p \tag{5}$$

The deviation between categories of samples is given in Equation (6)

$$D(\lambda_p) = \sum_{p=1}^{n} \lambda_p d(a_p,b_p) \tag{6}$$

Structure the model for maximizing the deviation between categories as follows:

$$\max D(\lambda_p) = \sum_{p=1}^{n} \lambda_p d(a_p,b_p) \tag{7}$$

Such that

$$\sum_{p=1}^{n} \lambda_p^2 = 1, \lambda_p \geq 0, \ p = 1,2,...n. \tag{8}$$

Using Lagrangian function method, solve the model and the weight of each feature is obtained as given in Equation (9)

$$\lambda_p = \frac{d(a_p, b_p)}{\sum_{p=1}^{n} d(a_p, b_p)} \tag{9}$$

Precomputed Linear Kernel for WFSVM: In precomputed kernel, the kernel values are computed using linear kernel function [14] that is $K(x_i, x_j) = x_i^T.x$. The precomputed kernel matrix is used in training and testing files. In that case, the SVM does not need the original training and testing files. Assume there are L training instances $x_1, x_2, \ldots x_L$. Let $K(x,y)$ be the kernel value of two instances x and y. The input formats of training and testing files are:

New training instances for x_i:

0:i 1:K(x_i, x_1)...............L:K(x_i, x_L)

New testing instances for any x:

? 0:1 1:K(x, x_1)..............L:K(x x_L)

 That is, in the training file the first column must be the class label of x_i. In testing, ? can be any value. All kernel values including zeros must be explicitly provided. Any permutation or random subsets of the training/testing files are also valid.

 For SVM without weights the kernel matrix constructed above is used in training and testing as it is but for WFSVM the diagonal of the kernel matrix i.e. K(x_1, x_1), K(x_2, x_2) .... K(x_n, x_n) are replaced with the weights of the features calculated using Equation (9).

2.5   Classification

The classification of breast tissue type is implemented and validated with:

1) Traditional SVM using different kernel types

2) WFSVM using precomputed Linear Kernel with relevant weights in the diagonal of kernel matrix and without weights substitution.

For both approaches, the difference lies in choosing the kernel function or constructing the kernel function only. But the Binary SVM classification algorithm given below remains same [8]. The classification of images into their category includes two phases: Training phase and testing phase.

Training Phase: In this phase, from the training images, the low level features are extracted with these clinical features are added. For WFSVM, Linear kernel matrix is constructed with weights / without weights and its model file is created. For traditional SVM, the model file is created from the features for specific kernel types (Linear, Polynomial and RBF).

Algorithm – Binary SVM

Step 1: Input sample set T = { (x_i, y_i) }i=1 to l where x_i is the feature vector and y_i is the classes.

Step 2: Construct the kernel matrix using the features.

Step 3: Select appropriate penalty parameter and positive component.

Step 4: Structure the decision function using Equation (10)

$$f(x) = \mathrm{sgn}(\sum i = 1 \ to \ l \ y_i p_i \times K(x_i, x) + b*) \tag{10}$$

where $b*$ is the positive component.

The algorithm for SVM based on weighted feature (WFSVM) [5] is the same as traditional SVM but the diagonal of the kernel matrix is replaced with the weights of the features.

Testing Phase: The trained WFSVM and SVM are tested with the features of test set. From the testing set of MIAS database features are extracted, kernel matrix is constructed without weights in the diagonal and then given as input to the WFSVM for classification. For SVM the test features are given directly to validate the classification with different kernel types.

2.6   Performance Evaluation

The performance of the system is measured using the quantitative metrics such as Sensitivity, Specificity and Accuracy as given in Equations (11)-(13).

$$\text{Sensitivity} = TP / (TP + FN) \tag{11}$$

$$\text{Specificity} = TN / (TN + FP) \tag{12}$$

$$\text{Accuracy} = (TP + TN) / (TP + TN + FP + FN) \tag{13}$$

where TP (True Positive)   - correctly classified positive cases.

TN (True Negative)   - correctly classified negative cases.

FP (False Positive)   - incorrectly classified negative cases.

FN (False Negative)   - incorrectly classified positive cases.

3   Results and Performance Evaluation

The mammogram images are a kind of X-ray image with a size of 1024*1024 pixels with 256 level grayscale. Pre-processing techniques such as noise removal and background removal are applied on the mammogram images and the resultant images are shown in Fig 2.

After preprocessing, eight statistical features and twelve texture features are extracted from the preprocessed image, and clinical report features are added directly to form a feature set for classification. From this feature space SVM and WFSVM are performed.

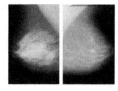

Fig. 2. Benign   Malignant   Noise removal   Background removal

For traditional SVM, the training feature space is used to build a train model file and then the test features are validated. This analysis is carried out for different kernel functions where equal number of samples is used in training and testing for both the classes. The training is carried out for different feature space with various kernel types by changing the *c, g* and *e* values and tested with the test features, resulted values are given in Table 1. From these results, it has been inferred that texture features are resulting with good accuracy than the other features.

Table 1. Performance Analysis of Support Vector Machine with Feature type

Feature type	Kernel type	Testing(58) misclassified samples		Accuracy in %	Number of support vectors
		B(34)	**M(24)**		
Statistical features	Lin	0	22	60	48
	Poly	0	24	58	53
	RBF	0	24	58	51
Texture features	Lin	0	1	98	14
	Poly	0	2	96	14
	RBF	0	2	96	10
Statistical, Texture and Clinical features	Lin	0	6	90	8
	Poly	0	8	86	8
	RBF	0	11	81	39

Lin– Linear, Poly– Polynomial, RBF– Radial Basis Function
B – Benign, M – Malignant.

For WFSVM, the relevant features are identified and maximum weight is assigned using the principle of maximizing deviations between the classes. The precomputed kernel matrix is constructed from the features of training dataset and the diagonal is replaced with the weighted features for training, from which the train model file is created. Then the kernel matrix is constructed from the features of test dataset is given as input to the train model file and the classification accuracy is tested. In this approach, to prove the importance of relevant features the constructed kernel matrix is validated without substituting the weights in the diagonal also. In both the cases, equal number of samples is used in training and testing. The detailed result of various analysis are tabulated in Table 2.

Table 2. Performance Analysis of Weighted Feature Support Vector Machine with Feature type

Feature type	Kernel type(4) – Precomputed linear kernel	Testing(58)- misclassified samples		Accuracy cy in %	Number of support vectors
		B(34)	M (24)		
Statistical features	With weights	0	24	58	44
	Without weights	1	21	62	51
Texture features	With weights	0	6	90	2
	Without weights	0	13	78	12
Statistical, Texture and Clinical features	With weights	0	8	86	14
	Without weights	1	10	81	8

B – Benign, M – Malignant.

From the results of Table 2, the Precomputed kernel with weights of texture features are resulted with high classification accuracy with less number of support vectors was inferred.

In Table 1 and Table 2, the misclassifications of Benign and Malignant classes are given. i.e. False Negative and False Positive. From these values, True Positive and True Negative can be calculated. The quantitative metrics are analyzed for texture features and shown in Table 3. For analysis, texture features is selected since it has resulted with high accuracy than other combinations. The value of sensitivity indicates that Benign samples are classified correctly but specificity indicates the more misclassifications in Malignant. The reason for this variation in specificity is the number of malignant cases taken for testing is less since large numbers of patient records are not available in the MIAS dataset.

Table 3. Performance Metrics Analysis for Texture Features

Approach used	Accuracy	Sensitivity	Specificity	No of support vectors
SVM – Linear	98	100	96	14
WFSVM- With weights	90	100	75	2
WFSVM-Without weights	78	100	46	12

4   Conclusions and Future Work

In this paper, the efficiency of segregating the mammogram tissue as Benign or Malignant is analyzed using two approaches, such as WFSVM and Traditional SVM with statistical, texture and clinical features. The character of background tissue which dominates the benign and malignant classes are also analyzed and it is inferred that malignant class falls majorly under the background tissue type dense glandular with tissue shape calcification. In real time applications, when a single patient record is given as input for testing, then it is classified efficiently using WFSVM since relevant features are assigned with more weights than the other features, whereas in traditional SVM all features are assigned with equal weights. To justify the need of WFSVM, the system was tested without updating the weight values in the diagonal also, which yields less accuracy in classification. Considering the feature set, texture features are resulted with high accuracy in traditional SVM and WFSVM with less number of support vectors. In future research, the approach used can be tested with DDSM (Digital Database for Screening Mammography) dataset where more number of patient records is available. The WFSVM can be constructed for other kernel types also. This project can be expanded by incorporating other learning techniques to achieve the task of ensemble learning and understanding in mammogram images.

References

1. Jaffar, M.A., Ahmed, B., Hussain, A., Naveed, N., Jabeen, F., Mirza, A.M.: Multi domain features based classification of Mammogram Images using SVM and MLP. In: Fourth International Conference on Innovative Computing, Information and Control, pp. 1301–1304 (2009)
2. Verma, B.: Impact of multiple clusters on Neural classification of ROIs in Digital Mammograms. In: International Joint Conference on Neural Networks, pp. 3220–3223 (2009)
3. Sheshadri, H.S., Kandaswamy, A.: Breast tissue classification using statistical feature extraction of Mammograms. Journal of Medical Imaging and Information Sciences 23(3), 105–107 (2006)
4. Wang, K., Wang, X., Zhong, Y.: A Weighted Feature Support Vector Machines method for semantic image classification. In: International Conference on Measuring Technology and Mechatronics Automation, vol. 1, pp. 377–380 (2010)
5. Wang, T., Tian, S., Huang, H.: Feature Weighted Support Vector Machine. Journal of Electronics and Information Technology 31(3), 514–518 (2009)
6. Wang, L., Khan, L.: Automatic image annotation and retrieval using weighted feature selection. Journal of Multimedia Tools and Applications 29(1), 55–71 (2006)
7. Sun, B., Song, S.-J., Wu, C.: A New Algorithm of Support Vector Machine based on Weighted Feature. In: International Conference on Machine Learning and Cybernetics, vol. 3, pp. 1616–1620 (2009)
8. Lee, Y., Lin, Y., Wahb, G.: Multi-category Support Vector Machines, Technical report, University of Wisconson-Madison (2001)
9. MIAS database, http://peipa.essex.ac.uk/info/mias.html
10. International Agency for Research on Cancer, http://www.iarc.fr
11. Breast Cancer Scenario in India, http://www.breastcancerindia.net/bc/statistics/stati.htm
12. National Center for Biotechnology Information, http://www.ncbi.nlm.nih.gov
13. Mammogram accuracy report by Radiologist, http://www.reuters.com/article/2007
14. LIBSVM, http://www.csie.ntu.edu.tw/~cjlin/libsvm/
15. Dhawan, A.P.: Medical Image Analysis. IEEE Press, A John Wiley &Sons Inc. (2003)

INZEDS: An Integrated Explosive Detection System Using Zigbee Based Wireless Sensor Network and Nanotechnology

R. Divya and G.S.S.K. Pooja Santoshi

Department of Information Technology,
Sri Sairam Engineering College,
West Tambaram, Chennai-44,
India
{divyalavan,poojasantoshigssk}@gmail.com

Abstract. In today's scenario, explosives detonated in population dense public places are highly destructive. An Explosive detection mechanism which enables detection of explosives amidst dense population is thus the need of the hour. The current detection systems such as ion mobility spectrometer, X-ray imaging have many disadvantages. There exists no system that continuously monitors an area for presence of explosives. Thus a new system that would monitor an area continuously for the presence of explosives is proposed. This paper uses powerful nanosensor to detect several kinds of explosives from any distance. It is made up of arrays of silicon nanowires forming a nanotransistor to detect explosives. The nanowires are coated with an electron-rich molecular layer that binds to the explosive due to the electron transfer from the electron-rich amino groups of the layer to the electron-poor explosive. This change in the charge distribution leads to an abrupt change in the conductivity of the nanowires that indicates the presence of explosive. This information will be passed using Zigbee Wireless Standards to the security agency that is nearest to the explosive position. The main advantages of the proposed scheme are its small size, reasonable operational area, higher throughput and lesser probability of false alarms.

Keywords: Explosive Detection, Nano technology, Zigbee, Nanowires.

1   Introduction

Terrorism is the perennial problem of the world. There have been 115 terrorist attacks in India till date and around 30000 innocent people have lost their lives. Given the devastation that bombs can cause, and the risk they pose to national security, the development of an explosive detection system is absolutely necessary. No autonomous system is being used by any security forces to inform them about the presence of explosives in an area.

An explosive is a chemical mixture that causes a sudden, instantaneous release of gas, heat and pressure accompanied by a loud noise when subjected to a certain amount of shock, pressure, or temperature.

P.V. Krishna, M.R. Babu, and E. Ariwa (Eds.): ObCom 2011, Part II, CCIS 270, pp. 330–336, 2012.

1.1 Overview of Proposed Paper

The proposed Explosive detection system uses Nanotechnology based sensors to give higher probability of detection and lesser false alarms. The sensor is built using arrays of silicon nanowires that form an electronic device called a nano-transistor ,to detect explosives from any distance. The nanowires are coated with a molecular layer that binds to the explosive molecules in the form of charge-transfer complexes. The binding process involves the transfer of electrons from the electron-rich amino groups of the molecular layer to the electron-poor explosive molecules. This change in the charge distribution on the surface of the nanowires modulates the electric field and leads to an abrupt change in the conductivity of the nanowires, which can be easily measured.

To alert the security agencies about the presence of an explosive in the area, Zigbee wireless standard is chosen. Though the wireless technologies Bluetooth, USB, Wi-Fi are available, ZigBee devices are chosen as they have the ability to form a mesh network between nodes. Meshing is a type of daisy chaining from one device to another. This technique allows the short range of an individual node to be expanded and multiplied, covering a much larger area.

2 Current Systems

The current systems for explosive detection have a constraint on their operational limits. The existing techniques to detect explosives include X-ray imaging, Ion Mobility Spectrometers, Amplifying Fluorescent Polymers, Fluorescent Sensors and Laser Sensors. In FIG 1 an X-ray imaging device is shown. In X-ray imaging, specially designed X-ray machines can detect explosives by looking at the density of the items being examined. Thus this technique requires the items being examined to be in close proximity with the detector. But since explosive devices can be installed and hidden in objects of daily life by the use of tiny electric and electronic elements, in addition to the application of X-ray imaging, the use of other technologies becomes necessary. Ion mobility spectrometry is an analytical technique used to separate and identify ionized molecules in the gas phase based on their mobility in a carrier buffer gas.FIG 2 shows an ion mobility spectrometer. Though ion mobility spectrometers are fast, sensitive, and reliable, they are expensive, bulky, require manual attention, and operate only when a suspicious material is brought to them for analysis. Amplifying Fluorescence Polymers rely on the adsorption of the explosive molecule on the surface of the polymer that leads to a change in the fluorescence characteristic. AFP's with TNT adsorbed on the surface continuously fluorescence under the ultraviolet light source. But this has a serious limitation that it can detect only presence of TNT and cannot operate in open space. For a fluorescent sensor, using the intensity of the fluorescent light to read the signal is more error-prone and noisier than measuring a wavelength. Since laser sensors have to be present more or less right on top of the explosives the technique is not ideal for monitoring a larger area. The difficulty with the detection of explosives such as TNT is their extremely low volatility. Methods available for the analysis of air samples are expensive and time-consuming, and require large, bulky instruments, laborious sample preparation, and expert handling.

Fig. 1. X-Ray Imaging

Fig. 2. Ion Mobility Spectrometer

2.1   Summary of Limitations of Existing Systems[4]

1. Always requires manual operation.
2. Bulkier in size.
3. Traditional systems are power consuming.
4. Cannot detect explosives from a distance.
5. Limited operational area.

Thus it is evident that **"there exists no system that continuously monitors an area for presence of explosives."**And hence there is a need for an inexpensive, simple explosive detection method that allows for quick, easy, and robust high-throughput analysis. The main objective of the proposed scheme is to design a customized system that will afford increased detection capabilities with higher probability of detection and lower false alarms. The proposed Explosive Detection System uses powerful nanotechnology based sensor to detect several kinds of explosives from any distance and alerts the security agencies about the presence of explosives using Zigbee based wireless sensor network. The explosive detection system with nanowires is superior to all other explosive detection methods. Nanotechnology based sensors have strong potential for meeting all the requirements for an effective solution for the trace detection of explosives.

3   Proposed Project

The proposed explosive detection system **continuously** monitors an area for presence of explosives using Nanosensor from any distance based on the binding of explosive molecules on nanowires to form charge transfer complexes .The sensor then sends the information to one of the security agencies stored in the database that is nearest to the position of the explosive which is based on the Shortest Path Algorithm and the information is propagated using ZigBee wireless standards.

3.1   Explosive Detection Using Nano-Technology

The powerful electronic sensor detects numerous types of explosives from any distance. [5]The sensor is made up of arrays of silicon nanowires that form an electronic device called a nanotransistor, which is supersensitive to the surrounding electrical environment. The sensor is also highly portable, extremely sensitive, and more reliable at detecting explosives. The sensor is built using the principle of a nanoscale field-effect transistor. In contrast to a current-controlled classical transistor, a field-effect transistor is switched by means of an electric field. At the core of the device are nanowires made of the semiconductor silicon. These are coated with a molecular layer made from special silicon compounds that contain amino groups (NH2). Explosive molecules bind to these amino groups in the form of charge-transfer complexes. The binding process involves the transfer of electrons from the electron-rich amino groups to the electron-poor explosives. This change in the charge distribution on the surface of the nanowires modulates the electric field and leads to an abrupt change in the conductivity of the nanowires, which is easily measured.

To increase the chips' sensitivity, 200 individual sensors are attached that allow increased ability and sensitivity, in order to detect many different kinds of explosives quickly. It is thus able to analyze liquid and gaseous samples without prior concentration or other sample preparation at previously unattainable sensitivities. It is possible to analyze concentrations down to 0.1 ppt (parts per trillion); that is, one molecule of explosive in 10 quadrillion other molecules. Not only can the sensor detect explosives from a safe distance, but it is also portable, so that it can be mounted to a stationary object, such as a wall. The sensor also has the advantage of providing a definite identification of explosives and ensures that there are no detection errors or failures.

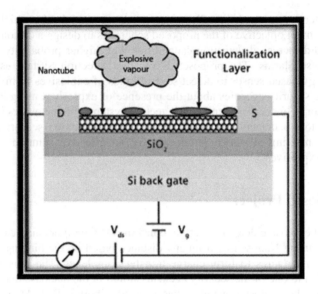

Fig. 3. Working of the Nanotransistor

3.2   Alert to Security Agencies Using Zigbee Based Wireless Sensor Network

i) Overview of Zigbee [1]

ZigBee, also known as IEEE 802.15.4, is a communications standard designed for low-power short-range communications between wireless devices. It is classified as a wireless personal area network (WPAN). ZigBee uses the IEEE 802.15.4 physical and MAC (medium access control) layers to provide standards-based, reliable wireless data transfer. ZigBee adds network structure, routing, and security (e.g., key management and authentication) to complete the communications suite. ZigBee is a standards-based technology for remote monitoring, control and sensor network applications. It allows users to be able to control devices without pointing at their devices. The ZigBee standard was created to address the need for a cost-effective, standards-based wireless networking solution that supports low data-rates, low-power consumption, security, and reliability. There are three categories of ZigBee devices:

- **ZigBee Network Coordinator:** Smart node that automatically initiates the formation of the network.
- **ZigBee Router:** Another smart node that links groups together and provides multi-hoping for messages. It associates with other routers and end-devices.
- **ZigBee End Devices:** Includes sensors, actuators, monitors, switches, dimmers and other controllers.

ii) Advantages of Zigbee

• Reliable and self healing
• Supports large number of nodes
• Easy to deploy
• Very long battery life
• Secure
• Low cost

iii) Zigbee Transmitter

The NanoSensor sends a signal to the microcontroller unit if an explosive is detected in that area. The high power transmission type ZMN2405HP Zigbee module is using the CC2430 transceiver IC from Texas Instrument comply to the IEEE 802.15.4 standards with a maximum transmission power of 100 mW - 250 mW. The module alone requires a 5VDC power supply, operating at a frequency of 2.4GHz to get the best of power consumption as low as 3uA.

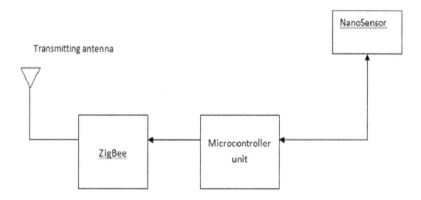

Fig. 4.1. Zigbee Transmitter

iv) Zigbee Receiver

The data from the sensor is received wirelessly by the Zigbee module at the receiver end. The module then transmits the data to the computer which searches for the nearest security agencies stored in the database and alerts them. It then waits for an acknowledgement. And then broadcasts the information to all other security agencies in the database if unacknowledged.

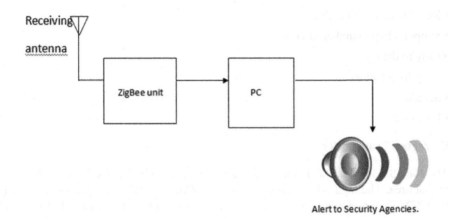

Fig. 4.2. Zigbee Receiver

4   Conclusion

Thus, in this paper an efficient Explosive detectionsystem is introduced. This system has many advantages over the traditional bomb detection systems such as smaller size, automated operation, distant detection, highly portable, higher efficiency in detection and lesser probability of false alarms. Nanosensors with increased sensitivity and selectivity and the ability to operate in a multimodal platform offer a potential paradigm for deploying a large number of sensors for detection. ZigBee networks provide smart, low-cost, low-power, low-maintenance monitoring and control systems. The overall advantages of the proposed system are low cost, reasonable coverage area and high throughput. Thus a integrated highly efficient explosive detection system can be designed at low cost to save human lives . Thus we have proposed that the integration of nanosensors and Zigbee based wireless network have potential to form an integrated explosive sensor system that can make the world bereft of terrorism.

References

1. The Zigbee Alliance website (2009), http://www.zigbee.org/
2. Yinon, Y. (ed.): Counterterrorist Detection Techniques of Explosives. Elsevier, Amsterdam (2007)
3. Woodfin, R.L. (ed.): Trace Chemical Sensing of Explosives. John Wiley & Sons, Hoboken (2007)
4. IJCSI International Journal of Computer Science Issues, vol. 8(4), No 2 (July 2011), ISSN 1694-0814, http://www.IJCSI.org
5. Singh, K.A.: Observatory Nano. Institute of Nanotechnology, U.K (2009)

Person Identification Using Palm Print Features with an Efficient Method of DWT

S. Sumathi[1] and R. Rani Hemamalini[2]

[1] Department of ECE, Sathyabama University,
Chennai-96, India
`sumathi_ba@rediffmail.com`
[2] Department of E&I, St.Peter's Engineering College,
Chennai-54, India
`ranihema@yahoo.com`

Abstract. In this paper, a new efficient method for individual identification, using palm print features based on Discrete Wavelet Transform (DWT) is proposed. Biometric system is designed to identify the people accurately, based on human physiological features. Palm print serves as reliable human identifier because the palm print patterns are not duplicated by others, even in monozygotic twins. Wavelet coefficients are used as features for identifying the individual and using Support Vector Machine (SVM) classifier for the classification purpose. Use reduced wavelet coefficients by specified window size placed at center of the image for palm print identification. Experiments are conducted for various window sizes and chose the best window size which gives good recognition rate and better result in substantial savings in storage and computation time. Experimental results show promising performance with the proposed methods from Hong Kong PolyU Multispectral Palm print database.

Keywords: Identification, Palm print, Discrete Wavelet Transform, Support Vector Machine.

1   Introduction

Biometrics be the most secure and convenient method to satisfy the need for identity recognition of individual in the society. For that physiological or behavioral characteristics of person are used for automatic identification of an individual Palm prints are potentially a good choice for biometric applications because they're invariant with a person, easy to capture, and difficult to duplicate. The palm print is regarded as one of the most unique, reliable, stable personal characteristics and performs effectively as a biometric. They offer greater security than fingerprints because palm veins are more complex than finger veins. Compared with the fingerprint, the palm provides a larger surface area so that more features can be extracted. The line features of a palm are stable throughout one's lifetime. Since palm print uses much lower resolution imaging sensor compared with fingerprints, the computation is much faster in both preprocessing and feature extraction stages.

P.V. Krishna, M.R. Babu, and E. Ariwa (Eds.): ObCom 2011, Part II, CCIS 270, pp. 337–346, 2012.
© Springer-Verlag Berlin Heidelberg 2012

Iris scanning biometric system can provides a high accuracy biometric system but the cost of iris scanning devices is high. Palm print biometric system is user-friendly because users can grant the access frequently by only presenting their hand in front of the camera. In face recognition system, users are required to remove their accessories such as spectacles or ear pendant during acquisition. Palm print biometric system achieves higher accuracy than hand geometry biometric system because the geometry or shape of the hand for most of the adults is relatively similar. Palm print contains geometry features, line features, point features, statistical features and texture features.

An online personal verification system by fusing palm print and palm vein information is presented in [1] based on GLMC entropy. A novel palm print and knuckle print tracking approach to automatically detect and capture these features from low resolution video stream is proposed in [2] and no constraint is imposed and the subject can place his/her hand naturally on top of the sensor without touching any device. A method of feature extraction of palm print using real- Gabor transform (RGT) is proposed [3], which converts the spatial domain information of palm print to joint spatial frequency domain. In critical sampling case, by calculating the compactly distributed coefficients of RGT, the sub-block energy distribution of palm print in spatial-frequency domain are extracted as recognition features.

A frequency domain feature extraction algorithm for palm-print recognition is proposed [4], which efficiently exploits the local spatial variations in a palm print image based on extracting dominant spectral features from each of these bands using two dimensional discrete cosine transform (2D-DCT). A novel approach is proposed, [5] to computing hand geometry measurements from frontal views of freely posed hands. These approaches offer advantages in hygiene, comfort and reliability. A novel fusion approach at the lowest level, i.e. the image pixel level is proposed [6]. It performs the Gabor transform on face and palm print images and combines them at the pixel level. A scanner-based personal authentication system by using the palm print features is proposed in [7]. The authentication system consists of enrollment and verification stages. In the enrollment stage, the training samples are collected and processed to generate the matching templates. In the verification stage, a query sample is matched with the reference templates to decide whether it is a genuine sample or not.

A new bimodal biometric system using feature-level fusion of hand shape and palm texture is presented in [8]. The combination is of significance since both the palm print and hand-shape images are proposed to be extracted from the single hand image acquired from a digital camera. A new method to authenticate individuals based on palm print identification and verification is described in [9] via multiple feature extraction. Palm print authentication based on intra-model feature fusion using wavelet is presented in [10].

2   Methodology

The proposed system is built based on Discrete Wavelet Transform of the image and by applying multiclass SVM for building the classifiers. In this section the theoretical background of both the approaches are introduced.

2.1   Discrete Wavelet Transform

Nowadays, wavelets have been used quite frequently in image processing. They have been used for feature extraction, de-noising, compression, face recognition, and image super-resolution. The decomposition of images into different frequency ranges permits the isolation of the frequency components introduced by "intrinsic deformations" or "extrinsic factors" into certain sub-bands. This process results in isolating small changes in an image mainly in high frequency sub-band images. Hence, discrete wavelet transform (DWT) is a suitable tool to be used for designing a classification system.

The 2-D wavelet decomposition of an image is performed by applying 1-D DWT along the rows of the image first, and, then, the results are decomposed along the columns. This operation results in four decomposed sub-band images referred to as low–low (LL), low–high (LH), high–low (HL), and high–high (HH). The frequency components of those sub-band images cover the frequency components of the original image as shown in Figure 1.

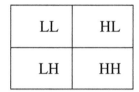

Fig. 1. The result of 2-D DWT decomposition

2.2   Support Vector Machine

Support vector machines (SVMs) are a set of related supervised learning methods that analyze data and recognize patterns, used for classification and regression analysis. The standard SVM is a non-probabilistic binary linear classifier, i.e. it predicts, for each given input, which of two possible classes the input is a member of. A classification task usually involves with training and testing data which consists of some data instances. Each instance in the training set contains one "target value" (class labels) and several "attributes" (features). SVM has an extra advantage of automatic model selection in the sense that both the optimal number and locations of the basis functions are automatically obtained during training. The performance of SVM largely depends on the kernel [11]. SVM is essentially a linear learning machine. For the input training sample set

$$(x_i, y_i), i = 1....n, x \in R^n, y \in \{-1,+1\} \tag{1}$$

the classification hyper plane equation is let to be

$$(\omega, x) + b = 0 \tag{2}$$

thus the classification margin is 2 / |ω| .To maximize the margin, that is to minimize |ω| ,the optimal hyperplane problem is transformed to quadratic programming problem as follows,

$$\begin{cases} \min \phi(\omega) = \dfrac{1}{2}(\omega,\omega) \\ s.t. \, y_i((\omega.x)+b) \ge 1, \quad i = 1,2....i \end{cases} \tag{3}$$

After introduction of Lagrange multiplier, the dual problem is given by,

$$\begin{cases} \max Q(a) = \displaystyle\sum_{i=1}^{n} a_i - \dfrac{1}{2}\sum_{i=1}^{n}\sum_{j=1}^{n} y_i y_j a_i a_j K(x_i.x_j) \\ \\ s.t. \displaystyle\sum_{i=1}^{n} y_i a_i = 0, \quad a_i \le 0, i = 1,2...., n \end{cases} \tag{4}$$

According to Kuhn-Tucker rules, the optimal solution must satisfy

$$a_i(y_i((w,x_i)+b))-1 = 0, i = 1,2...n \tag{5}$$

That is to say if the option solution is

$$a^* = (a_1^*, a_2^*, ..., a_i^*)^J, \quad i = 1,2...n \tag{6}$$

Then

$$w^* = \sum_{i=1}^{n} a_i^* y_i x_i$$

$$b^* = y_i - \sum_{i=1}^{n} y_i a_i^* (x_i, x_j), j \in \{j \mid a_i^* > 0\} \tag{7}$$

For every training sample point x_i, there is a corresponding Lagrange multiplier. And the sample points that are corresponding to $a_i = 0$ don't contribute to solve the classification hyperplane while the other points that are corresponding to $a_i > 0$ do, so it is called support vectors. Hence the optimal hyperplane equation is given by,

$$\sum_{x_o \in SV} a_i y_i (x_i, x_j) + b = 0 \tag{8}$$

The hard classifier is then,

$$y = \mathrm{sgn}\left[\sum_{x_i \in SV} a_i y_i (x_i, x_j) + b \right] \tag{9}$$

For nonlinear situation, SVM constructs an optimal separating hyperplane in the high dimensional space by introducing kernel function $K(x.y) = \emptyset(x).\emptyset(y)$, hence the nonlinear SVM is given by,

$$
\begin{cases}
\min \phi(\omega) = \dfrac{1}{2}(\omega, \omega) \\[2mm]
s.t. y_i((\omega.\phi(x_i)) + b) \geq 1, i = 1,2,....i
\end{cases}
\tag{10}
$$

And its dual problem is given by,

$$
\begin{cases}
\max L(a) = \displaystyle\sum_{i=1}^{i} a_i - \dfrac{1}{2}\sum_{i=1}^{i}\sum_{j=1}^{i} y_i y_j a_i a_j K(x_i.x_j) \\[4mm]
s.t. \displaystyle\sum y_i, a_i = 0, \quad 0 \leq a_i \leq c, i = 1,2,....l
\end{cases}
\tag{11}
$$

Thus the optimal hyper plane equation is determined by the solution to the optimal problem. A SVM classifier can predict or classify input data belonging to two distinct classes. However, SVMs can be used as multiclass classifiers by treating a K-class classification problem as K two-class problems. This is known as one vs. rest or one vs. all classification. The SVM classifier implementation is standard implementation. In the MATLAB environment the LIBSVM software is used. LIBSVM is integrated software for support vector classification, regression and distribution estimation. It supports multi-class classification.

3   Proposed Method

The proposed Palm print Identification Phase (PIP) consists of two stages. They are feature extraction stage and classification stage.

3.1   Feature Extraction Stage

The feature extraction stage in PIP is shown in Figure 2. Feature extraction is concerned with quantification of texture characteristics in terms of collection of quantitative measurement features, often referred as feature vector. First, the given palm print image is decomposed by using Haar wavelet transform. From 3-Level wavelet decomposition, 10 sub-bands are obtained. The selection of wavelet coefficients as features depends on the size of the window placed over the center of each sub-bands as shown in Figure 3.

The selected features from the 10 sub-bands are fused together in a serial manner starting from the detailed coefficients to approximate wavelet coefficients. For training purpose, window based wavelet features are extracted for 4 images from each object, totally 152 images and stored in a vector called as Feature Vector for training purpose.

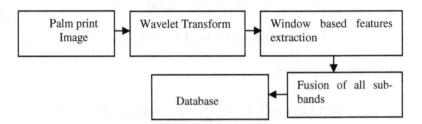

Fig. 2. Feature Extraction stage in PIP

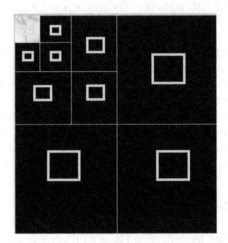

Fig. 3. Selection of Wavelet coefficients in PIP

3.2   Classification Stage

In the classification stage, the multi class SVM classifier with linear kernel is trained with the Feature vector calculated in the feature extraction stage. To recognize the user, the same wavelet features explained in the feature extraction stage are extracted from the user and tested with the SVM classifier. The classifier gives the class i.e. index of the retrieved image. Specifically, a threshold value is chosen, the correlation value between the user and the training images in the retrieved index whose absolute value exceeds the threshold are recognized while others are unrecognized. The correlation value is defined by,

$$r = \frac{\sum_m \sum_n (A_{mn} - \overline{A})(B_{mn} - \overline{B})}{\sqrt{\left(\sum_m \sum_n (A_{mn} - \overline{A})^2\right)\left(\sum_m \sum_n (B_{mn} - \overline{B})^2\right)}} \tag{12}$$

where $\overline{A}$ = mean2 (A) and $\overline{B}$ = mean2 (B). The moderate correlation value 0.5 is used for classification purpose.

4   Experimental Results

In order to execute the proposed method in the previous section we performed by using new data set with palm image from Hong Kong PolyU Multispectral Palm print database [12].

It consists of the palm image developed by the Biometric Research Centre at the Hong Kong Polytechnic University. The data base has been acquired, using real time multispectral palm print capture device which can capture palm print images under blue, green, red and near-infrared (NIR) illuminations and develop a large-scale multispectral palm print database. Multispectral palm print images were collected from 250 volunteers, including 195 males and 55 females. In this data base, each has his/her image taken under 4 illuminations, with 24 images of each illumination from 2 palms from each subject. Here we randomly choose 50 subjects each has 12 images, among these 6 images are taken for training and 6 images for testing chosen randomly. The sample Hong Kong PolyU Multispectral Palm print images are shown in Figure 4.

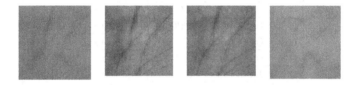

Fig. 4. Sample Multi spectral Palm Print Images

To show the effectiveness of the proposed system, many computer simulations and experiments conducted with IIT Delhi Palm Print data base and Hong Kong PolyU Multispectral Palm print database. The performance measures False Acceptance Rate (FAR) and False Rejection Rate (FRR) are calculated for various thresholds (0.1 to 1) and various window sizes (10 to 100%). The system is implemented in MATLAB version 7.6. The best window size of 60% which gives better success rate is chosen, FAR and FRR values of palm print identification phase are shown in Table 1 and 2 respectively and the graphical representations are shown in Figure 5 and 6 respectively. Table 3 shows the FAR and FRR values of selected parameters for PIP. To carefully analyze the table 1 and 2, a threshold of 0.8 with Blue illumination is chosen for identification of individual. For high security applications, the FAR is reduced to zero. Experiments conducted with IIT Delhi Palm print database, to analyze the result of various threshold and window sizes, a threshold of 0.5 with 60% window size is chosen for identification of individual. For security application the FAR is reduced to almost zero shown in Table 4.

Table 1. FAR values for various Thresholds with 60% window size

Th	RED	BLUE	GREEN	NIR
0.1	0.00612	0.00084	0.003810	0.001088
0.2	0.00612	0.00084	0.003810	0.001088
0.3	0.00612	0.00084	0.003810	0.001088
0.4	0.00612	0.00084	0.003708	0.001088
0.5	0.000510	0.000646	0.003401	0.001088
0.6	0.000340	0.000510	0.002653	0.001020
0.7	0.000034	0.000710	0.001633	0.000850
0.8	0.000000	0.000000	0.000612	0.000340
0.9	0.000000	0.000000	0.000000	0.000000
1	0.000000	0.000000	0.000000	0.000000

Table 2. FRR values for various Thresholds with 60% window size

Th	RED	BLUE	GREEN	NIR
0.1	0.00000	0.00000	0.00000	0.00000
0.2	0.00000	0.00000	0.00000	0.00000
0.3	0.00000	0.00000	0.00000	0.00000
0.4	0.00000	0.00000	0.00000	0.00000
0.5	0.00000	0.001667	0.005	0.00000
0.6	0.008333	0.023333	0.066667	0.001667
0.7	0.073333	0.083333	0.155	0.02
0.8	0.26167	0.26	0.26167	0.155
0.9	0.46	0.445	0.31333	0.40833
1	0.47	0.45667	0.31333	0.44667

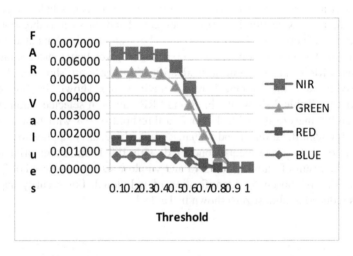

Fig. 5. Graphical representation of FAR for various threshold and 60% window size

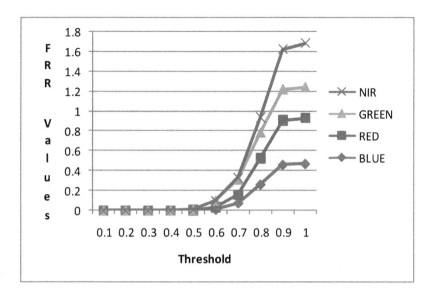

Fig. 6. Graphical representation of FRR for various threshold and 60% window size

Table 3. FAR and FRR values for selected threshold and illumination

	PIP
FAR	0.00000
FRR	0.26

Table 4. FAR and FRR values for selected threshold of IIT Palm Print Database

	PIP
FAR	0.0001
FRR	0.015

5   Conclusion

In this paper, a new efficient method is presented for the purpose of individual identification. The wavelet coefficients for palm print identification are reduced by using specified window size placed at center of the image. Experiments are conducted for various window sizes and the best window size of 60% which gives better success rate is chosen. Furthermore, the proposed approach considerably reduces the computation time and substantial savings in storage with 60% instead of 100%. The experimental results demonstrate that the proposed approach is an effective technique for individual identification with zero false acceptance rate.

In the future work we plan to extract palm print from hand images, take two modalities such as hand geometry and reduced coefficients of palm print for identification with score level fusion and also to exploit the model with serial fusion of different modalities.

References

1. Zhang, D., Guo, Z.: Online joint palmprint and palmvein verification. Journal of Expert Systems with Applications, 2626–2631 (2001)
2. Michael, G.K.O., Connie, T.: Robust Palm Print and Knuckle Print Recognition System Using a Contactless Approach. In: 5th IEEE Conference on Industrial Electronics and Applications, pp. 323–329 (2010)
3. Zhang, Y., Zhao, D.: Palm Print Recognition Based on Sub-Block Energy Feature Extracted by Real 2D-Gabor Transform. In: IEEE Conference on Artificial Intelligence and Computational Intelligence, pp. 124–128 (2010)
4. Imtiaz, H., Fattah, S.A.: A DCT-based Feature Extraction Algorithm for Palm-print Recognition. In: IEEE International Conference on Communication Control and Computing Technologies, pp. 657–660 (2010)
5. Jiang, X., Xu, W.: New Directions In Contact Free Hand Recognition. In: IEEE International Conference on Image Processing, pp. 389–392 (2007)
6. X.-Y. Jing, Y.-F. Yao.: Face and palmprint pixel level fusion and Kernel DCV-RBF classifier for small sample biometric recognition. Journal of Pattern Recognition, 3209 – 3224 (2007)
7. Han, C.-C., Cheng, H.-L.: Personal Authentication Using Palm Print Features. In: 5th Asian Conference on Computer Vision, pp. 1–6 (2002)
8. Kumar, A., Zhang, D.: Personal Recognition Using Hand Shape and Texture. IEEE Transactions on Image Processing, 2454–2461 (2006)
9. You, J., Li, W.: Hierarchical palmprint identification via multiple feature extraction. Journal of Pattern Recognition, 847–859 (2002)
10. Krishneswari, K., Arumugam, S.: Intramodal Feature Fusion Using Wavelet for Palmprint Authentication. International Journal of Engineering Science and Technology, 1597–1605 (2011)
11. Smola, A.J., Scholkopf, B., Muller, K.R.: The connection between regularization operators and support vector kernels. Neural Networks 11, 637–649 (1998)
12. Hong Kong PolyU Multispectral Palm print Database,
    http://www.comp.polyu.edu.hk/~biometrics/MultispectralPalmprint/MSP.htm
13. IIT   Database,   http://www4.comp.polyu.edu.hk/~csajaykr/IITD/Database_Palm.htm

PAPR Reduction Techniques for Multicarrier Systems

M.G. Sumithra and M. Sarumathi

Department of ECE, Bannari Amman Institute of Technology,
Sathyamangalam, Tamilnadu, India
mgsumithra@rediffmail.com, charu.nobel@gmail.com

Abstract. *OFDM* (Orthogonal Frequency Division Multiplexing) technique has been widely adopted in many wireless communication systems due to its high data-rate transmission ability and robustness to the multipath fading channel. One major drawback of the OFDM signal is the high peak-to-average power ratio (PAPR) problem. The high PAPR results in the in-band distortion and out-of-band radiation when the OFDM signal is fed into a nonlinear power amplifier (PA).Large fluctuations of OFDM signal amplitude represents a major drawback for amplification in mobile communication systems. This paper enumerate an idea about comparison of PAPR reduction schemes in terms of its performance. Clipping at nyquist and oversampled rate, and Partial transmit sequence method of PAPR reduction are considered here for comparison in terms of Complementary Cumulative Distribution Function (CCDF) and Bit error rate.

Keywords: Orthogonal Frequency-division multiplexing (OFDM), peak-to-average power ratio(PAPR), Clipping, Partial transmit sequence (PTS), Complementary Cumulative Distribution Function (CCDF).

1 Introduction

Multicarrier modulation systems, often also called as orthogonal frequency division multiplexing (OFDM), are competing well with single carrier systems. One of the advantages of OFDM system over the single carrier system is the better performance in fading phenomena of multipath environment. The OFDM system has a serious drawback which is denoted as high Peak to Average Power Ratio (PAPR)[1], [2]. The nature of modulation causes these high peaks.

When multiple sinusoids are added together to form the multicarrier signal, these peaks are generated. When all the peaks are added together, the peak appears. For example the peak magnitude would have a value of N, where the average might be quite low due to the destructive interference between the sinusoids. So the ratio between peak and average will be high which is usually undesirable for amplification stage and it usually strains the analog circuitry [3]. When the signal is introduced to the high power amplifier (HPA), high peaks could cause problems. Because HPA is a non-linear component and high PAPR signals would require high range of dynamic linearity from the analog circuits. So power amplifiers with higher linearity are more expensive and consume more power and normally have less efficiency. Even the best

P.V. Krishna, M.R. Babu, and E. Ariwa (Eds.): ObCom 2011, Part II, CCIS 270, pp. 347–356, 2012.
© Springer-Verlag Berlin Heidelberg 2012

power amplifier in case of linearity and efficiency has to operate with back-off to maintain this problem [3].

A reach variety of signals used in modern communication systems are characterized by large envelope fluctuations. This fact creates problems for distortion free and effective amplification because a power amplifier (PA) at the transmitter usually exhibits a nonlinear behavior with the respect to such signals. One of the solutions of the problem consists in decreasing envelope fluctuations of the signal before amplification. Variations of envelope of the signal are characterized by its peak-to average power ratio (PAPR). PAPR reduction is especially important for multicarrier transmission, for instance, in orthogonal frequency division multiplexing (OFDM) systems.

Among a great number of PAPR reduction techniques clipping [1], [2], [4] and Partial Transmit Sequence (PTS) are the simplest and most widely used method. This paper presents comparative analysis of clipping schemes (Nyquist and oversampled rate) and PTS scheme for PAPR reduction method in OFDM transmission.

2   OFDM system

2.1   OFDM System Architecture

A typical OFDM transmission system is shown in Fig. 1. At the transmitting end, first of all, input binary serial data stream is first processed by channel encoder, constellation mapping and serial to parallel (S/P) conversion. A single signal is divided into N parallel routes after N-point inverse fast Fourier transform (IFFT). Each orthogonal sub-carrier is modulated by one of the N data routes independently. By definition the N processed points constitute one OFDM symbol.

Next, convert modulated parallel data to serial sequence and then copy the last L samples of one symbol to the front as cyclic prefix (CP). At last, arrive at transmitter after process of digital to analog (D/A) conversion and radio frequency (RF) modulation. To recover the information in OFDM system, reception process is converse and self-explanatory. At the receiving end, digital down conversion is carried out, demodulate receiving signals.

At last, demodulated signals are fed into an analog to digital (A/D) converter, sample output and take timing estimation to find initial position of OFDM symbol. The CP added in transmission process is removed and N-Points fast Fourier transform (FFT) transformation will be conducted on the left sample points to recover the data in frequency domain. The output of baseband demodulation is passed to a channel decoder, which eventually recover the original data.

An OFDM symbol is made of sub-carriers modulated by constellations mapping. This mapping can be achieved from phase-shift keying (PSK) or quadrature amplitude modulation (QAM). For an OFDM system with N sub-carriers, the high-speed binary serial input stream is denoted as $\{a_i\}$. After serial to parallel conversion (S/P) and constellation mapping, a new parallel signal sequence $\{d_0, d_1, \cdots, d_i, \cdots, d_{N-1}\}$ is obtained, d_i is a discrete complex-valued signal.

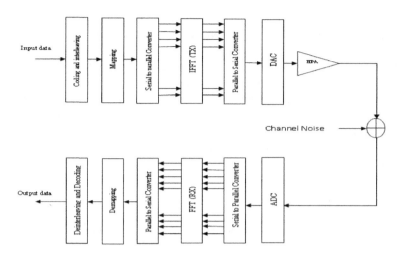

Fig. 1. Block diagram of OFDM system architecture

Here, $di \in \pm 1$ when BPSK mapping is adopted. When QPSK mapping is used, $di \in \pm 1, \pm j$. Each element of parallel signal sequence is supplied to N orthogonal sub-carriers $e^{j2\pi f_0 t}, e^{j2\pi f_1 t}, \ldots e^{j2\pi f_{N-1} t}$ for modulation, respectively. Finally, modulated signals are added together to form an OFDM symbol. Use of discrete Fourier transform simplifies the OFDM system structure.

An OFDM receiver consists of a group of decoders, which move different carrier frequencies to zero frequency and perform integration over one symbol period. Since sub-carriers are orthogonal to one another, only specified carrier can be demodulated, the rest irrelevant carriers do not have any impact on the results of the integration.

The frequency of an OFDM signal can be expressed as

$$f_i = f_c + i.\Delta f \tag{1}$$

where f_c stands for carrier frequency, Δf is the smallest interval between different sub-carrier frequencies. Δf is given by

$$\Delta f = \frac{1}{T} = \frac{1}{Nt_s} \tag{2}$$

where t_s is time interval of symbol sequence $\{ d_0, d_1, \cdots, d_i, \cdots, d_{N-1} \}$. Generally, we use complex baseband equivalent signal to describe OFDM output signal, which can be expressed as follows:

$$s(t) = \sum_{i=0}^{N-1} d_i e^{j2\pi\Delta ft} = \sum_{i=0}^{N-1} d_i e^{j2\pi\frac{1}{T}t}, t \in [0,T] \tag{3}$$

The real and imaginary parts of complex factor corresponding to in-phase components and quadrature components of OFDM symbols, respectively.

At the receiver, corresponding sub-carriers are applied to the input for demodulation. The process of demodulation for the *k-th* sub-carrier signal is described as follows: The output signal is multiplied by the *k-th* demodulation carrier expression $exp(-j\pi(2k-N)t/T)$, and then integrate the product over one OFDM symbol period T. The integration result is the transmitting signal corresponding to the *k-th* sub-carrier signal. It is known that modulation and demodulation in OFDM system can be achieved by IFFT and FFT, respectively. A data symbol in the "frequency domain" is transformed to "time-domain" by performing the *N* point IFFT operation, before being sent across to the wireless channel for transmission after radio frequency modulation.

2.2   PAPR of the OFDM Signal

PAPR of the signal s(t) on the time interval [O,T] is defined as:

$$PAPR = \frac{\max \ |s(t)|^2, 0 \le t \le T}{1/T \int_0^T |s(t)|^2 \ dt}.\tag{4}$$

Basically peak-to-average power ratio (PAPR) is the most popular parameter used to evaluate the dynamic range of the time-domain OFDM signal or signal envelop variation or the crest factor (CF) where

$$PAPR = CF^2 \tag{5}$$

Crest factor is another parameter which is widely used in the literature, and defined as the square root of the PAPR.

For example, the data sequence in (2) with length of N during the time interval of [0, T] is assumed as a modulated data for the multicarrier system.

$$A = (A_0, A_1, ...,A_{(N-1)}) \tag{6}$$

The OFDM signal with a large number of components may be considered as Gaussian due to the central limit theorem and consequently, its inphase (I) and Quadrature (Q) components are also Gaussian [6]. It means that square envelope of the signal is subjected to chi-square distribution with 2 degrees of freedom.

PAPR of the continuous signal approaches to that of its discrete version when the sampling frequency is increased. From this point of view, we can roughly consider PAPR of four times oversampled OFDM signal as an approximation for PAPR of the continuous signal. In this case Complementary Cumulative Distribution Function *(CCDF)* for PAPR

$$(CCDF(\gamma_0) = P_r\{PAPR > \gamma_0\}) \tag{7}$$

can be defined as probability that 4N chi-square distributed variables do not exceed the given level γ_0:

$$P(PAPR > \gamma_0) = 1 - \{1 - \exp(-\gamma_0)\}^{4N} \tag{8}$$

3   PAPR Reduction Techniques

3.1   Digital Clipping Method

There are many factors that should be considered before a specific PAPR reduction technique is chosen. These factors include PAPR reduction capability, power increase in the transmit signal, BER increase at the receiver, loss in data rate, computation complexity. Analyzing the above listed methods with respect to these parameters, it is clear that all these existing techniques reduce the PAPR with imposing one or more other limitations on the system performance. And some techniques do not even guarantee the reduction of PAPR. Hence a better reduction technique is required. Clipping technique provides a better solution for reducing PAPR without much affecting the system performance. It is a signal distortion technique, where the OFDM signal is clipped to a certain desired amplitude level[26].

The main idea behind the peak clipping is to monitor the OFDM signal to detect high peaks and find the amount by which the peak exceeds the cut-off value. A signal is then generated equal to the exceeding amount and finally the generated signal is subtracted from the original OFDM signal. Based on the amount of clipping the BER of the signal is varied. The signal is then amplified and transmitted through the channel. The amount of clipping can be selected based on the high power amplifier and the channel conditions[27].

One of the possible ways for the implementation of the above technique is to clip the signals in the digital form. Digital clipping may be produced on the signal at Nyquist rate and on an oversampled signal. In the first case clipping leads only to in-band distortions, while the second implementation causes also an out-of-band emission. This fact necessitates the use of a filter after the limiter. Filtering in its turn leads to a peak regrowth. On the other hand PAPR of the continuous signal may exceed that of its discrete version (sampled with Nyquist rate). So, the effects of peak regrowth and BER performances should be compared for both schemes.

The baseband part of the processing scheme is shown in Fig. 1. Clipping is applied to the I and Q components of the input signal. The input N-dimensional vector (in the frequency domain) is padded with M(N-1) zeroes in its middle (M is the oversampling factor).

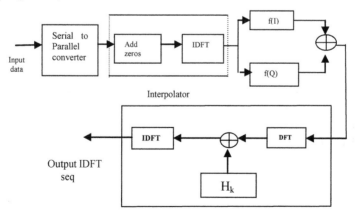

Fig. 2. Baseband part of the Processing Scheme Filter

The filter for attenuation of out-of-band emission is implemented in the frequency domain as a multiplier bank. For this purpose the digital signal is transformed again into the spectral domain and is multiplied next by the filter coefficients. Therefore, the processing scheme combines the nonlinear transformation in the time domain with linear filtering in the frequency domain as it was suggested in [1].

The clipping ratio (CR) parameter is defined as

$$CR = A_{max}/\sigma \tag{9}$$

Where A_{max} is the clipping level of the limiter ,σ is rms of the I and Q components.

3.2   Partial Transmit Sequence Method

Partial Transmit Sequence (PTS) algorithm was first proposed by Müller S H, Huber J B [21][22], which is a technique for improving the statistics of a multi-carrier signal. The basic idea of partial transmit sequences algorithm is to divide the original OFDM sequence into several sub-sequences, and for each sub-sequence, multiplied by different weights until an optimum value is chosen.

Fig. 2 is the block diagram of PTS algorithm. From the left side of diagram, we see that the data information in frequency domain **X** is separated into V non-overlapping sub-blocks and each sub-block vectors has the same size N. Hence, we know that for every sub-block, it contains N/V nonzero elements and set the rest part to zero.

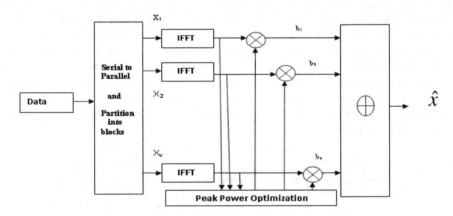

Fig. 3. Block diagram of Partial Transmit Sequence

Assume that these sub-blocks have the same size and no gap between each other, the sub-block vector is given by

$$\hat{X} = \sum_{v=1}^{V} b_v X_v \tag{10}$$

where $b_v = e^{j\varphi_v} (\varphi_v \in [0,2\pi])\{v=1,2,....V\}$ is a weighting factor been used for phase rotation. Select one suitable factor combination $b = [b_1, b_2, ...,b_v]$ which makes the result achieve optimum. The combination can be given by

$$b = [b_1b_2,b_3,......b_v]$$

$$= \arg\ \min_{(b_1,b_2 ..... b_v)} (\max_{1 \le n \le N} \ | \sum_{v=1}^{V} b_v X_v |^2) \tag{11}$$

In conventional PTS approach, it requires the PAPR value to be calculated at each step of the optimization algorithm, which will introduce tremendous trials to achieve the optimum value [21]. Furthermore, in order to enable the receiver to identify different phases, phase factor b is required to send to the receiver as sideband information (usually the first sub-block b_1, is set to 1). So the redundancy bits account for $(V-1) \log_2 W$, in which V represents the number of sub-block, W indicates possible variations of the phase. This causes a huge burden for OFDM system, so studying on how to reduce the computational complexity of PTS has drawn more attentions, nowadays.

4   Simulation Results

The Simulation results provide the performance comparison of clipping and Partial transmit sequence method in terms of CCD that evaluate the PAPR reduction.

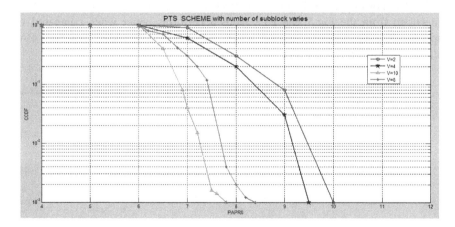

Fig. 4. CCDF of the Partial Transmit Sequence method

Fig.4 shows the performance comparison of partial transmit sequence method for different number of subblocks(V) in terms of complementary cumulative distribution function(CCDF). There is about 8.4dB reduction in PAPR of OFDM signal when PTS method is applied. When V=2, the PAPR is about 10 dB at CCDF=10^{-4}.when V=10, the PAPR is about 7.7dB at CCDF=10^{-4}. From this Fig.4, it is observed that when the

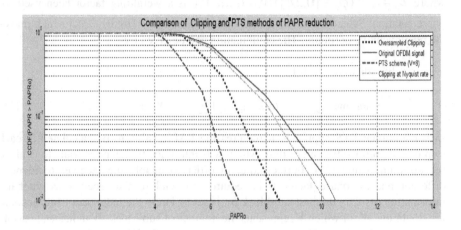

Fig. 5. Performance comparison of Clipping and PTS method in terms of CCDF

number of subblock increases then PAPR reduction will also be more. But the case is that increasing the number of subblocks causes increased complexity in the system.

Fig.5 enumerate comparative study on PAPR reduction between Clipping (Nyquist and Oversampled rate) and Partial transmit sequence(PTS) method in terms of CCDF. In PTS method, there is about 7.8dB reduction in PAPR of OFDM, but clipping scheme provides 2 – 4dB reduction only. For PTS method, PAPR is about 6.9dB at CCDF=10^{-2}.For clipping (Nyquist rate) method, its about 10.2dB at CCDF=10^{-2}.It is understood from the Fig.5 that PTS method performs better when compared with clipping (Nyquist and oversampled rate). PTS method provides improved PAPR reduction when compared with clipping schemes.

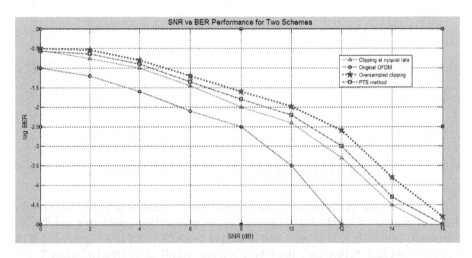

Fig. 6. SNR versus BER comparison for Clipping and PTS method

Fig.6 gives the comparison of SNR versus Bit error rate between clipping and PTS method. It is observed from the Fig.6 that PTS method for PAPR reduction introduces increased error rate when compared with clipping scheme (Nyquist and Oversampled rate). But the bit error rate of PTS is less when compared with original OFDM signal.

5   Conclusion

This paper analyses clipping (Nyquist rate and oversampled rate) and Partial transmit sequence(PTS) method of PAPR reduction in multicarrier transmission. It provides a comparative study of PAPR reduction techniques i.e (clipping and PTS) in terms of Complementary cumulative distribution function (CCDF) and Bit error rate(BER).It is observed that Partial transmit Sequence(PTS) method gives improved PAPR reduction when compared with clipping techniques. when the number of subblock increases, then PAPR reduction will also be more. But the case is that increasing the number of subblocks causes increased complexity in the system. Bit error rate employed with PTS will be more than clipping method, but it is comparatively better than original OFDM signal. As for increased PAPR reduction of multicarrier transmission, PTS method performs better than the clipping method.

References

1. Bauml, R.W., Fischer, R.F.H., Huber, J.B.: Reducing the peak to average power ratio of multi carrier modulation by selective mapping. IEEE Electronics Letters 32 (October 2006)
2. Foomooljareon, P., Fernando, W.A.C.: Input sequence envelope scaling in PAPR reduction of OFDM. In: IEEE 5th International Symposium on Wireless Personal Multimedia Communications, vol. 1 (October 2002)
3. Schulze, H., Luders, C.: Theory and Applications of OFDM and CDMA – Wideband wireless communications. John Wiley & Sons (2005)
4. Yin, H., Alamouti, S.: OFDMA: A Broadband Wireless Access Technology. In: IEEE Sarnoff Symposium (August 2007)
5. Bonaccorso, M., Buzenac, V.: Reducing the Peak to Average Power Ratio in OFDM Systems. Dix-septième colloque GRETSI, Vannes (September 2008)
6. Prasad, R.: OFDM for Wireless Communication System, Universal Communications, 1st edn. (2004)
7. Rana, M.M.: Clipping based PAPR reduction method for LTTE OFDMA Systems. In: IEEE IJECS-IJENS, vol. 10(05) (2000)
8. Paiement, R.V.: Evaluation of Single Carrier and Multicarrier Modulation Techniques for Digital ATV Terrestrial Broadcasting CRC Rep. Ottawa, ON, Canada, CRC-RP-004 (2004)
9. Sukanesh, R., Vijayarangan, V.: An overview of techniques for reduced peak to average power ratio and its selection criteria for orthogonal frequency division multiplexing radio systems. Journal of Theoretical and Applied Information Technology (February 2009)
10. Rappaport, T.S.: Wireless Communication: Principles and Practice, 2nd edn. Prentice Hall (2002)

11. Telladoj: Peak to average power reduction for multicarrier modulation. Ph.D. dissertation, Standard University (2000)
12. Wang, X., Tjhung, T.T., Ng, C.S.: Reduction of peak to average power ratio of OFDM system using a companding technique. IEEE Transactions on Broadcasting 25 (September 2002)
13. Wilkison, T.A., Jones, A.E.: Minimization of the peak to mean envelope power ratio of multicarrier transmission schemes by block coding. In: IEEE Vehicular Technology Conference, vol. 2 (July 2005)
14. Muller, S.H., Huber, J.B.: A novel peak power reduction scheme for OFDM. In: The 8th IEEE International Symposium on Personal, Indoor and Mobile Radio Communications, pp. 1090–1094 (February 1997)
15. Cimini Jr., L.J., Sollenberger, N.R.: Peak-to-Average power ratio reduction of an OFDM signal using partial transmit sequences. IEEE Electronic Letters 4(3), 86–88 (2000)
16. Xia, L., et al.: A novel method to design phase factor for PTS based on pseudo-random sub-block partition in OFDM system. In: 2007 IEEE 66th Vehicular Technology Conference, pp. 1269–1273 (September, October 2007)
17. Wen, Q., Xiao, Y., et al.: A modified partial transmit sequence scheme for PAPR reduction in OFDM system. In: IEEE 68th Vehicular Technology Conference, pp. 1–5 (September 2008)
18. Xia, L., Yue, X., et al.: Analysis of the performance of partial transmit sequences with different sub-block partitions. In: Proceedings of IEEE International Conference on Communication, Circuits and Systems, ICCCAS, vol. 2, pp. 857–858 (June 2006)
19. Kim, Y.K., Prasad, R.: What is 4G in 4G Roadmap and Emerging Communication Technologies, pp. 12–13. Artech House (2006)
20. University of Alberta, Home page - High capacity digital communications laboratory (2007), http://www.ece.ualberta.ca/~HCDC/mimohistory.html (accessed: July 12, 2009)

An Impact of Personality Traits and Recollection & Retention Skill in E-Learning

L. Arockiam[2,*], J. Charles Selvaraj[1,**], and S. Amala Devi[2,***]

Dept. of Computer Science
[1] A.A Government Arts College, Musiri
[2] St. Joseph's College, Tiruchirappalli,
Tamilnadu, India
larockiam@yahoo.co.in, chrls_selvaraj@yahoo.com,
ams.shane@gmail.com

Abstract. Many researches show that E-Learning is better than the traditional learning. Human factors such as Emotional Intelligence, Attention, Personality, Stress, IQ, Attitude and Cognitive factors such as recollection, retention, comprehension and recognition are some of the factors of E-learning process. The objective of this paper is to explore the relationship between Personality traits and Recollection & Retention (R&R) skill among students in E-learning. A case study was conducted by preparing customized questionnaires in order to examine the personality traits and R&R skills. The personality trait is quantified in terms of Extraversion, Neuroticism and Psychoticism. The relationships between personality traits and R & R skill were considered for the research.

Keywords: Cognitive Science, Personality Traits, Recollection, Retention, e- learning system.

1 Introduction

The E-learning environment is prominent and it affects the success of individual student's characteristics [1]. With the rapid development and increasing use of the World Wide Web, studying through the web interfaces becomes popular. Web-based learning environment can serve as motivational, instructional, modeling, feedback, and assessment tools to the E-learning process. These environments make considerable impact on the cognitive and social behavior of students [2].

E-learning content and course management is of high importance in higher education. Few researchers offered technical guidelines for designing interactive Web-based learning environment [3]. Most of the developmental approaches lack in two important considerations that are needed for implementing Web-based learning materials. They are (i) integration of the user interface design with human interaction and (ii) the evaluation framework to improve the overall quality of Web-based learning environments [4].

---

* Associate Professor.
** Assistant Professor.
*** Research Scholar.

P.V. Krishna, M.R. Babu, and E. Ariwa (Eds.): ObCom 2011, Part II, CCIS 270, pp. 357–366, 2012.

The organization of the web based learning materials such as size of text, inclusion of heading, physical layout and size of window are also affecting the E-learning process [5]. Shneiderman cites a number of cognitive aspects (e.g. short and long-term memory, problem solving, decision making, and searching) related to the user and the task that can have a significant impact on web page design [6].

There is a need to understand the cognitive factors and human factors of e-learning learners to improve the overall quality of the E-learning content. There are various human factors involved in the e-learning process such as Emotional Intelligence, personality, stress, IQ and attitude. These factors influence the E-learning process. Cognitive processes in e-learning incorporate the aspects such as attention, selection, comprehension, recollection, retrieval (retention), synthesis, memorization and abstraction.

This paper shows the correlation between personality traits of students and their respective R&R ability in an E-learning environment of immediate and after 24 hours performance.

2   Related Works

The Literature in the area of e-learning points out that the quality of educational software is significantly related to its interface quality and cognitive factors.

Seto Mulyadi conducted an experiment on Personality Development through Learning with Process Approach in E-learning in the year [7]. The main objective was to produce university graduates who have excellent intellectual giftedness and creative personality which can be only achieved if learning was done with process approach within E-leaning program, which integrate the elements of motion, audio, color, and image in the learning materials. With the e-learning programs, which integrate learning-by-doing methods, the student was trained to design learning materials that are not limited only to the theories but also to the applications. The learning method was believed to develop an advanced intellectual giftedness because the learning became more interesting and meaningful. Therefore, the learning material was mastered. The model of learning enabled the development of a creative personality.

Stephen R. Gulliver, et al from Informatics Research Centre, UK have done an experiment on Cognitive style and personality. The main purpose was to explore the relationship between cognitive style, user personality and perceived multimedia quality [8]. They have used Cognitive Style Analysis and an adapted Myers-Briggs questionnaire to assess cognitive style and user personality respectively. It also used an adapted Quality of Perception metric to assess user-perceived multimedia quality. They showed that personality type and user cognitive style affects information assimilation, self-perceived achievement and student level of confidence.

Essaid El Bachari, et al. did a research on Design of an Adaptive E-Learning Model Based on Learner's Personality in the year 2009. They presented an Adaptive e-learning model based personality learner's [9]. To recognize the learner's personality, the system used the Myers-Briggs Type Indicator's (MBTI) personality dimensions and proposed a Personalized Education System Learn Fit Framework that suggests a learning style matching with learner's preference in online learning education.

S. Fatahi, M. Kazemifard, et al. proposed a Design and Implementation of an E-Learning Model by Considering Learner's Personality and Emotions in the year 2009. They analyzed that People with different personalities show different emotions in facing an event [10]. In the case of teaching and learning, personality difference between learners plays an important role. In virtual learning the learners' personalities are various and the teaching method used for each learner should be different from the other learners. A new model was presented according to the learning model based on emotion and personality and the model of virtual classmate. Based on their knowledge base, the virtual teacher and classmate express suitable behaviors to improve the process of learning according to the learner's emotional status. The future work was to improve the parameters of culture, case based reasoning and agent's learning and to make the virtual teacher and classmate agents more credible for the user.

Amal Al-Dujaily et al. made a study on personality in designing adaptive e-learning systems in the year 2008. The aim of the study was to understand how learners with different personality respond to an e-learning content structure [11]. An experiment performed to explore the relationship between the learner's personality type and the learning sequence design. It was revealed that a different personality type had a markedly different effect on learning performance. They finally found that the task performances by the two different personality groups (introverted and extraverted) were significantly affected by the different learning sequence. Those findings strongly indicated that the personality type could be an influential indicator of learning performance when learners were taught by different learning material organizations. The empirical study showed that the personality type affected the learning process. The most important barrier was the number of participant. They plan to recruit more participants for re-confirming the understanding.

Du Jin, et al. have experimented on the Research of Mining Association Rules between Personality and Behavior of Learner under Web-Based Learning Environment in the year 2005. They found that discovering the relationship between behavior and personality of learner in the web-based learning environment was the key to guide learners in the learning process [12]. They proposed a new concept called personality mining to find the "deep" personality through the observed data about the behavior. A learner model which includes personality model and behavior model is proposed. They have designed and implemented an improved algorithm, which was based on Apriori algorithm widely used in market basket analysis, to identify the relationship. Finally they have discussed various issues like constructing the learner model, unifying the value domain of heterogeneous model attributes, and improving Apriori algorithm with decision domain. Experiment result indicated that the algorithm for mining association rules between behavior and personality was feasible and efficient. The future work was to analyze their behavior and how to adopt the proper study strategy and settle adaptive leaning material.

2.1   Web User Interface Design

The e-learning interface design should be a core, integrated component of the overall design of on-line units. The way people learn and the tasks they perform determine the design of an interface and the technological approach has no role in this. In this regard, design layout sites can affect the way students learn and interact on a particular unit [13].

User Interface Design (UID) is a central issue for the usability of a software product. The goal of effective UID is to create an environment for the user to successfully navigate and understand the content of the e-learning course. The quality of the UID directly influences the way the learner interacts with and processes the information presented in the UID [14].

There are three major factors that impact the complexity of a UID: (1) cognition, (2) content, and (3) form. These three factors exhibit how individuals perceive a web page, the content that is located at that web page, and the manner in which the web page is constructed [15].

2.2   Cognitive Architecture

A model of our cognitive architecture includes two major parts: working memory and long-term memory. Working memory provides temporary storage and transformation of verbal and pictorial information that is currently in the focus of our attention. Our working memory becomes overloaded if more than a few chunks of information are processed simultaneously [16] and [17]. Long-term-memory represents a large store of organized information with effectively unlimited storage capacity and duration. It contains a huge number of organized knowledge structures (schemas) that effectively determine our capabilities to function successfully in complex environments. Cognitive load theory considers learning design implications of the above human cognitive architecture [18] and [19].

2.3   Eysenck Personality Inventory

Eysenck Personality Inventory [20] suggests that individual differences could be expressed in terms of just three orthogonal higher order factors: extraversion, neuroticism and psychoticism. The Eysenck Personality Profiler has been employed in studies concerned with group obsessiveness as a moderator of dissimulation [21], the relationship between personality and intelligence.

In this instrument, extraversion comprises the three traits of sociability, activity and assertiveness; neuroticism comprises the three traits of anxiety, inferiority and unhappiness; and psychoticism comprises the three traits of risk-taking, impulsiveness and irresponsibility.

2.4   Recollection and Retention (R&R)

Recollection is defined in terms of subjects' ability to respond selectively on the basis of memory for some criterial feature such as the list in which an item was presented [22]. Recollection is the retrieval, or recall, of memory. Retrieval may take the form of recall (or) recognition, with recall being the higher order tasks because it requires learners to spontaneously remember an item of information rather than merely confirm its previous occurrence. The retrieval process can be increased by providing cues, Stimulant questioning, encouraging the use of external memory aids, etc [23]. Retention is an ability to recall or recognize what has been learned or experienced.

3   Methodology

The experiment conducted with a batch of students of MCA course. It is depicted in Fig.1.

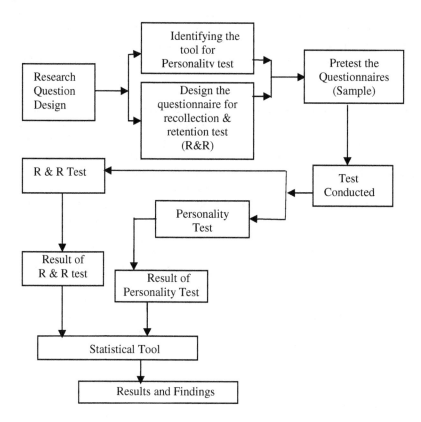

Fig. 1. Design methodology

The following objectives are considered in the experiment:

1. Is there any relation between personality traits and R&R ability in e-learning environment?
2. Is there any relation between personality traits and R&R ability immediately and after 24 hours in e-learning environment?
3. Which personality type has better R&R ability?

For the purpose of this study, 150 students pursuing M.C.A course were selected. They were all homogeneous in terms of their previous learning outcomes in other computer science course work and their level of knowledge in computer science programming skills are above average. An opinion test was conducted to find out their interest in participation. As a result, 100 students showed their willingness to participate. Among them, 80 students were selected who secured above 60% in both Under Graduation and Post Graduation and they belong to the same age group. Finally 50 students were short listed for further study who had secured above 40 in the pretest.

The web page selection is an important criterion for conducting the experiment. The R&R questionnaire is based on the web page content. Two new web pages are to be designed for the purpose of conducting the experiment. The web pages are designed with a collection of various web elements like different fonts, buttons, colors, etc.

The questionnaire is divided into two sections. Section 1 was designed to know the personality traits of each student and section 2 was designed to obtain R & R skill. In order to find the personality traits among the students, Eysenck Personality Inventory (EPI) was used. The EPI contained 48 "Yes" or "No" questions and also Demographic information such as age, gender, Place of Residence (rural, semi-urban, urban) educational Qualification and type of Family (Nuclear / Joint) were collected.

For the R&R test, a set of questions were reviewed by the academic experts. They suggested different criteria to customize the questionnaires. Based on those criteria, 20 questions regarding color, text and image on the web page were selected for the study.

The selected M.C.A students were explained the purpose of the experiment. A pretest was conducted to the students to verify the correctness of the personality questionnaire and R & R questionnaire. Experiment process consists of three different phases. In the first phase, the personality test was conducted for 30 minutes. In the second phase, the web page was shown to the students for 10 minutes. In the third phase, R & R test was conducted. All the three phases were completed by the students without any interaction. After 24 hours, the same R&R test was conducted to the same set of students.

4   Results and Discussions

Based on the results of EPI test, the students were categorized into three types of personality namely Extraversion, Neuroticism and Psychoticism.

From the results, it is found that 66%, 14%, 20% of students are categorized as Extraversion, Neuroticism and Psychoticism respectively as shown in Table 1. Figure 2 shows the graphical representation of the obtained results. The results show that most of the students belong to the extravert personality.

Table 1. Personality type

Personality Type	Number of Students (%)
Extraversion	66%
Neuroticism	14%
Psychoticism	20%

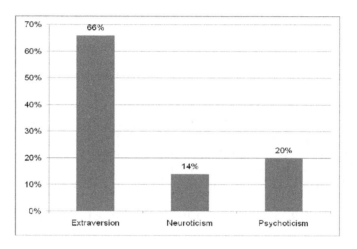

Fig. 2. Percentage of personality type

The relationship between personality traits and R & R skill are observed by using statistics calculator. From the observed result, the Extraversion personalities have positive correlation in the R & R test which was conducted immediately. Furthermore, the Neuroticism and Psychotism personality have negative correlation in the same test. It illustrates that the Extraversion personalities have better R & R skill when compared to other two personalities. The result is depicted in Table.2 and Fig 3.

Table 2. Relationships between personality traits and R & R (immediate test)

Personality Type	R & R
Extraversion	0.094239
Neuroticism	-0.19492
Psychotism	-0.00521

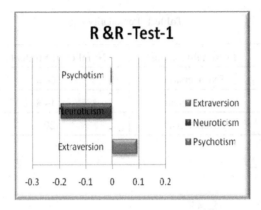

Fig. 3. Correlation between Personality traits and R&R Test-1 result immediately

After 24 hours, the second R & R was conducted to the same set of students. This result also shows that, the Extraversion personality type students have done the R & R test very well and also there is an improvement in Neuroticism personality students who have positive correlation in R&R when compared to the other Psychoticism personality types. The correlation between personality traits and R & R skill after 24 hours is shown in Table 3. It is shown as a pictorial representation in Fig 4.

Table 3. Relationships between Personality and R & R-Test-2 after 24 hours

Personality Type	R&R-Test-2
Extraversion	0.302963
Neuroticism	0.063758
Psychotism	-0.21664

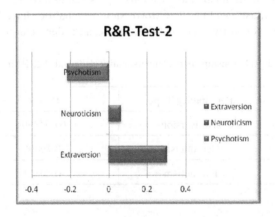

Fig. 4. Correlation between Personality traits and R&R –Test-2 after 24 hours

From the results, it is inferred that Extravert and Psychoticism students have better R & R skill in E-learning.

5   Conclusion

An experiment was conducted to find the impact of personality traits in R&R skill in E-learning. Students were classified based on their personality traits namely Extraversion (66%), Neuroticism (14%) and Psychoticism (20%). Extraversion and Psychoticism personality students have better R & R skill in E-learning. Further, it was found that there is a positive correlation between the R&R skill, immediately and after 24 hours. From this, it is inferred that students who performed better in the immediate test also performed better after 24 hours irrespective of the web page elements in e-learning. It is considered the contribution as a first step in exploring the relationship between personality traits and R&R skill in E-learning.

From the results of the case study, the extravert personality students have better R&R skills and also there was an improvement in Neuroticism personality students when compared to other personality type. Additional experimentation is needed to replicate and validate the results. Future research work will be performed to provide recommendations for the E-content designers which will suggest to use proper web page elements to increase the R & R skill of students with respective to their personality types.

References

1. Chen, N.S., Lin, K.M.: Factors affecting e-learning for achievement. In: IEEE International Conference on Advanced Learning Technologies, September 9-12 (2002)
2. Mayer, R.E.: Multimedia learning. Cambridge University Press, Cambridge (2001)
3. Chou, C.: Interactivity and interactive functions in web-based learning systems: a technical framework for designers, British Educational Communications and Technology Agency (2003)
4. Nam, C.S., Smith-Jackson, T.L.: Web–Based Learning Environment: A Theory Based Design Process for Development and Evaluation (2000)
5. Douglas, G., Riding, R.J.: The effect of pupil cognitive style and position of prose passage title on recall. Educational Psychology 13, 385–393 (2003)
6. Shneiderman, B.: Designing the User Interface, 3rd edn. Addison Wesley Longman, Inc. (1998)
7. Mulyadi, S.: Intellectual Giftedness and Creative Personality Development through Learning with Process Approach in E-learning Programme. International Journal of Business and Social Science 2(3) (special Issue - January 2011)
8. Gulliver, S.R., Ghinea, G.: Cognitive style and personality: impact on multimedia perception. Online Information Review 34, 39–58 (2010)
9. El Bachari, E., El Hassan Abdelwahed, El Adnani, M.: Design of An Adaptive E-Learning Model Based On Learner's Personality. Cadi Ayyad University, Marrakesh (2009)
10. Fatahi, S., Kazemifard, M., Ghasem-Aghaee, N.: Design and Implementation of an E-Learning Model by Considering Learner's Personality and Emotions (2009)

11. Al Dujaily, A., Ryu, H.: A study on personality in designing adaptive e- learning systems. Massey University, New Zealand (2008)
12. Jin, D., Qinghua, Z., Haifei, L., Wenbin, Y.: The Research of Mining Association Rules between Personality and Behavior of Learner under Web-Based Learning Environment. Xi'an Jiaotong University, China (2005)
13. Reyna, J.: Developing quality E-learning sites: designer approach (2008)
14. Wischmeyer, K.E.: Designing the E-learning User Interface, White Paper Assignement ITEC 860 fall (2004)
15. Germonprez, M., Zigurs, I.: Causal Factors for Web Site Complexity. 3(2), Article 5 (2005)
16. Baddeley, A.D.: Working memory. Oxford University Press, New York (1986)
17. Cowan, N.: The magical number 4 in short-term memory: A reconsideration of mental storage capacity. Behavioral and Brain Sciences 24, 87–114 (2001)
18. Clark, R.C., Nguyen, F., Sweller, J.: Efficiency in learning: Evidence-based guidelines to manage cognitive load. Wiley, San Francisco (2006)
19. Sweller, J., van Merriënboer, J., Paas, F.: Cognitive architecture and instructional design. Educational Psychology Review 10, 251–296 (1998)
20. Eysenck, H.J.: A short questionnaire for the measurement of two dimensions of personality. Journal of Applied Psychology 42, 14–17 (1958)
21. Eysenck, H.J., Barrett, P., Wilson, G., Jackson, C.: Primary trait measurement of the 21 components of the PEN system. European Journal of Psychological Assessment 8, 109–117 (1991)
22. Jacoby, L.L.: A process dissociation framework: Separating automatic from intentional uses of memory. Journal of Memory and Language 30, 513–541 (1991)
23. Yonelinas, A.P., Jacoby, L.l.: Noncriterial Recollection: Familiarity as Automatic. Irrelevant Recollection (1996)

Collaborative Approaches for Personalized Web Search Using Fuzzy Neural Networks

Selvakumar Kamalanathan and Sendhilkumar Selvaraju

Dept. of Information Science and Technology, College of Engineering Guindy,
Anna University, Chennai-600025
selvaa21@gmail.com, ssk_pdy@yahoo.co.in

Abstract. The Web is a vast and dynamic medium for accessing a great variety of information stored in various locations in the entire world. In recent days, the users are relying on Web and various Web search tools for retrieving the needed information. In order to easily get the exact information from the dynamic Web environment, search engines come into picture and they keep on developing. The currently existing search engines do not fulfill user's prerequisites, because of its traditional indexing and other techniques. Since users have their particular goal and intensions during their search process, it is fuzzy and is very tedious to predict. In order to achieve the user's specific goal and needs, personalized search mechanism can be introduced. Personalized Web search is a process of gathering information based on the user's interest which can be guessed from their actions performed during search. The main objective of this paper is to provide an overview of Fuzzy Neural Networks based approaches and hence an outline to how such approaches may be adopted for personalized Web search

Keywords: Web search, Personalization, Web mining and Fuzzy Neural Networks.

1   Introduction

As the amount of information on the Web continuously grows, Web search has become one of the most prominent information behaviors. Generally, it is considered to be a solitary activity for satisfying users' individual needs. Web search engine helps people to find what they need to know on the Web. With the development of Internet, people are getting more and more dependent on the Web search engine for their diverse information needs. Despite of the wide usage, there are still some challenges for search engine. Especially, when queries are submitted to a search engine, same results are returned to different users. To solve this problem, personalized Web search has been proposed. This approach may effectively obtain the users real-time information need, however obtaining this is a key issue. There have been many researches can be done in this area to improve the search results according to the user's interest or intension. Even though lot of effort can be taken in this area of research, the results are insufficient. People usually spend time to browse and read the irrelevant documents and continue to spend their valuable time until they find the

P.V. Krishna, M.R. Babu, and E. Ariwa (Eds.): ObCom 2011, Part II, CCIS 270, pp. 367–376, 2012.

satisfactory results [15]. The main reason of the inefficient search results is because it is very hard to understand user's search intentions.

Much work has been conducted in the history for personalizing Web search using keyword based approaches and user tag based approaches. There are also many researches has conducted in this domain based on the direct feedback collected from the users. The above two methods enforce additional burden on the user and makes the search a complex process. Implicitly user data may be collected from cookies, URL's (Uniform Resource Locator) and Weblogs which prove to be unethical. Moreover many factors like the time spend, use feedbacks and hit counts which were in the above mentioned approaches proved to be fuzzy in nature. Hence the need of the time is an automated search mechanism for inferring user's interests using Soft Computing techniques.

The Neural Networks integrated with the capability of processing fuzzy information is termed as Fuzzy Neural Networks (FNN) or Neuro-Fuzzy System (NFS). Both Neural Networks (NN) and Fuzzy Systems (FS) are dynamic, parallel processing systems that estimate input–output functions. They estimate a function without any mathematical model and learn from experience with sample data. A fuzzy system adaptively infers and modifies its fuzzy associations from representative numerical samples. Neural networks, on the other hand, can blindly generate and refine fuzzy rules from training data. Neural Networks is a computational model that is developed based on the biological neural networks. It is also called as Artificial Neural Networks (ANN). An ANN is made up of artificial neurons that are connecting with each other. Typically, an ANN adapts its structure based on the information coming to it.

A set of systematic steps called learning rules needs to be followed when developing an ANN. Further, the learning process requires learning data to discover the best operating point of the ANN. ANNs can be used to learn an approximation function for some observed data. Fuzzy Systems (FS) propose a mathematic calculus to translate the subjective human knowledge of the real processes. This is a way to manipulate practical knowledge with some level of uncertainty. It belongs to the family of many-valued logic. It focuses on fixed and approximate reasoning opposed to fixed and exact reasoning. A variable in fuzzy logic can take a truth value range between 0 and 1, as opposed to taking true or false in traditional binary sets. Since the truth value is a range, it can handle partial truth. Beginning of fuzzy logic was marked in 1956, with the introduction of fuzzy set theory by Lotfi Zadeh. Fuzzy logic provides a method to make definite decisions based on imprecise and ambiguous input data. It is also widely used for applications in control systems, since it closely resembles how a human make decision but in faster way.

Both ANN and Fuzzy System have its own pros and cons. It can be overcome while combining these two techniques. That is Neural networks and fuzzy systems can be combined to join its advantages and to cure its individual illness. Neural networks introduce its computational characteristics of learning in the fuzzy systems and receive from them the interpretation and clarity of systems representation. Thus, the disadvantages of the fuzzy systems are compensated by the capacities of the neural networks. These techniques are complementary, which justifies its use together. Soft Computing techniques are suitable for internet applications. Internet applications are also commonly known as Web applications. Web search is one of the most important features in Web applications. The Fuzzy Neural Networks concept play major role in various Web search applications such as: With the exponential growth in the number of Web pages, searching process becomes more difficult for users. The current information retrieval system, based on search engines and keywords, does not sufficiently take into account users' different interests. It is hard for a novice user to describe precisely their interests in a few words. In most cases, a user's interests are fuzzy, blended and cross multiple categories. The challenge is to identify an appropriate description of a user's complex multiple interests and to develop an adaptive information filtering system, which together are used in extracting the users needed information from the huge collection of Web contents using FNN concepts [18].

The success of Web search engines is related to their ability to satisfy Web users. To accomplish this, it is important to understand the underlying intents of these users in order to provide the most effective retrieval strategies. Mauro Rojas Herrera et.al proposed a model, which studies about the impact of using several features extracted from the document collection and query logs on the task of automatically identifying the users' goal behind their queries and other additional features (such as Anchor text based features, page content based features, URL based features Query based features and Log based features) using Support Vector Machine (SVM) concept [19] to perform the user classification.

Content recommendation in Web personalization from a perspective of psychology-based customer satisfaction can be achieved by using Neural Networks with Kano's approach [5]. It also avoids excessive server loading due to the large number of client request/server response pair and a large amount of user data to be stored. Furthermore, applying ANN to user clustering rather than traditional methods such as K-means methods leads this approach more adaptive to new users.

2   Soft Computing Approaches to Personalization

Personalized search aims to build systems that provide individualized collections of pages to the user, based on some form of model representing their needs and the context of their activities. Although personalized search has been under going for many years and many personalization algorithms have been proposed, it is still unclear whether personalization is consistently effective on different queries for different users and under different search contexts. Personalization requires collecting and using information about the user for showing the relevant content while searching. To achieve effective personalization, focus must be on the user needs, interests, preferences, expertise, nature of tasks performed by them etc. The users' data is collected in one of two ways either explicitly, by asking users to disclose information about them, or by gathering information without their awareness or consent. It is also a matter of interest for the marketing people, who take benefit of the transactional, demographic and users' choice data to provide service according to the requirement to improve the response rate [3], [15].

Personalization can be broadly categorized in two types: context oriented and individual oriented [9]. Context oriented personalization includes factors like nature of information available, information currently being examined, applications in use, when, and so on [3]. Individual oriented personalization uses user interests, query history, browser history, pages visited etc [13]. According to Gauch, there are five basic approaches to capture user's interest: software agents, logins, enhanced proxy servers, cookies and session ids. The first three techniques are more accurate but they require the active participation of the user. Cookies and session ids are less invasive, requiring no actions on the parts of users. Therefore, these are the easiest and most widely used [13]. However they proved to be unethical.

C. Lucchesez et al. [4] proposed a method, which utilizes user query sessions to perform Web content search using clustering techniques to analyze its inter-arrival time. Also this method uses a novel distance function that takes care of query lexical content and exploits the collaborative knowledge which can be collected. In this method three various approaches have been followed: 1) time-based, 2) content-based, and 3) heuristic-based methods that combine any of these two approaches will forms an cluster and identify the user needed content from the huge amount of Web content. It approaches clustering technique for splitting into task-based sessions a very large, long-term log of queries submitted to a Web Search Engine (WSE).

Chunlai Chai and Biwei Li [6] proposed a model which combines both fuzzy and genetic approach to form a hybridization of fuzzy sets with genetic algorithms approach. It is based on a hybrid technique that combines the strengths of rough set theory and genetic algorithm. The algorithm through the introduction of selection operators, crossover operators and mutation operators, improves the global convergence speed, and can effectively avoid prematurity. Which is based on user query and set of Web documents, both are compared using any boolean function to identify its relationship. Based on their relevant matching fuzzy set are formed and used for user's similarity measures with the help of genetic algorithm approach. The role of fuzzy sets in handling the different types of uncertainties/impreciseness in this work [12].

G. Castellano et.al proposed an application NEWER [11] (NEuro-fuzzy Web Recommendation), a Web personalization system designed to dynamically suggest interesting links to the current users according to their interests. In such a system, useful knowledge about usage access patterns is mined through the application of techniques underlying the Web Usage Mining methodology (WUM). WUM involves the application of data mining and machine learning techniques to discover usage patterns (or build user models) through the analysis of Web users historical navigational activities. It incorporate Neuro-fuzzy approach in order to determine categories of users sharing similar interests and to discover a recommendation model as a set of fuzzy rules expressing the associations between user categories and relevances of pages. This system have shown to greatly help Web users in navigating the Web, locating relevant and useful information, and receiving dynamic recommendations from Web sites on possible products or services that match their interest.

The weight assignment to hyperlinks is more exploited in [2] were each link gets a weight based on its position at the page, length of anchor text and on the tag where the link is inserted. In the links of a Web page are weighted based on the number of in-links and out-links of their reference pages. The resulting algorithm is named as 'weighted page rank'. These two page ranking algorithms do not take any extra information from the surfer for giving an accurate ranking. In a new approach of dissecting queries into crisp and fuzzy part has been introduced.

Cheng Chih Chang et al. [5] proposed model of a Web page ranking algorithm, which consolidates Web page classification with Web page ranking to offer flexibility to the user as well as to produce more accurate search result. The classification is done based on several properties of a Web page which are not dependent on the meaning of its content. The existence of this type of classification is supported by applying fuzzy c-means algorithm [8] and neural network classification on a set of Web pages. The typical interface of a Web search engine is proposed to change to a more flexible interface which can take the type of the Web page along with the search string. Also efficient approach when compared with the above said normal link based method, which is experimentally proved with set of bench mark examples.

G.Castellano et al. [11] proposed an algorithm called VDM (value difference metric) which divides the Web user accessing time using five integers from 0 to 4, to represent the following five levels of reading when people are browsing the Internet: passing, looking through, reading ordinarily, reading intensively and staying. So that it can build the initial data matrix to have the fuzzy clustering. The VDM algorithm eliminates the problem of traditional clustering and effectively reduces the computing space and time.

Chunyan Miao et al. [7] proposed a new approach that combines the on-line user's personal preferences, general user's common preference from user's most recent experiences, and expert's knowledge for personalized recommendations. The extended Fuzzy Cognitive Map (FCM) that represents current user's preference can be easily constructed instantly by fuzzy cognitive agents while interacting with the individual on-line users. The user's common preference together with expert's knowledge can also be represented by the fuzzy cognitive agents via extended FCM which its weights are learned from general user's most recent experience. In today's rapid changing environment, users may also change their preferences from time to time. Fuzzy cognitive agents have the ability of keep learning the users' common preference from their most recent behavior records and update its knowledge autonomously and frequently. The inference algorithm of the extended FCM can be regarded as a similarity function for recommending that information which closely matches both the current user's personal preferences and the general users' common preferences combined with the expert's knowledge.

The above approach had a new type of personalized recommendation agent, fuzzy cognitive agent [7], to give personalized suggestions based on the current user's preferences, general user's common preferences, and the expert's knowledge. Fuzzy cognitive agents are able to represent knowledge via extended fuzzy cognitive maps, to learn user's common preferences from most recent cases and to help customers to make inference/decisions through numeric computation instead of symbolic and logic deduction. This from the above study it can be understood that when Web mining approaches integrated with fuzzy neural networks techniques may improve the Web search process.

3   Generic Workflow for Personalized Web Search Using Soft Computing Techniques

Majority of the existing works learns user's behaviors using following: Content read by users, Links preferred by users and Navigational Behavior of the users. Content and Links are denotative in nature and the Navigational behavior is connotative factor from the user perspective. The factors which are collected from the users in direct form in known as denotative factors, otherwise it is called connotative factors.

Personalized Web search research depends greatly on the user data. Hence user data collection becomes an integral part of any personalized Web search research. User data collection may be done both on the client and server side. But data collection from the client side has many advantages than the server side data collection. Personalization depends on factors like page-view time, hit-counts, browsing speed (scrolling speed), favorites, query used, pages visited, links exploited and paths traversed [14]. Among these factors the first three may be captured more accurately from the client side. Since these factors are not correctly reflected in the server side. Page-view times recorded in the server logs are affected by networks delay. Moreover cache hits are not recorded in the server logs. Finally scrolling speed cannot be tracked from the server side. Because of such reasons, most of the data collection for personalized Web search may be performed from the client side. To achieve this, a specialized Web browser is required which might automatically keep track of the various factors that affect personalization.

Secondly the data collected may be classified according to the nature of personalization. For the purpose of performing Content based personalization, factors like bookmarks, tree lists and term lists in a Web Page may be used. For achieving link based personalization, factors like click streams, URLs (Uniform Resource Locator) are needed [20]. And finally to achieve a usage based personalization, factors like cursor tracking, page-view time and scrolling speeds are necessary. By this way the data collected may be classified into three groups as shown in Fig.1.

Thirdly, any personalized Web search required analysis of the data collected for the purpose of inferring few interesting factors like relationship between Web contents and the users, categorization of user interests into long and short term, and mapping between usage factors and its impact on the user's interests.

The Page re-ranking in one of the important process in personalized Web search. The ranking depends upon the user interaction in general, but the ranking process depends on the various characteristics of user interaction. There are various ranking techniques have its own advantages and limitations depending upon the application. The page re-ranking model depends on the user click through feedback process, clicking or downloading the URLs, Hyperlink Induced Topic Search (HITS), User feedback based, Social-tagging, Graph based, User's location and Social network based. The following Table 1. Summarizes the above mentioned techniques scope and its limitations.

Table 1. Scope and its limitations of various Page re-ranking techniques

Sl.No	Name of the Author(s)	Technique	Significance	Limitation
1	Harshit Kumar et al. (2008) [14]	User click through feedback process	Number of times page can be viewed	Only once the page hit can be considered
2	Sanjay Choudhary et al. (2009) [20]	Clicking or downloading the URLs	Certain amount of Weight can be added	Un ethical approach
3	Sanjay Choudhary et al. (2009) [20]	Hyperlink Induced Topic Search (HITS)	Authority and Hub based approach	Query depended, Suffered by Spam problem
4	Aliaa A.Youssif et al. (2009) [1]	User feedback	Accuracy as per user interest	Slower process
5	Shihn-Yuarn Chen et al. (2009) [21]	Social tagging	know the content of the resource	Not protective to corruption
6	EINAT MINKOV et al. (2001) [9]	Graph based	Information drawn from the graph structure	Favors older pages
7	Yumao Lu et al. (2010) [22]	User's location	Voice Web search	Applicable for only smart phone users
8	Kyung-Soon Lee et al. (2001) [16]	Social network	Exist multiple pages	Spam is a problem

According to the ranking output the users are recommended for the particular Web page. This recommendation can be done either by using content based or user profile. Visualization is one of the broad spectrum in personalized Web search [10]. The visualization technique exploits the research of ranking process by adopting various approaches like color representation, list according to the user application.

The following sub section provides the various scopes for research in the various stages of above mentioned work flow through personalized Web search.

3.1 Scope for Research

There are various scopes for research in personalized Web search starting from data collection till the feedback. Each process has its own insight into the research. Data can be collected depending upon the applications using standard or self defined tools. Before presenting the data to various tools standard and effective representation structures are still required. Any analysis specific or user's specific data structures may help the research community to end up with effective inferences from the collected data. Moreover semantic structures like ontology may used for highlighting

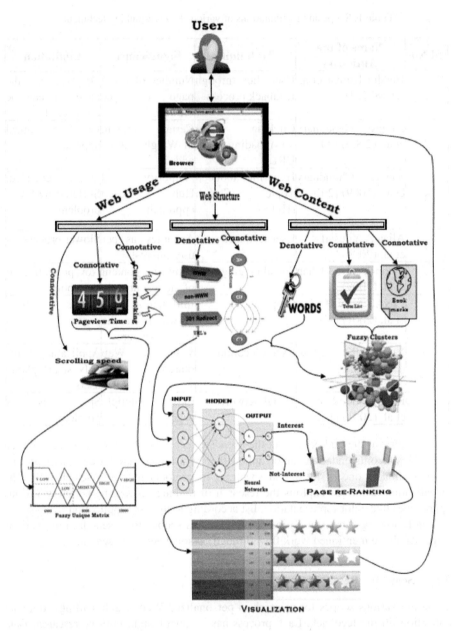

Fig. 1. Generic workflow for personalized Web search using Fuzzy Neural Systems in existing research works

the important relationships between the user and the browsed data. Preprocessing of the collected user data during Web search differs according to the need of the final analysis.

There are no hard and fast rules in choosing the right preprocessing techniques. Non-selection of appropriate preprocessing techniques might affect the analysis to a greater extend. Hence it would be a good step in the research to define a model that might instruct any personalized research system to use analysis specific preprocessing techniques. Factors that affect personalization are many in the history, however there is no specific model that highlights the relationship between the user analysis and the specific personalization factors that affect the analysis greatly.

The development of mathematical model is one of the main issues in the Web search since it involves various dynamic characteristics. In general the characteristics of Web search vary according to the users, which is random in nature. This randomness can be measured by using predefined statistical models. According to the statistical data evaluated the user interests can be predicted and the maximum search of the Web can be evaluated using the predicted data.

Interests of a user are fuzzier in nature and hence they affect the final re-ranking process. Interest prediction if accompanied with a mathematical model that might measure the interest decay will help the researcher to effectively deal with users recent/current interests. It is the current interest of any user which affects the re-ranking process to a greater extend. Moreover mathematical that proves the significance of the final results is indeed a great need of the time. More measures apart from traditional measures like Precision and Recall need to be derived for effective evaluation of the recommendation process.

The result of the recommendation process need to be finally projected to the user using effective visualization techniques. Instead of providing a text based results that just provides a URLs set, context of search and associated interests must be highlighted in the result colors.etc. Finally, all the above mathematical models can be adjusted based on the user's feedback. Thus an effective personalized search system may be developed if the above mentioned suggestions are considered in any research associated with personalization.

4   Conclusion and Future Work

Personalized Web search is an effective way of solving the problems of existing search engines. This paper has highlighted various key issues related with general Web search. Moreover this paper has provided an outline of the application of soft Computing techniques for Web mining. Finally this paper proposes a fuzzy neural networks based approach for solving various issues related with personalizing Web search.

References

1. Youssif, A.A., Darwish, A.A., Roshdy, A.: Development of Information Agent Reranking By Using Weights Measurement. International Journal of Computer Science & Security (IJCSS) 4(2), 256–264 (2009)
2. Rauber, A., Kaiser, M., Wachter, B.: Ethical Issues in Web Archive Creation and Usage-Towards a Research Agenda. Univ. of Brighton, Brighton (2008)

3. Alhenshiri, A., Watters, C., Shepherd, M.: User Behaviour during Web Search as Part of Information Gathering. IEEE (2011); ISSN:1530-1605/11 $26.00
4. Lucchesez, C., Orlandoy, S., Peregoz, R., Silvestriz, F., Tolomeizy, G.: Detecting Task-based Query Sessions Using Collaborative Knowledge. In: 2010 IEEE/WIC/ACM International Conference on Web Intelligence and Intelligent Agent Technology. IEEE (2010); ISSN:978-0-7695-4191-4/10 $26.00
5. Chang, C.C., Chen, P.-L., Chiu, F.-R., Chen, Y.-K.: Application of neural networks and Kano's method to content recommendation in Web personalization. Journal of Expert systems with Applications 36, 5310–5316 (2009)
6. Chai, C., Li, B.: A Novel Association Rules Method Based on Genetic Algorithm and Fuzzy Set Strategy for Web Mining. Journal of Computers 5(9) (September 2010)
7. Miao, C., Yang, Q., Fang, H., Goh, A.: Fuzzy Cognitive Agents for Personalized Recommendation. In: Proceedings of the 3rd International Conference on Web Information Systems Engineering (WISE 2002). IEEE (2009); ISSN: 0-7695-1766-8/02 $17.00
8. Mukhopadhyay, D., Biswas, P., Kim, Y.-C.: A Syntactic Classification based Web Page Ranking Algorithm. In: 6th International Workshop on MSPT Proceedings MSPT (2006)
9. Minkov, E., Cohen, W.W.: Improving Graph-Walk Based Similarity with Reranking: Case Studies for Personal Information Management. ACM Transactions on Computational Logic 2(3), 111–160 (2001)
10. Paulovich, F.V., Pinho, R., Botha, C.P., Heijs, A., Minghim, R.: PEx-WEB: Content-based visualization of Web search results. In: 12th International Conference Information Visualisation. IEEE (2008); ISSN:1550-6037/08 $25.00
11. Castellano, G., Fanelli, A.M., Torsello, M.A.: Mining usage profiles from access data using fuzzy clustering. In: Proceedings of the 6th WSEAS International Conference on Simulation, Modelling and Optimization, Lisbon, Portugal, September 22-24 (2006)
12. Castellano, G., Fanelli, A.M., Torsello, M.A.: NEWER:A system for NEuro-fuzzy Web Recommendation. Journal of Applied Soft Computing 11, 739–806 (2011)
13. Gauch, S., Speretta, M., et al.: User Profiles for Personalized Information Access. In: Brusilovsky, P., Kobsa, A., Nejdl, W. (eds.) Adaptive Web 2007. LNCS, vol. 4321, pp. 54–89. Springer, Heidelberg (2007)
14. Kumar, H., Park, S., Kang, S.: A Personalized URL Re-ranking Methodology Using User's Browsing Behavior. In: Nguyen, N.T., Jo, G.-S., Howlett, R.J., Jain, L.C. (eds.) KES-AMSTA 2008. LNCS (LNAI), vol. 4953, pp. 212–221. Springer, Heidelberg (2008)
15. Chawla, I.: An overview of personalization in Web search. IEEE (2011); ISSN: 978-1-4244-8679-3/11/$26.00
16. Lee, K.-S., Park, Y.-C., Choi, K.-S.: Re-ranking model based on document clusters. Journal of Information Processing and Management 37, 1–14 (2001)
17. Li, Z., Xia, S., Niu, Q., Xia, Z.: Research on the User Interest Modeling of Personalized Search Engine. Wuhan University Journal of Natural Sciences 12(5) (2007)
18. Sufyan Beg, M.M., Ahmad, N.: Web search enhancement by mining user actions. Journal of Information Sciences 177, 5203–5218 (2007)
19. Arora, M., Biswas, R.: Deployment of Neutrosophic Technology to Retrieve Answer for Queries Posed in Natural Language. IEEE (2010); ISSN:978-1-4244-5540-9/10/$26.00
20. Choudhary, S., Choudhary, J., Dehalwar, V.: A Re-ranking Strategy for Web Search Personalization. International Journal of Computer Science and its Applications (2009)
21. Chen, S.-Y., Zhang, Y.: Improve Web Search Ranking with Social Tagging (2009)
22. Lu, Y., Peng, F., Wei, X., Dumoulin, B.: Personalize Web Search Results with User's Location. In: SIGIR 2010, July 19-23. ACM, Geneva (2010)

Performance Analysis of Wavelet Based Transforms in JPEG

M. Arun Sankar and Philomina Simon

Department of Computer Science, University of Kerala
Kariavattom, Thiruvananthapuram-695581, Kerala, India
m.arunsankar@gmail.com, philominasimon@yahoo.com

Abstract. In this paper, a performance analysis of different transforms DCT, DWT and a combined approach of DCT and DWT is used to compress a digital image. JPEG is the first international digital image compression standard for continuous-tone still images, both grey scale and color. JPEG is a transform coder, which uses DCT as the default transform. It has been proved that we can easily plug in Discrete Wavelet Transform (DWT) to JPEG standard with minimal changes in the basic operations. The experimental results show that DWT based JPEG gives better quality at higher bit-rates than DCT based JPEG. Since the bit-rate is less, DCT-JPEG outperforms DWT JPEG. But the computational complexity of DWT-JPEG is much higher than that of DCT-JPEG. A combination of DCT and DWT transforms can be used to reduce the computational complexity and also to get better quality image than DCT-JPEG at higher bit-rates.

Keywords: Wavelet, Compression, JPEG, DCT, DWT, Encoding.

1   Introduction

Joint Photographic Experts Group's (JPEG) proposed a standard which aims to be generic to support a wide variety of applications for continuous tone images. To meet the differing needs of many applications, the JPEG standard includes two basic compression methods, each with various modes of operation [2]. A DCT-based method is specified for "lossy" compression and a predictive method for "lossless" compression. JPEG features a simple lossy technique known as the Baseline method [1], a subset of the other DCT-based modes of operation. The Baseline method has been the most widely implemented JPEG method till date and is sufficient for a large number of applications. JPEG also supports a Progressive mode of operation where data is compressed in multiple passes of progressively higher detail [1] [5] which allow a reasonable preview of image after receiving only a portion of the data.

Although DCT is the most widely used transform in image coding, there had been devoted much attention towards the dyadic Discrete Wavelet Transform (DWT), which has a versatile time-frequency localization due to a pyramid-like multi-resolution decomposition. A lot of researchers have studied the DWT in image

P.V. Krishna, M.R. Babu, and E. Ariwa (Eds.): ObCom 2011, Part II, CCIS 270, pp. 377–385, 2012.
© Springer-Verlag Berlin Heidelberg 2012

coding, obtaining a performance superior to JPEG or to most of other DCT-based coders. However, often, the improved performance carries along a large increase in coding complexity. For large resolution images, compression is necessary and it is desirable to find a compression scheme which avoids: buffering the image, performing multiple passes and very complex processing. Most of the efficient wavelet coders require buffering which are much more complex than JPEG and may require multiple passes through the image. These problems can be reduced by replacing JPEG's transform [3] [6].

This paper presents a review of literature and an analysis between the different transforms – DCT, DWT and combination of DCT and DWT in JPEG standard. This study is motivated by the lack of comparison in literature among the three given transforms. The comparison is done on the basis of PSNR measure of the compressed images and also on the computational complexity of these three transforms on TMS320C64xx processor from Texas Instruments. We have analysed the experimental results which shows that DWT based JPEG gives better quality at higher bit-rates than DCT based JPEG. But as the bit-rate is less, DCT-JPEG outperforms DWT-JPEG. But the computational complexity of DWT-JPEG is much higher than that of DCT-JPEG. Combination of DCT and DWT can be used to reduce the computational complexity and also to get better quality image than DCT-JPEG at higher bit-rates [7] [8].

The rest of this paper is organized as follows: A brief description of the JPEG standard is given in Section 2. Section 3 explains the Wavelet transforms in standard JPEG encoder. Section 4 discusses the experimental results and comparison of the transforms and Section 5 gives the conclusion.

2   JPEG Architecture

"JPEG" stands for Joint Photographic Experts Group, the name of the committee that created the JPEG standard and also other standards. JPEG Specification specifies two classes of encoding and decoding processes, lossy and lossless processes. Those based on the Discrete Cosine Transform (DCT) are lossy, thereby allows substantial compression to be achieved while producing a reconstructed image with high visual fidelity to the encoder's source image. The second class of coding processes is not based upon the DCT and is required to meet the needs of applications requiring lossless compression.

The block diagram for DCT based JPEG encoder is shown in Fig 2.1.

In the encoding stage, input samples of the components are grouped into 8 x 8 blocks and each block is transformed by the Forward DCT (FDCT) into a set of 64 values referred to as DCT coefficients. One of these values is referred to as the DC coefficient and the other 63 as the AC coefficients. Each of the 64 coefficients is then quantized using one of 64 corresponding values from a quantization table.

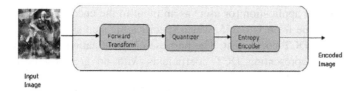

Fig. 2.1. Block diagram of JPEG Encoder

After quantization, the DC coefficient and the 63 AC coefficients are prepared for entropy encoding. The previous quantized DC coefficient is used to predict the current quantized DC coefficient and the difference is encoded. The 63 quantized AC coefficients are converted into a one-dimensional zigzag sequence. The quantized coefficients are then passed to an entropy encoding procedure which compresses the data further. Huffman or Arithmetic Encoding can be used for entropy coding.

Processing steps for DCT based coding can be summarized as follows:

2.1 8x8 FDCT and IDCT

During the input is given to the encoder, source image samples are grouped into 8x8 blocks, shifted from unsigned integers with range $[0, 2^{P-1}]$ to signed integers with range $[-2^{P-1}, 2^{P-1}-1]$ and input to the Forward DCT (FDCT), where a sample is an integer with precision P bits, with any value in the range 0 through 2^{P-1}. All samples of all components within an image should have the same precision P. At the output from the decoder, the Inverse DCT (IDCT) outputs 8x8 sample blocks to form the reconstructed image.

Each 8x8 block of source image samples is effectively a 64-point discrete signal which is a function of the two spatial dimensions x and y. The FDCT takes such a signal as its input and decomposes it into 64 orthogonal basis signals. The output of the FDCT is the set of 64 basis-signal amplitudes or 'DCT coefficients' whose values are uniquely determined by the particular 64-point input signal.

The DCT coefficient values can thus be regarded as the relative amount of the 2D spatial frequencies contained in the 64-point input signal. The coefficient with zero frequency in both dimensions is called the 'DC coefficient' and the remaining 63 coefficients are called the 'AC coefficients'. The FDCT processing step lays the foundation for achieving data compression by concentrating most of the signal in the lower spatial frequencies. For a typical 8x8 sample block from a typical source image, most of the spatial frequencies have zero or near-zero amplitude and need not be encoded. At the decoder the IDCT reverses this processing step. It takes the 64 DCT coefficients which at that point have been quantized and reconstructs a 64-point output image signal by summing the basis signals.

2.2 Quantization

After obtaining the output from the FDCT, each of the 64 DCT coefficients is uniformly quantized in conjunction with a 64-element Quantization Table, which can be specified by the application (or user) as an input to the encoder. Each element can be any integer value from 1 to 255, which specifies the step size of the quantizer for its corresponding DCT coefficient. The purpose of quantization is to achieve further compression by representing DCT coefficients with no greater precision than is necessary to achieve the desired image quality. Stated another way, the goal of this processing step is to discard information which is not visually significant. Quantization is a many-to-one mapping and therefore is fundamentally lossy. It is the principal source of lossiness in DCT-based encoders.

Quantization is a division of each DCT coefficient by its corresponding quantizer step size, followed by rounding to the nearest integer. De-quantization is the inverse function, means that the normalization is removed by multiplying by the step size, which returns the result to a representation appropriate for input to the IDCT. JPEG standard gives one quantization table each for luminance and chrominance block as an example. These tables are derived empirically based on psycho-visual thresholding.

2.3   DC Coding and Zig-Zag Sequence

After quantization, the DC coefficient is treated separately from the 63 AC coefficients. The DC coefficient is a measure of the average value of the 64 image samples. Because there is usually strong correlation between the DC coefficients of adjacent 8x8 blocks, the quantized DC coefficient is encoded as the difference from the DC term of the previous block in the encoding order. Finally, all of the quantized coefficients are ordered into the "zig-zag" sequence. This ordering helps to facilitate entropy coding by placing low-frequency coefficients which are more likely to be nonzero before high-frequency coefficients.

2.4   Entropy Coding

The final DCT-based encoder processing step is entropy coding. This step achieves additional lossless compression by encoding the quantized DCT coefficients more compactly based on their statistical characteristics. The JPEG proposal specifies two entropy coding methods - Huffman coding and Arithmetic coding. The Baseline sequential codec uses Huffman coding. It is useful to consider Entropy coding as a 2-step process. The first step converts the zig-zag sequence of quantized coefficients into an intermediate sequence of symbols. The second step converts the symbols to a data stream in which the symbols no longer have externally identifiable boundaries.

Huffman coding requires that one or more sets of Huffman code tables be specified by the application. The same tables used to compress an image are needed to decompress it. Huffman tables may be predefined and used within an application as defaults or computed specifically for a given image in an initial statistics-gathering pass prior to compression. The baseline encoding procedure may utilize up to two DC and two AC Huffman tables within one scan.

3   Transforms in JPEG

JPEG standard specifies DCT as the default transform. But it has been proved that we can plug in DWT into existing JPEG standard without much change in the basic building blocks of the coder [3].

3.1   DCT

JPEG uses Discrete Cosine Transform as the default transform for coding an image. Source image is grouped into 8x8 blocks and DCT is applied on each of these 8x8 blocks to de-correlate the image. The DCT coefficient values can be considered as the relative amount of the 2D spatial frequencies contained in the 64-point input signal. The coefficient with zero frequency in both dimensions is the 'DC coefficient' and the remaining 63 coefficients are called the 'AC coefficients.' The DC coefficient is a measure of the average value of the 64 image samples and the AC coefficients provide the details.

3.2   DWT

In the DWT, the coefficients are generated by applying a cascade of two-channel filter banks to the input image. DWT is known for its multi-resolution coding support for images. It also provides locality in both time-space domain and frequency domain. It has been proved that DWT performs well compared to DCT based image coding systems. But the disadvantage of using DWT based system is that it is really complex and requires buffering the whole image. It may also need multiple passes also for coding the image.

In any sub-band transform coding procedure, the coefficients can be grouped according to the sub-bands or according to spatial position or block. In DCT, it is common to group coefficients into blocks with common spatial location, different sub-bands; while using the DWT, it is common to have sub-band oriented grouping with common sub-band, different spatial locations.

Although JPEG uses DCT as the default transform, it can be easily replaced with DWT with minimal changes in the main building blocks [3].

Using the DWT; there are coefficients which belong to different sub-bands, but also multiple coefficients in the same sub-band for a given block. Hence, the scanning process as well as the quantizer selection may be changed when DWT is used as the transform in JPEG. The sub-bands are scanned from low to high frequency, obeying the following sub-band scan sequence: horizontal, then vertical, then diagonal. Vertical sub-bands are scanned horizontally, and vice-versa. The diagonal sub-bands are scanned in zigzag . A 3-level DWT is used to replace DCT in JPEG.

3.3   Combination of DCT and DWT

DWT transforms an image block in to 4 sub-bands – LL, LH, HL and HH. Among these four sub-bands, LL will be down-sampled replica of the original image. DWT can be applied in a recursive manner on LL sub-bands. For a 3-level DWT, an image block is transformed thrice on a recursive manner. Another modification possible here is that, after applying DWT on an 8x8 block instead of applying DWT again on LL sub-band, we can also use DCT in this sub-band. This helps to reduce the computational complexity while using a 3-level DWT.

4   Experimental Results and Discussion

Experiments are carried out with a set of four test vectors which includes a grey scale image, a low frequency image (image with all the pixel values equal to 200), a high frequency image (image with alternate 0 and 255 vertically and horizontally) and a natural image (Water lilies) for analyzing the behavior of different wavelets transforms. All these images are in YUV420 format. Performance analysis of JPEG with different transforms is carried out on quality level as well as on complexity level. Wavelet function used for DWT based transforms is LeGall (CDF 5/3) wavelet. LeGall is a reversible wavelet used in JPEG2000 for reversible encoding [4].

PSNR values for different bit-rates are calculated for assessing the quality of encoding. PSNR is calculated from the mean square error (MSE) which is given as:

$$MSE(f,l) = \frac{\sum\limits_{z=1}^{k}\sum\limits_{x=1}^{N}\sum\limits_{y=1}^{M}\left[I(x,y,z) - f(x,y,z)\right]^2}{k \times N \times M}$$

where I is the original color image, f is the reconstructed image of size N × M and K is the number of components. PSNR is given by:

$$PSNR(f,l) = 10\log_{10}\left(\frac{MAX^2}{MSE(f,l)}\right)$$

MSE values are used in the normalized form. For example, if the image is of 8bit then it has to be divided by 255*255. MAX is the maximum value of the pixel in the image. Higher the value of PSNR better is the similarity between two images.

PSNR comparison of grey scale image encoded using different transforms is given below:

Table 4.1. PSNR Comparison – Grey Scale

bpp	Grey Scale		
	DCT	DWT	DWT_DCT
0.2	100.696	74.2056	75.821
0.3	107.125	84.0041	86.0243
0.4	104.811	105.975	103.114
0.5	105.309	106.235	104.619
0.6	103.462	112.296	109.415

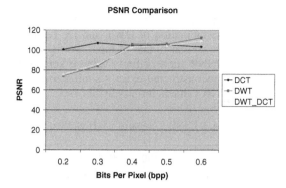

Fig. 4.1. PSNR Comparison – Grey Scale

It is evident from the graph that DWT based JPEG performs better compared to DCT-JPEG except for lower bit-rates. When the bit-rate is low, DCT outperforms DWT in quality. PSNR comparison of natural image encoded using different transforms is given below:

Table 4.2. PSNR Comparison –Water Liles

bpp	Water Lilies		
	DCT	DWT	DWT_DCT
0.2	103.885	88.0041	91.8855
0.3	103.923	97.9213	101.103
0.4	103.905	106.104	107.576
0.5	104.188	115.432	111.975
0.6	104.222	114.611	112.138

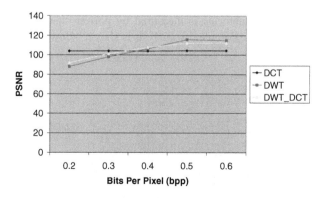

Fig. 4.2. PSNR Comparison – Water Lilies

Here also, the inference is same as that of grey scale images. PSNR comparison of high frequency image encoded using different transforms is given below:

While using DWT and combination of DWT and DCT, image "High Frequency" can be reconstructed exactly similar to that of input. So the PSNR value for this case is infinity. To plot this on PSNR curve, infinity value is kept as 200. Similarly, image "Low Frequency", can be reconstructed exactly similar to that of input with all the three transforms, so the PSNR value is infinity in all cases.

Table 4.3. PSNR Comparison – High Frequency

bpp	High Frequency		
	DCT	DWT	DWT_DCT
0.5	75.1241	200	200
0.6	87.1932	200	200
0.7	86.6031	200	200
0.8	98.0623	200	200

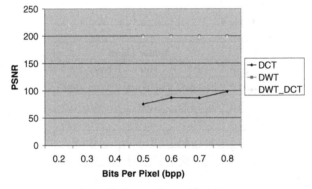

Fig. 4.3. PSNR Comparison – High Frequency

Complexity of the transforms is measured by porting them onto TMS320C64xx platform. The result of the complexity analysis is shown below:

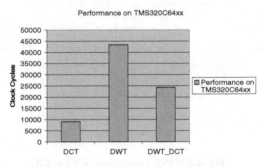

Fig. 4.4. Performance on TMS320C64xx

This graph clearly shows that the complexity using a 3-level DWT is much more than that of DCT or combination of DCT and DWT. It is also evident that the PSNR curve for DWT and combination of DCT and DWT are very close. But the complexity of combination of DCT and DWT is nearly one-half of the complexity of DWT.

The results can be summarized as shown below:

Table 4.4. Comparison of JPEG Transforms

Transform	Complexity	Analysis
DCT	Low	Better PSNR at low bit rate compared to DWT
DWT	High	Better PSNR at high bit rate compared to DCT
DWT+DCT	Moderate	Better PSNR at high bit rate compared to DCT

5   Conclusion

An Analysis of the performance and study of three transforms – DCT, DWT and Combination of DCT and DWT used in JPEG coder is discussed in this paper. The comparison is performed based on the quality and complexity analysis of these transforms. Result obtained shows that DWT based JPEG performs well compared to DCT-JPEG except for lower bit-rates. When the bit-rate is low, DCT outperforms DWT in quality. The complexity using a 3-level DWT is much more than that of DCT or combination of DCT and DWT. It is also evident that the quality of encoding with DWT and that with combination of DCT and DWT are very close. But the complexity of combination of DCT and DWT is nearly half of the complexity of DWT.

References

1. ITU-T.81, Digital compression and coding of continuous tone still images: requirements and guidelines. International Telecommunication Union (1992)
2. Wallace, G.K.: The JPEG still picture compression standard. IEEE Transactions on Consumer Electronics 38(1), xviii–xxxiv (1992)
3. de Queiroz, R., Choi, C.K., Huh, Y., Rao, K.R.: Wavelet Transforms in a JPEG-Like Image Coder. IEEE Transactions on Circuit and Systems for Video Technology 7(2), 419–424 (1997)
4. JPEG 2000 Final Committee Draft
5. In, J., Shiraizi, S., Kossentini, F.: JPEG compliant efficient progressive image coding. In: IEEE International Conference on Acoustics, Speech and Signal Processing, vol. 5, pp. 2633–2636 (May 1998)
6. Nayan, M.Y., Edirisinghe, E.A., Bez, H.E.: Baseline JPEG-like DWT CODEC for disparity compensated residual coding of stereo images. In: Proceedings - Eurographics UK Conference, pp. 67–74 (2002)
7. Dee, H.S., Jeoti, V.: On image compression: a DWT-DCT algorithm. In: Sixth International Symposium on Signal Processing and its Applications, vol. 2, pp. 553–556 (August 2001)
8. Kondo, H., Kou, H.: Wavelet image compression using sub-block DCT. In: Proceedings - Ninth IEEE International Conference Networks, pp. 327–330 (October 2001)

An Catholic and Enhanced Study on Basis Path Testing to Avoid Infeasible Paths in CFG

T. Bharat Kumar[1], N. Harish[1], and V. Sravan Kumar[2]

[1] Department of Computer Science and Engineering
[2] Department of Software Engineering,
Audisankara College of Engineering and Technology, Gudur, Nellore Dt.
bharathkumar_tarasi@yahoo.co.in, hari_divine@yahoo.com,
sravankumarreddy9@gmail.com

Abstract. Basis path testing is an imperative test method in white box testing it is also known as structured testing methodology. It fallows internal logic so, this approach generates and articulate set of independent paths present in the source code called as basis paths taken from the control flow graph (CFG) and uses the cyclomatic complexity. These basis paths are used to design the test cases while deriving these paths from the CFG some of paths may be infeasible. In this paper we promote an proposal to basis path testing with the base line method that how to avoid the generation of infeasible paths in a set of basis paths, and also discussed the different steps to be carried out in basis path testing with the assistance of real world example, showing how the test suits are generated according to the application.

Keywords: White box testing, control flow graph, basis path testing, method improvement, cyclomatic complexity, infeasible path, test cases.

1   Introduction

Testing is an integral part of the software engineering that performs in the later stages of SDLC process to find the accuracy of the software. In testing the software program quality measure is a keystone which ensures that project will work efficiently. The main goal of testing is to reveal the bugs and to ensure that the system built-up in such a way that it must meets the customer requirements. The testing can be done based on the validation & verification technique.

Verification: Checking whether the product is implemented accuracy for specific function

Vallidation: Checking that whether the product is reached customer needs. If software has been tested then the factors that will come after testing is are divided into three parts,

P.V. Krishna, M.R. Babu, and E. Ariwa (Eds.): ObCom 2011, Part II, CCIS 270, pp. 386–395, 2012.
© Springer-Verlag Berlin Heidelberg 2012

SNO	AREA	FOCUS ON	FACTORS
1	Functionality	exterior	Correctness, Usability, Reliability, Usability, Integrity
2	Engineering	interior	Efficiency, Testability, documentation, Structure, Interoperability
3	Adaptability	future	Flexibility, Portability, Reusability, Maintainability

All the above mentioned factors are must and should be tested and checked for each and every software to maintain the quality for the end user. The entire testing process is used to find the failures so that we can find the accurate software product. If there are no bugs then we can't say that that is an error free product. The tester who will test the product is by applying the different testing strategies at different levels in the SDLC. The basic testing of the product is based on the criteria they are Internal & External. So Software testing can be divided into functional testing and structural testing from the perspective of how to select test cases. Functional testing and structural testing play different roles in software testing. Structural testing, also known as white box testing or internal testing / structural testing/ open box testing/ Glass box testing/clear box testing/Logic-driven testing/design based testing. The clear box/glass box testing indicates that we have full visibility of the internal working of the software product specifically the logic & structure of the code.

By using the Basis path testing we are going to derive a set of feasible independent paths to design corresponding test cases by analysing cyclomatic complexity of the control structure. In this paper, we are going to design the control flow graph based on the code analysis, and we particularly concern about basis paths in the CFG and change an control flow graph to avoid selecting infeasible basis paths.

2   Motivation

White box testing methodology looks into the subsystem of an application. Whereas black-box testing concerns itself exclusively with the inputs and outputs of an application, white-box testing enables you to see what is happening inside the application. White box testing provides a degree of sophistication that is not available with black-box testing as the tester is able to refer to and interact with the objects that comprise an application rather than only having access to the user interface.

An example of a white-box system would be in-circuit testing where someone is looking at the interconnections between each component and verifying that each internal connection is working properly.

3   Literature Survey

This section discusses the basis path testing strategy, advantages. Throughout this section, basis path testing is illustrated using a different example of simple code. We know that White box testing monitors the internal logic of the data by the basis path testing. It identifies potential bugs by examining the internal logic. Using the methods of WBT, a tester can derive the test cases that guarantee that all independent paths within a module have been exercised at least once, exercise all logical decisions on their true and false values, execute all loops at their boundaries and within their operational bounds and exercise internal data structures. In this paper we are going to discuss each and every step which are involved in the basis path testing criteria with an real world example according to that example we are going to generate the test cases and removes the infeasible paths from the CFG that are not executed by the test cases.

4   Basis Path Testing

Basis path testing is proposed by "Thomas McCabe" in 1976. A basis path is a exclusive path through the software where no iterations are allowed - all possible paths through the system are linear combinations of them. Basis path testing is a cross between path testing and branch testing Path testing designed to execute all or selected paths through a computer program, Branch testing designed to execute each outcome of each decision point in a computer program. Basis Path Testing can be defined as "Testing that fulfills the requirements of branch testing & also tests all of the independent paths that could be used to construct any arbitrary path through the computer program". A path signifies the flow of execution from the start of a method to its exit. A method with N decisions has 2^N possible paths, and if the method contains a loop, it may have an infinite number of paths. The main motive of basis path testing is to cover the basic paths so that we can cover entire statements of the program by generating test suit that covers every statement in the program at least once which can also be takes place in the integration testing.

Steps in Basic Path Testing Includes

- 4.1   Flow Graph Notation
- 4.2   Derive Cyclomatic Complexity.
- 4.3   Determine the number of Independent paths
- 4.4   Deriving Test cases to exercise these paths

4.1   Flow Graph Notation

To know much more about basis path method we should have to draw a "Control flow graph" (CFG) or "program graph" of a code segment. A flow graph may be drawn when logical statement of code is complex.

Uses of Flow Graph

- ✓ This will allows you to trace program paths more readily.
- ✓ Provides you quick sketch about the code.
- ✓ Identify the number of decision points in the module without written representation.

We can implement the basis path without use of the CFG but there are several useful notations for understanding control flow.

There are some primitive used in the construction of CFG

- ✓ Sequence composition
- ✓ Branching statement
- ✓ While statement
- ✓ Repeat-Until statement

After understanding the basic primitives of CFG we have to concentrate on the procedural design of the CFG which are based on the simple terminology known as circle, node weight, edge/link, Link weight, Region

Let us take an example and an equivalent flow graph representation.

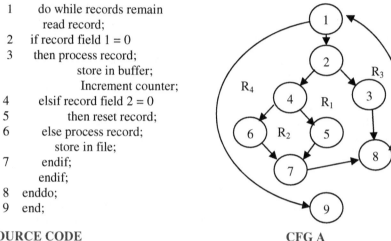

```
1     do while records remain
          read record;
2     if record field 1 = 0
3     then process record;
              store in buffer;
              Increment counter;
4     elsif record field 2 = 0
5         then reset record;
6     else process record;
          store in file;
7     endif;
      endif;
8     enddo;
9     end;
```

SOURCE CODE   **CFG A**

There is an another method which is differed from the basis path testing that is "*Baseline method* ".The former is a technique to derive a set of basis paths through the CFG generated from the tested component, and it is equal to the cyclomatic complexity in number. "Baseline" path is the first path, which is typically picked by the tester, and it should be, in the tester's judgment, the most important path to test . Backtrack the baseline path by flipping each decision node to generate new paths.

The idea is to start with a baseline path, then vary exactly one decision outcome to generate each successive path until all decision outcomes have been varied, at which time a basis will have been generated . Suppose that we have got a CFG from the program to be tested, with the baseline method to do the basis path testing, we can generally follow the next steps:

Step 1: Pick a functional baseline path, which is the most important path to test in the tester's judgment. In most cases, the baseline path we chose should satisfy the typical business logic and try to pass more decision nodes.

Step 2: To generate the next path, change the outcome of the first decision along the baseline path while keeping the maximum number of other decision outcomes the same as the baseline path. And begin again with the baseline but vary the second decision outcome rather than the first to generate the third path. Repeat the flip operation until all decision nodes has been done, and the basis path set is complete.

Baseline method is having the problem that often there are some paths are infeasible actually, when generating test cases, these paths cannot be executed at all.

In most CFGs, infeasible path mainly occurred on the condition that decision nodes are series connection, and variables involved in decisions.

Normally, we have two ways to deal with the infeasible paths:

Way1: Find out the out-degree which is greater than or equal to two node in the infeasible path and flip the following branch until getting a feasible path;

Way2: Modify the infeasible paths manually to meet the business logic.

These two methods are both based on the existing CFG and may require a lot of manual attempts. But actually, we want the changes in human intervention could be as few as possible when generating the basis paths. For this idea, we decided to start from the CFGs. For our improved method we should observe the following Ideology.

Rule 1: If one node forms many branches which are all depended on the results of the last judgment, we can just omit the end node of the former judgment part and the next determination Node, then append the following branches to the corresponding precondition node of itself.

Rule 2: The final "end-judge" node is the exit of a CFG. This node cannot be omitted.

Rule 3: If there are compound conditional statements, the CFG should be able to display the right condition of splitting the compound conditional statement into separate ones.

Here we discuss with an example that the triangle shape judgment program - to do some further analysis. The program fragment and the corresponding CFG B are shown as below and the basis paths from the base line method for the below control flow graph as fallows.

P1: $1\to2\to4\to5\to6\to8\to9\to11\to12\to14$	(baseline)
P2: $1\to3\to4\to5\to6\to8\to9\to11\to12\to14$	(node 1 flipped)
P3: $1\to2\to4\to5\to13\to14$	(node 5 flipped)
P4: $1\to2\to4\to5\to6\to7\to12\to14$	(node 6 flipped)
P5: $1\to2\to4\to5\to6\to8\to10\to11\to12\to14$	(node 8 flipped)

In the below example we can easily find that **P2** and **P3** are invalid for test those are the infeasible paths. For these two paths, since we have determined whether it is a triangle from node 1 to 4, the following path from node 5 is completely contradictory from the judge before.

These infeasible paths can be eliminated by the improved basis path testing method. Let's focus on the Triangle code fragment first, it can be divided into two parts: one part starts from the beginning to line 3 determines whether it is a triangle; and the second from line 5 to the end determines the shape of a triangle or prints out the non-triangle information. For the executable test paths, the results of the first part decide the branch choice of the second one. After clearing the role of each part, let's pay attention to the CFG generated.

```
void Triangle (int a, int b, int c)
{
        bool isTriangle;
1       if ((a < b + c) && (b < a + c) && (c < a + b))
2               isTriangle = true;
        else
3               isTriangle = false;
4
5       if (isTriangle)
        {
6               if (a == b && b == c)
7                       print ("Equilateral\n");
                else
8               if (a != b && b != c && a != c)
9                       print ("Scalene\n");
                else
10                      print ("Isosceles\n");
11      }
12
        else
13              print ("Not a triangle\n");
14      }
```

SOURCE CODE FOR FUNCTION TRIANGLE

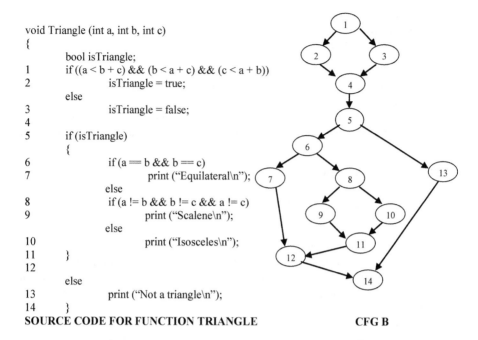

CFG B

We can see that node 4, 11, 12 and 14 all represent the end of a condition statement. Suppose we can allow the follow-up operations corresponds to the determine result of the previous part, these "end-judge" nodes should be omitted, thus we achieve the simplification of the CFG. Follow this idea, only in the determination of the premise of the triangle needs to judge the shape and non- triangle Just has to print a message. In this the CFG B could be modified CFG C In this CFG we merge the two "if" fragments together so that after the first judgment of node 1, we can ensure every path based on a reasonable Premise. In this condition, the Cyclomatic complexity and the number of basis path is reduced to 4 and all paths are feasible. Applying the baseline method again we can get these 4 paths as below:

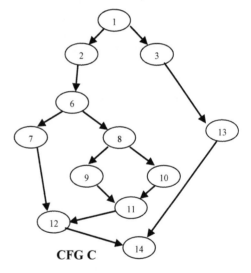

CFG C

P1: $1\rightarrow2\rightarrow6\rightarrow8\rightarrow9\rightarrow11\rightarrow12\rightarrow14$ (baseline);
P2: $1\rightarrow3\rightarrow13\rightarrow14$ (node 1 flipped);
P3: $1\rightarrow2\rightarrow6\rightarrow7\rightarrow12\rightarrow14$ (node 6 flipped);
P4: $1\rightarrow2\rightarrow6\rightarrow8\rightarrow10\rightarrow11\rightarrow12\rightarrow14$ (node 8 flipped).

Furthermore, for the compound conditional statements can be split into smaller single conditional statement, At the end of this section our improved basis path testing method can be applied not only for the program including simple if statement for judge, but for also the complex statement as well. We will not go into details here.

4.1. B   Cyclomatic Complexity

Cyclomatic complexity is an software McCabe's metric provides a quantitative measure of the global logical complexity of a structured program. It measures the amount of decision logic in a single software module. It defines two related purposes in the structured testing methodology.

First, it gives the number of recommended tests for software based on the number of independent paths in the basis set of program & also provides with an upper bound for the number of tests that must be conducted to ensure that all statements have been executed at least once.

Second, it is used during all phases of the software lifecycle, beginning with design, to keep software reliable, testable, and manageable. Cyclomatic complexity is based entirely on the structure of software's control flow graph. In simple the cyclomatic complexity is equals to the number of test cases to test all control statements and also the number of conditions in the program.

Computation of Cyclomatic Complexity

Cyclomatic Complexity has a foundation in graph theory and it will be found in one of the three ways.

1. The number of regions corresponds to the cyclomatic complexity including the outer region.
2. Cyclomatic complexity V(G) for a graph G is defined as
$$V (G)= E-N+2 \text{ or } E-N+2P$$

   Where, E = Number of flow graph edges   N = Number of flow graph nodes
   P = Number of Unconnected components of the graph
3. Cyclomatic complexity V(G) for a graph G is defined based on predicate node
$$V (G)= p+1$$
   Where, p= Number of predicated nodes present in the flow graph G

For example referencing the above mentioned flow graph A the cyclomatic complexity can be find in three ways as

1. Flow graph has four regions.
2. V(G) has Edges E= 11, Nodes N=9, un connected components P=1
$$V (G)=E-N+2P= 11-9+2(1)=4$$

3. V(G) has predicates p=3

$$V (G)= P+1=3+1=4$$

There is an limitation in calculating the V(G) based on the predicate formula is that it assumes that there are only two outgoing flows for each of such nodes. This will be explained as

Ex:

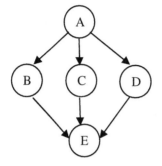

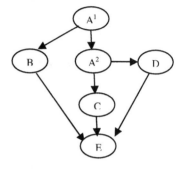

FLOW GRAPH   CFG D   **FLOW GRAPH   CFG E**

✓ According to the number of regions the below graph is having V(G)=3
✓ According to number of edges and the number of nodes the V(G) is

$$V (G)=E-N+2= 6-5+2=3$$

✓ According to number of predicated nodes V(G) is

$$V (G)=p+1=1+1=2$$

The above mentioned cyclomatic complexity according to the number of predicated nodes are wrong it is the limitation of this V(G) it will be overcome by split the predicate node into two sub-nodes as see in flow graph CFG D,E.

Risk analysis through the Cyclomatic complexity values

Cyclomatic complexity	Risk Evolution
1-10	A Simple program, without much risk
11-20	More complex, Moderate risk
21-50	Complex high risk program
Greater than 50	Un testable program(very high risk)

Advantages of Cyclomatic Complexity

✓ Tell us how many paths to look for in basis path testing
✓ Help pinpoint areas of potential instability
✓ Indicate a unit/component's testability & understand ability(maintainability)
✓ Provide a quantitative indication of unit/component's control flow complexity

4.1. C   Independent Paths

An independent path is any path through a program that introduces at least one new set of processing statements (i.e., a new **node**) or a new condition (i.e., a new **edge**). In terms of the flow graph an independent path must move along at least one edge that has not been traversed before the path is defined.

For example in the above referenced CFG A the set of independent paths

Path 1   : 1-9
Path 2   : 1-2-3-8-1-9
Path 3   : 1-2-3-4-5-7-8-1-9
Path 4   : 1-2-3-4-6-7-8-1-9

From the above example we can see that each and every path introduces an new edge.

4.1.D   Deriving Test Cases to Exercise These Paths

The basis path testing method can be applied to a source code. The following are the series of steps that can be used to derive the test cases for all the CFG's. It is important to note that some independent paths cannot be tested in stand-alone fashion. In such cases, these paths are tested as part of another path set.

Example

Consider the CFG A, the process for finding the independent paths is
Step 1: Using the design or code as a foundation, draw a corresponding flow graph.
Step 2: Determine the cyclomatic complexity of the resultant flow graph.
Step 3: Determine a minimum basis set of linearly independent paths. As mentioned in
          Above case..as

For example in the above referenced CFG A the set of independent paths

Path 1   : 1-9
Path 2   : 1-2-3-8-1-9
Path 3   : 1-2-3-4-5-7-8-1-9
Path 4   : 1-2-3-4-6-7-8-1-9
Step 4: Prepare test cases that will force execution of each path in the basis set.
Step 5: Run the test cases and check their results.

Advantages of Basis Path Testing

- ✓ Defines the number of independent paths thus the number of test cases needed to ensure
- ✓ Every statement will be executed at least one time
- ✓ Every condition will be executed on its true & false sides
- ✓ Focuses attention on program logic
- ✓ Facilitates analytical versus arbitrary test case design

5   Conclusion

Basis path testing is a extensively used technique of white box testing technology. Cyclomatic complexity theory proposed by McCabe and always generates the basis set of paths; it is used as basis for finding the number of independent paths and to express other paths. For it we completely depend on the Control flow graph(CFG) of the program, in this basis paths are dependent on the decision nodes and the results of the previous nodes. From this we can get many basis paths that depends on the cyclomatic number all the paths generated here are not feasible paths some of may infeasible paths. To circumvent this condition, we give an improved method that when generating the CFG, connect the causal paths of the two series judgment parts and omit the intermediate nodes and also we had mentioned the series of steps to be takes in the basis path testing with the necessary examples. In this ideology, we construct a communication between the paths and the following branch, to make sure that every basis path is feasible. With this comprehensive study the basis path testing may lead to simplify the testing process, and to improve software quality.

References

1. IEEE-610 IEEE Standards Software Engineering, vol.1, IEEE Standard Glossary of Software Engineering Terminology, IEEE Std. 610-1990 , The Institute of Electrical and Electronics Engineers (1999); ISBN 0-7381-1559-2
2. McCabe, T.J.: Structured Testing: A Software Testing Methodology Using the Cyclomatic Complexity Metric. NBS Special Publication, National Bureau of Standards (1982)
3. Beizer, B.: Software Testing Techniques. Van Nostrand Reinhold, New York (1990); ISBN 0-442-206720
4. Pressman, R.: Software Engineering, A practitioner's Approach, 7th edn. McGraw Hill, Boston (2005); ISBN 007-124083-7
5. Zhang, Z., Mei, L.: An Improved Method of Acquiring Basis Path for Software Testing. In: 5th International Conference on Computer Science and Education, ICCSE 2010, pp. 1891–1894 (2010)
6. Wu, J., Chen, C., Xiao, L.: Basis of Software Testing Technique. HuaZhong University of Science and Technology Press, Wuhan
7. Qingfeng, D., Xiao, D.: An Improved Algorithm for Basis Path Testing. School of Software Engineering Tongji University, Shanghai

Iris Authentication by Encoded Variant Length Iris Templates

S. Poornima[1] and S. Subramanian[2]

[1] Department of Information Technology, SSN College of Engineering,
Chennai, 603110, India
[2] Sri Krishna College of Engineering and Technology, Coimbatore, 641008, India
poornimas@ssn.edu.in

Abstract. Biometric-based personal verification and identification methods have gained much interest with an increasing emphasis on database security. Of all the physiological traits of the human body that help in personal identification, the iris is probably the most robust and accurate one by research. Iris recognition using texture based method is a robust biometric, that can operate in both verification and identification modes. The feature templates are the vital source for authentication which can be easily attacked. Hence securing this iris template is very essential. In this paper, a new encoded technique is been performed on the binary iris codes, generated from feature extraction method producing a non binary variant length codes which in turn securing the iris templates. Finally the hamming distance is calculated with a threshold in order to match the generated binary code of a given input with the database's encoded templates by decoding process. The iris code matching task is performed much faster by decoding process rather repeating the whole recognition process step by step for each individual data in the database for which the input to be authenticated or verified.

Keywords: Iris recognition, Iris localization, Hough transform, canny edge detector, Iris template.

1 Introduction

Humans have traditionally relied on the use of face, voice or gait information to recognize others. The identity of people at public places like airports is possessed using the documents such as passports or ID cards. Such identification measures are highly susceptible to failure since these documents can be forged or tampered with easily. Hence it is necessary to use an authentication scheme that is based on the human body and is unique to every individual. Biometrics seeks to link the identity of a person much more closely to the human body and some of its unique features [1]. Biometrics consists of several methods for uniquely recognizing humans based upon one or more intrinsic physiological (shape) or behavioral traits (behavior). Some of the physiological traits include fingerprint, face, retina, iris, DNA, Palm print, hand geometry, etc and behavioral traits includes typing rhythm, gait, and voice.

P.V. Krishna, M.R. Babu, and E. Ariwa (Eds.): ObCom 2011, Part II, CCIS 270, pp. 396–405, 2012.

A biometric system can operate in identification mode as well as verification mode which is called as identification system or verification system. A system using biometrics initially acquires the data, extracts relevant features and constructs a template from it, and then compares with a database of such templates linked to various identities [1], [2].Biometric identification can provide extremely accurate, secured access to information: fingerprint, signature, face, speech, vein, retinal and iris scans produce absolutely unique data sets when done properly. Password verification has many problems such as when people write them down, they may forget and make up easy-to-hack passwords. Automated biometric identification can be done very rapidly and uniformly, with a minimum of training. The identity of an individual can be verified without resort to documents that may be stolen, lost or altered. Normally any biometric recognition system is used for identification of an individual and verified with the available database to check whether the person is authorized or not. Nowadays, iris recognition system considered as the best authentication method compared to other biometric systems due to the unique characteristic feature of a human iris. Although numerous iris recognition algorithms have been proposed under Texture based, Feature based and Appearance based methods, the underlying processes that define the texture of irises have not been extensively studied [2], [3].

2   Related Works

Many authors had undergone their research for the biometric security issues based on various cryptographic techniques. In the paper [4], neither the key nor the original trait is stored, rather BE called biometric encrypted template is stored that contains the original template and as well as the key. In [5], the author analyzed the current image encryption algorithms and compression like Mirror-like image encryption and Visual Cryptography. In the paper [6], proposed a provably secure and blind biometric authentication protocol, which addresses the concerns of user's privacy, template protection, and trust issues. The protocol is blind in the sense that it reveals only the identity, and no additional information about the user or the biometric to the authenticating server or vice-versa. In [7], addition/subtraction operations and Reed-Solomon error-correcting algorithm are employed to directly encrypt and decrypt the data. In [8], algorithm was proposed to protect the identify code be transported securely, one-way coupled map lattice (OCML)chaos system be applied to generate pseudo-random number key stream, and the iris identify code was encrypted and decrypted based on the method of cipher text feedback.

3   Iris Recognition System

The iris recognition systems are used mainly in the areas where security is an important issue. The characteristics of a human iris is unique, plays a vital role in the identification of an individual. The most important feature of iris is that these characteristics can never be duplicated. Iris recognition has been successfully deployed in many large scale and small scale applications. The iris codes can be generated in many methods. In the present work (Fig.1), the wavelet-packet approaches are chosen, which is more efficient for iris code generation. A Haar wavelet method based on energy and intensity features is used for iris recognition. Each iris image is described by a subset of band filtered images (sub images) containing wavelet coefficients [1]. From these coefficients, which characterize the iris texture; we compute a compact iris feature code using the appropriate energies and intensities of these sub images to generate binary iris codes according to an adapted threshold .These binary iris codes are encoded to non binary iris code templates and stored in the database which provides a greater security. During the matching process, the iris codes are decoded and Hamming Distance is used to compare the iris codes between the input and template images in order to verify the match for authentication.

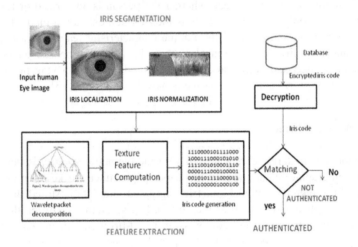

Fig. 1. Proposed Iris Recognition System

3.1   Iris Segmentation

The iris is an annular part between the pupil (inner boundary) and the Sclera (outer boundary) (Fig.2). The first and foremost step in iris recognition is to find the accurate pupil and iris boundary in input image. Iris segmentation takes place in two steps:

- Iris Localization
- Iris Normalization

Iris localization refers to the separation of iris from other parts of the eye. This will help to locate the unique portion of the eye, i.e. iris. The first step in iris localization is to detect the pupil which is the black circular part surrounded by iris tissues. The centre of pupil can be used to detect the outer radius of iris patterns. The important steps involved are pupil detection and outer iris localization. In case there are eyelids and eyelashes in the image or eye, they are eliminated by considering only the unique iris portion. Here, there are lots of iris localization algorithms available such as daugman'sintegro-differential operator, Wilde's method, Hough transform, canny edge detector, etc [2]. In the present work, the localization is carried out using canny edge detection to find the edges and Hough Transform to find the centre of the circular iris region. Canny zero-crossings correspond to the first directional derivative's maxima and minima in the direction of the gradient. Maxima in magnitude is a reasonable choice for locating edges [9]. A circle with radius r and centre (a, b) can be described with the parametric equation (1).

$$(x - [a)]^2 + (y - b)^2 - r^2 = 0 \tag{1}$$

When the angle θ sweeps through the full 360° range the points (x, y) trace the perimeter of a circle. This finds the inner boundary circle (pupil) and outer boundary circle (iris) through various stages in order to segment the iris from the eye (Fig.3).

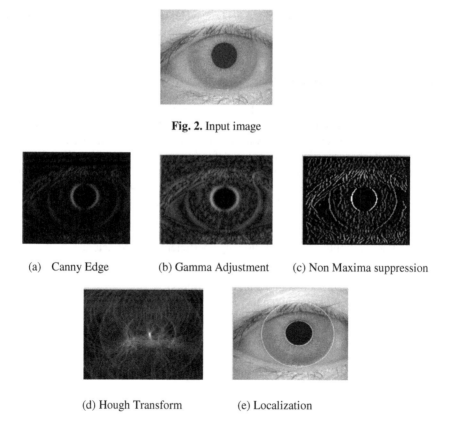

Fig. 2. Input image

(a)   Canny Edge   (b) Gamma Adjustment   (c) Non Maxima suppression

(d) Hough Transform   (e) Localization

Fig. 3. Iris Localization Steps

Two images of the same iris might be very different as a result of the size of the image, size of the pupil, orientation of the iris. To cope with this, [2] the image is

Fig. 4. Iris Normalization

normalized (Fig.4) by converting from Cartesian coordinates to polar coordinates which helps to remove the occlusions like eyelashes, etc.

3.2   Iris Feature Extraction

Different features can be extracted from iris to generate the iris code. Our work concentrates on texture features. Some of the texture based features are energy, mean, occlusion, angle, intensity, standard deviation etc. The two main features extracted here are energy and intensity. Different methods exist to perform the feature extraction as follows: wavelet transform, cosine transform, Fourier transform etc[10]. In our proposed system, energy is computed using wavelet transform. This extraction is done in three different steps: Wavelet Decomposition, Texture Feature Selection, Iris code generation.

3.2.1   Wavelet Decomposition

A wavelet transform is the representation of a function by wavelets. A wavelet is a mathematical function used to divide a given function or continuous-time signal into different scale components. Numerous transforms like Haar wavelet, Daubechies wavelet, Coiflet wavelet, Symlet wavelet, Biorthogonal wavelet, circular symmetric filters, and Gabor wavelets can be used for feature extraction [2]. Wavelet Packet Decomposition (WPD) is one of the wavelet transform and two-dimensional wavelet decomposition is performed to extract the iris features. Haar wavelet is the one type of WPD. Haar wavelet in a 3-level wavelet packet decomposition used to extract the texture features of the unwrapped images. This generates 64 wavelet packets numbered 0 to 63 [1], [3], [11]. The normalized image is passed through a series of low and high pass filters and the following coefficients are extracted:

    i) Approximation (a low and a low pass filters)
    ii) Horizontal (a low and a high pass filters)
    iii) Vertical (a high and a low pass filters)
    iv) Diagonal (a high and a high pass filters)

Decomposition step

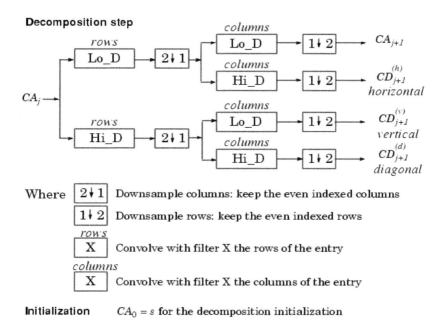

Where $\boxed{2\downarrow 1}$ Downsample columns: keep the even indexed columns

$\boxed{1\downarrow 2}$ Downsample rows: keep the even indexed rows

$\overset{\textit{rows}}{\boxed{X}}$ Convolve with filter X the rows of the entry

$\overset{\textit{columns}}{\boxed{X}}$ Convolve with filter X the columns of the entry

Initialization $CA_0 = s$ for the decomposition initialization

3.2.2   Texture Feature Computation

The various iris features based on texture are selected in order to form a template with reduced size based on region of interest and the texture features [1]. Some textual features of an iris are energy of an iris image, focus, intensity, occlusions, etc. Some of these features are selected for this proposed system.The mean energy distribution allows evaluating which packets are used to compute the normalized adapted threshold for our iris code generation [3]. The energy measure E_i for a wavelet packet subimage W_i can be computed as

$$E1 = \sum_{j,k} W1(j,k)2 . \tag{2}$$

Intensity represents the value of each individual pixel in the imageand its variance V [6] is computed by equation (3) using equation (4).

$$V(n) = \frac{\sum_{k=2}^{N-2} V(i,j) - (0.25 * T(i,j))}{N-4} \tag{3}$$

$$T(i,j) = V(i-1,j) + V(i-2,j) + V(i+1,j) + V(i+2,j) \tag{4}$$

$$E1 = E1 + V(n). \tag{5}$$

3.2.3 Iris Code Generation

Following the feature extraction, the unique binary iris code should be generated (Fig.5a). The normalized adapted threshold is calculated by equation (6). We definethe normalized adapted threshold S as follows:

$$S = Coef.\frac{\mu(E1, E2, ... E\lambda)}{Max(E1, E2, ... E\lambda)} \cdot \tag{6}$$

Let $E1...E\lambda$ be the appropriate wavelet packet energies of the packets $1...\lambda$ respectively and $\mu(E1, E2, ... E\lambda)$ represents the mean wavelet peak energy value, *Coeff* as a constant and λ is the number of the appropriate energies [3]. Finally the iris code $C\lambda$ is computed obtaining iris code according to energy appropriately, as defined in equation (7). Let $E\lambda$ be the appropriate energy of the peak λ.

$$C\lambda(j) = \begin{cases} 1 & if \frac{Ej}{E\lambda} > S \\ 0 & otherwise \end{cases} \tag{7}$$

3.3   Template Encoding

The generated binary iris codes are of 64 bit. These codes are encrypted in order to vary the length and value of each iris code using random values r1 and r2. The Encryption steps are as follows:

   1. Find iris code for the image.
   2. Find the number of zeros and ones.
           If (iris code is zero)
                   No. of zero's = (no of zero's*10) + r1
           If (one)
                   No. of one's = (no of one's*10) + r2
   3. Find the length of the encrypted code.
   4. Multiply the code with length.
   5. Add the length in front of the encrypted iris code array.
   6. Write into database.

The encrypted iris codes are non binary values with variant length and stored as a template in the database (Fig.5b).

3.4   Iris Code Matching

The given input to be authenticated and verified doesn't need to undergo the overall iris recognition process. The encrypted iris codes in the database are decoded by the following steps.

   1. Read the encrypted code from database.
   2. For each row get the first element of the code (length of encrypted code).
   3. Divide the remaining code in each row by length.
   4. Reverse the encryption process step 2.
   5. Find hamming distance with new image iris code.

Hamming distance was originally conceived for detection and correction of errors in digital communication [1], [2], [3].It is simply defined as the number of bits that are different between two bit vectors. It is implemented by the Boolean exclusive OR operator applied to the 64 bit vector that encodes any two iris codes by equation (8).

$$HDl,k = \sum_{j=0}^{j=N} Cl(j) \bigoplus \Box Ck(j) \qquad (8)$$

4   Experimental Results

The iris images for the test are collected from CASIA database v1 and v3 [12]. For an input image, the region of interest is segmented by various localization steps (Fig.3a to 3e) and normalized to polar coordinates (Fig.4). Specific texture features are extracted to generate iris codes. The generated iris codes from the extracted texture based features are of 64 bit binary codes. Those code templates are encrypted to vary its size, value and mode in order to safeguard from various hacking methods. Each encrypted iris codes are of non-binary, variant length and unique value. These codes are stored in the database. When the input is given for authentication, it doesn't require the entire recognition process to be performed repeatedly. It can be verified by decrypting the database codes and matches using hamming distance. This reduces the running time and the accuracy of the output. Threshold coefficients at various levels are tried duringiris code matching for both CASIAV1 and CASIAV3. The performance of the Biometric systems is often measured using the "Equal Error Rate (EER), False Rejection Rates (FRR) and False Acceptance Rate (FAR)"for any system. Lower the EER higher the accuracy. FRR occurs when users are granted access but should have been denied access. The FAR presents a greater security, because unauthorized access is granted.Lower the FAR and FRR, the performance is higher. The results of this system are listed in Table 1 which proves that the system is more effective for the very normal inputs, based on the setting of threshold coefficient. Also Table 2 proves that the proposed system is very effective even for reflected images.

```
1110000101111000
1000111000101010
1111001010001110
0000111000100001
0010101111000011
100100001000100
```

Fig. 5a. Binary Iris Codes

```
8,260,116,180,196,100,116,60,1756
32,2805,209,165,209,165,209,385,209,165
,209,165,209,165,209,165,209,165,209,16
5,429,165,209,165,429,165,209,165,209,1
65,209,165,429
16.1470.174.90.114.90.114.150.654.210.1
```

Fig. 5b. Encoded Variant Iris Codes

Table 1. Performance Results for CASIA v1

Coeff=1.4		Coeff<1.8		Coeff<2.4		Coeff<3.4		Coeff=3.5	
FAR	FRR	FAR	FRR	FAR	FRR	FAR	FRR	FAR	FRR
0.36	0	0.24	0	0.2	0	0.08	0	0	0

Table 2. Performance Results for CASIA v3

Coeff=1.4		Coeff<1.6		Coeff=1.7	
FAR	FRR	FAR	FRR	FAR	FRR
0.2	0	0.08	0	0	0

5   Conclusion

In the paper, the main focus is to develop a human authentication system based on human iris texture using wavelet packets decomposition and securing the iris template by encoding of templates. The proposed technique uses only appropriate packets with dominant energies to encode iris texture according to the adapted thresholds and coefficients. The effectiveness of this system was confirmed in the experimental results, which reveals that the verification results with an EER=0% has been obtained for packets combination, which means that our system is appropriate for very high security environments. This system is more effective and robust for any iris data set even with reflected images, which can further be improved for an image with more occlusions like cylindrical iris, iris with lens, etc. Also this system reduces the matching process time as a response of encoding concept which leads to effective performance of the recognition percentage and securing the iris code databases.

References

1. Bae, K., Noh, S., Kim, J.: Personal Authentication based on iris texture Analysis. IEEE Transactions on Computer Systems and Applications Analysis and Machine Intelligence 25, 12 (2008)
2. Bowyer, K.W., Hollingsworth, K., Flynn, P.J.: Image Understanding for Iris Biometrics: A Survey. Computer Vision and Image Understanding 110(2), 281–307 (2008)
3. Benhammadi, F., Kihal, N.: Personal Authentication Based on Iris Texture Analysis. IEEE Transactions on Pattern Analysis and Machine Intelligence 15, 537–543 (2008)
4. Mohapatra, A.K., Sandhu, M.: Biometric Template Encryption. International Journal of Advanced Engineering & Application, 282–284 (January 2010)

5. Ozturk, I., Sogukpınar, I.: IsmetOzturk and Ibrahim Sogukpınar: Analysis and Comparison of Image Encryption Algorithms. World Academy of Science, Engineering and Technology 3 (2005)
6. Upmanyu, M., et al.: Blind Authentication: A Secure Crypto-Biometric Verification Protocol. IEEE Transactions on Information Forensics and Security 5(2), 255–268 (2010)
7. Li, X., et al.: A Novel Cryptographic Algorithm based on Iris Feature. In: International Conference on Computational Intelligence and Security. IEEE (2008)
8. Yang, L., et al.: Iris Recognition System Based on Chaos Encryption. In: International Conference on Computer Design and Applications (ICCDA 2010), vol. 1, pp. 537–539. IEEE (2010)
9. Canny, J.F.: A computational approach to edge detection. IEEE Transactions on Pattern Analysis and Machine Intelligence PAMI-8(6), 679–698 (1986)
10. Boles, W., Boashash, B.: A human identification technique using images of the iris and wavelet Transform. IEEE Trans. on Signal Processing 46(4), 1185–1188 (1998)
11. Krichen, E., Anouar Mellakh, M., Salicetti, S.G., Dorizzi, B.: Iris Identification using wavelet packets. In: Int. Conf. on Pattern Recognition, pp. 335–338 (2004)
12. http://www.cbsr.ia.ac.cn/IrisDatabase/irislogin.html

Optimal and User Friendly Technique for Enhancing Security by Robust Password Creation Using Biometric Characteristic

Richa Golash[1], Chhaya Rani Ram Kinkar[1], and Akhilesh Upadhyay[2]

[1] Deptt. of EC Engg., Sagar Institute of Research Technology and Science – Bhopal, 462041 (M.P.), India
[2] Deptt. of EC Engg., Sagar Institute of Research and Technology – Bhopal, 462041(M.P.), India
{golash.richa,chhayakinkar,akhileshupadhyay}@gmail.com

Abstract. World is becoming technology dependent and with this Hacking of passwords has now become a regular phenomena. Researchers are going to create technique which contain properties like of iris recognition or face recognition, also have acceptability among the user and less complexity in processing. In this paper a new technique of creating biometric identity verification for dynamic system where number of user's increases or decreases, has been conceptualized. This technique is simple in use, simultaneously provides robustness to the overall system. In this 3 hand features are used as identity verification. A database in terms of hand geometry, finger length, finger width is created whenever a new user is registered and when the user gets login its identity is verified with the help of matching these features with the database, along with the password entered by keyboard.

Keywords: Biometric verification, Hand Geometry, Finger length, Finger width.

1 Introduction

As technology is growing day by day and online services using Internet are becoming indispensible way of life. Since these facilities, offered by the various organization like Banks, booking ticket of bus, rail, plane etc. are easy to use and also saves the time of the person, Therefore they have weaved up into our everyday routine. But everything has two faces and same is technology. It has been observed that due to lack of technical knowledge people are not able to make complex password [1]. According to Bell Lab's finding, a large percentage of passwords chosen by users were easy to decode in a short period of time.

These days Biometric authentication system has gaining more and more attraction. Which has used the fact every human being is unique in nature. Techniques have been developed where natural characteristic like face, thumb impressions are used as a code for the devices [2][11]. Biometric system works in two areas identification and identity verification [3] [4]. These two areas have different utility. Former is used for search purpose, where identity of the user is a priori unknown and the user's

P.V. Krishna, M.R. Babu, and E. Ariwa (Eds.): ObCom 2011, Part II, CCIS 270, pp. 406–413, 2012.

biometric data is matched against all the records in the database, as the user can be anywhere in the database or he/she actually does not have to be there at all. Later area is more generally used for system protection which based on the physical characteristic of the user and the user claims to be already enrolled in the system (as ID card or login name); in this case the verification of biometric data obtained from the user is compared to the user's data already stored in the database.

In Biometric verification system security threshold is the key issue. This depend on two parameter False rejection ratio (FRR) and False acceptance ratio (FAR) [5]. False rejection is when the system does not find the legitimate user's current biometric data similar to the master template stored in the database. False acceptance when an impostor is accepted as a legitimate user. System having high security level will have high FRR and low FAR.

Apart from security threshold any biometric verification system must have following characteristic [9] [12].

1. Uniqueness: Characteristic discriminating man from other man.

2. Permanence: The characteristics should be invariant with time.

3. Collectability: The characteristics must be measured quantitatively and obtaining the characteristics should be easy.

4. Performance: The achievable verification accuracy achieved by using the characteristic.

5. Acceptability: It indicates to what extend people are willing to accept the characteristic as a verification means for biometric system.

6. Circumvention: This refers to how difficult it is to fool the system by fraudulent techniques using the characteristic.

2   Types of Biometric System Techniques

A man has many distinguishable and unique features for eg. face, Iris, thumb impression, DNA etc.. Based on this, significant number technique have been developed like fingerprint, iris pattern, retina pattern, facial recognition, voice comparison, signature dynamics and hand writing[3][6]. In this some of the most prevailing techniques are analyzed with respect to a characteristic which can be globally accepted and have less complexity in maintaining its database.

2.1   Finger Print Recognition

Fingerprint identification is one of the oldest techniques originally started for identifying person as an author of the document. Presently Silicon technology Optical fingerprint, Ultrasonic technologies are in the market. Fingerprint readers are popular in mobile phones and laptop computers due to its compact size. The main drawback of accepting Fingerprint as a universal password format is Fingerprints are not compared and difficult to store as bitmaps. Matching techniques based on either minutiae matching or correlation matching. The problem with minutiae is that it is difficult to extract the minutiae points accurately when the fingerprint is of low quality. The correlation-based method techniques require the precise location of a registration point and are affected by image translation and rotation. Moreover the readability of a fingerprint depends on a variety of work and environmental factors like age, gender, occupation and race. A young, female, Asian mine-worker is seen as the most difficult subject[12]. More over factors like dust particle, water molecule will not produce bitmaps with a sufficient quality.

2.2   Iris Recognition

Iris recognition is one of the secured techniques. The iris pattern remains stable over a person's life, being only affected by several diseases. Since this technique require comparatively large memory space, therefore it is more useful for static system to avoid unauthorized penetration into the system of files, folders can be stopped [7] .

2.3   Face Recognition

Like iris recognition it is one of the authentic way of giving high security, but to create a database is a challenging task, also where number of users are more creating matching algorithm is difficult. Therefore is used for static system [8].

Similarly using Handwriting or voice [9] as the characteristic will also not be appropriate as they change with respect to time and other environmental factor. In this paper a new technique of creating biometric identity verification for dynamic system where number of user's increases or decreases, has been conceptualized. In this 3 Hand features are used to completely verify the identity of the user.

3   Process Description

This method comprises of two broad modules database generation and identity verification and each of these two contain three sub modules (i) Preprocessing (ii) Feature Extraction (iii) Generation of database or verification of identity.

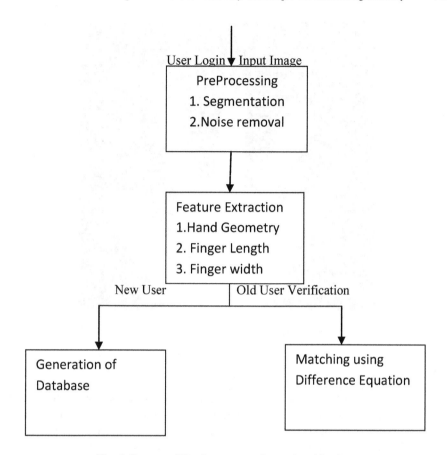

Fig. 1. Process of Database generation and verification

3.1   Pre Processing

When image of hand is captured using camera or scanner, the process to make the image ready to extract features is called preprocessing. The first step is the detection of hand region .In the proposed method this is done using color segmentation .Since color is one of the robust feature and highly invariant to rotation and scaling also it allows a simple and fast processing. Each pixel of the input image is classified as skin color or non skin color. Pixel of   Input image is in YCbCr color space or RGB color space format after segmentation converts to binary or monochromatic for where '1'represent white or lit pixel and '0' represent black or dark pixel.

Second step is noise removal, which consider the fact that hand is present (lower central part) in a portion of image and remaining is noise or black space. Here two types of noise has to be removed one which is away from the hand region and second which is present between the two fingers .These type of noise can be removed using binary search algorithm and convolution filter.

Fig. 2. Image of Hand after Preprocessing

3.2   Feature Extraction

In this proposed method feature extraction is the key element, on which the security system lies. Hand has many unique feature like hand geometry, finger length, finger width, thumb length, palm perimeter etc. [6]. Out of these we have selected three main features on which this technique is designed, are Hand Geometry, finger length, finger width and user database is created on this parameter.

The proposed method extracts geometric boundary of hand and for each finger one measurement of length and one measurements of width is taken. The thumb is not included in the feature extraction process. Therefore total 9 feature of any hand is collected and has to be verified.

Hand Geometry
After elimination of noise image contain black and white pixel. In order to extract geometric boundary of hand, the preprocessed image is converted to an image only the boundary of white pixel. Here Canny's edge detection algorithm [10] is used because of it properties that the thickness of the boundary is very low; also rate of false edge detection is very less.

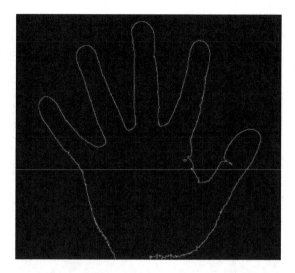

Fig. 3. Hand Geometry showing only edge

Finger Length

The proposed method considers the right hand therefore little finger is on left most position. To determine finger length, fingertip is determined. Traversing from the left most corner (0,0) of the image first white pixel(x1,y1) is find, which is the tip of little finger. Using line detection algorithm the bottom of the finger(x2,y2) is found by considering the fact that y coordinate does not decreasing after y2

-1	-1	-1
2	2	2
-1	-1	-1

Fig. 4. Kernel for Horizontal line

-1	2	-1
-1	2	-1
-1	2	-1

Fig. 5. Kernel for Vertical Line

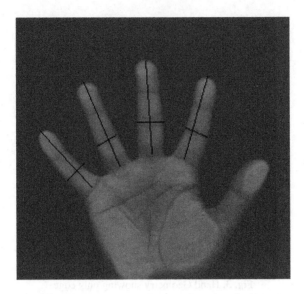

Fig. 6. Determination of Finger length and width

The length of the finger is then calculated by taking the distance between the top and bottom points.

Finger Width
We know that finger is into 3 parts. (x3,y3) and (x4,y4) is obtained by dividing line 'X' joining (x1,y1) and (x2,y2) into 3 parts .A line is drawn perpendicular to the line 'X' passing from (x4,y4) in both left and right direction. This line will traverse till they encounter a white pixel. Distance travelled wills the width of finger.

3.3   Generation of Database

In this method along with the Password given through Keyboard each user has to give its biological identity that is his hand features in terms of hand geometry, finger length, finger width. The features obtained from the input image are stored in the database in t matched against the images in the form of positive integers.

3.4   Matching or Verification

Verification or matching is the crucial responsibility of this method. When an image is input for verification it goes under the process of Preprocessing and feature extraction. The magnitude of the input image and the database image is then verified using difference formula.

Diff= mag.of database image – mag.of input image.

Since the magnitude of different features are of varying value. Even under the best of conditions it cannot be expected that the features obtained match exactly with the features of the previous image of the same individual [2][7]. Therefore a optimum level of difference which is known as threshold has to be set which balance the False rejection Ratio (FRR) and False acceptance Ratio (FAR).

4   Conclusion and Future

This paper has tried to present a novel technique of robust password creation along with integration of Keyboard typed password. Hand as biological characteristic is globally accepted therefore it will significantly be helpful in enhancing the security of password and identity of user. Future of this will be real time implementation of the technique.

References

1. Burge, M., Burger, W.: Ear biometrics, personal identification in networked society. Kluwer academic, Boston (1999)
2. Bulatov, Y., Jambawalikar, S., Kumar, P., Sethia, S.: Hand recognition using geometric classifiers (1999)
3. Individuality of handwriting: A validation study. In: roceedings of the Sixth International Conference on Document Analysis and Recognition, ICDAR 2001, p. 106. IEEE Computer Society, Washington, DC, USA (2001)
4. Bergadano, F., Gunetti, D., Picardi, C.: User authentication through keystroke dynamics. ACM Trans. Inf. Syst. Secur. 5(4), 367–397 (2002)
5. Oden, C., Yildiz, V.T., Kirmizitas, H., Buke, B.: Hand Recognition Using Implicit Polynomials and Geometric Features. In: Bigun, J., Smeraldi, F. (eds.) AVBPA 2001. LNCS, vol. 2091, pp. 336–341. Springer, Heidelberg (2001)
6. Kumar, A., Zhang, D.: Integrating shape and texture for hand verification. In: Proceedings of the Third International Conference on Image and Graphics (ICIG 2004), pp. 222–225. IEEE Computer Society, Washington, DC, USA (2004)
7. Verbitskiy, E., Tuyls, P., Denteneer, D., Linnartz, J.P.: Reliable biometric authentication with privacy protection. Presented at the SPIE Biometric Technology for Human Identification Conf., Orlando, FL (2004)
8. Pishchulin, L., Gass, T., Dreuw, P., Ney, H.: The Fast and the flexible: Extended pesudo two dimensional wrapping for face recognition. International Journal of Document analysis and Recognition (2010)
9. Tuske, Z., Golik, P., Schluter, R., Drepper, F.R.: Non stationary feature extraction for automatic speech recognition. International Journal of Document Analysis and Recognition (2009)
10. Canny, J.: A computational approach to edge detection. IEEE Transactions on Pattern Analysis and Machine Intelligence 08, 679–698 (1986)
11. Lu, G., Zhang, D., Wang, K.: Palmprint recognition using eigen palms features. Pattern Recogn. Lett. 24(9-10), 1463–1467 (2003)
12. Jain, A.K., Pankanti, S., Prabhakar, S., Ross, A.: Recent advances in fingerprint verification. In: AVBPA, pp. 182–191 (2001)

Raga Identification in CARNATIC Music Using Hidden Markov Model Technique

Surendra Shetty[1], K.K. Achary[2], and Sarika Hegde[3]

[1] Department of Computer Applications, NMAMIT, Nitte, Udupi District,
Karnataka, India-574110
hsshetty4u@yahoo.com
[2] Department of Statistics Mangalore University, Mangalagangothri,
Mangalore Karnataka, India-574199
kka@mangaloreunivarsity.ac.in
[3] Department of Computer Applications, NMAMIT, Nitte, Udupi District,
Karnataka, India-574110
sarika.hegde@yahoo.in

Abstract. *Raga* identification is very essential for automatic Music Information Retrieval (MIR) systems. One of the methods of classifying and organizing the songs of South Indian Classical music (Carnatic Music) is by identifying the *Raga* used to compose the music. *Ragas* can be defined as melody types, method of organizing tunes based on certain natural principles. As there are thousands of *ragas* classes defined in *carnatic* music system, the process of identifying *raga* of a song is a difficult task. In this paper, we have proposed a method where we divide the *raga* classes into number of groups based on the jump sequence of *swaras* used in the *raga*. So, using this method the *raga* identification process is solved in two levels where in the first level we identify the group to which song belongs and then in the next step identify the *raga*. Here in this paper, we describe the method used to group the *ragas* and then present the experimental analysis of the work done.

Keywords: *Raga* Identification, Music Information Retrieval, Hidden markov model.

1 Introduction

1.1 Motivation

Music Information Retrieval (MIR) is a process of searching and indexing an audio clip from a large database collection based on the content of the audio clip. One of the approaches to solve MIR is by High-Level Music Content Description where musical concepts such as melody or harmony are used to describe the content of music. The design of MIR for Indian Music collections would require the intelligence of retrieving the piece of audio sample based on the underlying *raga* used to compose the musical piece. Also, managing the vast audio collections of classical music will require greater human intervention for classifying the songs into different categories based on the concept of *Raga*. *Raga* is the most fundamental concept of Indian classical music both in *Hindustani* and *Carnatic Musical* traditions. *Raga* constitutes a separate object of knowledge organization having a specific relationship to song. This relationship ideally

P.V. Krishna, M.R. Babu, and E. Ariwa (Eds.): ObCom 2011, Part II, CCIS 270, pp. 414–423, 2012.

needs represented in order to expose to the user important (intra) musical meanings. Our approach attempts to illustrate the design of solving the *Raga* Identification into different clusters which further simplify the task of *raga* identification. This type of technique would be useful since the task is done without knowing the scale of the song and gives a solution to a *raga* system with thousands of categories.

1.2   Previous Works

The digital library of Carnatic music should contain the objects of knowledge organization and their interrelationships as conceived by indigenous practitioners and audiences, rather than by Western specialists or North Indian practitioners. Different methods have been proposed for melody extraction in Western music for content based music retrieval system. Classification of European folk music by geographic origin was experimented using Hidden Markov Model (HMM) [1]. The idea is to detect structure similarity between pieces from the observation of pitch sequences. The experiment results legitimate this approach as a way to draw a characterization of similarities between same origin pieces. A new extension to the variable duration HMM is proposed that is capable of classifying musical patterns that have been extracted from raw audio data into a set of predefined classes [2]. A *melakarta Raga* identification method is proposed where the input polyphonic music signal is analyzed and made to pass through a signal separation algorithm to separate the instrument and the vocal signal [3]. Recently Srinath Krishna [4] have developed a technique to identify *ragas* using HMM by considering the analysis of a music signal in its log-frequency domain.

1.3   *Raga*

Understanding and designing MIR system requires an intense knowledge of a '*Raga*', which is a very complex structure. In spite of its complexity, the *Raga* structure is clearly defined in a systematic way. *Raga* in simpler term is a combination and permutation of *swaras* or notes in western term decorated in such a way that when combined with the feel of the song creates pleasant melody for a listener. As the words in any language are formed with combination of letters to give a particular meaning so as *Raga* is a combination of *swaras* which creates melody. A *swara* is a basic unit of Indian music. *Hindustani* and *Carnatic Music* are two forms of Indian music, where the basic concepts of these two are same but differ by the set of *Ragas* defined in those. In *Carnatic Music*, there are seven *swaras,* named as *S, R, G, M, P, D, N*. Whereas the *swaras S* and *P* are always fixed (meaning, they do not have sharp or flat variants), the *swaras R, G, D and N* have three variants each listed as R1, R2, R3, G1, G2, G3, D1, D2, D3, N1, N2, N3 and the *swara M* has two variants listed as M1, M2 as shown in Table 1.

Basically, a '*swara*' is a set of harmonic frequencies. Any *swara* is sung with a particular pitch where, pitch is the subjective perception of frequency that the human ear detects and this is measured in Hz. As in Western music where there is a strong relationship between note and pitch, it is not true in case of Indian music. We cannot say that *swara* 'S' is always sung with a defined pitch. This is why the melody detection in Indian music becomes different and difficult from Western music. The relationship between pitch and *swara* is related based on the scale (*shruthi*) in which song is played. The singer can play the song based on the scale he/she is comfortable with. Table 2 shows the relationship between the pitch of the *swara* and the scale of the song. .

Table 1. List of *Swaras*

No.	Swara	Indicated Swara
1	S	S
2	r	R1
3	R	R2, G1
4	g	R3, G2
5	G	G3
6	m	M1
7	M	M2
8	P	P
9	d	D1
10	D	D2, N1
11	n	D3, N2
12	N	N3

Table 2. Scale-swara relationship

Swara	Ratio	Swara	Ratio
Sa	1	M	729/512
r	256/243	P	3/2
R	9/8	D	128/81
g	32/27	Dha	27/16
G	81/64	n	16/9
m	4/3	N	243/128

The set of *Ragas* in Carnatic Music are mainly categorized into 72 *Melakarta Ragas* based on the main seven *swaras* used out of the 16 *swaras* as shown in Table1. Using each of the *Melakarta raga*, new *ragas* are formed by omitting some of the *swaras* and defining the different style of ascending/descending pattern of these *swara* called as *Janya ragas*.

1.4   Problem Definition

Having defined the *Raga* and *Carnatic Music*, we define the problem statement of work. The goal of our work is, given a piece of *Carnatic Music*; identify the *Raga* of the song. The solution to the problem is difficult due to the following reasons.

1. As we have mentioned above that there are thousands of *ragas* defined in Carnatic music. So the classification problem has to deal with large number of classes at a time to make a decision about a given piece of music.
2. To know the *Raga*, we must know what *swaras* used in the song. It is not simple because after calculating the pitch we cannot relate it directly to a particular *swara* without knowing the scale of the song.

2   Proposed Solution

The solution to the problem is given in two steps. In the first level we manually divide the set of *ragas* into groups based on the sequence of *swaras* in the *raga* and design HMM model for each of the group. In the next level, HMM model is designed for each of the *raga*. The design of both the HMM model is done in the training step. In the testing phase, a given song is classified by first indentifying the group to which it belongs. This is done by testing the song against all the group HMM models created. After identifying the group we test the song against the *raga* HMM models belonging to the identified cluster. So using this method, the number of *raga* HMM models to be compared for classification are reduced drastically. The following diagram shows the block diagram of the solution to the problem of testing a new song for *raga* identification. Each HMM model gives the result as probability of matching the song with that model. The cluster model which gives the highest probability is selected as the matched cluster. The same approach is applied for *raga* HMM model. The *raga* HMM which gives the highest probability is selected as the identified *raga*.

In the Fig 1 below, we have indicated 'X' number of group models generated. So a new song will be tested against all these 'X' group models whichever gives the highest probability is selected as the identified cluster. We can see in the diagram that each of the group having some number *raga* models within it. So after identifying the group we need to compare the song against all the *raga* HMM models within the identified group. Training and testing HMM models requires the generation of observation and state sequence for a given song. The method for generating observation sequences is explained in the next section

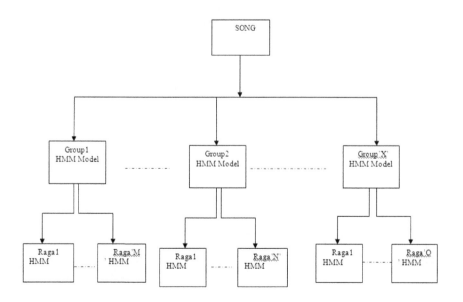

Fig. 1. Block diagram for *Raga* Identification using HMM

2.1   Grouping of *Ragas*

The *ragas* are grouped into groups based on the sequence of *swara* combination used in the *raga*. When a song is composed depending on the scale of the song , the range of 36 pitch values are decided and these 36 pitch values can be mapped to 36 *swaras* of three octaves that is lower, middle and higher octave. The choice of actual *swaras* used out of these 36 will differ for different *raga*. For any pair of *swara* that is used in the *raga*, compute the level of jump from one pitch (*swara*) to the next pitch (swara) in the octave which is used as an observation value for a *swara*. In the training phase when the *swara* is known, this observation value can be calculated by finding the difference of the position of *swara* in the octave. In the testing phase when the *swara* is not known this observation value can be calculated by finding the level of the ratio of the adjacent pitch values. For example if *raga* uses 7 *swaras* that is S, R2, G1, M1, P, D1 and N1. Then the total number of *swaras* that can be used in the song of that *raga* is 21 (practically all 21 *swaras* are not used) which is calculated as sum of 7 *swaras* of lower octave, 7 *swaras* of middle octave and the 7 *swaras* of higher octave shown as in the following table.

Table 3. Theoretical based jump values for the three octaves for a *raga*

LOWER OCTAVE							MIDDLE OCTAVE							HIGHER OCTAVE						
P_1	P_2	P_3	P_4	P_5	P_6	P_7	P_8	P_9	P_{10}	P_{11}	P_{12}	P_{13}	P_{14}	P_{15}	P_{16}	P_{17}	P_{18}	P_{19}	P_{20}	P_{21}
'S	'R$_2$	'G$_1$	'M1$_1$	'P	'D$_1$	'N$_1$	S	R$_2$	G$_1$	M$_1$	P	D$_1$	N$_1$	S'	R$_2$'	G$_1$'	M$_1$'	P'	D$_1$'	N$_1$'
2	1	2	2	1	2	2	2	1	2	2	1	2	2	2	1	2	2	1	2	2

In the table, the first line indicates the sequence of pitch values that we get after processing the input song. The second line indicates the sequence of *swara* used, which can be mapped from the pitch value. The third line indicates the level of jump for each of the *swara* which is just calculated by taking difference of position of the two *swara* in the octave. The observation sequence is generated by taking the sequence of observation values of one octave from the table, for example, 2 1 2 2 1 2 2. Practically, every song composed in this *raga* will use all the *swaras* middle octave are used in the song, but may omit few of the *swaras* of lower and higher octave. For ex, if we have used *swaras* starting from 'P to P', then observation sequence generated is given in Table 4.,

Table 4. Practical based observation values for the three octave for *raga1*

LOWER OCTAVE			MIDDLE OCTAVE							HIGHER OCTAVE				
P_5	P_6	P_7	P_8	P_9	P_{10}	P_{11}	P_{12}	P_{13}	P_{14}	P_{15}	P_{16}	P_{17}	P_{18}	P_{19}
'P	'D$_1$	'N$_1$	S	R$_2$	G$_1$	M$_1$	P	D$_1$	N$_1$	S'	R$_2$'	G$_1$'	M$_1$'	P'
1	2	2	2	1	2	2	1	2	2	2	1	2	2	1

For any octave of 7 consecutive *swaras*, the list of all possible jump sequence generated is given as in the following table.

Table 5. List of possible observation sequence for *raga1*

SEQUENCE OF *SWARA*		SEQUENCE OF PITCH		OBSERVATION SEQUENCE						
FROM	TO	FROM	TO							
'P	P	P_2	P_{12}	1	2	2	2	1	2	2
'D₁	D₁	P_6	P_{13}	2	2	2	1	2	2	1
'N₁	N₁	P_7	P_{14}	2	2	1	2	2	1	2
S	S'	P_8	P_{15}	2	1	2	2	1	2	2
R₂	R₂'	P_9	P_{16}	1	2	2	1	2	2	2
G₁	G₁'	P_{10}	P_{17}	2	2	1	2	2	2	1
M₁	M₁'	P_{11}	P_{18}	2	1	2	2	2	1	2
P	P'	P_{12}	P_{19}	1	2	2	2	1	2	2

These observations can be either generated using the sequence of *swaras* when the scale is known or it can be generated with the sequence of pitch values when the scale is not known. So the possible list of all sequence for the *raga* can be generated by just circular shifting the actual sequence by some number of positions. When we shift the sequence circularly it may happen that the new jump sequence generated may be the actual jump sequence for some other *raga*. In the case of unknown scale these two *ragas* in terms of jump sequence looks similar. For example if any *raga* say *raga2* with the *swara* combination as SR2G2M1PD2N2, then the Table 6 below shows the value for the observation sequence of this *raga*.

Table 6. Practical based observation values for the three octaves for *raga₂*

Lower Octave							Middle Octave							Higher Octave						
P1	P2	P3	P4	P5	P6	P7	P8	P9	P10	P11	P12	P13	P14	P15	P16	P17	P18	P19	P20	P21
'S	'R₂	'G₂	'M1₁	'P	'D₂	'N₂	S	R₂	G₂	M₁	P	D₂	N₂	S'	R₂'	G₂'	M₁'	P'	D₂'	N₂'
2	2	1	2	2	2	1	2	2	1	2	2	2	1	2	2	1	2	2	2	1

2.2   Design and Implementation

2.2.1   Date Preprocessing

In this step, we take an audio sample as input and convert it into sequence of pitches. Here the input song is converted into number of samples with a sampling rate 44.1 KHz. Initially, the number of samples are grouped into different frames where frame-size is 2048 samples i.e approximately 50ms. An autocorrelation method is used to calculate the fundamental frequency or pitch of the frame. After dividing the song into number of frames, we compute the pitch of all the frames. After calculating the pitch of all the frames, the adjacent same pitch values are grouped into one segment that corresponds to a *swara*. The difference in dealing with the songs with known scale and unknown scale is that the mapping of pitch value to *a swara* cannot be done if the scale is not known. Instead of mapping pitch value to a *swara* absolutely and then finding the *swara* combination, relative difference between the pitch values are used as a basis for feature extraction. So, the sequence of pitch values are considered as input for feature selection process.

2.2.2 Generation of Jump Sequence

Any HMM model is represented with three parameters $\Theta = \{ \pi, A, B \}$ and the set of states. In both the type of the HMM model, the sequence of states represents the sequence of *swaras*. The observation value used in both of the HMM model represents the level of jumps occurred from moving one state to another. The level of jump is nothing but the variation in pitch values which becomes an important factor as we do not know the scale of the song. So, if we have the adjacent pitch values and do not know the actual *swara*, we can still calculate the variation between the pitch values. For example, if we have sequence of 'n' pitch values as $p_1, p_2, p_3, \ldots, p_n$ then map it to the notes of an octave of any scale say 'p_1'. Then calculate the level of jumps between the adjacent pitch values by calculating the difference between the adjacent notes with respect to the octave. The figure shows the example of the process where we have sequence 7 pitch values.

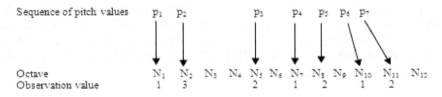

Fig. 2. Mapping of pitch values into Observation sequence

2.2.3 Hidden Markov Model for Group of *Ragas*

The grouping of *ragas* is done based on the combination of *swaras* which are used in the *raga*. As explained in the previous section even if the scale is not known, we can collect the distinct pitch values used in the song and map it to an octave. Creation of HMM model is done by training the model with the generated jump sequences of the input songs. To generate the jump sequence, we first get the unique pitch values which are used in the song. Here each of the pitch value represents the *swara*. Since in training phase we know the *Raga*, the lists of pitch values are mapped to the corresponding list of *swaras* to identify the states. Then compute the jump value for each of the state by calculating the level of difference with reference to the scale of an octave. For example, if we have the pair of *swaras* S R1, then the *swara* 'S' generates the jump value of 1. Since these two *swaras* are appears adjacent *swaras* in the octave. In the testing phase, the jump value is generated using the same method but there we do not know the state. So the jump value is generated by computing the level of jump between pair of pitch values. The jump value can range from 1 to 8 for any state assuming at least we get three *swaras* in one octave.

We collect the feature sequence consisting of the observation and state sequence for all the input songs used for training. And then generate the three tables those are Prior, Transition and emission tables. The prior table gives the probability of particular state being the first state in the state sequence. The transition table is created by calculating the probability of occurrence for each of the pair of states. The emission table is created by calculating the probability of occurrence of pair of state and the corresponding observation value.

2.2.4 Hidden Markov Model Method for *Raga* Identification

In the first step the entire audio signal is converted into sequence of pitch values which actually indicates the sequence of *swaras*. We consider sequence of nine *swara* at a time and represent this as state sequence and the observation sequence is created for this. In the case scale is not known, observation sequence is generated by considering the sequence of nine consecutive pitch values. Since any combination of *swara* out of the 36 possible values can occur as a pair, the observation value can range from -24 to +24. These values can be negative depending on when pitch goes down. The goal is to identify the *Raga* based on the sequence of ratios of adjacent pitch values. The set of states are the sequence of *swaras* and the observation sequence is the ratio level by which pitch changes (*swara* transition).

2.2.5 Experimental Results and Analysis

We collected monophonic songs of belonging to 21 *ragas*, the choice of which is made based on the availability of the songs. Since it is difficult to get the monophonic songs, we composed the songs by ourselves using the notations given for different the songs in the music books. These *ragas* were grouped into 5 clusters. The set of *ragas* and corresponding clusters are as listed below in Table 7.

From the table, we can observe that many *ragas* have been placed in Cluster1. That is just because of the choice of the *raga*. As we consider more and more *raga* and apply the above method we will get variety of clusters depending on the *swara* combination. Some of the *ragas* in cluster1 uses only five *swaras* in ascending sequence like *Arabhi, Begade, Dhanyasi, Shree-raga* which gives possibility of enhancing the system by further dividing cluster1 into sub clusters.

Each of the cluster and the *raga* is given a unique ID. In the first step we have selected few of the samples from each *raga* for the training set. Then the feature extraction method is applied for all the songs in the training set. The feature sequence constituting state and observation sequence are extracted for both the cluster and *raga* HMM models. These feature sequences are stored in separate files. Then each of the cluster and *raga* is trained individually where we generate prior, transmission and emission table which is later stored in files. The training is done in 2 steps, first initializing the table and then apply Expectation Maximization (EM) algorithm for updating the probabilities. Initialization is done by counting the relative frequency of occurrence of each pair of states and the pair state and the observation value. Updating the table is done by calculating the likelihood of each of the observation sequence in the training dataset with the HMM model.

Table 7. List of clusters along with the *ragas* under each cluster

GROUP	RAGA	JUMP SEQUENCE
GROUP1	1. THODI 2. ANANDABHAIRAVI 3. REETHIGAULA 4. SHREE-RAGA 5. KHARAHARAPRIYA 6. KAMBHOJI 7. HARI-KAMBHOJI 8. KHAMAJ 9. SHAHANA 10. ARABHI 11. BILAHARI 12. BEGADE 13. SHANKARABHARANA 14. KALYANI 15. DHANYASI	1 2 2 2 1 2 2
GROUP2	16. SAAVERI	1 3 1 2 1 3 1
GROUP3	17. HINDOLA 18. MOHANA 19. MADHYAMAVATHI	2 3 2 3 2
GROUP4	20. SHREE-RANJINI	2 1 2 4 1 2
GROUP5	21. HAMSADHWANI	2 2 3 4 1

For the testing purpose, we select the songs randomly from the available dataset and give it to the feature extraction module which generates the required observation sequence. The observation sequence is first tested with the different group models in the database and then the *raga* models within the database. The following table shows the result of the classification accuracy for the songs belonging to different clusters and the songs belonging to different *ragas*. Cluster identification accuracy is 85% and the *raga* identification within the cluster is 65%.

3   Conclusion

Here we have implemented a system for *Raga* Identification in two levels which simplifies the process by reducing the total number of HMM model comparisons. The accuracy of classification result is promising where it is also affected by the proper pitch calculation method for a given signal. We have used autocorrelation method for the pitch calculation. The designed solution presents a new way of solving the *raga* identification problem. This is just described at the fundamental level by considering only 21 *ragas*. The system can be enlarged further by testing and training for more number of *ragas* and clusters. Instead of grouping the *ragas* manually based on jump sequence and then applying classification, we can apply automatic clustering on the feature sets i.e jump sequences and test how the *ragas* are clustered. Even the clustering of *ragas* can be more refined by further sub-clustering each of the clusters based on the ascending/descending sequence of pitch values or *swaras*. But the method proposed here is a promising method to give the solution for the complete problem of *Raga* Identification in Indian Classical Music.

References

1. Chai, W., Vercoe, B.: Folk Music Classification Using Hidden Markov Models. In: Proceedings of International Conference on Artificial Intelligence (June 2001)
2. Pikrakis, A., Theodoridis, S., Kamarotos, D.: Classification Musical Patterns Using Variable Duration Hidden Markov Models. In: Proceedings EUSIPCO, pp. 1281–128 (2004)
3. Sridhar, R., Geetha, T.V.: Raga Identification of Carnatic Music for Music Information Retrieval. International Journal of Recent Trends in Engineering 1(1), 571–574 (2009)
4. Krishna, A.S., Rajkumar, P.V., Saishankar, K.P., John, M.: Identificaton of Carnatic *ragas* using Hidden Markov Models. In: Proceedings of 9th IEEE International Symposium on Applied Machine Intelligence and Informatics, Smoleniu, Slovakia, January 27-29 (2011)
5. Rabiner, L.R.: Fundamentals of Speech Recognition. Prentice Hall, PTR USA; ISBN,-10:013051572
6. Padmanabha Acharya, S.K., Veda, P.: Kasargod, India (Published by S.K. Padmanabha Acharya)

Automatic Lesion Detection in Colposcopy Cervix Images Based on Statistical Features

P.S. RamaPraba[1] and H. Ranganathan[2]

[1] Sathyabama University, Chennai, India
pazrama@yahoo.co.in
[2] Sakthi Mariamman Engineering College, Chennai, India

Abstract. Colposcopy is a medical diagnostic procedure to examine an illuminated, magnified view of the cervix by a colposcope. Colposcopic images are acquired in raw form, contains major cervix lesions, regions outside the cervix and parts of the imaging devices such as speculum. In this paper, a preprocessing method that removes the irrelevant information from the cervical images based on Mathematical morphology and clustering based on Gaussian Mixture Modeling is presented. The detection of specularities in cervix image is based on intensity and saturation information from the HSI colour space is presented. A novel approach to detect the lesion in the cervix image based on statistical features and Bayes classifier is presented. The detection of lesion is achieved by extracting the statistical features such as mean, standard deviation and skewness and the features are used as an input to the Bayes classifier. Segmentation results are evaluated on 240 images of colposcopy.

Keywords: Colposcopy, Cervigram, Gaussian Mixture Model, K means Clustering, Morphological Operations, Statistical Features.

1 Introduction

Cervical cancer is the most common form of cancer in women under 35 years of age, worldwide. Colposcopic images are characterized by color, texture and relief information. Thus, their automatic analysis is difficult. However, the diagnosis of experts about some much debated images is often different, because of the very high specialization required. An integrated analysis tool for helping gynecologists to build their colposcopic diagnosis is proposed in [1]. Moreover, specific preprocessing methods and different segmentation methods are available like principal component analysis and multidimensional histogram analysis.

In cervigram, the lesions are of varying sizes and complex, non-convex shapes. A new methodology that enables the segmentation of non-convex regions, thus providing a major step forward towards cervigram tissue detection and lesion description is presented in [2]. The framework transitions from pixels to a set of small coherent regions, which are grouped bottom-up into larger, non-convex, perceptually similar regions, utilizing a new graph-cut criterion and agglomerative clustering. A multistage scheme for segmenting and labeling regions of anatomical interest within

P.V. Krishna, M.R. Babu, and E. Ariwa (Eds.): ObCom 2011, Part II, CCIS 270, pp. 424–430, 2012.

the cervigrams is presented in [3]. In particular, focus on the extraction of the cervix region and fine detection of the cervix boundary; specular reflection is eliminated as an important preprocessing step and in addition, the entrance to the endocervical canal is detected.

Colposcopic image classification based on contour parameters using different artificial neural network and the KNN classifier is proposed in [4]. A set of original spatial and frequency parameters is extracted from 283 samples to characterize the attribute of contour. The spatial parameter is the number of the region around the edges and the frequency parameters are amplitude of first peak, frequency of the end of first peak, area under first peak and area under other peaks. Then the Principal Component Analysis is performed to test the parameters. Segmentation and classification of cervix lesions by pattern and texture analysis is presented in [5]. The acetowhite region, a major indicator of abnormality in the cervix image, is first segmented by using a non-convex optimization approach. Within the acetowhite region, other abnormal features such as the mosaic patterns are then automatically classified from non-mosaic regions by texture analysis.

A cost-sensitive 2v-SVM classification scheme to cervical cancer images to separate diseased regions from healthy tissue is proposed in [6]. Multiplier classifier scheme is used instead of the traditional single classifier to test the NCI/NLM archive of 60000 images. The phase correlation method followed by a locally applied algorithm based on the normalized cross-correlation is presented for image registration in [7]. During the parameterization process, each time series obtained from the image sequences is represented as a parabola in a parameter space. A supervised Bayesian learning approach is proposed to classify the features in the parameter space according to the classification made by the colposcopist.

Cervical Intraepithelial Neoplasia (CIN) is detectable and treatable precursor pathology of cancer of the uterine cervix. A non-parametric technique, based on the transformation and analysis of the distortion-rate curve is proposed in [8] to assess the model order. This technique provides good starting points to infer the GMM parameters via the expectation- maximization (EM) algorithm, reducing the segmentation time and the chances of getting trapped in local optima.

2   ROI Segmentation of Cervical Images

The segmentation of cervix from the colposcopy cervix image is shown in Figure 1. An ROI segmentation image processing system substantially masks non-ROI image data from a digital image to produce a ROI segmented image for subsequent digital processing. A colposcopy cervical image contains major cervix lesions, regions outside the cervix and parts of the imaging device.   In this method, only the major cervix lesion is segmented for further processing.   The major cervix lesion is a reddish, nearly circular section approximately centered in the image. This feature is used to identify the ROI region.

For ROI segmentation, first the given cervix image in RGB colour space is converted into Lab colour space due to the fact that Lab colour space is a good choice for representing the colour. The Euclidean distance of a pixel from the image center is extracted for all pixels and it is represented as Euclidean distance array d.

The Gaussian Mixture Model (GMM) parameters μ and σ are calculated by (1) for the Euclidean distance array and the colour channel a from the Lab colour space.

$$a(x, y) = \frac{a - \mu_a}{\sigma_a} \quad and \quad d(x, y) = \frac{d - \mu_d}{\sigma_d} . \tag{1}$$

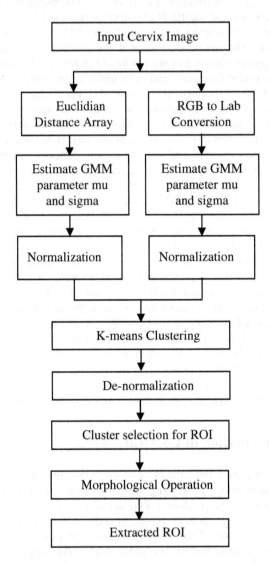

Fig. 1. Block diagram of ROI Segmentation of cervical images

By using the GMM parameters, Euclidean distance array and the colour channel a from the Lab colour space are normalized and aggregated into a single array which is given to K-means clustering algorithm as an input. Here the value K is set to 2.

Among the 2 cluster, the cluster which has the smallest d and largest a is chosen as ROI after the cluster centroids are de-normalized. Finally, morphological opening is used to remove the small regions and fill the holes to get the required ROI image that contains only the cervix lesion.

3   Specular Reflection of Cervical Images

Specular reflections (SR) appear as bright spots heavily saturated with white light. These occur due to the presence of moisture on the uneven cervix surface, which acts like mirrors reflecting the light from the illumination source. The block diagram for removal of specular reflection in the segmented cervix image is shown in Figure 2.

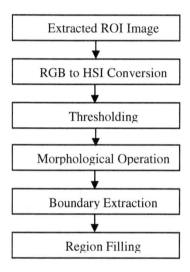

Fig. 2. Block diagram for removing Specular Reflection on ROI cervix images

The segmented cervix image in RGB colour space is converted into *HSI* colour space due to the fact that *HSI* colour space represents the colour similarity how the human eye senses colours. The *HSI* color model represents every color with three components, hue (H), saturation (S) and intensity (I). Specularities always have very intense brightness and low saturation values. Hence, the I and S component in the *HSI* colour space is used to find the SR region and the conversion formulae are given in (2) and (3) respectively.

$$I = \frac{R + G + B}{3},\tag{2}$$

$$S = 1 - \frac{\min(R, G, B)}{3},\tag{3}$$

The initial SR regions are identified by applying thresholding technique on image pixels. The threshold values are defined in (4)

$$I > 0.8 * I_{max}[] \quad S > 0.6 * S_{max}[]. \tag{4}$$

After thresholding, morphological dilation is performed on the thresholded image by using square structuring element of width 5 to get SR regions. Boundaries are extracted from the SR regions by using 8-connected neighborhood. Finally, the SR regions are smoothly interpolates inward from the pixel values on the boundaries by solving Laplace's equation.

4   Lesion Detection

The Lesion detection mainly consists of two stages namely feature extraction stage and classification stage. In the feature extraction stage, the statistical features are extracted from the normal and abnormal region and these features are given to the Bayes classifier for detecting the lesion.

4.1   Feature Extraction Stage

The statistical features, mean (μ), standard deviation (σ) and skewness are extracted from each channel of RGB cervix images for every 32x32 overlapping tile. The features of each channel is fused together to form the feature vector. The feature extraction stage is shown in Figure 3.

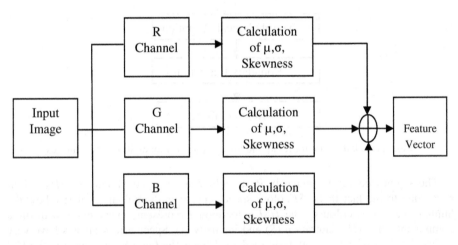

Fig. 3. Feature Extraction Stage

4.2   Classification Stage

For training the classifier, 20 normal and 20 abnormal cervix images marked by the experts are taken. The normal and abnormal region in cervix images is divided into 32x32 overlapping tiles. The statistical features are extracted from the tiles and stored in the database which will be used for training the classifier. Then the Naïve Bayes classifier is created by fitting the training data in the database. The classification stage is shown in Figure 4.

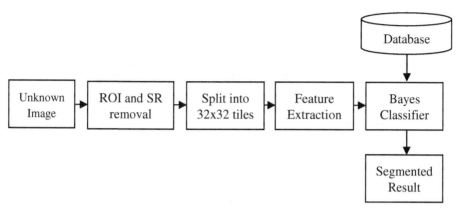

Fig. 4. Classification Stage

5   Experimental Results

The performance of the proposed method is tested on 200 normal colposcopy cervix images and 40 abnormal colposcopy cervix image obtained from Government Kasturibaigandhi Hospital (KGH), Chennai, India. Experimental result of 3 cervix images by the proposed system is shown in Figure 5. The First row image in the

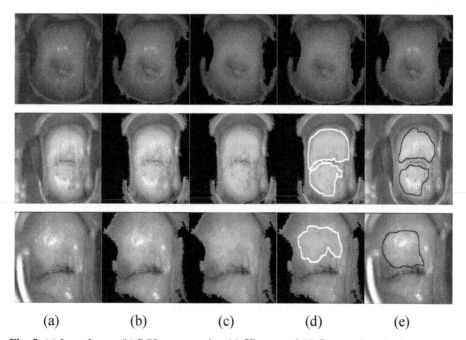

(a)   (b)   (c)   (d)   (e)

Fig. 5. (a) Input Image (b) ROI segmentation (c) SR removal (d) Proposed method (e) Marked by expert

figure is normal cervix image. The proposed method correctly classified the normal cervix image as normal and there is no mark by the proposed method and the expert also. The proposed method correctly detects the lesion in the posterior and anterior lib of the second row image and also marked by the experts. The lesions are detected for third row images and also similar to the experts' results.

6   Conclusion

In this paper, a fully automatic method for removal of irrelevant information such as regions outside the cervix, speculum in colposcopy cervix images based on mathematical morphology and clustering based on Gaussian Mixture Modeling and also the lesion is detected based on statistical features is presented. The purpose of the recommended process is mainly to prepare the colposcopy cervix images for further analysis. The proposed algorithm is tested on a large set of images totally 240 images and good results are achieved.

In most of the cases, the proposed method detects the lesions very well. However, some of the region outside the lesion edges is also detected as lesion. This is due to that the lesion edges and the region outside lesion edges are classified as abnormal by the classifier based on the features. Still, the work is going on to get the better result.

References

1. Claude, I., Pouletaut, P.: Integrated color and texture tools for colposcopic image segmentation. In: IEEE International Conference on Image Processing, pp. 311–314 (2001)
2. Gordon, S., Greenspan, H.: Segmentation of Non-Convex Regions within Uterine Cervix Images. In: IEEE International Symposium on Biomedical Imaging, pp. 312–315 (2007)
3. Greenspan, H., Gordon, S.: Automatic Detection of Anatomical Landmarks in Uterine Cervix Images. IEEE Transaction on Medical Imaging, 454–468 (2009)
4. Claude, I.W.: Contour features for colposcopic image classification by artificial neural networks. In: IEEE International Conference on Pattern Recognition, pp. 771–774 (2002)
5. Tulpule, B., Yang, S.: Segmentation and Classification of Cervix Lesions by Pattern and Texture Analysis. In: IEEE International Conference on Fuzzy System, pp. 173–176 (2005)
6. Artan, Y., Huang, X.: Combining Multiple 2ν-Svm Classifiers For Tissue Segmentation. In: IEEE International Symposium on Biomedical Imaging, pp. 488–491 (2003)
7. Acosta-Mesa, H.G., Barbara, Z.: Cervical Cancer Detection Using Colposcopic Images: a Temporal Approach. In: IEEE International Conference on Computer Science, pp. 158–164 (2005)
8. Srinivasan, Y., Corona, E.: A Unified Model-Based Image Analysis Framework for Automated Detection of Precancerous Lesions in Digitized Uterine Cervix Images. IEEE Journal of Selected Topics In Signal Processing, 101–111 (2009)

An Efficient Algorithm for Automatic Malaria Detection in Microscopic Blood Images

J. Somasekar[1], A. Rama Mohan Reddy[2], and L. Sreenivasulu Reddy[3]

[1] Department of CSE, Gopalan College of Engineering and Management, Bangalore,
Karnakata, India-560 048
[2] Department of CSE, S.V.U. College of Engineering, S.V. University, Tirupati,
Andhra Pradesh, India-517 502
{somasekar_nitk,ramamohansvu}@yahoo.com
[3] Department of CSE, MITS, Madanapalle, Chittoor, Andhra Pradesh, India- 517 325
sreenivasulu.lingam@gmail.com

Abstract. An interactive automatic method for detection of malaria from microscope blood images is presented. The user is required to select image from data set and the algorithm detects whether the blood is infected with malaria or not automatically. This method will help in reducing the time taken for diagnosis and the chance for human errors. A general framework to perform detection of malaria parasite, which includes an image pre-processing, extracting infected blood cells, morphological operation and highlighting the infected cells, is described. We have evaluated our algorithm using a dataset of 76 microscopic blood images from different patients (both infected and uninfected).Experimental results show that the proposed algorithm achieves 94.87% sensitivity and 97.3% specificity for the malaria parasite detection. This methodology may serve as a rapid diagnostic tool for malaria, even in microscopically negative cases. We also present future work.

Keywords: Image processing, Malaria parasites, Microscopic diagnosis, Erythrocytes, Morphological Operations.

1 Introduction

Malaria is one of the most common infectious diseases and a great public health problem worldwide, particularly in Africa and south Asia. According to the World Health Organization, it caused more than 1 million deaths arising from approximately 300 to 500 million infections every year [1], mostly in children under five years of age. Several international organizations have set up ambitious objectives for large-scale malaria control. The target set by the World Health Organization (WHO) in 2005 is to offer malaria prevention and treatment services by 2010 to at least 80% of the people who need them [2]. By doing so, it aims to reduce at least by half the proportion of people who become ill or die from malaria by 2010 and at least by three quarters by 2015 compared to 2005.

P.V. Krishna, M.R. Babu, and E. Ariwa (Eds.): ObCom 2011, Part II, CCIS 270, pp. 431–440, 2012.
© Springer-Verlag Berlin Heidelberg 2012

The definitive diagnosis of malaria infection is done by searching for parasite in blood slides through a microscope. Although there are newer techniques [3], manual microscopy examination of blood smears [4] (invented in the late 19th century), is currently "the gold standard" for malaria diagnosis. Diagnosis using a microscope requires special training and considerable expertise [5]. It was shown in several studies that manual microscopy is not a reliable screening method when performed by non experts due to lack of training especially in the rural areas where malaria is endemic [6]. The sample malaria microscopic blood image as shown in figure 1.

Detection is the most important task whereas the species identification is necessary for an appropriate treatment. There are so many numbers of vision studies address the automated diagnosis of malaria [7]-[12]. However, none of these works provide a complete solution (100%) to detect malaria parasite in microscopic blood images. This paper is the most comprehensive work up-to-date from a computer vision perspective addressing the entire required essential task for the diagnosis. Two main contributions of this study must be highlighted. First we propose a malaria parasite detection method and finally, we compare our proposed method with previous five methods for malaria detection and then conclude that the detection can be performed successfully with more accuracy.

1.1   Motivations and Objectives

Malaria laboratory diagnosis becomes a hard task particularly in its final stages where microscopic specialists   make efforts to specify disease stage parasite morphology. In addition, laboratory diagnosis is time consuming. As we know, computer is a useful tool in many applications particularly in clinical and technical medical activities. So it is reasonable to use computer advantages such as speed and accuracy to make malaria diagnosis.

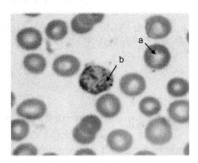

Fig. 1. The microscopic image [13] of (a) normal, and (b) malaria infected cells

The main objectives of our system includes extremely fast detection of the parasite within seconds, highly accurate in true detection, simple to execute and operate and serves as a reliable second opinion to pathologists and microbiologists.

1.2   Literature Review

In the literature, detection of malaria methods are available such as: T.Jelinek[14], Boray Tek[15] Vishnu.V [16], and Gatti.S [17] using image processing techniques. Apart from these various detection algorithms are available by using various classification techniques and are described as follows.

D. Ruberto et. al. [18] follow morphological method for detection of parasites in Giemsa stained blood slides. Different objects in blood are identified using their dimensions and color. The parasites are detected by means of an automatic thresholding based on morphological approach, using Granulometrices to evaluate size of RBCs and nuclei of parasite. A segmentation method using morphological operators combined with the watershed algorithm.

Silvia Halim et. al. [19], proposed a technique for estimating parasitemia. An approach of template matching is used for detection of RBCs. Parasites are detected using variance based technique from grayscale images and second approach is based on color co-occurrence matrix which is based on the individual color index of pixel and color indices of its eight neighboring pixel.

Tomasz Markiewicz et. al. [20], presents the feature characterization and assessment of the blasts that leads to the best performance of the recognizing and classifying system. The cells are classified by using the geometrical, textural and statistical features. The features categorized by using linear SVM network using SVM classifier.

Nicola Ritter et. al. [21] used stained blood images to present unsupervised blood cell segmentation. Algorithm finds all objects cells, cell groups and cell fragments that do not intersect the image border, and identifies the points interior to each object, finds an accurate one pixel wide border for each object, separates objects that just touch. Statistical analysis based by borders that have clusters of pixels is used to refine the borders by pruning stubs and thinning the border to one pixel width.

Gloria Diaz et. al. [22], presents a method for quantification and classification of erythrocytes in stained thin blood films infected with Plasmodium falciparum. These approaches still do remained some drawbacks which are need to be improved. For example, S.Gatti et. al. [17] approach having highest sensitivity 94.4% so far. Our proposed method yields sensitivity of 94.87%.

The organization of the rest of this paper is as follows. Section 2 introduces the proposed method; section 3 described the experiments and then presents the evaluation results. Section 4 provides the conclusion and future works.

2   Methodology

The basic aim our system is to read microscopic blood image from dataset and detect whether the blood is infected with malaria or not. The digitized images of erythrocytes are obtained from various sources [23][24] and stored in the computer for further processing. The sequence of procedures for detecting the malaria in blood images is given in Figure 2.

In microscopic image processing, it is usually necessary to perform high degree of noise reduction in an image before performing higher-level processing steps, such as extracting parasite components. The median filter is a non-linear digital filtering technique, often used to remove noise from images. The median filter is given by

$$g(x,y)=median \ (f(s,t))$$

$$(s,t)\varepsilon S_{xy}$$

Where $g(x,y)$ is the restored image at point (x,y) of the original image $f(x,y)$ and S_{xy} represents the set of coordinates in a rectangular sub image window [24].

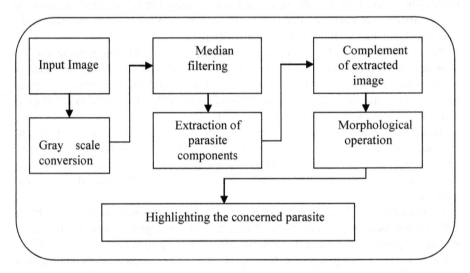

Fig. 2. General workflow of the proposed malaria detection method

Applying the median filter for smoothing and noise removal led to better results than using the averaging or Gaussian low pass filters. Median filtering is known to be better able to remove the outliers without reducing the sharpen of the image.

The basic aim of next step is to extract the cells which are infected with malaria. The extracted components of a parasite and its histogram are shown in figure 3. The proposed algorithm for extracting parasite components can be summarized in algorithm 1.

Each resulting image of extracted parasite components was then processed with morphological operator so that the holes inside the blood cells can be removed. The basic idea in binary morphology is to probe an image with a simple, pre-defined shape, drawing conclusions on how this shape fits or misses the shapes in the image [25]. This simple "probe" is called structuring element and is itself a binary image. Let E be a Euclidean space or an integer grid, and A a binary image in E. The erosion of the binary image A by the structuring element B is defined by:

$$A \ominus B = \{z \ \varepsilon \ E / B_z \subseteq A\}$$

Here B_z is the translation of B by the vector Z. .i.e., $B_z = \{b+Z/b \ \varepsilon \ B\}$ for all $Z \ \varepsilon \ E$

Algorithm 1: Extraction of Parasite components algorithm

***STEP1*:** [Initialization]
    Count= sum= sum1= add= add1= P=0, W=0.5
    Set T= Arithmetic mean of maximum and minimum intensity value of
the image
    ***STEP2*:** If the intensity of the pixel value is greater than 190 then
replace it with 180.
    ***STEP3*:**
Repeat
Count=Count+1
FOR each x FROM 1 to m
FOR each Y FROM 1 to n
IF (Im(x,y)>=T)
THE N
SET sum=sum+Im(x,y) and sum1=sum1+1
ELSE
SET add=add+Im(x,y) and add1=add1+1
END FOR
Total=sum/sum1
Total1=add/add1
P= (Total+Total1)/2
D=absolute value of (T-P)
UNTIL (D>=W);
    ***STEP4*:**
If the intensity value of the pixel is more than or equal to P value then
replace it by 1.

The concerned parasite can be highlighted by using the resultant image after morphological operation applied. The various results of applying the proposed method and its evaluation, comparison with other previous methods are presented in the next section.

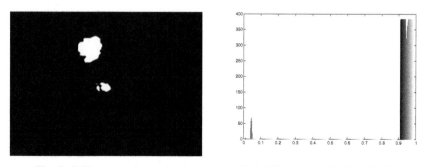

Fig. 3. (left) extracted parasite components,(right) histogram of infected cells

3   Results and Discussions

To evaluate the performance of the proposed algorithm, we made some experiments using MATLAB version 7.10.0.499(R2010a). The tested images were selected from the malaria image library [23].

The proposed method is applied to several microscopic blood images as indicated in the figures given below. Part (a) and part(b)of figures 4 to 5 shows a raw images and the gray level images after applied 5X5 median filter respectively and the final detection result is given in part(c). We can notice that the result of these tests is positive where the algorithm detects the infected cells.

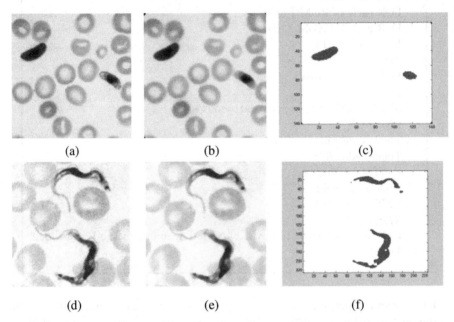

(a)   (b)   (c)

(d)   (e)   (f)

Fig. 4. Positive malaria test. (a,d) original blood microscopic images, (b,e) gray scale images after applied median 5X5 filter, (c,f) final detection results

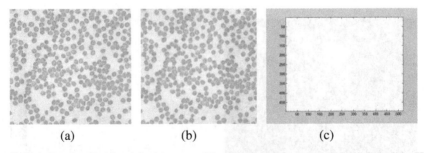

(a)   (b)   (c)

Fig. 5. Uninfected cell. (a) original images, (b) gray scale images after applied median 5X5 filter, (c) final result

In order to evaluate the performance of our method we apply it to some uninfected images. Figure 5 show the result of testing uninfected blood cells. In this figure, the result is satisfactory where the system indicated that the cell is not infected, i.e. negative test.

Table 1. Results of applying our method to the whole data set we have

Blood Images	No. of test images	Detection Results	
		Malaria	Non-Malaria
Malaria	39	37	2
non-malaria	37	1	36
	Sensitivity=94.87%, Specificity=97.3%		

However, in some cases, the proposed method indicated that the result is negative while the cell is infected with malaria as indicated in figure 6.

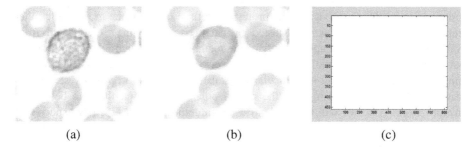

(a)   (b)   (c)

Fig. 6. Infected cell. (a) Original image, (b) gray scale image, (c) final result

In fact, these erroneous results can be caused due to white blood cells, other impurities which carry the same colour as malaria parasite. There are two measures [26] used to judge the quality of the method in the case of malaria detection which are sensitivity and specificity. Sensitivity is the   percentage of malaria detection among all malaria cases and the specificity is defined as percentage of detecting non-malaria among all non-malaria cases.

On applying the proposed algorithm to the malaria images data set, the resulting accuracy is enhanced with 94.87% sensitivity and 97.3% specificity. Table 1 shows the results of applying the proposed method to the whole data set we have (76 blood images). Among those 73(39 infected and 37 uninfected) images are detected correctly by the proposed system, true positive and only 3 images were missed (false negative). In addition, a comparative study has been made with five well known previous methods. Table 2 shows a quantitative comparison between the proposed method and five of other methods found in the literature survey.

Table 2. Quantitative comparison between our method and some of other methods

Method	Sensitivity (%)	Specificity (%)	Data Used
T.Jelinek[14]	92.5	98.3	Not-mentioned
Boray Tek[15]	74	98	9 images
Vishnu.V [16]	83	98	55 images
Gatti.S [17]	94.4	94.5	Not-mentioned
Halim[19]	92	95	Not-mentioned
Our Method	**94.87**	**97.3**	**76 images**

4 Conclusions and Future Work

An efficient method for detection of malaria parasite from microscopic blood images has been introduced in this paper. This automated computer based system is interactive, hence is faster and accurate than manual process. The results are promising and the sensitivity of the proposed method outperforms most of the other reported methods. The work is tested primarily based on images collected from various sources [23]. The applicability of the method can be noted in telepathology in areas lacking trained pathologists. Further work still needs to be done in order to improve the accuracy (and in particular the sensitivity) of the proposed system. This can be achieved by investigating the use of other features and that can be one of feature work. Also we will try to identify the infecting species [23] (five species of malaria namely P.falciparum, P.knowlesi, P.malariae,P.ovale and P.vivax) and degree of parasitemia in future.

Acknowledgement. The authors would like to acknowledge the support from Ching-Hao La, National Chung Hsing University, Taiwan.

References

[1] Korenromp, E., Miller, J., Nahlen, B., Wardlaw, T., Young, M.: World Malaria report, Technical Report, World Health organization, geneva (2005)
[2] World Malaria Report, World Health organization (2008); ISBN: 978-92- 4-1563697, http://whqlibdoc.who.int/publications/2008/9789241563697_eng.pdf
[3] Hanscheid, T.: Current strategies to avoid misdiagnosis of malaria. Clin. Microbiol. Infect. 9, 497–504 (2003)
[4] WHO, Basic Malaria Microscopy. Part I. Learner's Guide, World Health Organization (1991)

[5] Kettelhut, M.M., Chiodini, P.L., Edwards, H., Moody, A.: External quality assessment schemes raise standards: evidence from the UKNEQAS parasitology subschemes. J. Clin. Pathol. 56, 927–932 (2003)

[6] Bates, I., Bekoe, V., Asamoa-Adu, A.: Improving the accuracy of malaria-related laboratory tests in Ghana. Malar. J. 3, 38 (2004)

[7] Tek, F.B., Dempster, A.G., Kale, I.: Malaria parasite detection in peripheral blood images. In: Proc. Med. Imaging Understand. Anal. Conf., Manchester, UK (2006)

[8] Tek, F.B., Dempster, A.G., Kale, I.: Malaria parasite detection in peripheral blood images. In: Proc. Br. Mach. Vis. Conf., Edinburgh, UK (2006)

[9] Halim, S., Bretschneider, T., Li, Y., Preiser, P., Kuss, C.: Estimating malaria parasitaemia from blood smear images. In: Proc. IEEE Int. Conf. Control Autom. Robot Vis., Singapore (2006)

[10] Sio, S.W.S., Sun, W., Kumar, S., Bin, W.Z., Tan, S.S., Ong, S.H., Kikuchi, H., Oshima, Y., Tan, K.S.W.: Malariacount: an image analysis-based program for the accurate determination of parasitemia. J. Microbiol. Methods 68, 11–18 (2007)

[11] Ross, N.E., Pritchard, C.J., Rubin, D.M., Duse, A.G.: Automated image processing method for the diagnosis and classification of malaria on thin blood smears. Med. Biol. Eng. Comput. 44, 427–436 (2006)

[12] Tek, F.B., Dempster, A.G., Kale, I.: Computer vision for microscopy diagnosis of malaria. Malar. J. 8, 153 (2009)

[13] Edison, M., Jeeva, J.B., Singh, M.: Digital analysis of changes by plasmodium vivax malaria in erythrocytes. Indian Journal of Experimental Biology 49, 11–15 (2011)

[14] Jeinek, T., Grobusch, M.P., Schwenke, S., Steidl, S., Von Sonnenburg, F., Nothdurft, H.D., Klein, E., Loscher, T.: Sensitivity and specificity of dipstick test for rapid diagnosis of malaria in nonimmune travellers. Journal of Clinical Microbiology 37(3), 721–723 (1999)

[15] Boray Tek, F., Dempster, A.G., Kale, I.: Malaria Parasite Detection in Peripheral Blood Images. In: Proceedings of the British Machine Vision Conference (BMVC 2006), UK, pp. 347–356 (2006)

[16] Makkapati, V.V., Rao, R.M.: Segmentation of malaria parasites in peripheral blood smear images. In: International Conference on Acoustics, Speech and Signal Processing (ICASSP), pp. 1361–1364 (April 2009)

[17] Gatti, S., Bemuzzi, A.M., Bisoffi, Z., Raglio, A., Gulletta, M., Scaglia, M.: Multicentre study, in patients with imported malaria, on the sensitivity and specificity of a dipstick test (ICT Malaria P.f./P.v.) compared with expert microscopy. Ann. Trop. Med. Parasitol. 96(1), 15–18 (2002)

[18] Di Ruberto, C., Dempster, A., Khan, S., Jarra, B.: Automatic thresholding of infected blood images using granulometry and regional extrema, pp. 441–444. IEEE (2000)

[19] Halim, S., Bretschneider, T.R., Li, Y., Preiser, P.R., Kuss, C.: Estimating malaria parasitaemia from blood smear images. In: Proceedings of the 9th International Conference on Control, Automation, Robotics and Vision, pp. 1–6 (December 2006)

[20] Markiewicz, T., Osowski, S.: Automatic Recognition of the Blood Cells of Myelogenous Leukemia Using SVM. In: Proceedings of International Joint Conference on Neural Networks, Canada, pp. 2496–2501 (August 2005)

[21] Ritter, N., Cooper, J.: Segmentation and Border Identification of Cells in Images of Peripheral Blood Smear Slides. In: The Thirtieth Australasian Computer Science Conference (ACSC 2007), Conferences in Research and Practice in Information Technology (CRPIT), Australia, vol. 62 (2007)

[22] Diaz, G., Gonzalez, F.A., Romero, E.: A Semi automatic method for quantification and classification of erythrocytes infected with malaria parasites in microscopic images. Journal of Biomedical Informatics 42, 296–307 (2009)

[23] DPDx-Malaria Image Library, http://www.dpd.cdc.gov/dpdx/html/imagelibrary/malaria_il.htm

[24] Gonzalez, R.C., Woods, R.E.: Digital Image Processing, 2nd edn. Prentice Hall (2002)

[25] Zgang, Y.-B., Zhou, K.: Study on automotive style recognition with the image erosion technology. In: International Conference on Consumer Electronics, Communications and Networks, April 16-18, pp. 4438–4441 (2011)

[26] Mohamed, S.S., Youssef, A.M., Sadaany, E.F.E.L., Salama, M.M.A.: LLE based TRVS image features dimensionality reduction for prostate cancer diagnosis. In: The International Congress for Global Science and Technology (ICGST), GVIP Special Issue on Cancer Diagnosis (2007)

Isolated Tamil Digit Speech Recognition Using Template-Based and HMM-Based Approaches

S. Karpagavalli[1], R. Deepika[1], P. Kokila[1], K. Usha Rani[1], and E. Chandra[2]

[1] Department of Computer Science (PG), PSGR Krishnammal College for Women, Coimbatore
karpagam@grgsact.com,
{dpi.feb88,saikokila87,dhanalakshmi27}@gmail.com
[2] DJ Academy for Managerial Excellence, Coimbatore

Abstract. For more than three decades, a great amount of research was carried out on various aspects of speech signal processing and its applications. Highly successful application of speech processing is Automatic Speech Recognition (ASR). Early attempts to ASR consisted of making deterministic models of whole words in a small vocabulary and recognizing a given speech utterance as the word whose model comes closest to it. The introduction of Hidden Markov Models (HMMs) in the early 1980 provided much more powerful tool for speech recognition. And the recognition can be done for continuous speech using large vocabulary, in a speaker independent manner. Two approaches like conventional template-based and Hidden Markov Model usually performs speaker independent isolated word recognition. In this work, speaker independent isolated Tamil digit speech recognizers are designed by employing template based and HMM based approaches. The results of the approaches are compared and observed that HMM based model performs well and the word error rate is greatly reduced.

Keywords: Automatic Speech Recognition, Speaker Independent, Template-based approach, Hidden-markov model.

1 Introduction

Speech Recognition is also known as Automatic Speech Recognition (ASR), or computer speech recognition is the process of converting acoustic signal captured by microphone or telephone to a set of words.

Fundamentally, the problem of speech recognition can be stated as follows. When given with acoustic observation $O = o_1 o_2 ... o_t$, the goal is to find out the corresponding word sequence $W = w_1 w_2 ... w_n$ that has the maximum posterior probability $P(W|O)$ can be written as

P.V. Krishna, M.R. Babu, and E. Ariwa (Eds.): ObCom 2011, Part II, CCIS 270, pp. 441–450, 2012.

$$\hat{W} = \underset{w \in L}{\operatorname{argmax}} P(W|O) \tag{1}$$

Equation 1 can be expressed using Bayes rule as

$$\hat{W} = \underset{w \in L}{\operatorname{argmax}} \frac{P(O|W)\,P(W)}{P(O)} \tag{2}$$

Since the P (O) is the same for each candidate sentence W, thus equation 2 can be reduced as

$$\hat{W} = \underset{w \in L}{\operatorname{argmax}} P(O|W)\,P(W) \tag{3}$$

Where $P\ (W)$, the prior probability of word W uttered is called the language model and $P\ (O|W)$, the observation likelihood of acoustic observation O when word W is uttered is called the acoustic model [1].

The various components of the speech recognition system are Acoustic Front End, Acoustic Model, Pronunciation Dictionary, Language model and Decoder. The Schematic representation of the Speech Recognition Architecture is shown in figure 1.

2   Related Work

Speech recognizers for Spanish digit using template based and HMM based approaches are analyzed by Lucas D.Terrissi, Juan C. Gomez, University of Rosario, Argentina, [2005]. They have applied various template selection techniques and incorporated dynamic time warping for time aligning [2].

Arabic digit speech recognition System was developed by H Satori, M Harti, N Chenfour [2007]. This system is developed using the open source framework Sphinx-4, from the Carnegie Mellon University, a speech recognition system based on discrete hidden markov models (HMMs). In their work an in house Arabic speech corpus was developed and used for training and testing [3]. In the proposed work, a comparison between template-based and HMM-based approaches for isolated Tamil digit recognition is carried out. Template based approach with DTW time align algorithm implemented in Matlab environment. HMM based approach carried out using Sphinx Train and Sphinx-4 of Carniegie Mellon University. Both recognizers have been tested on a speech corpus generated from the Tamil speech utterances of digit from zero to nine spoken by 20 native speakers of Tamil Language.

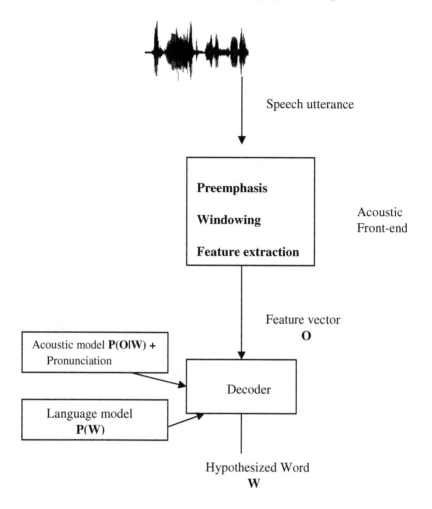

Fig. 1. Speech Recognition Architecture

3   Feature Extraction

The feature extraction is the first stage to extract feature vectors from the speech signals. Most speech recognition systems use the so–called Mel frequency Cepstral coefficients (MFCC) and its first and sometimes second derivative in time to better reflect dynamic changes. These are coefficients based on the Mel scale that represent sound. The word Cepstral comes from the word Cepstrum, which is a logarithmic scale of the spectrum (and reverses the first four letters in the word spectrum). It is shown in figure 2. First, the speech data are divided into 25 ms windows (frames).

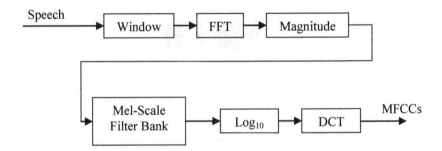

Fig. 2. Block Diagram of MFCC feature extraction method

A new frame is started every 10 ms making this the sampling period and causing the windows to overlap each other. Next, the fast Fourier transform is performed on each frame of speech data and the magnitude is found. The next step involves filtering the signal with a frequency-warped set of log filter banks called Mel-scale filter banks [4][5]. The log filter banks are arranged along the frequency axis according to the Mel scale, a logarithmic scale that is a measure of perceived pitch or frequency of a tone [6], thus simulating the human hearing scale. The Mel scale yields a compression of the upper frequencies where the human ear is less sensitive. Next, the logarithm is taken of the log filter bank amplitudes. Finally, the MFCCs are calculated using the discrete cosine transform (DCT). To further enhance speech recognition performance, an extra set of delta and acceleration coefficient features are sometimes calculated with MFCCs. These features are the first and second time derivatives of the original coefficients, respectively.

For template-based approach, 20 speakers uttering 3 times each digit is recorded with the sampling rate16 kHz using Audacity tool and MFCC feature vector of 39 dimensions (12-MFCC, 12-ΔMFCC, 12-$\Delta\Delta$MFCC, P, ΔP, $\Delta\Delta$P where P is stands for raw energy of the speech signal) are extracted using Matlab code. For HMM based approach, SphinxTrain tool used the 13 dimensional MFCC and Sphinx-4 used 39 dimensions of MFCC feature vector for processing.

4   Methodology

Basically there exist three approaches for speech recognition that include Acoustic Phonetic approach, Pattern Recognition approach and Artificial Intelligence approach. The pattern-matching approach has become the predominant method for speech recognition in the last six decades.

The pattern-matching approach involves two essential steps namely, pattern training and pattern comparison. The essential feature of this approach is that it uses a well-formulated mathematical framework and establishes consistent speech pattern representations, for reliable pattern comparison, from a set of labeled training samples via a formal training algorithm. A speech pattern representation can be in the form of a speech template or statistical models like HMM and can be applied to a sound like a phoneme, a word, or a phrase. In the pattern-comparison stage of the approach, a direct comparison is made between the speech to be recognized and each possible pattern learned in the training stage in order to determine the identity of the unknown according to the goodness of match of the patterns [4][12]. A schematic representation of pattern recognition approach for the proposed work is presented in Figure 3.

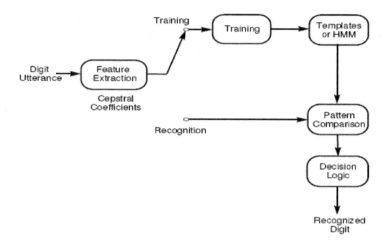

Fig. 3. Pattern Recognition Approach

5   Template-Based Approach

Template based approaches, in which unknown speech is compared against a set of prerecorded words (template) in order to find the best match. This has the advantage of using perfectly accurate word models; but also it has the disadvantages like suitable for small vocabulary and more computational time.

5.1   Time Alignment and Normalization

An utterance, which is to be recognized, however, is more complex than a steady sound, and thus a speech pattern almost always involves a sequence of short-time acoustic representations. The pattern-recognition approach for speech recognition compares the sequences of acoustic features. The problem associated with spectral sequence comparison for speech comes from the fact that different acoustic renditions, or tokens, of the same speech utterance are seldom realized at the same speed (speaking rate) across the entire utterance. Speaking rate variation as well as duration variation should not contribute to the linguistic dissimilarity score when comparing different tokens of the same utterance. Thus there is a need to normalize out speaking rate fluctuation in order for the utterance comparison to be meaningful before a recognition decision can be made. That can be achieved using Dynamic Time Warping (DTW), a dynamic programming algorithm that performs a non-linear time alignment to normalize the speaking rate fluctuations [2] [4].

5.2   Template Selections and Matching

The choice of the template will affect the performance of the recognizer. In this work, an utterance with medium duration from all the utterances of a particular digit is considered as template for that digit. Similarly template for each digit is selected and stored in the repository. The test data will undergo time alignment and will be matched against templates of each digit in the system's repository. The best matching template is the one for which there is the lowest distance path aligning the test input pattern to the template. A simple global distance score for a path is simply the sum of local distances that go to make up the path [7] [8].

The results of template based approach for each Tamil digit is summarized in Table 1. Isolated Tamil digit recognition accuracy is different for each word. The digit 0 (Pujjiyum) and digit 6 (ARu) has been correctly recognized for all the test data. The digit 7 (Aezhu) has the lowest accuracy, may be due to the pronunciation variation. The word 'Aezhu' has the special phone 'Zhu' which is not usually pronounced correctly by the native speakers of Tamil. The average accuracy rate is 87.8% while considering the results for all digits of Tamil.

Table 1. Results of template based approach for each Tamil digit

Tamil word	Pujjiyam உஜ்ஜியும்	Onru ஒன்று	Irandu இரண்டு	mUnRu மூன்று	Naanku நான்கு	aiNthu ஐந்து	Aru ஆறு	Aezhu ஏழு	ettu எட்டு	Onpathu ஒன்பது
Accuracy	100%	86%	94%	82%	91%	80%	100%	70%	80%	95%

6   Hidden Markov Model

HMM is very rich in mathematical structure and hence can form the theoretical basis for use in a wide range of application. The introduction of Hidden Morkov Models (HMMs) in the early 1980 provided much more powerful tool for speech recognition. The elements of HMM is characterized by following:

1. Number of state N
2. Number of distinct observation symbol per state
3. State transition probability,
4. Observation symbol probability distribution in state
5. The initial state distribution

The Three Basic Problems for HMMs are,

Problem 1: Evaluation Problem -Given the observation sequence $O = O_1\, O_2 \cdots O_T$, and model $\lambda = (A,B,\pi)$, how do we efficiently compute $P(O|\lambda)$, the probability of observation sequence given the model.

Problem 2: Hidden State Determination (Decoding) -Given the observation sequence $O = O_1 O_2 \cdots O_T$, and model $\lambda = (A,B,\pi)$ how do we choose corresponding state sequence $Q = q_1 q_2 \cdots q_T$ which is optimal in some meaningful sense.

Problem 3: Learning -How do we adjust the model parameter $\lambda = (A,B,\pi)$, to maximize $P(O| \lambda)$. Problem 3 is one in which we try to optimize model parameter so as to best describe as to how given observation sequence comes out.

Solution to three problems of HMM are Forward Algorithm for Evaluation Problem, Viterbi Algorithm for Decoding Hidden State Sequence $P(Q,O| \lambda)$ and Baum-Welch Algorithm for Learning [1] [9][10].

For HMM based approach training is carried out in SphinxTrain and model is implemented in Sphinx-4. Sphinx-4 is a flexible, modular and pluggable framework to help foster new innovations in the core research of hidden Markov model speech recognition systems. Automatic speech recognition involves many tasks that include speech corpus preparation, building pronunciation dictionary, acoustic model and language model.

6.1   Development of Speech Corpus

Tamil digit speech corpus was created in a noise free lab environment, as standard speech corpora are not available for Tamil language. For training 20 speakers uttering 20 times each digit is recorded with the sampling rate 16 kHz using Audacity tool. For testing 10 speakers uttering 4 times each digit is recorded. And the necessary transcription files are prepared.

6.2   Building Language Model and Dictionary

Language models mainly describe the linguistic restrictions present in the language and to allow reduction of possible invalid phoneme sequences. Language model estimate the probability of sequences of words. Common language models are bi-gram and trigram models. These models contain computed probabilities of groupings of two or three particular words in a sequence, respectively. In this work, Statistical tri-gram language models were built using the CMU Statistical Language Modeling toolkit for word-based model.

6.3   Building the Acoustic Model

The HMM based acoustic model trainer from CMU, *SphinxTrain*, has been employed. Sphinx Train supports Mel frequency Ceptral Co-efficient (MFCC) features. The features are extracted from the training wav files recorded with sampling rate 16 kHz of 16 bits depth [11]. Pronunciation dictionary, filler dictionary, transcription files, MFCC feature files are used for training. Number of states in the HMM is 15 and context independent training was carried out. The training procedure comprises the following processes.

Flat-start monophone training: Generation of monophone or CI seed models with nominal values, and re-estimation of these models using reference transcriptions. This is also called flat initialization of CI model parameters.

Baum-Welch training of monophones: Adjustment of the silence model and reestimation of single-Gaussian monophones using the standard Viterbi alignment process.

After these processes, context independent word model was generated. *SphinxTrain* generates the parameter files of the HMM namely, the probability distributions and transition matrices of all the HMM models. The word model is implemented on Sphinx-4, which is a state-of-art HMM based speech recognition system.

7   Results and Discussion

The hypothesis word sequences from the decoder are aligned with reference sentences. The performance of the speech recognizers are measured in terms of Word Error Rate (WER) and Word Recognition Rate (WRR). Word errors are categorized into number of insertions, substitutions and deletions. Finally, the word error rate and word recognition rate are computed by the following equations (4) (5),

$$\text{Word Error Rate (\%)} = (100)\frac{\text{Insertion (I)} + \text{Substitution(S)} + \text{Deletion(D)}}{\text{No of Reference Words (N)}} \qquad (4)$$

$$\text{WRR} = 1 - \text{WER} = \frac{N\text{-}S\text{-}D\text{-}I}{N} \qquad (5)$$

Other performance measures are speed and memory footprints. The results of HMM based approach are given in Table 2.

Table 2. Results of HMM based Approach for Tamil digits

Words	400
Errors	32 (Sub: 11 Ins: 16 Del: 5)
Accuracy	92%
Time	Audio: 564.06s Processing 61.55s
Speed	0.11 X real time
Memory	Average: 25.27MB Max: 35.38MB

Comparison of the performance of Template based approach and HMM based approach is presented in Table 3. It is clearly observed that statistical model (HMM) outperforms the conventional template based approach for Tamil digit speech recognizer.

Table 3. Comparison of the performance of Template based approach and HMM based approach

Model	Word Recognition Rate
Template	87.8%
HMM	92%

8   Conclusion

The goal of automatic speech recognition research is to address the various issues relating to speech recognition. Various methodologies are identified and applied to ASR area which led to many successful ASR applications in limited domains. But in Tamil language, speech recognition applications are very less. In our work, we tried to design small vocabulary, isolated, speaker independent Tamil digit recognizers using template based approach and HMM based approaches. It is being observed that, in HMM based approach Tamil digit recognition rate is high with less computational time and memory.

References

1. Jurafsky, D., Martin, J.H.: Speech and Language Processing - An Introduction to Natural Language Processing, Computational Linguistics, and Speech Recognition. Pearson Education (2002)
2. Terissi, L.D., Gomez, J.C.: Template-based and HMM-based Approaches for Isolated Spanish Digit Recognition. Intelligencia Artificial.Revista Iberoamericana de Intelligencia Artificial 9(26) (2005)
3. Satori, H., Harti, M., Chenfour, N.: Arabic Speech Recognition System based on CMUSphinx. In: International Symposium on Computational Intelligence and Intelligent Informatics (March 2007)
4. Rabiner, L., Juang, B.-H.: Fundamentals of Speech Recognition. Prentice-Hall, Inc., Engelwood (1993)
5. Kamm, T., Hermansky, H., Andreou, A.G.: Learning the Mel-scale and Optimal VTN Mapping. In: Center for Language and Speech Processing, Workshop (WS 1997). Johns Hopkins University (1997)
6. Hornback, J.R., Lieutenant, S.: Speech Recognition Using The Mellin Transform, MS Thesis report, Air Force Instituite of Technology, Wright-Patterson Air Force Base, Ohio (2006)
7. Li, D., Strik, H.: Structure-Based and Template-Based Automatic Speech Recognition-Comparing parametric and non-parametric approaches. Microsoft Research, One Microsoft Way, Redmond, WA, USA, CLST, Department of Linguistics, Radboud University, Nijmegen
8. Hachkar, Z., Farchi, A., Mounir, B., El Abbadi, J.: A Comparison of DHMM and DTW for Isolated Digit Recognition System for Arabic Language. International Journal of Computer Science and Engineering 3(3) (March 2011); ISSN : 0975-3397

9. Jacob, B., Sondhi, M.M., Huang, Y.: Springer Handbook of Speech Processing, XXXVI (2008)
10. Rabiner, L.R.: A Tutorial on Hidden Markov Models and Selected Applications in Speech Recognition. Proceedings of the IEEE 77(2), 257–286 (1989)
11. Thangarajan, R., Natarajan, A.M., Selvam, M.: Word and Triphone based approaches. Continuous Speech Recognition for Tamil Language 4(3) (March 2008)
12. Anusuya, M.A., Katti, S.K.: Speech Recognition by Machine: A Review. International Journal of Computer Science and Information Security 6(3), 181–205 (2009)

An Improved Algorithm for Medical Image Compression

M. Moorthi[1] and R. Amutha[2]

[1] Research Scholar, SCSVM University, Kanchipuram, India
Assistant Professor, Prathyusha Institute of Technology and Management and Technology,
Chennai, India
[2] Professor, SSN College of Engineering, Chennai, India
msskm10@gmail.com, ramutha@svce.ac.in

Abstract. The objective of image compression is to reduce of the image data in order to be able to store or transmit data in efficient form. One of the medical standards is the DICOM (Digital Imaging and Communications in Medicine) Standards Committee exists to create and maintain international standards for communication of biomedical diagnostic and therapeutic information in disciplines that use digital images and associated data. The important issues to be considered with the DICOM communication are memory requirement, bandwidth constraint and battery resource constraint.

In the proposed method, first Segmentation is applied to get two different clusters (ROI and Non ROI). Integer Wavelet Transform based compression is applied for Higher Energy clusters and JPEG is applied for another cluster. In the reconstruction part both the reconstructed clusters are fused by fusion technique. Since Lossless and lossy compression methods are used to get high compression ratio and high quality image. Efficient edge information is obtained by using Fusion.

Keywords: Image compression, Segmentation, Integer wavelet decomposition, encryption, decryption, decompression, Compression ratio.

1 Introduction

Multimedia supports the non-interactive or interactive use of image, video, audio and text data. The multiple modalities of these elements are disseminated in some way. And these information sources are delivered via more than one device. Multimedia can be also accessed over a network such as the Internet. Due to the advancement of the Internet, people are living in a connected world. Besides, with the availability of enormous digitized multimedia contents from Internet, the research of multimedia applications becomes more and more important.

The DICOM standards are used in cardiology, dentistry, endoscopy, mammography, ophthalmology, orthopedics, pathology, pediatrics, radiation therapy, radiology, surgery, etc. The main objective of DICOM standard is to improve workflow efficiency between imaging systems and other information systems in healthcare environments worldwide.

Image segmentation is an important process to extract information from complex medical images. First Segmentation is applied to get two different clusters (ROI and

P.V. Krishna, M.R. Babu, and E. Ariwa (Eds.): ObCom 2011, Part II, CCIS 270, pp. 451–460, 2012.
© Springer-Verlag Berlin Heidelberg 2012

Non ROI). The JPEG [1] standard is the most successful and popular image format. It is used for compressing Non ROI parts.

The JPEG2000 standard used for compressing ROI part and improves the compression ratio [2], [3], [4]. We then compress the ROI to a higher quality than the rest of the image by scaling the wavelet coefficients corresponding to the ROI .we repeat wavelet coefficient trees corresponding to the ROI and code them to higher bit rates than the background trees. Spatial regions in images that are most important to the end user are called regions of interest (ROIs). Targets can be identified and tracked using only small sections of surveillance images. An objective of this paper is to design a faster and reliable compression technique with high compression ratio and preserve edge information.

2   Existing Method

The existing methods are 1. JPEG Codec 2. JPEG 2000 Codec.

2.1   JPEG Codec

JPEG gives good compression results for lossy compression with the least complexity. The processing at encoding side can be explained as:

Step1: The source image is partitioned into non-overlapping 2-D blocks of 8x8,
Step2: The pixels in each block are level shifted by subtracting a value of 128
Step3: DCT is applied to generate an array of 2-D transformed coefficients.

The 8-point 2-D DCT to generate 8x8 data matrices is calculated as:

$$F(u,v) = \frac{1}{4} \cdot C(u)C(v) \left[\sum_{x=0}^{7} \sum_{y=0}^{7} f(x,y) \cos \frac{(2x+1) \cdot u\pi}{16} \cos \frac{(2y+1) \cdot v\pi}{16} \right] \qquad (1)$$

Where $C(x) = 1/\sqrt{2}$ if x is 0, and $C(x) = 1$ for all other cases. Also, $f(x, y)$ is the 8-bit image value at coordinates (x, y), and $F(u, v)$ is the new entry in the frequency matrix.   Where k,l = 0,1,...........,7

Step4: The coefficients are quantized using uniform scalar quantizer.
Step5: The 2-D DCT array of quantized coefficients is reordered using a zigzag pattern to form a 1-D sequence.
Step 6: The final step at the encoder is to use entropy coding such as Huffman coding on both AC and DC (DPCM coded before) coefficients to achieve extra compression and making them more immune to error.

The processing at decoding side can be explained as:

1. At the decoder side, after the encoded bit stream is entropy decoded,
2. The 2-D array of quantized DCT coefficients is recovered using de-zigzags, reordered and each coefficient is inverse quantized.
3. The resulting array of coefficients is transformed back using 2-D inverse DCT

The 8-point 2-D IDCT is calculated as:

$$f(x,y) = \frac{1}{4}\left[\sum_{x=0}^{7}\sum_{y=0}^{7}C(u)C(v)F(u,v)\cos\frac{(2x+1)\cdot u\pi}{16}\cos\frac{(2y+1)\cdot v\pi}{16}\right] \quad (2)$$

Where m, n = 0,1,...........,7. $c(u),c(v) = \begin{cases} 1/\sqrt{2}, k \& l = 0 \\ 1, otherwise \end{cases}$

4. Adding 128 to each pixel value to yield an approximation of the original 8x8 block or sub-image.
5. The reconstructed chrominance component is bilinear interpolated to the original size.

2.2   JPEG 2000 Codec

The JPEG2000 encoding and decoding procedure is as follows:

1. The image is decomposed into components.
2. The image and its components can be decomposed into rectangular tiles. The tile-component is the basic unit of the original or reconstructed image.
3. The wavelet transform is applied to each tile, decomposing it into different resolution levels. The 1-D DWT is given as the inner product of the signal x(t) being transformed with each of the discrete basis functions.

$$W_{m,n} = < x(t), \psi_{m,n}(t) > \quad ; \quad m, n \in Z \quad (3)$$

Where $\psi_{m,n}(t) = 2^{m/2} \psi(2^m t - n)$; m, n $\in Z^1$ such that $-\infty < m, n < \infty$, 'Z' refers to the set of integers.
4. These decomposition levels are made up of sub-bands of coefficients that describe the frequency characteristics of local areas of the tile-component.
5. Sub-bands of coefficients are quantized and partitioned into rectangular arrays of "code-blocks". Each of the transform coefficients $a_b(u,v)$ of the sub band b is quantized to the value $q_b(u,v)$ according to the formula
6. Bit-planes of the coefficients of a "code-block" are entropy coded.
7. Markers are added to the bit stream to allow error resilience. The code stream has a main header at the beginning.

8. Similarly, we obtained reconstructed signal $\hat{x}[n]$ from synthesis stage. To reconstruct the original signal, the low pass and high pass coefficients are up sampled by a factor of 2 and pass through another low pass and high pass filter banks. Each coefficient is inverse quantized and Inverse transform is applied. The 1-D inverse DWT is given as:

$$x(t) = \sum_{m}\sum_{n}W_{m,n}\psi_{m,n}(t) \quad ; \quad m, n \in Z \quad (4)$$

3   Proposed Method

The algorithm of proposed method is given below

Step1: Read the medical image

Step2: Apply segmentation algorithm to get Non ROI and ROI parts.

Step3: ROI is compressed using Integer Wavelet Transform based compression algorithm.

Step4: Non ROI is compressed using JPEG algorithm.

Step5: Fusing ROI and Non ROI parts.

Its flow diagram is given below

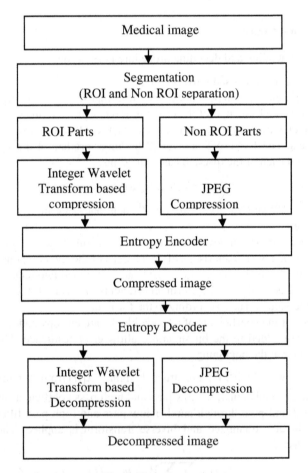

Fig. 1. Flow diagram

Image segmentation is typically used to locate objects and boundaries (lines, curves, etc.) in images.DCT based coders are still considered better due to their lower complexity, fast computation and good coding efficiency. Integer Wavelet Transform based compression supports excellent low bit rate performance without sacrificing the performance at high bit rate. Entropy encoding which is a way of lossless compression that is done an image after the quantization stage.

3.1   Segmentation

Segmentation refers to the process of partitioning a digital image into multiple regions (sets of pixels). The goal of segmentation is to simplify and/or change the representation of an image into something that is more meaningful and easier to analyze. We get ROI and Non ROI Parts of an image using manual segmentation

3.2   ROI Compression

A ROI part of an image is compressed by Integer wavelet transform based compression algorithm. The block diagrams of proposed method encoder and decoder is given in Figure 2.

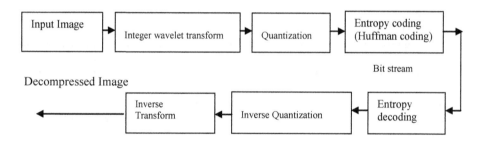

Fig. 2. Encoder and decoder of proposed method

3.2.1   Integer Wavelet Transform

The wavelet transform of image is implemented using the lifting scheme [5]. The lifting operation consists of three steps. First, the input signal x[n] is down sampled into the even position signal $x_e(n)$ and the odd position signal $x_o(n)$, then modifying these values using alternating prediction and updating steps.

$$x_e(n) = x[2n] \quad \text{and} \quad x_o(n) = x[2n+1] \tag{5}$$

The block diagram of forward lifting and inverse lifting is shown in figure.

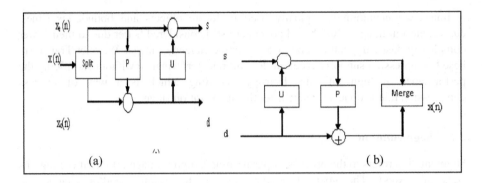

Fig. 3. The Lifting Scheme. (a) Forward Transform (b) Inverse Transform.

A prediction step consists of predicting each odd sample as a linear combination of the even samples and subtracting it from the odd sample to form the prediction error. An update step consists of updating the even samples by adding them to a linear combination of the prediction error to form the updated sequence.

The prediction and update may be evaluated in several steps until the forward transform is completed.

The inverse transform is similar to forward. It is based on the three operations undo update, undo prediction, and merge. This section illustrates the lifting approach using the Haar Transform [6]. The Haar transform is based on the calculations of the averages (approximation co-efficient) and differences (detail co-efficient). Given two adjacent pixels a and b, the principle is to calculate the average $s = \dfrac{(a+b)}{2}$ and the difference $d = a - b$. If a and b are similar, s will be similar to both and d will be small, i.e., require few bits to represent. This transform is reversible, since $a = s - \dfrac{d}{2}$ and $b = s + \dfrac{d}{2}$. Consider a row of 2^n pixels values $S_{n,l}$ for $0 \le l < 2^n$. There are 2^{n-1} pairs of pixels $S_{n,2l}, S_{n,2l+1}$ $for l = 0,2,4,.....,2^{n-2}$. Each pair is transformed into an average $S_{n-1,l} = (S_{n,2l} + S_{n,2l+1})/2$ and the difference $d_{n-1,l} = S_{n,2l+1} - S_{n,2l}$. The result is a set $S_{n-1} of 2^{n-1}$ averages and a set $d_{n-1} of 2^{n-1}$ differences.

3.2.2   Quantization

The coefficients are quantized and partitioned into rectangular arrays of "code-blocks". Each of the transform coefficients $a_b(u,v)$ of the sub band b is quantized to the value $q_b(u,v)$ according to the formula

$$q_b(u,v) = sign(a_b(u,v)) \left\lfloor \frac{|a_b(u,v)|}{\Delta_b} \right\rfloor \qquad (6)$$

Where Δ_b is the quantization step.

3.2.3   Entropy Encoding

It uses a model to accurately determine the probabilities for each quantized value and produces an appropriate code based on these probabilities so that the resultant output code stream will be smaller than the input stream. Various entropy encoding schemes are:

1. Huffman Coding
2. Arithmetic Coding
3. LZW Coding

Huffman coding gives a greater compression compared to other entropy encoding.
Huffman coding is done as follows:

1. The data is listed with their probabilities.
2. The two data with the smallest probabilities are located.
3. The two data are replaced by a single set containing both, whose probability is the sum of the individual probabilities.
4. These steps are repeated until the list is left with only one member

3.3   Non ROI Compression

A Non ROI part of an image is compressed by JPEG algorithm.

3.4   Fusion

Finally fusing ROI compressed parts on Non ROI compressed parts of an image. Thereby size of medical image is reduced and increased the quality of medical image

4   Quality Measures

In order to measure the quality of the image or video data at the output of the decoder, mean square error (MSE) and peak to signal to noise ratio (PSNR) ratio are often used. MSE is calculated as:

$$MSE = \sigma_q^2 = \frac{1}{N} \sum_{j,k} (f[j,k] - g[j,k])^2 \qquad (9)$$

Where the sum over j, k denotes the sum over all pixels in the image and N is the number of pixels in each image. The PSNR in terms of decibels (dBs) is given by:

$$PSNR = 10 \log_{10} \left(\frac{255^2}{MSE} \right) \tag{10}$$

The compression ratio calculated as

$$\textbf{Compression ratio} = \frac{\text{input data size}}{\text{Output data size}} \tag{11}$$

The term 'compression ratio' is used to characterize the compression capability of the system.

5   Results

The following shows the input, ROI, Compressed image, and Decompressed image using Integer Wavelet transform based compression and JPEG algorithms for different images.

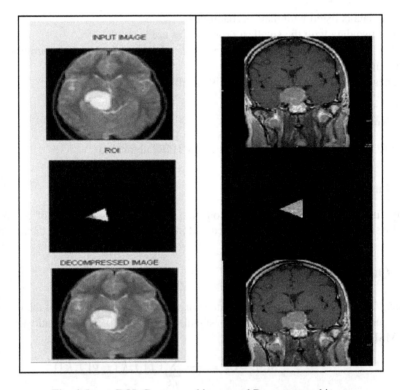

Fig. 4. Input, ROI, Compressed image and Decompressed image

6   Performance Evaluation

The performance of the proposed algorithm is done based upon the quality measures such as MSE, PSNR, CR, Encryption time and Decryption time results for medical image(CT image) and is tabulated as follows,

Table 1. Performance Evaluation in terms of quality measures for different methods

Performance Method	CR	BIT RATE	MSE	PSNR	Enc-Time	Dec-Time
ROI+JPEG 2000	1.88	0.46	4145	11.95	0.31	0.46
ROI+IWT+ JPEG2000	1.76	0.21	4567	11.5	0.06	0.21
Proposed Method	1.76	0.14	14.17	36.61	0.04	0.14

The following graph shows that CR vs PSNR values for different methods

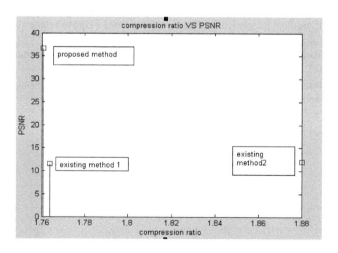

Fig. 5. Compression ratio vs PSNR

7   Conclusion

In this paper, both Lossless and Lossy compression algorithms were used. Lossless compression is used to compress the segmented ROI and Lossy compression is used to compress the Non-ROI. The Proposed method has the advantages of not requiring codebook design and it is not limited in the size of the blocks used for classification. Moreover the implicit size of the codes, for a given bpp, extends over the support of the entire image. Finally the images are fused and decompressed. Image fusion will join ROI and Non-ROI parts of an image and hence there is no information lost. Thus, the results proved to be better in compression performance provided by ROI based algorithms in terms of visual quality and higher PSNR and compared with previous methods.

References

[1] Talukder, K.H., Harada, K.: Haar Wavelet Based Approach for Image Compression and Quality Assessment of Compressed Image. IAENG International Journal of Applied Mathematics (2007)

[2] Lakhani, G.: Modified JPEG Huffman Coding. IEEE Trans. Image Processing 12(2), 159–169 (2003)

[3] Wang, K., Wu, J., Pian, Z., Guo, L., Gao, L.: Edge Detection Algorithm for Magnetic Resonance Images Based on Multiscale Morphology. In: IEEE International Conference on Control and Automation, Guangzhou, China, May 30 - June 1 (2007)

[4] Li, G., Zhang, J., Wang, Q., Hu, C., Deng, N., Li, J.: Application of Region Selective Embedded Zero tree Wavelet Coder in CT Image Compression. In: IEEE Engineering in Medicine and Biology 27th Annual Conference, Shanghai, China, September 1-4 (2005)

[5] Miaou, S.-G., Chen, S.-T.: Automatic quality control for wavelet-based compression of volumetric medical images using distortion-constrained adaptive vector quantization. IEEE Trans.Medical Imaging 23(11) (November 2007)

[6] Wallace, G.K.: The JPEG Still Picture Compression Standard. Communications of the ACM 34(4), 30–44 (1991)

[7] Daubechies, I., Sweldens, W.: Factoring Wavelet Transforms into Lifting Steps. J. Fourier Analysis and Applications 4, 247–268 (1998)

[8] Salomon's, D.: Data Compression, 2nd edn.

Malware Obfuscator for Malicious Executables

Sachin Jain

Department of Computer Engineering,
Malaviya National Institute of Technology,
Jaipur, Rajasthan, India
sachin.1nm@gmail.com

Abstract. Computer viruses are a type of malware that have created threats to millions of computer systems connected over the Internet. Generally all malicious programs try to exploit vulnerabilities to infect the system. The traditional signature based scanner detects malicious samples by comparing malware with signature repository. The signature based method can detect known malware but fails to detect variants of malware. Malware writers make use of self–modifying code to replicate and thwart detection. Such kind of malware is known as metamorphic malware and is very difficult to detect. These malware make use of code obfuscation techniques to generate new variants. Metamorphic malware uses a engine which change the code by incorporating obfuscation methods like junk code insertion, dead code insertion, instruction permutation etc. In this research work, an assembly code morpher is designed which has the ability to morph malware source programs generated using malware constructors and viruses downloaded from VX Heavens. The proposed method also computes the similarity between base malware and its known variants.

Keywords: Metamorphism, Obfuscation, Metamorphic Generators, Morpher.

Computer viruses cause damage to the host machine by monitoring system vulnerabilities and attaching them to a host program for its propagation. The damage could be on system files, boot sectors, documents or macros of some application. Internet is the primary source of malware and they are installed unknowingly by a naïve users while browsing over the Internet. Once the system is infected, malware multiplies by infecting files, installing bots or by setting up multiple connections on attackers machines. The early detection of malware is extremely essential to minimize the damages incurred on the computer systems.

Antivirus vendors utilize signature based scanners for detecting malware. The scanners detect malware by comparing the malware with the signature database to flag alarms for all suspicious samples. The signature based malware scanners fails to detect unknown malware samples as they lack program semantics. Viruses are proliferating and malware writers are making use of sophisticated techniques for evading detection. One such method is code morphing while replication. In this way all malware variants generated appear syntactically dissimilar

P.V. Krishna, M.R. Babu, and E. Ariwa (Eds.): ObCom 2011, Part II, CCIS 270, pp. 461–469, 2012.

and functionally similar. Thus, the scanners employing signatures for detecting malware fail to detect the morphed malware variants.

In this paper, there is explanation about the method which involve in designing a code morpher for malware variants. The assembly code morpher generates the obfuscated malware variants of the base malware created from malware constructors and samples downloaded from VX Heavens [1]. The obfuscation techniques incorporated by the proposed morpher are (a) junk code insertion (b) instruction permutation (c) equivalent instruction substitution and (d) control flow obfuscation. The similarity between the base malware and its known variants are computed using Manhattan distance. Each base malware is morphed using proposed code morpher to generate variants and the similarity is computed between the base malware and generated variants. Comparative analysis is performed on known variants and generated variants (using morpher) to estimate the randomness and complexity of obfuscation incorporated by malware constructors and the proposed morpher.

Paper Organization: In Section 2, there is description about the previous work carried out by researchers in the field of malware invariant detection. Section 3 gives overview of proposed code morpher for creating malware variants. In Sub section 3.6, comparison on similarity between the base malware and variants created using malware constructors and proposed morpher is done. Finally concluding remarks and directions for future scope is covered in Section 4.

1   Related Work

Tiny Mutation Engine (TMC) [2] earliest of all mutation engines. This engine has a compiler and the source code embedded in encrypted form. On execution, the virus decrypts its source code, inserts dead code and recompiles the code. Zombie Code Mutation Engine [3] uses a buffer where the instructions are copied randomly. These instructions are permuted using jmp instructions such that structure of original code is modified. LEXOTAN [4], disassembles the source code, added dead code, and implemented REGSWAP, which shuffled the registers. ZPERM has the REAL PERMUTATION ENGINE (RPME), which can be linked to other viruses and enables random permutation of the virus code, with insertion of dead code and branching using jmp instructions [5]. METAPHOR [6], by Mental Driller, is the most advanced metamorphic virus. It may infect both Windows and Linux executables. Metamorphic techniques used by Metaphor are dead code insertion, permutation of registers, code permutation, instruction modification etc.

2   Proposed Code Morpher

In this section, there is describtion about the metamorphic code morpher that generates the morphed variants of given malware assemblies. Assembly code of virus is divided into blocks. For this procedures/subroutine are extracted from malware assembly code and apply various obfuscation techniques to transform the original code. The transformation is applied on the instruction until there is encounter of instructions like `call`, `retn`, `jmp`, `endp`. Blocks of code are randomly shuffled and some garbage code is inserted which does not alter the semantic of original source program. The sequence of operations performed by proposed morpher is shown in figure 3. The basic idea is to generate variants that are structurally different from each other as well as its base malware. The primary reason for generating morphed variants is that the signature based detector will fail to detect such malware since each variant will have a different pattern that may vary from the signature of its parent. Figure 2 shows the idea behind metamorphism and figure 1 depicts structurally different malware variants of the same base malware. All malware variants of same base malware will have different signatures and thus the signature based scanners will fail to detect them.

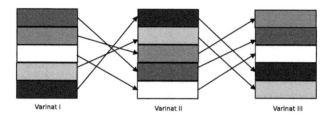

Fig. 1. Three different variants of same malware. Blocks of instructions are shuffled in each generation.

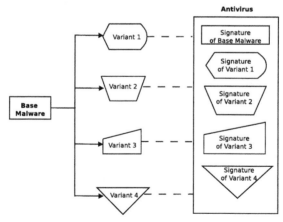

Fig. 2. Base and its variants, each malware variant have different structure and signature

2.1   Framework for Designing Assembly Code Morpher

In this section, there is discussion about the proposed method for generating malware variants using code morpher. Primarily, all metamorphic engines make use of code obfuscation techniques for generating variants. Obfuscation tries to maximize code obscurity, so that users are unable to extract program functionality. Various obfuscation techniques are adopted by malware writers for generating obfuscated variants of same parent code, which are (a) encryption (b) compression (c) dead code insertion (c) junk code insertion (d) equivalent code insertion (e) instruction permutation (f) conditional flow obfuscation. Following steps have been adopted by us to generate morphed malware variants.

  (i)   Collect generated assembly code.
 (ii)   Extract individual subroutines from the assembly code.
(iii)   Generate a random line number (using random number generator) within the extracted procedure. This is the point where the obfuscation transformation is be performed.
(iv)   Using the obfuscation module, various transformations like (a) junk code insertion (b) equivalent code insertion (c) instruction permutation and (d) control flow obfuscation is performed.
 (v)   Finally, a morphed malware variant is obtained which is syntactically different from the input malware sample.

Figure 3 shows the steps involved in generating morphed assemblies of the original base code of malware. In the following subsections, there is describtion about different obfuscation transformations used in proposed code morpher.

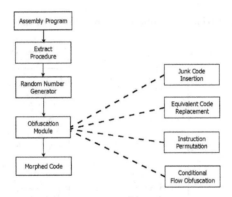

Fig. 3. Proposed method for generating malware variants for a given assembly code of base malware

2.2   Junk Code Insertion

The assemblies of malware code are broken in blocks and junk code is inserted by selecting a random line number generated using the random number generator. These codes do not change the behavior of the program. Thus, the data and the flow of malware samples are not affected. These codes expand the number of instructions present in a block. Some of the junk code used are listed in Table 1. The left hand side of the Table depicts the instructions and the right hand side depicts the meaning of each instruction.

Table 1. Different types of instructions used as junk code by proposed assembly code morpher

Instructions	Meaning
NOP	No Operation
CLD	No Operation
PUSHFD POPFD	No Operation
PUSHAD POPAD	No Operation
MOV REG, REG	REG := REG
ADD REG, 0	REG := REG + 0
OR REG, 0	REG := REG |0
AND REG, -1	REG := REG & -1
PUSH REG POP REG	No Operation
XCHG REG, REG	No Operation
XOR REG, 0	No Operation
SUB REG, 0	No Operation
SBB REG, 0	No Operation
ADC REG, 0	No Operation
SHL REG, 0	No Operation
SHR REG, 0	No Operation
AND REG, 1	REG := REG & 1

2.3   Instruction Permutation

Instruction permutation obfuscation consists of reordering consecutive instructions having two operands. For permuting instructions, two instructions are considered at a time and are swapped if the data flow of operands these two instructions is not dependent on each other. The algorithm 1 shows instruction permutation obfuscation.

2.4   Equivalent Instruction Replacement

Some malware like Win95Zperm [5] and Win32.Evol [7] make use of equivalent instruction substitution as an obfuscation mechanism. In proposed code morpher, there is use of a dictionary of instructions which can be possibly replaced by equivalent instructions. Instruction replacement can either expand or shrink the size of code of offspring. Proposed morpher basically increase the size of the

Algorithm 1. Instruction Permutation Algorithm used by Proposed Morpher

Input: Instructions with two operands i.e. $Instr_1$ and $Instr_2$
Output: Permuted instructions

    if (*Destination Operands* of $Instr_1$ and $Instr_2$ are **not equal**) **and**
    (*destination operand* of $Instr_1$ instruction is **not equal to** *source operand* of $Instr_2$
    instruction) **and**
    (*source operand* of $Instr_1$ instruction is **not equal to** *destination operand* of $Instr_2$
    instruction) **then**
        swap($Instr_1$, $Instr_2$)
    else
        Instructions $Instr_1$ and $Instr_2$ cannot be permuted
    end if

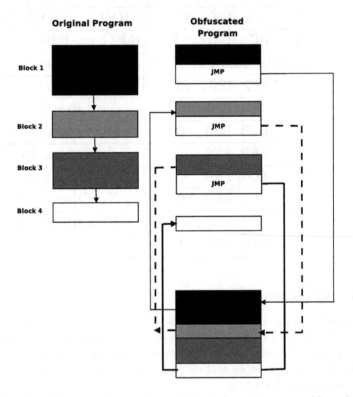

Fig. 4. Proposed method for generating malware variants for a given assembly code of base malware

generated variants. Table 2 depicts the instruction and their equivalent set of instructions.

Table 2. List of equivalent instruction set used in the proposed code morpher

Instructions	Equivalent Instructions
ADD REG, -1	NEG REG; NOT REG or NOT REG; NEG REG
ADD REG, 0	NOP
ADD REG, 1	INC REG or NOT REG; NEG REG or NEG REG; NOT REG
AND REG, -1	NOP
XOR Reg,-1	NOT Reg
XOR Mem,-1	NOT Mem
MOV Reg,Reg	NOP
SUB Reg,Imm	ADD Reg,-Imm
SUB Mem,Imm	ADD Mem,-Imm
AND REG, 0	MOV REG, 0
AND REG, REG	CMP REG, 0
JMP REG	PUSH REG; RET
MOV REG, REG	NOP
AND Mem,0	MOV Mem,0
XOR Reg,Reg	MOV Reg,0
SUB Reg,Reg	MOV Reg,0
OR Reg,Reg	CMP Reg,0
AND Reg,Reg	CMP Reg,0
MOV REG1, REG2	PUSH REG2; POP REG1 or XCHG REG1, REG2
NOP	PUSHFD; POPFD or PUSHAD; POPAD or PUSH REG; POP REG
XOR Reg,0	MOV Reg,0
XOR Mem,0	MOV Mem,0
ADD Reg,0	NOP
ADD Mem,0	NOP
OR Reg,0	NOP
OR Mem,0	NOP
AND Reg,-1	NOP
AND Mem,-1	NOP
AND Reg,0	MOV Reg,0
TEST Reg,Reg	CMP Reg,0
LEA Reg,[Imm]	MOV Reg,Imm
LEA Reg,[Reg+Imm]	ADD Reg,Imm
LEA Reg1,[Reg2]	MOV Reg1,Reg2
LEA Reg1,[Reg1+Reg2]	ADD Reg1,Reg2
MOV Reg,Reg	NOP

2.5   Control Flow Obfuscation

The assembly code of the program is divided into some blocks by generating random line number. After each block, unconditional jump instruction jmp is inserted and remaining statements of block are added as target to this unconditional jmp instruction. In this way, complete program is linked using multiple jmp instructions. Normally the antivirus would scan the program and fail to

Table 3. Manhattan distance between NGCVK base malware and its variants (generated using malware constructor and morphed using proposed code morpher)

	Variants created from NGVCK virus constructor					Variants generated Morpher				
	B1.asm	B2.asm	B3.asm	B4.asm	B5.asm	B1.asm	B2.asm	B3.asm	B4.asm	B5.asm
B1.asm	0.0	0.2775	0.205	0.0268	0.0267	0.0	0.2459	0.2108	0.0548	0.2685
B2.asm	0.0	0.522	0.5066	0.5418	0.5242	0.0	0.0984	0.1626	0.0493	0.4122
B3.asm	0.0	0.1368	0.0341	0.1506	0.1299	0.0	0.1675	0.116	0.2171	0.066
B4.asm	0.0	0.0297	0.0215	0.6118	0.0324	0.0	0.0882	0.1734	0.4125	0.1315
B5.asm	0.0	0.0692	0.1779	0.0463	0.0444	0.0	0.154	0.0118	0.294	0.0336

Table 4. Manhattan distance between G2 base malware and its variants (generated using malware constructor and morphed using proposed code morpher)

	Variants created from G2 virus constructor					Variants generated Morpher				
	B1.asm	B2.asm	B3.asm	B4.asm	B5.asm	B1.asm	B2.asm	B3.asm	B4.asm	B5.asm
B1.asm	0.0	0.0085	0.0085	0.0034	0.0068	0.0	0.0305	0.1861	0.0735	0.1733
B2.asm	0.0	0.061	0.0041	0.0061	0.0102	0.0	0.0106	0.1331	0.0564	0.201
B3.asm	0.0	0.0043	0.0113	0.0028	0.0112	0.0	0.0519	0.1083	0.0845	0.0944
B4.asm	0.0	0.0	0.0	0.027	0.054	0.0	0.0333	0.1051	0.0794	0.0487
B5.asm	0.0	0.0362	0.0	0.0181	0.0362	0.0	0.0067	0.1195	0.0598	0.0233

Table 5. Manhattan distance between PSMPC base malware and its variants (generated using malware constructor and morphed using proposed code morpher)

	Variants created from PSMPC virus constructor					Variants generated Morpher				
	B1.asm	B2.asm	B3.asm	B4.asm	B5.asm	B1.asm	B2.asm	B3.asm	B4.asm	B5.asm
B1.asm	0.0	0.0025	0.0051	0.0051	0.0025	0.0	0.0358	0.1237	0.1027	0.0842
B2.asm	0.0	0.008	0.0	0.004	0.008	0.0	0.0287	0.175	0.0221	0.0886
B3.asm	0.0	0.0046	0.0	0.0	0.0	0.0	0.0528	0.1899	0.0743	0.1181
B4.asm	0.0	0.0077	0.0038	0.0	0.0038	0.0	0.0287	0.0524	0.1301	0.076
B5.asm	0.0	0.0	0.0063	0.0031	0.0063	0.0	0.0585	0.1755	0.0157	0.1484

Table 6. Manhattan distance between Vx Heaven's base malware and its variants (downloaded from malware repository and morphed using proposed code morpher)

	Variants downloaded from Vx Heaven					Variants generated Morpher				
	B1.asm	B2.asm	B3.asm	B4.asm	B5.asm	B1.asm	B2.asm	B3.asm	B4.asm	B5.asm
B1.asm	0.0	0.0085	0.0085	0.0034	0.0068	0.0	0.0305	0.1861	0.0735	0.1733
B2.asm	0.0	0.061	0.0041	0.0061	0.0102	0.0	0.0106	0.1331	0.0564	0.201
B3.asm	0.0	0.0043	0.0113	0.0028	0.0112	0.0	0.0519	0.1083	0.0845	0.0944
B4.asm	0.0	0.0	0.0	0.027	0.054	0.0	0.0333	0.1051	0.0794	0.0487
B5.asm	0.0	0.0362	0.0	0.0181	0.0362	0.0	0.0067	0.1195	0.0598	0.0233

trace the complete flow of such a program. These malicious codes would thus go undetected. Blocks of instructions can also be linked using conditional jump statements. In proposed morpher, conditional jump statements are used to link part of original blocks of malicious program. Figure 4 depicts the original program broken into different blocks. Each block of malware is of varying size as the number of instructions in blocks are different. The second part of the same figure shows obfuscated program using multiple unconditional jump instructions.

2.6   Experimental Setup and Result Analysis

Experiments are performed in controlled environment i.e. virtual machine installed on Windows XP machines. The computer system have Intel Core 350M processor, 4GB RAM installed on it. Malware is generated using NGVCK, G2, PSMPC virus constructor. Similarly, malware samples are also taken from VX Heaven. Five base virus is created by selecting different infection modes. For each base malware, five variants are created. Similarity score is computed for a base virus and its variants using Manhattan distance. Using proposed morpher, five variants are created for each base virus by selecting the obfuscation transformation described in previous subsections. Manhattan distance is computed between the base malware and generated variants. Results are tabulated in Table 3 and Table 5. It can be observe that the distance of generated variants (using proposed morpher) to its base is large compared to the original variants generated using malware constructors. Thus, it can be argue that the obfuscation performed by proposed morpher is more and comparable to existing malware constructors.

3   Conclusions

In this paper, basic assumption was that the base malware and its variants preserve same functionality by bringing change in the structure of code. The variants are created using code obfuscation methods. In order to understand the basic functionality of the parent and offspring, an assembly code morpher is designed using obfuscation techniques like junk code insertion, instruction permutation, equivalent code replacement and code reordering using conditional flow obfuscation. The similarity analysis of base malware and its variants created using virus constructors was computed using Manhattan distance. Likewise, the similarity score of the generated variants and the base malware of the constructor was computed. It is observed that the basic obfuscation performed by our proposed morpher was comparatively more that the variants created by the malware constructors. In future, I would like to incorporate both semantic and syntactic knowledge of the program for identifying malware variants and differentiating them from benign samples.

References

1. Vx heavens, http://vx.netlux.org/lib
2. Tiny mutation engine, http://vxheavens.com/vx.php?id=et04
3. Zombie's code mutation engine–computer virus engines,
   http://vx.netlux.org/vx.php?id=ez00
4. The molecular virology of lexotan32: Metamorphism illustrated,
   http://www.openrce.org/articles/full_view/29
5. Ször, P., Ferrie, P.: Hunting for metamorphic. In: Virus Bulletin Conference, pp. 123–144 (2001)
6. Metamorphism in practice or "how i made metaphor and what i've learnt",
   http://vxheavens.com/lib/vmd01.html
7. Lakhotia, A., Kapoor, A., Uday, E.: Are Metamorphic Viruses Really Invicible. In: Virus Bulletin Conference (2005)

A Better RGB Channel Based Image Steganography Technique

Gandharba Swain[1] and Saroj Kumar Lenka[2]

[1] Research Scholar-CSE, Siksha 'O' Anusandhan University,
Bhubaneswar-751030, Odisha, India
gswain1234@gmail.com
[2] Professor, Department of CSE, MITS University,
Lakshmangarh-332311, Rajasthan, India
lenka.sarojkumar@gmail.com

Abstract. In this paper a new RGB channel based steganographic technique is proposed. The RSA algorithm is used for encryption and decryption. In a RGB image each pixel (24 bits) is having R-channel 8 bits, G-channel 8 bits and B-channel 8 bits. R, G and B stands for red, green and blue respectively. Out of these three channels, the one which is having the maximum value summed over for all the pixels will be decided as the indicator channel. Out of the remaining two channels (say channel1 and channel2) in each pixel, one channel is used for embedding four bits of the cipher text, depending on its value satisfying one of the four defined conditions. At the receiver side the reverse operation will be performed to retrieve the message. The experimental results show that the performance of this technique is satisfactory.

Keywords: Steganography, cryptography, encryption, decryption, RGB, channel based, RSA.

1 Introduction

Steganography is a technique for secret communication between two parties. In steganography the secret information is hidden inside a carrier file such that the change in appearance of the carrier file should not be apparent to normal human eye. If we use cryptography with in steganography the security becomes two fold.

The word steganography is originally derived from Greek words Steganos which means "covered" and Graptos which mean "writing". It has been used in various forms for thousands of years. In Ancient Greece they used to select messengers and shave their head, they would then write a message on their head. Once the message had been written the hair was allowed to grow back. After the hair grew back the messenger was sent to deliver the message, the recipient would shave off the messengers hair to see the secret message. During world war-2 also this concept was used. With the boost in computer power, the internet and with the development of digital signal processing (DSP), information theory and coding theory, steganography

P.V. Krishna, M.R. Babu, and E. Ariwa (Eds.): ObCom 2011, Part II, CCIS 270, pp. 470–478, 2012.

has gone digital. In the realm of this digital world steganography has created an atmosphere of corporate vigilance that has spawned various interesting applications, thus it is continuously evolving.

Steganography can be categorized into four categories [1]. Those are: Steganography in image, steganography in audio, steganography in video and steganography in text. The image steganography algorithms can be categorized into two categories, namely, spatial domain and frequency domain. In each of these categories we can have adaptive and dynamic methods. Adaptive methods are image statistics based, where as dynamic methods are message bit dependent.

When hiding information inside images usually Least Significant Bit (LSB) method is used. In the LSB method the 8th bit of every byte of the carrier file is substituted by one bit of the secret information. This method works fine in the image carriers because if the least significant bit is changed from 0 to 1 or vice versa, there is hardly any change in the appearance of the color of that pixel. The LSB method usually does not increase the file size, but depending on the size of the information that is to be hidden inside the file, the file can become noticeably distorted. Instead of hiding a fixed number of bits in the LSBs of each pixel, one can also embed different number of bits in LSBs of different pixels based on pixel value range calculation [2]. In [3] a two way block matching procedure and the hop embedding scheme is proposed to embed a secret image inside a cover image. Kumar and Roopa proposed the same block matching procedure and the hop embedding scheme with improved tamper proofing, so that it is not possible for any intruder to modify the content of the embedded data in the cover image [4].

In general if the pixels are located in edge areas they can tolerate larger changes than those in smooth areas. The range of changeable pixel value in smooth areas is small, where as in edge areas it is large, so that the stego image maintains a good perceptual quality. Wu and Tsai [5] proposed a pixel value differencing method, where a cover image is partitioned into non overlapping blocks of two consecutive pixels. A difference value is calculated from the value of the two pixels in each block. Secret data is embedded into a cover image by replacing the difference values of the two pixel blocks of the cover image with similar ones, in which bits of embedded data are included. Zhang and Wang [6] found that pixel value differencing steganography is vulnerable to histogram based attacks and proposed a modification for enhanced security. Chang and Tseng [7] employed two sided, three sided and four sided side match schemes. The two sided side match method uses the information of the upper and left neighboring pixels in order to make estimates. The three sided side match method utilizes upper and left neighboring pixels; and one of the other neighboring pixels. The four sided match method uses the upper, left, right and below neighbors.

In RGB images each pixel is represented by 3 bytes to represent the intensities of red, green and blue channels in that pixel. Parvez and Gutub [8] presented a technique based on RGB intensity values of the pixel. They took one of the channels as indicator channel and used one or both of the remaining two channels to conceal data bits. The last two bits of the indicator channel tells whether the data bits are hidden in the other two channels or not. In [9] Tiwari and Shandilya proposed two techniques based on RGB concept. In the first technique they modified the technique of Pervez and Gutub, by changing the indicator for every subsequent pixels. The second technique is a random number generation based, in which a random number generated determines the number of least significant bits that is used to hide the secret data. In [10] Kaur et al. proposed a RGB based technique in which embedding was done upto 4 bits in the channels other than the indicator channel based upon the last four bits of the indicator channel.

In [8] an RGB based algorithm is proposed where the indicator channel is randomly chosen, and 2 bits are embedded in a channel other than the indicator. In this proposed algorithm the indicator channel is chosen based on the sum of color values and embedding is done, as 4 bits in each selected channel satisfying some conditions. In section-2 the proposed algorithm is discussed. In section-3 the experimental results are narrated and in section-4 the paper is concluded.

2   RGB Channel Based Steganography

2.1   Algorithm at Sender

Step-1: Receive the secret message. Apply RSA Algorithm and convert it to cipher text. Now get it in binary.

Step-2: Receive the RGB Image. Convert to binary. Calculate the sum of R channels of all the pixels, sum of G channels of all the pixels and sum of B channels of all the pixels. The channel having maximum sum is the indicator channel. Four bit data is to be hidden in one of the channels other than the indicator, in the following manner.

Step-3: Suppose, the two channels other than the indicator channel are channel1 and channel2.

If R is the Indicator channel, then G is channel1 and B is channel2.

If G is the Indicator channel, then R is channel1 and B is channel2.

If B is the Indicator channel, then R is channel1 and G is channel2.

Step-4: Divide the cipher text into groups of four bits each.

Step-5: Take the next pixel, take the next four bits of cipher text. Do any of the following 4 sub steps.

(a). If (channel1 value $\leq$ 63 and channel2 value > 63) Embed the 4 bits of cipher in channel1 and set 8th bit of indicator channel to 0.

(b). If (channel1 value > 63 and channel2 value $\leq$ 63) Embed the 4 bits of cipher in channel2 and set 8th bit of indicator channel to 1.

(c). If (Channel1 value $\leq$ 63 and channel2 value $\leq$ 63)
Then, If Channel1 value $\leq$ Channel2 value, Embed in channel1 and set 8th bit of indicator channel to 0. Otherwise Embed in channel2 and set 8th bit of indicator channel to 1.

(d). If Channel1 value > 63 and channel2 value > 63) do not embed in this pixel.

Step-6: If embedding of cipher text is not yet over go to step-5.

Step-7: Stop

Table 1. Example of embedding

	Before Embedding			After Embedding		
	Red (Channel1)	Green (**Indicator Channel**)	Blue (Channel2)	Red (Channel1)	Green (**Indicator Channel**)	Blue (Channel2)
Pixel1	10010110	10001110	00011110	10010110	10001111	00010010
Pixel2	00001111	01010101	11001100	00001010	01010100	11001100
Pixel3	10111101	11110000	11001100	10111101	11110000	11001100

As an example suppose we have the three pixels as in table1 and the Green channel is the indicator channel. Suppose the cipher text stream is: 0010 1010 1111 0000. In pixel1 channel1 is 10010110 = 150 which is greater than 63 and channel2 is 00011110 = 30 which is less than 63. Thus the four bits of cipher 0010 is embedded at 4 LSBs of channnel2 and the 8th bit of indicator is set to 1, it becomes 10001111. In pixel2 channel1 is less than 63 and channel2 is greater than 63, the next 4 cipher bits i.e, 1010 are embedded in channel1 and 8th bit of indicator is set to 0, it becomes 01010100. In pixel3 both the channel1 and channel2 are greater than 63, so no embedding is done. After embedding the pixels are also shown in table1.

Now you may question that if we are changing the last 4 bits of a channel, its value will change a lot, how does it work? Look at table2. The channel having decimal value in range 0 to 15, if we change the last 4 bits its value will also fall in range 0 to 15. Similarly the channel having decimal value in range 16 to 31, if we change the last 4 bits its value will also fall in range 16 to 31. The channel having decimal value in range 32 to 47, if we change the last 4 bits its value will also fall in range 32 to 47 and the channel having decimal value in range 48 to 63, if we change the last 4 bits its value will also fall in range 48 to 63. Thus a channel value will suffer a maximum displacement of 16, which will not make much change in the total pixel value which is 24 bits.

2.2   Algorithm at Receiver

Step-1: Receive the Stego Image. Transform to binary. Detect the indicator channel; this information is hidden in some reserved location of stego image. Detect the starting pixel and ending pixel locations with in which the cipher is embedded, these information is also hidden in the reserved location of the image.

Step-2: Suppose, the two channels other than the indicator channel are channel1 and channel2.

If R is the Indicator channel, then G is channel1 and B is channel2.
If G is the Indicator channel, then R is channel1 and B is channel2.
If B is the Indicator channel, then R is channel1 and G is channel2.

Step-3: Begin with start pixel (from where embedding continues)

Step-4: If both channel1 value and channel2 value are > 63 skip this pixel and go to step-5, otherwise do sub step 4(a) and go to step-5.

(a). If 8th bit of indicator channel is 0, take last four bits of channel1, otherwise take the last four bits of channel2. Concatenate these 4 bits to a variable named as CIPHER. Initially the variable CIPHER is blank.

Step-5: Take the next pixel. If it is the pixel following the end marker (it is the last pixel up to which embedding is done), go to step-6, otherwise go to step-4.

Step-6: Now apply RSA algorithm to decrypt the cipher text stored in the variable CIPHER.

Step-7: Stop

Table 2. Change in value of a channel after changing it's last 4 bits

Channel value	Channel value after changing its 4 LSBs
00000000	00000001 or 00000010 or 00000011 or 00000100 or 00000101 or 00000110 or 00000111 or 00001000 or 00001001 or 00001010 or 00001011 or 00001100 or 00001101 or 00001110 or 00001111
0	Channel value 0 changes to 1 or 2 or 3 or 4 or 5 or 6 or 7 or 8 or 9 or 10 or 11 or 12 or 13 or 14 or 15
00000001	00000000 or 00000010 or 00000011 or 00000100 or 00000101 or 00000110 or 00000111 or 00001000 or 00001001 or 00001010 or 00001011 or 00001100 or 00001101 or 00001110 or 00001111
1	Channel value 1 changes to 0 or 2 or 3 or 4 or 5 or 6 or 7 or 8 or 9 or 10 or 11 or 12 or 13 or 14 or 15
00000010	00000000 or 00000001 or 00000011 or 00000100 or 00000101 or 00000110 or 00000111 or 00001000 or 00001001 or 00001010 or 00001011 or 00001100 or 00001101 or 00001110 or 00001111
2	Channel value 2 changes to 0 or 1 or 3 or 4 or 5 or 6 or 7 or 8 or 9 or 10 or 11 or 12 or 13 or 14 or 15
...	...
00001111	00000000 or 00000001 or 00000010 or 00000011 or 00000100 or 00000101 or 00000110 or 00000111 or 00001000 or 00001001 or 00001010 or 00001011 or 00001100 or 00001101 or 00001110
15	Channel value 15 changes to 0 or 1 or 2 or 3 or 4 or 5 or 6 or 7 or 8 or 9 or 10 or 11 or 12 or 13 or 14

3   Results and Discussion

The technique is experimented and results are observed for more than 50 images. Some sample observations are shown. In fig.1, (a) is the original Statue image and (b) is it's stego image with 20027 bytes of cipher data embedded in it, (c) is the original Player image and (d) is it's stego image with 30116 bytes of cipher data embedded into it. Similarly, (e) is the original Leena image and (f) is it's stego image with 30079 bytes of cipher data embedded into it. If you see the stego images, you can not observe any change in quality.

(a). Original Statue image   (b). Stego Statue image

(c). Original Player image   (d). Stego Player image

(e). Original Leena Image   (f). Stego Leena image

Fig. 1. Original images and their stego images

Moreover, there are some basic notes that should be observed by a steganographer [1]. Those are: (i) In order to eliminate the attack of comparing the original image with the stego image, we can freshly create an image and destroy it after generating the stego image. The images available in World Wide Web should not be used. (ii) In order to avoid any human visual perceptual attack, the generated stego image must not have visual artifacts. (iii) Smooth homogeneous areas must be avoided, e.g., cloudless blue sky over a blanket of snow, and however chaotic areas with naturally noisy back grounds and salient rigid edges can be targeted. (iv) The secret data must be a composite of balanced bit values, since in general; the expected probabilities of bit 0 and 1 for a typical cover image are the same. In such cases encryption provides such a balance.

The performance of various steganographic methods can be rated by the three parameters: security, capacity, and imperceptibility [11]. Security: Steganography may suffer from many active or passive attacks, thus a secured steganographic algorithm should survive from passive or active attacks. Capacity: Capacity means the amount of information that can be hidden. To be useful in conveying secret message, the hiding capacity provided by steganography should be as high as possible, which may be given in measurements such as the size of secret message, or bits per pixel etc. Imperceptibility: Stego images should not have severe visual artifacts. It means the resultant image should look innocuous enough.

This proposed algorithm is also a secured one. Table 3 represents the peak signal to noise ratio (PSNR) with different message length for different images. PSNR is measured in decibels (dB). PSNR values falling below 30 dB indicate a fairly low quality, i.e., distortion caused by embedding can be obvious; however, a high quality stego-image should strive for atleast 40 dB [1]. The PSNR is as defined below.

$$PSNR = 10 \log_{10} \left(\frac{C_{max}^{2}}{MSE} \right),$$

Where C_{max} = the maximum pixel value which is 255 for 8-bit images. MSE called the mean square error is as defined below.

$$MSE = \frac{1}{MN} \sum_{x=1}^{M} \sum_{y=1}^{N} \left(S_{xy} - C_{xy} \right),$$

Where x and y are the image coordinates, M and N are the dimensions of the image, C_{xy} is the cover image and S_{xy} is the generated stego image.

Table 3. Observed PSNR for various images with different Payload

Image	Image size KBs	Maximum embedding capacity (bits)	Amount of cipher embedded (bytes)	PSNR (dBs)
Statue	1433	1626288 (198.52 KB)	20027	47.84
Leena	768	1003028 (122.44 KB)	30079	42.75
Player	3290	3720284 (454.14 KB)	30116	49.61

The capacity is very high, in Statue image it is 198.52 kilo bytes which is 14% of the image size. In Leena image it is 122.44 kilo bytes which is 16% of the image size. In Player image it is 454.14 kilo bytes which is 14% of the image size.

If you can observe the stego images in fig.1, you can not find any visual artifacts, showing the presence of steganography.

The table 4 shows the comparison of our proposed scheme with the different algorithms proposed by other researchers. Compared to other algorithms suggested by different experts in this field; this is also a stronger one.

Table 4. Comparision with other schemes

Scheme	Mimimum Observed PSNR	Capacity	Imperceptibility
Wang and Chen. [3]	44.20	high	good
Kumar and Roopa [4]	44.15	medium	good
Wu and Tsai [5]	37.90	medium	good
Zhang and Wang [6]	36.00	medium	good
Chang and Tseng [7]	33.53	medium	good
Proposed Scheme	42.75	high	good

4 Conclusion

In this paper a new RGB based steganography is proposed. It provides two levels of security, one at cryptography level and the other at steganography level. The embedding capacity is very high. The channels where data is embedded is different for different pixels, it will make the intrusion difficult. The proposed scheme is a novel approach. This technique is one of the efficient approaches. Capacity and PSNR is better as compared to some of the existing algorithms. No visual artifacts can be observed from the corresponding stego images.

Acknowledgments. Gandharba Swain is working as an Associate Professor in GMR Institute of Technology. He would like to thank the management of GMR Institute of Technology for providing the necessary computing facilities.

References

1. Cheddad, A., Condell, J., Curran, K., Kevitt, P.M.: Digital Image Steganography: Survey and Analysis of Current Methods. Signal Processing 90, 727–752 (2010)
2. Jain, Y.K., Ahirwal, R.R.: A Novel Image Steganography Method with Adaptive Number of Least Significant Bits Modification Based on Private Stego Keys. International Journal of Computer Science and Security 4(1), 40–49 (2010)

3. Wang, R., Chen, Y.: High Payload Image Steganography Using Two-Way Block Matching. IEEE Signal Processing Letters 13(3), 161–164 (2006)
4. Kumar, P.M., Roopa, D.: An Image Steganography Framework with Improved Tamper Proofing. Asian Journal of Information Technology 6(10), 1023–1029 (2007)
5. Wu, D.C., Tsai, W.H.: A Steganograhic Method for Images by Pixel Value Differencing. Pattern Recognition Letters 24(9-10), 1613–1626 (2003)
6. Zhang, X., Wang, S.: Vulnerability of Pixel-Value Differencing Steganography to Histogram Analysis and Modification for Enhanced Security. Pattern Recognition Letters 25, 331–339 (2004)
7. Chang, C.C., Tseng, H.W.: A Steganographic Method for Digital Images Using Side Match. Pattern Recognition Letters 25(12), 1431–1437 (2004)
8. Parvez, M.T., Gutub, A.A.: RGB Based Variable-Bits Image Steganography. In: Proceedings of IEEE Asia Pacific Services Computing Conference, pp. 1322–1327 (2008)
9. Tiwari, N., Shandilya, M.: Secure RGB Image Steganography from Pixel Indicator to Triple Algorithm- An Incremental Growth. International Journal of Security and Its Applications 4(4), 53–62 (2010)
10. Kaur, M., Gupta, S., Sandhu, P.S., Kaur, J.: A Dynamic RGB Intensity Based Steganography Scheme. World Academy of Science, Engineering and Technology 67, 833–838 (2010)
11. Li, B., He, J., Huang, J., She, Y.Q.: A Survey on Image Steganography and Steganalysis. Journal of Information hiding and Multimedia Signal Processing 2(2), 142–172 (2011)

LSB Array Based Image Steganography Technique by Exploring the Four Least Significant Bits

Gandharba Swain[1] and Saroj Kumar Lenka[2]

[1] Research Scholar-CSE, Siksha 'O' Anusandhan University,
Bhubaneswar-751030, Odisha, India
gswain1234@gmail.com
[2] Professor, Department of CSE, MITS University,
Lakshmangarh-332311, Rajasthan, India
lenka.sarojkumar@gmail.com

Abstract. In this paper a new LSB (least significant bit) array based image steganographic technique using encryption by RSA algorithm is proposed. In the image each pixel is 8 bits. The four arrays, namely the LSB, LSB1, LSB2 and LSB3 are formulated separately by collecting the bits from the 8th (LSB), 7th, 6th and 5th bit locations of the pixels respectively. The cipher text is divided into four blocks. The first block is mapped and slided over the LSB array and embedded at maximum matching portion of LSB array. Similarly the second, third and fourth blocks are embedded at maximum matching portion of LSB1, LSB2 and LSB3 arrays respectively. Where the blocks are embedded, the start indices are captured and embedded at a separate place in the image. The retrieving process at the receiver is the reverse of the sender. The performance of this technique is compared with other techniques.

Keywords: Steganography, cryptography, encryption, decryption, LSB, LSB array based.

1 Introduction

Steganography is a technique for secret communication between two parties. In steganography the secret information is hidden inside a carrier file such that the change in appearance of the carrier file should not be apparent to normal human eye. The word steganography is originally derived from Greek words Steganos and Graptos which mean "Covered and writing" respectively. It has been used in various forms for thousands of years. In Ancient Greece they used to select messengers and shave their head, they would then write a message on their head. Once the message had been written the hair was allowed to grow back. After the hair grew back the messenger was sent to deliver the message, the recipient would shave off the messengers hair to see the secret message. During world war-2 also this concept was used. With the boost in computer power, the internet and with the development of

P.V. Krishna, M.R. Babu, and E. Ariwa (Eds.): ObCom 2011, Part II, CCIS 270, pp. 479–488, 2012.
© Springer-Verlag Berlin Heidelberg 2012

digital signal processing (DSP), information theory and coding theory, steganography has gone digital. In the realm of this digital world steganography has created an atmosphere of corporate vigilance that has spawned various interesting applications, thus it is continuously evolving.

Steganography can be categorized into four categories [1]. Those are: Steganography in image, steganography in audio, steganography in video and steganography in text. The image steganography algorithms can be categorized into two categories, namely, spatial domain and frequency domain. In each of these categories we can have adaptive and dynamic methods. Adaptive methods are image statistics based, where as dynamic methods are message bit dependent.

To a computer an image is simply a file that shows the different colors and intensities of light on different areas of an image. When hiding information inside images usually Least Significant Bit (LSB) method is used. In the LSB method the 8th bit of every byte of the carrier file is substituted by one bit of the secret information. Instead of hiding a fixed number of bits in the LSBs of each pixel, one can also embed different number of bits in LSBs of different pixels based on pixel value range calculation [2].

In [3] techniques of error control coding, image restoration and those similar to spread spectrum communication are combined. The fundamental concept is the embedding of the secret information within noise, which is then added to a digital cover image. This noise is typical of the noise inherent to the image acquisition process and, if kept at low levels, is not perceptible to human eye or by computer analysis without access to the original image. To successfully decode the image, image restoration techniques and error control coding are used.

In [4] the authors have studied the effect of applying popular steganography algorithms on different statistical models of natural images. On one hand they observed that some popular stego-algorithms consistently bias these statistics for some of the most fundamental models. On the other hand the intrinsic variability of these statistics is so high, for the class of images studied, that this bias induced by hiding "unnatural" information is not sufficient in general to move the results outside of the "natural" range, unless knowledge of the embedding algorithm is available and exploited.

In [5] a two way block matching procedure and the hop embedding scheme is proposed to embed a secret image inside a cover image. Kumar and Roopa represented the same block matching procedure and the hop embedding scheme with improved tamper proofing, so that it is not possible for any intruder to modify the content of the embedded data in the cover image [6]. In image steganography, a pixel can carry secret bits by adding/subtracting one to/from the gray value. This kind of ±1 steganography can hide a longer message than simple LSB embedding. Zhang et al. [7] proposed a double layered embedding method to further improve the embedding efficiency of ±1 steganography.

In [8] a text in image steganography is proposed. This technique presents a way for labeling different colors to identify dark areas of image and then embed the text in those areas. Instead of dark areas darker and brighter pixels can also be exploited to hide the secret data bits [9]. In [10] a text in image steganography is proposed by mapping the binary values of characters of the text message to various pixels of the image.

In general if the pixels are located in edge areas they can tolerate larger changes than those in smooth areas. The range of changeable pixel value in smooth areas is small, where as in edge areas it is large so that the stego image maintains a good perceptual quality. Wu and Tsai [11] proposed a pixel value differencing method, where a cover image is partitioned into non overlapping blocks of two consecutive pixels. A difference value is calculated from the value of the two pixels in each block. Secret data is embedded into a cover image by replacing the difference values of the two pixel blocks of the cover image with similar ones, in which bits of embedded data are included. Zhang and Wang [12] found that pixel value differencing steganography is vulnerable to histogram based attacks and proposed a modification for enhanced security. Chang and Tseng [13] employed two sided, three sided and four sided side match schemes. The two sided side match method uses the side information of the upper and left neighboring pixels in order to make estimates. The three sided side match method utilizes upper and left neighboring pixels; and one of the other neighboring pixels. The four sided match method uses the upper, left, right and below neighbors.

Juneja and Sandhu [14] proposed a technique based upon LSB array, in which they have taken all the LSB bits of the different pixels as an array called LSB array, mapped the encrypted message block to this LSB array, where maximum matched, there steganographed. In fact a number of images can be experimented; the image in which the percentage of match is maximum can be used.

In this paper a new technique is proposed in which, this LSB array concept is extended to have 4 arrays namely LSB, LSB1, LSB2 and LSB3, so that 4 different blocks of cipher text can be matched. Thus the hiding capacity can be four times than that of the scheme in [14]. In section-2 the proposed algorithm is discussed. In section-3 the experimental results and its merits are narrated. In section-4 it is concluded.

2   LSB Array Based Steganography

2.1   Algorithm at Sender

Step-1: Input the secret message.

Step-2: Apply RSA algorithm to encrypt the secret message. Divide the cipher text into four blocks namely block0, block1, block2 and block3.

Step-3: Input the image. Transform it to binary.

Step-4: The first hundred bytes carries the image characteristics. Next to store the information like length of the blocks and the start index from the arrays where the blocks are matched, reserve from 101th byte upto 5000th byte. Then start from 5001th byte onwards upto the last byte or upto a desired byte depending upon the length of your secret message.

Take the 8th bits (LSBs) of these pixels, now it is an array of bits called LSB array. Take the 7th bits of these pixels, it is an array called the LSB1 array. Take the 6th bits of these pixels as an array called LSB2 array. Take the 5th bits of all these pixels as an array call it as LSB3 array.

Step-5: Map block0 with the LSB array. Start from the first location of LSB array, go on sliding the block0 on the LSB array, where it matches maximum, embed there and note down the start index in LSB array where steganographed. Say it is index0. Similarly find index1 from LSB1 array after embedding block1, index2 from LSB2 array after embedding block2 and index3 from LSB3 array after embedding block3.

Step-6: Embed these four indices and the block lengths in the reserved pixels i.e pixel number 101 to 5000, using 7th and 8th bits of all those pixels.

Step-7: Stop

2.2   Algorithm at Receiver

Step-1: Receive the stego image.

Step-2: Compute the LSB, LSB1, LSB2 and LSB3 arrays.

Step-3: Retrieve index0, index1, index2 and index3 from the reserved pixels.

Step-4: Retrieve block0 from LSB array from the location starting with index0. Retrieve block1 from LSB1 array from the location starting with index1. Retrieve block2 from LSB2 array from the location starting with index2. Retrieve block3 from LSB3 array from the location starting with index3.

Step-5: Concatenate all these 4 blocks, thus we get the cipher.

Step-6: Apply RSA algorithm to decrypt it to get the plain text which is the secret message.

Step-7: Stop.

3   Results and Discussion

Three sample observations are discussed in this section. In fig.1, (a) is the original Leena image, (b) is it's histogram, (c) is the Stego Leena image with 2504 bytes of cipher text embedded and (d) is it's histogram. First 100 bytes(pixels) are not disturbed. Then the bytes 101th to 5000th of the image are reserved, for hiding the length information of the message blocks, and the matched block start indices. So the LSB, LSB1, LSB2, and LSB3 arrays are formulated from pixel number 5001 onwards in all the three observations.

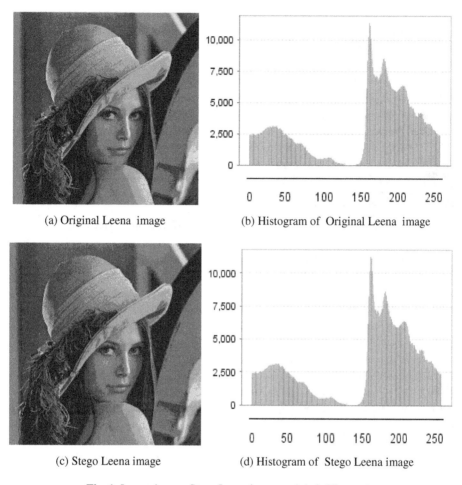

(a) Original Leena image

(b) Histogram of Original Leena image

(c) Stego Leena image

(d) Histogram of Stego Leena image

Fig. 1. Leena image, Stego Leena image and their Histograms

In fig.2, (a) is the original Tree image, (b) is it's histogram, (c) is the stego Tree image with 5016 bytes of cipher text embedded and (d) is it's histogram.

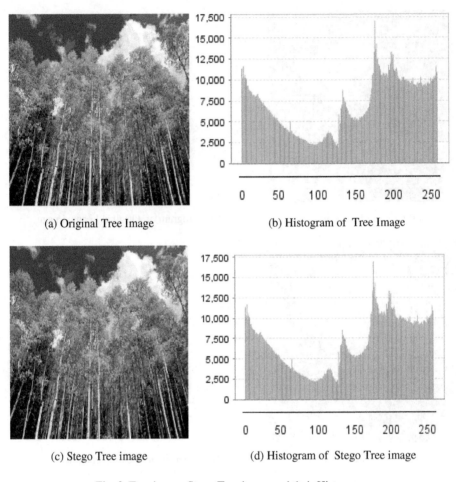

(a) Original Tree Image   (b) Histogram of Tree Image

(c) Stego Tree image   (d) Histogram of Stego Tree image

Fig. 2. Tree image, Stego Tree image and their Histograms

In fig.3, (a) is the original Road image, (b) is it's histogram, (c) is the stego Road image with 7529 bytes of cipher text embedded and (d) is it's histogram.

It is not necessary to formulate the LSB array starting from byte number 5001 upto the last byte of binary image for faster execution point of view. In all these three observations the arrays are formulated from byte number 5001 upto the byte number 25000. So the length of the LSB array, LSB1 array, LSB2 array and LSB3 array will be 20000 bits. The cipher text is divided into 4 blocks such as block0, block1, block2 and block3. The arrays are LSB, LSB1, LSB2, LSB3. Block0 is matched into LSB array, Block1 is matched into LSB1 array, Block2 is matched into LSB2 array and Block3 is matched into LSB3 array. The start indices of matched portion in the arrays are as shown in table-1 for all the three observations.

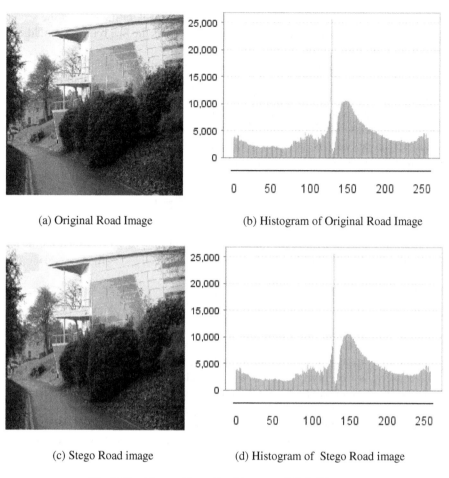

(a) Original Road Image (b) Histogram of Original Road Image

(c) Stego Road image (d) Histogram of Stego Road image

Fig. 3. Road image, Stego Road image and their Histograms

Table 1. Matching Indices

Block Name	Array Name	Start index of the matched portions in the arrays		
		Leena	Tree	Road
Block0	LSB	6984	2771	1993
Block1	LSB1	671	3368	24
Block2	LSB2	43	3	668
Block3	LSB3	1780	90	1107

The performance of various steganographic methods can be rated by the three parameters: security, capacity, and imperceptibility [15]. To be secure a Steganographic technique should survive from passive or active attacks. Capacity means the amount of information that can be hidden, it should be as high as possible, which may be given in measurements such as bits per pixel, or the ratio of the secret message to the cover medium, etc. Imperceptibility means the Stego image should not have severe visual artifacts.

This proposed algorithm is highly secure because of the matching pattern and storing of the start indices. One can see the histograms of the images and their stego images, there is no change. Table2 records the peak signal to noise ratio (PSNR) at different payloads for different images. PSNR is measured in decibels (dB). PSNR values falling below 30 dB indicate a fairly low quality, i.e., distortion caused by embedding can be obvious; however, a high quality stego-image should strive for 40 dB and above [1]. The PSNR is as defined below.

$$PSNR = 10 \log_{10} \left(\frac{C_{max}^2}{MSE} \right),$$

Where C_{max} = the maximum pixel value, 255 for 8-bit images. MSE called the mean square error is as defined below.

$$MSE = \frac{1}{MN} \sum_{x=1}^{M} \sum_{y=1}^{N} \left(S_{xy} - C_{xy} \right),$$

Where x and y are the image coordinates, M and N are the dimensions of the image, C_{xy} is the cover image and S_{xy} is the generated stego image.

The capacity is very high, upto 4 bits in a pixel, after leaving the reserved pixels, 50% capacity of the remaining size will be the maximum available space for payload to be embedded. For example in the Leena image 768 kilo bytes, which is 786432 bytes, then 786432-5000=736432 bytes space is available. If you can observe the stego images in fig.1, fig.2 and fig.3, you can not find any visual artifacts, showing the presence of steganography.

Table 2. Estimated PSNR for different images

Image Name	Image size In KBs	Cipher text Size in bytes	PSNR In decibels
Leena	768	2504	53.78
Trees	1749	5016	54.53
Road	1050	7529	50.50

The table3 shows the comparison of the proposed scheme with the different algorithms proposed by other researchers. Compared to other algorithms suggested by different experts in this field; this is also a stronger one.

Table 3. Comparision with other schemes proposed by other Researchers

Scheme	Mimimum Observed PSNR	Capacity	Imperceptibility
Wang and Chen [5]	44.20	high	good
Kumar and Roopa [6]	44.15	medium	good
Wu and Tsai [11]	37.90	medium	good
Zhang and Wang [12]	36.00	medium	good
Chang and Tseng [13]	33.53	medium	good
Proposed Scheme	50.50	high	good

4   Conclusion

A LSB array based algorithm is proposed. It provides two levels of security one at cryptography level and the other at steganography level. The algorithm is a secure one. Offers high capacity and provides no visual artifacts in the stego image. In this algorithm the most interesting thing is the maximum matching portion in the different arrays and the hiding of the start indices of the matched portion of the arrays in a different place in the image. The observed PSNR is better than the different existing algorithms as shown in table3.

Acknowledgment. Gandharba Swain is working as an Associate Professor in GMR Institute of Technology. He would like to thank the management of GMR Institute of Technology for providing the necessary computing facilities.

References

1. Cheddad, A., Condell, J., Curran, K., Kevitt, P.M.: Digital Image Steganography: Survey and Analysis of Current Methods. Signal Processing 90, 727–752 (2010)
2. Jain, Y.K., Ahirwal, R.R.: A Novel Image Steganography Method with Adaptive Number of Least Significant Bits Modification Based on Private Stego Keys. International Journal of Computer Science and Security 4(1), 40–49 (2010)
3. Marvel, L.M.: Spread Spectrum Image Steganography. IEEE Transactions on Image Processing 8(8), 1075–1083 (1999)
4. Martin, A., Sapiro, G., Seroussi, G.: Is Image Steganography Natural. IEEE Transactions on Image Processing 14(12), 2040–2050 (2005)
5. Wang, R., Chen, Y.: High Payload Image Steganography Using Two-Way Block Matching. IEEE Signal Processing Letters 13(3), 161–164 (2006)
6. Kumar, P.M., Roopa, D.: An Image Steganography Framework with Improved Tamper Proofing. Asian Journal of Information Technology 6(10), 1023–1029 (2007)
7. Zhang, W., Zhang, X., Wang, S.: A Double Layered Plus-Minus One Data Embedding Scheme. IEEE Signal Processing Letters 14(11), 848–851 (2007)

8. Motameni, H., Norouzi, M., Jahandar, M., Hatami, A.: Labeling Method in Steganography. Proceedings of World Academy of Science, Engineering and Technology 24, 349–354 (2007)
9. Swain, G., Lenka, S.K.: A Hybrid Approach to Steganography Embedding at Darkest and Brightest Pixels. In: Proceedings of the International Conference on Communication and Computational Intelligence (INCOCCI 2010), pp. 529–534 (2010)
10. Al-Husainy, M.A.F.: Image Steganography by mapping Pixels to Letters. Journal of Computer Science 5(1), 33–38 (2009)
11. Wu, D.C., Tsai, W.H.: A Steganograhic Method for Images by Pixel Value Differencing. Pattern Recognition Letters 24(9-10), 1613–1626 (2003)
12. Zhang, X., Wang, S.: Vulnerability of Pixel-Value Differencing Steganography to Histogram Analysis and Modification for Enhanced Security. Pattern Recognition Letters 25, 331–339 (2004)
13. Chang, C.C., Tseng, H.W.: A Steganographic Method for Digital Images Using Side Match. Pattern Recognition Letters 25(12), 1431–1437 (2004)
14. Juneja, M., Sandhu, P.S.: Designing of Robust Steganography Technique Based on LSB Insertion and Encryption. In: Proceedings of International Conference on Advances in Recent Technologies in Communication and Computing, pp. 302–305 (2009)
15. Li, B., He, J., Huang, J., She, Y.Q.: A Survey on Image Steganography and Steganalysis. Journal of Information hiding and Multimedia Signal Processing 2(2), 142–172 (2011)

Isolated Kokborok Vowels Recognition

Abhijit Debbarma

RK Mahavidyalaya,
Department of Information Technology,
Kailashahar, North Tripura, India
db.abhi@gmail.com

Abstract. Vowels form the basic block for word formation. It is the main constituent block for word pronunciation. In this paper we try to analyze the Kokborok vowels signals. Kokborok is the official language of Tripura, India. A Linear predictive coding coefficient (LPCC) feature is extracted and analyzed to recognize the vowels. Kokborok uses the English vowels format with additional vowel 'w'. We have found satisfactory recognition rate for the Kokborok vowels based on LPC analysis.

Keywords: Kokborok, LPC, Vowels Recognition.

1 Introduction

Vowels form the main constituent of the word formation. Kokborok language uses the English vowels format viz. /a/, /e/, /i/, /o/, /u/ and additional vowel /w/ which is not used in English and is a commonly used vowel in Kokborok language. Kokborok being from the Tibeto-Burman language family has some phoneme that has no English phoneme representation. Today many speech recognition systems are available for rich language like English. Based on this working model we are designing an isolated vowels recognition system on a Kokborok Vowels.

This paper tries to study the Kokborok vowels computationally. Linear Predictive Code using Durbin's Algorithm is used to compute the feature parameters of the vowels. Euclidian Distance measure is being used to compute the nearest matching vowels. A satisfactory recognition is found using the method. A recognition rate of 98% is being observed with the vowels /w/ being the most mismatches. A similar work has been done on the Kokborok language [6] but not on the vowels. This being the first known work on Kokborok vowels will surely through some light in the future work on the language.

1.1 Kokborok Language

Kokborok [3] is the language of the Tripuri people spoken in the state of Tripura situated in the North Eastern part of India and also adjoining areas of Chittagong Hill Tract in Bangladesh. This language belongs to the Tibeto-Burman language family

P.V. Krishna, M.R. Babu, and E. Ariwa (Eds.): ObCom 2011, Part II, CCIS 270, pp. 489–493, 2012.
© Springer-Verlag Berlin Heidelberg 2012

and shows close affinity with other North Eastern language like Boro, Garo etc. Earlier Kokborok has its own script used by the Tripura Royal Family, but presently it uses either the Bengali script or Romans Script for writing of which the later has greater acceptance among the educated Tripuri intellectuals. Kokborok has been recognized as the official language of Tripura State.

1.2   Kokborok Vowels and Consonants

Kokborok Vowels:
'A' as in Father, ama (mother)
'E' as in end, kechen (looser)
'I' as in Inside, bini (his/her)
'O' as in hot, bolong (forest)
'U' as in put, buwa (teeth)
'W' as in bwkha, (heart)

Kokborok Consonants:
B C D G H J K L M N P R S T Y along with combined consonants CH, KH, PH, TH, NG.

The consonant letter 'C' is not used by some writer and is replaced by consonant 'K' and English consonant 'F' is not used in Kokborok writing and is with combined consonant 'PH'

2   Data Preparation and Procedure

Isolated vowels are recorded using the CoolEdit software [5]. The wav files recorded have the specification of 16 kHz, PCM 16 bit Mono. A total of 60 vowels were recorded with each vowels recorded 10 times each in the given format. After the recording the data were further process before the final computation using LPC.

2.1   DC Shift Correction

The speech signal gives error measures at times due to the atmospheric influence or human error and the voltage interference in the current. To overcome this error in speech signal we perform he DC Shift correction of the speech signal.

2.2   Normalization

Normalization of the speech signal is required as the speech signal are recorded at different times have difference in amplitude. To Normalize the whole speech signal, normalization technique is performed on the speech signal for further processing.

2.3   End Point Detection

The end point detection of speech is essential to separate the speech signal for the noise present in the wav files. We perform the end point detection as in [1] using the zero crossing rate (ZCR) and energy.

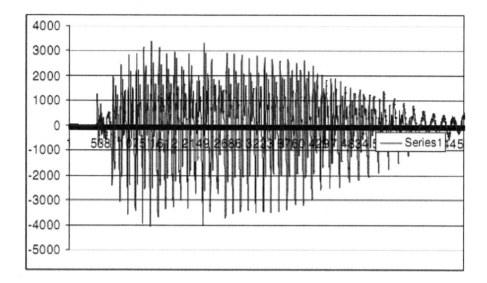

Fig. 1. Signal view of vowel /w/

3   LPC Feature Extraction

Linear Predictive Coding (LPC) is a good tool for analysis of speech signals. [2] One of the more powerful analysis techniques is the method of linear prediction. LPC has become an important and widely accepted speech parameter. LPC analysis helps in computing present speech samples based on the approximation of past speech samples. A unique speech parameters, coefficient is determined based on the concept. The pre-emphasised speech signal is blocked into number of frames with window size 320.

$$w(n) = 0.54 - 0.46 \cos\left(\frac{2\pi n}{N-1}\right), \quad 0 \le n \le N-1. \tag{1}$$

Autocorrelation is applied on each frame of speech signal. The highest autocorrelation value p is the order of the LPC analysis.

$$r_\ell(m) = \sum_{n=0}^{N-1-m} \tilde{x}_\ell(n)\tilde{x}_\ell(n+m), \qquad m = 0, 1, \dots, p, \qquad (2)$$

Each frame of the windowed signal is then auto correlated. The highest autocorrelation value p is the order of the LPC analysis. The next processing step is the LPC analysis, which converts each frame of p+1 autocorrelations [2] into an LPC parameter set in which the set consists of LPC coefficients. The formal method of converting from autocorrelation coefficients to a LPC parameter set is known as DURBIN's method [2]. By applying the above described procedures for each frame a set of LPC coefficients is computed.

$$E^{(0)} = r(0)$$

$$k_i = \left\{ r(i) - \sum_{j=1}^{L-1} a_j^{(i-1)} r(|i-j|) \right\} \bigg/ E^{(i-1)}, \quad 1 \leq i \leq p$$

$$(3)$$

$$a_i^{(i)} = k_i$$

$$a_j^{(i)} = a_j^{(i-1)} - k_i a_{i-j}^{(i-1)}$$

$$E^{(i)} = \left(1 - k_i^2\right) E^{(i-1)}.$$

The above equation are solve for p = 1 to p where p=12. Where

$$a_m = \text{LPC coefficients} = a_m^{(p)}, \qquad 1 \leq m \leq p$$

$$k_m = \text{PARCOR coefficients}$$

$$(4)$$

$$g_m = \text{log area ratio coefficients} = \log\left(\frac{1-k_m}{1+k_m}\right).$$

The 12 LPC cepstral coefficients are thus obtained by recursion method used:

$$a_m = \text{LPC coefficients} = a_m^{(p)}, \qquad 1 \leq m \leq p$$

$$k_m = \text{PARCOR coefficients}$$

$$(5)$$

$$g_m = \text{log area ratio coefficients} = \log\left(\frac{1-k_m}{1+k_m}\right).$$

Please note that, if your email address is given in your paper, it will also be included in the meta data of the online version.

4   Weighted Euclidean Distance

Weighted Euclidean distance [4] is used to find the nearest distance measure among the vowels based on the cepstral coefficient computed.   A codebook is generated based on the above mention rules consisting of a set of cepstral coefficients for the Kokborok vowels. The weight are computed from the cepstral coefficient taking the standard deviation. The test speech signal again goes through the same process and obtains the coefficient parameter. The test signal then goes through the Euclidean distance measure with the generated codebook. The vowels matching the codebook will give the minimum distance.

5   Experiments and Results

The experiments were conducted based on the above algorithm to compute the LPC coefficient, the test wav file is compared based on the Euclidian distance that is nearest in distance to the vowels. The training file consists of 20 speaker's isolated vowels split from a word and recorded individually using Cooledit software as per earlier stated recorder 20 times each i.e 400 each vowels. A database of 3000 vowels size is being experimented in laboratory environment for the recognition purpose.

An overall accuracy rate of 98% was obtained for vowels recognition. The vowels /w/ is found to be having most mismatch in our experiments. Only 70% recognition rate was obtained for this vowel, and is found to be mismatch with other vowels and more commonly with /o/, /a/ and /e/.

As a future work a more elaborate data set is to be experimented and vowels from the continuous spoken words is to be analyzed. A further volume of experiment with sufficient data will serve the best purpose of the recognizer.

References

1. Rabiner, L.R., Sambur, M.R.: An Algorithm for Determining the Endpoints of Isolated Utterances. The Bell System Technical Journal 54(2), 297–315 (1975)
2. Rabiner, L., Juang, B.H.: Fundamentals of Speech Recognition. Prentice-Hall, Englewood Cliffs
3. Chowdhury, K.K.: Kokborok the promising language of North East, Tipura, India
4. Planner, B.: An Introduction to speech recognition, Workshop, SMG, Venice, University of Munich (2000)
5. CoolEdit Software, http://www.adobe.com/special/products/audition/syntrillium.html
6. Abhijit, D.: Speech Recognition for Kokborok Language. In: International Conference BEATS 2010, NIT Jalandhar, December 17-19 (2010)

A Spatio-Temporal Framework for Moving Object Detection in Outdoor Scene

Deepak Kumar Rout[1] and Sharmistha Puhan[2]

[1] Department of Electronics & Telecommunication Engineering
[2] Department of Computer Science & Engineering,
C.V. Raman College of Engineering,
Bidya Nagar, Mahura, Janla, Bhubaneswar, India – 752054

Abstract. This paper addresses the problem of video object detection under illumination variation condition. Since it is a very general case in outdoor environment, hence many attempts have been made to design a robust and efficient algorithm, which takes care of any such case of illumination variation. In this paper we have proposed an effective spatio-temporal framework based algorithm which computes the inter-plane correlation between three consecutive Red, Blue and Green planes of three consecutive video sequences by using a correlation function. The correlation matrix obtained is then used to construct an image which gives a rough estimate of the object to be detected. This image is then fused with the moving edge image in a deterministic framework to detect the final moving object in the video. The algorithm is tested in different outdoor and indoor situations and found to be very much efficient in terms of the misclassification error.

Keywords: Illumination variation, Three frame differencing, Inter Plane Correlation, Object detection, Data fusion.

1   Introduction

Video object detection is a primary task in many machine vision systems. It is important to segment the motion areas effectively for recognition, tracking as well as behavior understanding. Change detection is a special case of motion segmentation with only two regions, namely changed and unchanged regions (in the case of static cameras) or global and local motion regions (in the case of moving cameras). A lot of work has been carried out starting from simple techniques such as frame differencing and adaptive median filtering, to more sophisticated probabilistic modeling techniques. Background subtraction is a commonly used class of techniques for segmenting objects of interest in a scene for applications such as surveillance. Many background subtraction methods exist in literature [1]. Although these methods are simpler and have less computational complexity, but when the reference frame is not available many of them fails to yield good result. The problem becomes more difficult when the video sequences suffer from uneven lightening and illumination variation. Cavallaro et.al.[2] have proposed a color edge based detection scheme for object detection. Specifically the color edge detection scheme has been applied to the

P.V. Krishna, M.R. Babu, and E. Ariwa (Eds.): ObCom 2011, Part II, CCIS 270, pp. 494–502, 2012.
© Springer-Verlag Berlin Heidelberg 2012

difference between the current and a reference image. This scheme is claimed to be robust under illumination variation. Jiglan Li[3] has proposed a novel background subtraction method for detecting foreground objects in a dynamic scene based upon the histogram distribution. Lu wang et al.[4] have proposed a new method that consistently performs well under different illumination conditions, including indoor, outdoor, sunny, rainy and dim cases. This method uses three thresholds to accurately classify pixels as foreground or background. These thresholds are adaptively determined by considering the distributions of differences between the input and background images and are used to generate three boundary set that represents the boundaries of the moving objects. Ivanov et al.[6] have proposed a new method of fast background subtraction based upon disparity verification that is invariant to run-time changes in illumination. The algorithm is easily implemented in real-time on conventional hardware because no disparity search is performed at run time. This method uses two or more cameras, which requires the off-line construction of disparity fields mapping the primary background image to each of the additional difference background image by assuming the background is fixed. Segmentation is performed at run time by checking color intensity values at corresponding pixels. With more than two cameras, the method gives more robust segmentation and also the occlusion shadows are eliminated. Kim et al. [7] have proposed an image segmentation method for separating moving objects from the background in image sequences. The method utilizes the spatio-temporal information for localization of moving objects in the image sequence by taking two consecutive image frames in the temporal direction and then comparing the two variance estimates to get the change detection mask which indicates moving areas and nonmoving areas. Deng et al.[8] have proposed a method for unsupervised segmentation of color-texture regions in images and videos. This method shows the robustness of the JSEG algorithm on real images and video. The method consists of two independent steps: color quantization and spatial segmentation. Trucco et al.[9] have given a survey on video tracking, the problem of following moving targets automatically over a video sequence. Xiaofeng et al.[5] proposed a novel background subtraction method for moving objects detection based on three frames differencing. Although they dealt with both slow and fast moving object detection under illumination variation, they convert the color video to gray level image sequences and then applied their technique. Since the algorithm used gray level video sequences hence it lost the color information present in the video, which otherwise could results in better segmentation results.

In this paper, an algorithm has been devised to detect moving objects in a video sequence in outdoor scene. The problem is addressed when the reference frame is not available and the motion of the object is fast or slow enough to be missed by temporal segmentation. An efficient three frame differencing method is proposed, which takes care of all type of cases irrespective of the availability of reference frame and irrespective of the speed of the moving object. It could be seen that at improper lightening and illumination variation condition, the proposed spatio-temporal framework based three frame differencing method gives very good results.

The rest of the paper is organized as follows:

Section-2 describes the overview of the Xiaofeng method. Proposed spatio-temporal framework has been discussed in section-3 and section-4 illustrates the experimental results. The paper ends with a conclusion in section-5.

2   Overview of the Xiaofeng Method[5]

This algorithm finds the background subtraction result and then determines the three frame difference result and thereafter fuses them together in a deterministic framework. The overview of the algorithm is shown in Figure-1. It first converts the color video sequences to gray level sequence by the following transform

$$f(x, y) = 0.299f(x, y, z)_R + 0.587f(x, y, z)_G + 0.144f(x, y, z)_B \qquad (1)$$

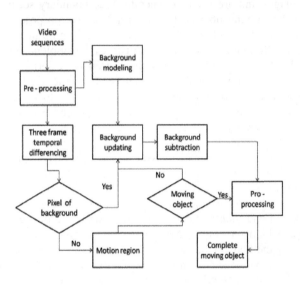

Fig. 1. Flowchart of the Xiaofeng algorithm

The background is then modeled as Gaussian distributed and is subsequently updated using three frame differencing result. The algorithm used is given below.

1. Read three consecutive frames, say $f_{k-1}(i, j)$, $f_k(i, j)$ and $f_{k+1}(i, j)$.
2. Get the gray scale difference between the two consecutive images,
$$IZ_{k,k-1} = |I_{k-1}(i, j) - I_k(i, j)|$$
$$IZ_{k+1,k} = |I_k(i, j) - I_{k+1}(i, j)| \qquad (2)$$
3. If $IZ_{k,k-1}$ and $IZ_{k+1,k} < Th + (1/N\sum|I_k(i, j) - I_{k+1}(i, j)|)$
$$\text{then } B(i, j) = I_{k+1}(i, j)$$
$$\text{else } M(i, j) = I_{k+1}(i, j) \qquad (3)$$

where $B(i,j)$ is the background pixel and $M(i,j)$ is the foreground pixel. The threshold 'Th' is chosen manually and the term $(1/N\sum|I_k(i, j) - I_{k+1}(i, j)|)$ is used to make the threshold adaptive to any slight variation of illumination. The object regions in video sequences can be obtained by thresholding the absolute differences between the pixels of background image $B(i, j)$ and video image $I_k(i, j)$.
$$\Delta I_k(i, j) = |I_k(i, j) - B(i, j)|$$

$$DB_k(i, j) = \begin{cases} 1 & if \quad \Delta I_k(i, j) / B(i, j) \ge Th' \\ 0 & otherwise \end{cases} \qquad (4)$$

where, Th' is the threshold to binarize the detected region and $DB_k(i, j)$ is the binary image. The moving object can be detected by merging the motion regions obtained from the equations (3) and (4) by the following equation

$$\mathrm{Re}_k(i, j) = \begin{cases} 255 & if \quad DB_k(i, j) \cup M(i, j) = 1 \\ 0 & otherwise \end{cases} \qquad (5)$$

where $Re_k(i,j)$ is the object region extracted.

3   Proposed Spatio-Temporal Framework

Detection of a moving object in a video can be done by temporal segmentation methods. Many existing work explain about the methodologies. Although it works up to some extent but, fails to detect exact moving area in a scene. This is because of the fact that, the temporal difference can detect the relatively changed information in successive frames. If the object is moving very fast then, up to some extent it can yield good results but, if the object is moving with a slow speed, then, the temporal segmentation methods result in cavities inside the object body. Many such cases have been solved by the use of morphological operations like erosion and dilation. Such operations are basically supervised operations. Thus, each time the new object enters into the scene, the morphological filter parameters need new assignments. Morphological filtering some times result in larger or smaller object size than the actual size of the object, which unnecessarily add to misclassification error. To make this more effective and robust, we have proposed a spatio-temporal framework based method, which takes care of the object shape, size as well as the cavities inside the object body.

In this paper we have first constructed a crude moving region by the help of the inter-plane similarity matrix. This gives the idea of the moving region in the scene. Then, a moving edge estimate for the same sequence is computed using Canny's edge detector. This gives the exact shape of the object to be detected. These two results are then fused together by a simple logical operator to yield the object of interest. The overview of the proposed algorithm is shown in Figure-2.

Here, we proposed a three plane similarity approach, which takes care of the spatial information, as well as temporal information to decide whether a pixel belongs to object class or background class.

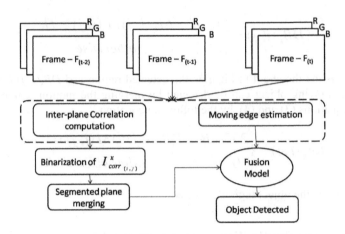

Fig. 2. Overview of the proposed algorithm

Initially, the video sequences are extracted from the video. Each video sequence is a color image frame, which contains color information. Here, we have used the RGB color model. Thus, each video sequence is then splitted to different color planes, called Red plane, Green plane and Blue plane, notated as P_{red}, P_{green}, P_{blue}. Three consecutive video sequences are taken and the R, G and B planes are then extracted. The three consecutive X (X could be R, G or B) planes are considered to compute the inter-plane similarity $I^X_{corr(i,j)}$, using the inter plane correlation computing functions which is given by

$$I^x_{corr_{(i,j)}} = \frac{\sum\limits_{allm,n} \left(\mu^X_{(i,j)}-C^X_{(m,n)}\right)_{f_{t-2}} \left(\mu^X_{(i,j)}-C^X_{(m,n)}\right)_{f_{t-1}} \left(\mu^X_{(i,j)}-C^X_{(m,n)}\right)_{f_t}}{\sqrt{\sum\limits_{m,n}\left(\mu^X_{(i,j)}-C^X_{(m,n)}\right)^2_{f_{t-2}} \sum\limits_{m,n}\left(\mu^X_{(i,j)}-C^X_{(m,n)}\right)^2_{f_{t-1}} \sum\limits_{m,n}\left(\mu^X_{(i,j)}-C^X_{(m,n)}\right)^2_{f_t}}} \qquad (6)$$

where, $\mu^X_{(i,j)}$, is the mean intensity value of (mxn) window in the X-plane. $C^X_{(m,n)}$ is the intensity value of the pixel in the X-plane. After computation of the $I^X_{corr(i,j)}$ values a matrix of dimension equal to the dimension of the image is constructed called I_{corr} . The values of elements of I_{corr} generally vary from 0 to 1. Less is the value less is the correlation between consecutive planes and hence, more is the probability that the pixel belongs to object class. Higher is the value, more is the temporal similarity and hence, less is the probability that the pixel belongs to object class. Thus, a threshold (T_{cor}) for the correlation is chosen in such a way that below which it corresponds to the object class and above which it corresponds to the background. The selection of such a threshold basically depends upon the amount of overall illumination variation and the change in overall intensity between the three consecutive frames. In this paper, we have selected this threshold manually by trial and error basis. Thus the result obtained by this can be given as

$$F_{CDM}(i, j) = \begin{cases} foreground & if \quad I_{corr(i,j)} \le T_{cor} \\ background & otherwise \end{cases} \tag{7}$$

The result obtained here is a crude result which contains the expected foreground region and not the exact region. In order to get the exact region the moving edge is determined. Canny's edge detector is used to get the edge information in each of the consecutive video sequences. The results are then further improvised by the fusion of the obtained object area along with the moving edge image which gives a better view of the object boundary, to give a far better result of foreground region under illumination variation condition. The algorithm is as follows

1. Take the color video sequence and extract the three color planes
2. Canny's edge detector is used to get the static as well as moving edge pixels. These moving edge pixels are used to construct the contour of the object, P_{cdme}. Thus the region inside the contour is the foreground and outside the contour is the background

The results obtained from the first and second steps are now fused by the following method to obtain the final foreground region.

If $P_{cdme}(i,j) \in C_{obj}$ and $F_{cdm}(i,j) \in C_{obj}$ then $pixel_{(i,j)} \in Object$
Else
    If $P_{cdme}(i,j) \in C_{obj}$ and $F_{cdm}(i,j) \in C_{back}$ then $pixel_{(i,j)} \in Object$
    Else
        If $P_{cdme}(i,j) \in C_{back}$ and $F_{cdm}(i,j) \in C_{obj}$ then $pixel_{(i,j)} \in Background$
        Else
            If $P_{cdme}(i,j) \in C_{back}$ and $F_{cdm}(i,j) \in C_{back}$ then $pixel_{(i,j)} \in Background$

where C_{obj} is the object class and C_{back} is the background class. $pixel_{(i,j)}$ is the corresponding pixel under consideration. The final foreground obtained is then combined with the original image sequence to get the video object plane (VOP).

4   Experimental Results

The proposed method has been tested in different situations. In particular, the sequences acquired in two different outdoor contexts are: walk video, where a man is moving slowly in the scene; hand video, which has been taken outside of a room with the wall as background. The experiments were performed on a dual core system with 3GHz processor speed and with a DRAM of capacity 2GB. The processing time is strictly dependent on the quality of moving points and on the image dimension which is 640x480. Although the window size depends upon the object shape and extent of illumination variation, in our experiment and simulations we have taken the window size to be 5X5, as it gives very good result, in accordance to the time complexity and accuracy. The thresholds used in all the algorithms are chosen manually. In case of the two videos shown here, the different threshold selected by trial and error basis is given in Table-1.

Table 1.

Video	*Th*	*Th'*	*Tcor*
Walk	45	70	0.23
Hand	28	56	0.18

The Figure-3(a) show the original sequences of walk video. Figure-3(b) and Figure- 3(c) show the VOP resulted by the Xiaofeng method and our proposed method respectively. It can be seen that some silhouette present in the result of Xiaofeng method where as our proposed method gives far better result. Similar kind of observation is being made from Figure-4, which shows the hand video sequence. The resultant image shown in Figure-4(c) is quite better than the images obtained by Xiaofeng method which is shown in Figure-4(b). The table-2 shows the percentage of misclassification error in case of Xiaofeng method and our proposed method. Here, it is clearly observed that our proposed method yields very good result. Our proposed method yields such a better result as compared to Xiofeng method because of the spatio-temporal framework which computes the inter-plane correlation, use of color information and use of moving edge information between the three consecutive video sequences. The percentage of misclassification error was calculated by comparing the segmented video frames obtained with their corresponding manually constructed ground truth sequences with the help of GIMP software. This was done only for a comparison and analysis purpose. The algorithm was tested with different video sequences. Here we have provided two video results.

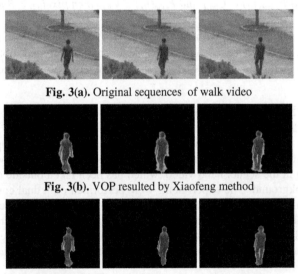

Fig. 3(a). Original sequences of walk video

Fig. 3(b). VOP resulted by Xiaofeng method

Fig. 3(c). VOP resulted by our proposed method

Fig. 4(a). Original sequences of hand video

Fig. 4(b). VOP resulted by Xiaofeng method

Fig. 4(c). VOP resulted by our proposed method

The results contain three sequences where as the Table-2 contains the data for four frames.

Table 2. Computation of misclassification error

Video	Frame No.	PME Xiofeng Method	PME Proposed Method
walk	532	7.16821	1.88145
	534	7.89876	1.95763
	536	6.75216	1.87342
	538	8.77261	2.01923
hand	629	10.97665	3.81768
	630	09.84132	3.98129
	631	10.99876	2.79981
	632	10.83243	3.80278

5   Conclusion

In this paper, the problem of moving object detection under illumination variation has been addressed. The Xiaofeng method can be used to deal with the slight illumination variation and detection of slow as well as fast moving object. Although it yields good result but the silhouettes present around the object. Thus the proposed method is used to detect the object perfectly. The inter-plane correlation is used to tackle the problem of illumination variation. The algorithm can further be modified to tackle the stop and go motion detection, shadow elimination problems. The thresholds used are all chosen manually which can be made adaptive to the video sequence to make the algorithm more efficient in different environment and situations.

References

1. Elhabian, S.Y., El-Sayed, K.M., Ahmed, S.H.: Moving Object Detection in Spatial Domain using Background Removal Techniques State of Art. Recent Patents on Computer Science 1(1), 32–54 (2008)
2. Cavallaro, Ebrahimi, T.: Change Detection based on Color Edges. In: IEEE International Symposium on Circuits and Systems ISCAS 2001, vol. 2, pp. 141–144 (2001)
3. Li, J.: Moving Object Segmentation Based on Histogram for Video Surveillance. Journal of Modern Applied Science 3(11) (November 2009)
4. Wang, L., Yung, N.H.C.: Extraction of moving objects from their background based on multiple adaptive thresholds and boundary evaluation. IEEE Tran. on Intelligent Transportation System 11(1), 40–51 (2010)
5. Lian, X., Zhang, T., Liu, Z.: A Novel Method on Moving Objects Detection Based on Background Subtraction and Three Frames Differencing. In: Proc. of IEEE International Conference on Measuring Technology and Mechatronics Automation, pp. 252–256 (2010)
6. Ivanov, Y., Bobick, A., Liu, J.: Fast Lighting Independent Background Subtraction. In: Proc. IEEE Workshop on Visual Survillance, Bombay, India, pp. 49–55 (January 1998)
7. Kim, M., Choi, J., Kim, D., Lee, H.: A VOP Generation Tool: Automatic Segmentation of Moving Objects in Image Sequences based on Spatio-Temporal information. IEEE Transaction on Circuits and Systems for Video Technology 9(8), 1216–1226 (1999)
8. Deng, Y., Manjunath, B.S.: Unsupervised Segmentation of Color-Texture Regions in Images and Video. IEEE Transactions on Pattern Analysis And Machine Intelligence 23, 800–810 (2001)
9. Trucco, E., Plakas, K.: Video Tracking: A Concise Survey. IEEE Journal of Oceanic Engineering 31(2), 520–529 (2006)
10. Babacan, S.D., Pappas, T.N.: Spatiotemporal Algorithm for Background Subtraction. In: Proc. of IEEE International Conf. on Acoustics, Speech, and Signal Processing, ICASSP 2007, Hawaii, USA, pp. 1065–1068 (April 2007)

Two New Approaches of Independent Component Analysis

V. Salai Selvam[1], S. Shenbagadevi[2], V. Padhma[1], D. Sujatha[1], and R. Sharmila[1]

[1] Sriram Engineering College, Thiruvallur, Tamil Nadu, India
[2] Anna University, Chennai, Tamil Nadu, India
vsalaiselvam@yahoo.com, s_s_devi@annauniv.edu,
padhmavasugi@gmail.com,
{sujathad79,sharmilar96}@yahoo.in

Abstract. In many practical applications or experiments the signals of interest are often recorded at a sampling rate much higher than the required Nyquist rate (twice the signal bandwidth of interest), resulting redundant and irrelevant signal information in the data. This redundant and irrelevant signal information causes the ICA process to "concede" some source components and to consume more processing time and memory. The methods proposed overcome these problems. The performances of the proposed methods are first evaluated using the inference-to-signal ratios (ISRs) and the correlations (CRs) between the simulated source signals and their estimates obtained by the proposed methods and the direct application of ICA and the speed of convergence (SOC) of the proposed methods and the direct application of ICA. Then the methods are tested using real time scalp EEG records as well.

Keywords: Modified Wavelet ICA, Wavelet Transform, Resample ICA, EEG.

1 Introduction

The Independent Component Analysis (ICA) is a method of separating (independent) sources from their (linear) mixtures [1]. Several efficient algorithms [2]-[4] have been proposed to successfully implement the process of ICA to separate the sources from their mixtures. Any ICA algorithm generally makes the following assumptions [2]: (i) the sources are statistically independent and (ii) the number of sources is less than or equal to the number of independent observations of their mixture. Then the algorithm decorrelates the (mixed) signal values to find the sources based on some measure of statistical independence such as mutual information, differential entropy and higher-order cumulants [3]. In many practical situations signals (e.g., biological signals such as EEG and ECG) are often acquired at sampling rates much higher that their Nyquist rates [5] (over-sampled) for a better visual presentation of the signal and the features such as spectra extracted from it though the bandwidth of interest is often very small. However, over-sampling results in redundant and irrelevant signal information. The redundant and irrelevant information in the over-sampled data affect the end results of the ICA process by "conceding" some source components under the identity of

P.V. Krishna, M.R. Babu, and E. Ariwa (Eds.): ObCom 2011, Part II, CCIS 270, pp. 503–513, 2012.

artifacts. The presence of redundant and irrelevant information also requires more processing time and memory during the ICA process. A simple filtering process, due to its inherent property, might eliminate the signal information less correlated to the desired signal information to some extent but it does not remove the redundant information. This paper proposes two methods to solve the addressed problems.

2   Methods

Two methods namely the **Resample-ICA** (RICA) and the **Modified Wavelet-ICA** (MwICA) are presented in the following sections. In both methods, the Second Order Blind Identification with Robust Orthogonalization (SOBI-RO) ICA algorithm [4] is used as this is the most powerful ICA algorithm among many popular ICA algorithms [3].

2.1   First Method: Resample-Independent Component Analysis (RICA)

In RICA the sampling rate of the (over-sampled) mixed signals is changed to just twice the signal bandwidth (of interest) thereby reducing the redundant and irrelevant information and hence speeding up the process of ICA. Fig. 1 shows the block diagram representation of the first method proposed. In the process of changing the sampling rate by a rational factor, I/D, where I and D are integers, the sampling rate of the signal is first increased by an integer factor, I by inserting zeros, then the signal is lowpass-filtered and finally the sampling rate of the filtered signal is reduced by an integer factor, D by discarding samples [5]. The frequency response of the lowpass filter is given in [5]. A T_A-second epoch of a signal sampled at a rate, f_s Hz (i.e., samples per second) will be having $N_p = T_A f_s$ samples (data points). If the signal is resampled by a rational factor, I/D to have a new sampling rate of $f_s' = (I/D)f_s$ Hz (samples per second), then there will be $N_p' = T_A f_s' = T_A (I/D)f_s = (I/D)N_p$ samples (data points). If $f_s' < f_s$, then $N_p' < N_p$ since the signal duration is the same, T_A seconds. If the signal's bandwidth (of interest) is B, then the values of I and D are chosen such that f_s' is as close as possible to $2B$.

2.2   Second Method: Modified Wavelet Independent Component Analysis (MwICA) [6]

The Wavelet Transform (WT) is a multiresolution tool to decompose a signal into its subbands [7] whereas the Independent Component Analysis (ICA) is a tool to separate source signals from their linear mixtures [1]. The common feature between these two techniques is the process of decorrelation. The effective combination of these two most popular signal processing techniques has recently attracted the researchers all over the world [8]-[10]. One such popular combination is known as the Wavelet-Independent Component Analysis (wICA) [8]. In this paper a new approach to an effective combination of these two popular techniques, named as Modified Wavelet-Independent Component Analysis (MwICA), which is a modified version of the wavelet-ICA (wICA) method presented in [9] and [10], has been proposed.

The Continuous Wavelet Transform (CWT), its properties and limitations are well discussed in [7] [11]-[15]. The discrete of version of CWT, known as the Discrete Wavelet Transform (DWT) and its practical implementation (decomposition and reconstruction) using iterated filter banks are available in [7] [11][12]. In this figure H (H') and G (G') represent the lowpass and highpass decomposition (reconstruction) filters and the down (up) arrow represents the process of downsampling (upsampling) by 2. The input signal is convolved with the filters G and H. Then the signal is shifted to the left by one data point and the convolution process of the resulting signal with the filters G and H is repeated. This process of shifting and convolving is repeated until the entire signal is covered [11]. The output of the highpass section is called the detail coefficients representing the finer details in the signal and the output of the lowpass section is called the approximation coefficients representing the coarse approximation of the signal [13]. The process is known as the multiresolution decomposition (reconstruction) [7]. After every level of decomposition the signal bandwidth is halved beginning with a bandwidth of [0 to $f_s/2$] where f_s is the sampling rate of the signal [14] and the number of data point is also approximately halved [15]. Thus the wavelet decomposition level, L is chosen such that the bandwidth of the Lth approximation level is as close to the signal's bandwidth of interest, B as possible i.e., $f_s/2^{(L+1)} \approx B$. The unique feature of the WT, which the decimation cannot cope with, is its (energy) compactness [7]. Though the (energy) compactness is the feature of any transform [16], the WT provides an opportunity to go for the best possible (energy) compactness through a proper selection from several choices of wavelets [13]. The (energy) compactness of the transform means the concentration of as much signal energy (information) in as few coefficients as possible [7] [16]. This property of the WT is utilized to reduce the number of data points in the oversampled mixed signals prior to the ICA process thereby improving the process of decorrelation by the ICA in the source separation task. Fig. 2 (a) to (d) depict the entire process of MwICA.

3   Materials

The proposed methods are first tested with a simulated data set. The simulation of data set is done according to [17] with some modification. The desired source signals, $s_i(n)$, $i=1, 2, 3,..., N$, are generated as a sum of sinusoids using Equation (1).

$$s_i(n) = \sum_{k=1}^{N_s} A_k \sin\left(\frac{2\pi f_k n}{f_s}\right), \quad \begin{matrix} i = 1, 2, 3, \cdots, N \\ n = 0, 1, 2, \cdots, N_p \end{matrix} \tag{1}$$

where N_s is the number of sinusoids, A_k and f_k is the amplitude and frequency of kth sinusoid and N_p is the number of samples in each trial of $s_i(n)$. The M mixtures, $x_j(n)$ for $j=1, 2, ..., M$, of these N source signals, $s_i(n)$ for $i=1, 2, 3,..., N$, are obtained using Equation (2).

$$x_j(n) = \sum_{i=1}^{N} a_{ji} s_i(n), \quad \begin{matrix} j = 1, 2, 3, \cdots, M \\ n = 0, 1, 2, \cdots, N_p \end{matrix} \quad \& \quad X = AS \tag{2}$$

where $X=[x_1(n),\ x_2(n),\ x_3(n),\ ...,\ x_M(n)]^T$ is the mixed signal matrix, $A=[a_{ji}]$ is the uniform random mixing matrix and $S=[s_1(n),\ s_2(n),\ s_3(n),\ ...,\ s_N(n)]^T$ is the source signal matrix. A source signal in a desired frequency band is simulated by setting f_1 and f_{Ns} in Equation (2) equal to lower and upper bounds of the desired frequency band. The simulated source signals and mixed signals will resemble the human EEG activities if the frequencies and amplitudes of the sinusoids are selected in the desired bands of EEG. The MATLAB is used for the simulation of data, the implementation of the proposed methods and the evaluation of the performances of the proposed methods. Then the methods are tested using real time scalp EEG records.

4   Result and Discussion

Six different cases of simulations are considered for the demonstration of the proposed methods. The performances of the proposed methods are measured by the inference-to-signal ratios (ISRs) and the correlations (CRs) between the original simulated source signals and their estimates obtained by the proposed methods and the direct application of ICA algorithm, and the speed of convergence (SOC) of the ICA algorithm i.e., the time taken for the ICA algorithm to estimate the demixing matrix (i.e., the process of decorrelation). This time is evaluated using the MATLAB functions *tic* and *toc*. The ISR and CR between the ith source signal, S_i and its estimate, S_i' is computed using Equation (3) and (4), respectively [18]. In Equation (4), m_i' and m_i are the mean values of S_i' and S_i, respectively and σ_i' and σ_i are the standard deviations of S_i' and S_i, respectively.

$$ISR = 20\log_{10}\left[\frac{\left\|S_i' - S_i\right\|}{\left\|S_i\right\|}\right] \tag{3}$$

$$CR = \frac{E\left\{S_i'S_i\right\} - m_i'm_i}{\sigma_i'\sigma_i} \tag{4}$$

In Case 1, two-second epochs of five (linear) mixtures of five source signals, S_i, $i=1$, 2, 3, 4, and 5 in three frequency bands, [1-2] Hz, [2-3] Hz, [3-4] Hz, [4-5] Hz and [5-6] Hz, respectively at f_s=256 Hz are generated. Thus B is approximately 8 Hz. Here, $I=1$ and $D=16$ such that $f_s'=(I/D)f_s=2B$ i.e., 16 Hz and $L=4$ such that $[0-(f_s/2)/2^L]=[0-B]$ i.e., [0-8] Hz. In Case 2, two-second epochs of ten (linear) mixtures of ten source signals, S_i, $i=1, 2,...,$ and 10 in ten frequency bands, [1-2] Hz, [2-3] Hz, [3-4] Hz, [4-5] Hz, [5-6] Hz, [6-7] Hz, [7-8] Hz, [8-9] Hz, [9-10] Hz and [10-11] Hz, respectively at f_s=256 Hz are generated. Thus B is only [1-12] Hz or approximately 16 Hz. Here, $I=1$ and $D=8$ such that $f_s'=(I/D)f_s=2B$ i.e., 32 Hz and $L=3$ such that $[0-(f_s/2)/2^L]=[0-B]$ i.e., [0-16] Hz. In Case 3, two-second epochs of 30 (linear) mixtures of 30 source signals, S_i, $i=1, 2,...,$ and 30 in thirty frequency bands, from 1 Hz to 31

Hz in steps of 1 Hz, respectively at f_s=256 Hz are generated. Thus B is only [1-31] Hz or approximately 32 Hz. Here, I=1 and D=4 such that $f_s'=(I/D)f_s=2B$ i.e., 64 Hz and L=2 such that $[0-(f_s/2)/2^L]=[0-B]$ i.e., [0-32] Hz. Case 4, 5 and 6 are the Cases 1, 2, and 3 respectively with the sampling rate doubled i.e., f_s=512 Hz. Grouping the cases based on the sampling rate, f_s and the number of sources, we have the following groups: {Case 1, Case 2, Case 3} with f_s=256 Hz, {Case 4, Case 5, Case 6} with f_s=512 Hz, {Case 1, Case 4} with 5 sources, {Case 2, Case 5} with 10 sources and {Case 3, Case 6} with 30 sources. Table 1 and 2 summarize the mean and variances of ISR for these groups. Table 3 summarizes the SOC in seconds for these six cases. From these tables, it is evident that the oversampling not only results in the poor performance of the source separation process (low ISRs and CRs in the direct application of ICA algorithm) by the ICA but also increases the time consumption (higher SOCs in the direct application of ICA algorithm) and the process of resampling and wavelet decomposition prior to the application of ICA improves the process of decorrelation in the ICA-based source separation task. The results show that the RICA and the MwICA outperform the plain ICA in the process of source separation especially when the sources are closer in frequency. The bold numbers in Tables indicate lowest values. Finally the three methods just discussed are applied to decompose a 16-channel bipolar montage EEG signal (corrupted by muscular and ECG artifacts) to show that the MwICA outperforms both the RICA and plain ICA in the source-separation process. The method, MwICA is very effective in separating Gaussian and non-Gaussian artifacts. The results of ICA for the real-time EEG signals are shown in Fig.3 (a) to (j). It can be easily seen how the MwICA outperforms in eliminating muscular and ECG artifacts. The cerebral components recovered by MwICA are much *purer* than those by other two methods.

Table 1. Mean and variance of ISR

		RICA	MwICA	ICA
Mean (dB)	f_s=256 Hz	-17.242	**-17.43**	-13.39
	f_s=512 Hz	**-16.337**	-15.54	-10.939
Variance (dB)	f_s=256 Hz	73.029	**52.322**	112.67
	f_s=512 Hz	**35.736**	38.558	79.721

Table 2. Mean and variance of ISR

		RICA	MwICA	ICA
Mean (dB)	5 Sources	**-20.9473**	-19.3203	-17.5254
	10 Sources	-17.3147	**-17.4287**	-12.5507
	30 Sources	-14.8171	**-14.8396**	-9.0691
Variance (dB)	5 Sources	60.0029	**41.9640**	185.6181
	10 Sources	50.5217	**30.8913**	92.6506
	30 Sources	46.3745	47.9290	**46.2993**

Table 3. SOC in seconds for the six cases

	Case 1	Case 2	Case 3	Case 4	Case 5	Case 6
RICA	**0.0060**	**0.02336**	**0.31967**	0.006	0.0226	**0.3156**
MwICA	**0.0060**	0.02566	0.32312	**0.0059**	**0.0221**	0.31929
DICA	0.0083	0.02914	0.51808	0.011	0.0375	0.75941

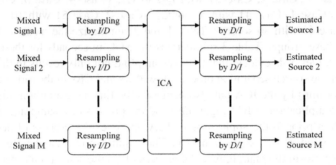

Fig. 1. First Method: Use of resampling technique for the application ICA of over-sampled signals

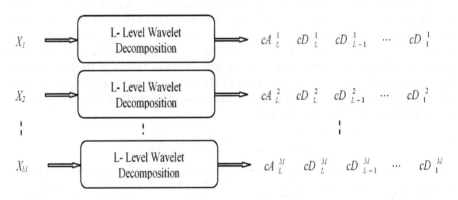

Fig. 2(a). L-level wavelet decomposition of mixed signals where X_i stands for (T_A-second epoch of) ith (observation of) mixture of N (=M) source signals, S_k, $k=1, 2,...,N$, having bandwidth of $[0-B]$ Hz and oversampled at $f_s>2B$ Hz and cA^i_j (cD^i_j) stands for jth level approximation (detail) coefficients of ith mixture. L is chosen such that $f_s/2^{L+1} \approx 2B$.

$$\begin{bmatrix} cD^1_L & cD^1_{L-1} & \cdots & cD^1_1 \\ cD^2_L & cD^2_{L-1} & \cdots & cD^2_1 \\ \vdots & \vdots & \vdots & \vdots \\ cD^M_L & cD^M_{L-1} & \cdots & cD^M_1 \end{bmatrix} \xrightarrow{\begin{array}{c}\text{Demixing}\\\text{by}\\W\end{array}} \begin{bmatrix} dcD^1_L & dcD^1_{L-1} & \cdots & dcD^1_1 \\ dcD^2_L & dcD^2_{L-1} & \cdots & dcD^2_1 \\ \vdots & \vdots & \vdots & \vdots \\ dcD^M_L & dcD^M_{L-1} & \cdots & dcD^M_1 \end{bmatrix}$$

Fig. 2(d). Demixing of detail coefficients of all mixtures where cD^i_j stands for jth level detail coefficients of ith mixture and dcD^i_j for jth level detail coefficients of ith estimated signal, S'_i. This step is only optional if any finer details are desired to be added to estimated source signals, S'_i. In Fig. 2 (c), Z^i_j is to replaced with corresponding dcD^i_j.

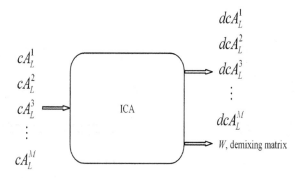

Fig. 2(b). ICA of Lth level approximation coefficients from all mixtures where cA^i_j stands for jth level approximation coefficients of ith mixture, dcA^i_j for jth level approximation coefficients of ith estimated source signal and W for $M{\times}M$ ($=N{\times}N$) estimated demixing matrix. The demixing matrix, W may be used to demix the detail coefficients as shown in Fig. 2 (d) to add finer details to estimated source signals.

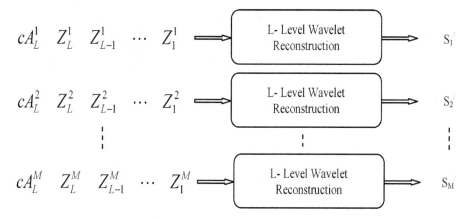

Fig. 2 (c). L-level wavelet reconstruction using only Lth level approximation coefficients where cA^i_j stands for jth level approximation coefficients of ith estimated source signal, Z^i_j for zeros for jth level detail coefficients of ith estimated source signal and S'_i, $i=1,2,...,N$ ($=M$) for ith estimated source signal.

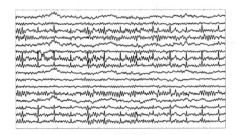

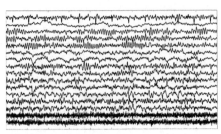

Fig. 3(a). Original 16-channel bipolar montage with (mild) muscular and (strong) ECG artifacts

Fig. 3(b). Estimated source components using direct application of (SOBI-RO) ICA

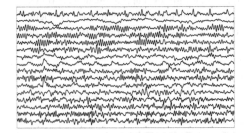

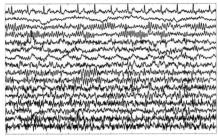

Fig. 3(c). Estimated source components using RICA

Fig. 3(d). Estimated source components using MwICA

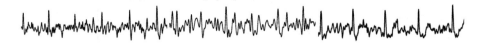

Fig. 3 (e). ECG artifact separated using direct application of ICA. ECG recovered by direct application of ICA does not well correlate with actual ECG recording.

Fig. 3 (f). ECG artifact separated using RICA. RICA oversmooths the ECG component.

Fig. 3 (g). ECG artifact separated using MwICA. ECG recovered by MwICA correlates well with actual ECG recording.

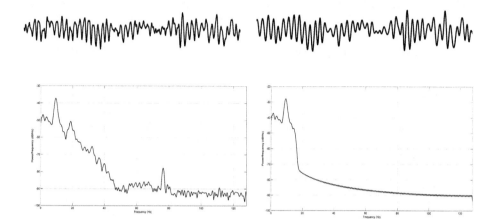

Fig. 3 (h). A source component (alpha + beta + muscular artifact) recovered by direct application of ICA (above) and its power spectrum (below)

Fig. 3 (i). The same component (alpha-oversmoothed) recovered by RICA (above) and its power spectrum (below)

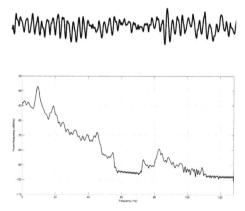

Fig. 3 (j). The same component (alpha + beta, artifact-smoothed) recovered by MwICA (above) and its power spectrum (below)

5   Future Development

Instead of wavelet decomposition, it will be more interesting to use wavelet packet decomposition since this has more precise control over the decomposition of the signal into frequency bands.

Acknowledgments. We would like to thank Dr. N. Kumaravel, Professor and Head, Department of Electronics and Communication Engineering, Anna University, Chennai, India – 600 025 for his consistent encouragement in all our research activities. We would like to thank the private clinics who provided us the required EEG data.

References

[1] Hyvarinen, A.: The fixed-point algorithm and maximum likelihood estimation for independent component analysis. Neural Process. Lett. 10, 1–5 (1999)

[2] Hyvarinen, A., Oja, E.: Independent component analysis: Algorithms and applications. Neural Networks 13, 411–430 (2000)

[3] Albera, L., Comon, P., Parra, L.C., Karfoul, A., Kachenoura, A., Senhadji, L.: ICA and biomedical applications. In: Comon, P., Jutten, C. (eds.) Handbook of Blind Source Separation, Independent Component Analysis and Applications, pp. 793–832. Academic Press, New York (2009)

[4] Belouchrani, A., Abed-Meraim, K., Cardoso, J.F., Moulines, E.: A blind source separation technique using second-order statistics. IEEE Trans. Signal Process 45, 434–444 (1997)

[5] Proakis, J.G., Manolakis, D.G.: Digital Signal Processing Principles, Algorithms, and Applications. Prentice Hall, New Delhi (2000)

[6] Selvam, V.S., Shenbagadevi, S.: Brain Tumor Detection Using Scalp EEG with Modified Wavelet-ICA and Multi Layer Feed Forward Neural Network. In: Proceedings of the 33rd Annual International Conference of the IEEE Engineering in Medicine and Biology Society, August 30 - September 3 (accepted, 2011)

[7] Stark, H.G.: Wavelets and Signal Processing An Application-Based Introduction. Springer, Berlin (2005)

[8] Azzerboni, B., Finocchio, G., Ipsale, M., La Foresta, F., Morabito, F.C.: A New Approach to Detection of Muscle Activation by Independent Component Analysis and Wavelet Transform. In: Marinaro, M., Tagliaferri, R. (eds.) WIRN 2002. LNCS, vol. 2486, pp. 109–116. Springer, Heidelberg (2002)

[9] Azzerboni, B., La Foresta, F., Mammone, N., Morabito, F.C.: A New Approach Based On Wavelet-ICA Algorithms for Fetal Electrocardiogram Extraction. In: Proceedings - European Symposium on Artificial Neural Networks (ESANN 2005), pp. 193–198 (2005)

[10] Taelman, J., Huffel, S.V., Spaepen, A.: Wavelet-Independent Component Analysis to remove Electrocardiography Contamination in surface Electromyography. In: Conf. Proc. IEEE Eng. Med. Biol. Soc., pp. 682–685 (2007)

[11] Quiroga, R.Q., Sakowitz, O.W., Basar, E., Schurmann, M.: Wavelet Transform in the analysis of the frequency composition of evoked potentials. Brain Research Protocols 8, 16–24 (2001)

[12] Vetterli, M., Herley, C.: Wavelets and Filter Banks: Theory and Design. IEEE Trans. Signal Process 40, 2207–2232 (1992)

[13] Misiti, M., Oppenheim, G., Poggi, J.M.: Wavelet Toolbox 4 User's Guide. The Mathorks Inc., Natick (2007)

[14] Costa, F.B., Silva, K.M., Dantas, K.M.C., Souza, B.A., Brito, N.S.D.: A Wavelet-Based Algorithm for Disturbances Detection using Oscillographic Data. In: IEEE Power and Energy Society General Meeting – Conversion and Delivery of Electrical Energy in the 21st Century, pp. 1–8 (2008)

[15] Unser, M., Blu, T.: Wavelet Theory Demystified. IEEE Trans. Signal Process 51, 470–483 (2003)
[16] Jain, A.K.: Fundamentals of Digital Image Processing. Prentice Hall, Englewood Cliffs (1989)
[17] Yeung, N., Bogacz, R., Holroyd, C.B., Cohen, J.D.: Detection of synchronized oscillations in the electroencephalogram: An evaluation of methods. Psychophysiology 41, 822–832 (2004)
[18] Vorobyov, S., Cichocki, A.: Blind noise reduction for multisensory signals using ICA and subspace filtering, with application to EEG analysis. Biol. Cybern. 86, 293–303 (2002)

GAB_CLIQDET: - A Diagnostics to Web Cancer (Web Link Spam) Based on Genetic Algorithm

S.K. Jayanthi[1,*] and S. Sasikala[2]

[1] Department of Computer Science,
Vellalar College for Women, Erode, India
[2] Department of Computer Science,
KSR College of Arts and Science, Tiruchengode, India
sasi_sss123@rediff.com

Abstract. Web spam significantly deteriorates the quality of search engine results. The web cancer refers to the taxonomy of variations in web contaminations. The way that how cancer has been treated inspired the thought to lead the research towards finding a solution to the spamdexing by approaching it in a different scenario. The motivation is based on the logical perspective of approaching the web spam problem as cancer caused to the internet, and the solution could be derived by formulating the algorithms for treating the web cancer based on notable oncology, radiology achievements in medicine. The algorithms could be classified into different levels such as benign, meta state treatments in cancer, compared with newly created link spam, link farm and cliques. This paper proposes an algorithm GAB_CLIQDET (Genetic Algorithm Based Cliques Detection) to detect the web spam inspired by cancer diagnostics. The diagnostics is based on various parameters implied from the cancer insights. This approach performs well as shown through experiments.

Keywords: Search engine. Link spam, Content spam, Cliques, HITS, Hub.

1 Introduction

Traditional information retrieval algorithms were developed for relatively small and coherent document collections such as newspaper articles or book catalogs in a library. Very little, if any, of the content in such systems could be described as "spam." In comparison to these collections, the Web is massive, changes more rapidly, and is spread over geographically distributed computers [1]. Distinguishing between desirable and undesirable content in such a system presents a significant challenge, as every day more people are using search engines more often. Search engine spamming, also known as spamdexing, encompasses malicious attempts to influence the outcome of ranking algorithms, for the purpose of getting an undeservedly high rank. Obtaining a higher rank is strongly correlated with traffic,

---

* Corresponding author.

P.V. Krishna, M.R. Babu, and E. Ariwa (Eds.): ObCom 2011, Part II, CCIS 270, pp. 514–523, 2012.
© Springer-Verlag Berlin Heidelberg 2012

and a higher rank often translates to more revenue. Thus, there is an economic incentive for Web site owners to invest on spamming search engines, instead of investing on improving their Web sites. This paper attempts to detect the link spam in websites with the GAB_CLIQDET, a procedure based on genetic algorithm.

1.1   Cancer and Spam

In link spam the properties of cancer such as invasion of affected cell in organs happens as invasion of link spam in WebPages and as a whole in websites. In traditional cancer diagnosis, pathologists manually examine biopsies to make diagnostic assessments. The assessments are largely based on visual interpretation of cell morphology and tissue distribution, lacking of quantitative measures. In link spam diagnosis the sample clique structure is examined and the corresponding site could be blacklisted. In link spam analysis, the visual interpretation of the website structure could be used (i.e.), a completely connected structure say clique, could be seen in this link spam affected sites. The simulated structure of a web crawl is offered in Fig. 3, Fig. 4 and Fig. 5, which resembles a Ideal website, resembling Normal cell Network (Fig. 3), Partially affected website like benign cancer cell network (Fig. 4) and Complete spam similar to meta state cancer cell network (Fig. 5). Therefore, they are subject to considerable inter-observer variability. Here in this paper an algorithm has been proposed examining web graph nodes to make diagnostic assessments in spamdexing.

1.2   Role of Genetic Algorithm

A genetic algorithm (GA) is a search heuristic that mimics the process of natural evolution. This heuristic is routinely used to generate useful solutions to optimization and search problems. This could be implied to foresee the spam occurrence in web. The reason why GA has been chosen for the link spam detection relies on the natural evolution behavior like selection, crossover and mutation could be repeated with different feature values of link in web.

1.3   Cliques in Websites

Clique cluster groups the set of nodes that are completely connected to each other. Specifically if it is added, connections between objects in the order of their distance from one another a cluster if formed when the objects forms a clique. A clique in a graph is a maximal complete subgraph of three or more nodes. These are nodes that are also adjacent to all of the members of the clique. The mathematical definition can be written as; Given a graph $G = (V, E)$ and an integer k, a clique is a subset U of V with $|U|$ with k such that every pair of vertices in U is joined by an edge. Then, it is called U a k-clique of the graph G. Some examples of cliques with four, five vertices are given in Fig. 1. Llink structure analysis is an important factor in ranking web pages. As a result, link spam is used frequently, and appropriate measures to deal with it are needed. The goal of the paper is to examine detect link spam.

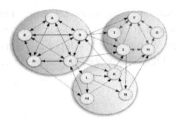

Fig. 1. Web cliques in link farm

2   Web Spam Clusters and Characteristics

The biological properties of the cancer network are seems to be similar to the link farm or cliques present in website. As it could be seen that the cancer originates at one place and spread in different adjacent organs (meta-state), the link spam origins at one website and tends to be spread over the internet with variety of techniques. This thought acts as a motivation for this paper. The properties of network both biological and internet nodes has been discussed in this section. The scientific community has recently seen a renaissance of graph theory especially in mathematics and physics thanks to theory breakthroughs in the works of [2] and [3], exponentially increasing computing power providing new tools for research and investigations. It is believed that graph theory will enable to detect differences between spam and natural networks.

2.1   Comparison of the Indegree and the Outdegree

It is defined the number of links pointing into and out of a web graph (or a subset, e.g. clusters) as indegree or outdegree distribution. Looking for sub graphs with a low outdegree distribution could be an attempt to detect a link farm.

2.2   Degree Distribution

The degree of a vertex is the same as the number of edges connected to this vertex. It is defined pk as a subset of the vertices with degree k of a network. Hence pk expresses the probability that a randomly chosen vertex of the network has a degree of k. If one draws histograms of the degree values of every vertex in a network, the resulting chart describes the degree distribution of the network. Spam networks are expected to show a different degree distribution than ideal webs.

2.3   Betweenness Centrality

A geodesic path is the shortest path (least edges) from one vertex to another. There is usually more than one geodesic path between two vertices. The betweenness centrality is a local value of a vertex. Per definition the betweenness centrality of a vertex i equal the number of geodesic paths running through i. The number of geodesic paths between two vertices i and j, C(ij) and the number of those geodesic paths between i and j, which run through a vertex k Ck(ij) determine the value of gk(ij) with gk(ij) = C(ij)/Ck(ij). The betweenness centrality BC of k is defined as the sum of gk(i,j) of all pairs of vertices with a geodesic path, BC=gk as mentioned in equation (1).

$$g_k = \sum_{i=j} gk(i,j) = \sum_{i=j} \frac{C_{k(i,j)}}{C(i,j)} \tag{1}$$

In cancer cells the correlation between the affected cells and normal cells deviate and betweenness centrality is low like benign state cancer, whereas in complete spam that resembles the metastate cancer, the centrality is high. It means, like invasion of cancer cells in other organs, the link exchanges create a tightly knitted network with different websites. This structure could be seen in pornographic websites.

2.4 Degree Correlations

The degree correlations describe the relations of vertices with focus on their degree, e.g. whether high degree vertices are more likely to connect to other high degree vertices or low degree ones. Spam-networks, which are determined to boost specific pages or sites, will show noticeable correlations similar to cancer cells and normal cells correlations.

2.5 Diameter and Shortest Path

The diameter of a graph equals the length of the shortest path between the two most distant vertices. The comparison of diameter values of giant components deserves special attention.

3   Related Literatures

Many studies on web spam are carried out in previous works. [5] Proposed a technique of information retrieval based on Markov models, this paper laid down the random selection of nodes for navigation thought for this paper. [6] Proposed a method of detecting link spam based on fuzzy classification. [7] Classified web spam into two categories, one is various techniques to raise the search result rankings, and another is hiding techniques to make the spam activities invisible to users. [8] introduced link bombs and explores its effects in internet. [9] took advantage of the fact that link spam tends to result in drastic changes of links in a short period and proposed using temporal information such as Inlink Growth Rate and Inlink Death Rate in detection of link spam. Clustering the spam is done through a clear means of examining the web structure and it is elaborated in the next part of the paper.

4   Extraction of Web Spam

In traditional cancer diagnosis, pathologists manually examine biopsies to make diagnostic assessments. The assessments are largely based on visual interpretation of cell morphology and tissue distribution, lacking of quantitative measures. Therefore, they are subject to considerable inter-observer variability. Here in this paper an algorithm has been proposed examining web graph nodes to make diagnostic assessments in spamdexing. The GAB_CLIDET algorithm performs the extraction of cliques form the web graph and the threshold value for the comparison may vary time to time based on the diversification process implied in the algorithm with genetic algorithm mutation and crossover. The algorithm has been listed here:

```
1. Pseudo code: CLIQUE_GA_PROCESS

   Input sub graph sequence formation
   Enumeration (Sub graph selection)
           Add new nodes randomly chosen from the graph
           Extraction of the clique; Choose randomly a
           position 1≤ R_POS ≥ N;
           for i=R_POS to N; if ni Belongs to the
           subgraph then either delete ni   or
           for j=i+1 to N; delete nj or if it belongs to
           the subgraph and nj is not connected  with nj
           for j=1 to i-1; delete nj or if it belongs to
           the subgraph and nj is not connected with nj
           for i=R_POS-1 downto 1; if ni   belongs to the
           subgraph then either delete ni   or
           for j=i-1 downto 1; delete ni or if it belongs
           to the subgraph and
           nj is not connected with n
   Clique_Manipulation
           Choose randomly a position 1≤ R_POS ≥ N;
           for j=R_POS to N;
           add nj  if it is connected with all the nodes
           of the subgraph (obtained so far)
           for j=1 to R_POS-1; add nj  if it is
           connected with all the nodes of the subgraph
           (obtained so far)
2. Pseudo code: GAB_CLIQDET
           begin
           x = 0
           initialize P(t)
           apply CLIQUE_GA_PREPROCESS to P(x)
           evaluate P(x); while (not termination-
           condition) do
           begin
            x = x + 1
            select P(x) from P(x - 1); apply
            diversification procedure to P(x)
            alter P(x) (via Mutation and crossover)
            apply CLIQUE_GA_PREPROCESS to P(x)
            evaluate P(x)
           end
           end
```

The working scenario has been depicted in Fig. 2. Maximal cliques are extracted from the sites inspected and it is also noticed that many of them are duplicated nodes which leads the user to wherever they start the navigational pattern of the website remains cyclic and the observations are listed as a table in Table 1. Results were simulated with GATree tool [10], an open source implementation of the Genetic Algorithm and enlisted in Fig. 6. Sample dataset is listed in Appendix A.

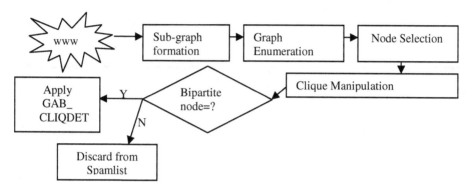

Fig. 2. Working method of the proposed system GAB_CLIQDET

5   Observations and Discussion

In order to evaluate the effectiveness of this proposed method, the results are compared with PageRank algorithm. The simulated result shows that the spam could easily be trapped with the GAB_CLIQDET (Fig. 3, Fig. 4, and Fig. 5). The Fig 6 show that the comparison between the precision of the [3] and GAB_CLIQDET, that this proposed method outperforms well than the former one. The Table 1 represents the taxonomy of the spam types present in the analyzed samples and it could be seen that the clique interchange of the domain implies maximum in marketing and sexually explicit sites. The porn sites interchange links to improve their visibility in the search results and that leads all the interconnected websites to be present at the top of the results. This resembles the metastate cancer in which the interconnected sites are also spam. All affected cells in metastate cancer should either be removed or to be treated. Likewise, all websites of link exchange are either to be discarded or it may be blacklisted. One more observation is that the same website doesn't retains at same rank for consistent period of the time and one more interesting thing is the website owners imply the cloaking mechanism also. Same content offered in different name. In Fig. 3 genuine website crawled with yellow layout and it represents genuine web pages and in Fig. 4, a partial spam with red color cross mark is detected with an utility whereas in Fig. 5, a complete spam is detected in which no crawl in webpages is done based on the GAB_CLIQDET.

Table 1. Spam classification of maximum cliques

Classification Type	*Sites*	*Ratio*
Non-Spam	70	24.05
Commercial Advertisements	93	31.96
Link Exchanges and Farms	5	1.71
Sexually Explicit	123	42.26
Total	**291**	**100%**

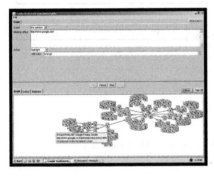

Fig. 3. Genuine Website   **Fig. 4.** Partial-spam Website

The Table 1 represents the taxonomy of the spam types present in the analyzed samples and it could be seen that the clique interchange of the domain implies maximum in marketing and sexually explicit sites. The porn sites interchange links to improve their visibility in the search results and that leads all the interconnected websites to be present at the top of the results. One more observation is that the same website doesn't retains at same rank for consistent period of the time and one more interesting thing is the website owners imply the cloaking mechanism also. Same content offered in different name. In Fig. 3 genuine website crawled with yellow layout and it represents genuine web pages and in Fig. 4, a partial spam with red color cross mark is detected with an utility whereas in Fig. 5, a complete spam is detected in which no crawl in webpages is done.

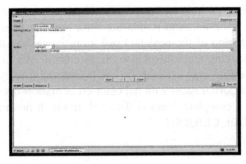

Fig. 5. Complete Spam

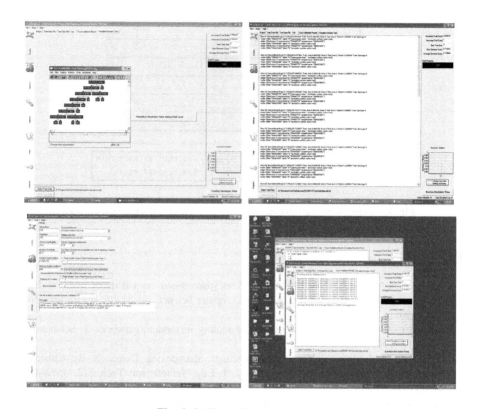

Fig. 6. GATree – Simulated results

6   Conclusion

The precision and recall of the results evaluated has been offered in Fig. 7 and the results of GAB_CLIQDET are compared with the algorithm KCPM [4]. The objective of this paper was to determine the implications that search engine spam possessed in Web sites. This paper proposes a novel strategy that can be used to filter the spam which has the link spam, farm and cliques, with the help of approaching the problem in cancer inspection perspective. For that the web graph has been created to study the topology of the web site to determine the occurrence of the spam. It is not necessary to consider how difficult a spamming technique could be almost all of them are designed to have the effect of manipulating the factors that are used, or believed to be used, by popular search engines in their ranking algorithms. As certain outgoing spam links are intentionally hidden by spammers, some of these pages would be able to bypass the earlier Algorithms. Hence, this is suggested to improve the efficiency in link spam detection by analyzing additional link farms based on some constraints as such motioned in the algorithm with GA based NLP strategy. One of the possible improvements is by integrating the weight of web page content relevancy into GAB_CLIQDET and formulating a collaborative constraint based filter.

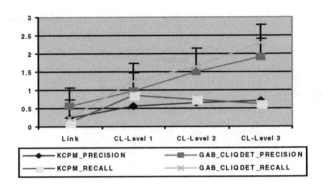

Fig. 7. Comparison of Precision and recall of GAB_CLIQDET and KCPM

References

1. Sasikala, S., Jayanthi, S.K.: Perceiving LinkSpam based on DBSpamClust. In: IEEE International Conference on Network and Computer Science, pp. 31–35. IEEE Press, New York (2011)
2. Barabási, A.-L., Albert, R.: Emergence of scaling in random networks. J. Science 286, 509–512 (1999)
3. Sasikala, S., Jayanthi, S.K.: Dblc_Spamclust: Spamdexing Detection By Clustering Clique-Attacks In Web Search Engines. I. J. Eng. Science and Tech. 272, 4572–4580 (2011)
4. Sasikala, S., Jayanthi, S.K.: Cliques-Attacks Detection in Web Search Engine for Spamdexing using K-Clique Percolation Technique. In: 3rd International Conference on Machine Learning and Computing, pp. 364–369. IEEE Press, New York (2011)
5. Sasikala, S., Balaji, S.: SIGNET: Web Information Retrieval with NE Disambiguation Based on HMM and CRF. In: 3rd International Conference on Machine Learning and Computing, pp. 438–443. IEEE Press, New York (2011)
6. Sasikala, S., Jayanthi, S.K.: Link Spam Detection based on Fuzzy C-Means Clustering, I. J. Next-Generation Networks 198, 1–10 (2010)
7. Gyongyi, Z., Garcia-Molina, H.: Web Spam Taxonomy. In: First Workshop on Adversarial Information Retrieval on the Web, pp. 39–47. Citeseer (2005)
8. Adali, S., Liu, T., Magdon-Ismail, M.: Optimal link bombs are uncoordinated. In: 1st International Workshop on Adversarial Information Retrieval on the Web, pp. 46–56. Citeseer (2005)
9. Wu, B., Davison, B.D.: Undue influence: Eliminating the impact of link plagiarism on web search rankings. In: Proceedings of the 21st Annual ACM Symposium on Applied Computing, Dijon, France, pp. 1099–1104 (2006)
10. Kalles, D., Papagelis, A.: http://www.gatree.com/wordpress/

Appendix A: Sample Dataset

@RELATION spam
@ATTRIBUTE Type {spam, normal}
@ATTRIBUTE PR real
@ATTRIBUTE inlink real
@ATTRIBUTE outlink real
@ATTRIBUTE flag {S, N}
@DATA
spam,1.00000,34,39, S
spam,1.00000,34,43, S
norma,l 0.00000,34,52,N
norma,l 0.00000,34,52,N
norma,l 0.00000,34,52,N
spam,1.00000,46,34,S
norma,l 0.00000,46,54,N
spam,1.00000,34,48,S
spam,1.00000,34,39,S
spam,1.00000,34,43,S
norma,l 0.00000,34,36,N
norma,l 0.00000,34,35,N
norma,l 0.00000,34,35,N
spam,0.75000,34,42,S

Grammar Checking System Using Rule Based Morphological Process for an Indian Language

Lata Bopche[1], Gauri Dhopavkar[1,2], and Manali Kshirsagar[1]

[1] Yeshwantrao Chavan College of Engineering, Nagpur, M.S., India
[2] Research Scholar, G.H. Raisoni College of Engineering, Nagpur, M.S., India
{gaurid.manoj,lata_bopche}@gmail.com,
manali_kshirsagar@yahoo.com

Abstract. This paper describes a novel method for "Hindi" grammar checking. This system utilizes a full-form lexicon for morphology analysis and rule-based systems. In this approach, we propose a system which uses a set of rules which is matched against the input "Hindi" sentence which has at least been POS tagged. This approach is similar to the statistics-based approach, but all the rules are developed manually in our approach.

Keywords: Stemmer, Hindi, WordNet, Morphological Analyzer, Rule based Grammar Checker.

1 Introduction

Grammar checking is one of the most widely used tools within natural language engineering applications. Most of the word processing systems available in the market incorporate spelling, grammar, and style-checking systems for English and other foreign languages. Morphological analyzer tool is used in grammar checking systems for analyzing text and POS tagging.

The morphological strength of Indian Languages warrants the use of thorough morphological analysis. It should be the first step towards any Indian language processing task. It means taking a word as input and providing the grammatical information about word. It provides information about a word's semantics and the syntactic role it plays in a sentence. It is essential for Hindi as Hindi has a rich system of inflectional morphology as like other Indo- Aryan family languages. There are basically three ways to implement a grammar checker.

Syntax-Based Checking, as described in [Jensen et al,1993]. In this approach, a text is completely parsed, i.e. the sentences are analyzed and each sentence is assigned a tree structure. The text is considered incorrect if the parsing does not succeed.

P.V. Krishna, M.R. Babu, and E. Ariwa (Eds.): ObCom 2011, Part II, CCIS 270, pp. 524–531, 2012.
© Springer-Verlag Berlin Heidelberg 2012

Statistics-Based Checking, as described in [Attwell, 1987]. In this approach, a POS-annotated corpus is used to build a list of POS tag sequences. Some sequences will be very common (for example *determiner, adjective, noun* as in *the old man*), others will probably not occur at all (for example *determiner, determiner, adjective*). Sequences which occur often in the corpus can be considered correct in other text, uncommon sequences might be errors.

Rule-Based Checking, as it is used in this system. In this approach, a set of rules is matched against a text which has at least been POS tagged. This approach is similar to the statistics-based approach, but all the rules are developed manually.

In Section 2, we discuss previous work. In Section 3 we explain our model and its implementation and snapshots of the outcome of the system are also included for analysis. Section 4 concludes this paper.

2   Literature Survey

Many researchers have developed various systems for "grammar checking" for Indian languages. Some of the efforts are as below:

Bangla Grammar Checking System: In their work related to Bangla Grammar Checking System, authors, Md. Jahangir Alam, Naushad UzZaman, and Mumit Khan explain a statistical grammar checker, which considers the n-gram based analysis of words and POS tags to decide whether the sentence is grammatically correct or not [1]. They employed this technique for both Bangla and English and also described limitation in their approach with possible solutions.

Punjabi Grammar Checking System: Punjabi grammar checking system was developed by Mandeep Singh Gill and Guripreet Singh Lehal, Punjab University [2]. The grammar checking system was developed for detecting various grammatical errors in Punjabi texts. This system utilizes a full form of lexicon for morphological analysis, and applies rule-based approaches for part-of-speech tagging and phrase chunking. The system follows a novel approach of performing agreement checks at phrase and clause levels using the grammatical information exhibited by POS tags in the form of feature value pairs. The system can detect and suggest rectifications for a number of grammatical errors, resulting from the lack of agreement, order of words in various phrases etc., in literary style Punjabi texts.

Architectural and System Design of the Nepali Grammar Checker
This paper describes the architectural and system design of the Nepali Grammar Checker, which is in due course of research and development. The development follows a modular approach with the Grammar Checker consisting of independent modules. These modules then in turn serve as a pipeline for the over all integrated system. The Grammar Checker aims to check the grammatical errors such as nominal and verbal agreement, parts of speech inflections, phrase and clause structure and the different categories of sentence patterns for Nepali.

GB Theory Based Hindi To English Translation System
Alka Choudhary, et.al[4], in the above paper focused on Government and Binding (GB) theory, which emphasizes common phrase structure for all the languages. In this paper, a machine translation system based on GB theory is proposed. The system takes Hindi as source language and English as target language.

Architectural and System Design of the Nepali Grammar Checker
Bal Krishna Bal and Prajol Shrestha in the above titled paper describe the architectural and system design of the Nepali Grammar Checker. The development follows a modular approach with the Grammar Checker consisting of independent modules. These modules then in turn serve as a pipeline for the over all integrated system. The authors claim that this Grammar Checker checks the grammatical errors such as nominal and verbal agreement, parts of speech inflections, phrase and clause structure and the different categories of sentence patterns for Nepali.[3]

A Rule-Based Afan Oromo Grammar Checker [8]
Debela Tesfaye in the above titled paper describe the architectural and system design of the Afan Oromo grammar checker. Afan Oromo grammar checker has been developed and tested on real-world errors. Most of the false flags are related to compound, complex and compound complex sentences as most of the rules are constructed for simple sentences. More rules that handles the types of sentences can be added to the existing rules in order to improve the performance of the grammar checker. There are also sentences that exhibits grammatical errors but not flagged by the checker.

3   Our Approach

For checking grammar of a Hindi sentence we have implemented a novel algorithm.

3.1   Hindi Morphology

Morphology involves the study of inner structure of words and their forms in different uses and constructions. It can be mainly divided into two branches – derivational morphology and inflectional morphology. Derivational morphology involves the processes by which new lexemes are built from existing ones mainly through the addition of affixes. As an example in Hindi म + मेरा = ममेरा (Pronoun to Adjective), like in English – go + at = goat (verb to noun) etc. Inflectional morphology involves the processes by which various inflectional forms are formed from a lexical stem. As an example in Hindi – inflectional forms of noun अतिथि (guest) are अतिथि (masculine-singular-direct), अतिथि (masculine- oblique-singular), अतिथि (masculine-direct-plural), (masculine-oblique-plural). Hindi is very rich in inflectional morphology can be witnessed from the fact that in English usually there are maximum of 7-8 inflected word forms of noun but in Hindi it can be up to 40 and even more than that.

Input Word:- राम लड़का है|

Output:-   राम [N]लड़का[N] है[VC]

Morphological Analysis Done at Two Levels

i)   Word Level Morphological Analyzer

ii)   Phrase Level Morphological Analyzer

3.1.1   Word Level Morphological Analyzer

- Identifies the structural component of the word

- Provides Person, Number, Case, Aspect, Gender, Modality and Tense information

3.1.2   Phrase Level Morphological Analyzer

Phrase Level Morphological Analyzer provides the grammatical information about the complete sentence.

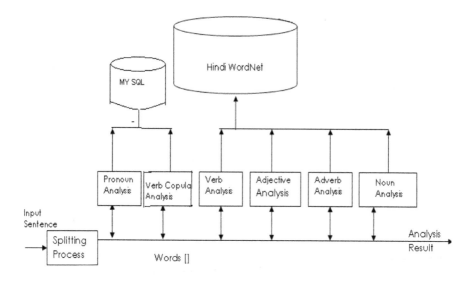

Fig. 1. Detailed Architecture of Phrase Level Morphological Analyzer

Phrase Level Morphological Analyzer Architecture is Divided into the Following Modules

•Splitting Process

This module splits the Hindi sentence and counts the number of words present in the sentence. It stores all the words in the word [] array and counts the word in count variable.

•Pronoun Analysis

Pronoun analysis uses the PronounLookUpTable; here the entire possible pronouns are stored at the time of searching   any   word   present   in   the PronounLookUpTable i.e. pronoun.

•Noun Analysis

Nouns are categorized into 20 different paradigms based on

1. Vowel ending.
2. Valid suffix of a word.
3. Gender, Number, Person and Case information.

Noun analysis uses the NounLookUpTable and Hindi WordNet. In NounLookUpTable noun is divided into two types i.e. Singular and Plural. Apply stemming process on the word then search the root word in Hindi WordNet .If the word is found in the noun list of the Hindi WordNet, it is identified as a noun. Noun analysis finds the gender, number and case information of a word.

•Verb Analysis

The Verb Group represents the following grammatical properties:

1. Aspect: Durative, Stative, Infinitive, Habitual and Perfective etc.
2. Modal: Abilitive, Deontic, Probabilitative etc.
3. Gender: Male, Female, Dual.
4. Person: 1st, 2nd and 3rd.

Verb analysis uses the VerbLookupTable and Hindi WordNet. In VerbLookUpTable, verb is divided into two types i.e. Singular and Plural. Apply stemming process on the word and find the root word in Hindi WordNet. If word is found in the verb list of the Hindi WordNet i.e. the word is identified as a verb.

•Adjective Analysis

The adjective Group represents the following grammatical properties:

1. Aspect: Durative, Stative, Infinitive, Habitual and Perfective etc.
2. Modal: Abilitive, Deontic, Probabilitative etc.
3. Gender: Male, Female, Dual.
4. Person: 1st, 2nd and 3rd.

Adjective analysis uses the "AdjectiveLookUpTable" and Hindi WordNet. In "AdjectiveLookUpTable" adjectives are divided into two types i.e. Singular and Plural. Apply stemming process on the word and find the root word in Hindi WordNet. If word is found in the Adjective list of the Hindi-WordNet, i.e. the word is identified as an Adjective.

•Adverb Analysis

The adverb Group represents the following grammatical properties:

1. Aspect: Durative, Stative, Infinitive, Habitual and Perfective etc.
2. Modal: Abilitive, Deontic, Probabilitative etc.
3. Gender: Male, Female, Dual.
4. Person: 1st, 2nd and 3rd.

Adverb analysis uses the "AdverbLookUpTable" and Hindi WordNet. In "AdverbLookUpTable" adverbs are divided into two types i.e. Singular and Plural. Apply stemming process on the word and find the root word in Hindi WordNet. If word is found in the Adverb list of the Hindi WordNet i.e. the word is identified as an Adverb.

•Verb Copula Analysis

Verb copula analysis uses the VerbCopulaLookUpTable; here all the possible verb copula words are stored. At the time of searching any word in the VerbCopulaLookUpTable, identify the word as a verb copula.

•Tense Analysis

Tense analysis is performed at the phrase level morphological analyzer. Identify the tense of an input sentence using last word present in the sentence. We have used tense analysis table shown in below.

Following are the Tables Used in our Hindi Grammar Checker System

- GrammaticalPatternTable
- PronounLookUpTable
- VerbCopulaLookUpTable
- NounLookUpTable
- VerbLookUpTable
- AdverbLookUpTable
- AdjectiveLookUpTable

System stores all the grammatical patterns in GrammaticalPatternTable, Pronouns in the PronounLookUpTable, Noun in NounLookUpTable, Adverb in AdverbLookUpTable, Adjective in AdjectiveLookUpTable, Verb in VerbLookUpTable. We have used Hindi WordNet for Noun, Verb, Adjective, Adverb, and Verb. In Lookup Table for Noun, Verb, Adjective, Adverb, Verb contain only singular and plural. Only these tables are used for finding singular or plural after that searching word in Hindi WordNet.

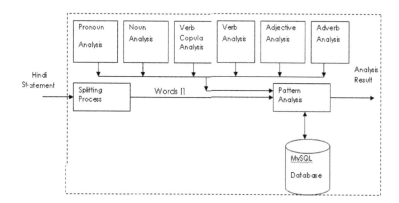

Fig. 2. Detail Architecture of Grammar checking system

Proposed Algorithm

Step 1: Input Hindi statement.

Step 2: Splitting word from Hindi sentence. (word[ ])

Step 3: Count number of words. (count)

Step 4:- Retrieve Records from GrammaticalPatternTable (Table having Number of Pattern Element=count (Pattern))

Step 5: i=0

Step 6: if i<Pattern.Length, then Get Pattern Element from Pattern Array (PatternElement) i=i+1 else return null.

Step 7: j=0

Step 8: if j<PatternElement (j) then p=PatternElement(j) mainId=p.getMainId()
SubId=p.GetSubId()
mainType=getMainType(mainId)
Subtype=getSubType (subId)
j=j+1 else
return Pattern[i]

Step 9: If MainType=WordMainType And SubType=WordSubType
Then Goto step 7 else Goto step 5

Using grammar checking algorithm match the syntax of an input sentence with available pattern. If pattern match as then it display result with the rule id and pattern.

As Hindi WordNet does not provide Hindi verb Copula and pronoun list, we have stored the entire verb copula in the verb copula lookup table, all pronouns in pronoun lookup table. Phrase Level Morphological analyzer is a part of a system.

Sample Rules used in Our System

Rule Id	Grammatical Pattern	
4	<Pronoun=हम> <Noun=PLURAL> <Verb Copula=हैं>	▲
5	<Pronoun=वे> <Noun=SINGULAR> <Verb Copula=है>	≡
6	<Pronoun=वह> <Noun=PLURAL> <Verb Copula=है>	
7	<Pronoun=वह> <Noun=SINGULAR> <Verb Copula=था>	▼

Output of Our System

Result: 1: Given Statement is Proper Statement as Per the Following Grammatical Pattern rule.
Rule Id: 1
Pattern : <Pronoun=मैं> <Noun=SINGULAR> <Verb Copula=हूँ>

4   Conclusion

Thus, as mentioned in above sections, **Grammar Checking System using Rule Based Morphological Process for Indian Language (Hindi)** is successfully implemented for simple Hindi sentences. The results are very promising. The advantage of this system is the time required for grammar checking and analyzing the complete sentence is less than other existing systems. The reason of better performance is that the system only checks those patterns which have same number of words present in input sentence and does not consider all the patterns stored in database. Performance of system can be further improved by adding more rules in data base manually.

References

1. Alam, J., UzZaman, N., Khan, M.: N-gram based Statistical Grammar Checker for Bangla and English. In: Ninth International Conference on Computer and Information Technology (ICCIT 2006), Dhaka, Bangladesh (2006)
2. Gill, M.S., Lehal, G.S.: A Grammar Checking System for Punjabi. In: Coling 2008: Companion volume-Poster & Demonstrations, Manchester, pp. 149–152 (August 2008)
3. Bal, B.K., Pandey, B., Khatiwada, L., Rupakheti, P.: Nepali Grammar Checker. Research Report on the Nepali grammar checker PAN/L10n/PhaseII/Reports by Madan Puraskar Pustakalaya, Lalitpur, Nepal (2008)
4. Choudhary, A., Singh, M.: GB Theory Based Hindi To English Translation System. IEEE (2009); ISSN: 978-1-4244- 4520-2/09/$25.00
5. Shrivastava, M., Agrawal, N., Singh, B.M.S., Bhattacharya, P.: Morphology Based Natural Language Processing tools for Indian Languages. In: The 4th Annual Inter Research Institute Student Seminar in Computer Science, Indian Institute of Technology, Kanpur, April 1-2 (2005)
6. Goyal, V., Lehal, G.S.: Hindi Morphological Analyzer and Generator. In: ICETET 2009, GHRCE, Nagpur (2009)
7. Akshar, B., Chaitanya, V., Sangal, R.: Natural Language Processing: A Paninian Perspective. Prentice-Hall of India, New Delhi (1995)
8. Tesfaye, D.: A rule-based Afan Oromo Grammar Checker (IJACSA) International Journal of Advanced Computer Science and Applications 2(8) (2011)
9. Mozgovoy, M.: Dependency-Based Rules for Grammar Checking with Language Tool. In: Proceedings of the Federated Conference on Computer Science and Information Systems, pp. 209–212 (2011); ISBN: 978-83-60810-22-4

Object Recognition with Wavelet-Based Salient Points

R. Ahila Priyadharshini[1], S. Arivazhagan[1], and S. Jeypriya[2]

[1] Department of ECE,
Mepco Schlenk Engineering College, Sivakasi
{ahilaprem,s_arivu}@yahoo.com
[2] Department of ECE,
Kamaraj College of Engineering and Technology, Virudhunagar
jeypriyas14@gmail.com

Abstract. In this paper, an efficient method to recognize various objects using wavelet based salient points with the help of Moment features is presented. In the detection of salient points, a salient point detector is presented that extract points where variations occur in the image, whether they are corner-like or not. The detector is based on wavelet transform with full level decomposition to detect global variations as well as local ones. This method provides better retrieval performance when compared with other point detectors. After detecting the salient points, patches are extracted over those points. The patches have the advantage of being robust with respect to occlusion and background clutter in images. Then the features are extracted using Basic Moments method for the detected patches in order to give them to a classifier. Support Vector Machines scale relatively well to high dimensional data. SVM classifier recognizes the objects (positive images) from the background (negative images) and vice-versa. The experimental evaluation of the proposed method is done using the well-known and complex Caltech database with complex images. The results obtained here proved that the proposed method is able to successfully recognize the objects with good recognition rate along with the background using wavelet based salient points with full level decomposition under challenging conditions.

Keywords: Salient points rotation invariance, saliency value, efficiency, stability, wavelets, tracking, negative images, positive images.

1 Introduction

The human visual system allows us to identify and distinguish thousands or possibly millions of objects quickly and effortlessly, even in complex cluttered surroundings and in the presence of partial occlusions. Duplicating this ability with computers has many practical applications. Computer programs that tackle it must cope with a lot of difficulties. They must be able to recognize arbitrary objects, the object to be recognized may be occluded by other objects and therefore be only partially visible, the object can appear at any position and with any size in the image and the appearance of the object is not restricted to any "prototypical" appearance [1]. The proposed method

P.V. Krishna, M.R. Babu, and E. Ariwa (Eds.): ObCom 2011, Part II, CCIS 270, pp. 532–541, 2012.
© Springer-Verlag Berlin Heidelberg 2012

allows for recognizing objects under these challenging circumstances and provides excellent results on Caltech database.

1.1 Recent Work

Generic object recognition systems do not include any information about specific objects [2, 3]. Rather they learn to recognize arbitrary objects by inspecting a set of training images and train a model based on these. This model is then used to recognize objects in unseen images. For each of the training images a set of features are derived. Each feature describes properties of either the whole image (global feature) or a part of the image (local feature). Usually, local features are most successful in capturing the content of complex images.

In the most promising approaches to object recognition and classification, an object is assumed to consist of several parts which can be modeled more or less independently [1].

A recently popular approach which is helpful in recognizing the objects accurately is the calculation of local features at points of interest. Here, the detector used is based on wavelet transform to detect global variations as well as local ones. Various approaches differ mainly in the type of feature used, the way the object parts are modeled and in the detection framework.

Opelt and Pinz [2] presented an approach where weak hypotheses are combined using boosting. As features, local descriptions of regions of discontinuity and of homogeneity are used. Regions of discontinuity are detected by several interest point detectors, while for determining regions of homogeneity the authors proposed a new segmentation algorithm.

Schmid and Mohr [4] used the Harris corner detector to identify interest points, and then created a local image descriptor at each interest point from an orientation-invariant vector of derivative-of-Gaussian image measurements.

Another approach to object recognition was proposed by Deselaers and Keysers [5], where image patches are clustered using the EM algorithm for Gaussian mixture densities and images are represented as histograms of the patches over the (discrete) membership to the clusters.

Ferrari & Tuytelaars [6] present an approach to object recognition which they report to work even under very adversarial conditions like a high amount of background clutter, dominant occlusion and viewpoint changes.

A comparison of learning and classifying techniques, such as, nearest neighbor methods, support vector machines, and convolutional networks is given by LeCun & Huang [7]. These techniques are studied for challenging conditions: complex images with high amount of "clutter", varying pose, and lighting.

An approach is used to compute salient points of images incrementally, i.e., the salient point detector can operate with a coarsely quantized input image representation [8]. The experiments demonstrate the feasibility of incremental approaches for salient point detection in various classes of natural images.

An unsupervised salient object detection system that able to extract potential exogenous regions of interests may be used in robotic navigation system [9]. A comparison is done with existing extraction methods and results are presented.

A method [10] is developed to detect salient points at different scales in a given image. The principle of this approach was to consider a salient point as an outlier. The contribution here was twofold. Experimental results carried out on real and synthetic images illustrated the performances of this new detection scheme.

The main contribution of this work is:

An efficient method in the detection of salient points and extracting patches is proposed in [11].

The paper is structured as follows. The next section discusses the outline of the proposed method. In Section 3, salient point detection, in particular their benefits to represent complex images are discussed. Section 4 deals with extraction of patches and Section 5 deals with the steps involved in extracting the features using Basic Moment method. Section 7 gives the recognition results for single class object recognition by Moment features for the whole database and for randomly taken images. Finally Section 8 gives the conclusion of the proposed method.

2   Outline of the Proposed Method

The first step is to detect salient points using interest point detectors. The interest points are found in regions of high variance.Here the detector used is based on wavelet transform to detect global variations as well as local ones. A salient point extraction algorithm is used to implement the salient point extraction. The patches are extracted around each of these salient points [12]. Then the features are extracted and classified by SVM classifier.

3   Salient Point Detection Algorithm

The salient point detection using wavelet based full level decomposition is an efficient method since the image is decomposed upto the last level so that the points can be extracted in a detail manner where variations occur in the image, whether they are corner-like or not.

The wavelet transform is a multiresolution representation, which expresses image variations at different scales [13].A salient point extraction algorithm is used to implement the salient points extraction described before.

The main steps are:

- For each wavelet coefficient, find the maximum child coefficient.
- Track it recursively in finer resolutions.
- At the level where the maximum value of the tracked pixel, set the saliency value of the tracked pixel: the sum of the wavelet coefficients tracked.
- The most prominent salient points are finally chosen based on the saliency value present in the track.

3.1   Finding Maximum Child Coefficients

Since wavelets used here has a compact support, it is easy to find out from which signal points each wavelet coefficient at the scale 2^j was computed, and the wavelet coefficients can be obtained for the same points at the finer scale 2^{j+1}. Indeed there is a set of coefficients at the scale 2^{j+1} computed with the same points as a coefficient $W_{2^j} f$ at the scale 2^j. This occurs because of the pyramidal algorithm and the compact support of the wavelet. This set of coefficients is the children $C(W_{2^j} f(n))$ of the coefficient $W_{2^j} f(n)$. The children set in one dimensional for a given wavelet coefficient can be expressed as,

$$C(W_{2^j} f(n)) = \{W_{2^{j+1}} f(k), 2n \le k \le 2n + 2p - 1\} \tag{1}$$

The children set in two dimensional for a given wavelet coefficient can be expressed as,

$$C(W_{j^d} f(x, y)) = \{W_{j+1^d} f(k, l)\} \tag{2}$$

where, $2x \le k \le 2x + 2y - 1, 0 \le x \le 2^j N$
$2y \le l \le 2y + 2p - 1, 0 \le y \le 2^j M$
$1 \le d \le 3$

Each wavelet coefficient $W_{2^j} f(n)$ is computed with $2^{-j} p$ signal points. It represents their variation at the scale 2^j. Its children coefficients give the variations of some particular subsets of these points (with the number and the size of subsets depending on the wavelet). The most salient subset is the one with the highest wavelet coefficient at the scale 2^{j+1}, that is the maximum in absolute value of $C(W_{2^j} f(n))$.

3.2   Tracking Procedure

In this salient point extraction algorithm, the maximum value obtained in the first step is considered, and look at its highest child. Applying recursively this process, a coefficient $W_{2^{-1}} f(n)$ at the finer resolution $1/2$ is selected. Hence, this coefficient only represents $2p$ signal points. To select a salient point from this tracking, among these $2p$ points the one with the highest gradient is chosen. Its saliency value is set as the sum of the absolute value of the wavelet coefficients in the track.

$$saliency = \sum_{k=1}^{-j} |C^{(k)}(W_{2^j} f(n))| \tag{3}$$

where, $0 \le n \le 2^j N, -\log_2 N \le j \le -1$

In the Fig.5, if $W_{1/2} f(1)$ is the maximum child of $W_{1/4} f(0)$, look at it recursively. Since it corresponds to the finer scale, we select the point with the higher gradient between C and D, for instance D.

The tracking of the wavelet coefficients for each orientation (horizontal, diagonal, vertical) is shown clearly in Fig.1. Finally, the tracked point and its saliency value are computed for every wavelet coefficient. The most prominent salient points are finally chosen based on the saliency value present in the track. Fig.2 represents the points extracted using wavelets with full level decomposition method.

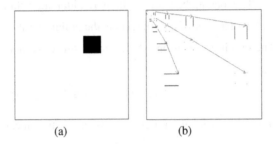

(a)   (b)

Fig. 1. (a) An image (b) The wavelet transform and the track of the wavelet coefficients for each orientation

Fig. 2. (a) Categories in Caltech database (b) Detected Salient Points

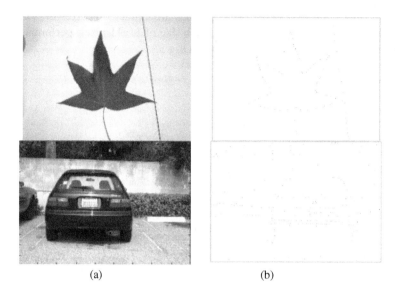

(a)   (b)

Fig. 2. (*Continued*)

4   Patch Extraction

The variability of images can be modeled as a collection of smaller sub-images, usually called patches. A patch –based approach to recognition has several advantages in the presence of variability [14]. It is also evident that this approach can handle occlusions as well. If parts of an object are occluded in an image, the remaining visible parts may still be used to recognize the object correctly or to learn about the appearance of an object from this instance. Further advantages include that changes in the geometrical relation between image parts can be modeled to be flexible or can even be ignored and the algorithm can focus on those image parts that are most important to recognize the object [15]. Another advantage of patch-based methods as considered here is that patches containing different local variations can be simultaneously chosen from various training images from the same class to explain a test image patch set. Thus it is possible to approximate image transformations that were not present in the training data.

4.1   Patch Size

If the objects appear across all images at roughly the same size, then all patches are extracted at the same chosen patch size. Anyway, this assumption is unlikely to hold in many cases. A possibility to address this scale difference of the objects is to extract the patches at different scales. The sizes are chosen to represent a small, middle and large object parts. In these experiments patches are extracted at sizes of 7x7, 11x11 and 15x15 pixels and encountered that a patch size of 11x11 pixels performs well [1], [2]. The result of patch extraction is shown in Fig 3.

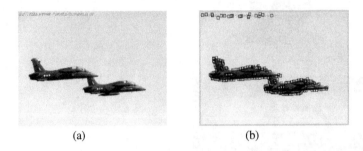

(a)   (b)

Fig. 3. (a) An Airplane Image (b) Extracted Patches

5   Feature Extraction

For extraction of features, basic moment method is used. An essential issue in the field of pattern analysis is the recognition of objects regardless of their position, size, illumination and orientation, basic moment method is mostly used. In object recognition, the hard part is the same   object can look incredibly different in different viewpoints. In order to overcome this complexity in object recognition, the method best suited for this purpose is moment method.

The formula for calculating the Moments is shown in eqn. (4)

$$M = \sum_x \sum_y I(x, y)^\alpha x^p y^p \qquad (4)$$

where,
I(x, y) - extracted patches intensity values
α- degree of moment
p, q- order of moment

In basic moment method degree is kept as one and order has to be varied upto ten and for each and every patch ten moments is taken and these are given as input to SVM classifier. So, depending upon the number of patches for each and every image, the total number of moments will get added up. These features for a set of training images are given to SVM classifier so that these features can be trained up.

6   Experimental Results

Here the two-class problem is considered for classification. The training images are obtained from Caltech database. Negative images that do not contain the object of interest are also tested to verify the robustness of the algorithm.

6.1   Single Class Object Recognition

In case of single class object recognition, the task is to determine whether an object is present in a given image or not [16]. For this purpose, sets of images containing certain objects (Airplanes, Motorbikes, Leafs, Faces and Cars) and a set of background images not containing any of these objects in Caltech database [17] are considered. There are a set of background images especially given for Car dataset containing only roads. The images are of various sizes and for the experiments they were converted to gray scale.

The airplane dataset consists of 1074 images; bike dataset contains 826 images; leaf dataset contains 186 images; face dataset contains 450 images, whereas there are 1155 images in car dataset. 150 images from both object category and background are used for training and the remaining images are used for testing. Negative images that do not contain the object of interest are also tested to verify the robustness of the algorithm. Also, the images are randomly taken from each and every category for testing. Table 1 gives the recognition rate for whole database and Table 2 gives the recognition rate for randomly taken images. Comparatively, the recognition rate obtained from randomly taken images is better than the recognition rate obtained from whole database.

Table 1. Recognition Rate for whole database

Category	Number Of Images In Training Set		Number Of Images In Testing Set		Recognition Rate(%)	
	Positive Images	Negative Images	Positive Images	Negative Images	Positive Images	Negative Images
Bike	150	150	676	750	92	70
Leaf	100	100	86	800	90	91.4
Face	150	150	300	750	95	83
Car	150	150	1005	1220	83	80
Air plane	150	150	924	750	84	86

Table 2. Recognition Rate for randomly taken images

Category	Number Of Images In Training Set		Number Of Images In Testing Set		Recognition Rate(%)	
	Positive Images	Negative Images	Positive Images	Negative Images	Positive Images	Negative Images
Bike	150	150	150	150	93	75
					95	73
					94.5	76
Leaf	100	100	50	50	94	96
					96	98
					98	96
Face	150	150	150	150	94.6	82
					96	85
					97.3	83
Car	150	150	150	150	85	85
					88	85
					90	84
Air Plane	150	150	150	150	91.3	88
					89.5	92
					90.6	90

7   Conclusion

In this paper, the proposed method focuses on recognizing various objects in "complex" images, which proves to be a challenging task, as several factors complicate this successful method, among them clutter, occlusion and object transformations like translation and scaling. In this method, salient points are detected using wavelet transform with full level decomposition which can be used in emerging multimedia applications. After detecting the salient points, patches are extracted over those points. Then the features are extracted using Basic Moments method for the detected patches in order to give them to a classifier. SVM classifier recognizes the objects (positive images) from the background (negative images) and vice-versa. The proposed method will greatly increase the stability, uniqueness, accuracy and decreasing the computational complexity since few points are enough to recognize the objects. The results on these tasks of Caltech database proved that the proposed method is able to successfully recognize the objects with good recognition rate along with the background using wavelet based salient points with full level decomposition under challenging conditions.

References

1. Hegerath, A.: Patch-based Object recognition. Diploma thesis, Human Language Technology and Pattern Recognition Group, RWTH Aachen University, Aachen, Germany (March 2006)
2. Opelt, A., Pinz, A., Fussenegger, M., Auer, P.: Generic Object Recognition with Boosting. IEEE Transaction on Pattern Analysis and Machine Intelligence 28(3), 416–431 (2006)
3. Agarwal, S., Roth, D.: Learning a Sparse Representation for Object Detection. In: Heyden, A., Sparr, G., Nielsen, M., Johansen, P. (eds.) ECCV 2002. LNCS, vol. 2353, pp. 113–127. Springer, Heidelberg (2002)
4. Schmid, C., Mohr, R.: Local gray value invariants for image retrieval. IEEE PAMI, 530–534 (1997)
5. Deselaers, T., Keysers, D., Ney, H.: Features for Image Retrieval-A Quantitative Comparison. In: Rasmussen, C.E., Bülthoff, H.H., Schölkopf, B., Giese, M.A. (eds.) DAGM 2004. LNCS, vol. 3175, pp. 228–236. Springer, Heidelberg (2004)
6. Ferrari, V., Tuytelaars, T., Van Gool, L.: Simultaneous Object Recognition and Segmentation by Image Exploration. In: Pajdla, T., Matas, J(G.) (eds.) ECCV 2004. LNCS, vol. 3021, pp. 40–54. Springer, Heidelberg (2004)
7. LeCun, Y., Huang, F.J., Bottou, L.: Learning Methods for Generic Object Recognition with Invariance to Pose and Lighting. In: Proc. CVPR (2), pp. 97–104 (2004)
8. Andreopoulos, Y., Patras, I.: Incremental Refinement of Image Salient-Point Detection. IEEE Transactions on Image Processing 17(9) (September 2008)
9. Nguyen, V.A., Phuan, A.T.L.: A Multi-Processed Salient Point Detection System for Autonomous Navigation. In: 2008 10th Intl. Conf. on Control, Automation, Robotics and Vision Hanoi, Vietnam, December 17-20, pp. 2170–2175 (2008)
10. Ayadi, W., Benazza-Benyahia, A.: Wavelet Based Statistical Detection of Salient Points by the Exploitation of the Interscale Redundancies. In: Proceedings of International Conference of Image Processing (2009)
11. Loupias, E., Sebe, N., Bres, S., Jolion, J.-M.: Wavelet-based Salient Points for image retrieval. In: Proceedings of International Conference on Image Processing, vol. 2, pp. 518–521 (2000)
12. Schmid, C., Mohr, R., Bauckhage, C.: Comparing and Evaluating Interest Points. In: International Conference on Computer Vision, pp. 230–235 (January 1999)
13. Stollnitz, E., De Rose, T., Salesin, D.: Wavelets for Computer Graphics: A Primer, part 1. IEEE Computer Graphics and Applications 15(3), 76–84 (1995)
14. Harris, C., Stephens, M.J.: A Combined corner and edge detector. In: Alvey Vision Conference, pp. 147–152 (1988)
15. Deselaers, T., Keysers, D., Ney, H.: Improving a Discriminative Training Approach to Object Recognition using Image Patches. In: Kropatsch, W.G., Sablatnig, R., Hanbury, A. (eds.) DAGM 2005. LNCS, vol. 3663, pp. 326–333. Springer, Heidelberg (2005)
16. Paredes, R., Keysers, D., Lehmann, T.M., Wein, B.B., Ney, H., Vidal, E.: Classification of Medical Images using Local Representations. In: Proc. Bildverarbeitung fur die Medizin, Leipzig, Germany, pp. 171–174 (2002)
17. http://www.robots.ox.ac.uk/~vgg/data3.html

The Role of ICTs in Knowledge Management (KM) for Organizational Effectiveness

R. Subashini, S. Rita, and M. Vivek

VIT Business School,
VIT University, India
rsubashini@vit.ac.in,
{ritasamikannu,vivekm974}@gmail.com

Abstract. Knowledge Management (KM) has become the key factor for the success of all organizations. ICTs are technologies which facilitate the management to share knowledge and information. Thus, ICTs have a prominent role on Knowledge Management initiatives. In the current business environment, the implementation of Knowledge Management projects has become easier with the help of technological tools. The value of Knowledge Management is more when made available to the right people at the right time. Thus, knowledge sharing is facilitated through information and communication technologies including computers, telephones, e-mail, databases, data-mining systems, search engines, video-conferencing equipment and many more. The purpose of this study is to identify the significant role of information and communication technologies (ICTs) in Knowledge Management (KM) initiatives that lead to organizational effectiveness. This paper moves towards an understanding of the overall importance of ICTs to knowledge management that paves way to achieve organizational effectiveness. Finally, an integrated model linking ICTs, Knowledge Management processes and organizational effectiveness is done and thereby the relationship between ICTs and KM processes is conceptualized.

Keywords: Information and Communication Technologies, Knowledge Management, Processes, Organizational Effectiveness.

1   Introduction

Stair and Reynolds (1998) states that '"Knowledge is the awareness and understanding of a set of information and ways that information can be made useful to support a specific task or reach a decision". Davenport and Prusak (1998) states that "Knowledge involves the link people make between information and its potential applications and, as such, knowledge is closer to action than either information or data". Knowledge Management is basically the process involved in blending the organizations internal and external information appropriately to the right person at the right time. Information and Communication Technologies (ICTs) covers an enormous

P.V. Krishna, M.R. Babu, and E. Ariwa (Eds.): ObCom 2011, Part II, CCIS 270, pp. 542–549, 2012.

diversity of heterogeneous technologies that facilitate the organizations for sharing of knowledge and information. Information Technology strengthens the self action of employees and also makes the effective use of organizational resources.

1.1   Knowledge Hierarchy

Tiwana (2000) states that knowledge is a "fluid mix of framed experience, values, contextual information, expert insight, and grounded intuition that provides an environment and framework for evaluating new experiences and information". According to Bellinger et al., (2004), the knowledge hierarchy levels are given as follows:

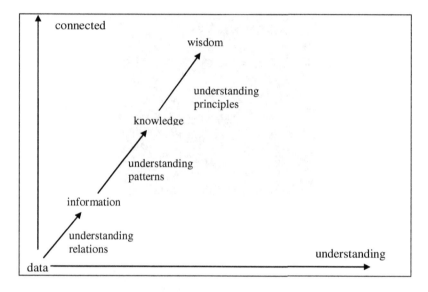

Fig. 1. Knowledge Hierarchy (Source: Bellinger et al., 2004)

1.2   Knowledge Management (KM)

Knowledge management increases the ability to learn from its environment by adapting to new tools and technologies (Liautaud and Hammond, 2001). Knowledge Management has been recognized as an essential component of a proactively managed organization wherein a robust technological infrastructure plays a crucial role. We are living in a knowledge economy (Bartlett and Ghosal, 1993; Davenport and Prusak 1995; Drucker, 1997; Nonaka, Toyama and Konno, 2001; Stewart 2001). Rosenberg (2001) states Knowledge Management as the "creation, archiving and sharing of valued information, expertise and insight within and across communities of people and organizations with similar interests and needs". The overall objective of knowledge management is to create knowledge assets and thereby achieve organizational effectiveness.

KM efforts encompass two distinctive types of knowledge, explicit and tacit. Explicit knowledge can be transferred with the help of ICTs and can be kept in a storage-able form (papers, products, digital documents, print, audio, etc.).Tacit knowledge is commonly referenced as the knowledge that is contained inside human heads and is therefore inexpressible.

As stated by Nonaka and Takeuchi (1995), the SECI model (Socialization, Externalization, Combination, and Internalization) has become the cornerstone of knowledge creation and transfer theory. In this model, based upon the users learning tendency knowledge is continuously converted and created.

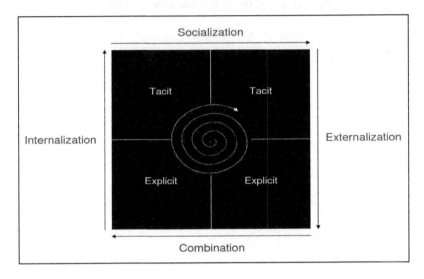

Fig. 2. SECI Model (Source: Nonaka & Takeuchi, 1996)

The various dimensions of KM implementation can be in organizational, managerial and technological form. For effective KM implementation there should be a conducive work environment, proper organization structure, leadership-enriched culture that supports KM, right systems, tools and technologies to support KM.

1.3   Information and Communication Technologies (ICTs)

ICTs can be used to support knowledge management activities by allowing people to search for and identify people with expertise that they are looking for. This can be done through producing databases of expertise, searchable web portals or electronic yellow pages. Here, knowledge is shared via inter-personal communication and interaction even in geographically dispersed, large multi-national organizations. The use of ICTs collaboration and communication tools may also be via a wide range of virtual/ web-based platforms, forums, such as e-mail, instant messaging, discussion boards, intranets, chat rooms, blogs and many more. The creation of communities of practice also represents a means of developing and encouraging rich forms of communication and knowledge sharing that are ICT-mediated.

2   Role of ICTs in Knowledge Management

The availability of ICTs (for example: World Wide Web) has paved way for KM movement wherein the knowledge base can be speedily accessed and adds more value to the user. Firstly, the role of KM in organizations should be understood. To be concise, KM paves way to

- Identify knowledge that is pivotal to the organization
- Analyze knowledge existing in the organization
- Focus on what form this knowledge is stored
- Tools to best transfer this knowledge to relevant people
- Build an effective KM system
- Implement enablers (ICTs, Organizational structures, Leadership, Culture) to make KM work for organizational effectiveness.
- So, it enables the firm to better protect and exploit what it knows and helps firms to learn from past mistakes and successes. It promotes a long term focus on developing the right competencies and skills. KM also enhances the firm's ability to innovate and also protect its key knowledge and competencies from being lost or copied.

To find, create, assemble and to apply knowledge the IT Components are useful. Thus, few of the various uses of ICTs to KM are

- Find Knowledge (Employee skills directories-Yellow pages)
- Quick storage and retrieval of data/use of explicit knowledge (Knowledge repositories)
- Distribution of knowledge (Databases, Discussion lists, Notes databases)
- Delivery (Web, Networks, Intranets, E-mail)
- Mobilizing tacit knowledge through communication networks (Video conferencing)
- Promote Paperless Office and thereby save paper
- Reuse and revalidate knowledge (past project record databases, Community of practice)
- Create new knowledge to meet the changing needs in organizations (DSS tools)

Thus, the collaborative knowledge management platform should have efficient protocols with various platforms and operating system environment that has easy-to-use client interface. A few essential technology components with respect to World Wide Web are Client software, Server software, Server Hardware, Gateways, GroupWare, Web client interface.

3   ICTs, KM, Organizational Effectiveness: An Integrated Model

Information is not knowledge and knowledge is not just information. For information to make any sense, learn and become knowledge, the interaction with networks and peers is required. Thus, putting information in context helps to learn and get inputs via websites, databases and other types of electronic communication platforms.

Based on the vast literature survey on KM, the researchers have confined the KM processes (as in Figure 3) to Knowledge Discovery, Knowledge Organization, Knowledge Sharing, Knowledge Re-use, Knowledge Creation and Knowledge Acquisition.

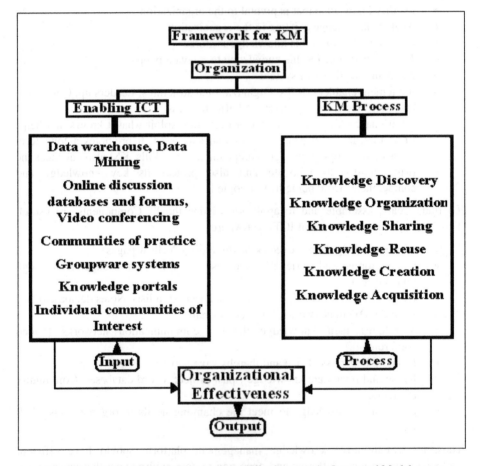

Fig. 3. ICTs, KM and Organizational Effectiveness: An Integrated Model

The systems approach mentioned above with the technology enablers as input, KM processes as Process and Organizational effectiveness as output is an integrated model which depicts the relationship between ICTs, KM that paves way for high firm performance.

- Knowledge can be discovered with the help of technology enablers. With the help of Information Technology (IT), data/hidden data and information can be gathered and analyzed. Identification of experts/communities via social networks can be made too. The main technological tool in Knowledge Discovery would be Data Mining.
- Botha et al. (2008) states that "Knowledge Organization involves activities that classify, map, index, and categorize knowledge for navigation, storage, and retrieval". So, the knowledge user should be in a position to identify, retrieve and understand the knowledge base. For this purpose, corporate yellow pages, groupware systems, video-conferencing (to support formal and even informal forms of communication) can be used.
- Based on the area of business Knowledge Sharing happens. For example, processing the marketing related information and collecting feedback are some KM initiatives. ICTs can be used in this case for speedy data/information analysis. Knowledge exchange protocols can be of use.
- As stated by Fruchter and Demian (2002) Knowledge Re-use is of two types:
    - Internal: Where the knowledge producer uses his own knowledge at some future point.
    - External: Where the knowledge consumer uses someone else's knowledge.

The support of ICTs via groupware systems can be used to enhance communication.

- Knowledge Creation depends on an environment which supports more interaction among people. The organization should also be technologically resourced so that experimentation can also be made. Knowledge portals as forms of ICTs can be the enabler here.

- The knowledge that can be obtained from external sources is Knowledge Acquisition. As stated by Gamble & Blackwell (2001) "External knowledge sources are important and one should therefore take a holistic view of the value chain". Effective knowledge acquisition with the help of technological tools can be made through sources like suppliers, competitors, partners/alliances, customers, external experts, individual communities of practice.

4   Conclusion and Future Research

In the present day of competitive business environment, Knowledge management has gained high importance and is the key success factor of an organization. Although not intended to represent all possible areas, the integrated model ties in technology drivers, knowledge management processes and organizational effectiveness. As Bielawski & Metcalk (2003) rightly pointed, "KM can include the key documents expertise directories, lessons-learned databases, best practices and communities of practice that reflect and deliver knowledge to learners at a particular time of need". Thus, the role of ICTs in KM is highly pivotal to achieve organizational effectiveness. Mostly ICTs are very much helpful with respect to explicit knowledge. As many researchers have well identified that the tacit knowledge is crucial for an organization to succeed, in future the research on the role of ICTs in tacit knowledge management can be focussed more.

References

1. Bartlett, C.A., Ghosal, S.: Beyond the M-form: toward a managerial theory of the firm. Strategic Management Journal 14, 23–46 (1993)
2. Castillo, J.: A note on the concept of tacit knowledge. Journal of Management Inquiry 11(1), 46–57 (2002)
3. Crossan, M.M., Lane, H.W., White, R.E.: An organizational learning framework: from intuition to institution. Academy of Management Review 24(3), 522–537 (1999)
4. Davenport, T.H., Prusak, L.: Working Knowledge: How Organisations Manage What They Know, p. IX. Harvard Business School Press, Boston (1995)
5. Davenport, T.H., Prusak, L.: Working Knowledge: How Organizations Manage What They Know. Harvard Business School Press, Boston (1998)
6. Drucker, P.F.: Looking Ahead: Implications of the Present. Harvard Business Review, 18–33 (1997)
7. Geisler, E.: Tacit and explicit knowledge: empirical investigation in an emergency regime. International Journal of Technology Management 47(4), 273–285 (2009)
8. Grant, R.M.: Toward a knowledge-based theory of the firm. Strategic Management Journal 17, 109–222 (1996)
9. Hall, R., Andriani, P.: Managing knowledge for innovation. Long Range Planning 35, 29–48 (2002)
10. Herschel, R.T., Nemati, H., Steiger, D.: Tacit to explicit knowledge conversion: knowledge exchange protocols. Journal of Knowledge Management 5(1), 107–116 (2001)
11. Howells, J.: Tacit knowledge, innovation and technology transfer. Technology Analysis and Strategic Management 8(2), 91–105 (1996)
12. Nissen, M.: An extended model of knowledge-flow dynamics. Communications of the Association for Information Systems 8 (2002)
13. Nonaka, I.: A dynamic theory of organizational knowledge creation. Organization Science 5(1), 14–37 (1994)
14. Nonaka, I., Takeuchi, H.: The Knowledge-Creating Company: How Japanese Companies Create the Dynamics of Innovation. Oxford University Press, Oxford (1995)
15. Nonaka, I., Takeuchi, H., Umemoto, K.: A Theory of Organisational Knowledge Creation. International Journal of Technology Management 11(7/8), 833–845 (1996)
16. Nonaka, I., Toyama, R., Konno, N.: SECI, Ba and Leadership: United Model of Dynamic Knowledge Creation. In: Nonaka, I., Teece, D. (eds.) Managing Industrial Knowledge, pp. 13–41. Sage Publications, London (2001)
17. Ouchi, W.G., Wilkins, A.L.: Organizational culture. Annual Review of Sociology 11, 457–483 (1985)
18. Pillania, R.K.: Role of Top Management in KM. The Indian Experience Productivity 47(2), 56–65 (2006)

19. Smith, K.G., Collins, C.J., Clark, K.D.: Existing knowledge, knowledge creation capability, and the rate of new product introduction in high-technology firms. Academy of Management Journal 48(2), 346–357 (2005)
20. Spender, J.C.: Making knowledge the basis of a dynamic theory of the firm. Strategic Management Journal 17, 45–62 (1996)
21. Stenmark, D.: Turning Tacit Knowledge Tangible. In: Proceedings of the 33rd Annual Hawaii International Conference on System Sciences, pp. 1–9. IEEE Computer Society (2000)
22. Stewart, A.T.: The Wealth of Knowledge, New York, Doubleday (2001)
23. Weichoo, C.: Perspectives on Managing Knowledge in Organizations (1998), http://choo.fis.utoronto.caf.com

JPEG Compression and Decompression for Color Images Using Lattice Based Structures

T.A. Sangeetha[1], A. Saradha[2], and Ilango Paramasivam[3]

[1] Mother Teresa Women's University, Kodaikanal, India
tasangeetha1979@rediffmail.com
[2] Department of Computer Science & Engineering, IRTT Erode, India
saradha_irtt@yahoo.com
[3] School of Computing Science and Engineering, VIT University, Vellore, India
pilango@vit.ac.in

Abstract. Digital color images are compressed using common standards such as JPEG. The compression technique is used in various applications such as imaging and equalization of channels. But the decompression technique is not having enough sources to handle various problems. The process of sampling and sub sampling is done by both compression and decompression. In this paper the images with color planes (3-D) is used and its coefficient is taken for compression with discrete cosine transform of quantization technique. The settings for color plane with JPEG is chosen for an image(1)the color space (2)sampling and sub sampling(3)quantization technique. Here JPEG Compression history settings are used for an image with JPEG operation. The features like smoothness and lattice structures are taken for images to find and develop the solution of JPEG decompression which uses JPEG compression history estimation. Here the method used for JPEG compression and decompression which denotes the above point is effective and equalize the give color images.

Keywords: Quantizing, Lattice structures, Sampling, Compression, Decompression, Standards.

1   Introduction

Collection of pixels forms digital images where each and every pixel is referred as 3-D vector. The same process is done for color images. The values of vector represent the color of pixel to choose a color space for example RGB etc [1]. The settings for JPEG Compression and decompression are color space, sampling and quantization. The above three concepts use JPEG as common standards for compression and decompression with discrete cosine transform by quantization. Here, in JPEG operation, images are not directly represented in JPEG compression history because JPEG images are stored in MS-power point or MS-word with MS-clip gallery using computer graphics then it is decompressed and stored internally [2]. The settings of JPEG compression are taken away after decompression when its images are converted to lossless compression format example BMP (bit map) and TIFF (Tagged file formats) file formats.

P.V. Krishna, M.R. Babu, and E. Ariwa (Eds.): ObCom 2011, Part II, CCIS 270, pp. 550–555, 2012.

In many applications if needed compression history is used according to its nature. The file size of BMP and TIFF image file is larger than previous JPEG file. With the help of JPEG settings, compressing the images such as BMP and TIFF gives reduced file size without any distortion [3]. The errors received from BMP files while compression for example such as blocking are cleared by JPEG compression history. So this process is also used as authentication character for message conversion and free of error images by settings which are used in digital cameras. While compressing the images during JPEG operations quantization table is noted for gray scale images with compression history. The compression history estimation is explored in gray scale. So, in this paper compression history estimation is used for color images [4].

First of all statistical operation of compression history estimation is derived. The previous JPEG compressed image with DCT coefficient by JPEG's Quantization gives a periodic structure. The statistical periodic structure gives single color (i.e. grey scale) plane quantization table is performed. Further study of statistical periodic structure is extended to compression history estimation algorithm for color images. This gives maximum priority of color image compression history denoting color space, sub sampling, interpolation and quantization tables [5]. To transform current image's representation to affine and color space quantization by JPEG compression a structure called lattice with compression history estimation algorithm is used. The affine color transform is determined by the basic concepts of DCT coefficients with 3-D vector. The lattice structure is observed from its theoretical manner. The lattice vector consists of non-zero format vectors and gives uniqueness of such basic vector sets by lattice algorithms [15]. By this we can get color image's compression history called the affine color transform and quantization tables. Here the description is shown in compression history estimation algorithm with an effective way. Therefore the given algorithm below recompresses an image with minimum distortion and gives a small file size in the color planes [6, 10].

1.1   Color Spaces and Transform

The receptors in human retina produce sensational color perception if the incident light is activated on it. The spectrum of light is called as color. The human retina has three types of receptors called as trichromatic theory. It is nothing but three parameters to specify any color which is viewed as 3-D vector [7]. The reference coordinate system is called as color space with 3-D vector .According to the color there are many coordinate systems.

The CIE XYZ color space is defined to specify all visible colors using positive X, Y, and Z values [10, 11]. Other colors include different varieties of *RGB* (Red (*R*), Green (*G*), and Blue (*B*)) and *YCbCr* (luminance *Y*, and chrominance *Cb* and *Cr*) color spaces [8, 9]. These color spaces are related to each other and to reference color spaces such as the CIE XYZ via linear or non-linear color transformations.

1.1.1. JPEG Overview
The overview of JPEG compression and decompression is given in the figure 1.1 [11]. Consider a color image that is currently represented in the F color space,

F 1, F 2, and F 3 denote the three color planes. The F space is denoted as the *observation color space [12,18]*. Here the image was previously JPEG-compressed in the G color space—termed *compression color space*.

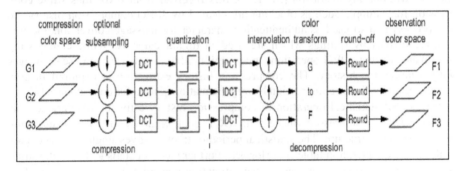

Fig. 1. Overview of JPEG compression and decompression

1.1.1.1. Independent Operations of G Space (G1,G2,G3) Planes is Processed by JPEG Compression is Given as Follows:

1. Down sample each color plane optionally which is termed as sub sampling.
2. Each color plane is divided into 8×8 blocks and it is split to take the DCT of each block.
3. Quantize the DCT coefficients at each frequency to the closest integer multiple of the quantization step-size corresponding to that frequency.

1.1.1.2. JPEG Decompression Performs the Following Operations:

1. Take the inverse DCT of the 8×8 blocks of quantized coefficients.
2. Interpolate the down sampled color planes by repetition followed by optional spatial smoothing with a low-pass filter. The popular IJG JPEG implementation [12] uses an impulse response filter to smooth in the horizontal and vertical directions.
3. Transform the decompressed image to the desired color space F using the appropriate G to F transformation.
4. Round-off resulting pixel values to the nearest integer so that they lie in the 0–255 range.

1.2   Compression History Estimation (CHEst) for Gray-Scale Images

JPEG compression and decompression replicates the steps for a single color plane but without sub sampling and interpolation in the gray scale images [13, 17]. Due to JPEG's quantization operations, the discrete cosine transform (DCT) coefficient histograms of previously JPEG-compressed gray-scale images exhibit a near-periodic structure with the period determined by the quantization step-size. But here the same periodic structure with quantization of maximum priority with sampling, interpolation, and quantization is used for color images [15, 20].

1.2.1. Algorithm
The estimation of quantization of step-sizes is given as follows:

1. Compute set of the desired frequency DCT coefficients D from the previously compressed image.
2. Estimate the parameter λ from the observations with N the number of coefficients in the set D.
3. Assuming all quantization step-sizes are equally used with suitable parameters.

1.3   JPEG Recompression

If the TIFF or BMP image's file-size needs to be reduced, the approach is applied with features like color space, sub sampling factor, and quantization table for JPEG compression [16, 21]. There are some of the choices for the color transformations include RGB to YCbCr, RGB to ITU, RGB to YCC, and sRGB to 8-bit CIELab. The common sub sampling factors are 2×2, 1×1, 1×1 and 1×1, 1×1, 1×1. The quantization tables are often adjusted by Quality Factor (QF). The QF is a reference number between 1 to 100 used by the IJG JPEG implementation, QF=100 set all the quantized steps which are in unity and thus yields the best quality of JPEG is achieved. The combination of the above choices yields a JPEG image file with a certain file-size. Smaller file-sizes are typically accompanied by increased distortions in the recompressed image. In this section, the demonstration shows using CHEst to recompress a previously JPEG-compressed color image offers significant benefits over a recompression approach to reduce the distortion.

1.4   JPEG Recompression on Using CHEst

To perform recompression using the CHEst information, transform the observed image into the compression color space using the estimated sRGB to 8-bit CIELab color transformation. Then, the effect of the smoothing decompression on a and b color planes is processed [19]. After performing 2×2, 1×1, 1×1 sub sampling using the IJG JPEG implementation [12], JPEG-compress the 8-bit CIE Lab color planes with the estimated quantization tables. Our recompression yields a JPEG image with file-size 32.31 kilobytes (KB) with an SNR of 22.58 dB; the SNR is computed in dB with respect to the image in the perceptually-uniform CIE Lab color space by the theoretical study.

For comparison, recompress the image using a variety of settings; JPEG-compress the test BMP image using the RGB to YCbCr, RGB to ITU, YCbCr , RGB to YCC, and sRGB to 8-bit CIE Lab color transforms using 2×2, 1×1, 1×1 and also using 1×1, 1×1, 1×1 sub sampling . For each chosen color transform and sub sampling, varied quantization tables using the QF value and noted the resulting JPEG image's file-size (in KB) and the incurred distortion in SNR (in dB in the CIELab space)[22]. Each curve illustrates the behavior of file-size versus SNR as it vary the QF for a particular choice of color space; curves are obtained using 2×2, 1×1, 1×1 sub sampling and using 1x1, 1x1, 1x1 sub sampling. The curves demonstrate a "knee-point" trend—the SNR remains flat for a broad range of file-sizes, but decreases rapidly for small changes in file-size thereafter. The file- size SNR pair (32.31 KB, 22.58 dB) associated with the image recompressed using dictionary- based CHEst results is marked with symbol. Both the plots confirm that exploiting the dictionary-based CHEst enables us to strike a desirable file-size versus distortion trade-off [14, 15] and attained the nearly minimum file-size without introducing any significant additional distortion.

1.5   JPEG Recompression Using Lattice Based Chest

To perform recompression using the lattice-based CHEst information, transform the observed image to the estimated *space*. Using the inverse of estimated *transformation,JPEG* compress the three planes with the estimated quantization calculations to obtain an image with file-size according to the use of its applications.

2   Conclusion

In this paper, smoothness and lattice structures are explained which inherent in images to develop solutions for JPEG Compression History Estimation (CHEst). Here, it is shown that JPEG Compression and *Decompression* methods for color images that effectively combines and balances. The motivation for the hybrid approach from the realization that decompression techniques rely on sampling quantization are inadequate to handle the wide variety of practically encountered decompression problems. Compression estimation can be potentially employed in a wide variety of applications, including imaging, decompression, and channel equalization. Theoretical analysis of an idealized compression algorithm reveals that the balance between the amount of sampling and sub sampling is simultaneously determined by the compression and decompression process with the CHEst history estimation and algorithms. In future it can be taken with some forms of periodic structures, techniques and algorithms.

References

[1] Wallace, G.K., Pennebaker, W.B., Mitchell: JPEG. Van No strand Reinhold, NY (1993); Nelson, M.: The JPEG Still Picture Compression Standard. Communications of ACM 34 (4) 31-44 (1991)

[2] Rosenholtz, R., Zakhor, A.: Iterative procedures for reduction of blocking effects in transform image coding. IEEE Trans. Cir. Sys. For Video Tech. 2 (1992)

[3] Minami, S., Zakhor, A.: An optimization approach for removing blocking effects in transforms. Trans. Cir. Sys. For Video Tech. 5, 74–82 (1995); IEEE Trans Image Processing 5, 1363–1368 (1996)

[4] Yang, Y., Galatsanos, N.P., Katsaggelos, A.K.: Regularized reconstruction to reduce blocking artifacts of block discrete cosine transform compressed images. IEEE Trans. Cir.Sys. for Video Tech. 3, 837 (1993)

[5] Aburdene, G.R., Kozick, M.F., Harris, R.J., Commun, R.F., Rochester, N.Y.: Differential block coding of bilevel images Robertson. IEEE Transactions on Image Processing 5(9), 1368–1370 (1996)

[6] Fan, Z., de Queiroz, R.L.: Identification of bitmap compression history: JPEG detection and quantizer estimation. IEEE Transactions on Image Processing 12(2), 230–235 (2003)

[7] Chou, J., Crouse, M., Ramachandran, K.: A simple algorithm for removing blocking artifacts in block-transform coded images. IEEE Signal Processing Lett. 5 (February 1998)

[8] watson, A.B.: Image compression using discrete cosine transformer. Mathematica Journal 4(1), 81–88 (1996)

[9] Fan, Z., de Queiroz, R.L., Fan, Z.: Identification of Bitmap Compression History: JPEG Detection and Quantizer Estimation. IEEE Transactions on Image Processing 12(2) (2003)

[10] Sharma, G., Trussell, H.J.: Digital color imaging. IEEE. Trans Image Processing 6(7), 990–1001 (1997), html/colormultimedia/, http://www4.ncsu.edu/eos/users/h/hjt/ of color signals, Scanners. IEEE Trans. Image Processings

[11] Poynton, C.A., Wiley, J.: A technical introduction to digital video. J. Wiley, New York (1950)

[12] Jayant, N.: signal compression. International Journal of High Speed Electronics and Systems 8(1), 1–12 (1997)

[13] Smith, S.W.: The Scientist and Engineer's Guide to Digital Signal Processing, 2nd edn.

[14] Neelamani, R.: Inverse Problems in Image Processing. Rice University, Texas (2003)

[15] Neelamani, R., Dash, S., Baranink, R.G.: On nearly orthogonal lattice bases and random lattices (September 18, 2006)

[16] Neelamani, R., de Queiroz, R., Fan, Z., Dash, S.: The pixel with respect to a chosen color space; for example, RGB, YCbCr(1) the color space used to independently compress the image's. Recentl Derived the Geometric Conditions for a Lattice Basis

[17] Eschbach, Fan, Z., Eschbach, R.: JPEG decompression with reduced artifacts. In: Proc. SPIE, vol. 2186, p. 50 (1994); doi:10.1117/12.173932

[18] Bauschke, H.H., Hamilton, C.H., Macklem, M.S., McMichael, J.S., Swart, N.R.: IEEE Transactions on Image Processing 12(7), 843–849 (2003); ISSN:1057-7149 (Date of Current Version: July 15, 2003)

[19] Filler, T., Pevny, T., Craver, S.: Identification of bitmap compression history: jpeg detection and quantizer Information. In: 13th International Conference, Prague, Czech, p. 297 (2011)

[20] Sharma, G., Trussell, J.: Digital color imaging. IEEE Transactions on Image Processing 6(7) (1997)

[21] Clarke, R.R.: Transform coding of images, p. 432. Academic Press Press Professional, Inc., San Diego (1985); ISBN: 0-12-175730-7, ISBN: 0-12-175730-7 (1986)

[22] Neelamani, R., de Queiroz, R.L., Fan, Z., Dash, S., Baraniuk, R.G.: JPEG compression history estimation for color images, 15(6), 1365–1378 (2006)

Detection of Car in Video Using Soft Computing Techniques

T. Senthil Kumar[1], S.N. Sivanandam[2], and G.P. Akhila[3]

[1] Assistant Professor (SG), Computer Science Department,
Amrita School of Engineering,
Amrita Vishwa Vidyapeetham, Coimbatore
t_senthilkumar@cb.amrita.edu
[2] Professor-Emeritus, Karpagam College of Engineering,
Coimbatore
[3] M.Tech (Computer Vision and Image Processing) Second Year
Amrita Vishwa Vidyapeetham, Coimbatore

Abstract. The features indicate the characteristics of the object. The features vary from object to object like colour, size, shape, texture etc. Natural images can be decomposed into constituent objects, which are in turn composed of features. The corners or edges of the object can be considered as part of feature extraction. The edges / corner detection is also complex for certain objects as it has varied characteristics due to other objects in representation. The other examples of features include motion in image sequences, curves, boundaries between different image regions, properties of region. Feature extraction is the process of transforming of high-dimensional data into a meaningful representation of reduced dimensionality. The identified features are beneficial to mitigate the computational complexity and improve the accuracy of a particular classifier. This paper suggests mechanism for selection of appropriate technique for detecting object like car in video.

Keywords: Feature, Classifier, Edge detection, Eigen value.

1 Introduction

The provided input may be a image or a video. In video it is splitted into frames and each frame is analyzed for extracting features. The features are mapped on to a feature space. The extracted features are then analyzed and the relevant features could be taken using appropriate feature reduction techniques. The feature reduction allows the application domain space to be handled on a reduced complexity as the number of features analyzed is reduced.

Feature extraction requires reducing amount of resources required for analyzing large data set. The number of variables always plays a vital role in analyzing complex data. There is a need for a large amount of memory and programming involved in generating training sets. The trained data needs to be analyzed for better results. The selection of an appropriate classifier plays a vital role in feature analysis. The dimensionality reduction techniques include: Principle Component Analysis, Multi learning subspace learning, Non linear dimensionality reduction, Multi linear PCA etc.

P.V. Krishna, M.R. Babu, and E. Ariwa (Eds.): ObCom 2011, Part II, CCIS 270, pp. 556–565, 2012.
© Springer-Verlag Berlin Heidelberg 2012

2   Feature Extraction Techniques

2.1   Feature Extraction Algorithms with Different Rules

This algorithm of feature extraction [2] uses principal component analysis (PCA), minimum noise fraction (MNF) transform and their kernel versions. The rules for feature selection are energy and signal-to-noise (SNR). A local singularity measure is introduced to select the most singular component transformed for anomaly detection. Kernel PCA (KPCA) with Local singularity (LS) rules shows good single extreme feature. Detection performance of KPCA with LS rule is much better than the other methods. KPCA is stronger than others in terms of for feature extraction. Kernel based feature extraction is more effective. The demerits of these methods are detection performance with multi-components which is worse than with one component and issues undertaken by the assumption that reliable ground truth target maps are available.

2.2   Feature Extraction Algorithm Based on K Nearest Neighbor Local Margin

The algorithm which is used for feature extraction is K nearest neighbor local margin maximization [3]. The comparison is done using with LDA (Linear Discriminant Analysis), PCA (Principal Component Analysis) and MMC (Maximum Margin Criterion). Many feature extraction algorithms have been proposed in the last decades. Principle Component Analysis (PCA), as a well-known unsupervised feature extraction method, aims to extract a subspace in which the reconstruction error can be minimized, or equivalently the variance of the total projected data points can be maximized. Linear Discriminant Analysis (LDA) maximizes the between class scatter matrix and simultaneously minimize the within-class scatter matrix. The objective of PCA is not to select useful features but to reserve the data information as much as possible. The LDA suffers from the small sample size problem that provides singularity characteristics for the scatter matrix.

This method performs better in high dimensionality. It reduces error rate and complexity by selecting only limited   K nearest neighbors for each point. The main disadvantage of this algorithm is what it will not work with high dimensional data.

2.3   Feature Extraction Using Extended Optical Flow Algorithm

General optical flow algorithm [4] detects noisy and irrelevant features. The extended version of this algorithm extracting low level features. To overcome the problem due to complex scenes it introduces a frame jump technique along with thresholding of unwanted features. Frame jump restricts to detecting only useful features by removing other features detected by the existing Optical Flow algorithm. This method eliminates noisy and irrelevant features. It minimizes correspondence problem by eliminating multiple features on the same point.

For analyzing the human activities in videos, one of the major steps involved is extraction of concise low level features. There have been many algorithms that concentrate on feature extraction techniques including Optical Flow, Point Trajectories, Background Subtracted Blobs and Filter Responses to serve a variety of applications. Extraction of unambiguous feature data is complicated by several factors such as occlusions, noise and background clutter.

Frame Jump[3] helps for eliminating noisy and irrelevant features by determining Euclidean distance of separation of various features and correspondingly filter useful low level features for extraction. Data such as coordinate position, speed and direction of the moving features pertaining to human actions are comfortably extracted using our technique. The notable increase in the accuracy for classifying human actions accounts for the effectiveness of extracting such data.

The useful features are defined as features that show considerable movement in their position spatially with respect to a sequence of images. The sequence of images constitutes variety of human actions. The change in the motion while performing an action helps us distinguish the useful features from noisy features that are spatially distant from human body. The detection and separation of these two types of features is performed by Frame Jump technique. The Frame Jump technique coupled with the threshold of noisy features is employed in Optical Flow algorithm to extract low level feature data. The demerits of this method is that when integrate with other feature tracking algorithm it will increase the possibility of classifying variety of human actions.

2.4   A Data-Driven Intermediate Level Feature Extraction Algorithm

The algorithm which is used to extract feature is iterative refinement algorithm [5].The approach works by classifying the edge data prior to fitting which is not required. The algorithm is efficient because of robustness, accuracy and robust performance with complex data including surfaces. The method depends on correct choices of initial estimates and restricted to a set of images. The time required to obtain initial estimates depends on parameters such as window size and sampling pattern based on empirical threshold value.

2.5   Nonlinear Discriminant Algorithm for Feature Extraction and Data Classification

This algorithm [6] combines Fisher's criterion function with a preliminary Perceptron-like nonlinear projection of vectors in pattern space. Nonlinear Discriminant Algorithm(NLDA) training required less iteration than MLP. NLDA features gave better classification result than MLP features. Unequal class sizes may provide bad results. The demerit of this method is that, it depends on the model selection criteria.

High iteration numbers suggests a very complicated geometry for MLP error surfaces. Around 30000 iterations were required to be completed to converge to MPLS values.

The features of MLP and NLDA networks have been analyzed using their mean error probabilities [6]. The proposed network model used one hidden layer architecture and one output in the NLDA case and two outputs for MLP's.

2.6   Modified Multiple Discriminant Analysis and Difference Principal Component Analysis

Multiple discriminant analysis (MMDA) and difference principal component analysis (DPCA) [7] are popularly used for feature detection. The algorithms can be enhanced and applied for confusing patterns. This algorithm is proved to be efficient for working with complex shapes.

2.7   A Polygonal Line Algorithm

This algorithm works by using local linear models. The algorithm uses robust and nonlinear curve estimation for multivariate data types. It reduces the computational complexity for large samples. The accuracy of this algorithm depends on number of line segments and sample size. The data sets are analyzed and their equivalent eigen values and vectors are extracted [8]. The extracted values are used for analyzing the features. The demerit of this method is that it depends on number of line segments and sample size.

2.8   On Image Matrix Based Feature Extraction Algorithm

Image matrix based feature extraction is applied in Two dimensional principal component analysis and two dimensional linear discriminant analysis [9]. The algorithm is efficient as it reduces the computational cost. The algorithm works by mapping the 2D Image vertices on to a one-dimensional vector space. The disadvantage of this approach includes the large size of vector space and computational effort.

2.9   Feature Extraction Algorithm Based on Local Picture Computation

The algorithm [10] works by converting the picture on to a geometric space. The parameters of the picture include picture size, perimeter, picture shape and texture. The picture feature components are being generated. The approach works based on generating effective feature values. The picture localization is performed both locally and globally. The merits effective extraction of feature value during computation. The algorithm is not strongly influenced by noise effects. The effective picture information becomes lost during noise.

2.10   Feature Extraction Algorithm Using Reference Vectors

The algorithm extracts a reference feature vector from a image [11]. The reference vector is calculated based on correlation matrices. The approach works better based on user preferences. The method is computationally less complex as reference vector is used for feature extraction. The reference data are considered as constituents of a coordination system. The demerit of this method is that, it takes long time for calculation of reference vector.

2.11 Rotation Invariance Image Matching Method Using Harris Corner Detection

Improved Harris Corner Detection and descriptor of SIFT method [12] are applied to extract features from images. First, Harris corner detection method is used for finding the interest points from the two images to be matched, in which an extreme tactics is adopted for exactly determining the interest points. A sub-block checking method is adopted for eliminating the cluster to reduce the number of interest points. Second, it describes an approach to depict the characteristics of interest points which are gained by rotating the area centered the interest point. Thirdly, the matching method is introduced calculating the similar information among these points. This method produces good results for matching two images that has different angle and error rate is low when matching two images. This method depends on the proper assigning of threshold value.

First, Gaussian filter smooth image processing is adopted to eliminate noisy points. Then, Edge detection algorithm can be used for solving this problem. The Robert, sobel, prewitt methods are the operators based on gradient, which can make sure of the direction of edge according with the gradient orientation, as these methods are chosen based on gradient. Sobel operator shows good results in edge extraction, and inhabits the noisy better than the other two methods.

2.12 Linear Feature Extraction Technique

Linear feature extraction Technique [13] uses Bayesian error probability. This approach is easy to implement. It preserves the shape of the class conditional densities after transformation and classified the problem with known conditional densities. This approach will give better result only when classes are known before classification. The proposed optimization procedure significantly improves the classification performance when it is initialized by popular LFE (Linear Feature Extraction) matrices such as the Fisher linear discriminant analysis. The proposed algorithm is enhanced to apply when the class conditional densities are estimated from given training data.

The main assumptions are: (1) the number of classes, C, is known before classification, (2) the given classes are disjoint and exhaustive; i.e., a pattern x belongs to exactly one of the C classes, and (3) all the class conditional densities and the class prior probabilities are exactly known. The improvement has been validated experimentally for three popular LFE algorithms.

2.13 Nonlinear Feature Extraction Algorithm with Distance Transformation

Distance information is taken as the basis for feature extraction. This algorithm does not uses classification based approaches. The number of parameters used in the approach may be larger and may reduce the performance of the algorithm.

3   Advantages and Disadvantages of Different Methods

Sl.No.	Author	Method	Merit	Remarks	Performance Parameter
1.	Zhenlin Liu, Yanfeng Gu, Ye Zhang	Feature Extraction Algorithms with Different Rules	-KPCA with LS rule shows good single extreme feature. -Detection performance of KPCA with LS rule is greatly better than the other methods. -KPCA is stronger than others in terms of ability to feature extraction. -Kernel based feature extraction is more effective	-Detection performance with multi-components is worse than with one component. -Issues undertaken by th assumption that reliable ground truth target map are available	-Receiver Operating Characterstics(ROC
2.	Feng Pan, Jiandong Wang, Xiaohui Lin	Based on K Nearest Neighbor Local Margin	-Perform better in High dimensionality -Reduces the complexity by selecting only limited K nearest neighbors for each point. -Lower error rate	-Algorithm will fail, if work with high dimensional data set	- Error Rate
3.	Ashok Ramadass, Myunghoon Suk, B.Prabhakaran	Extended optical Flow Algorithm	-Eliminate noisy and irrelevant features. -Extract low level feature data -Minimize correspondence problem by eliminating multiple features on the same point.	-Threshold should be set by user	-Accuracy of classification
4.	David Shi Chen	Data-Driven Intermediate Level Feature Extraction Algorithm	-It reconstructs curves from edge data -It performs well against outliers and is computationally efficient. -Data classification and parameter estimation is easier. -Higher Accuracy -The approach provides reconstruction of surfaces from range data.	-Depends upon correct choices of initial estimates. -Restricted to the class of edge images where curves are well defined. -Selection of threshold value is empirical. -Time required to obtain initial estimates depends on parameters such as window size and sampling pattern	-Goodness-of-fit measure
5.	Carlos Santa Cruz and Jos´e R. Dorronsoro	A Nonlinear Discriminant Algorithm for Feature Extraction and Data Classification.	-The training iteration is less for NLDA -The classification feature results are better than MLP.	-Model Selection Criteria	-Error Rate

6.	Jiang Gao and Xiaoqing Ding	On Improvement of Feature Extraction Algorithms for Discriminative Pattern Classification	-The features are extracted from a small category set.	-The discriminative features are extracted using nonlinear and bilinear transformation.	-Classification Error Rate
7.	Feng Zhang	Polygonal Line Algorithm	-The approach produces better curve estimation. -It reduces complexity. -Decrease noise effect in estimation accuracy	-Accuracy depends on factors such as number of line segments and sample size	- Estimation error
8.	Liwei Wang, Xiao Wang, and Jufu Feng	On Image Matrix Based Feature Extraction Algorithms Two Dimensional Principal Component Analysis (2DPCA) and Two Dimensional Linear Discriminant Analysis (2DLDA)]	-The computational effort and singularity in feature extraction is reduced.	-Feature extraction depends on the dimensionality	-Model have been proposed
9.	Yoshio Hayashi And Yasuzo Suto	A Feature Extraction Algorithm Based on Local Picture Computation	-It extracts effective feature values from a binary picture on the basis of local picture computation.	-The noise is introduced due to picture sampling. -For picture sampling density being too high, algorithm will be strongly influenced by noise effects. -For picture sampling density being too low, effective pictorial information will become lost.	-Error Probability
10.	Asako Ohno, Hajime Murao	Feature Extraction Algorithm Using Reference Vectors	-Appropriate data selection is important as it uses reference vector. -Easy to implement	-Takes long time for calculation of reference vector	-Similarity

11.	Xin Zhang,Guojin He,Jiying Yuan	A rotation invariance Image matching method based on Harris corner detection	-Produces good results for matching two images that has different angle. -Low error rate for matching two images	-Confirming the proper threshold is very important	-Invariance to rotataion
12.	Moataz El Ayadi and Konstantinos N. Plataniotis	Linear Feature Extraction Algorithm (LFE) characterized by Bayesian Error Probability (BEP)	-Easy to implement -Preserve the shape of the class conditional densities after transformation. -Classified the problem with known conditional densities.	-Classes are known before classification. -Enhance the proposed algorithm to apply when the class conditional densities are estimated from given training data.	-Bayesian Error probability(BEP)
13.	Warren L. G. Koontz And Keinosuke Fukunaga	A Nonlinear Feature Extraction Algorithm Using Distance Transformation	-Less memory is required. -Mapping algorithm is highly flexible. -Algorithm is non iterative.	-This proposed algorithm not intended to compete with algorithms for classification	-Classification error

4   Conclusion

The paper analyzes the different approaches available for feature extraction techniques for extracting objects in video. The existing techniques are applied for data sets like human behavior, vehicle and face. This could be used for detecting object like car. The observations from survey have provided the following inferences:

i.   The performance of feature extraction technique depends on key point extraction mechanism.
ii. There is a little amount of research being done on brand analysis of cars.
iii. Kernel PCA along Local Singularity rule outperforms PCA Minimum noise fraction (MNF) technique.
iv. The feature extraction techniques could be measured using Error rate techniques.
v.   Hue statistics can be a better solution for feature extraction technique as there is large variance in data analysis.

References

1. Pineda-Torres, I.H., Gokcen, I., Buckles, B.P.: Image Feature Set for Correspondence Mappings. International Journal of High Performance Computing Applications 16(3), 273–283 (2002)
2. Liu, X.Z., Gu, Y., Zhang, Y.: Comparative Analysis of Feature Extraction Algorithms with Different Rules for Hyper spectral Anomaly Detection. In: 2010 First International Conference on Pervasive Computing, Signal Processing and Applications, vol. 7, pp. 293–297 (2010)

3. Pan, F., Wang, J., Lin, X.: Feature Extraction Algorithm Based on K Nearest Neighbor Local Margin. In: CCPR 2009, Chinese Conference on Pattern Recognition, vol. 7, pp. 1–5 (December 2009)
4. Ramadass, A., Suk, M., Prabhakaran, B.: Feature Extraction Method For Video based Human Action Recognitions: Extended optical Flow Algorithm. In: 2010 IEEE International Conference on Acoustics Speech and Signal Processing (ICASSP), vol. 7, pp. 1106–1109 (June 2010)
5. Chen, D.S.: A Data-Driven Intermediate Level Feature Extraction Algorithm. IEEE Transactions On Pattern Analysis And Machine Intelligence 11, 749–758 (2002)
6. Cruz, C.S., Dorronsoro, J.R.: A Nonlinear Discriminant Algorithm for Feature Extraction and Data Classification. IEEE Transactions on Neural Networks 9, 1370–1376 (1998)
7. Gao, J., Ding, X.: On Improvement of Feature Extraction Algorithms for Discriminative Pattern Classification. In: Proceedings 15th International Conference on Pattern Recognition, vol. 2, p. 7 (August 2002)
8. Zhang, F.: A Polygonal Line Algorithm based Nonlinear Feature Extraction Method. In: ICDM 2004, pp. 281–288 (2004)
9. Wang, L., Wang, X., Feng, J.: On Image Matrix Based Feature Extraction Algorithms. IEEE Transactions n Systems, Man and Cybernetics 36, 194 (2006)
10. Hayashi, Y., Suto, Y.: A Feature Extraction Algorithm Based on Local Picture Computation. IEEE Transactions on Systems, Man and Cybernetics 7, 743 (2007)
11. Ohno, A., Murao, H.: A Similarity Measuring Method for Images Based on the Feature Extraction Algorithm using Reference Vectors. In: Second International Conference on Innovative Computing, Information and Control, ICICIC 2007, p. 454 (2007)
12. Zhang, X., He, G., Yuan, J.: A rotation invariance Image matching method based on Harris corner detection. In: 2nd International Conference on Image and Signal Processing, CISP 2009, p. 1 (October 2009)
13. Ayadi, M.E., Plataniotis, K.N.: Improving Classification Performance Of Linear Feature Extraction Algorithms. In: 2010 IEEE International Conference on Acoustics Speech and Signal Processing (ICASSP), p. 2166 (March 2010)
14. Koontz, W.L.G., Fukunaga, K.: A Nonlinear Feature Extraction Algorithm Using Distance Transformation. IEEE Transactions on Computers 21, 56 (1972)
15. Xu, L.-Q., Li, Y.: Video Classification Using Spatial-Temporal features and PCA. In: ICME 2003, vol. 3, pp. 485–488 (March 2003)
16. Harris, C., Stephens, M.J.: A combined corner and edge detector. In: Alvey Vision Conference, pp. 147–152 (1988)
17. Moravec, H.: Obstacle avoidance and navigation in the real world by a seeing robot rover,Technical Report CMU-RI-TR-3, Carnegie-Mellon University,Robotics Institute, Stanford University (September 1980)
18. Schmid, C., Mohr, R., Bauckhage, C.: Evaluation of interest point detectors. International Journal of Computer Vision 37(2), 151–172 (2000)
19. Freund, Y.: Boosting a weak learning algorithm by majority. Information and Computation, 256–285 (1995)
20. Freund, Y., Schapire, R.E.: Experiments with a new boosting algorithm. In: Proceedings of the Thirteenth International Conference Machine Learning, pp. 148–156 (1996)
21. Schapire, R.: The boosting approach to machine learning: An overview. In: MSRI Workshop on Nonlinear Estimation and Classification (2001)
22. Freund, Y., Schapire, R.E.: A short introduction to boosting. Journal of Japanese Society for Artificial Intelligence 14(5), 771–780 (1999)

23. Sivaraman, S., Trivedi, M.M.: A General Active-Learning Framework for On-Road Vehicle Recognition and Tracking. IEEE Transactions on Intelligent Transportation System 11, 2 (2010)
24. Yeh, Y.-J., Hsu, C.-T.: Online Selection of Tracking Features Using AdaBoost. IEEE Transactions on Circuits and Systems for video technology 19 (March 2009)
25. Viola, P., Jones, M.: Rapid object detection using a boosted cascade of simple features. In: Conf. CVPR 2001, Dearborn, MI, USA (2001)
26. Hiromoto, M., Sugano, H.: Partially Parallel Architecture for AdaBoost-Based Detection With Haar-Like Features. IEEE Transactions on Circuits and Systems for Video Technology 19 (January 2009)
27. Sivanantha Raja, A., Sankaranarayanan, K.: Use of RGB Color Sensor in Colorimeter for better Clinical measurement of Blood Glucose. BIME Journal ICGST 2006 06 (December 2006)
28. Bradsky, G., Kaebler, A.: Learning OpenCV computer vision with the OpenCV library
29. Bradski, G.R., Pisarevsky, V.: Intel's Computer Vision Library: Applications in calibration, stereo, segmentation, tracking, gesture, face and object recognition (2000)
30. Jain, A.K., Vailaya, A.: Image retrieval using color and shape. Pattern Recogniton, 1233–1244 (August 1996)
31. Freund, Y., Schapire, R.E.: A decision-theoretic generalization of on-line learning and an application to boosting. In: 2nd European Conference on Computational Learning Theory (1995)
32. Schapire, R.E., Singer, Y.: Improved boosting using confidence-rated predictions. Machine Learning 37, 297–336 (1999)

A Survey of Different Stages for Monitoring Traffic Rule Violation

R. Aarthi, C. Arunkumar, and S. Padmavathi

Department of Information Technology,
Amrita Vishwa Vidyapeetham, Coimbatore 641112, India
{r_aarthi,c_arunkumar,s_padmavathi}@cb.amrita.edu

Abstract. A traffic surveillance system is a controlled system that helps to monitor and regulate the traffic. In this paper, a method for extracting the license number of the vehicle that is exceeding the speed limit is proposed. A Study is conducted by covering various stages of monitoring system such as vehicle detection in the video, tracking the vehicle for speed calculation and extracting the vehicle number in the number plate that can be used in places with high public vicinity.

Keywords: vehicle detection, classification, tracking, speed calculation and license plate localization component.

1   Introduction

The vision application is to mainly focus on handling complicated real-time video data for automatic recognition and monitoring. The robust system should not depend on the climatic conditions and hardware devices. Development of technologies helps the researchers to analyze more complex data in much robust way. One of the major contributions of technology in the vision system is that it has an impressive role in several Intelligent Transportation applications. The Intelligent transport system (ITS) helps in vehicle count, a much larger set of traffic parameters such as vehicle classifications, lane changes, etc., can be measured

According to the Insurance Institute for Highway Safety [12], 22% of all traffic accidents around the world are caused by drivers violating rules. Traditionally, vehicle speed monitoring or detection is done using radar technology. The disadvantage of traditional method is that it produces noise in the result and radar sensor can only track one vehicle at any point of time. In this paper, analysis is done to identify a robust and efficient method for monitoring traffic and detect violation of traffic rule in vision based method. The procedure is divided into sub categories for simplification. The architecture diagram of the proposed model is depicted in Figure.1.This paper is organized as follows: Section 2 - study on vehicle detection is done. In Section 3 - vehicle type detection is discussed followed by vehicle tracking and speed estimation in Section 4 & 5. In Section 6 various number plate extraction methods are discussed.

P.V. Krishna, M.R. Babu, and E. Ariwa (Eds.): ObCom 2011, Part II, CCIS 270, pp. 566–573, 2012.

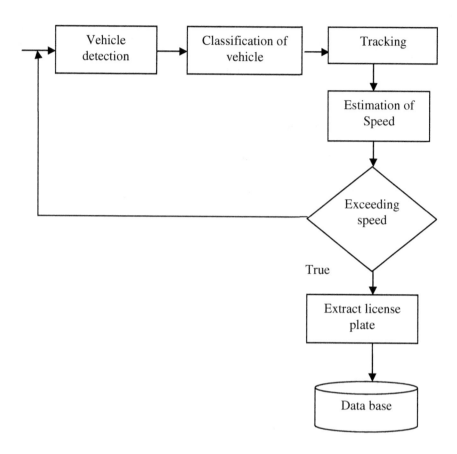

Fig. 1. Architecture of the proposed system

2   Vehicle Detection

Object detection involves capturing the frames from the video taken through surveillance cameras. These frames are then examined for detecting the object of our interest (vehicle) in the frame. In optical flow method [1], image difference between two consecutive frames is taken to obtain the binary image. The maximum and minimum value of each row and column helps in deciding the presence of moving object. The algorithm produces better results for stationary cameras. But, the performance is degraded in the real time system.

The 3D model based algorithm [2] uses shape and appearance of specific objects. The image pixels are grouped, if they are connected in edge image. The connected pixels are then verified with the predefined model of the object in the database. The disadvantage is that it is unrealistic to expect detailed models for all vehicles that could be found on the roadway. This method fails even if the vehicle occludes partially with each other and the processing time increases as linearly as the size of the image. This method is good with the well defined vehicle model dataset. As the improvement of [1], the image difference method [3] is done by dividing the image region into square regions called grids. Then the dissimilarity in the gray levels is considered row and column wise. The method has 95% efficiency in a real time video under any environmental conditions. Table.1 shows comparison between vehicle detection methods.

Table 1. Comparison of vehicle detection algorithms

Method Constraints	Optical Flow method	3D model Based method	Image difference method
Real-time Capability	No	Holds good for some condition	Yes
Process time	Very High	Increase with size of image	Less
Adaptability to environment	No	No	yes
Detection capability	----	85%	95%
Requirement of prior knowledge	No	Yes	No

3   Vehicle Type Detection

In [4], detection and classification of the vehicles based on length and width is discussed. Camera calibration plays a major role in estimating these attributes. The dimensions used for classifying vehicles fall into two categories: Cars and Non-cars(Van, Tractor-trailers etc.,) Since the classification is based on the dimension of the vehicle, the computed height might be the combination of the vehicle's width and height due to camera orientation. It is difficult to separate the width and height using vehicle boundaries or camera parameters. It is also observed that combined width and height value for computing the height the average dimensions of a truck are slightly larger than the dimensions of a car.

Sub region strategy [5] method detects the vehicles by using scene division that divides the scene into 16 parts as 4*4 grids. k-means clustering is used for classifying the moving objects with the 5 features listed below.

Area: Size of the object in pixels

Velocity: Time derivative of centriod of the objects

Area': Time derivative of area

Compactness: Equal to area / perimeter^2

Angle: Angle between motion direction and direction of major axis of silhouette

Compactness is used to distinguish a vehicle from pedestrians and bicycles. Area' is useful for classifying pedestrians from vehicle and bicycle. Angle helps to classifying pedestrians and vehicle. The approach is based on each grid

$$P_i(v) = \eta(v, \mu_i, \Sigma_i) \quad i = 1,2,3.$$ (1)

Where v = (area, speed, compactness)
   Using Bayesian rules the following equation can be derived:

$$p(category = i \mid v) \alpha \, p_i(v)^* \, p_i i = 1,2,3.$$ (2)

Where p(category=i|v) and p_i are posterior and prior probability of each category respectively
   If the number of moving objects passing a subregion has not reached a threshold N, Classification is simply realized by comparing the distance between the feature vector and every cluster and the Gaussian distribution is estimated in the following way:

$$\mu_i = 1/N(\sum_{r=1}^{N}) v_{i,r}, i = 1,2,3.$$ (3)

$$\sigma_{ij}^2 = 1/N(\sum_{r=1}^{N} (v_{i,r} - \mu_i)^*(v_{j,r} - \mu_i) \, i, j = 1,2,3.$$ (4)

The category is determined by the posterior probability and the classifier is refined at the same time to be robust to condition change:

$$P_{k,new} = (1 - \beta)P_{k,old} + \beta(M_{k,t})k = 1,2,3.$$ (5)

$$\mu_{new} = (1 - \gamma)\mu_{old} + w_t.$$ (6)

$$\sigma_{i,j,new}^2 = (1 - \gamma)\sigma_{i,j,old}^2 + \gamma(v_{i,t} - \mu_t)(v_{j,t} - \mu_t).$$ (7)

Where β and y are the refinement rate

Table 2. Comparison of vehicle type detection algorithms

Method	Classification by dimension of vehicle	Sub region strategy
Constraints		
Heavy Vehicle	Yes	No
Cars	Yes	No
Pedestraints	No	Yes
Limitations	Cars may actually be longer and wider than trucks cannot be identified	Heavy vehicles like trucks are not detected

4   Vehicle Tracking

This step focuses to track the vehicle within the focusing field. This enables the user to calculate the speed of the vehicle. In the SVM based algorithm [6], it does not use a template to identify the vehicle type. It requires an additional method to identify the model of the vehicle and to point out the position. Hence it reduces the efficiency.

In the HMM model [7] (a mathematical probabilistic model), tracking of the vehicle is done faster because of a feature called the Self Organizing Map(SOM). The SOM is presented in a tabular format that contains the position of the control points of the b-spline which forms the shape of the bonnet of the car. Hence this obtained SOM can be used as a template and can be checked with the acquired image of the car so as to identify the exact make and model of the car. This template check is performed by the HMM algorithm.

5   Vehicle Speed Calculation

The video sequences are used to measure the speed of the vehicle [8]. Speed in each image is calculated using the position of reference points, given the time stamp. As the vehicle proceeds, calculations are performed and from each calculation the summary will be made as the final step to give the average speed of the vehicle between two marks. The equations to find the vehicle speed are shown below.

Distance between vehicle and starting point is measured in Kilometre

$$\text{Distance} = Df*(D/Dx)*(pn-p0) . \tag{8}$$

Time that vehicle spent in order to move to pn in unit of hour

$$\text{Time} = Tf*(tn-t0) . \tag{9}$$

Where,

   D   :The real distance between two marking points.
   Dx :The distance between two marking points measured in
        pixels
   X   :The width of the video scene measured in pixel
   Y   :The height of the video scene measured in pixel
   p0 :The right most of the vehicle position at time t=0
        measured in unit of pixels
   pn :The right most of the vehicle position at time t=n
        measured in unit of pixels
   t0   :The time stamp saved at time t=0 measured in unit of
        milliseconds
   tn   :The time stamp saved at time t=n measured in unit of
        milliseconds
   Df :The distance conversion factor from meter to kilometer, which is
(1/(1000*60*60))
   Tf :The time conversion factor. Converting millisecond to hour , which is (1/1000)

In automatic vehicle speed detection [9] projection rules are applied to map from the in-camera coordinates to the real world coordinates. Fig.3.Camera is at a height H above the road with its optical axis tilted at an angle θ from the road's forwarded direction. Mapping is done between the image domain and real- world domain based on geometrical optics.

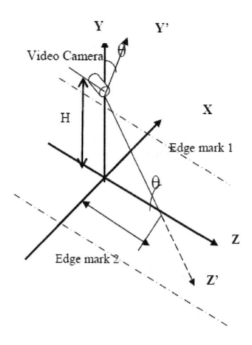

Fig. 2. Projection map

6   Number Plate Localization

The license plate localization involves segmenting the portion of the number plate region out of the car image. Input for this module is car image that is segmented in the frame and the output is a segmented region of number plate. There are various algorithms used under certain constraints. The comparison of the different algorithms is as follows:

The number plate reading using computer vision [10] method uses the signature of the number plate area in a horizontal cross section of the image. The signature of the number plate can be observed in the bottom cross section. There are strong grey level variations at regular intervals. The algorithm searches for maxima and minima of the cross section. This method is good for a standard type of number plate.

Optical character recognition method [11] is applicable only for the vehicles that have number plates with yellow color background. In this method, the yellow pixels in the image are assigned with white pixels. Then the change from black to white is observed and the region of the number plate is segmented. License plate recognition system [12] uses weight based density map method that assigns a weight for each pixel. The region whose pixel values are more will be segmented and identified as number plate region. There are 3 stages in this method. They are color subtraction, edge detection and density map method. This method is applied for varieties of number plate.

Table 3. Comparison of number plate localization algorithms

Method ⟍ Characteristics	Computer vision method	OCR method	Robust video based License plate recognition
Constraints	Standard vehicle template	Number plate with yellow background	No constraints
Efficiency	Less	Less	97%
Detect any type of number plate	No	No	Yes
Database for Comparison	Required	Not Required	Not Required

7   Conclusion

A study on various stages of real time traffic monitoring system is done. The image difference method for vehicle detection holds better for video. Vehicle type can be identified by dimension method by reducing the complexity of the problem. Then the vehicle is tracked to calculate the speed of the vehicle. HMM model combined with project rule can improve the result. If the vehicle exceeds the speed limit, then the number on the number plate is extracted and stored in a database. Robust license plate recognition method might bring better results.

References

1. Wei, S., Chen, Z., Dong, H.: Motion Detection based on temporal difference method and optical flow field. In: IEEE Second International Symposium on Electronic Commerce (2009)
2. Surgailis, T., Valinevicius, A., Zilys, M.: Traffic image processing systems. In: IEEE Second International Conference on Advances in Circuits (2009)
3. Junwei, W., Enrong, M.: Analysis and realization of a kind of grid arithmetic in detecting moving vehicle based on Image sequence (2003)

4. Gupta, S., Masoud, O., Martin, R.F.K., Papanikolopoulos, N.: Detecting and classification of vehicle, vol. 3(1) (2002)
5. Zhang, Z., Cai, Y., Huang, K., Tan, T.: Real-time moving object classification with automatic scene division. IEEE (2007)
6. Gao, D., Zhou, J., Xin, L.: SVM based detection moving vehicles for automatic traffic. In: IEEE Trasportation System Conference Proceedings, Oakland, CA USA (2001)
7. Lee, H., Kim, D., Bang, S.Y.: Real-time Automatic vehicle management system using vehicle tracking and car plate number identification. IEEE (2003)
8. Porpanomchai, C., Kongkittisan, K.: Vehicle speed detection system
9. Wu, S., Liu, Z., Li, J., Gu, C., Si, M., Tan, F.: An algorithm for automatic vehicle speed detection using video camera. In: Proceedings of 4th International Conference on Computer Science and Education (2009)
10. Barroso, J., Dagles, E.L., Rafael, A., Bular-Cruz, J.: Number plate reading using computer vision. In: ISIE-1997 Guimaras Portugal (1997)
11. Tahir, M., Asif, M.: Automatic number plate recognition system for vehicle identification using optical character recognition. In: Proceeding of ICISIP (2005)
12. Bremanth, R., Chitra, A., Seetharaman, V., Sudhan, V., Nathan, L.: A robust "Video based license plate recognition system. In: Proceedings of ICISIP (2005)

Common Ground Method of Current Injection
in Electrical Impedance Tomography

Tushar Kanti Bera and J. Nagaraju

Department of Instrumentation and Applied Physics, Indian Institute of Science Bangalore
Bangalore – 560012, Karnataka, India
solarjnr@isu.iisc.ernet.in

Abstract. Surface electrodes are essentially required to be switched for boundary data collection in electrical impedance tomography (EIT). Parallel digital data bits are required to operate the multiplexers used, generally, for electrode switching in EIT. More the electrodes in an EIT system more the digital data bits are needed. For a sixteen electrode system, 16 parallel digital data bits are required to operate the multiplexers in opposite or neighbouring current injection method. In this paper a common ground current injection is proposed for EIT and the resistivity imaging is studied. Common ground method needs only two analog multiplexers each of which need only 4 digital data bits and hence only 8 digital bits are required to switch the 16 surface electrodes. Results show that the USB based data acquisition system sequentially generate digital data required for multiplexers operating in common ground current injection method. The profile of the boundary data collected from practical phantom show that the multiplexers are operating in the required sequence in common ground current injection protocol. The voltage peaks obtained for all the inhomogeneity configurations are found at the accurate positions in the boundary data matrix which proved the sequential operation of multiplexers. Resistivity images reconstructed from the boundary data collected from the practical phantom with different configurations also show that the entire digital data generation module is functioning properly. Reconstructed images and their image parameters proved that the boundary data are successfully acquired by the DAQ system which in turn indicates a sequential and proper operation of multiplexers.

Keywords: electrical impedance tomography, common ground current injection, surface electrodes, practical phantom, inhomogeneity, image reconstruction, resistivity image, EIDORS.

1   Introduction

Electrical Impedance Tomography (EIT) [1] reconstructs the conductivity or resistivity distribution of a conducting domain (Ω) from the surface potential developed by a current signal injected at the domain boundary ($\partial\Omega$). EIT is a non-invasive, non-radiating, non-ionizing and inexpensive imaging modality. As a result, EIT has been extensively researched in clinical diagnosis [2-11], biotechnology [12] and other nondestructive methods (landmine detection [13], semiconductor wafer

P.V. Krishna, M.R. Babu, and E. Ariwa (Eds.): ObCom 2011, Part II, CCIS 270, pp. 574–587, 2012.
© Springer-Verlag Berlin Heidelberg 2012

characterization and [14], nondestructive testing of other materials like brick walls [15] and rocks [16]). But, due to poor signal to noise ratio (SNR) [3] of the boundary potential data and poor spatial resolution [17] the EIT systems has not yet been accepted as the regular medical imager.

Practical phantoms [18-29] are essential to assess the performance of an EIT systems for their validation, calibration and comparison purposes. It is, also, highly recommended to conduct a profound study on the system's efficiency, reliability and factor of safety prior to use the EIT system for the diagnostic imaging of human subjects. Reconstructed image quality mainly depends on the boundary data accuracy and the reconstruction algorithms [30-33]. Boundary data accuracy again depends upon the surface electrode array, phantom geometry and the analog instrumentation used. In EIT, the impedance images are reconstructed from the surface potentials developed by a constant current signal injected to the boundary of the domain to be imaged. The surface electrodes are required to be switched in a particular fashion for current injection and voltage measurements. Parallel digital bits are essentially required to operate the multiplexers which are, generally, used for electrode switching in modern EIT systems. For a 2^N-electrode EIT system, 4N digital bits are required to switch the electrodes in a particular current pattern. More the electrodes in an EIT system more the digital data bits are needed. A sixteen electrode system requires 16-bit parallel digital data bits to operate the multiplexers in a particular current pattern such as opposite or neighbouring current injection method. In this paper a common ground current injection technique is proposed for EIT and the resistivity imaging is studied. Common ground methods needs only two analog multiplexers each of which need only 4-bit parallel digital data to switch the surface electrodes. Hence only 8-bit parallel digital data are required to be generated by the electronic hardware such as DAQ card or any microcontroller. Results show that the data acquisition system sequentially generates the parallel digital data bits required for multiplexer operating in common ground current injection method. Boundary data profile and resistivity images of the practical phantoms also proved that the entire digital data generation module functioned properly and hence the surface electrodes are switched in a accurate sequence. Reconstructed images and their image parameters proved that the boundary data are successfully acquired by the DAQ card which in turn indicates a sequential and proper operation of multiplexers and data acquisition system.

2   Materials and Methods

2.1   Current Injection Methods in EIT

In EIT a low frequency constant sinusoidal current is injected to the domain under test through the pairs of two electrodes called current electrodes (E_C). The potentials developed at the domain boundary are measured on the other electrodes called voltage electrodes (E_P). In general, the differential potentials are measured across the different electrodes to avoid the error due to the contact impedance [34]. In the present study, however, in spite of the problem of skin impedance, to obtain the greatest sensitivity to changes in the resistivity of the body [35], voltages from current carrying electrodes are also measured. The method in which the current is injected to the object under EIT imaging system is called the current patterns or current injection protocols. The famous four different current injection protocols as reported by the researchers are neighboring or adjacent current injection method [36], opposite method [37], cross method [37] and adaptive method or trigonometric method [38].

2.2   Common Ground Current Injection Method

A simple current injection method named common ground current injection protocol (Fig.-1) required only two multiplexers for a 16-electrode EIT system is proposed and the resistivity imaging is studied with the boundary data collected from the practical phantoms. In common ground current injection protocol, the current signal is injected through a particular electrode by connecting the positive terminal of the current injector to that electrode keeping its ground point connected to the ground point of the electronic instrumentation (Fig.-1). The boundary potentials developed are measured on all the surface electrodes (E_1 through E_{16}) by connecting the positive terminal of the voltage acquiring probes (positive terminal of the DAQ analog input ports used for data acquisition) to the voltage electrodes (E_1 through E_{16}). The negative terminal of the voltage acquiring probes (negative terminal of the DAQ analog input ports used for data acquisition) is connected to the same ground point i.e. the ground point of the electronic instrumentation. Though, sometimes, it is not preferred to measure the potential data on the current electrodes for contact impedance problem, but in the present study, however, the boundary potentials are also measured on the current carrying electrodes to obtain the greatest sensitivity to changes in the resistivity of the body, as reported and suggested by Cheng et al. [35].

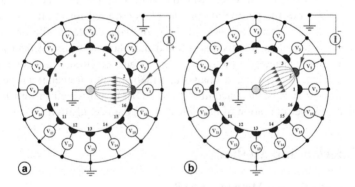

Fig. 1. Common ground current injection: (a) projection-1, (a) projection-2

Hence, the common ground method (Fig.-1) in the 16-electrode EIT system yields sixteen current projections (P_1 through P_{16}) and each current projection produced sixteen boundary voltage data (V_1, V_2, V_3, ..., V_{15}, V_{16}) collected from sixteen voltage electrodes (E_1, E_2, E_3, ..., E_{15}, E_{16}) respectively (Fig.-1). In first current projection (P_1), the current is injected through the electrode E_1 and sixteen voltage data (V_1, V_2, V_3, ..., V_{15}, V_{16}) collected from sixteen electrodes (E_1, E_2, E_3, ..., E_{15},

E_{16}) respectively (Fig.-1a). Similarly, in the current projection-2 (P_2), the current is injected through the electrode 2 (E_2) and sixteen voltage data (V_1, V_2, V_3, …, V_{15}, V_{16}) are collected from the corresponding sixteen voltage electrodes; E_1, E_2, E_3, …, E_{15} and E_{16} (Fig.-1a). Similarly in the projections P_3, P_4, P_5, …, P_{15} and P_{16} , the current signal is injected to the electrodes E_3, E_4, E_5, …, E_{15} and E_{16} (Fig.-1) respectively. For all the projections, sixteen voltage data (V_1, V_2, V_3, …, V_{15}, V_{16}) are collected from the corresponding sixteen voltage electrodes; E_1, E_2, E_3, …, E_{15}, E_{16}.

2.3   EIT Phantom

A reconfigurable practical phantom (Fig.-2a) is developed with a shallow glass tank (150 mm diameter) and sixteen stainless steel electrodes [39-44]. All the electrodes are equally spaced on the tank inner wall and fixed on tank wall using steel clips (Fig.-2a). Sixteen identical electrodes (rectangular shape, 34 mm × 10 mm) are cut from a 50 μm thick high quality stainless steel (type 304) sheet to avoid the localized pitting corrosion leading to the creation of small holes. The electrode array fixed with the steel clips is found easily adjustable, replaceable and reconfigurable for developing a phantom with a new configuration. All the electrodes are connected to the EIT electronic hardware through the low resistive flexible multi-strand copper wires and steel crocodile clips (Fig.-2a). All the wires are chosen with equal lengths to obtain the identical impedance paths through all the connecting wires.

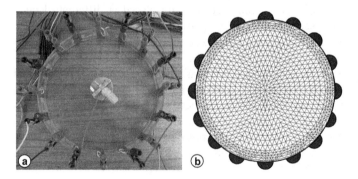

Fig. 2. (a) Practical phantom, (b) FEM mesh used for image reconstruction

The phantom tank is filled with a 0.9% (w/v) NaCl solution and a cylindrical stainless steel rod (25 mm dia.) called common mode electrode (CME) [39-44] is placed at the phantom center (Fig.-2a). The CME is connected to the ground point of the EIT electronics to reduce the common mode error of the circuits. The surface electrodes at the phantom boundary act as the EIT sensors and allow the electronic hardware to send the current signal to the phantom and sending back the voltage signals to the measuring instruments. A liquid resistivity measurement setup [39, 45] is developed and the bathing solution resistivity is measured using an impedance analyzer (QuadTech 7600) with a test signal of 1 mA, 50 kHz. The resistivity of the 0.9% (w/v) NaCl solution is found as 0.61 Ωm for 1 mA 50 kHz current signal.

2.4   Instrumentation

EIT instrumentation is developed with a constant current injector [40, 46], electrode switching module, signal conditioner and a data acquisition system for current injection and the boundary data collection. Constant current injector consists of a sinusoidal signal generator and a constant current source. Automatic electrode switching module is developed with two 16:1 multiplexers which are very high speed CMOS analog multiplexer/demultiplexer ICs (CD4067BE). Signal conditioner block is developed with a 50 Hz notch filter and a narrow band pass filter with a center frequency of 50 kHz. A USB based high speed data acquisition system is developed with NI USB-6251 DAQ card for boundary data acquisition through the multiplexer board connected to the surface electrodes. Data acquisition software is written in LabVIEW and it is used to interface the EIT electronic hardware with the PC.

2.5   Boundary Data Collection

1 mA, 50 kHz sinusoidal current signal is injected to the phantom boundary with and without inhomogeneity and the electrode potentials (V_m: m = 1, 2, 3, ... , 16) are collected using the common ground current injection protocol (Fig-5). Nylon cylinders are placed inside the NaCl solution (Fig.-2a) in different electrode positions and the boundary potentials are measured by injecting a constant current (1 mA, 50 kHz) to the phantom boundary using common ground current patterns. For all the phantom configurations, inhomogeneities are placed at different electrode positions maintaining a distance of 7 mm away from the phantom boundary. Nylon cylinders are put as the inhomogeneity near electrode no. 4, 5 and 6 and the constant current signal is injected. The current flux (Fig.-1) generated due to the current conduction produces potentials in the phantom domain (Ω). The boundary potentials developed at the surface electrodes are collected for all the inhomogeneity configurations using common ground current injection protocol and sent to the PC for the analysis and image reconstruction. As discussed earlier, due to the reciprocity, the boundary data collected for the first eight current projections (P_1, P_2, P_3, ..., P_8) are found sufficient to produce impedance image and that is why the potential data for other eight current projections (P_9, P_{10}, P_{11}, ..., P_{16}) are not collected. Therefore, the RMS potential on all the electrodes is measured for first eight current projections and the voltage data set (containing 128 voltage data) are saved as a *.txt* file in PC for computation. As shown in Fig.-1, the boundary potentials (V_1 through V_{16}) developed at the surface electrodes (E_1 through E_{16}) for the first eight current projections are collected.

2.6   Image Reconstruction and Image Analysis

Boundary data are collected for different phantom configurations and the resistivity image are reconstructed in Electrical Impedance and Diffuse Optical Reconstruction Software (EIDORS) [47-48]. Forward problem [44] is solved with the phantom domain (diameter of 150 mm) discretized with a FEM based triangular element mesh (Fig.-2b). The FEM mesh contains 1968 triangular elements and 1049 nodes [24].

The inverse solution is also conducted with the same FEM mesh (Fig.-2b). Images reconstructed for different phantom configurations are analysed with the different image parameters. CNR [49], PCR [49], COC [49], DRP [49], IR_{Mean} [49] and IR_{Max} [49] are calculated from the resistivity profiles of the reconstructed images obtained for all the phantom configurations to assess the reconstruction.

3   Results and Discussion

Boundary potentials developed for homogeneous medium (NaCl solution only) are collected for opposite and common ground method by injecting 1 mA, 50 kHz sinusoidal current of constant amplitude. Results show that, the boundary potential profiles obtained are found of similar fashion both for opposite and common ground current injection methods. Results also show that, either for homogeneous medium or for inhomogeneous medium, the potential profiles obtained with opposite and common ground current injection, are found of similar fashions. It is observed that the first voltage data in the first projection in common ground method is less than the corresponding data point in the potential profile obtained with opposite method. Results show that, the 18th data (i.e. the second peak of the boundary data profile as shown in the Fig.-3) of the boundary potential matrix obtained for common ground current injection method is found slightly more compared to the other seven peaks (i.e. 1st data, 35th data, 52nd data, 69th data, 86th data, 103rd data and 120th data). It is also observed that, for both the opposite and common ground methods, the voltage peaks in the boundary potential data profile obtained from a homogeneous medium are found at the similar except at the first peak (1st data point).

It is reported that [24], in opposite method, only first 128 voltages measured for first eight projections are independent data and hence are sufficient to reconstruct the inhomogeneities due to the reciprocity principle. Similarly, it is also noticed that, for common ground method, first 128 voltages obtained for first eight projections are independent and hence are found sufficient to reconstruct the inhomogeneities. Hence, only first 128 voltage data are collected (Fig.-3) for imaging study and consequently the acquisition time reduced to 50 % of the full acquisition time.

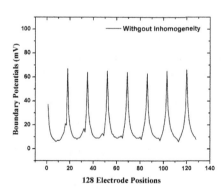

Fig. 3. Boundary potentials for homogeneous medium with common ground method

Fig.-4, Fig.-5 and Fig.-6 show the resistivity imaging of the phantoms with nylon cylinders (35 mm diameter) as the inhomogeneity near electrode no. 4 (Fig.-4a), 5 (Fig.-5a) and 6 (Fig.-6a) using common ground current injection. 1 mA 50 kHz current is injected and the RMS boundary potentials (Figs.-4b, 5b and 6b) are measured using data acquisition system. Figs.-4b, 5b and 6b show the boundary data profiles of their corresponding phantom configurations as shown in Figs.-4a, 5a and 6a respectively. In common ground method, all the potential profiles show that, the maximum potential (V_{ei}) of the boundary data obtained for a phantom with inhomogeneity placed at K^{th} electrode occurs at $[((K-1) \times 16) + K]^{th}$ data point in the boundary potential data matrix [V_m]. It is reported [24] for the opposite method, the maximum potential (V_{ei}) in the [V_m] matrix is the potential of the electrode near the object when the positive terminal of the current source is connected to the same electrode. Similarly, in common ground method also, it is observed that the maximum potential point (V_{ei}) in V_m matrix is the potential of the electrode near the inhomogeneity when the positive terminal of the current source is connected to the same electrode. This is because of the highest voltage drop occurred across the current path along the nylon cylinder (inhomogeneity) and the electrode due to the high resistance of inhomogeneity and the high electrode contact impedance. It is also observed that for all the inhomogeneity positions, boundary data are successfully generated and collected by the system. Boundary potentials measured with nylon inhomogeneity are found satisfactory for all the at electrode positions (Figs.-4a, 5a and 6). Potential curves with nylon cylinder at the electrode E_m (m: = 1, 2, 3, ... , 16) show that the highest voltage peak is appeared at the mth projection (Figs.-4a, 5a and 6a) which clearly indicates the presence of inhomogeneity at m^{th} electrode position.

Potential profile obtained with the inhomogeneity at electrode 4 (Fig.-4a) shows that the highest voltage peak is found at the 4th projection (Fig.-4b) which clearly indicates the presence of inhomogeneity at 4th electrode position. Potential curves with inhomogeneity at electrode 5 (Fig.-5a) also show that the high voltage peak is appeared at the 5th projection (Fig.-5b) which indicates the presence of object near the 5th electrode. Similarly in the boundary data (Fig.-6b) obtained for the phantom with the inhomogeneity at electrode 6, it is observed that the highest voltage peak appeared at the 6th projection. It indicates that the inhomogeneity is at the 6th electrode.

Figs.-4c, 5c and 6c show the resistivity images of the phantoms with inhomogeneity near electrode number 4, 5 and 6 respectively. It is observed that, for all the phantom configurations, the inhomogeneities are successfully reconstructed with almost their proper shape and position. The resistivity of the NaCl solution (bathing medium) is also reconstructed (Figs.-4c, 5c, and 6c) with minimum amount of background noise. The resistivity of the NaCl solution (bathing medium) is measured as 0.61 Ωm in impedance analyzer [24]. It is observed that the average background resistivity (neglecting the background error near inhomogeneity) in the reconstructed images is found as 0.29 Ωm (Fig.-4c) for the phantom with inhomogeneity at electrode no. 4. On the other hand the average background resistivities (neglecting the background error near inhomogeneity) for the phantoms with inhomogeneity near electrode no. 5 and 6 are found as 0.50 Ωm and 0.49 Ωm (Figs.-5c and 6c) respectively.

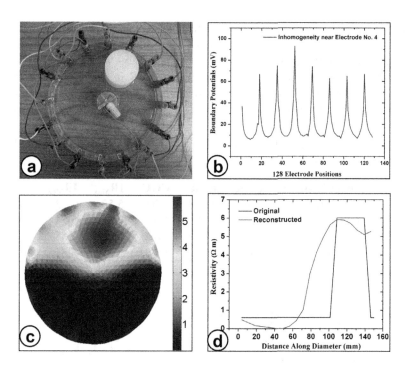

Fig. 4. (a) Practical phantom with nylon cylinder at electrode no. 4, (b) boundary potentials, (c) resistivity image, (d) DRP

The resistivity of the inhomogeneity is found to be almost ten times more than the bathing solution resistivity (Figs.-4c, 5c and 6c). Average reconstructed resistivity of the inhomogeneities (IR_{Mean}) near electrodes 4, 5, and 6 are found as 5.42 Ωm, 5.54 Ωm and 5.58 Ωm respectively (Table-1). Hence all the resistivities are found as very closer to the original inhomogeneity resistivity. The maximum resistivity of the reconstructed inhomogeneities (IR_{Max}) near electrodes 4, 5 and 6 are 5.53 Ωm, 6.06 Ωm and 6.02 Ωm (Table-1). All these resistivity values are almost similar to the original inhomogeneity resistivity. Hence it is observed that, common ground current injection method, all the resistivity images (Figs.-4c, 5c and 6c) of nylon inhomogeneity at different electrode positions in the practical phantom, are reconstructed successfully from the boundary data with their proper background resistivities.

Image analysis studies (Table-1), show that the CNR of the reconstructed image for the inhomogeneity near electrodes 4 (Fig.-4c) is 2.45 (Table-1). On the other hand CNR of the images for the inhomogeneity near electrodes 5 and 6 (Figs.-5c and 6c) are found as 2.72 and 2.85 (Table-1) respectively. Hence it is concluded that, for the present resistivity imaging study with common ground method, the average CNR in the reconstructed images for inhomogeneities near all the electrodes is 2.67 (Table-1) which indicates an efficient image reconstruction [24].

PCR of the reconstructed image for the phantom with inhomogeneity near electrode 4 is 73.18 % (Table-1). On the other hand, for the phantom with inhomogeneities near electrodes 5 and 6, PCRs are found as 76.09 % and 77.59 % respectively (Table-1). Therefore, in common ground method, the average PCR in the reconstructed images for all the in homogeneity positions is found as 75.62 % (Table-1) which indicates an efficient image reconstruction.

Table 1. CNR, PCR, COC, IR_{Max} and IR_{Mean} of the reconstructed images for different inhomogeneity positions

Object Positions	CNR	PCR	COC	IR_{Max}	IR_{Mean}
Electrode-4	2.45	73.18	3.70	5.53	5.42
Electrode-5	2.72	76.09	3.88	6.06	5.54
Electrode-6	2.85	77.59	4.02	6.02	5.58
Average	**2.67**	**75.62**	**3.87**	**5.87**	**5.51**

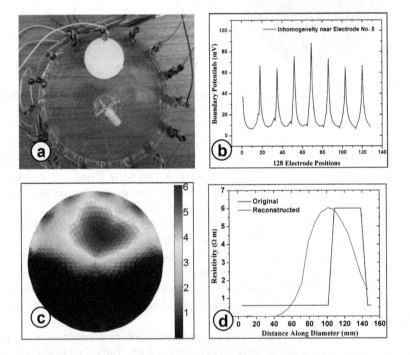

Fig. 5. (a) Practical phantom with nylon cylinder at electrode no. 5, (b) boundary potentials, (c) resistivity image, (d) DRP

It is also observed that the COC of the reconstructed image (Fig.-4c) for the inhomogeneity near electrode 4 is 3.70 (Table-1). On the other hand COCs of the images (Figs.-5c and 6c) for the phantoms with inhomogeneities near electrodes 5 and 6 are found as 3.88 and 4.02 (Table-1) respectively. Hence it is noted that, for the present resistivity imaging study with common ground method, the average COC in the reconstructed images for inhomogeneities near all the electrodes is 3.87 (Table-1) which indicates an successful image reconstruction. Figs.-4d, 5d and 6d show the DRP of the resistivity images of the phantoms with inhomogeneity near electrode number 4, 5 and 6 respectively. It is observed that, for the common ground method, all the DRPs (Figs.-4d, 5d and 6d) almost follow the DRP of the original object but with a little shift of object centre.

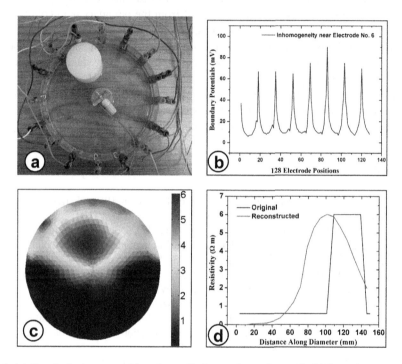

Fig. 6. (a) Practical phantom with nylon cylinder at electrode no. 6, (b) boundary potentials, (c) resistivity image, (d) DRP

4   Conclusions

A common ground current injection method is proposed for EIT and the resistivity imaging is studied with practical phantoms. Common ground methods needs only two analog 16:1 multiplexers for a 16-electrode EIT system: one for current electrode switching and other for voltage electrode switching. Each of the multiplexers needs only 4-bit parallel digital data to switch the surface electrodes. Hence only 8-bit parallel digital data are found sufficient to operate the multiplexers for surface electrode switching of the 16-electrode EIT system. Experimental studies show that the analog instrumentation successfully generated the 1 mA 50 kHz sinusoidal constant current signal suitable for injecting it to the phantom boundary. Results show that the USB based data acquisition system sequentially generates digital data required for multiplexer operation in common ground current injection. It is observed that all the sets of 8-bit parallel digital data required for multiplexer operation are sequentially generated by the D/O ports of the DAQ card controlled by the LabVIEW based computer software. Boundary data collected from practical phantom show that the multiplexers are operating in the required sequence and the surface electrodes are switched as per the current injection logic. The voltage peaks obtained at the accurate positions in the boundary data matrix also proved the sequential operation of multiplexers. Resistivity images reconstructed from the boundary data collected from the practical phantom with different configurations show that the entire digital data generation module is functioning properly in common ground method. Reconstructed images and their image parameters proved that the boundary data are successfully acquired by the DAQ system which in turn indicates a sequential and proper operation of two multiplexers. Hence, the common ground current injection method is found suitable to work with two 16:1 multiplexers operating with only 8-bit parallel digital data for surface electrode switching of a 16-electrode EIT system.

References

[1] Webster, J.G.: Electrical impedance tomography. Adam Hilger Series of Biomedical Engineering. Adam Hilger, New York (1990)
[2] Li, Y., Rao, L., He, R., Xu, G., Wu, Q., Yan, W., Dong, G., Yang, Q.: A Novel Combination Method of Electrical Impedance Tomography Inverse Problem for Brain Imaging. IEEE Transactions on Magnetics 41(5) (May 2005)
[3] Brown, B.H.: Medical impedance tomography and process impedance tomography: a brief review. Measurement Science & Technology 12, 991–996 (2001)
[4] Bagshaw, A.P., Liston, A.D., Bayford, R.H., Tizzard, A., Gibson, A.P., Tidswell, A.T., Sparkes, M.K., Dehghani, H., Binnie, C.D., Holder, D.S.: Electrical impedance tomography of human brain function using reconstruction algorithms based on the finite element method. NeuroImage 20, 752–764 (2003)
[5] Murphy, D., Burton, P., Coombs, R., Tarassenko, L., Rolfe, P.: Impedance Imaging in the Newborn. Clin. Phys. Physiol. Meas. 8(suppl. A), 131–140 (1987)
[6] Tyna, H.A., Iles, S.E.: Technology review: The use of electrical impedance scanning in the detection of breast cancer. Breast Cancer Research 6(2), 69–74 (2004)
[7] Moura, F.S., Aya, J.C.C., Fleury, A.T., Amato, M.B.P., Lima, R.G.: Dynamic Imaging in Electrical Impedance Tomography of the Human Chest With Online Transition Matrix Identification. IEEE Transactions on Biomedical Engineering 57(2) (February 2010)
[8] Ferraioli, F., Formisano, A., Martone, R.: Effective Exploitation of Prior Information in Electrical Impedance Tomography for Thermal Monitoring of Hyperthermia Treatments. IEEE Transactions on Magnetics 45(3) (March 2009)
[9] McArdle, F.J., Suggett, A.J., Brown, B.H., Barber, D.C.: An assessment of dynamic images by applied potential tomography for monitoring pulmonary perfusion. Clin. Phys. Physiol. Meas. 9(suppl. A), 87–91 (1988)
[10] Hoetink, A.E., Faes, T.J.C., Marcus, J.T., Kerkkamp, H.J.J., Heethaar, R.M.: Imaging of Thoracic Blood Volume Changes During the Heart Cycle With Electrical Impedance Using a Linear Spot-Electrode Array. IEEE Tran. on Med. Imaging 21(6), 653 (2002)

[11] Ferrer, A.R.Z., Castro, G.M., Gaona, G.A., Aguillon, M.A., Rosell, F.P.J., Carrera, B.J.: Electrical Impedance Tomography: An Electronic Design, with Adaptive Voltage Measurements and A Phantom Circuit for Research in The Epilepsy Field. In: Proceedings of the 19th International Conference – IEEE/EMBS, USA, October 30-November 2, pp. 867–868 (1997)

[12] Linderholm, P., Marescot, P., Loke, M.H., Renaud, P.: Cell Culture Imaging Using Microimpedance Tomography. IEEE Transactions on Biomedical Engineering 55(1), 138–146 (2008)

[13] Church, P., McFee, J.E., Gagnon, S., Wort, P.: Electrical Impedance Tomographic Imaging of Buried Landmines. IEEE Transactions on Geoscience and Remote Sensing 44(9), 2407–2420 (2006)

[14] Djamdji, F., Gorvin, A.C., Freeston, I.L., Tozer, R.C., Mayes, I.C., Blight, S.R.: Electrical impedance tomography applied to semiconductor wafer characterization. Meas. Sci. Technol. 7(3), 391–395 (1996) (Printed in the UK)

[15] Hola, J., Matkowski, Z., Schabowicz, K., Sikora, J., Wojtowicz, S.: New Method of Investigation of Rising Damp in Brick Walls by means of Impedance Tomography. In: 17th World Conference on Nondestructive Testing, Shanghai, China, October 25-28 (2008)

[16] Yang, J.S., Par, M.K., Kim, H.J.: Nondestructive Imaging of Rock Sample Using Electrical Resistance Tomography: Theoretical Approach. Journal of the Earth system 41(4), 265–270 (2004)

[17] Hou, W.D., Mo, Y.L.: Increasing image resolution in electrical impedance tomography. Electronics Letters 38, 701–702 (2002)

[18] Holder, D.S., Hanquan, Y., Rao, A.: Some practical biological phantoms for calibrating multifrequency electrical impedance tomography. Physiol. Meas. 17, A167–A177 (1996)

[19] Griffiths, H.: A Cole phantom for EIT. Physiol. Meas. 16, A29–A38 (1995)

[20] Schneider, I.D., Kleffel, R., Jennings, D., Courtenay, A.J.: Design of an electrical impedance tomography phantom using active elements. Med. Biol. Eng. Comput. 38, 390–394 (2000)

[21] Bera, T.K., Nagaraju, J.: A Simple Instrumentation Calibration Technique for Electrical Impedance Tomography (EIT) Using A 16 Electrode Phantom. In: The Fifth Annual IEEE Conference on Automation Science and Engineering (IEEE CASE 2009), Bangalore, August 22-25, pp. 347–352 (2009)

[22] Kim, B.S., Kim, K.Y., Kao, T.J., Newell, J.C., Isaacson, D., Saulnier, G.J.: Dynamic electrical impedance imaging of a chest phantom using the Kalman filter. Physiol. Meas. 27(5), S81–S91 (2006)

[23] Paulson, K., Breckon, W., Pidcock, M.: A hybrid phantom for electrical impedance tomography. Clin. Phys. Physiol. Meas. 13(suppl. A), 155–159 (1992)

[24] Bera, T.K., Nagaraju, J.: Resistivity Imaging of A Reconfigurable Phantom With Circular Inhomogeneities in 2D-Electrical Impedance Tomography. Measurement 44(3), 518–526 (2011), doi:10.1016/j.measurement.2010.11.015

[25] Kao, T.J., Saulnier, G.J., Isaacson, D., Szabo, T.L., Newell, J.C.: A Versatile High-Permittivity Phantom for EIT. IEEE Transactions on Biomedical Engineering 55(11), 2601 (2008)

[26] Jun, S.C., Kuen, J., Lee, J., Woo, E.J., Holder, D., Seo, J.K.: Frequency-difference EIT (fdEIT) using weighted difference and equivalent homogeneous admittivity: validation by simulation and tank experiment. Physiol. Meas. 30, 1087–1099 (2009)

[27] Bera, T.K., Nagaraju, J.: A Chicken Tissue Phantom for Studying An Electrical Impedance Tomography (EIT) System Suitable for Clinical Imaging. Sensing and Imaging: An International Journal, doi:10.1007/s11220-011-0063-4

[28] Griffiths, H.: A phantom for electrical impedance tomography. Clin. Phys. Physiol. Meas. 9(suppl. A), 15–20 (1988)

[29] Hahn, G., Just, A., Dittmar, J., Hellige, G.: Systematic errors of EIT systems determined by easily-scalable resistive phantoms. Physiol. Meas. 29, S163–S172 (2008), doi:10.1088/0967-3334

[30] Yorkey, T.J.: Comparing reconstruction methods for electrical impedance tomography. PhD thesis, University of. Wisconsin at Madison, Madison, WI 53706 (1986)

[31] Lionheart, W.R.B.: EIT reconstruction algorithms: pitfalls, challenges and recent developments. Review Article, Physiol. Meas. 25, 125–142 (2004); PII: S0967-3334(04)70421-9

[32] Bera, T.K., Biswas, S.K., Rajan, K., Nagaraju, J.: Improving Conductivity Image Quality Using Block Matrix-based Multiple Regularization (BMMR) Technique in EIT: A Simulation Study. Journal of Electrical Bioimpedance 2, 33–47 (2011), doi:10.5617/jeb.170

[33] Bera, T.K., Biswas, S.K., Rajan, K., Nagaraju, J.: Improving Image Quality in Electrical Impedance Tomography (EIT) Using Projection Error Propagation-Based Regularization (PEPR) Technique: A Simulation Study. Journal of Electrical Bioimpedance 2, 2–12 (2011), doi:10.5617/jeb.158

[34] Malmivou, J., Plonsey, R.: Principles and Applications of Bioelectric and Biomagnetic Fields, ch. 26, Section 26.2, p. 2. Oxford University Press (1995)

[35] Cheng, K.S., Simske, S.J., Isaacson, D., Newell, J.C., Gisser, D.G.: Errors due to measuring voltage on current-carrying electrodes in electric current computed tomography. IEEE Trans. Biomed. Eng. 37(60), 60–65 (1990)

[36] Brown, B.H., Segar, A.D.: The Sheffield data collection system. Clin. Phys. Physiol. Measurement 8(suppl. A), 91–97 (1987)

[37] Hua, P., Webster, J.G., Tompkins, W.J.: Effect of the measurement method on noise handling and image quality of EIT imaging. In: Proc. Ninth Int. Conf. IEEE Eng. in Med. and Biol. Society, vol. 2, pp. 1429–1430. IEEE, New York (1987)

[38] Gisser, D.G., Isaacson, D., Newell, J.C.: Current topics in impedance imaging. Clin. Phys. Physiol. Measurement 8(suppl. A), 39–46 (1987)

[39] Bera, T.K., Nagaraju, J.: A Stainless Steel Electrode Phantom to Study the Forward Problem of Electrical Impedance Tomography (EIT). Sensors & Transducers Journal 104(5), 33–40 (2009)

[40] Bera, T.K., Nagaraju, J.: A Study of Practical Biological Phantoms with Simple Instrumentation for Electrical Impedance Tomography (EIT). In: Proceedings of IEEE Internl. Instrumentation and Measurement Technology Conference (I2MTC 2009), Singapore, pp. 511–516 (2009)

[41] Bera, T.K., Nagaraju, J.: Studying the Boundary Data Profile of A Practical Phantom for Medical Electrical Impedance Tomography with Different Electrode Geometries. In: Dössel, O., Schlegel, W.C. (eds.) Proceedings of The World Congress on Medical Physics and Biomedical Engineering, WC 2009, Munich, Germany, September 7-12. IFMBE Proceedings 25/II, pp. 925–929 (2009), doi:10.1007/978-3-642-03879-2_258

[42] Bera, T.K., Nagaraju, J.: A Reconfigurable Practical Phantom for Studying the 2 D Electrical Impedance Tomography (EIT) Using a FEM Based Forward Solver. In: 10th International Conference on Biomedical Applications of Electrical Impedance Tomography (EIT 2009), School of Mathematics, The University of Manchester, UK, June 16-19 (2009),
http://www.maths.manchester.ac.uk/eit2009/abstracts/bera.pdf

[43] Bera, T.K., Nagaraju, J.: A Study of Practical Biological Phantoms with Simple Instrumentation for Electrical Impedance Tomography (EIT). In: Proceedings of IEEE International Instrumentation and Measurement Technology Conference (I2MTC 2009), Singapore, May 5-7, pp. 511–516 (2009), doi:10.1109/IMTC.2009.5168503

[44] Bera, T.K., Nagaraju, J.: A FEM-Based Forward Solver for Studying the Forward Problem of Electrical Impedance Tomography (EIT) with A Practical Biological Phantom. In: Proceedings of IEEE International Advance Computing Conference 2009 (IEEE IACC 2009), Patiala, Punjab, India, March 6-7, pp. 1375–1381 (2009), doi:10.1109/IADCC.2009.4809217

[45] Bera, T.K., Nagaraju, J.: Electrical Impedance Spectroscopic Study of Broiler Chicken Tissues Suitable for The Development of Practical Phantoms in Multifrequency EIT. Journal of Electrical Bioimpedance 2, 48–63 (2011), doi:10.5617/jeb.174

[46] Bera, T.K., Nagaraju, J.: A Multifrequency Constant Current Source for Medical Electrical Impedance Tomography. In: Proceedings of the IEEE International Conference on Systems in Medicine and Biology 2010 (IEEE ICSMB 2010), Kharagpur, India, December 16-18, pp. 278–283 (2010), doi:10.1109/ICSMB.2010.5735387

[47] Polydorides, N., Lionheart, W.R.B.: A Matlab toolkit for three-dimensional electrical impedance tomography: a contribution to the Electrical Impedance and Diffuse Optical Reconstruction Software project. Meas. Sci. Technol. 13, 1871–1883 (2002)

[48] Vauhkonen, M., Lionheart, W.R.B., Heikkinen, L.M., Vauhkonen, P.J., Kaipio, J.P.: A MATLAB package for the EIDORS project to reconstruct two dimensional EIT images. Physiol. Meas. 22, 107–111 (2001)

[49] Bera, T.K., Nagaraju, J.: Studying the Elemental Resistivity Profile of Electrical Impedance Tomography (EIT) Images to Assess the Reconstructed Image Quality. In: Venugopal, K.R., Patnaik, L.M. (eds.) ICIP 2011. CCIS, vol. 157, pp. 621–630. Springer, Heidelberg (2011)

OO Metric Studies of Behavioral Diagrams

Lavu Jayasudha[*], Sriraman Kothuri[**], and M. Venkata Rao[***]

Dept. of CSE, Vignan's Lara Institute of Technology and Science, Vadlamudi,
Guntur Dt., A.P., India
{lavu.jayasudha,er.k.sriraman,mvrao239}@gmail.com

Abstract. Using the Unified Modeling Language (UML), static aspects at conceptual level are represented in structural diagrams such as class diagrams, while dynamic aspects are represented in behavioral diagrams such as state chart diagram, activity diagram, sequence diagrams and collaboration diagrams. And metric measures for those, improves the quality of design. The earlier work focuses on metrics for class diagrams. The main goal of this paper is to focus on the definition of mea -sures that applied to guarantee the validity of design through {NEntryA, NExitA, NA, NT, NS} State chart diagrams, {NM} Inter-action diagrams, and {NOA, NOUC, NOUCA}Use-Case diagrams. This measure of metric validates intrinsic understandability of all behavioral UML diagrams.

Keywords: Software metrics, UML behavioral diagrams, complexity metrics, theoretical validation.

1 Introduction

UML stands for Unified Modeling Language, a collection of graphical modeling techniques to describe software intensive system. Each technique of UML focuses on particular aspect of the software such as use cases, structural relation, interaction and communication. An UML model contains the information about a system and UML diagram displays a particular view of the system.

The fig. 1. depicts the concept of UML model, which defines the concepts for a particular system/domain. Using the Unified Modeling Language (UML) static aspects at conceptual level are mainly represented in structural diagram such as class diagram, while dynamic aspects are represented in behavioral diagrams such as state-chart diagram, activity diagrams, sequence diagrams and collaboration diagrams. There exist several complexity metrics for structural diagram (class diagram) such as WMC, CBO, LCOM, DIT, and NOC etc. [1] [3] [5] [7] [8] [9] [10] [11] [12] .

UML diagrams can be classified as shown in fig. 2.

---

[*]   Assisstant Professor.
[**]   Associate Professor.
[***] Professor & Principal.

P.V. Krishna, M.R. Babu, and E. Ariwa (Eds.): ObCom 2011, Part II, CCIS 270, pp. 588–595, 2012.

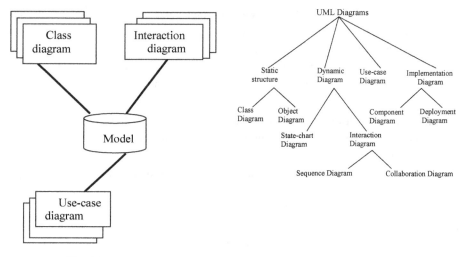

Fig. 1. UML Model   **Fig. 2.** Classification of UML Diagram

2   Metrics for Dynamic Diagram

Since metrics for static structure diagram is already discussed, it is started with metrics for dynamic diagram, in which we illustrate the metrics for *State chart diagram*. [3][5][7][8][11][12]

2.1   State Chart Diagram

A state chart diagram shows the behavior of classes in response to external stimuli. This diagram models the dynamic flow of control state to state within a system. In other words, a state chart diagram is a hierarchical diagram, which consists of nested state that represents a full state machine. It has concept of action and activity. An action is an atomic processing and it can't be interrupted and it normally occurs quickly whereas activity can be interrupted and it takes longer time. The complexity of a state-chart diagram is determined by different elements that compose it, such as states, transitions, activities, actions, etc. We can't define a single measure for the complexity of UML state chart diagrams, since a single measure of complexity cannot capture all possible aspects or view points of complexity instead several measures are needed, each one focusing on different state chart diagram elements.[2][4][9] [13]

Metrics for State Chart Diagram
For State-chart diagram we consider the following metrics: [9]

1. Number of Entry Actions (NEntryA)
2. Number of Exit Actions (NExitA)
3. Number of Activities (NA)
4. Number of States (NS)
5. Number of Transitions (NT)

Number of Entry Actions (NEntryA): The total number of entry actions, i.e. the actions performed each time a state is entered. It is measured by counting the total number of entry actions.

Number of Exit Actions (NExitA): The total number of exit actions, i.e. the actions performed each time a state is left. It is measured by counting the total number of exit actions.

Number of Activities (NA): The total number of activities (do/activity) in the state chart diagram. It is measured by counting the total number of activities in the state chart diagram.

Number of States (NS): The total number of simple states, considering also the simple states within the composite states. It is measured by counting total number of states present in the state chart diagram.

Number of Transitions (NT): The total number of transitions, considering common transitions (the source and the target states are different), the initial and final transitions, self-transitions (the source and the target state is the same), internal transitions (transitions inside a state that respond to an event but without leaving the state). It is measured by counting the total number of arcs in the state chart diagram.

To illustrate how we measure the above defined metrics, consider the state chart diagram:

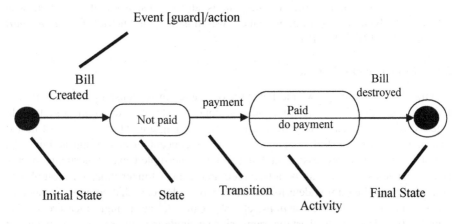

Fig. 3. State Chart Diagram

The fig.4. depicts how system starts from the initial state and it enters into state labeled receive order. When it enters this state, it checks whether the ordered items are available or not if all items are available, it moves into dispatch state and deliver the ordered items and then it moves into final state which indicates that system will halt, otherwise if all items are not available, it enters into pending state and it remains in pending state until all items become available. When all items arrive it goes into dispatch state where it do activity of delivering items and finally goes into final state.

The total number of states (NS) in fig.4. is 5.

The total number of transition (NT) is measured by counting all arcs present in the state chart diagram. So NT for fig.4. will be 6 and for fig. 3 will be 3.

The total number of activity (NA) in fig. 4. will be 1.

NentryA and NexitA for fig.4 will be 2 since there are only two actions performed that are checking the availability of items.

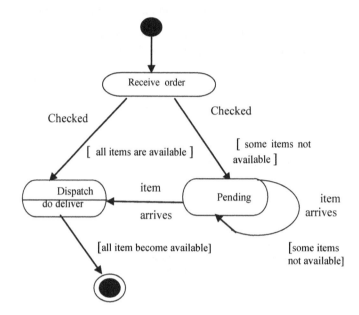

Fig. 4. State chart diagram

2.2   Interaction Diagram

Interaction diagram is one of the most important diagrams that is used in the design process. That is why it is often called vital design tool. There are two types of interaction diagram as we mentioned above that are: *sequence diagram* and *collaboration diagram.*

Sequence Diagram: It is used to describe interaction among classes in terms of an exchange of message over time. It can be used to document the dynamic aspect of an object model.

The fig. 5 illustrates the sequence diagram for library book renewal process, which depicts the exchange of messages between object-classes.

Collaboration Diagram: A collaboration diagram describes interactions among objects in terms of sequenced messages. Collaboration diagrams represent a combination of information taken from class, sequence, and use-case diagrams describing both the static structure and dynamic behavior of a system. By considering fig.5 we can easily construct collaboration diagram for library book renewal process as shown in fig. 6.

Metrics for Interaction Diagram

There is no specific metrics has been proposed for interaction diagram but we can propose one metrics called "Number of Messages (NM)". Since interaction diagram are usually used to represent the message communication between object-classes.

Number of Messages (NM): The metrics is defined as the total number of messages in the interaction diagram. It is measured by counting the total number of messages in the interaction diagram.

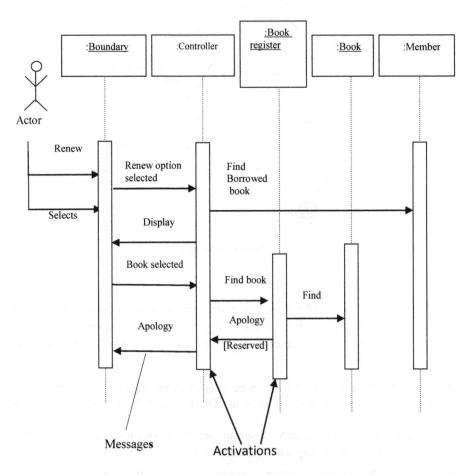

Fig. 5. Sequence diagram for Library Book renewal process

To illustrate how we measure this metrics consider fig.6. which depicts the collaboration diagram for Library book renewal process in which the total number of messages is 8. So,NM = 8.

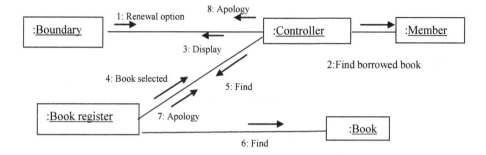

Fig. 6. Collaboration diagram for Library Book renewal

2.3   Use-Case Diagram

Use case diagrams model the functionality of a system using actors and use cases. Use cases are services or functions provided by the system to its users.

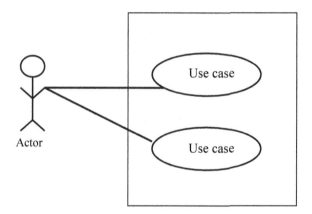

Fig. 7. Structure of Use Case Diagram

Fig.7 shows the structure of use case diagram. In which Actor is the user of the system and use case represents the system function.

Metrics for Use Case

Use case diagram is modeled by actors and use case so based on that there are three metrics that can be used to measure the complexity of use case diagram:

1. NOA (Number Of Actor)
2. NOUC (Number of Use Case)
3. NOUCA (Number Of Use Cases per Actor)

Number of Actor (NOA): This is defined as the number of actors in use case diagram. It is measured by counting the total number of actors present in the use case diagram.

Number of Use Case (NOUC): The number of use cases in the use case diagram. It is measured by counting the total number of use cases present in the use case diagram.

Number of Use Cases Per Actor (NOUCA): It is count of the number of use cases per actor. This metrics is measured by counting the total number of actors in the use case diagram and dividing it by number of use cases.

Example: To illustrate how we measure the above-defined metrics let us consider a Use Case diagram. In the fig.8. total number of actors and use cases are 4 and 3 respectively. So,

NOA=4
NOU=3   and
  NOUCA=4/3=1.33

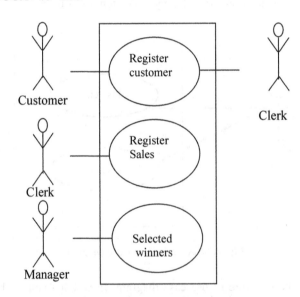

Fig. 8. Use case diagram for example

3   Conclusions and Future Work

It is well known that software product metrics are very useful to evaluate the different characteristics that affect the quality of OO software, for example the maintainability. On the other hand, it is necessary to make a family of experiments that allow the extension of conclusions as much as possible to increase the external validity of the results, including experiments with professionals and also data about real projects. Besides we are conscious of the necessity to make laboratory packages with the information of the empirical studies, to encourage their external replication and obtain a body of knowledge about the utility of metrics. This can contribute to metrics being useful for OO software designers to make better decisions in the early phases of OO software development, which is the most important goal for any measurement proposal to pursue if it aims to be useful.

References

1. Briand, L., Arisholm, S., Counsell, F., Houdek, F., Thévenod-Fosse, P.: Empirical Studies of Object-Oriented Artifacts, Methods, and Processes: State of the Art and FutureDirections. Empirical Software Engineering 4(4), 387–404 (1999)
2. Briand, L., El Emam, K., Morasca, S.: Theoretical and empirical validation of software product measures. Technical report ISERN-95-03, International Software Engineering Research Network (1995)
3. e Abreu, F.B., Carapuça, R.: Object-Oriented Software Engineering: Measuring and controlling the development process. In: 4th Int. Conference on Software Quality (1994)
4. Calero, C., Piattini, M., Genero, M.: Empirical validation of referential integrity metrics. Information and Software Technology 43, 949–957 (2001)
5. Chidamber, S., Kemerer, C.: A Metrics Suite for Object Oriented Design. IEEE Transactions on Software Engineering 20(6), 476–493 (1994)
6. Darcy, D.P., Kemerer, C.F.: OOMETRICS in practice. IEEE Software (November/December 2005)
7. ISO 9126.:Software Product Evaluation-Quality Characteristics and Guidelines for their Use, ISO/IEC Standard 9126, Geneva (2001)
8. Lorenz, M., Kidd, J.: Object-Oriented Software Metrics: A Practical Guide. Prentice Hall, Englewood Cliffs (1994)
9. Genero, M., Miranda, D., Piattini, M.: Defining and Validating Metrics for UML Statechart Diagrams (2006)
10. Esperanza Manso, M., Genero, M., Piattini, M.: No-Redundant Metrics for UML Class Diagram Structural Complexity
11. Marchesi, M.: OOA Metrics for the Unified Modeling Language. In: Proceedings of the 2nd Euromicro Conference on Software Maintenance and Reengineering, pp. 67–73 (1998)
12. Object Management Group: UML Revision Task Force, OMG UML Specification, v. 1.3, doc. ad/99-06-08 (1999)
13. Poels, G., Dedene, G.: DISTANCE: A Framework for Software Measure Construction. Research Report DTEW9937, Dept. Applied Economics, Katholieke Universiteit Leuven, Belgium, p. 46 (1999) (submitted for publication)

Retracted: Optimizing a Tone Curve for Backward-Compatible High Dynamic Range Image and Video Compression

S. Aravind Kumar

Anand Institute of Higher Technology, M.E- Computer Science and Engineering,
Kazhipattur, Chennai 601103
saravind123@gmail.com

Abstract. High dynamic range (HDR) is a techni que that allow a great dynamic range of luminance between the lightest and darkest area of an image. For video compression, the HDR sequence is reconstructed by inverse tone-mapping a compressed Standard dynamic range (SDR) version of the original HDR content. In this paper, we show that the appropriate choice of a Tone-mapping operator (TMO) can significantly improve the reconstructed HDR quality. It is used to compress a large range of pixel luminance in to smaller range that is suitable for display on devices with limited dynamic range. we formulate a numerical optimization problem to find the tone-curve that minimizes the expected mean square error (MSE) in the reconstructed HDR sequence. We also develop a simplified model that reduces the computational complexity of the optimization problem to a closed-form solution. It is also shown that the LDR image quality resulting from the proposed methods matches that produced by perceptually-based TMOs.

Keywords: Bit-depth scalable, High dynamic range, video compression, tone-mapping.

1 Introduction

Natural scene contain far more visible information that can be captured by the majority of digital imagery and video devices High dynamic range (HDR) video encoding goes beyond the typical color space restrictions and attempts to encode all colors that are visible and distinguishable the human eye. The main motivation is to create a video format that would be future-proof, independent of a display technology, and limited only by the performance of the human visual system (HVS). HDR images preserve colorimetric or photometric pixel values (such as CIE XYZ) within the visible color gamut and allows for intra-frame contrast exceeding 5–6 orders of magnitude (10^6:1), without introducing contouring, banding or posterization artifacts caused by excessive quantization. High dynamic range video formats are unlikely to be broadly accepted without the backward-compatibility with these devices. Such backward-compatibility can be achieved if the HDR video stream contains 1) a backward-compatible 8-bit video layer which could be directly displayed on existing

P.V. Krishna, M.R. Babu, and E. Ariwa (Eds.): ObCom 2011, Part II, CCIS 270, pp. 596–605, 2012.

devices, and 2) additional information which along with this 8-bit layer can yield a good quality reconstructed version of the original HDR content. Finally, a HDR residual signal can also be extracted and encoded in the bit stream as an enhancement layer.

This paper is organized as follows: an overview of related work is presented in Section 2. In Section 3, the proposed tone-mapping approach that considers tone-mapping together with compression is discussed in detail. Section 4 demonstrates and analyzes the performance of the proposed methods. Finally, we draw our conclusions in Section 5.

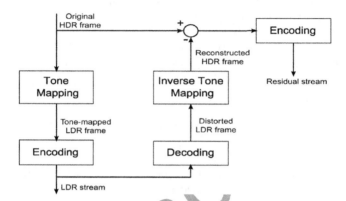

Fig. 1. General structure of the scalable approach used for backward-compatible HDR video encoding. The base layer encodes an 8-bit LDR representation of the HDR input. The enhancement layer encodes the difference (residual) between the inverse tone-mapped base layer and the original HDR source.

2   Related Work

Backward compatible HDR video encoding has received significant interest recently. A color space of encoding HDR content based on the luminance threshold sensitivity of the human visual system. They concluded that 10–12 bit luma encoding is sufficient to encode the full range of visible and physically plausible luminance levels. Their encoding, however, is not backward-compatible with the existing video decoding hardware. For still image compression, backward compatibility can be achieved by encoding a tone-mapped copy of the HDR image together with a residual or a ratio image that allows the reconstruction of the original HDR image. A tone-mapping curve was encoded together with the tone-mapped and residual video sequences. The residual video sequence was additionally filtered to remove the information that is not visible to the human eye.

3   Problem Statement and Proposed Solution

In this section, we present the challenges of obtaining a good quality reconstructed HDR representation in a backward-compatible HDR video encoding system and describe in detail the approach we propose towards overcoming these challenges. The performance of a backward-compatible HDR video and image encoding system depends on the coding efficiency of the LDR base layer and the HDR enhancement layer.

3.1   Tone-Mapping Curve

The global tone-mapping curve is a function that maps HDR luminance values to either the display's luminance range, or directly to LDR pixel values. The tone-mapping curve is usually continuous and non-decreasing. The two most common shapes for the tone curves are the sigmoidal ("S-shaped") or a compressive power function with an exponent 1 (gamma correction).

To keep the problem analytically tractable, we parameterize the tone-mapping curve as a piece-wise linear function with the nodes (l_k, v_k), as shown in Fig. 2. Each segment k between two nodes (l_k, v_k) and (l_{k+1}, v_{k+1}) has a constant width in HDR values equal to δ (0.1 in our implementation). The tone-mapping curve can then be uniquely specified by a set of slopes.

$$S_k = \frac{V_{k+1} - V_k}{\delta} \tag{1}$$

which forms a vector of tone-mapping parameters . Using this parameterization, the forward tone-mapping function is defined as

$$V(l) = (l - l_k).S_k + V_k \tag{2}$$

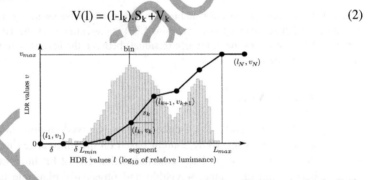

Fig. 2. Parameterization of a tone-mapping curve and the notation. The bar-plot in the background represents an image histogram used to compute p(l).

where is the LDR pixel value, is the segment corresponding to HDR value, that is $l_k \leq l < l_{k+1}$. The inverse mapping function is then

$$\bar{l}(v; S_k) = \left\{ \sum_{l \in S_0}^{v - v_k} l.pL\,(l) \right.$$

for

$$S_k < 0, S_k = 0 \text{ where } S_k \in \{ S_1 \ldots S_N \} \tag{3}$$

When the slope is zero ($S_{k=0}$), $\bar{l}(v; S_k)$ is assigned an expected HDR pixel value for the entire range S_0 in which the slope is equal zero. $P_L(l)$ is the probability of HDR pixel value .

3.2   Statistical Distortion Model

As mentioned earlier in Section 3, accurately computing the distorted HDR values would be too computationally demanding. Instead, we estimate the error $\left\|\bar{l} - l\right\|_2^2$ assuming that the compression distortions follow a known probability distribution P_C. Under this assumption, the expected value of the error $\left\|\bar{l} - l\right\|_2^2$ is

$$
E\left[\left\|\bar{l} - l\right\|_2^2\right] = \sum_{l=l_{\min}}^{l_{\max}} \sum_{\bar{v}=0}^{v_{\max}} \left(\bar{l}(v; s_k) - l\right)^2
$$
$$
\cdot pc(v(l) - \bar{v} / v(l)) \cdot p_L(l) \tag{4}
$$

Where $pc(v - \bar{v} / v)$ is the probability that the encoding error equals $v - \bar{v}$. Consequently, the continuously relaxed objective function is written as

$$
\varepsilon(S_K) = \sum_{l=l_{\min}}^{l_{\max}} \sum_{\bar{v}=0}^{v_{\max}} \left(\bar{l}(v; s_k) - l\right)^2 \cdot pc(v - \bar{v}).p_L(l) \tag{5}
$$

The only unknown variable is the probability distribution of the compression error $pc(v - \bar{v})$, which can be estimated for any lossy compression scheme.

3.3   Optimization Problem

The optimum tone curve can be found by minimizing the $\varepsilon(S_K)$ function with respect to the segment slopes

$$
S_K \; \arg\min \varepsilon(S_K) \tag{6}
$$

where $s_1 \dots s_N$ Subject to :

$$
s_{\min} \leq s_K \leq s_{\max} \quad \text{for} \quad k=1\dots N
$$
$$
\sum_{k=1}^{N} s_K . \delta = v_{\max}. \tag{7}
$$

The first constraint restricts slopes to the allowable range, while the second ensures that the tone curve spans exactly the range of pixel values from 0 to V_{max}. The minimum slope s_{min} ensures that the tone-mapping function is strictly increasing and thus invertible and $\bar{l}(\bar{v}; s_K)$ can be computed. The lack of this assumption introduces discontinuity and local minima, impeding the use of efficient solvers. Since s_{min} is set to a very low value (below $0.5/\delta$), this assumption has no significant effect on the resulting tone-curves, which are rounded to the nearest pixel values. With s_{max}. we can write

$$\bar{l}(v+1; s_k) - \bar{l}(v; s_k)_{>\log_{10}(1.01)} \tag{8}$$

$$s_K = (\log_{10}(1.01))^{-1} \tag{9}$$

So that

3.4   Closed-Form Solution

The distortion model in (5) gives a good estimate of compression errors, but poses two problems for practical implementation in an HDR compression scheme: 1) it requires the knowledge of the encoding distortion distribution pc , and 2) the optimization problem can only be solved numerically using slow iterative. l in the distortion model (5) using the inverse mapping function in (3), this gives

$$\varepsilon(S_k) \approx \sum_{l=l_{min}}^{l\ max} \sum_{\bar{v}=0}^{v_{max}} pc\ (v - \bar{v}).\ p_L(l).(\frac{v-\bar{v}}{S_k})^2 \tag{10}$$

After reorganizing we get

$$\varepsilon(S_k) \approx \sum_{l=l_{min}}^{l\ max} \sum_{\bar{v}=0}^{v_{max}} pc(v - \bar{v}).$$

$$= \sum_{l=l_{min}}^{l_{max}} \frac{pL(l)}{S_k^2}.\ Var(v-\bar{v}) \tag{11}$$

Since the variance of $(v - \bar{v})$ does not depend on the slopes , it does not affect the location of the global minimum of $\varepsilon(S_k)$. The tone-curves found using the accurate model from (5) and a simplified model from (11) were almost the same. The most important consequence of using the simplified model from (11) is that the optimal tone-curve does not depend on the image compression error, as long as the compression distortions are not severe enough to invalidate the local linearity assumption.

The constrained optimization problem defined in (6) can now be re-written as follows:

$$\underset{s1......sN}{\arg\min} \sum_{k=1}^{N} \frac{p_k}{s_k^2} \qquad \text{Subject to } \sum_{k=1}^{N} s_k = \frac{v_{max}}{\delta} \qquad (12)$$

Where $p_k = \sum_{l=l_k}^{l+1} p_L(l)$ and l_k and l_{k+1} define the lower and the upper bounds of a segment, respectively. This problem can be solved analytically by calculating the first order Karush-Kuhn-Tucker (KKT) optimality conditions of the corresponding Lagrangian, which results in the following system of equations:

$$\begin{cases} \dfrac{-2p_1}{s_1^3} + \lambda = 0 \\[2mm] \dfrac{-2p_2}{s_2^3} + \lambda = 0 \\[2mm] \vdots \\[2mm] \dfrac{-2p_N}{s_N^3} + \lambda = 0 \\[2mm] \displaystyle\sum_{k=1}^{N} s_K - \frac{v_{max}}{\delta} = 0 \end{cases} \qquad (13)$$

where λ is the Lagrange multiplier. The solution to the above system of equations results in the slopes s_k given by

$$s_k = \frac{v_{max} \cdot p_K^{1/3}}{\delta \cdot \displaystyle\sum_{k=1}^{N} p_k^{1/3}}. \qquad (14)$$

Note that the expression derived in (14) does not consider the upper bound constraint imposed on s_k in (7). Let be the set of the index of a segment with a slope that exceeds the upper bound. We overcome the upper bound violation using the following adjustment:

$$S_k = \begin{cases} \dfrac{\left(v_{max} - \sum_{i \in X} \delta_{max\delta}\right)}{\delta . \displaystyle\sum_{j \notin X}^{N} p_j^{1/3}} . p_k^{1/3} & \text{for } S_k \in I \end{cases} \qquad (15)$$

4   Experimental Results and Discussion

In this section we first validate the proposed methods: optimization using the statistical model proposed in Section III-B and the closed-form solution based on a simplified model derived in Section III-D. Then, our models are further analyzed based on the generated tone curve and the distortion of the reconstructed HDR content. The performance of our models is also evaluated by comparing it with existing tone-mapping methods.

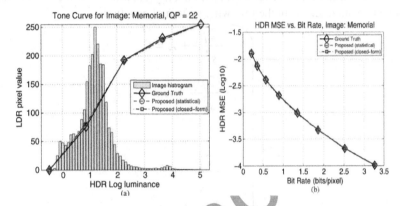

Fig. 3. Validation of the proposed models by comparison with the ground-truth solution. The top figure, (a), shows the tone curves computed using the statistical model, the closed-form solution and the ground-truth optimization for the image "Memorial". The x axis denotes the HDR luminance in the log-10 scale, and y axis is the LDR pixel value. (b) demonstrates the result of HDR MSE (in log10 scale) versus bit rate. The lower the MSE value, the better the image quality.

4.1   Model Validation

In this section, we validate that the statistical model of Section 3.2 results in a tone curve that truly reflects the ground-truth results. Ground-truth results are achieved using the ideal scheme illustrated in Fig. 3(a), where the actual H.264/AVC encoder and decoder are employed to find the truly optimal piecewise linear tone curve. To make the experiment computationally feasible, we divided the tone curve into four segments of equal width.

4.2   Dependence of the Tone Curves on QP

Next, we verify that the proposed statistical model can be well approximated by the closed-form solution which produces a tone curve that is independent of QP. The probability distribution of the H.264/AVC compression errors, which is a function of QP, is included in the statistical model proposed in Section III-B. The figures show that the tone curves are not significantly affected by the variation of QP.

4.3   Further Analysis of the Closed-Form Solution

The tone curve resulting from the closed-form solution given by (14) can be genera-lized as follows:

$$s_k = \frac{v_{max} \cdot p_k^{1/t}}{\delta \cdot \sum_{k=1}^{N} p_k^{1/t}}$$

(16)

In our closed-form solution, is set to be equal to 3. Note that when t=1, (16) is iden-tical to the histogram equalization operation.

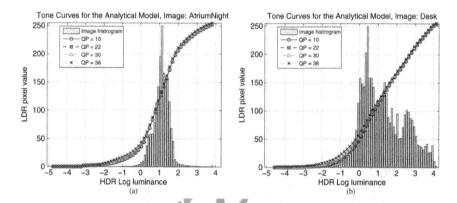

Fig. 4. Tone curves generated using the statistical model with different QP values for the im-ages "AtriumNight" and "Desk". The notation of the axis is the same as Fig. 3(a). The smaller the value of QP, the better the compression quality. 87 and 88 segments are used for "Atrium-Night" and "Desk" respectively.

A particular quality metric. Fig. 4 shows the resulting average performance over 40 HDR images. The left row in the figure indicates that our closed-form solution (t=3) is largely better than the histogram equalization method (t=1) and outperforms all other cases for HDR MSE. This can be expected, since our approach explicitly mini-mizes MSE. From a practical point of view, HDR content is usually prepared for high-quality visual experience where only light or medium compression quantization is allowed. In this sense, the results demonstrated in Fig. 4 indicate that our closed-form solution guarantees good performance.

The linear combination of the tone-curves produced by our method and these algo-rithms. Moreover, our study shows that the overall quality of images tone-mapped with our method is comparable to other tone-mapping algorithms and none of the tone-mapped images we generated was considered as unacceptable. This means that for the applications that do not require a finely adjusted backward-compatible layer, our method can be used directly.

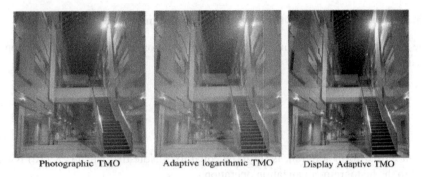

Photographic TMO   Adaptive logarithmic TMO   Display Adaptive TMO

Fig. 5. Rate-distortion curves, tone curves and tone-mapped images for the image "Atrium-Night". The first row demonstrates the resulting tone-curves with different TMOs, followed by the results for MSE and SSIM versus bit rates; the second row shows tone-mapped LDR images using the proposed statistical model and the closed-form solution. The third row shows the tone-mapped images using the existing tone-mapping methods. All the tone-mapped images shown are compressed. The compression quantization parameters used for "AtriumNight" is 10. The number of segments used for the histogram is 87.

Photographic TMO   Adaptive logarithmic TMO   Display Adaptive TMO

Fig. 6. Rate-distortion curves, tone curves and tone-mapped images for the image "Coby". The notation is the same as Fig.6. The compression quantization parameters used for "Coby" is 22. The number of segments used for the histogram is 36.

Statistical (proposed)   Close-form (proposed)   Photographic   Logarithmic   Adaptive Display

Fig. 7. Distortion maps of the LDR images relative to the original HDR images. The LDR images evaluated have not been compressed. In each of the distortion maps, three colors denote three different types of distortions: green for loss of visible contrast; blue for amplification of invisible contrast; red for reversal of visible contrast. The higher intensity of a color correlates with higher distortion of that type.

5   Conclusion

In this project, we showed that the appropriate choice of a tone-mapping operator (TMO) can significantly improve the reconstructed HDR quality. We developed a statistical model that approximates the distortion resulting from the combined processes of tone-mapping and compression. Using this model, we formulated a constrained optimization problem that finds the tone-curve which minimizes the expected HDR MSE. The resulting optimization problem, however, suffers from high computational complexity. Therefore, we presented a few simplifying assumptions that allowed us to reduce the optimization problem to an analytically tractable form with a closed-form solution. The closed-form solution is computationally efficient and has a performance compatible to our developed statistical model. Moreover, the closed-form solution does not require the knowledge of QP, which makes it suitable for cases where the compression strength is unknown. Although our models are designed to minimize HDR MSE, the extensive performance evaluations show that the proposed methods provide excellent performance in terms of SSIM and the LDR image quality, in addition to an outstanding performance in MSE.

References

[1] Seetzen, H., Heidrich, W., Stuerzlinger, W., Ward, G., Whitehead, L., Trentacoste, M., Ghosh, A., Vorozcovs, A.: High dynamic range display systems. ACM Trans. Graph (Proc. SIGGRAPH) 23(3), 757–765 (2004)

[2] IEC61966-2-4, Colour Measurement and Management—Part 2–4: Colour Management—Extended-Gamut YCC Colour Space for Video Applications— xvYCC (2006)

[3] Mantiuk, R., Krawczyk, G., Myszkowski, K., Seidel, H.-P.: Perception- motivated high dynamic range video encoding. ACM Trans. Graph. (Proc. SIGGRAPH) 23(3), 730–738 (2004)

[4] Ward, G.: Real pixels. Graphics Gems II, 80–83 (1991)

[5] Bogart, R., Kainz, F., Hess, D.: Openexr image file format. In: Proc. ACM SIGGRAPH 2003, Sketches Applicat. (2003)

[6] Larson, G.W.: Logluv encoding for full-gamut, high-dynamic range images. J. Graph. Tools 3(1), 15–31 (1998)

[7] Gao, Y., Wu, Y.: Applications and Requirement for Color Bit Depth Scalability. Tech. Rep., ISO/IEC JTC1/SC29/WG11 and ITU-T SG16 Q.6, JVT-U049 (October 2006)

[8] Sullivan, G.J., Yu, H., Sekiguchi, S.-I., Sun, H., Wedi, T., Wittmann, S., Lee, Y.-L., Segall, A., Suzuki, T.: New standardized extensions of mpeg4-avc/h.264 for professional-quality video applications. In: Proc. ICIP, vol. 1, pp. I-13–I-16 (2007)

[9] Winken, M., Marpe, D., Schwarz, H., Wiegand, T.: Bit-depth scalable video coding. In: Proc. ICIP, vol. 1, pp. I-5–I-8 (2007)

Short - Text Mining Approach for Medical Domain

R. Kavitha, A. Padmaja, and P. Subha

Department of Computer Science and Engineering,
Vel Tech Dr. RR & Dr. SR Technical University,
Chennai, India
rkavitha1984@gmail.com, alapadmaja@yahoo.com,
subha_cse2003@yahoo.co.in

Abstract. The growing amount of published articles in medicine represents a massive source of knowledge, which can only efficiently be accessed by a new creation of automated information extraction tools. By discovering predictive relationships between different pieces of extracted data from the medicine field, data-mining algorithms can be used to improve the precision of information extraction. Medical text retrieval refers to text retrieval techniques applied to biomedical resources and articles available in the biomedical domain. In this paper we propose an approach to extract the important medical text from the published medical articles. The medical text here means the disease and the treatment keywords. Here we extract the relationship between the disease and the treatment. The three relations that we extract are cure, prevention and side-effect. The amount of published medical articles, and therefore the underlying medical knowledge base, is expanding at an increasing rate. So retrieval of the reliable information is a difficult task. To overcome that we propose this method and also we develop an expert system to develop medical diagnosis applications and the medication management which serves a good purpose for the laypeople as well as for the people who do research in the medical field. This paper presents a technique for using data mining algorithm to increase the accuracy of medical text extraction.

Keywords: Disease, Semantic, Treatment, Medical.

1 Introduction

Text mining aims to extract useful knowledge from textual data or documents. Although text mining is often considered as a subfield of data mining, some text mining techniques have originated from other disciplines, such as information retrieval, information visualization, computational linguistics, and information science. Examples of text mining applications include document classification, document clustering, entity extraction, information extraction and summarization. Compared with well-structured sources such as wikipedia, forums are more valuable in the sense that they contain first hand patient experiences with richer information in terms of which treatments are better than others and why. Besides this, on forums, patients explain their symptoms much more freely than those mentioned on relatively

P.V. Krishna, M.R. Babu, and E. Ariwa (Eds.): ObCom 2011, Part II, CCIS 270, pp. 606–612, 2012.
© Springer-Verlag Berlin Heidelberg 2012

formal sources like Wikipedia. Relevant feedback requires the extraction and computation of certain features that can distinguish different elements of a document collection. We focus on three semantic relations: Cure, Prevent, and Side Effect. The contributions of this paper consists in the fact that better results are obtained compared to previous studies and the fact that our research settings allow the integration of biomedical and medical knowledge. The aim of this paper is to show which Natural Language Processing and Machine Learning techniques are suitable for the task of identifying semantic relations between diseases and treatments in short biomedical texts. The value of our work stands in the results we obtain and the new feature representation techniques.

The proposed work develops an expert system for medical diagnosis with the extracted text from the medical articles. Expert system or knowledge-based systems are the common type of AI systems in routine clinical use. They contain medical knowledge, usually about a very specifically defined task, and are able to reason with data from individual patients to come up with reasoned conclusions. Although there are many variations, the knowledge within an expert system is typically represented in the form of a set of rules. Machine learning systems can create new medical knowledge. Learning is seen to be the essential characteristic of an intelligent system. Consequently, one of the driving ambitions of AI has been to develop computers that can learn from experience. The resulting developments in the AI sub-field of machine learning have resulted in a set of techniques which have the potential to alter the way in which knowledge is created.

In a recent report, the Institute of Medicine recognized that NLP is potentially a very powerful technology for the medical domain because it enables a new level of functionality for health care applications that would not be otherwise possible. The contributions that we bring with our work stand in the fact that we present an extensive study of various ML algorithms and textual representations for classifying short medical texts and identifying semantic relations between two medical entities: diseases and treatments. From an ML point of view, we show that in short texts when identifying semantic relations between diseases and treatments a substantial improvement in results is obtained when using a hierarchical way of approaching the task.

There are many different types of clinical task to which expert systems can be applied.

Medical Diagnosis: When a patient's case is complex, rare or the person making the diagnosis is simply inexperienced, an expert system can help come up with likely diagnoses based on patient data.

Therapy planning: Systems can either look for inconsistencies, errors and omissions in an existing treatment plan.

Image recognition and interpretation: Many medical images can now be automatically interpreted, from plane X-rays through to more complex images like CT and MRI scans.

Medication Management: According to the patients reviews the medicines are provided to the patient. It can be very useful for the paramedical companies.

2   Literature Survey

Feldman et al. (2002) used a rule-based system to extract relations that are focused on genes, proteins, drugs, and diseases. Friedman et al. (2001) go deeper into building a rule-based system by hand-crafting a semantic grammar and a set of semantic constraints in order to recognize a range of biological and molecular relations. In biomedical literature, rule-based approaches have been widely used for solving relation extraction tasks. The main sources of information used by this technique are either syntactic: part-of-speech (POS) and syntactic structures; or semantic information in the form of fixed patterns that contain words that trigger a certain relation.

The most relevant work for our study is the work of Rosario and Hearst (2004). The authors of this paper are the ones that created and distributed the data set used in our research. The data set is annotated with disease and treatments entities and with 8 semantic relations between diseases and treatments. The main focus of their work is on entity recognition that is the task of identifying entities, diseases and treatments in biomedical text sentences. The authors use Hidden Markov Models and maximum entropy models to perform both the task of entity recognition and of relation discrimination. Their representation techniques are based on words in context, part-of- speech information, phrases, and terms from MeSH1, a medical lexical knowledge-base.

The biomedical literature contains a wealth of work on semantic relation extraction, mostly focused on more biology-specific tasks: subcellular- location (Craven 1999), gene-disorder association (Ray and Craven 2001), and diseases and drugs relations (Srinivasan and Rindflesch 2002, Ahlers et al., 2007). Text classification techniques combined with a Naïve Bayes classifier and relational learning algorithms are methods used by Craven (1999). Hidden Markov Models are used in Craven (2001), but similarly to Rosario and Hearst (2004), the research focus was entity recognition. A context based approach using MeSH term co-occurrences are used by Srinivasan and Rindflesch (2002) for relationship discrimination between diseases and drugs. A lot of work is focused on building rules used to extract relation.

One of the drawbacks of using methods based on rules is that they tend to require more human-expert effort than data-driven methods . The best rule-based systems are the ones that use rules constructed manually or semi automatically extracted automatically and refine manually. A positive aspect of rule-based systems is the fact that they obtain good precision results, while the recall levels tend to be low. Published medical text extraction refers to text mining applied to texts and literature of the published medical and molecular biology domain. It is a rather recent research field on the edge of natural language processing, bioinformatics, medical informatics and computational linguistics. There is an increasing interest in text mining and information extraction strategies applied to the published medical and molecular biology literature due to the increasing number of electronically available publications stored in databases.

The increasing research in Complementary and Alternative Medicine and the importance placed on practicing evidence-based medicine require ready access to the published medical scientific literature. In this paper we try to employ an algorithm that extracts the published medical texts for the published medical database based on the some data mining algorithm. Our approach first identifies the disease keywords and the treatment related for the given disease contained in the published medical articles and then finding the relationship between these keywords.

With the growth of the biomedical technology, enormous biomedical databases are produced. It creates a need and challenge for data mining. Data mining is a process of the knowledge discovery in databases and the goal is to find out the hidden and interesting information. The technology includes association rules, classification, clustering, and evolution analysis etc. Clustering algorithms are used as the essential tools to group analogous patterns and separate outliers according to its principles that elements in the same cluster are more homogenous while elements in the different ones are more dissimilar. Furthermore, data mining algorithms do not need to rely on the pre-defined classes and the training examples while classifying the classes and can produce the good quality of clustering, so they fit to extract the biomedical text better.

Structuring of unstructured text has been studied by many works in the literature. Automatic information extraction and wrapper induction techniques have been used for structuring web data. Sarawagi (2008) and Laender et al. (2002) offer comprehensive overviews of information extraction and wrapper induction techniques respectively. The main difference between our work and main stream work on extraction is that we extract sentences as units, which is shallower but presumably more robust. Heinze et al. (2002) state that the current state-of-theart in NLP is suitable for mining information of moderate content depth across a diverse collection of medical settings and specialties. Zhou et al. (2006), the authors perform information extraction from clinical medical records using a decision tree based classifier using resources such as WordNet 1, UMLS 2 etc. They extract past medical history and social behaviour from the records.

3   Method and Dataset

Our work is divided into two important tasks. First task is to identify the sentence that is having the disease and treatment key phrase. Second work is to extract the relation in the identified sentence. Here we concentrate on three relations: Cure, Prevent, and Side Effect. We are proceeding this task by using techniques based on NLP and supervised techniques. We decided to focus on these three relations because these are the ones that are better represented in the original data set and in the end will allow us to draw more reliable conclusions. Also, looking at the meaning of all relations in the original data set, the three that we focus are the ones that could be useful for wider research goals and are the ones that really entail relations between two entities. In the supervised ML settings the amount of training data is a factor that influences the performance; support for this stands not only in the related work performed on the same data set, but in the research literature as well.

4   Proposed Model

Clustering is the process of organizing objects into groups whose members are similar in some way. It can be considered the most important unsupervised learning problem which deals with finding a structure in a collection of unlabeled data. A cluster is therefore a collection of objects which are "similar" between them and are "dissimilar" to the objects belonging to other clusters. Hard clustering is the techniques in which any pattern can be in only one cluster at any time. Soft clustering is the technique which permits patterns to be in more than one cluster at any time. There are various clustering approaches that can be applied to cluster the published medical keywords extracted from full text articles, some of them are k-means, k-median, Hierarchical Clustering Algorithm, Nearest Neighbor Algorithm etc.

K-means (MacQueen, 1967) is one of the simplest unsupervised learning algorithms that solve the well known clustering problem. The procedure follows a simple and easy way to classify a given data set through a certain number of clusters (assume k clusters) fixed a priori. The main idea is to define k centroids, one for each cluster. These centroids should be placed in a cunning way because of different location causes different result. So, the better choice is to place them as much as possible far away from each other. The next step is to take each point belonging to a given data set and associate it to the nearest centroid. When no point is pending, the first step is completed and an early group age is done. At this point we need to re-calculate k new centroids as bar centers of the clusters resulting from the previous step. After we have these k new centroids, a new binding has to be done between the same data set points and the nearest new centroid. A loop has been generated. As a result of this loop we may notice that the k centroids change their location step by step until no more changes are done. In other words centroids do not move any more.

- Place K points into the space represented by the objects that are being clustered. These points represent initial group centroids.
- Assign each object to the group that has the closest centroid.
- When all objects have been assigned, recalculate the positions of the K centroids.
- Repeat Steps 2 and 3 until the centroids no longer move. This produces a separation of the objects into groups from which the metric to be minimized can be calculated.

The proposed algorithm will take complete list of all the published medical articles and the output will be the files containing the clusters created using k mean algorithm on keywords.

Input: List of published medical articles.
Output: Clusters.
Algorithm
1. Read the articles containing the disease and the treatment keyword in the list of published medical articles.
2. Read the full medical article.
3. Extract the keywords from the article using KEA algorithm
4. Build a medical lexicon
5. Refer to the published medical lexicon and discard the irrelevant keywords
6. Put the data in following relation so that the full text can be retrieved later using keywords only

7. Go to step 1 and repeat till all the articles in the list of published medical articles are processed.
8. Use the k-means algorithm to create clusters on keywords.
9. Save the article clusters with a unique articles IDs.

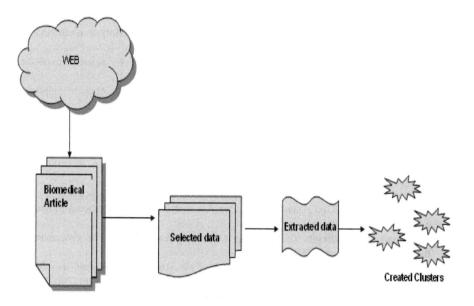

Fig. 1. Architecture Design

The relation created step 6 will be used at the time of retrieval. Whenever the published medical database is searched for any word the cluster containing the matching keywords is returned. The respective full text and other details corresponding to the returned cluster can be retrieved using this relation. The figure 1 depicts the design of the proposed model. The input to be given to the model is the medical articles and the final output is the clusters which are saved with a unique ID. For each relation different clusters are created and are saved.

5   Conclusion

Extraction of text from published medical article is an essential operation. Although there have been many text extraction methods developed, this paper presents a novel technique that employs keyword based text clustering to further enhance the text extraction process. The development of the proposed algorithm is of practical significance; however it is challenging to design a unified approach of text extraction that retrieves the relevant text articles more efficiently. The proposed algorithm, using data mining algorithm, seems to extract the text with contextual completeness in overall, individual and collective forms, making it able to significantly enhance the text extraction process from published medical literature.

References

[1] Han, J., Kamber, M.: Data Mining Concepts and Techniques. Morgan Kaufmann, CA (2001)
[2] Badgett, R.G.: How to search for and evaluate medical evidence. In: Seminars in Medical Practice (1999)
[3] Richardson, J.: Building CAM databases: the challenges ahead. J. Altern. Complement Med. (2002)
[4] Kantardzic, M.: Data Mining: Concepts, Models, Methods, and Algorithms. John Wiley & Sons (2003); ISBN 0471228524. OCLC 50055336
[5] Miller, H., Han, J.: Geographic Data Mining and Knowledge Discovery (2003)
[6] Aery, M., Ramamurthy, N., Aslandogan, Y.A.: Topic identification of textual data. Technical report, The University of Texas at Arlington (2003)
[7] Rosario, B., Hearst, M.A.: Classifying semantic relations in bioscience text. In: Proceedings of the 42nd Annual Meeting on Association for Computational Linguistics, p. 430 (2004)
[8] Srinivasan, P., Rindflesch, T.: Exploring text mining from Medline. In: Proceedings of the AMIA Symposium (2002)
[9] Feldman, R., Regev, Y., Finkelstein-Landau, M., Hurvit, E., Kogan, B.: Mining biomedical literature using information extraction. Current Drug Discovery (2002)
[10] Sarawagi, S.: Information extraction. Foundations and Trends in Databases (2008)

Multilevel Security in Cloud Computing Environment Using Graceful Codes

K. Govinda[1] and E. Sathiyamoorthy[2]

[1] School of Computer Science & Engg.,
VIT University, Vellore, India
kgovinda@vit.ac.in
[2] School of Information Technology & Engg.,
VIT University, Vellore, India
esathiyamoorthy@vit.ac.in

Abstract. Cloud is an emerging style of Information Technology infrastructure designed for rapid delivery of computing resources. Business or consumer services are delivered in a simplified manner, providing unbounded scale, differentiated quality, and with a user focus designed to foster rapid innovation and efficient decision making. Cloud computing is a potentially cost-efficient model for provisioning processes, applications and services while making IT management easier and more responsive to the needs of the business. These services - computation services, storage services, networking services, whatever is needed - are delivered and made available in a simplified way - "on demand" regardless of where the user is or the type of device they're using. Security is a major concern in this domain. Security has become a research area in this field involving both academic and industrial communities. This paper describes multilevel cryptography technique for data encryption and decryption using graceful codes.

Keywords: Cryptography, Permutations, Graceful Codes, Edge labeling and Vertex labeling.

1   Introduction

Cloud security have the ability of Massive scalability in which the work done on different computers can be allocated or gathered on a single platform of limited platforms rather than on hundred of platforms and can be approached easily from the specific computer. It is true that every organization have hundreds or thousands of systems of computing the data but cloud computing is the best plat form of providing the ability to scale to tens of thousands of systems, as well as the ability of scaling massively the storage space. Cloud security is also having the ability of Elasticity. Users can rapidly increase and decrease their computing resources as needed as well as renovate resources and also produce new recourses for different uses when the previous ones are no longer required. Cloud computing can provide you the best platform of Self-provisioning the resources. Users can self-provision the resources

P.V. Krishna, M.R. Babu, and E. Ariwa (Eds.): ObCom 2011, Part II, CCIS 270, pp. 613–618, 2012.
© Springer-Verlag Berlin Heidelberg 2012

like as additional systems capability of processing, software and data storage as well as enhances the network resources. In short it is the best plat form to share your resources to others. The attractive attribute of cloud computing is the elasticity of resources. This allows the user to increase and decrease the computing resources as they want. They can increase the storage capacity, processing etc. There is always an awareness of the baseline of computing resources but predicting future needs is difficult, especially when demands are constantly changing. Cloud computing is said to be very flexible and cost-efficient. But when the data is not proven it cannot be safeguard for public clouds, tools for thwarting outside threats and trusted compliance standards, security is always the largest hurdle for cloud computing.

Many different cryptographic algorithms have been developed in recent past, some of which are worth mentioning like the R.S.A or the D.E.S, which are looked upon as very safer for secure communication. But one thing common to all is the repetition of data values in the cipher coded text, or which in a different language might be called as patterns. An intelligent intruder might easily recognize these patterns and thus can generalize the coding algorithm after a deep analysis. This might pose a serious threat to data communication.

The rest of this paper is organized as follows: the second section discusses cloud overview and section three discusses different cloud service model, the fourth section describes the purpose of cryptography, the section five describes types of cryptography, the proposed model is discussed in section six, section seven describes the architecture, implementation and results are shown in section eight and nine, followed by conclusion

2   Proposed Method

The method put forward in this paper ensures the security level by encrypting the encrypted code. We start off the encryption process by first encrypting the given text by a particular algorithm to get the graceful code and we then we move on to permute the graceful code to get final permuted cipher text which is sent over the network. This second round of encryption ensures that the occasional repetition that might have crept in during the encryption is eliminated. In the end we will show a sample code snapshot that we have worked with to check our encryption algorithm.

Let's start with an example to explain our algorithm. Assuming that the text to be encrypted is "THIS IS A TEST." After our proposed model's encryption, it may look something like this:

ASVBDHJKHMGDXMKDMVXJKSNCXHLBKILHJEWBNDUCI

Here it is very difficult to find out what is the length of encrypted 'T' and what the length is of encrypted 'H'. Also, as is obvious from the encrypted text, no one can find any repeating pattern so that he can try a normal attack. To clarify our point, let us assume that a letter 'X' is encrypted to 'AGDBSSB'. If we use the normal algorithms, a pattern will emerge because of repetition if we start the encryption process by encrypting of ASCII values. To avoid this hack, we do the permutation of the generated cipher text. The permutation ensures that no pattern emerges to avoid the generally possible attacks. This second level of permutation converts our G-code into unique and recurring permutations. The second level of encryption which essentially is a 'permutation', maps each and every character into a set of unique values that differentiates them from other sets. This form the part of multilevel graceful code cryptography.

3   Architecture

As is obvious from the proposed model, there are 2 (or n) levels in encryption. The encryption process starts with the conversion of the number text/given text to graceful code. This is followed by permutations (n rounds of permutation if we need much deeper encryption level which has already been agreed upon by both the parties involved).

On the decryption site, the process is followed in reverse. First the permutations are done and then the conversion of graceful code to the original text is done.

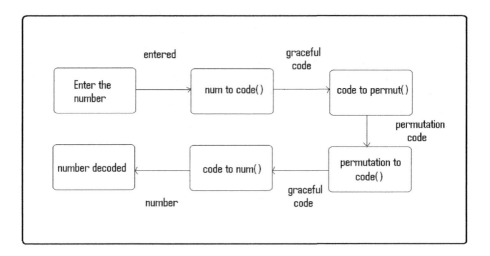

Fig. 1. Architecture

4   Implementation

We start the encryption process from the first level of encryption. We can represent the first level of encryption by the following graph. The graceful code generated in this case, the set being (0,1,4,6), is (0,4,1,0,1,0) which is the intermediate encrypted code generated in our algorithm.

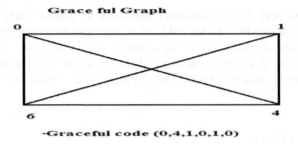

Grace ful Graph

-Graceful code (0,4,1,0,1,0)

Fig. 2. Graceful Graph

Code for this graceful graph will be of the form (a1, a2, a3, a4, a5, a6) where

$a_1 = \min\{ e_1 = (0,1) \} = 0$
$a_2 = \min\{ e_2 = (4,6) \} = 4$
$a_3 = \min\{ e_3 = (1,4) \} = 1$
$a_4 = \min\{ e_4 = (0,4) \} = 0$
$a_5 = \min\{ e_5 = (1,6) \} = 1$
$a_6 = \min\{ e_6 = (0,6) \} = 0$

The graceful code thus is (0,4,1,0,1,0). But as indicated earlier, this set will lead to repetition of this pattern everywhere whenever the set (0,1,4,6) appears. To ensure that this repetition is not apparent in our cipher text, we will go for n rounds of repetition (we consider here only one round of repetition). We perform the permutation round in the way shown below. We perform the permutation on the very same graph by subtracting the edges. Example:

1 => (1-0)
2 => (6-4)
3 => (4-1)
4 => (4-0) and so on

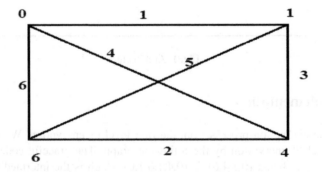

Grace ful Graph

-Graceful code (0,4,1,0,1,0)

Fig. 3. Graceful Graph with unique edge label

Now, the value thus obtained is unique for all data sets and has independent unique values inside its own set. While implementing this algorithm over a network, these values will be sufficiently large that mapping the values back for intruders will become a tedious task.

5   Result

Below I present a few snapshots of the algorithm presented.

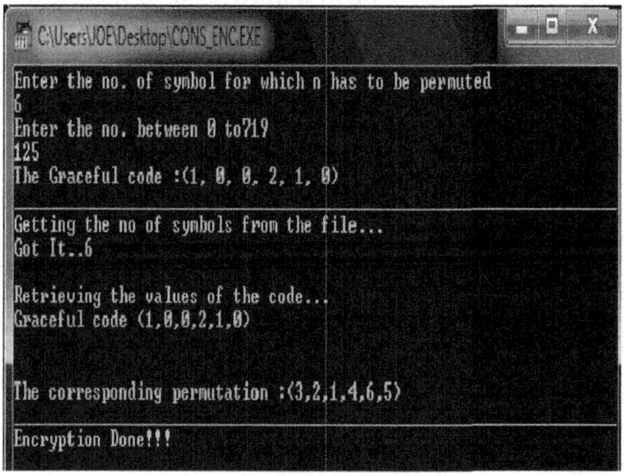

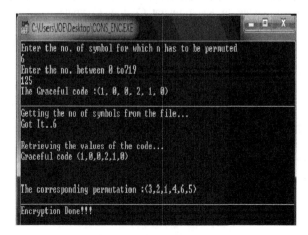

Fig. 4. Encryption Process

The above snapshot show the encryption process. The graceful code generated as well as the final cipher text are clearly demonstrated. It is also clearly visible that the cipher generated also has no repeating pattern which could be vulnerable to attack.

Fig. 5. Decryption Process

The above snapshot shows the decryption algorithm. It is also to be observed that the graceful code obtained from the cipher text is same as the one in the encryption part. We call it graceful in the sense that it is elegant and ingeniously simple and ciphers the data to two levels of encryption.

6   Conclusions

Cryptography as well known ensures confidentiality and data integration. Our proposed algorithm affirms to these main objectives as it makes attacks very tedious and cumbersome. The model proposed fuses best of two known cryptographic algorithms and proposes a new algorithm to ensure security. The n-level architecture ensures that the deeper one encrypts his text, the stronger cipher he gets.

References

1. Smith, T.F., Waterman, M.S.: Identification of Common Molecular Subsequences. J. Mol. Biol. 147, 195–197 (1981)
2. William, S.: Cryptography and Network Security: Principles and Practice, 2nd edn., pp. 23–50. Prentice-Hall, Inc. (1999)
3. Basic Cryptographic Algorithms, http://www.itsc.state.md.us/oldsite/info/InternetSecurity/Crypto/CryptoIntro.htm#Algorithms
4. Hebert, S.: A Brief History of Cryptography, http://cybercrimes.net/aindex.html
5. Gary, K.: An Overview of Cryptography, http://www.garykessler.net/library/crypto.html
6. Bondy, J.A., Murty, U.S.R.: Graph Theory with Application, 1st edn. Macmillan Press Ltd. (1976)
7. Balasubramanium, K., Chandramowliswaran, N., Ramachandran, N., Arun, S., Kumar, P.: Mathematical properties of trees generation code and Algorithm to generate all free code for given number of edge. In: Kyoto Interat. Conf. on Computational Geometry and Graph Theory
8. Koblitz, N.: A course in Number theory and Cryptography, 2nd edn. Springer, Heidelberg
9. Stalling, I.W.: Cryptographic and Network Security- Principles and Practices. Prentice
10. Arun, S.: Project Report on Graceful Labelings, Dept of Computer Science and Engineering, SCSVMV (Deemed University) Kanchipuram (November 2006)
11. Mell, P., Grance, T.: Draft nist working definition of cloud computing 15 (August 21, 2009)
12. Cloud security Alliance. Securitybestpracticesforcloudcomputing (2010b), http://www.cloudsecurityalliance.org
13. http://www.thelatestnews.in/reliance-cloud-computing-simplify-the-life-of-small-and-big-businesses/21270.htm

Let's Play with Images and Private Data Using Stick of Randomness

Manish Mahajan and Navdeep Kaur

Deptt. of IT at CEC, Landran Mohali, Punjab
{manishmahajan4u,cecm.infotech}@gmail.com

Abstract. Steganography is the process of hiding one message or file inside another message or file. For instance, steganographers can hide an image inside another image, an audio file, or a video file, or they can hide an audio or video file inside another media file or even inside a large graphic file. Steganography differs from cryptography in that while cryptography works to mask the content of a message, steganography works to mask the very existence of the message. With the war on terrorism and the hunt for those responsible for the September 11 attacks mounting, steganography is increasingly in the news. Some experts theorize the al Qaeda terrorists used the Internet to plan the attacks, possibly using steganography to keep their intentions secret [13]. The aim of this study was to investigate the various steganograhy methods & how they are implemented .LSB is a very well known method in this field. In binary images we are very much restricted in the scope as there are only 4 bits or 8 bits to represent a pixel so we are very much restricted to most popular LSB methods .But in coloured images there are generally up to 24 bits images with three different RGB channels, if using RGB colour space .So , we can explore a lot many new methods which can manipulate or use various channels of colouerd images in regular or arbitrary pattern to hide the information. Using this concept we have explored the various existing methods of data hiding in coloured images & taken an intersection between the arbitrary pixel manipulation & LSB method to propose our work which uses arbitrary channel of a pixel to reflect the presence of data in one or two other channels. We are sure that this work will show an attractive result as compared to the other present algorithms on the various parameters like security, imperceptibility capacity & robustness.

Keywords: Steganography, stegoimage, information reflector.

1   Introduction

The word steganography means "covered or hidden writing" [9]. The object of steganography is to send a message through some innocuous carrier (to a receiver while preventing anyone else from knowing that a message is being sent at all. Computer based stenography allows changes to be made to what are known as digital carriers such as images or sounds. The changes represent the hidden message, but result if successful in no discernible change to the carrier. The information may be

P.V. Krishna, M.R. Babu, and E. Ariwa (Eds.): ObCom 2011, Part II, CCIS 270, pp. 619–628, 2012.
© Springer-Verlag Berlin Heidelberg 2012

nothing to do with the carrier sound or image or it might be information about the carrier such as the author or a digital watermark or fingerprint [9].

Cryptography and steganography are different. Cryptographic techniques can be used to scramble a message so that if it is discovered it cannot be read. If a cryptographic message is discovered it is generally known to be a piece of hidden information (anyone intercepting it will be suspicious) but it is scrambled so that it is difficult or impossible to understand and de-code. On the other hand the goal of steganography is to conceal data. There are a few features and restrictions to successfully hide data. "The goal is for the data to remain "hidden." . The word "hidden" has two meanings here, (1) the data can be "hidden" and not visible to the human eye (2) the data can be visible and still not visible to the human eye. If the focus is deterred from the data, the data will not be seen, which means that it is "hidden". Steganography hides the very existence of a message so that if successful it generally attracts no suspicion at all. Using steganography, information can be hidden in carriers such as images, audio files, text files, videos and data transmissions [9]. When the message is hidden in the carrier a stego-carrier is formed for example a stego-image. Hopefully it will be perceived to be as close as possible to the original carrier or cover image by the human senses. Images are the most widespread carrier medium [10]. They are used for steganography in the following way. The message may firstly be encrypted. The sender (or embedder [12]) embeds the secret message to be sent into a graphic file [11] (the cover image [12] or the carrier). This results in the production of what is called a stego-image. Additional secret data may be needed in the hiding process e.g. a stegokey. The stego-image is then transmitted to the recipient [11]. The recipient (or extractor [12]) extracts the message from the carrier image. The message can only be extracted if there is a shared secret between the sender and the recipient. This could be the algorithm for extraction or a special parameter such as a key [11] (the stegokey). A stegoanalyst or attacker may try to intercept the stego-image. Figure 1 below shows the steganographic system.

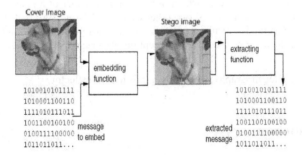

Fig. 1. Steganographic system

One of the commonly used techniques is the LSB where the least significant bit of each pixel is replaced by bits of the secret till secret message finishes [2,4,5,6]. The risk of information being uncovered with this method as is very much prone to 'sequential scanning' based techniques [1], which are threatening its security. The random pixel manipulation technique attempts at overcoming this problem, where pixels, which will be used to hide data are chosen in a random fashion based on a stego-key. However, this key should be shared between the entities of communication as a secret key. Moreover, some synchronization between the entities is required when changing the key [1]. This will put key management overhead on the system. Another technique is the Stego Color Cycle (SCC). This SCC technique uses the RGB images to hide the data in different channels. That is, it keeps cycling the hidden data between the Red, Green and Blue channels, utilizing one channel at a cycle time. The main problem of this technique is that, hiding the data in the channels is done in a systematic way. So, being able to discover the data in the first few pixels will make the discovery of the technique easy. StegoPRNG is also a different technique that uses the RGB images. However in this technique, a pseudo random number generator (PRNG) is used to select some pixels of the cover image. Then, the secret will be hided in the Blue channel of the selected pixels. Again this technique has the problem of managing the key, and problem of capacity since it uses only the Blue channel out of the three channels of their available channels [6]. Our suggested technique tries to solve the problem of the previous techniques by using an arbitrary channel of a pixel to act as an information reflector which reflects the presence of data in one or two other channels.

The flow of this paper is as follows: Section 2 represents the various parameters that should be taken into consideration while designing a technique for steganograhy. Section 3 gives as outline about the proposed method.

2   Parameters

2.1   Imperceptibility: (Security or Transparency)

The unauthorized user should not be even able to percept that data is being transferred in image i.e. by message hiding in image there should not be any changes in images that are easily visible to human eye. This should be as much a high as possible.

2.2   Capacity

By capacity we mean how much data or how much length of message a cover image can carry. For efficient transmission this parameter should also be as higher as possible.

2.3   Stoutness

By stoutness we mean that how much the stego image can withstand with the accidental or intentional changes for e.g. compression. We mean that there should be no change in hidden data.

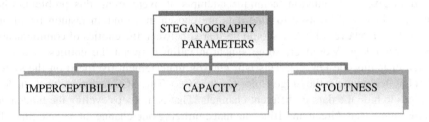

Fig. 2. Various Steganography parameters

The above outlined fig 2 shows the various parameters that are responsible for deciding the strength of some steganography technique. These 3 parameters are not independent rather they are very much dependent upon each other. For e.g. if we want to increase the imperceptibility of a stego image then we will choose some random pixels to store the secret message but due to this the capacity of stego image will definitely be decreased & the stoutness will also increase to some extent. In this way we can say that these 3 parameters are interdependent & change in one will definitely change the value of other two parameters to some extent.

3   Random Channel Reflector Method

In this paper we are representing a technique that is based upon using arbitrary channel of a pixel as an information reflector. Here we use one of the RGB channels of a pixel of a coloured image as a reflector to represent whether the hidden information bits are present in one or both of the other channels. In this method firstly we check the least significant bit of the reflector channel, if it is 1 it means the secret text is in both the other channels so we can insert or retrieve the least 2 significant bits of both the channels in the order Ist channel followed by 2nd channel. But if the least significant bit of reflector channel is 0, it means that the secret text is only in one of the other channels. Then we check the most significant of reflector channel, if it is 0 then the secret data is in least two significant bits of IST channel else if MSB value is 1 then the secret data is in 2nd channel. So accordingly we retrieve or insert the 2 LSBs of Ist or 2nd channel as our secret data. The Ist or 2nd channel will be two channel other than the reflector channel in the order red, green and blue as shown in table 1.For choosing the reflector channel we will use the pseudo random number generator which should be in synchronization at both transmitter & receiver ends.

Also we will use the first 8 bytes of cover image as header to carry the information about the message like size of secret message in bytes or may be some other relevant information. In addition to this while inserting as well as while extracting the secret message we will maintain a special pointer that will be incremented according to the length of total message.

Table 1. Relation between reflector & other two channels

REFLECTOR	IST CHANNEL	2ND CHANNEL
RED	GREEN	BLUE
GREEN	RED	BLUE
BLUE	RED	GREEN

Table 2. Relation showing the secret information channel

LSB OF REFLECTOR	MSB OF REFLECTOR	SECRET DATA
0	0	2 LSBs OF IST CHANNEL
0	1	2 LSBs OF 2nd CHANNEL
1	DON'T CARE	2 LSBs OF BOTH CHANNELS

3.1 Algo for Hiding the Secret Data

STEP 1   Find the total length of message in bytes considering 8 bit code for every Character.

STEP 2   Use the first 8 bytes of the cover image as header & store the length of the Message in this header & set the pointer at the first bit of message. The pixels after the 8th byte will be used for hiding information.

STEP 3   Use the pseudo random number generator to generate the numbers which will be used to choose the information reflecting channel.

STEP 4   If the LSB of reflecting channel is 0 then check the MSB of reflecting channel & goto step5 else goto step6.

STEP 5   If the MSB of reflector channel is 0 then hide the two bits secret data in Ist channel according to table 1 but if MSB value is 1, then hide the 2 bits of data in 2nd channel by replacing 2 LSBs in accordance to table 1 & increment the pointer by 2. Then goto step7.

STEP 6   Now as LSB of reflector channel is 1 it means we have to insert data in both the other two channels, so first take the 2 bits & insert it with LSBs of Ist channel & then take the next 2 bits & replace it with LSBs of 2nd channel according to table 1.Also increment the pointer by 4.

STEP 7   Now check the pointer value if it is equal to the no of bits of message length then goto step8 else take the next pixel of image & goto step3.

STEP8   Exit

3.2 Algo for Extracting the Secret Data

STEP 1   Firstly read the header of stego image & get the hidden message length in Bytes & set the pointer to 1.

STEP 2   Use the pseudo random number generator synchronized with transmitting end to generate the numbers which will tell the information reflecting channel.

STEP 3   If the LSB of reflecting channel is 0 then check the MSB of reflecting channel & goto step4 else goto step5.

624   M. Mahajan and N. Kaur

STEP 4 If the MSB of reflector channel is 0 then retrieve the two bits secret data in IST channel but if MSB value is 1, then retrieve the 2 bits of data in 2nd channel in accordance to table 1 & Increment the pointer by 2.Then goto step 6
STEP 5   Now as LSB of reflector channel is 1 it means data resides in both the other two channels so first retrieve the 2 bits from IST channel & then retrieve 2 bits from 2nd channel in order according to table 1.Also increment the pointer by 4.
STEP 6   Now check the pointer value if it is equal to the no of bits of message length then goto step7 else take the next pixel of image & goto step2.
STEP 7   Exit.

3.3   Application Example of the Method

Secret message:-1011001110000110

First Pixel

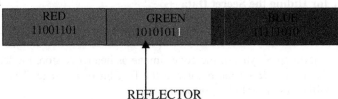

REFLECTOR
LSB = 1 So From Table 1 & 2 both red & blue channel will carry 2 bits of data

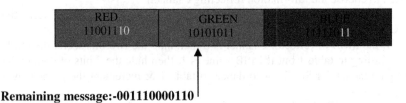

Remaining message:-001110000110

Next Pixel

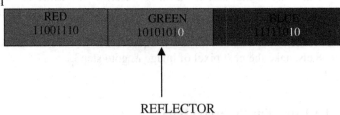

REFLECTOR

LSB = 0, MSB =1 so from Table 1 & 2 blue channel will carry 2 bits of data

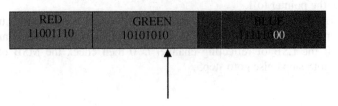

Remaining message: - 1110000110

Next Pixel

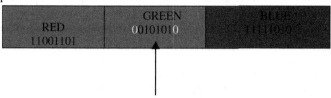

REFLECTOR

LSB = 0, MSB =0 so from Table 1 & 2 red channel will carry 2 bits of data

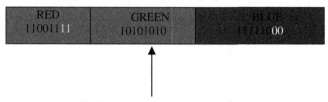

Remaining message: - 10000110

In this way message will be hidden in every Pixel of an image till the end of the message.

4   Comparisons and Results

4.1   Capacity

In the proposed scheme each pixel of the cover image will carry 2 or 4 bits of data depending upon the LSB of the reflecting channel. On the average approximately 50% of the pixels will have bit value 1 for LSB of reflecting channel & 50% will have bit value 0 for LSB of reflecting channel. So 50% pixels may contain 4 bits of data & 50% will contain 2 bits of data .So if a cover image is of size 256 X 256 with each pixel of 3 bytes, one byte for each channel, then the size of the image will be 196608 bytes. Now if 8 bytes are being used as header then remaining 196600 bytes may carry secret data. On the average if 50% pixels will carry 4bits (half byte) & 50% pixels will carry 2 bits (1/4byte) of secret data then if A represents the number of pixels containing 4 bits & B represents the no of pixels containing 2 bits of secret data

A= (50/100)*196600   = 98300pixels
B= (50/100)*196600   = 98300pixels
A containing 4 bits (half byte) per pixel so data contained in A pixels will be
Adata=98300*(1/2) =49150bytes
Similarly B containing 2 bits (1/4 byte) per pixel so data containing in B pixels will be
Bdata= 98300*(1/4)   =24575bytes

So total data capacity will be Tdata= 49150+24575= 73725bytes of secret data.
%ge hiding capacity of cover image is (73725/196608)*100 = 37.5 %(approx)

For a secret message of length 11733 character (or 93864bits) the no of pixels used is 31296 pixels of cover image of size 256X256 with pixel depth of 24bits i.e. 196608bytes image .

So the no of pixels unutilized are 196608-31296=165312 pixels so %ge of unutilized pixels is 84% (approx)

But earlier in LSB techniques 1 or 2 bits of each pixel are replaced so for the same message & same cover image they require 46940 pixels (approx) i.e. 76% pixels are unutilized only.

Table 3. Comparison of capacity in terms of unused pixels for LSB & proposed Technique

Technique	Image Size (bytes)	Message size(bits)	Pixels Utilized	%ge Unused Pixels
LSB	196608	93864	46940	76.1%
PROPOSED METHOD	**196608**	**93864**	**31296**	**84%**

For random pixel manipulation the capacity may be still lower because pixels are chosen randomly based on certain key.

So it is clear from the discussion that this technique is having high capacity than previous existing techniques.

4.2   Imperceptibility

i) In the proposed method as we are using only 2 or 4 LSB bits of a pixel, even in case of 4 bits 2 LSB bits of 2 different channels so the distortion in image may be very less .This technique may be very much suitable in images with high pixel depth for e.g.24bits per pixel, as 8 bits are being used for each channel allowing 0-255 colours in each channel. As we are replacing 2 LSBs of any channel the max value change in colour may be from 0 to (+/-) 3 [(+/-) 7 for 3 LSB)] for a channel (for e.g. for colour value 187 the max change will be -3 i.e. 184) so in a channel with such high range of possible colour values this small (+/-) 3 or 7 change may not make any major difference & may not be easily distinguishable to human visual system.

ii) Besides according to Gonzalez LSB plane of image contains the fine information about image not any visually perceptual information so stego images with this proposed method may not be easily detected by the unauthorized user.

iii) Additionally if an unauthorized user may be able to know that the stego image is carrying certain hidden data even then he will not be able to read the data because data is not stored in same channel in very pixel rather it is stored in different channels in different pixels i.e. too not in any fixed pattern . To read the message unauthorized user must know the algorithm as well as have access to random number generator in synchronization with transmitter & receiver so as to get the reflector channel. So even after getting an idea about the hidden message in a stego image an unauthorized user must know so many things to read the message.

So from the above discussion we can say that the imperceptibility parameter of our proposed scheme is strong enough to save the secret message from eavesdropper.

4.3 Stoutness

i) In the proposed technique if some unauthorized user tries to distort the secret data then in our method data resides in one or two channels of a pixel which has been decided randomly ,so it is possible that the unauthorized user may distort the channel other than the data carrier so our data will be safe.

ii) Even if the secret data channel will be distorted our secret data will be in 2 LSBs & out of 256values (0-255) same LSB pair will be repeated after every 4 numbers. For e.g.183=10110111, 187=10111011, 191=10111111 & so on. So in 256 values 64 values will have same LSB pair so there will be 25% chances that even after distorting the data channel our secret data will not be hampered.

In fact the last two parameters i.e. imperceptibility & stoutness clearly depends upon the type of image & the type of message. The image with large no of variations may have high degree of imperceptibility & stoutness.Sothe images that are more suitable for the proposed scheme are cartoon images & geographical images having high colour range & higher degree of variations & edges.

5   Conclusion

In this paper we have proposed the steganograhy method based upon choosing the random channel firstly for reflection & then accordingly choosing channel for secret data.

We have tried to check this method on basic goodness criteria of any steganography algorithm i.e. capacity, imperceptibility & stoutness but still it may have many shortcomings that need to be worked upon in future. In general, this proposed algorithm may open new directions in steganography research leading to interesting results.

References

1. Venkatraman, S., Abraham, A., Paprzycki, M.: Significance of Steganography on Data Security. In: International Conference on Information Technology: Coding and Computing (ITCC 2004), Las Vegas, April 5-7 (2004)
2. Hempstalk, K.: Hiding Behind Corners: Using Edges in Images for Better Steganography. In: Proceedings of the Computing Women's Congress, Hamilton, New Zealand, February 11-19 (2006)
3. Johnson, N.F., Jajodia, S.: Exploring Steganography: Seeing the Unseen. IEEE Computer 31(2), 26–34 (1998)

4. Kessler, G.C.: An Overview of Steganography for the Computer Forensics Examiner. Forensic Science Communications 6(3) (July 2004)
5. Artz, D.: Digital Steganography: Hiding Data within Data. IEEE Internet Computing: Spotlight, 75–80 (May-June 2001)
6. Bailey, K., Curran, K.: An Evaluation of Image Based Steganography Methods. Multimedia Tools & Applications 30(1), 55–88 (2006)
7. Gutub, A., Ghouti, L., Amin, A., Alkharobi, T., Ibrahim, M.K.: Utilizing Extension Character 'Kashida' With Pointed Letters For Arabic Text Digital Watermarking. In: Inter. Conf. on Security and Cryptography - SECRYPT, Barcelona, Spain, July 28-31 (2007)
8. Gutub, A., Fattani, M.: A Novel Arabic Text Steganography Method Using Letter Points and Extensions. In: WASET International Conference on Computer, Information and Systems Science and Engineering (ICCISSE), Vienna, Austria, May 25-27 (2007)
9. Johnson, N.F., Duric, Z., Jajodia, S.: Information Hiding, and Watermarking - Attacks & Countermeasures. Kluwer (2001)
10. Andreas, W., Pfitzmann, A.: Attacks on Steganographic Systems. In: Pfitzmann, A. (ed.) IH 1999. LNCS, vol. 1768, pp. 61–76. Springer, Heidelberg (2000)
11. Zöllner, J., Federrath, H., Klimant, H., Pfitzmann, A., Piotraschke, R., Westfeld, A., Wicke, G., Wolf, G.: Modeling the Security of Steganographic Systems. In: Aucsmith, D. (ed.) IH 1998. LNCS, vol. 1525, pp. 344–354. Springer, Heidelberg (1998)
12. Birgit, P.: Information Hiding Terminology. In: Anderson, R. (ed.) IH 1996. LNCS, vol. 1174, pp. 347–350. Springer, Heidelberg (1996)
13. http://www.crime-research.org/library/Jack2.htm

EJS Algorithm for Job Scheduling in Grid Environment

K. Manikandan, Jacob P. Cherian, and Nikhil Scaria

School of Computing Science & Engineering, VIT University, Vellore - 632014,
Tamil Nadu, India
kmanikandan@vit.ac.in,
jacobpc29@yahoo.co.in,
nikhil@intellwiz.com

Abstract. Grid computing is a term referring to the combination of computer resources from multiple administrative domains to reach a common goal. The use of powerful computing resources transparently available to the user via a networked environment is the aim of grid computing. Grid systems enable the sharing and aggregation of geographically distributed resources for solving large-scale problems in science, engineering, and commerce. There are several scheduling algorithms presently available in grid system for resource and job scheduling. Scheduling onto the Grid is NP-complete problem [11], so there is no best scheduling algorithm for any grid computing system. An alternative is to select an appropriate scheduling algorithm to use in a specific grid environment. It depends on the characteristics of the tasks, machines and network connectivity. By this research paper, our aim is to analyze the existing algorithms and propose an optimal algorithm for job scheduling in grids.

Keywords: Grid computing, Job Scheduling, Optimal scheduling.

1   Introduction

Grid Computing is an emerging technology. It allows the management of heterogeneous, geographically distributed and dynamically available resources in an efficient way, extending the boundaries of what we consider as distributed computing. Grid Computing provides highly scalable, highly secure and extremely high-performance mechanisms in a seamless manner. For running applications, resource management and job scheduling are the most crucial problems in grid computing systems. In recent years, the researchers have proposed several efficient scheduling algorithms that are used in grid computing to allocate grid resources with a special emphasis on job scheduling. The scheduling and management of jobs and resources are having a crucial role in developing a dynamic grid environment.

2   Literature Survey

2.1   Basic Grid Model

Figure 1 represents the basic Grid Model [11]. It contains dynamically available nodes interconnected via a high speed network. The important building blocks in a

P.V. Krishna, M.R. Babu, and E. Ariwa (Eds.): ObCom 2011, Part II, CCIS 270, pp. 629–638, 2012.
© Springer-Verlag Berlin Heidelberg 2012

grid model are users, grid broker, grid information service (GIS) [11] and dynamically available resources. Whenever a user needs higher computational power for a job, GIS can be used forth. The jobs are submitted to the grid broker. The grid broker will identify the appropriate resources required for each job. The jobs are split into different tasks and each task may be assigned to a particular node. The grid broker identifies the resources based on the data available with the GIS tables. The GIS tables are updated frequently as the resources are available dynamically in a grid. The process of scheduling and management of different jobs are entrusted upon the grid broker. It implements different algorithms for efficient and scalable usage of grid environment. The broker can be termed as the intelligent part of a grid system [7].

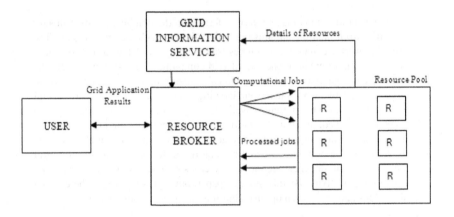

Fig. 1. Basic Grid Model

2.2   Task Scheduling

Why Scheduling? In a grid system, there are a distributed set of resources and dynamically arriving jobs. Each job is having certain properties like burst time, memory required, OS Platform needed etc. The Scheduler should allocate the job to a processor which satisfies all the job requirements.

3   Existing Approaches towards Scheduling

There are many existing algorithms for job scheduling in a grid environment. For analysis purposes, we have considered a few of them and noted the drawbacks of the existing algorithms.

3.1   HRN Algorithm [11]

Highest Response Next Scheduling [6] provides more responses with time, memory and CPU requirements. Here, jobs are allotted to a no: of processors based on job's priority and processor's capability. Each job will be assigned with some priority values. This scheme is adaptive for local jobs and remote jobs without any loss of performance and also highly adaptive for grid environment. HRN with priority will effectively utilize the available resource and complete all the jobs quickly than FCFS. It has a higher turnaround time, which is not generally desirable and the memory wastage is also high.

3.2   ORC Algorithm [11]

The Optimal Resource Constraint algorithm [7] allocates the jobs according to processor's capability. It applies best fit algorithm followed by Round Robin (RR) scheduling which distributes the jobs among the available processors. ORC gives better performance than other algorithms in terms of turnaround time and average waiting time. It improves the efficiency of load balancing and dynamic capability of the grid resources. It avoids starvation problem. However, the communication overhead involved is very high.

3.3   Grouping-Based Fine-Grained Job Scheduling in Grid Computing (GFJS)

The grouping strategy in job scheduling model [11] is based on resource characteristics. The grouping algorithm combines Greedy algorithm and FCFS algorithm to improve the processing of fine-grained jobs. The total overhead of fine-grained job scheduling can be reduced by grouping the light weight jobs during the scheduling process for deployment over the resources. Algorithm maximizes the utilization of the resource. It reduces the network latency and total processing time. It does not consider memory size constraint. The Pre-processing time of job grouping is very high.

3.4   Job Schedule Model Based Algorithm (JSMB)[11]

This is a job schedule model based on Maximum Processor Utilization and Throughput (MPUT).Since this scheduling algorithm maximizes CPU utilization and throughput at the same time and minimizes turnaround time, it is highly recommended over real time systems. Grid nodes are divided into Supervisor grid node, Supervisor backup node, and execute grid nodes [8]. Each type of nodes are having their own functionalities in the environment. It uses backup node at the condition of failure of the supervisor node so it provides reliability with good load balance. Communication overhead is high. It does not consider any constraints on jobs and resources.

4   Proposed System

Considering the drawbacks of many grid scheduling algorithms, EJS Model for grid scheduling environment is proposed. The model is based on clustering of computing resources across a distributed environment. The job allocation is considered to be dynamic in nature i.e. each job is assigned to a cluster as and when it is arrived, based on the availability of resources and other parameters.

4.1   Terminology

CPF: Cluster Power Factor, is a term defined in the EJS context which is a value which describes the overall computing power of a cluster. CPF value can be obtained by considering parameters like no: of processors, operating system being used, memory capacity, etc.

Fault Factor: The Fault Factor '∂' is defined as the ratio of total faulty processors to the total no: of processors in the cluster.

Rate Factor: The Rate Factor is the fraction by which the rate of arrival of jobs to the system should be controlled.

Grid Factor: The Grid Factor 'γ' is a measure of utilization of grid resources at an instant of time's'.

R (i): Defines the reliability of a node. It is the ratio of total jobs successfully completed at node 'i' to the total jobs submitted to node 'i'.

4.2   Cluster Grouping

Cluster is a collection of processors which may be characterized by their properties. A cluster can be heterogeneous or homogeneous in nature. The grouping of processors or nodes can be performed based on various factors. A group of nodes having similar OS, memory capacity, etc can be grouped together. Similarly a group of nodes specialized in executing a specific set of tasks can be grouped together. However, clustering of the grid environment can be entrusted upon the Grid Broker. Once clustering is performed, each cluster will be having a value CPF$_{start}$ based on the cluster's computing ability. The initial value of CPF for any cluster is the maximum value of CPF for that cluster which can be computed in terms of any set of desired parameters. Once the initial CPF values of clusters are set, the clusters are ready to accept incoming jobs.

4.3   EJS Model

The proposed EJS Model is shown in Figure 2. It consists of a CPF Evaluator Module, Resource Broker, EJS Scheduler and a Cluster Pool. The incoming jobs arrive at the CPF Evaluator Module. This module calculates the approximate value of CPF that is required by the job to complete its execution. Once the CPF of the job is calculated, it is allocated to the EJS Scheduler which runs EJS Algorithm for scheduling of the jobs.

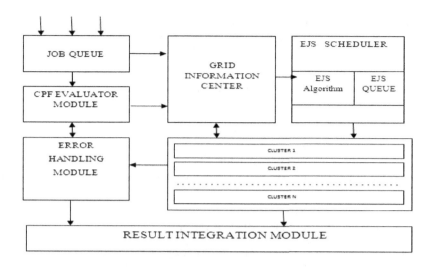

Fig. 2. Proposed EJS Scheduler

4.4   Fault Handling

Faults are common in any distributed environment. There is no guarantee that every job submitted to the system will be executed successfully. Some processors may crash at any point of time and the fate of the job executed by the faulty processor is uncertain. When a processor crashes at any particular point of time, the Fault Handling Sub System starts playing the role of a 'Grid Protector'. It should ensure that the failure of one processor should not lead to the breakdown of the entire cluster. The job can be completed at some other node or the faulty processor should be rectified. When a processor becomes faulty, the CPF value of the cluster to which it belongs decreases according to the equation:

$$CPF_{faulty} = \delta * CPF_{start} \text{ , where}$$

$$\partial = 1 - (no\ of\ faulty\ processors)/(total\ no\ of\ processors)$$

CPF_{faulty} is the maximum value of CPF for the cluster when faulty processors are present. The new value of CPF for the cluster is updated by the CPF Evaluator Module and GIC is updated with this value. Once the faults are rectified, the maximum CPF value for the cluster will increase to the previous value.

4.5   Rate Control by EJS

Let 'R' be the initial rate at which the jobs are arriving. As long as the initial CPF value i.e. CPF_{start} is maintained by each cluster there is no need to control the rate of the incoming jobs. However when faulty processors are present in one or more clusters, the system cannot handle jobs at the previous rate. Hence the rate at which jobs arrive at the system should be controlled according to the equation:

$$\beta = \frac{\Sigma(CPF)}{\Sigma(CPF\ initial)}$$

$$R_{new} = \beta * R$$

Where, numerator is the sum of maximum CPF values of all the clusters at an instant when the faulty processors exist and the denominator is the summation of the initial CPF values for all the clusters.

4.6   Node Reliability and Overall Grid Usage

The reliability of a node is of great importance in scheduling of important tasks. High-Priority jobs cannot be allocated to a node which is un-reliable. The reliability of a node is given by:

$$R\ (i) = \frac{Total\ Jobs\ Successfully\ Completed\ At\ Node\ i}{Total\ No{:}Of\ Jobs\ Submitted\ To\ Node\ i}$$

If the reliability of a node is below a particular value (say threshold value), no jobs should be assigned to that node. Un-reliable nodes can decrease the throughput and reduce the overall efficiency of the system.

The overall grid usage is termed as 'grid factor' and is calculated for time instant 'i' according to the equation:

$$\gamma i = \frac{\Sigma\ Utilized\ Time}{\Sigma(Idle\ Time + Utilized\ Time)}$$

The overall grid usage is a measure of efficiency of the grid system.

4.7   EJS Algorithm

The Efficient Job Scheduling (EJS) Algorithm is the heart of EJS Model. The CPF value required for each job should be known in advance. The EJS scheduler is updated with the CPF values by the Grid Information Center. For any job to be assigned to a cluster, its required CPF value should be less than the current CPF value of the cluster. Once a job is allocated to a cluster, the CPF value of the cluster will decrease according to:

$$CPF = 1 - (Mem\_Utilization * Cluster\_Utilization)$$

$$Mem\_Utilization = \frac{Used\ Memory}{Available\ Memory}$$

$$\text{Cluster\_Utilization} = \frac{No:Of\ Processors\ Allocated}{Total\ No:Of\ Processors}$$

Pseudo code

1. Start
2. Calculate current CPF for each cluster
3. Calculate the CPF required for the job, CPF_{job}
4. Generate the set of clusters (S) to which the job can be assigned
5. Select the cluster having the minimum load
6. While there are faulty processors do:

    a. $CPF_{faulty} = \delta * CPF_{start}$

    b. $\beta = \dfrac{\sum(CPF)}{\sum(CPFinitial)}$

    c. $R_{new} = \beta * R$

7. If $CPF_{job} <= CPF_i$ then
        a. Allocate the job to the cluster
        b. Update CPF Values
        c. Go to 8
    Else
        a. i++; $i \varepsilon S$
        b. Go to 6;

8. Queue the Job;
9. Do Until Queue Is Empty or No More Jobs Arrive

Where N= No: Of Clusters, CPF_i = CPF value of Cluster 'i'.

The essence of the algorithm lies in the fact that before a job is allotted to a processor or resource, the actual load on the cluster is calculated and jobs are allocated such that the overall load is balanced across the different clusters.

5   Results and Analysis

From the analysis, it is clear that, the GFJS is having the lowest processing time. But GFJS is having some disadvantages like higher pre-processing time and exclusion of memory size constraints. If these disadvantages are removed, it can act as an optimal scheduling algorithm. This algorithm works on basis of grouping strategy. So, the pre-processing time for grouping cannot be avoided. Proper load balancing is not guaranteed in most algorithms. Based on the sample runs it was found that EJS works more efficiently than all the analyzed algorithms. The graph plotted by taking some test samples is shown. From figure 3, it is clear that the scheduling based on clustering, are showing higher performance. A scheduler has been designed which adopts all the advantages of the discussed algorithms and incorporates the memory constraint.

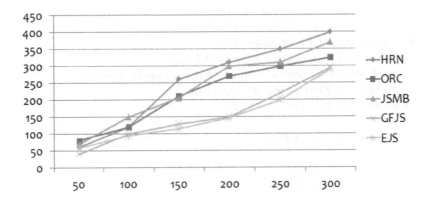

Fig. 3. Comparison of algorithms [Processing time(Y) v/s No. of Jobs(X)]

The load scheduling between the clusters is also analyzed and found to be equally distributed. The jobs are distributed among the clusters in equal weightage. Figure 4 shows the load balancing across the clusters.

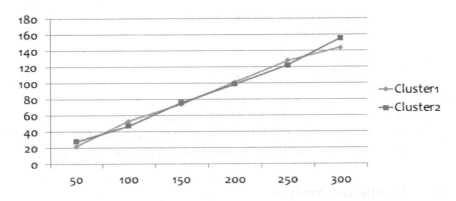

Fig. 4. Load Sharing [Allocated jobs to a cluster(Y) v/s Total no. of jobs(X)]

The grid factor gives the overall grid usage which is the efficiency of the entire system. Figure 5 shows the variation of grid factor with the no: of jobs.

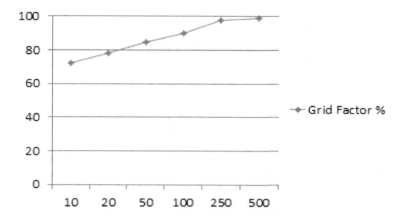

Fig. 5. Grid Factor(Y) v/s No: Of Jobs (X)

An EJS software simulator was developed and the graphs were obtained by performing sample runs on the simulator. Fig 6 shows the screenshot of the EJS Simulator.

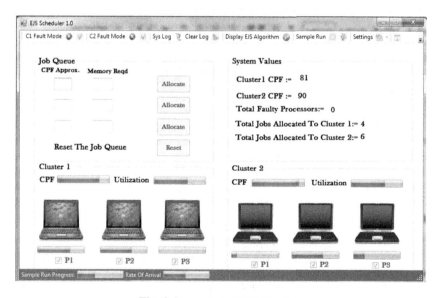

Fig. 6. Screenshot of EJS Simulator

6   Conclusion and Future Work

Different scheduling models exist for the grid environment. Research is still going on in the field of Grid Computing. More efficient algorithms for job scheduling can be devised provided more functionalities and characteristics of the grid environment are developed and recognized.

The advantages of using the proposed EJS model can be summarized as follows.

1. Allocation of jobs based on memory consideration and CPU Utilization.
2. Improved response time and turnaround time for jobs.
3. Perfect Load balancing across the clusters.

The system can be extended in future by making the following modifications. Currently our model is not addressing these issues.

1. The Algorithm can be modified to consider Inter Cluster Dependencies
2. Modifications in CPF function can be made including other parameters which may affect the Grid Computing Power.

References

1. Sharma, R., Soni, V.K., Mishra, M.K., Bhuyan, P.: A Survey of Job Scheduling and Resource Management in Grid Computing. World Academy of Science Engineering & Technology (2010)
2. Ranganathan, K., Foster, I.: Simulation studies of computation and data scheduling algorithms for data grids. Journal of Grid Computing 1(1), 53–62 (2003)
3. Caramia, M., Giordani, S., Iovanella, A.: Grid scheduling by on-line rectangle packing. Networks 44(2), 106–119 (2004); Smith, B.: An approach to graphs of linear forms (unpublished work style)
4. Gao, Y., Rong, H., Huang, J.: Adaptive grid job scheduling with genetic algorithms. Future Generation Computer Systems 21, 151–161 (2005)
5. Weng, C., Lu, X.: Heuristic scheduling for bag-of-tasks application in combination with QoS in the computational grid. Future Generation Computer Systems 21, 271–280 (2005)
6. Somasundaram, K., Radhakrishnan, S., Gomathynayagam, M.: Efficient Utilization of Computing Resources using Highest Response Next Scheduling in Grid. Asian Journal of Information Technology 6(5), 544–547 (2007)
7. Somasundaram, K., Radhakrishnan, S.: Node Allocation In Grid Computing Using Optimal Resource Constraint (ORC) Scheduling. IJCSNS International Journal of Computer Science and Network Security 8(6) (June 2008)
8. Santoso, J., van Albada, G.D., Nazief, B.A.A., Sloot, P.M.A.: Hierarchical Job Scheduling for Clusters of Workstations. In: ASCI 2000, pp. 99–105. ASCI, Delft (2000)
9. Moise, D., Moise, I., Pop, F., Cristea, V.: Resource CoAllocation for Scheduling Tasks with Dependencies, in Grid. In: The Second International Workshop on High Performance in Grid Middleware HiPerGRID (2008)
10. Foster, I., Kesselman, C.: The Grid: Blueprint for a New Computing Infrastructure, 2nd edn. Elsevier Inc., Singapore (2004)

Clustering of Concept-Drift Categorical Data Implementation in JAVA

K. Reddy Madhavi[1], A. Vinaya Babu[2], and S. Viswanadha Raju[2]

[1] SSITS, Rayachoty
kreddymadhavi@gmail.com
[2] JNT University, Hyderabad
avb1222@gmail.com,
Viswanadha_raju2004@yahoo.co.in

Abstract. Identification of useful clusters in large datasets has attracted considerable interest in clustering process. Clustering categorical data is a hard choice when compared to the numerical data, because the similarity measures in the traditional clustering algorithms uses distances between points to generate clusters that are not appropriate for Boolean and categorical attributes. Since data in the World Wide Web is increasing exponentially that affects on clustering accuracy and decision making, change in the concept between every cluster occurs named concept drift. To detect the difference of cluster distributions between the current data subset and previous clustering result, an algorithm called Drifting Concept Detection(DCD) which uses sliding window and node importance has been presented and implemented in JAVA language by considering "usenet" dataset in which every data point is the message and the node is the word. Hence it is challenging in the problem of clustering concept-drift categorical data. In this paper, few concepts have been implemented to produce the appropriate clustering results by minimizing the clustering process as the time evolving data comes into the sliding window every time that minimizes I/O costs and number of concept drifts decreases if sliding window size increases.

Keywords: Categorical data, Concept drift and Sliding window.

1 Introduction

Data mining refers to extracting or mining knowledge from large volumes of data [10]. The most distinct characteristic of data mining is that it deals with very large and complex datasets (gigabytes or even terabytes) often contain millions of objects described by tens, hundreds or even thousands of various types of attributes or variables (interval, ratio, binary, ordinal, nominal etc.). This requires the data mining operations and algorithms to be scalable and capable of dealing with different types of attributes. One of the major functionality of data mining is clustering which is often a critical component of the data mining or information retrieval process. Clustering is

P.V. Krishna, M.R. Babu, and E. Ariwa (Eds.): ObCom 2011, Part II, CCIS 270, pp. 639–654, 2012.

an unsupervised learning and clusters are generated based on the principle of low-interclass similarity and high-intraclass similarity [12, 19]. Most existing clustering algorithms either can handle both categorical as well as numerical but are not efficient when clustering large data sets or can handle large data sets efficiently but are limited to numeric attributes. Many clustering algorithms to handle with categorical attributes exist but not concentrating on time evolving data. However we are interested on clustering of categorical data that change with time.

The rest of the paper is organized as follows: section 2 concentrates on relevant research, section 3 focuses on drifting concepts detection, section 4 provides implementation with results and discussion and section 5 concludes with future work.

2   Relevant Research

Many clustering algorithms exist and is difficult to provide a crisp categorization of clustering methods because these categories may overlap, but few of them were included in the relevant research.

2.1   Partitioning Methods

These methods classifies the database D of n objects into k partitions or groups where each partition represents a cluster, $k \leq n$, where each group must contain at least one object and each object must belong to exactly one group. K-Means [15,16] method measures cluster similarity in regard to the mean value of the objects in a cluster, which can be viewed as the cluster's centroid or center of gravity by using square-error criterion, which is sensitive to outliers. k-Medoids or PAM (Partition around medoids) is a representative-object based technique finds representative objects called medoids in clusters. It is more robust than k-means in the presence of noise and outliers but does not scale well for large data sets. CLARA (Clustering LARge Applications) is sampling-based method. It draws multiple samples of the data set, applies PAM on each sample, and gives the best clustering as the output. Its efficiency depends on sample size [14]. CLARANS (Clustering Large Applications based upon RANdomized Search) combines the sampling technique with PAM[18]. While CLARA has a fixed sample at each stage of the search, CLARANS dynamically draws a random sample of neighbors in each step of a search. CLARANS uses efficient spatial access methods [4]. CLARANS has been experimentally shown to be more effective than both PAM and CLARA. But all these methods are limited to numerical data. For handling categorical data: k-modes [11] is used by replacing means of clusters with modes.

2.2   Hierarchical Methods

These methods works by grouping data objects into a tree structure called a dendrogram that shows how objects are grouped together step by step. The quality of a pure hierarchical clustering method suffers from its inability to perform adjustment once a merge or split decision has been executed, that is, the method cannot backtrack and correct. Hierarchical clustering methods can be further classified as: Agglomerative which follows bottom-up merging and Divisive which follows top-down splitting.

An agglomerative hierarchical clustering algorithm that uses the average distance as its measure to compute distance between clusters is advantageous in that it can handle categorical as well as numerical data. The computation of the mean vector for categorical data can be difficult or impossible to define. These methods do not scale well, because each decision to merge or split requires the examination and evaluation of a good number of objects or clusters. To improve the clustering quality of hierarchical methods integrate hierarchical clustering with other clustering techniques, resulting in multiple-phase clustering. Three such methods are introduced. BIRCH (Balanced Iterative Reducing and Clustering Using Hierarchies) is designed for clustering a large amount of numerical data by integration of hierarchical clustering (at the initial microclustering stage) and other clustering methods such as iterative partitioning (at the later macroclustering stage). BIRCH applies a multiphase clustering technique: a single scan of the data set yields a basic good clustering, and one or more additional scans can (optionally) be used to further improve the quality. It handles only numeric data and sensitive to the order of the data record [25].ROCK (RObust Clustering using linKs) is a hierarchical Clustering Algorithm for Categorical Attributes [9]. Links are the number of common neighbors between two objects. It takes a more global approach to clustering by considering the neighborhoods of individual pairs of points. Traditional measures like Jaccard coefficient (Similarity function) for categorical data may not work well. Hence ROCK uses the link-based approach in addition to object similarity [20, 21] that can correctly distinguish the two clusters of transactions. Link is a better measure than Jaccard coefficient. This method uses sampling-based clustering, draws random sample, cluster with the links and label data in disk. CHAMELEON: It is a hierarchical clustering algorithm that uses dynamic modeling to determine the similarity between pairs of clusters [13]. It was derived based on the observed weaknesses of two hierarchical clustering algorithms: ROCK and CURE. ROCK emphasizes cluster interconnectivity and ignores cluster proximity. CURE considers cluster proximity yet ignore cluster interconnectivity [8]. In Chameleon, cluster similarity is assessed based on how well-connected objects are within a cluster and on the proximity of clusters. That is, two clusters are merged if their interconnectivity is high and they are close together. It applies to all types of data as long as a similarity function can be specified.By viewing all these methods it has been observed that clustering categorical attributes is an important task in data mining that has been handled in popular algorithms such as ROCK, CHAMELEON, COOLCAT[1] and CACTUS[6]. This prior work does not adequately address the problem of categorical data that evolve with time. However, we concentrate on clustering of categorical data with time-evolving trends.

After generation of initial clusters based on any existing EM (Expectation-Maximization) algorithm, new data enters into the database. To add an importance of this new data to the clusters, that data can be handled properly. So, basically, we need a way to identify those elements of the stream in a timely manner that is no longer consistent with the current concepts. Instead of sampling the data stream randomly, we can use the sliding window model to analyze stream data. The basic idea is that rather than running computations on all of the data seen so far, or on some sample, we can make decisions based only on recent data. More formally, at every time t, a new data element arrives. This element "expires" at time t+N, where N is the window size or length. The sliding window model is useful for stocks or sensor networks, where only recent events may be important. It also reduces memory requirements because only a small window of data is stored. The intuition behind it is to incorporate new examples yet eliminate the effects of old ones. We can repeatedly apply a traditional classifier to the examples in the sliding window. As new examples arrive, they are inserted into the beginning of the window. The corresponding numbers of examples are removed from the end of the window and the classifier is reapplied. This technique, however, is sensitive to the window size, N. If N is too large, the model will not accurately represent the concept drift (drift means changes with time). On the other hand, if w is too small, then there will not be enough examples to construct an accurate model.

3   Drifting Concept Detection (DCD)

Clustering data can be viewed as follows: there are a series of categorical data points D, where each data point is a vector of q attribute values, i.e., $p_j=(p_j^1,p_j^2,...,p_j^q)$ and A = $\{A_1,A_2,..., A_q\}$, where A_a is the ath categorical attribute, $1 \le a \le q$. The window size N is to be given so that the data set D is separated into several continuous subsets S_t, where the number of data points in each S^t is N. The superscript number t is the identification number of the sliding window and t is also called time stamp. Here in we consider the first N data points of data set D. This makes the first data sliding window or the first sliding window S^0. Our intention is to cluster every data sliding window and relate its clusters with previous clusters formed by the previous data sliding windows, that is, giving the drifting concepts between S^t and S^{t+1} and also analyze the relationship between different clustering results. Several notations and representations like node representation and value of threshold [22] are used in our work to ease the process of presentation and are explained below.

3.1   Node Representation

Among the several representations for categorical or mixed data, in our work we can take two sorts of data representations.

1.   The node is represented by its frequency. For example: A node with attribute name "LAPTOP" which is a categorical part and the number of occurrences in the document '32'   is a numerical part is represented as: Node [LAPTOP: 32]. This representation eventually reduces the ambiguity that may prevail among the attributes because introducing the categorical part into the node eliminates the risk of confusion.

2. Use a data description file that describes the data attributes recognized with a transitive relation. This is the simplification of the above mentioned representation. The only difference is that categorical part is kept in another file.

The importance of the node is evaluated with two important concepts:

1. The node is important in the cluster when the frequency of the node is high in this cluster.
2. The node is important in the cluster if the node appears prevalently in this cluster rather than in other clusters.

3.2   Value of Threshold

The major obstacle in the decision function is to find out the threshold, which decides the number of the cluster elements and the quality of the cluster. This can have a simple solution that is to set the thresholds (λ) identical for all the clusters, i.e., $\lambda_1=\lambda_2=\ldots=\lambda_n=\lambda$. Still it is a problem to set the main λ (threshold) that is to be applied to all the clusters. Hence an intermediate solution is chosen to identify the threshold (λ_i). The smallest resemblance value of the last temporal clustering is used as the new threshold for the new clustering.

3.3   Our Method

The major aspect of our work is to find the difference between the clusters of a sliding window to the clusters formed from the new sliding window. This eventually can be called as the DCD which is used to generate code. This algorithm detects the difference of cluster distribution between the current data subset S^t and the last clustering result $C^{[tr,t-1]}$ and to decide whether the result is required or not in S^t. Hence the incoming data points in the sliding window S^t should be able to be allocated into the corresponding proper cluster at the last clustering result. Such process of allocating the data points to the proper cluster is named as "data labeling" [2]. After obtaining temporal clustering results by data labeling, these clusters are compared with the last clustering results, which are base for the formation of the new clusters. This leads to the "Cluster Distribution Comparison" step (see section4). Data labeling even detects the outlier data points as few data points may not be assigned to the cluster called "outlier detection" (see section4). If the comparison between the last clusters and the temporal clusters availed from the new sliding window data labeling produce the enough differences in the cluster distributions, then the latest sliding window is considered as a concept-drifting window. A re-clustering is done on the latest sliding window. This includes the consideration of the outliers that are obtained in the latest sliding window and forming new clusters which are the new concepts that help in the new decisions.

In our work we perform very simple and effortless steps to find the concept drift, with the number of temporal clusters formed and the number of outliers obtained. The only burden is to overcome the re-clustering of the data if there is a concept drift and updating of the NIR table if there is no concept drift. NIR is related to the idea of conceptual clustering [5,7], which creates a conceptual structure to represent a concept (cluster) during clustering. The minimal resemblance of all the data points in the previous clusters is calculated with the NIR (Node Importance Representative) values [23, 24] and summation of those weights gives the threshold value of the particular cluster in the previous sliding window. To reduce the clustering on every sliding window of data, we check for the similarity in the data points of the present sliding window to that of the clustering results of the previous sliding window with the help of the NIR and MARDL. By using the previous sliding window cluster result's NIR values, threshold values are calculated. If a data point is chosen from the present sliding window the maximal resemblance is calculated, then cluster to which the data point is related is compared with the corresponding threshold of the cluster.

4   Implementation

In this paper, an implementation of the clustering over the concept drifting categorical data is done using JAVA [3, 17]. There are 5 classes performing this task. Data set contains 15 data points and every data point has 14 binary attribute values shown in fig 4.1. Presence of an attribute in the data point is shown as '1' and the absence with '0'. This data set of 15 data points is divided into 3 sliding windows, each containing 5 data points. Now we find concept drift between these sliding windows. As we need to cluster the initial data sliding window, we use a string clustering (any convenient clustering algorithm can be used). The initial clustering of the first data sliding window results in the formation of two clusters, i.e., the data sliding window with five data points $S^1 = \{p_1, p_2, p_3, p_4, p_5\}$ where S^1 is the first data sliding window. The two clusters formed with this algorithm are denoted by C_1, C_2. File "data.txt" contains all the attributes in an order@: A{0,1},B{0,1}, C{0,1},D{0,1}, E{0,1},F{0,1}, G{0,1},M{0,1},N{0,1},P{0,1},T{0,1},X{0,1},Y{0,1}andZ{0,1}@DATA:{1,0,1,0,0, 0,0,1,0,0,0,0,0,0},{0,0,0,0,0,0,0,1,0,1,0,1,0,0},{1,0,0,1,0,0,0,1,0,0,0,0,0,0},{0,0,0,0,0, 0,0,1,0,1,0,0,1,0},{1,0,1,0,0,0,0,1,0,0,0,0,0,0},{0,1,0,0,1,0,1,0,0,0,0,0,0,0},{0,0,0,0,0, 0,0,1,0,1,0,1,0,0},{0,1,0,1,1,0,0,0,0,0,0,0,0,0},{0,0,0,0,0,0,0,1,0,1,0,0,1,0},{0,1,0,1,0, 1,0,0,0,0,0,0,0,0},{0,0,0,0,0,0,0,1,0,1,0,0,1,0},{0,0,0,0,0,0,0,1,0,1,0,1,0,0},{0,0,0,0,0, 0,0,0,1,0,1,0,0,1},{0,0,0,0,0,0,0,1,0,1,0,1,0,0},{0,0,0,0,0,0,0,1,0,1,0,0,1,0}

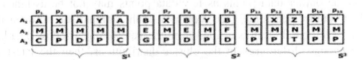

Fig. 4.1. Sample Dataset

Finding the NIR of every node present in the incoming data sliding window is most important because it decides the concept drift between the two consecutive sliding windows with respect to every cluster that is formed in the previous data sliding window which has been already clustered. In cluster $C_1 = \{p_2, p_4\}$ there are two data points as mentioned, and in cluster $C_2 = \{p_3, p_5, p_1\}$ there are three data points. i.e., C_1 contains 2 data points the nodes that occur in this cluster can be uniquely given as 'M','P','X','Y'. Hence the node $\{[A_1=M]\}$ occurs two times i.e., $|I_{1,\{[A1=M]\}}|=2$ and occurs 3 times in the C_2. The weight of the node $F(I_{1,\{[A1=M]\}})=1-\{$equation$\} = 0.2922$. Hence the importance of the node in C_1 is $w(c_1{}^1, \{[A_1=M]\}) = 0.2922*2/2 = 0.2922$, and in cluster 2, it is $w(c_1{}^1, \{[A_1=M]\}) = 0.2922*3/3 = 0.2922$, In addition, the weight of the node $\{[A_1=P]\}$, $F(I_{1,\{[A1=P]\}})=1-\{$equation$\} = 1$. Therefore, the importance of the node $\{[A_1=P]\}$ in C_1 is $w(c_1{}^1, \{[A_1=P]\}) = 1*2/2 = 1$, and in C_2 is $w(c_1{}^1, \{[A_1=P]\}) = 1*0 = 0$. Similarly the importance values of all the nodes is found and are placed in the NIR table. And cluster C_2 contains three data points, the nodes that are present in this cluster uniquely are 'A','C','D','M'. Importance of all these nodes is calculated same as for cluster C_1. The NIR of cluster C_i of the pairs $(I_{ir}, w(C_i, I_{ir}))$ for all the nodes in C_i can be represented by using three fields i.e., first field denotes node, second field denotes value of that node in cluster C_1 and third field denotes value of that node in cluster C_2. The NIR of all the distinct nodes in every cluster can be viewed as: $\{(A,1,0), (B,0,0), (C,0.67,0), (D,0.33,0), (E,0,0), (F,0,0), (G,0,0), (M,0.029,0.029), (N,0,0), (P,0,1), (T,0,0), (X,0,0.5), (Y,0,0.5), (Z,0,0)\}$

4.1   Outlier Detection

For the same data set, the NIR values for both clusters are computed. A common threshold $(\lambda_1 = \lambda_2)$ value of 0.5 is considered for the next incoming sliding window and data labeling is performed to identify the clusters to which the data points belong to. The first data point in the next sliding window i.e., p_6 is decomposed into the different nodes and the three resulting nodes are ($p_6 = \{B,E,G\}$ in S^2) $\{[A_1=B]\}$, $\{[A_2=E]\}$, $\{[A_3=G]\}$. The resemblance of p_6 in C_1 of the first sliding window is zero, and in C_2 is zero, since the maximal resemblance is less than the threshold that is being considered. Hence the data point is considered as an outlier. In addition, the resemblance of p_7 in C_2 is 0.029, and in C_1 it is 1.529(0.5+0.029+1). The maximal resemblance value is larger than the threshold 0.5. Therefore, p_7 labeled to C_2. With the same process data point containing nodes ($p_8=\{B,E,D\}$ in S^2) and ($p_{10}=\{B,F,D\}$ in S^2) are labeled as outliers. And the data point ($p_9=\{Y,M,P\}$ in S^2) is labeled as C_2. Temporal clusters formed at sliding window S^2 are: Cluster C_1: { } ;   Cluster C_2: $\{(X,M,P),(Y,M,P)\}$;   Outliers:$\{(B,E,G), (B,E,D),(B,F,D)\}$

4.2   Cluster Distribution Comparison

As we have discussed in previous section temporal clustering results, labeling resulted in forming one cluster and three outlier data points. We compare the temporal results to that of the previous clusters formed. Ratio of outliers to that of the cluster data points is verified to the outlier threshold (θ) and if the ratio exceeds the threshold, then the sliding window is considered to be drifting the concept. As there is concept drift occurred in this aspect we apply. This resulted re-clustering of temporal clusters of S^2 are: Cluster C_1: $\{(X,M,P),(Y,M,P)\}$;   Cluster C_2: $\{(B,E,G),(B,E,D),(B,F,D)\}$. NIR values of every node with respect to the clusters C_1, C_2 of sliding window S^2 are represented in the form (Node, C_1, C_2) are:{(A,1,0), (B,0,0), (C,0.67,0), (D,0.33,0), (E,0,0), (F,0,0), (G,0,0), (M,0.029,0.029), (N,0,0), (P,0,1), (T,0,0), (X,0,0.5), (Y,0,0.5), (Z,0,0)}.Temporal clusters formed at sliding window S^3 are: Cluster C_1 : {(X,M,P),(Y,M,P),(X,M,P),(Y,M,P)};   Cluster C_2 : {   };   Outliers:{(Z,N,T)}. This has a cluster variation as the data points in C_1 in previous sliding window are 4, hence we have a cluster variation value of 0.8 which is larger than 0.3 cluster variation threshold, thus sliding window 4 is re-clustered using the initial clustering technique this gives a single cluster as the result. Re-clustering of temporal clusters of S^3 are: Cluster C_1:{(X,M,P),(Y,M,P),(X,M,P),(Y,M,P)};   Cluster C_2:{(Z,N,T)}.   Actual clusters formed after concept drifts and NIR values for last sliding window are as follows:{(A,0,0), (B,0,0), (C,0,0), (D,0,0), (E,0,0), (F,0,0), (G,0,0), (M,1,0), (N,0,1), (P,1,0), (T,0,1), (X,0.5,0), (Y,0.5,0), (Z,0,1)}.Hence this result is checked with the previous clustering result, and it satisfies all the thresholds like, no outliers (θ) outlier threshold is satisfied, both the previous and the present clusters have same number of data points in their clusters, thus cluster variation threshold is satisfied, and finally, both previous and present results have the same number of clusters, thus cluster difference threshold is satisfied.

4.3   Methods for an Implementation of Concept-Drift

In this paper we implemented a drifting mechanism using JAVA, which is a platform independent, robust and user friendly language. Methods used in this implementation are discussed in the sub-sections.

4.3.1   Initial Clustering Method
This Method "cluster (number)" is used to cluster data; Here we pass number as the parameter, which specifies the threshold for the clustering of the present sliding window. Pseudo code for this method is shown in Fig 4.2.

4.3.2   Sliding Window Method
In this method the largest dataset is sliced into small parts, called sliding windows, which are used for further processing. Basically these sliding windows are used for initial clustering and for data labeling. This window is used to represent the user data. Here we supply the data set as an argument, and this data set is divided into sliding windows of a particular size as mentioned by the user.

CLUSTER(n)

```
public static void cluster(int n)
{
for(int j=0;j<attnum;j++
        {
          double raj=sliding window[i][j]*sliding
          window[k5][j];
          sum=sum+raj;
        }
        sim[i][k5]=sum;
for(int k6=0;k6<dp;k6++)
        {
          if(i==k6){
               sim[k6][i]=0;
                 }
          if(sim[k6][i]>th){
               rel[k6][i]=1;
                 }
          else {
               rel[k6][i]=0;
                 }
        }
for(int j=0;j<Main.dp;j++)
        {
          if(cluster[i][j]>0){
          System.out.println(cluster[i][j]+",");
          k5++;}
        }
}
```

Fig. 4.2. Method for initial clustering

```
Sliding window(input-filename)
public void sliding
window(java.lang.String filename)
{
while ((c = in.read()) != -1)
        {
            array1[k]=c;
            k++;
        }
for(int k2=0;k2<k;k2++)
        {
            if(k3==dp)
            {
            k3=0;k9++;
            }
            if(array1[k2]==13)
            {
            k3++;
            g=0;
            }
            else{
            if(array1[k2]==44){}
            else{
            if(array1[k2]==10){}
            else{
            if(array1[k2]==95){}
            else{
            sliding window[k9][k3][g]=array1[k2];
            g++;
            }}}}
        }
}
```

Fig. 4.3. Method used in class for sliding window

Here we read the file(data set) until reaches the end of the file. During the process data points are read into arrays called sliding window array. Finally these sliding windows are written into the text files. Pseudo code for this method is shown in Fig 4.3.

4.3.3   NIR Method

This Method takes the sliding window(sliding window method) as the parameter and divide the data points into nodes. The importance of every node is calculated with respect to the previous clusters. In this method we used two methods called nodeSplit Method, which splits the data point into nodes and weight method, which calculates the weight of the nodes. Pseudo code for this method is shown in Fig 4.4.

```
NIR(cluster,sliding windownumber)
```

```java
public void nodeSplit(int[][][] rr, int l1, int l2)
{
        for(int i4=0;i4<Main.dp;i4++)
          {
          for(int j=0;j<Main.attnum;j++)
          {
                if(rr[l1-1][i4][j]==49)
                {
                node[k1]= Main.datadesc[j];
                k1++;
                }else{}
          }
          }
}

private void weight(double[] ct, int l,int t,

int ctnum,int l2)
{
        for(int j1=0;j1<InitialCluster.h1;j1++)
        {
        plogp=plogp+(NIR1.p[d][j1]*Math.log10
        (NIR1.lp[d][j1]));
        }
        w=f*(ct[d]/InitialCluster.Precluscount1[l-2]);
        weight1[ctnum][d]=w;
}
```

Fig. 4.4. Method for NIR values

4.3.4   Templabel Method

This templabel method also called **data label method,** by using this we can assign the labels. This method takes the sliding window number as the parameter and assign the labeling of the cluster number to every data point in the sliding window. Pseudo code for this method is shown in Fig 4.5.

```
label(sliding window number)
public void templabel(int r1)
{
        for(int j=0;j<Main.dp;j++)
        {
          for(int i=0;i<InitialCluster.h1;i++)
          {
                if(k[j]<=NIR.resemblance[i][j])
                {
                  k[j]=NIR.resemblance[i][j];
                  k1[j]=i;
                }
          }
        }
}
```

Fig. 4.5. Method for DataLabel

4.3.5   DCD Method

DCD also called **driftC method,** which detects the drift in the concept of the present sliding window with respect to previous sliding window. The main functionality of this as follows.

IF the number of outliers is large with respect to the temporal clusters formed **then** there is a concept drift in the sliding window

ELSE IF the number of data points is varying with that of the previous sliding windows **then** there is a drift in the concept. Pseudo code for this method is shown in Fig 4.6.

In this implementation we used **usenet** data, which contains 1500 data points for experimentation. The **"usenet"** is a dataset, which contains the combination of the messages passed through this web. Here the data point is the message and the node is the word. This dataset contains 100 attributes; which are binary. 1 indicates the presence of the attribute and 0 for absence. Every attribute is separated with a comma (,). The dataset may also contain attribute description about the data is present or in the other. If the attribute description is in the same file then the data should be separated from the attribute description. For maximum utilization of system resources, the larger dataset may be split into parts or sliding windows which further reduces the burden of over load on the system main memory and manages the system calls. The data may be obtained in any format and converted into plain text, separating attribute values with attribute names, which are taken at the preprocessing stage. The dataset is obtained from the http://mlkd.csd.auth.gr/concept_drift.html.

driftC(sliding window number)

```
public static void driftC()
{
      if((outnum1/Main.dp1)>outlierth)
      {
      drift_count++;
      InitialCluster.cluster(DataLabeling.m1);
      }
      else{
      for(int k4=0;k4<InitialCluster.h1;k4++)
      {
      InitialCluster.Precluscount1[k1]=
      InitialCluster.Precluscount1[k1]+

InitialCluster.Precluscount1[k1+1];
      double k2=
      (double)InitialCluster.Precluscount1[k4]/
            (double)InitialCluster.dp_in_ctr1;
      double k3=(double)DataLabeling.k2[k4]/
            (double)DataLabeling.i7;
      if(Math.abs(k3-k2)>clustervarth)
      {
      clustervari=1;
      }
      else{
      clustervari=0;
      }
      cv=cv+clustervari;
      }
      }
      if(cv/InitialCluster.h1>clusterdiffth)
      {
      drift_count++;
      }
}
```

Fig. 4.6. Method for driftC in class DCD

4.4   Experimental Results

Based on the sliding window size the concept may drift according to the data points present in the sliding window.

Input:

    Dataset   : Usenet.txt, with 1500 data points and 100 attributes.
    Sliding window size : 50 windows

Output   : 30 concept drifts are formed

Results are shown in Table 4.1 and its relevant graph in Fig 4.7

Table 4.1. Number of the drifts occurred for sliding window size 50

Drift no.	Sliding window no.	No. of clusters
1	1	18
2	2	30
3	3	33
4	4	26
5	5	27
6	6	26
7	14	22

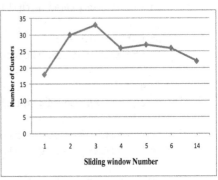

Fig. 4.7. Sliding window Vs clusters

Input:

Dataset   : Usenet.txt, with 1500 data points and 100 attributes.

Sliding window size   : 60 windows

Output   : 25 concept drifts are formed

Results are shown in Table 4.2 and its relevant graph in Fig 4.8.

Table 4.2. Number of drifts occurred at sliding window size 60

Drift no.	Sliding window no.	No. of clusters
1	1	19
2	2	34
3	5	36
4	15	24

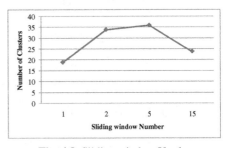

Fig. 4.8. Sliding window Vs clusters

The above two tables and graphs show that as the size of sliding window increases, the number of concept drifts decreases.

5   Conclusion and Future Work

In this paper, the method to handle the generation of clusters for time-evolving data was implemented using sliding window model with node importance values and setting threshold. To implement clustering of concept-drift categorical data, we worked on "usenet" dataset and JAVA language. The number of the outliers formed in the sliding window decides the drift in the concept. If the number of the outliers is more as compared to that of the cluster points then sliding window is said to be drifting the concept. Drift also occurs if the maximum numbers of the clusters are varied with respect to their number of clusters and the number of the cluster point in the same cluster label of the previous sliding window. It was shown that number of drifts is less if sliding window size is more.

Since our work considers large categorical dataset with huge number of attributes, it takes more time to achieve result and a low memory system cannot handle the total data, resulting in reduced sliding window size. If sliding window size is small, then the data has to be clustered very frequently and the results are to be analyzed in less time gap which can be considered as drawback that may be overcome with the implementation of the hierarchical clustering approaches in the data selection. Hence, a Leader- subleader algorithm may also be used to concentrate on the short range of the data.

References

1. Barbara, D., Li, Y., Couto, J.: COOLCAT: An entropy-based algorithm for categorical clustering. In: Proceedings of the Eleventh International Conference on Information and Knowledge Management, McLean, VA (2002)
2. Chen, H.L., Chen, M.S., Chen, L., Su.: Frame work for clustering Concept –Drifting categorical data. IEEE Transaction Knowledge and Data Engineering 21(5) (2009)
3. Eckel, B.: Thinking in Java (1998)
4. Ester, M., Kriegel, H.P., Xu, X.: Knowledge Discovery in Large Spatial Databases: Focusing Techniques for Efficient Class Identification. In: Egenhofer, M.J., Herring, J.R. (eds.) SSD 1995. LNCS, vol. 951, pp. 67–82. Springer, Heidelberg (1995)
5. Fisher, D.H.: Knowledge Acquisition via Incremental Conceptual Clustering. Machine Learning (1987)
6. Ganti, V., Gehrke, J., Ramakrishnan, R.: CACTUS: Clustering categorical data using summaries. In: Proceedings of the ACM-SIGKDD International Conference on Knowledge Discovery and Data Mining, San Diego, CA (1999)
7. Gluck, M.A., Corter, J.E.: Information Uncertainty and the Utility of. In: Proc. Seventh Ann. Conf. Cognitive Science Soc. (1985)
8. Guha, S., Rastogi, R., Shim, K.: Cure: An efficient clustering algorithm for large databases. In: Proc. 1998 ACM-SIGMOD Int. Conf. Management of Data (SIGMOD 1998), Seattle, WA, pp. 73–84 (June 1998)
9. Guha, S., Rastogi, R., Shim, K.: ROCK: A robust clustering algorithm for categorical Attributes. In: Proc. 1999 Int. Conf. Data Engineering (ICDE 1999), Sydney, Australia, pp. 512–521 (March 1999)
10. Han, J., Kamber, M.: Data Mining: Concepts and Techniques. Morgan Kaufmann (2001)
11. Huang, Z.: Extensions to the k-means algorithm for clustering large data sets with categorical values. Data Mining and Knowledge Discovery 2, 283–304 (1998)
12. Kantardzic, M.: Data Mining: Concepts, Models, Methods and Algorithms. Wiley-Interscience, Hoboken (2003)
13. Karypis, G., Han, E.H., Kumar, V.: CHAMELEON: A hierarchical clustering algorithm using dynamic modeling. Computer 32, 68–75 (1999)

14. Kaufman, L., Rousseeuw, P.J.: Finding Groups in Data: An Introduction to Cluster Analysis. John Wiley & Sons (1990)
15. Lloyd, S.P.: Least Squares Quantization in PCM. IEEE Trans. Information Theory 28, 128–137 (1982); (original version Technical Report, Bell Labs 1957)
16. MacQueen, J.: Some methods for classification and analysis of multivariate observations. In: Proc. 5th Berkeley Symp. Math. Statist. Prob., vol. 1, pp. 281–297 (1967)
17. Naughton, P., Schildt, H.: Java, The Complete Reference (December 1996)
18. Ng, R., Han, J.: Efficient and effective clustering method for spatial data mining. In: Proc. 1994 Int. Conf. Very Large Data Bases (VLDB 1994), Santiago, Chile, pp. 144–155 (September 1994)
19. Prasanna Lakshmi, K., Reddy Madhavi, K., Anitha, T.: Generation of clusters for duplicate records using Union-Find Algorithm. In: International Conference on Advanced Computing Technologies- GRIET, Hyderabad, India, 12-17 (2008)
20. Reddy Madhavi, K., Vinay Babu, A., Rajini Kanth, T.V., Rathnamma, M.V.: Finding Interesting Relationships among Documents in DDB. International Journal of Engineering Science and Technology 3(4), 3071–3077 (2011)
21. Reddy Madhavi, K., Vinay Babu, A., Rajini Kanth, T.V., Geetha, C.: Finding Closed Correlated Documents in DDB using all-conf. International Journal of Engineering Science and Technology 3(5), 4036–4042 (2011) ISSN : 0975-5462
22. Viswanadha Raju, S., Venkateswara Reddy, H., Sudhakar Reddy, N.: A Threshold for Clustering Concept – Drifting Categorical Data. In: ICMLC 2011. IEEE Computer Society (2011)
23. Viswanadha Raju, S., Sudhakar Reddy, N., Venkateswara Reddy, H., Sreenivasulu, G., Nageswara Raju, C.: POur-NIR: Modified Node-Importance Representative for clustering of categorical data. International Journal of Computer Science and Information Security 9(4) (April 2011); ISSN 1947-5500
24. Viswanadha Raju, S., Venkateswara Reddy, H., Sudhakar Reddy, N., Sreenivasulu, G., Sunitha, K.V.N.: Our - NIR: Node Importance Representative for Clustering of Categorical Data. International Journal of Computer Science and Technology 2(2) (June 2011); ISSN: 2229 - 4333 (Print), IISSN:0976 - 8491 (Online)
25. Zhang, T., Ramakrishnan, R., Livny, M.: BIRCH: an efficient data clustering method for very large databases. In: Proc. 1996 ACM-SIGMOD Int. Conf. Management of Data (SIGMOD 1996), Montreal, Canada, pp. 103–114 (June 1996)

A Weighted Particle Swarm Optimization Technique for Optimizing Association Rules

G. Maragatham and M. Lakshmi

Computer Science & Engg. Dept., Sathyabama University
600 119, Chennai, India
maragathamhaarish@gmail.com, hodcse@sathyabamauniversity.ac.in

Abstract. The Process of finding out correlations among the data items in the databases forms the core concept in Association Rule Mining. The Association rule Mining algorithms helps in decision making process. Since it plays a vital role in this area, the rules generated by the algorithms should be of less in number and precise. Association rule algorithms, such as Apriori, scrutinize a long list of transactions in order to decide which items are most commonly purchased together. The challenge of digging out association patterns from data draws upon research in databases, machine learning and optimization to bring advanced intelligent solutions. But even though it provides some robustness, the rules generated from the algorithm may be redundant in some cases. So in order to overcome the problems we need to optimize the rules generated from these algorithms. Here we consider the Utility based Temporal Association Rule Mining method for generating the association rules and the Particle Swam Optimization algorithm is used to optimize the generated rules. The main processes in this proposed approach are calculation of the support and confidence from the input data, the Rule generation, Initialization, updation of the velocity, position of the rules and evaluation of fitness function. This paper attempts to use the PSO technique to optimize the utility based temporal rules by filtering out the redundant rules and thereby reducing the problem space.

Keywords: Association Rule Mining, Utility based Temporal Association rule mining, Particle Swam Optimization.

1 Introduction

Data mining is the task of discovering meaningful new correlations, patterns and trends by sifting through large amounts of data stored in repositories using machine learning, statistical analysis, modeling techniques and database technology. It is the source of inexplicit, purely valid, and potentially useful and important knowledge from large volumes of natural data [2]. When the data consist of continuous values, it becomes hard to mine the data and some special techniques need to be prepared. Association rule is basically used for searching the useful patterns and relation between items found in the database of transactions [3]. The inferred knowledge must be not only precise but also readable, comprehensible and ease of understanding.

P.V. Krishna, M.R. Babu, and E. Ariwa (Eds.): ObCom 2011, Part II, CCIS 270, pp. 655–664, 2012.
© Springer-Verlag Berlin Heidelberg 2012

There exists various data mining tasks such as AR's, sequential patterns, Classification, clustering, time series, etc., and there have been plenty of techniques and algorithms for these tasks and diverse types of data in data mining [1]. Due to the widespread use of data mining methods. Association rules have advantages of simplicity, uniformity, transparency, and simplicity of deduction that have made them one of the most extensively accepted approaches for symbolizing real world medical knowledge [9]. The advantage of using an optimization method such as PSO is that it does not rely unambiguously on the gradient of the problem to be optimized, so the method can be readily employed for a host of optimization problems [12].

Further, the association rules are at times very bulky. It is nearly impracticable for the end users to understand or validate those outsized complex association rules, thereby restricting the worth of the data mining results [10]. A fuzzy method is used in order to distinguish the important rules from the less important ones for each class while the Association Rule Mining algorithm for Classification (ARMC) combines the weighted voting and the decision list algorithms [14]. For creating association rules using Apriori, Hegland [11] reviewed the most well known algorithm and discuss alternatives for distributed data, addition of constraints and data taxonomies. The appraisal ends by means of an outlook on tools which have the prospective to deal with long itemsets and significantly minimizes the amount of (uninteresting) itemsets returned. The algorithms for performing association rule mining are NP-complete and [8] revealed that association rule mining can be abridged to finding a CLIQUE in a graph which is NP-complete. The main inspiration for using Evolutionary Algorithms in the detection of sophisticated forecast rules is that they perform a global search and cope better with attribute interaction than the greedy rule induction algorithms often used in data mining. The improvements applied in EAs are replicated in the rule based systems used for classification [4]. The PSO with association rules is discussed in [5],[21]. Application of PSO to Economic Dispatch problem is given by Kwang Y. Lee [13].

In the field of data mining a numerous methods proposed for different resolutions, amongst the association rule mining define a role of its kind. As we conversed above, there are a number of algorithms and techniques available for refining the basic association rule mining. We proposed a method to generate the association rule and to optimize the rules with PSO (Particle Swarm Optimization) Algorithm. The purpose of PSO algorithm is to filter out the redundant rules from the set of rules and to provide an optimized solution to the user.

2   Related Works

Mining ARM from large databases is discussed by Agrawal in [6] &[7]. Hamid Reza Qodmanan et al. [15] discussed the application of multi objective genetic algorithm to association rule mining. They focused their attention especially on association rule mining. This paper proposed a method based on genetic algorithm without taking the minimum support and confidence into account. Andrea Bellandiet al. [16] described some improvements of their previous work that realized an integrated framework for extracting constraint-based multi-level association rules with an ontology support.

Ziqiang Wang et al. [17] proposed a classification rule mining algorithm based on particle swarm optimization (PSO) to efficiently mine the classification rule from databases. The experimental results showed that the proposed algorithm achieved higher predictive accuracy and much smaller rule list than other classification algorithm.

R.J. Kuo et al. [18] proposed an algorithm for association rule mining in order to improve computational efficiency as well as to automatically determine suitable threshold values. Mourad Ykhlef [19] derived an algorithm based on Quantum Swarm Evolutionary approach which gave better results compared to genetic algorithms. Association rule mining aims to extract the correlation or causal structure existing between a set of frequent items or attributes in a database.. The search for association rules was an NP-complete problem. The complexities mainly arise in exploiting huge number of database transactions and items. They proposed a new algorithm to extract the best rules in a reasonable time of execution but without assuring always the optimal solutions. Veenu Mangat [20] presented a swarm intelligence based technique for mining rules over a medical database.Carvalho A and Pozo A [22] described a multi-objective particle swarm optimization (MOPSO) algorithm that handles with numerical and discrete attributes. Guo-rongcai, Shao-zi Li and Shui-li Chen [23] presented a fuzzy association rules mining algorithm by using nonlinear particle swarm optimization (NPSO) to determine appropriate fuzzy membership functions that covered the domains of quantitative attributes.

3 Familiarization of Concepts

We are using utility based temporal association rule mining [24] and the Particle swarm optimization (PSO) in our proposed approach. These techniques are used to trigger the concept behind our proposed approach. Let us have a detailed look at these techniques.

3.1 Utility Based Temporal Miner

This method is one among the key concept that we use for generating the association rules for the dataset. This basics of the algorithm is presented by us in [24]. The input database D has a set of partitions, $D = \{ P_1, P_2, \ldots P_n \}$ where each partition has a set of transactions $T = \{ T_1, T_2 \ldots, T_s \}$ and has a set of items; $X_D = \{ x_1, x_2, \ldots, x_n \}$. Each item in the partition P_k contains different utility values. The transaction weighted utility value of an item and item set is calculated by considering both internal utility if item in the transaction and external utility of the item in the corresponding transaction. [24]. Each rule is generated adhering to the support and confidence framework of sec. 5.1.

3.2 Particle Swarm Optimization

Kennedy and Eberhart proposed the particle swarm optimization (PSO) algorithm in 1995. The PSO algorithm has become an evolutionary computation technique and an important heuristic algorithm in recent years. The main concept of PSO originates from the study of fauna behavior. The role of PSO algorithm is vibrant in the optimization of solutions which obtained through different methods. The PSO considers every solution in the search space as "Particles". All particles have fitness values, which are evaluated by the fitness function to be optimized. The particles also have velocities which direct the flight of the particles. Particles fly through the problem space by following the current optimum particles.

The working of PSO algorithm begins with population of candidate solutions called particles, the population can be considered as swarm. In PSO the particles are moved around the search space according to some mathematical formulae. The movement of the particle is governed by the particles best known position and the swarm's best known position. A fitness function is defined over the problem to be optimized and the maximization of the fitness value determines the optimum solutions. In the following algorithm values x_i^n, x_i^o are new position and old position of the particles respectively, and in similar way v_i^n, v_i^o are the new velocity and old velocity of the particles. The process continues up to a termination criteria . Finally we get the value of g, the best known position of the swarm as a global minimum, from that value we optimize the different problem which are subjected for optimization.

Algorithm

define fitness $f : R^n \rightarrow R$. where R is the SearchSpace

Define S as the set of Particles

$x_i, v_i \in R$, x and v are the position and velocity of the particle respectively.

set p_i as the best known position of particle and g_i be best known position of Swarm.

For $i = 1,\ldots, S$

    Initialize particle's positions

    $x_i \rightarrow$ best_position   // assign initial position as best position

    select r_p, r_g // Random numbers ranging [0,1]

    update velocity

$$v_i^n = v_i^o + r_p(p_i - x_i) + r_g(g - x_i)$$

    update position

$$x_i^n = x_i^o + v_i^n$$

    if($f(x_i) < f(p_i)$)

        update particle's best known position : $x_i \rightarrow p_i$

        if($f(p_i) < f(g)$)

            update swarm's best known position.

repeat untill end of loop

Now g represents the best known position

4   Architecture of the Proposed System

The system starts with a dataset as input , which is given to the UTARM technique
for generating rules. These rules are considered as initial swarm population for the
second phase. This phase is used to optimize the rules generated by first phase for
effective decision making process.

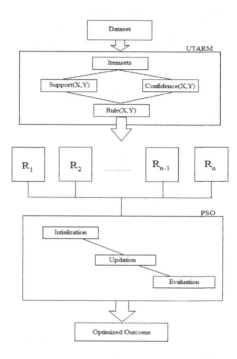

Fig. 1. Architecture of the proposed system

5   Proposed Approach : Weighted PSO Approach

Optimization of rule generated by different association rule mining algorithm has
become a serious task, because of the redundancy present in the generation of rules.
Different methods are introduced for this optimization problem. In our method, we
use the PSO algorithm for optimizing the Utility based Temporal Association Rule
Mining. In our method we incorporate the PSO algorithm in to the Association rule
mining method. The advantage of the PSO algorithm reflects in the speed of the
accuracy of the optimization of the rules and also the use of utility based temporal
mining is an added advantage for the rule optimization. Since UTARM generate rules
according to the Utility measure, which consequently speed up the process.

The advantage of PSO is that it generates position and velocity for each of the rules that are present. As the algorithm proceeds and after a number of iteration the velocity and the position of the rules are assigned to their best known values thus the optimization process can be executed quickly and accurately. As discussed in the above sections, there are two concepts which triggers our proposed approach and they are i) Rule Generator   ii) PSO. The Rule generation algorithm is discussed by us in [24]. In [24] we considered a synthetic data set for Rules generation. Whereas, In this paper we considered a retail dataset. For optimizing the generated rules we have considered PSO technique. In the second phase, the fitness function is defined by us using support and confidence which are based on utility and temporal concepts.

5.1   Rule Generation (I Phase)

The process starts with supplying the input data to the first phase. We have a dataset D, which consists of a number of Item set.

$$D = \{ I_1, I_2, \dots\dots, I_n \} \tag{1}$$

Each of the itemsets consists of a number of items. The main function that are inevitable for our proposed approach are the support and the confidence of the itemsets, which are used to find the rules.

$$I = \{ x_1, x_2 \dots\dots\dots, x_n \} \tag{2}$$

$$\text{support}\,(\,I\,,p_i\,) = f\,(\,I,\,P_i\,) * \sum_{x_i \in I}\left(E_u\,(\,x_i,P_i\,) * \sum_{x_i \in I, T_q \in P_i} I_u\,(\,x_i,T_q\,)\right) \tag{3}$$

The support function, which is defined , is derived from FTU_support defined on the UTARM method. The support function defines how much the items in the itemset give support to each other and this support function incorporates utility value with it. The confidence function is given below.

$$\text{conf}(\,X \Rightarrow Y\,) = \frac{\text{support}(\,X \Rightarrow Y\,)}{\text{support}(X)} \tag{4}$$

Eventhough the rules provide information for decision making , there are some redundant rules generated. To remove this redundancy, PSO technique is adapted. The rules generated are stored in the rule array in R.

$$R_D = \{ r_1, r_2, \dots\dots, r_n \} \tag{5}$$

5.2   Optimization (II Phase)

PSO is the main method which controls the second phase of our approach. We give the set of rules as input to the PSO algorithm, according to the PSO concept each rules are considered as particles and the set of rules is considered as the Swarm. There are mainly three process are happening in the PSO processing, they are listed below.

Initialization: It can be considered as the first step in the optimization phase. The input data contains a set of rules. As per PSO algorithm each rule has been considered as particles in the swarm, where the swarm mentioned here is the set of rules, R. So each rule has a position and a velocity. We initialize the position and velocity of each rule with a random vector value.

$$X(r_i), V(r_i) \Rightarrow [0,1], r_i \in R, i = 1,2,\ldots\ldots,n \tag{6}$$

The random values ranges between the lower and upper bounds. After the initialization process we will update best position with the initial position and also the best position of the swarm with its initial value.

$$x_i(r_i) \rightarrow bp(r_i) \tag{7}$$

Where, $x_i(r_i)$ is the initial position defined for the rule and $bp(r_i)$ is the best known position of the rule.

Updation: This step consists of the updating the position and velocity of each rule. The velocity can updated using the following equation.

$$v(r_i)^{new} = v(r_i)^{old} + r_p \left(b_p(r_i) - x_i \right) + r_s \left(s_p - x_i \right) \tag{8}$$

Where r_p is the random vector defined for the particle and r_s is the random vector defined for the Swarm. x_i is the position of the particle. This updated velocity is used to calculate the new position of the particle.

$$x_i^{new} = x_i^{old} + v(r_i^{new}) \tag{9}$$

After updating the position and velocity of the particles, we assign the best known position to the particle and to the swarm according to the updated positions and velocities. After updating, we subject these values into the optimization function called fitness function.

Evaluation: This step includes the key function in our proposed approach. We define the optimization function as the fitness unction. The fitness function provides the fitness value for each rule and that fitness value of the rule shows how important that rule is. The evaluation of fitness values of all the rules gives the optimized outcome of our proposed approach. The fitness function can be given as,

$$fitness(r_i) = bp(r_i) * conf(r_i) * log(support(r_i)) \tag{10}$$

We find the fitness value of all the rules in the problem space. In our approach, the fitness function is considered as a global maximum. i.e., the maximum the fitness value, the better the result will be.

6   Results

We have conducted an experimental set for checking the efficiency of the proposed method. The experimental setup includes Intel core i3 processor running with 3GB RAM and a 500 GB Hard disk. We have selected the retail dataset for the evaluation of our proposed system. The dataset [25] is described by Tom Brijs and contains the retail market basket data from an anonymous Belgian retail store. We have selected three partitions from the retail dataset and each containing 100 transactions.

6.1 Performance Evaluation

Population size vs. number of items:

In this section we perform the evaluation of the retail dataset according to its population size and the number of items, which are used for the optimization. The fig.2 represents the performance of the proposed approach over the different population under a certain range of support values.

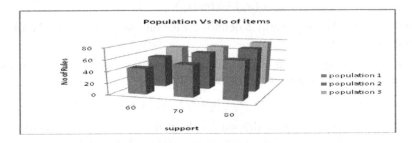

Fig. 2. Population vs. No of items

Population size vs. time:

This section denotes the performance evaluation of different population over the time taken for optimizing each of the particles in the populations.

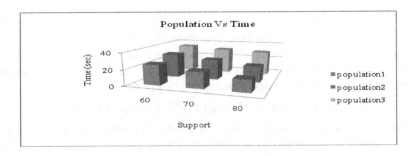

Fig. 3. Population vs. Time for Execution

7 Conclusion

In order to provide efficient decision making process, the optimization concept is used. The fitness function used in this article is based on support and confidence, which are computed based on the aspects of considering both temporal and utility factors. Generating more rules may be misleading, some rules may be duplicated. With optimized less rules, efficient decision making can be done. Therefore PSO concept is adapted using the proposed fitness function. The experimental results have been encouraging.

References

1. Dewang, R., Agarwal, J.: A New Method for Generating All Positive and Negative Association Rules. International Journal on Computer Science and Engineering (IJCSE) 3(4), 1649–1657 (2011)
2. Olafsson, S., Li, X., Wu, S.: Operations research and data mining. European Journal of Operational Research 187(3), 1429–1448 (2008)
3. Agrawal, R., Imielinksi, T., Swami, A.: Database mining: a performance perspective. IEEE Transactions on Knowledge and Data Engineering, 914–925 (1993)
4. Arunadevi, J., Rajamani, V.: Optimization of Spatial Association Rule Mining using Hybrid Evolutionary algorithm. International Journal of Computer Applications 1(19), 86–89 (2010)
5. Ykhlef, M.: A Quantum Swarm Evolutionary Algorithm for mining association rules in large databases. Journal of King Saud University – Computer and Information Sciences 23, 1–6 (2011)
6. Agrawal, R., Imielinski, T., Swami, S.: Mining association rules between sets of items in large databases, pp. 207–216 (1993a)
7. Agrawal, R., Imielinski, T., Swami, S.: Mining association rules between sets of items in large databases. In: Proceedings of the ACM SIGMOD International Conference on Management of Data, Washington DC, pp. 207–216 (1993b)
8. Angiulli, F., Ianni, G., Palopoli, L.: On the complexity of mining association rules. In: Proceedings of SEBD, pp. 177–184 (2001)
9. Mangat, V.: Swarm Intelligence Based Technique for Rule Mining in the Medical Domain. International Journal of Computer Applications 4(1), 19–24 (2010)
10. Kotsiantis, S., Kanellopoulos, D.: Association Rules Mining: A Recent Overview. GESTS International Transactions on Computer Science and Engineering 32(1), 71–82 (2006)
11. Hegland, M.: Algorithms for Association Rules. In: Mendelson, S., Smola, A.J. (eds.) Advanced Lectures on Machine Learning. LNCS (LNAI), vol. 2600, pp. 226–234. Springer, Heidelberg (2003)
12. Pedersen, M.E.H., Chipperfield, A.J.: Simplifying Particle Swarm Optimization. Applied Soft Computing, 1–32 (2009)
13. Lee, K.Y.: Application of Particle Swarm Optimization to Economic Dispatch Problem: Advantages and Disadvantages. In: IEEE PSCE (2006)
14. Zemirline, A., Lecornu, L., Solaiman, B., Ech-Cherif, A.: An Efficient Association Rule Mining Algorithm for Classification. In: Rutkowski, L., Tadeusiewicz, R., Zadeh, L.A., Zurada, J.M. (eds.) ICAISC 2008. LNCS (LNAI), vol. 5097, pp. 717–728. Springer, Heidelberg (2008)
15. Qodmanan, H.R., Nasiri, M., Minaei-Bidgoli, B.: Multi objective association rule mining with genetic algorithm without specifying minimum support and minimum confidence. An International Journal Expert Systems with Applications 38(1), 288–298 (2011)

16. Bellandi, A., Furletti, B., Grossi, V., Romei, A.: Ontological support for Association Rule Mining. In: Proceedings of the 26th IASTED International Conference on Artificial Intelligence and Applications, pp. 110–115 (2008)
17. Wang, Z., Sun, X., Zhang, D.: A PSO-Based Classification Rule Mining Algorithm. In: Proceedings of the 3rd International Conference on Intelligent Computing: Advanced Intelligent Computing Theories and Applications, pp. 377–384 (2009)
18. Kuo, R.J., Chao, C.M., Chiu, Y.T.: Application of particle swarm optimization to association rule mining. Applied Soft Computing 11(1), 326–336 (2011)
19. Ykhlef, M.: A Quantum Swarm Evolutionary Algorithmfor mining association rules in large databases. Journal of King Saud University – Computer and Information Sciences 23, 1–6 (2011)
20. Mangat, V.: Swarm Intelligence Based Technique for Rule Mining inthe Medical Domain. International Journal of Computer Applications 4(1), 19–24 (2010)
21. Wang, H.-S., Yeh, W.-C., Huang, P.-C., Chang, W.-W.: Using association rules and particle swarm optimization approach for part change. International Journal of Expert Systems with Applications 36(4), 8178–8184 (2009)
22. Carvalho, A., Pozo, A.: Non-Ordered Data Mining Rules Through Multi-Objective Particle Swarm Optimization: Dealing with Numeric and Discrete Attributes. In: Proceedings of the Eighth International Conference on Hybrid Intelligent Systems, pp. 495–500 (2008)
23. Cai, G.-R., Li, S.-Z., Chen, S.-L.: Mining Fuzzy Association Rules by Using Nonlinear Particle Swarm Optimization. AISC, vol. 82, pp. 621–630 (2010)
24. Maragatham, G., Lakshmi, M.: A Strategy for Mining Utility based Temporal Association Rules. In: Proceedings of the 2nd International Conference on Trendz in Information Sciences and Computing, TISC-2010 Organized by Sathyabama University in association with IEEE and Cognizant (2010)
25. Frequent itemset repository, http://fimi.ua.ac.be/data

Enhancement of Infrared Images Using Triangular Fuzzy Membership Function and Truncated Interval Thresholding

S. Arun Bharathi, S. Logesh, and P.V.S.S.R. Chandra Mouli

School of Computing Science and Engineering, VIT University
Vellore 632014, Tamilnadu, India
{arunbharathi90,mouli.chand}@gmail.com,
logesh_s@hotmail.com

Abstract. Image Enhancement is a preliminary step in basic image processing routines in general and is a crucial step in infrared (IR) images in specific. In most of the IR images, the target and the background fall into almost similar intensity levels. In order to increase the contrast of the target from its background, the preprocessing step is mandatory. In this paper, we proposed a fuzzy based approach for enhancing the infrared images so that the target can be detected in normal and cluttered images. The proposed method is robust and the experimental results show the efficacy of the proposed method.

Keywords: Image Enhancement, Infrared Images, Infrared Image Enhancement, Fuzzy Sets, Triangular Membership Function, Truncated Thresholding.

1 Introduction

IR light is an invisible form of radiation given off by all objects in day time as well as night time. IR is an electromagnetic radiation having wavelength longer than visible light. These images have major applications in defense / military and for other civilian purposes. Tracking, night vision, target recognition are some of the defense related applications whereas whether forecasting, spectroscopy are some of the civilian applications wherein IR sensors are heavily used. Every object in the Universe emits infrared radiation across a spectrum of wavelengths but only certain range is of great interest. Accordingly, IR band is divided into sub bands. The International Commission on Illumination (CIE) recommended the division of IR radiation into three bands [1] namely IR-A ($0.7m - 1.4m$), IR-B ($1.4m - 3m$) and IR-C ($3m - 1000m$).

Another sub division which is commonly used [2] is Near-Infrared (NIR, $0.7m - 1.4m$), Short-wavelength Infrared (SWIR, $1.4m - 3m$), Mid-wavelength Infrared (MWIR, $3m - 5m$), Long-wavelength Infrared (LWIR, $8m - 15m$) and finally Far-Infrared (FIR, $15m - 1000m$). No precise boundary has been defined between the visible light and IR light.

P.V. Krishna, M.R. Babu, and E. Ariwa (Eds.): ObCom 2011, Part II, CCIS 270, pp. 665–673, 2012.
© Springer-Verlag Berlin Heidelberg 2012

Usually the IR images captured are dark objects on a background. In many cases, the difference in contrast between the target and the background is minimal. Most of the times, the images are cluttered. So, for successful target detection, the enhancement of images is must. Image enhancement is a subjective process. There are no standard metrics for evaluating the results obtained. The results are based on human perception. Still, some common measures like minimum and maximum intensity levels, mean, standard deviation etc are the metrics often used by researchers for comparison of the enhanced image with the original image.

This paper is organized as follows: In Section 2, the literature survey related to the present topic has been reviewed. In Section 3, the usage of Fuzzy sets and Fuzzy logic in image processing is briefly reviewed. The proposed method is discussed in Section 4. Experimental results and analysis of results are presented in Section 5. Section 6 concludes the work.

2   Literature Review

Histogram modification, noise removal, edge enhancement and amplitude scaling are the four main categories of image enhancement [3]. Bit slicing, histogram equalization and contrast improvement through look up tables combined with noise reduction are further used for enhancement of images [4]. In particular case of IR images, motion estimation is also used for the enhancement [5], [6]. Logarithmic model is used for enhancement in dynamic ranges [7]. In [8], histogram projection, histogram equalization and histogram weighted hybrid mapping and median filtering are used for IR image enhancement. The results are evaluated by psychological experiments.

A two-stage process based on global and local contrast enhancement is proposed in [9]. The authors initially enhanced the global contrast using adaptive plateau histogram equalization which is popularly known as APHE. This is followed by wavelet transform for local contrast enhancement. Histogram shaping on local regions and adaptive Wiener filter for noise removal is used in [10]. Adaptive unsharp masking (AUM) is proposed in [11] for image enhancement. Adaptive thresholding using error-diffusion algorithm is used in [12] for edge enhancement. A qualitative model for FAR IR scenes using spatiotemporal homomorphic filtering is used in [13]. An adaptive version of [13] is proposed in [14]. The IR images are enhanced using autoregressive moving average filter in [15]. The IR image enhancement based on human visual system is proposed in [16] using multifractal theory. Balanced contrast limited adaptive histogram equalization and contrast enhancement (BCLAHE-CE) techniques are used in [17] for better visualization of IR images. In [18], the authors made a comparative study of different IR image enhancement techniques for sea-surface targets. They observed that BCLAHE-CE provides good results for different scenarios in subjective and quantitative tests. In [19], the same authors proposed IR image enhancement for sea-surface targets based on local frequency cues. They transformed the image block-wise into Fourier domain and clustering was done based on expected number of regions to be enhanced in frequency domain.

3 Fuzzy Sets in Image Processing

The pixel values of an image possess uncertainty due to the grayness ambiguity, uncertain knowledge and geometrical fuzziness. To remove this uncertainty, fuzzy theory is introduced and it is applied to solve image processing problems. Fuzzy image processing [20] is the collection of approaches that understand, represent and process the images, their segments and their features as fuzzy sets.

Definition 1. *A fuzzy set is denoted by an ordered set of pairs, the first element denotes the element and the second represents its membership value.*

Fuzzy theory is applied in image enhancement, image segmentation, object detection etc., Many researchers have applied the fuzzy set theory for image processing problems. An image I of size $M \times N$ with L gray levels can be considered as an array of fuzzy singletons, each having a membership denoting its degree of brightness relative to some brightness values [20]. The notion of fuzzy sets for an image is written as

$$I = \bigcup_{mn} \frac{\mu_{mn}}{g_{mn}} \tag{1}$$

where $m = 1 \ldots M$, $n = 1 \ldots N$, g_{mn} is the intensity of $(m,n)^{th}$ pixel and μ_{mn} is the membership value.

The membership function characterizes the whole image or local portions of the image. Fuzzy based image processing system is in general a rule based system. In this work, we have used fuzzy concepts for enhancing the image thereby inference can be made. The major steps involved in enhancement of an image using fuzzy concepts are (i) image fuzzification, (ii) modification and (iii) defuzzification. The fuzzification process transforms the image domain data into fuzzy domain i.e. to a membership plane. The modification step tries to modify the fuzzified data. Decoding the result of modification is done in Defuzzification. The decision making process is carried out in inference rule making.

4 Proposed Methodology

The block diagram of the proposed methodology is given in Figure 1.

The input IR image is transformed into fuzzy domain. We have employed the triangular membership function and defined five sets Very Dark, Dark, Gray, Bright and Very Bright. Graphical representation of the membership function is shown in Fig.
reff2.

where min and max are the minimum and maximum intensities of the image,

$$mid = \frac{(min + max)}{2}, T_1 = \frac{(min + mid)}{2}, T_2 = \frac{(mid + max)}{2} \tag{2}$$

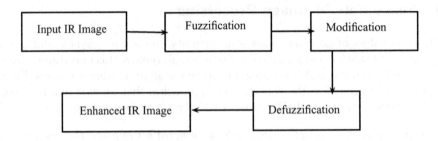

Fig. 1. Block Diagram of the Proposed Methodology

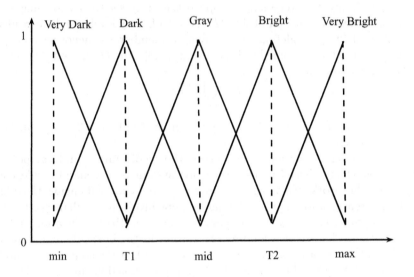

Fig. 2. Triangular Fuzzy Membership function

A variation to Fuzzy histogram hyperbolization [20] has been introduced in this paper for contrast enhancement of the given input image. The steps of the original histogram hyperbolization given in [20] is given below:

(i) Initialization of parameters - min, max, mid, T_1 and T_2 as they are defined in equation (2).

(ii) Transform the spatial data to fuzzy data (Fuzzification using triangular membership function)

The pseudo code for fuzzification process is given as

```
for i=1:M
for j=1:N
 if min <= I(i,j) && I(i,j) < T1
```
$$FD(i,j) = 2 * (\frac{(B(i,j)-min)}{(mid-min)})^2$$

```
elseif B1<= I(i,j) && I(i,j) < mid
```
$$FD(i,j) = 1 - 2 * (\frac{(B(i,j)-mid)}{(mid-min)})^2$$

```
elseif md<= I(i,j) && I(i,j) < T2
```
$$FD(i,j) = 1 - 2 * (\frac{(B(i,j)-mid)}{(max-mid)})^2$$

```
else B2<= I(i,j) && I(i,j) < max
```
$$FD(i,j) = 2 * (\frac{B(i,j)-mid)}{max-mid})^2$$

```
  end
end
end
```

In the above pseudo code, the range of comparison is done using unsigned intensity pixel values represented in $I(i,j)$. On fuzzification, the spatial data is normalized to $[0,1]$ and hence the image is converted to double format for practical implementation which is represented in $B(i,j)$. $FD(i,j)$ represents the fuzzified data.

(iii) Modify the fuzzified data The modification is done by squaring the fuzzification data obtained in the previous step.

```
for i=1:M
for j=1:N
   MD(i,j)=pow(Fd, 2);
end
end
```

where M and N represent the rows and columns of the image I respectively, $MD(i,j)$ represents the modified fuzzy data.

(iv) Defuzzification process to revert back the fuzzified data to spatial data. The enhanced data is obtained using the formula

$$ED(i,j) = \frac{(L-1)}{e^{-1}-1}(e^{(-1*MD(i,j))-1}) \tag{3}$$

where L represents the maximum gray level of the image.

In the case of Infrared images, most of the intensity distribution is spread over the darker region and hence the thresholds calculated may not yield good results all the time. To change the process of selecting the threshold value, we introduced truncated thresholding. The process is described below.

1. Mark the intensity level for which the maximum peak is obtained in the histogram (say k). 2. To the intensity level, 1/3rd of the intensity value is calculated (k/3). [Empirically chosen and found that it works well in all cases]. 3. Now calculate k-k/3 and k+k/3 and mark the positions in the histogram and draw lines to the peak obtained in step-1. 4. Thus a triangle is formed and the threshold values T1 and T2 are taken as the intensity values k-k/3 and k+k/3.

This is termed as centroid method because once the triangle is formed, the peak is treated as the centroid of the triangle. If two or more intensity levels have the peaks the mean value is chosen. Similarly on calculation of T1 or T2, if the intensity value falls beyond the histogram then the boundary values are chosen in such cases.

5   Experimental Results and Analysis

5.1   Experimental Setup

The experiments are carried out on the IR images available in [21]. The dataset contains 62 classes of information. The experiments are carried out in MATLAB environment using Intel Core 2 Duo processor T 7250 @2.00 GHz, 1 GB RAM.

5.2   Experimental Description

The images are of size 480×512 grayscale. Images are taken by a camera which was set on the top of Ambler description of the position of the camera varies from image to image. The description of one sample image as mentioned in the website is given below:

The length between the camera and the nearest corner of the box: $5.18m$. The length between the camera and the ground: $4.6m$. The horizontal length between the camera and the box: $3.18m$. The height of the box: $0.505m$. The width and the depth of the box: $0.5m$.

5.3   Results

The results are shown in Table. 1 and Fig. 3 respectively. The images are of size 480×512 grayscale. Images are taken by a camera which was set on the top of Ambler description of the position of the camera varies from image to image.

5.4   Subjective Comparison

Table. 1 shows the results of original and proposed enhanced results of two sample images. In Table. 1, two sample original images, and the enhanced results are shown with the corresponding histograms. The enhanced image is in fuzzy domain with intensity range in [0, 1]. The objects are clearly visible for the human visual system in the enhanced version of the image over the corresponding original versions. Similar results obtained for all the 62 classes of images where each class containing approximately 12 test images.

5.5   Quantitative Comparison

The results are compared quantitatively using standard deviation. Standard deviation for the enhanced images is quite high compared to that of original images. The high value in the standard deviation representing the maximum deviation from the mean image and hence the histogram is distributed over the entire range thus improving the visibility. Fig. 3 shows the graphical representation of standard deviation values for 100 original and enhanced images.

Table 1. Enhancement Results of two sample images their histogram distributions

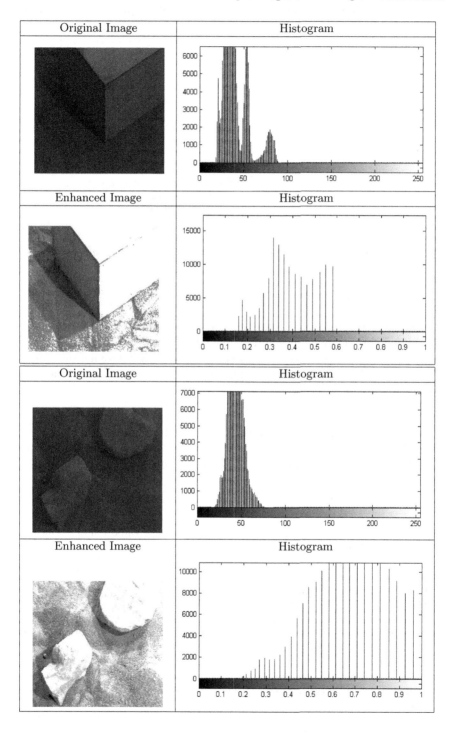

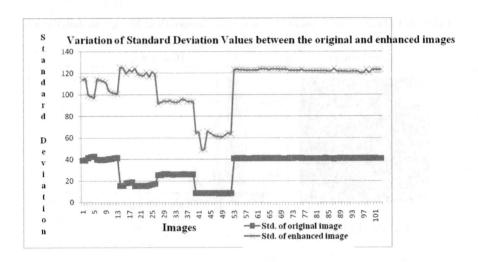

Fig. 3. Variation of Standard Deviation values for original and enhanced images

6   Conclusion

In this paper, we proposed a novel method for enhancement of infrared images using triangular membership function defined over fuzzy sets. The novelty lies in extending the fuzzy concepts for infrared images and in improving the threshold value selection by centroid method. The experimental results shows the robustness of the proposed method.

Acknowledgements. This work is supported by the Defence Research and Development Organization (DRDO), New Delhi India for funding the project under the Directorate of Extramural Research & Intellectual Property Rights (ER &IPR) No. RRIP/ER/1103978M/01/1347 sanctioned on 28th July 2011.

References

1. Henderson, R.: Wavelength Considerations. Instituts for Umformund Hochleistungs (retrieved on October 18, 2007)
2. James, B.: Unexploded Ordnance Detection and Mitigation, pp. 21–22. Springer, Heidelberg (2009)
3. Pratt, W.K.: Digital Image Processing. Wiley (2001)
4. McCauley, H., Auborn, J.E.: Image enhancement of infrared uncooled focal plane array imagery. In: Proceedings of SPIE, vol. 1479, pp. 416–422 (1991)
5. Irani, M., Peleg, S.: Motion analysis for image enhancement: resolution, occlusion and transparency. Journal of Visual Communication and Image Representation 4, 324–335 (1993)
6. Zhao, W., Zhang, C.: Scene-based nonuniformity correction and enhancement: pixel statistics and sub pixel motion. Journal of Optical Society of America 25, 1668–1681 (2008)

7. Jourlin, M., Pinoli, J.-C.: Image dynamic range enhancement and stabilization in the context of logarithmic image processing model. Signal Processing 41, 225–237 (1995)
8. Aviram, G., Rotman, S.R.: Evaluating the effect of infrared image enhancement on human target detection performance and image quality judgement. Optical Engineering (Bellingham) 38, 1433–1440 (1999)
9. Shao, M., Liu, G., Liu, X., Zhu, D.: A new approach for infrared image contrast enhancement. In: Proceedings of SPIE, vol. 6150, pp. 1–6 (2006)
10. Pace, T., Manville, D., Lee, H., Cloud, G., Puritz, J.: A multi resolution approach to image enhancement via histogram shaping and adaptive wiener filtering. In: Proceedings of SPIE, vol. 6978, pp. 1–11 (2008)
11. Polesel, A., Ramponi, G., Mathews, V.J.: Image enhancement via adaptive unsharp masking. IEEE Transactions on Image Processing 9, 505–510 (2000)
12. Eschbach, R., Knox, K.T.: Error-diffusion algorithm with edge enhancement. Journal of Optical Society of America 8, 1844–1850 (1991)
13. Highnam, R., Brady, M.: Model-based image enhancement for far infrared images. IEEE Transactions on Pattern Analysis and Machine Intelligence 19, 410–415 (1997)
14. Tang, M., Ma, S., Xiao, J.: Model based adaptive enhancement of far infrared image sequences. Pattern Recognition Letters 21, 827–835 (2000)
15. Qidwai, U.: Infrared Image enhancement using H bounds for surveillance applications. IEEE Transactions on Image Processing 17, 1274–1282 (2008)
16. Yu, T., Li, Q., Dai, J.: New enhancement of infrared image based on human visual system. Chin. Opt. Lett. 7, 206–209 (2009)
17. Branchitta, F., Diani, M., Corsini, G., Porta, A.: Dynamic range compression and contrast enhancement in infrared imaging systems. Optical Eng (Bellingham) 47, 76401 (2008)
18. Karah, A.O., Aytac, T.: A comparison of different infrared image enhancement techniques for sea-surface targets. In: IEEE Conference on Signal processing, Communications and Applications, pp. 765–768 (2009)
19. Karah, A.O., Erman Okman, O., Aytac, T.: Adaptive enhancement of sea-surface targets in infrared images based on local frequency cues. Journal of Optical Society of America 27(3), 509–517 (2010)
20. Hassanein, A.E., Bader, A.: A comparative study on digital mammography enhancement algorithms based on fuzzy theory. International Journal of Studies in Informatics and Control 12(1), 21–31 (2003)

Seizure Detection Using Parameter Estimation and Morlet Wavelet Transform

P. Grace Kanmani Prince[1] and R. Rani Hemamalini[2]

[1] Electronics and Control Engineering Department,
Sathyabama University, Chennai
cog_grace@yahoo.co.in
[2] Head of the Department, Electronics and Instrumentation,
St. Peter's University, Chennai
ranihema@yahoo.com

Abstract. The EEG signals prove to be an efficient tool in analyzing Epileptic seizure. The parameters like mean, standard deviation and their confidence interval of the seizure EEG signal are compared with the normal EEG signal. The seizure EEG signals have higher values of parameter estimates when compared to the normal EEG signals. In this paper Morlet wavelet transform is also performed on the EEG signals. Significant variations are observed in the Morlet coefficient of the seizure EEG when compared to the normal EEG signal.

Keywords: Epileptic Seizure, EEG signals, parameter estimation, wavelet transform.

1   Introduction

The definition for epileptic seizure was proposed by International League Against Epilepsy (ILAE) and the International Bureau for Epilepsy (IBE). It states that Epileptic seizure is 'a transient occurrence of signs and/or symptoms due to abnormal excessive or synchronous neuronal activity in the brain' [1]. The symptoms vary from patient to patient. Some may have vivid symptoms such as vibrant shaking of the body, sudden fall, excessive sweat etc. Some patients may have subtle symptoms like loss of memory or loss of awareness for few seconds. Around 1 % of the world's population is affected by epileptic seizure. Numerous researches are being carried out to analyze and treat epileptic seizure. In earlier days seizure was thought that it was harmless except for the injuries caused due to the symptoms such as sudden fall etc. But the recent studies have proved that repeated seizures can cause damage to the brain. Repeated seizures can also cause permanent loss of memory because of the damage caused in the hippocampus of the brain which is responsible for consolidating the long term memory and the short term memory. Ones seizure occurs it is likely to cause the occurrence of seizure in the future too [2]. Therefore it is very vital to detect seizure at the earliest even before the symptoms intensify. Automatic detection of seizure is also used for designing smart devices to warn the patient before the seizure occurs or at least to warn the patient at the onset of the seizure.

P.V. Krishna, M.R. Babu, and E. Ariwa (Eds.): ObCom 2011, Part II, CCIS 270, pp. 674–679, 2012.
© Springer-Verlag Berlin Heidelberg 2012

The most effective marker for diagnosis of epileptic seizure is the analysis of variation in EEG signal. Various methods are used to analyze the EEG data. This paper deals with the analysis of EEG signals by comparing the parameter estimates such as mean and standard deviation and their confidence intervals of the seizure EEG signal with the normal EEG signals. Wavelet transforms also proves to be an efficient tool in the time frequency analysis of non-stationary signals. In this paper Morlet wavelet transform has been used to analyze the time frequency variations of the EEG signals for the detection of seizure.

Section 2 deals with the comparison of parameter estimation between normal EEG signal and seizure EEG signals. Section 3 covers the details of analysis and results of EEG signals using continuous Morlet transform for seizure detection. Section 4 gives the concluding remarks of the paper.

2   Parameter Estimation

The EEG signals are low frequency and low amplitude signals. The frequency of the EEG signal acquired from the scalp of a normal person under standard clinical recording environment usually is in the range of 1Hz to 20Hz. The amplitude varies from 10µV to 100 µV. The EEG of the epileptic seizure patient is characterized by sharp waves and spikes. The mean and standard deviation values of the EEG signal of a normal person is lower when compared with the EEG signal of the epileptic patient.

Table 1. Comparison of Parameter Estimates of EEG signals

Parameter Estimates / EEG Signals	Mean(μ)	Standard Deviation (σ)	Confidence Interval of μ	Confidence Interval of σ
Normal EEG	-2.6965	34.9907	-7.5633 / 2.1702	31.8719 / 38.7915
Seizure EEG1	-49.2587	101.877	-63.4286 / -35.0889	92.7969 / 112.9439
Seizure EEG2	15.4080	66.4681	6.1631 / 24.6528	60.5435 / 73.6880
Seizure EEG3	-123.711	143.109	-143.6161 / -103.8067	130.3538 / 158.6549

The confidence interval is also found out to ensure the significance of the variation that is present between a normal and seizure EEG signals. In this paper 95% of confidence interval is used for calculation [3]. The EEG signal considered for this analysis was acquired from a local hospital. The mean, standard deviation and their confidence interval are studied for a normal signal and compared with three other seizure signals.

It can be seen from the above table that seizure EEG has a higher mean, standard deviation and confidence interval of both mean and standard deviation.

3   EEG Analysis Using Morlet Wavelet Transform

The wavelet transform is widely used for time frequency analysis. Fourier transform analysis gives only the details of the frequencies present in the signal. Wavelet transform provides the information of the frequencies with respect to time. In wavelet transform the wavelet is applied at the beginning of the signal that is at t=0 and then moved across the signal. The scale for the wavelet is initially chosen as s=1. The correlation between the mother wavelet and the selected portion (window) of the signal to which the mother wavelet is applied is found and integrated over time. The result thus obtained after the integration is then normalized to have a uniform energy level across the signal. Then the same procedure is repeated with increased scales till a favorable result is obtained. Since the wavelet transform for the given EEG signals are obtained by a computer the scale and the length of the window are incremented in small steps and it gives a better result [4]. The equation for continuous wavelet transform is given by equation 1.

$$C(a,b) = \frac{1}{\sqrt{a}} \int_{-\infty}^{\infty} x(t) w\left(\frac{t-a}{a}\right) dt \tag{1}$$

Where 'a' is the translation, 'b' is the scale, 'x' is the signal, 'w' is an equation which represents the mother wavelet and t is time.

The wavelet transform chosen for this particular EEG analysis is the Morlet wavelet transform. Figure 1 shows the Morlet wavelet which is the mother wavelet. The Morlet wavelet transform is a sine wave which is enveloped by the Gaussian window [5].

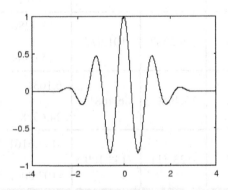

Fig. 1. Morlet Wavelet

The equation for Morlet wavelet is given by

$$w(t) = e^{-ti\theta} \cdot e^{-\frac{t^2}{2\sigma}} \qquad (2)$$

Where 'w' is the wavelet, θ is the modulation parameter and σ is the scaling parameter.

The Morlet wavelet transform is applied to the EEG waves for the analysis and detection of epileptic seizure. The results Morlet wavelet transform when applied to four different EEG signals are shown in the following figures. Figure 2 shows the result for a normal EEG signal. Figures 3a to 3c gives the result for Morlet wavelet transform of seizure EEG signal.

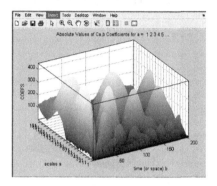

Fig. 2. Morlet wavelet transform applied to a normal EEG signal

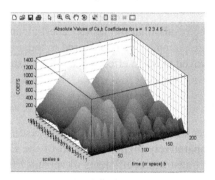

Fig. 3a. Morlet wavelet transform applied to a seizure EEG signal 1

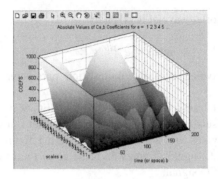

Fig. 3b. Morlet wavelet transform applied to a seizure EEG signal 2

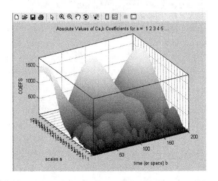

Fig. 3c. Morlet wavelet transform applied to a seizure EEG signal 3

It is observed from the results that the Morlet coefficients are significantly higher for EEG signals of seizure patients when compared to the normal EEG. Hence Morlet wavelet transform has proved to be an effective tool for seizure detection.

4   Conclusions

The results of this paper shows that the parameters estimates of EEG signals of seizure patients are comparatively higher than that of the EEG signal of the normal person. Also the Morlet transform coefficients of seizure EEG signal is much higher than the normal EEG signals. These methods can be used in automatic seizure detection using EEG signals.

References

1. Fisher, R., van Emde Boas, W., Blume, W., Elger, C., Genton, P., Lee, P., Engel, J.: Epileptic seizures and epilepsy: definitions proposed by the International League Against Epilepsy (ILAE) and the International Bureau for Epilepsy (IBE). Epilepsia 46(4), 470–472 (2005)

2. Carroll, L.: Mounting Data on Epilepsy Point to Dangers of Repeated Seizures, http://www.nytimes.com/2003/02/18/health/mounting-data-on-epilepsy-point-to-dangers-of-repeated-seizures.html
3. Sanei, S., Chambers, J.: EEG signal processing. Wiley-Interscience (2007)
4. Poliker, R.: The Wavelet Tutorial (1999)
5. Torrence, C., Compo, G.P.: A Practical Guide to Wavelet Analysis. American Meteorological Society

Evaluation of Classifier Models Using Stratified Tenfold Cross Validation Techniques

Swarnalatha Purushotham and B.K. Tripathy

SCSE VIT University, Vellore – 632 014, Tamilnadu, India
{pswarnalatha,tripathybk}@vit.ac.in

Abstract. One of the important datamining function is prediction. Many predictive models can be built for the data. The data may be continous, categorical or combination of both. For either of the above type of data many similar predictive models are available. So it is highly important to choose the possible best accurate predictive model for the user data . For this the models are evaluated using resampling techniques. The evaluated models gives statistical results respectively. These statistical results are analysed and compared . The appropriate model that gives maximum accuracy for the user data is used to do predictions for further data of same type. The predictions thus made by the suitable model can be visualized which forms the decision reports for the user data. A proposal is made to apply fuzzy rough set techniques for evaluation of classifier models [7].

Keywords: Dataset, Stratified Tenfold Cross Validation, Accuracy, Class label, Training data, Test data, Model induction, Model deduction.

1   Introduction

In today's Competitive Corporate world, Research field and Medicine it is highly necessary to make predictions for the huge available data in order to classify them into different categories. These data are taken in the form of dataset which is a collection of data in rows and columns, where each row is a set of data or instance. Prediction identifies to which class or value each instance belong to. The prediction is a single dependent value which is either a categorical or a continuous one for a single set of independent data or instance. Classification and Regression models are needed respectively to do such prediction. These models are built on a sample population and then used to do the prediction in the target population of the same domain. But again several classification and regression models are available. So it is very important for us to choose the appropriate Predictive model among several similar models, such that it produces the reliable predictions for the supplied data. For this predictive models are first constructed on a dataset and evaluated using resampling techniques which gives quantifiable statistical results. Finally Statistical analysis is done to obtain the possible best model. In this paper Classification models are taken into evaluation and analysis. These models does the categorical or nominal prediction only.

P.V. Krishna, M.R. Babu, and E. Ariwa (Eds.): ObCom 2011, Part II, CCIS 270, pp. 680–690, 2012.

Wherever Times is specified, Times Roman or Times New Roman may be used. If neither is available on your word processor, please use the font closest in appearance to Times. Avoid using bit-mapped fonts if possible. True-Type 1 or Open Type fonts are preferred. Please embed symbol fonts, as well, for math, etc.

Application of the Rough-set theory[11] which is a model that may be used to deal with categorical or nominal prediction of the data which involves uncertainty, may be applied to extract fuzzy-rules, reason with uncertainty and vagueness.

In a fuzzy rough set model, the membership function of the fuzzy set enables efficient handling of overlapping partitions of rough sets that deal with categorical or nominal prediction involving vagueness and incompleteness in class definition [7]. The integration of probabilistic and possibilistic membership functions of the FCM (fuzzy c-means) may provide the suitable model of the data.

2 Methodologies

Machine learning is the core technique in modeling. The goal of machine learning, is to build computer systems that can adapt and learn from their experience. Thus bringing in the concept of artificial intelligence. This technique is used in model induction or model training. A classifier is a function that maps an unlabelled instance to a label using internal data structures. An inducer or induction algorithm builds a classifier from a given dataset. In this paper we are not interested in the specific method for inducing classifiers, but assume access to a dataset and an inducer of interest [10].

Supervised learning is a machine learning technique for learning a function from training data. The training data consist of pairs of input objects (typically vectors), and desired outputs. The output of the function can be a continuous value (called regression), or can predict a class label of the input object (called classification). The task of the supervised learner is to predict the value of the function for any valid input object after having seen a number of training examples. This is model deduction.

For evaluation resampling techniques such as cross validation, bootstrap and holdout method are available. Resampling refers to repeated random sub sampling of data from the original dataset into training and test data. In our evaluation we use cross validation [9] to split the given data into training data and test data which are independent of each other. After splitting, build the model with training data and evaluate with the test set to get the accuracy rate and various supporting statistical results, which is helpful in comparing models and find the best classifier for the data.

2.1 Rough Sets

The notion of rough sets was introduced by Pawlak [6] in the year 1982 as an extension of the crisp sets. We provide below the definition of a rough set.

Let U ($\neq \emptyset$) be a finite set of objects, called the universe and R be an equivalence relation over U. By U/R we denote the family of all equivalence classes of R (or classification of U) referred to as categories or concepts of R and $[x]_R$ denotes a category in R containing an element x∈U. By a Knowledge base, we understand a relation system k= (U, R), where U is as above and R is a family of equivalence relations over U.

For any subset P ($\neq\varnothing$) ⊆ R, the intersection of all equivalence relations in P is denoted by IND (P) and is called the indiscernibility relation over P. The equivalence classes of IND (P) are called P- basic knowledge about U in K. For any Q∈R, Q is called a Q-elementary knowledge about U in K and equivalence classes of Q are called Q-elementary concepts of knowledge R. The family of P-basic categories for all $\varnothing \neq P$ ⊆R will be called the family of basic categories in knowledge base K. By IND (K), we denote the family of all equivalence relations defined in k. Symbolically, IND (K) = {IND (P): $\varnothing \neq P \subseteq R$}.

For any X⊆U and an equivalence relation R∈IND(K), we associate two subsets, $\underline{R}X = \bigcup\{Y \in U / R : Y \subseteq X\}$ and $\overline{R}X = \bigcup\{Y \in U / R : Y \cap X \neq \varnothing\}$, called the R-lower and R-upper approximations of X respectively. The R-boundary of X is denoted by $BN_R(X)$ and is given by $BN_R(X) = \overline{R}X - \underline{R}X$. The elements of $\underline{R}X$ are those elements of U which can be certainly classified as elements of X employing knowledge of R. The borderline region is the undecidable area of the universe. We say X is rough with respect to R if and only if $\underline{R}X \neq \overline{R}X$, equivalently $BN_R(X) \neq \varnothing$. X is said to be R-definable if and only if $\underline{R}X = \overline{R}X$, or $BN_R(X) = \varnothing$. So, a set is rough with respect to R if and only if it is not R-definable.

2.2   Fuzzy Sets

In his seminal paper published in 1965 [12], Lotfi A. Zadeh introduced the concept of Fuzzy sets, which uses the concept of graded membership of elements instead of dichotomous membership of crisp sets. Next, we define fuzzy sets below.

The most commonly used range of values of membership functions is the unit interval [0, 1]. We shall denote the membership function of a fuzzy set A by μ_A, which is defined as $\mu_A : U \rightarrow [0, 1]$, such that for each $x \in U, \mu_A(x) = \alpha, 0 \leq \alpha \leq 1$.

The membership function assigns values to elements in a specified range. This value indicates the grade of membership of the elements. The higher membership value indicates greater degree of membership.

Each fuzzy set is completely and uniquely defined by one particular membership function. The fuzzy membership functions are not only dependent upon the concept but also upon the context.

2.3   Fuzzy Rough Sets

In the beginning when rough sets were introduced by Pawlak in the early 1980s, these two theories were supposed to be rival theories. But it was established by Dubois and Prade [1] that instead of being rival theories, these two theories complement each other. In fact they combined these two concepts to develop the hybrid models of fuzzy rough seta and rough fuzzy sets.

The notion of fuzzy rough sets was introduced by Dubois and Prade [1] as follows. Let (U, R) be an approximation space. Then for any $X \in F(U)$, the lower and upper approximations of X with respect to R are given by

$$(\underline{R}X)(x) = \inf{}_{y \in [x]_R} X(y), \text{ for all } x \in U \text{ and} \tag{1}$$

$$(\overline{R}X)(x) = \sup{}_{y \in [x]_R} X(y), \text{ for all } x \in U. \tag{2}$$

3 Evaluation

Assume that there is a contest to design the best classifier on some sample data. The person running the contest must reserve test cases for judging the winner. These cases are not seen by any contestant until the end of the contest, when the classifiers are compared. The classifier that makes the fewest mistakes, i.e., the classifier with the lowest error rate, is declared the winner. Note that these hidden test cases are a special group of test cases. They are used strictly for determining the exact true error rate. During the contest, the contestants must proceed with the classifier design as if these test cases didn't exist. Having large numbers of hidden test cases is atypical of most real-world situations. Normally, one has a given set of samples, and one must estimate the true error rate of the classifier. Unless we have a huge number of samples, in a real-world situation, large numbers of cases will not be available for hiding. Setting aside cases for pure testing will reduce the number of cases for training. More the training data the performance of the classifier is better and also more the no of test data the estimation can be better.

Training and testing the data mining model requires the data to be split into at least two groups. If you do not use different training and test data, the accuracy of the model will be overestimated [3]. The resampling technique is applied to create mutually exclusive repeated training and test partitions. The particular resampling methods that should be used depend on the number of available samples. Here are the guidelines:

- For sample sizes greater than 100, use cross-validation. Either stratified 10-fold cross-validation [10] or leaving-one-out is acceptable.
- For samples sizes less than 100, use leaving-one-out.

10-fold is far less expensive computationally than leaving-one-out and can be used with confidence for samples numbering in the hundreds. This technique can be used as a standard estimation technique as various theoretical proof suggest that this method has low variance and better reliable accuracy for dataset of all sizes and it is unbiased.

Data is split into k subsets of equal size. The instances for each subset or fold are randomly selected. Each subset in turn is used for testing and the remainder for training a particular model. This training and testing is done for k times such that each subset is used once as the test set. The disadvantage of this method is that the training algorithm has to be rerun from scratch k times, which means it takes k times as much computation to make an evaluation. Thus we get k error estimates. In stratified tenfold cross validation, each fold is stratified so that they contain approximately the same proportion of class labels as the original dataset. By this variance among the estimates are reduced and the average error estimate is reliable. The test set is a group of labeled instances that were not used in the training process. So when the test set is deduced on a trained model, the model classifies the instances (model deduction). These classified instances are compared with actual labels and from this we deduce the accuracy and several misclassification details. The misclassification details are mentioned in detail in later part of the paper.

Accuracy of a classifier is defined as the number of correctly classified instances divided by total no of test instances taken. Error rate is calculated as (1- accuracy rate).

3.1   Significance Tests

Given a classier and an estimate of its error, the true error might be substantially higher or lower than the estimate. When the sampling distribution is skewed (asymmetric), as is usually the case for error rates, a correctly defined confidence interval is more informative than the standard deviation. Another way is to specify a confidence interval, a region which contains the relatively plausible values of the true error. One way to do this is to give the standard deviation of the estimate's sampling distribution. Statistical Inference is obtained from the evaluation methods. The topics dealt with in this module, a different aspect of statistical inference and hypothesis testing- "using sample information to answer questions about the population and the Inferred classifier".

One such question is whether the classifier correctly predicts the classes. The various methods for estimating error can be thought of as alternative methods for assessing the truth of the hypothesis that the classifier's predictions are correct. If we knew or assumed that the population data were free of any measurement, observation, or labeling errors, then the occurrence of a single prediction error would serve to refute the hypothesis. If we know or can reasonably assume that the population data are imperfect, as is typically the case, then a single prediction error is not sufficient to refute the hypothesis (it could be that the prediction is right and the data are wrong). In the latter circumstance, we must accept or reject the hypothesis based on an inference regarding the strength of the contradictory evidence relative to the reliability of our data.

Another hypothesis that we frequently wish to test is that the true errors of two alternative classifiers are different, i.e., that one classifier predicts more accurately than the other. This question is more conveniently posed as a test of the null hypothesis [2] that the true errors are equal. Again, typically we must accept or reject the hypothesis based on an inference regarding the strength of the contradictory evidence relative to the reliability of our data.

Thus, the ability to answer the following two questions is particularly important:

(1) How reliable is our estimated error, e.g., within what interval is the true error to be found with a 95% (or 99%) likelihood?
(2) Given another classifier having a different estimated error, how confident can we be that its true error is different from that of the first classifier?

3.2   Confidence Interval

With the estimated accuracy rate we can expect that the future true performance of this classifier will be around close to the estimated accuracy rate. But how far it is close? Within 5% TO 10%. So we have to perform various statistical analyses [2] on the results to get the confidence internal of the estimated accuracy rate. For this we use the Bernoulli trial, binomial distribution of Bernoulli trial and standard normal deviation method to find the confidence interval. With the confidence interval given for a particular classifier, the future predictions on the same model can deviate within these intervals, so that we can believe the predictions are mostly accurate.

If x is the number of correct predictions then accuracy, $f = x/N$, where N is the number of test instances. The true accuracy of model, p should be predicted. Accuracy has a normal distribution with mean p and variance, $p(1-p)/N$. For large enough N, f follows a normal distribution, $\Pr[-z \leq X \leq z] = c$. (c is confidence interval). It is necessary to reduce the random variable f to have 0 mean and unit variance. The normal distribution equation is shown described as $\Pr[-z < (f-p)/\sqrt{p(1-p)/N} < z] = c$. (c is the confidence interval).

With c=90% we find the corresponding z value from table and substitute in the following quadratic equation to find the true accuracy rate-p.

$$p = [f + z^2/2*N \pm z \sqrt{(f/n - f^2/N + z^2/4*N^2)}] / [1 + z^2/N] \qquad (3)$$

Thus, the confidence interval is obtained.

3.3   Model Comparison

When comparing two learning schemes by comparing the average error rate over several cross validations, we are effectively trying to determine whether the mean of set of samples- samples of cross validation estimate that is significantly greater than or significantly less than the mean of the other. The job for a statistical device known as the t- test, or Student's t test [5]. Because the same cross-validation split can be used for both methods to obtain a matched pair of results, one for each scheme, giving a set of pairs for different Cross validation splits, a more sensitive version of the t- test known as paired t – test can be used. The following procedural step explains the required models.

3.4   Procedure for Model Comparison

The individual samples are taken from the set of all possible cross-validation estimates. We can use a paired t-test because the individual samples are paired.

The same CV is applied twice. Let x1, x2, ..., x k and y1, y2, ..., yk be the 2k samples for a k-fold CV. The distribution of the means is as follows,

Let mx and may be the means of the respective samples. If there are enough samples, the mean of a set of independent samples is normally distributed .The estimated variances of the means are $\sigma x^2/k$ and $\sigma y ^2/k$. If μx and μy are the true means then mx - $\mu x/\sqrt{} \sigma x^2/k$, my - $\mu y /\sqrt{} \sigma y ^2/k$, are approximately normally distributed with 0 mean and unit variance. Let md=mx-my, The difference of the means (md) also has a Student's distribution with k-1 degrees of freedom. Let $\sigma d ^2$ be the variance of the difference. The standardized version of md is called t-statistic t= md/ $(\sqrt{}\sigma d^2)/k$. Fix a significance level α. Look up the value for z that corresponds to $\infty/2$. If t$\leq$-z or t$\geq$z then the difference is significant i.e., the null hypothesis can be rejected. There is significantly some difference between the accuracy of two predictive models else, null hypothesis is accepted. There is no real difference between the two predictive models.

3.5   Model Selection

A classic metric for reporting performance of machine learning algorithms is predictive accuracy. Accuracy reflects the overall correctness of the classifier and the overall error rate is (1 - accuracy). If both types of errors, i.e., false positives and false negatives, are not treated equally, a more detailed breakdown of the other error rates becomes necessary.

Accuracy has many disadvantages as a measure. These are its basic shortcomings:

- It ignores differences between error types
- It is strongly dependent on the class distribution (prevalence) in the dataset rather than the characteristics of examples.

Apart from accuracy, the misclassification cost should also be considered because a patient with a disease symptom predictive negative is of more risk compared to a patient with no such symptoms but predicted positive. Performance of a learning scheme includes many such statistics such as precision, recall (sensitivity), F-measure, true positive rate, false positive rate etc. Even these parameters are used to compare classifiers. This is considered to be second supervised learning.

The accuracy rate and its confidence interval are taken into consideration. The interval should not be very large as it suggests that the true accuracy rate can deviate widely. The following figure is confusion matrix showing the deviation of predictions from the actual class.

	C.P (C+)	C. N (C-)
P. P (R+)	T. P (TP)	F. P (FP)
P. N (R-)	F. N (FN)	T. N(TN)

Fig. 1. Confusion Matrix

C.P-Class Positive, C.N-Class Negative, P.P-Prediction Positive, P.N-Prediction Negative, T.P-True Positives, F.N-False Negatives, F.P-False Positives, T.N- True Negatives.

From the confusion matrix other statistics such as true positive rate or sensitivity or recall (the accuracy among positive instances and specificity among negative.) and true negative rate is calculated.

$$Sensitivity = TP/TP+FN = True\ Positive\ Rate \qquad (4)$$

$$Specificity = TN/TN+FP = True\ Negative\ Rate \qquad (5)$$

In the evaluation of information retrieval systems, the most widely used performance measures are recall and precision.

$$Calculation\ of\ Recall = TP/TP+FN = Sensitivity = True\ Positive\ Rate \qquad (6)$$

$$Calculation\ of\ Precision = TP/TP+FP \qquad (7)$$

Based on these misclassification costs and significance tests made the best appropriate model is selected.

3.6   Model Deduction

The best model from the above evaluation method is taken and it is supplied with a new test file whose instance class labels have to be predicted. The best model gives the appropriate prediction for the new data of the same domain, with the attribute type, name being the same with the original data on which the model was built. The predicted class value for each instance is displayed for the given test file. Fig 2 explains the model induction and deduction.

Task Classification

S.Id.	Var1	Var2	Var3	Class
1.	Yes	Large	125K	No
2.	No	Medium	100K	No
3.	No	Small	50K	No
4.	Yes	Medium	110K	No
5.	No	Large	95K	Yes
6.	No	Small	55K	Yes
7.	No.	Small	90K	Yes

Training Set

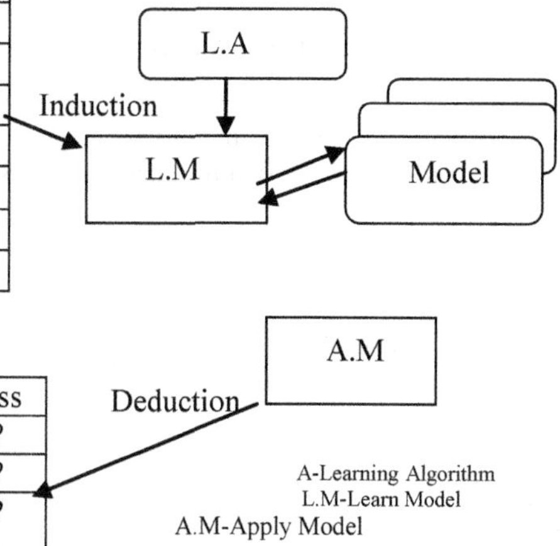

S.Id.	Var1	Var2	Var3	Class
8.	No	Small	55K	?
9.	Yes	Medium	100K	?
10	Yes	Large	95K	?

Test Set

Induction

L.A

L.M   Model

Deduction

A.M

A-Learning Algorithm
L.M-Learn Model
A.M-Apply Model

Fig. 2. Model induction and model deduction

4   Experimental Results

The dataset is taken as Comma Separated file format or Attribute Relation file format(*.arff). The same dataset is used to build different classifier models. The trained models are evaluated on the same resampling technique called stratified tenfold Cross Validation. The dataset used in our experiment is Iris dataset [4] which has 150 instances having three class labels (setosa/versicolor/virginica), each distributed in equal proportion. Three classifier models are taken into consideration namely Decision Stump, BF tree and J48. Their respective inducer algorithms are used to build the classifiers. All these models can predict nominal data. Cross validating these models produces the following output,

- Stratified cross validated estimates such as no of correctly and incorrectly classified instances, average accuracy rate, kappa static.
- Detailed accuracy by each class such as recall, precision, false positive rate, F-measure.
- Confusion matrix showing misclassification details as shown below for the iris dataset classification

a	b	c	<--	classified as
50	0	0 | a	=	Iris-setosa
0	46	4 | b	=	Iris-versicolor
0	5	45 | c	=	Iris-virginica

The following table shows comparative statistical details of three classifier models. The recall, precision and false positive rate are given for the three class labels – setosa, versicolor, virginica respectively under each misclassification.

Table 1. Statistical Comparison Chart for Three Models

Model	Accuracy rate (Confidence Interval)	Recall	Precision	False Positive Rate
J48	0.98 (0.94– 0.98)	0.98 0.94 0.96	1.0 0.94 0.96	0.0 0.03 0.03
Decision Stump	0.67 (0.62-0.72)	1.0 1.0 0.0	1.0 0.5 0.0	0.0 0.5 0.0
BF Tree	0.94 (0.92– 0.97)	1.0 0.93 0.91	1.0 0.91 0.92	0.0 0.06 0.05

After all these evaluation, the best predictive model is selected according to the interest of the application in which the model is going to be applied. In our experiment results J48 is chosen as the appropriate model because of higher accuracy, narrow confidence interval for the true accuracy rate, higher recall and deduced for a new test file whose class labels are to be predicted. Fig 3 shows unclassified instances of iris test dataset and fig 4 shows the classified iris set after model deduction.

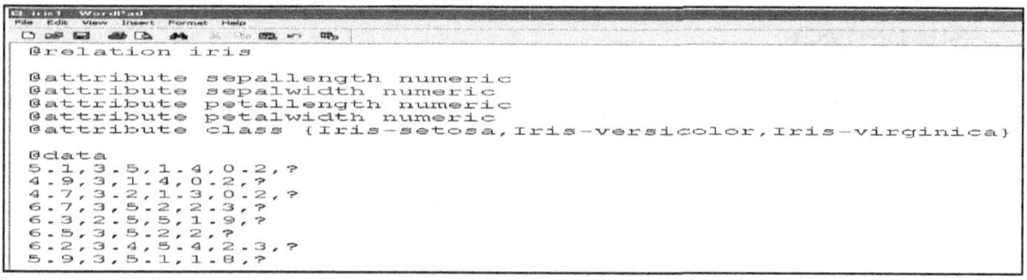

```
@relation iris

@attribute sepallength numeric
@attribute sepalwidth numeric
@attribute petallength numeric
@attribute petalwidth numeric
@attribute class {Iris-setosa,Iris-versicolor,Iris-virginica}

@data
5.1,3.5,1.4,0.2,?
4.9,3,1.4,0.2,?
4.7,3.2,1.3,0.2,?
6.7,3,5.2,2.3,?
6.3,2.5,5,1.9,?
6.5,3,5.2,2,?
6.2,3.4,5.4,2.3,?
5.9,3,5.1,1.8,?
```

Fig. 3. Iris test set unclassified

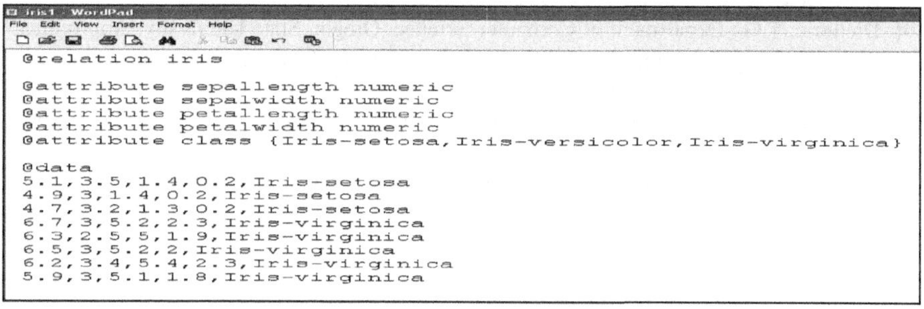

```
@relation iris

@attribute sepallength numeric
@attribute sepalwidth numeric
@attribute petallength numeric
@attribute petalwidth numeric
@attribute class {Iris-setosa,Iris-versicolor,Iris-virginica}

@data
5.1,3.5,1.4,0.2,Iris-setosa
4.9,3,1.4,0.2,Iris-setosa
4.7,3.2,1.3,0.2,Iris-setosa
6.7,3,5.2,2.3,Iris-virginica
6.3,2.5,5,1.9,Iris-virginica
6.5,3,5.2,2,Iris-virginica
6.2,3.4,5.4,2.3,Iris-virginica
5.9,3,5.1,1.8,Iris-virginica
```

Fig. 4. Iris test set classified by J48 Model

5 Conclusion

By this evaluation system the classifiers are compared statistically by significance tests [6] and provide an improved comparison schemes which gives more insight into the true error rate and misclassification costs. This provides a better evaluation methodology to choose the appropriate predictive model for the data and can make possible reliable predictions. For better results , we have proposed in this paper to apply rough-set theory which along with fuzzy set theory is used to deal with appropriate possible prediction models for the data which involves vagueness, etc.,.

References

[1] Dubois, D., Prade, H.: Rough fuzzy sets model. International Journal of General Systems 46(1), 191–208 (1990)

[2] Kibler, D., Langley, P.: Machine learning as an experimental science. In: Proc. of 1988 Euro. Working Session on Learning, pp. 81–92 (1988)

[3] Wolpert, D.: On the connection between insample testing and generalization error. Complex Systems 6, 47–94 (1992)

[4] Written, I.H., Frank, E.: Data Mining -Practical Machine Learning Tools and Techniques With Java Implementations, p. 371

[5] Gascuel, O., Caraux, G.: Statistical significance in inductive learning. In: Proc. of the European Conf. on Artificial Intelligence (ECAI), New York, pp. 435–439 (1992)

[6] Pawlak, Z.: Rough sets. International Jour. of Information and Computer Science 11, 341–356 (1982)

[7] Maji, P., Pal, S.K.: Rough Set Based Generalized Fuzzy C-Means Algorithm and Quantitative Indices. IEEE Transactions on Systems, Man, and Cybernetics-Part B, Cybernetics 37(6), 1529–1540 (2007)

[8] Murphy, P.M.: UCI repository of machine learning databases – a machinereadable data repository. Maintained at the Department of Information and Computer Science, University of California, Irvine (1995), Anonymous FTP from, ftp.ics.uci.edu. inthedirectorypub/machine-learning-databases

[9] Kohavi, R.: Computer Science Department, A Study of Cross-Validation and Bootstrap for Accuracy Estimation and Model Selection, Stanford University, Stanford, CA 94305, ronnyKGCS,Stanford EDU, KOHAVI, pp. 1137–1143

[10] Dietteric, T.G.: Department of Computer Science, Oregon State University, Approximate Statistical Tests for comparing Supervised Classification Learning Algorithms, Corvaellis OR 9733, December 30 (1997)

[11] Pawlak, Z.: Rough Sets, Theoretical Aspects of Reasoning about Data. Kluwer, Dordrecht (1991)

[12] Zadeh, L.A.: Fuzzy Sets. Information and Control 11, 338–353 (1965)

Hybrid Approach for Construction of Summaries and Clusters of Blog Data for Improved Blog Search Results

K. Saravanakumar and K. Deepa

VIT University, Vellore, Tamilnadu, India
{ksaravanakumar,deepa.k}@vit.ac.in

Abstract. The data are noisy in blogs, because blog entries are unstructured and might cover a wide variety of topics. However, because of the number of blogs exist, manually viewing and examining them is a difficult and time-consuming task. Intuitively, you could apply existing text and Web mining techniques to blog analysis and mining. But, because of the existence of various challenges, we can't directly apply these techniques. The bloggers update their information content on the blogs much more frequently than Web masters update traditional Web pages, often daily or even hourly. Above all, bloggers cover very diverse topics, so maybe only one paragraph in a particular entry could relate to someone's topic of interest. In this paper we propose an architecture which takes a query from the user, process through blog parser and extract content from the blog page. Then we identify the sentences which should be taken for further processing using a blog analyzer and finally summarizing the content based on the analysis results. The process is repeated for all the blogs and results in the summarized output of clustered blogs.

Keywords: Information Retrieval, Blog mining, text summarization.

1 Introduction

Blogs, the blend of the terms web and log, are frequently updated, and is a type of website or part of website, which is a part of fast growing Internet. Blogs are given much importance, because they offer every users of WWW a place to post their thoughts easily and thus become a journal. Nowadays, Blogs are the right place for the internet users to convey their ideas, opinions, problems, etc. This kind of growth of blogs opened up a lot of new opportunities in social study. Numerous researchers have examined weblogs, especially addressing their social aspects. Bloggers read other different blogs and leave comments and also send trackbacks as they update their blogs based on others. Users might mention other blogs in their postings, and express their suggested contacts in blogs. These activities present a record of multiple relationships among blogs, which is an interesting source of information to identify the user behavior, their interests and information diffusion. While in the previous days, researchers in the area of social study had to extend huge efforts in data collection. Today, it is very easy to get the data from internet as most of them available free. An example could be the

P.V. Krishna, M.R. Babu, and E. Ariwa (Eds.): ObCom 2011, Part II, CCIS 270, pp. 691–700, 2012.
© Springer-Verlag Berlin Heidelberg 2012

collection of public thoughts from the blogosphere by issuing articles and comments on a specific subject during specified time. However, the size of the results we get as opinions highly need analysis and summarization. In [8], the blogs are used for product reviews, by getting user persuasions. It may be cumbersome to get such analysis from different user to present to the buyer. Hence, [8] discusses a strategy to analyze blogs related to computers only.

In this paper, we are proposing an unsupervised approach which selects topic-related words and searches the related topic in the blogosphere. This topic related search proposed in [1] uses the number of topic-related words in a paragraph as an identifier for the strength of containing a reason. Each reason is then evaluated for the semantic orientation by the system. In our architecture it undergoes different steps for extraction of fact and summarized information from blogs. The Blog parser extracts the content of the blog. The Blog analyzer generates the semantic dependency graph between the sentences in the blog. The three main tasks in Blog analyzer are reason extraction, sentiment classification, and reason clustering. However, a reason can be expressed in many different ways. Sometimes, a reason can span across sentences to explain. That is why we use paragraphs as the unit for recognizing reasons. Sentiment classification, or polarity identification, is more difficult than that for a single sentence because there are more ways to express positions [1]. The reason for clustering is about providing better classification for the reasons extracted from blogs about a topic.

Summarizer module scores each sentence in the blog and picks top 30 percent of high scored sentences. In [2, 10] paradigms proposed for extracting salient sentences from text using features like word and phrase frequency position in the text and key phrases to summarize scientific documents. Many approaches addressed the problem by building systems depending of the type of the required summary. In [2], the summarization is categorized as extractive, which is mere extraction of sentences, and abstractive which produces grammatical summary. The later usually requires advanced language generation techniques.

For the successful evaluation which can lead the research direction in the future, there are many different evaluations systems exist, like, TREC, DUC and MUC. They have created large sets of training documents and have established baselines for performance evaluation. However, we are still missing a universal strategy to evaluate summarization systems is still absent. Fact Extractor module processes each sentence and evaluates whether it contains any fact. Clustering is an important method for searching and extracting useful knowledge from massive blog text data in a huge number of the blog websites spread in the world [3]. A blog document consists of three text blocks i.e. title, body, and comments. They play different roles in presenting the topics and opinions of blog pages. For blog data, the features groups are formed through extracting the features from each text block. In clustering, the features groups are treated differently to reflect their roles in page characterization. We collect the output of the above module and cluster the obtained information of different blogs. The rest of the paper organized with related work as the second topic, followed by the proposed framework. The obtained results are discussed in experimental results section. Finally, it is concluded with the future work.

2   Related Work

Blog analysis can be done by three main tasks which are reason extraction, sentiment classification, and reason clustering. For editorial reviews, reason extraction is more or less same to the subjective or objective separation problem. The population of words in a given paragraph can be utilized as the mean of how strong the given paragraph could contain a reason. In [1], LODR score is used to find the topic related words. In Sentiment classification, the lexicons in General Inquirer are compiled by experts to give their properties as labels. They have included a total of 11788 words in the vocabulary, while only 4206 words are labeled with positive or negative tags, which are their properties. To evaluate the opposed words to more grade level, they used Turney's point wise mutual information (PMI) as the similarity measure of two words in [1]. This comparison would be used to verify the effectiveness of words identified. Processing comments on the blog is another very useful source of information which plays a very important role in judging about the prestige of the blog as well as the rating of the blog. Some of the comments which are harsh should lead towards the decline in the rating of the product and vice-versa should also hold true.

For the special characters of blog pages, blogger's role may be used to represent semantic meaning between blogger and query. In [5], described a way to extract the blog role and role features from semantic dictionary WorldNet then we compute document relevance probability by the blogger role and the classical retrieval by iterative algorithm. Matrix factorization [4, 9] is another common tool researcher's use for knowledge discovery in blogs. This technique involves decomposing a matrix into some canonical form. Many different matrix decompositions exist, such as LU decomposition, singular value decomposition (SVD), Cholesky decomposition, and QR decomposition, and each is useful for particular problems.

Blogs which are retrieved as an effect of a given query must be ranked and given to the user to have a better outlook [6]. Ranking blogs is quite similar to ranking Web pages. We have well known algorithms Page Rank and Hypertext Induced Topic Selection (HITS) for Webpage ranking that exploit the link structure between such pages. These algorithms focus on a directed graph setting that describes resources via nodes and hyperlinks. The link based algorithms might not do well for blogs because blogs aren't properly structured and completely linked to one another on their relatedness. Bloggers may try to exploit such a system to hike the rank of their blog. Clustering assigns a set of observations to subsets, referred to as clusters, such that observations in the same cluster are similar according to pre specified criteria. The text block structure information is considered in blog clustering in [14], where they have used mean TFIDF method as the feature selection method. In this, a weight is manually assigned to the different feature groups like title, body, etc. before clustering. But, it is known difficult task. Partition algorithms typically determine all clusters at once but can also act as divisive algorithms in hierarchical clustering [6]. Clustering techniques might involve users to note the number of groups the technique should produce from the input data set. An important measure in clustering is to select an appropriate distance measure, which can ascertain how algorithm calculates groups' similarity.

3   Proposed Framework

We have proposed a framework for the summarized output pertaining to a query of different blogs is shown in the Figure 1. The framework comprises the following.

3.1   Blog Parser

Blog parser takes the URL of a blog and extracts the text out of the blog web page. The blog parser considers the content that is present in the paragraph tags in the html code of the blog page as most of the compiled information could be found in there and also to define a boundary to avoid complication. All the advertisement contents and other noise information such as member information, contributions, and other related blog information, etc. are eliminated from the page to improve the validity of the extracted data.

3.2   Blog Miner

Blog miner finds the candidate words in each sentence in the extracted paragraph. To find the candidate words, the words other than the common conjunctions like is, a, an, was, the etc. (listed as stop words to improve the accuracy in weighing a word), in the paragraph is extracted and counted the number of times it has appeared in the paragraph. The frequency of each word in a given document is attached to that word. We count the frequencies of all the words and find the maximum and minimum values and we calculate the average frequency using the Gaussian function.

$$X - \left(\frac{\mu}{\sum^{\square}\square} \right) \tag{1}$$

Where X is number of words and μ is the mean of words and $\sum$ is the variance. Average frequency helps to improve the selection of relevant candidate words over just selection of a word as candidate word. Figure 2 shows the architecture of the words processing in the Blog miner. After calculating the average frequency, we extract the words that have the frequency greater than or equal to the average frequency from each sentence of extracted text. This might help in identifying the important words which are called as candidate words. It can be a flaw in case the document contains unnecessary repetition of the words.

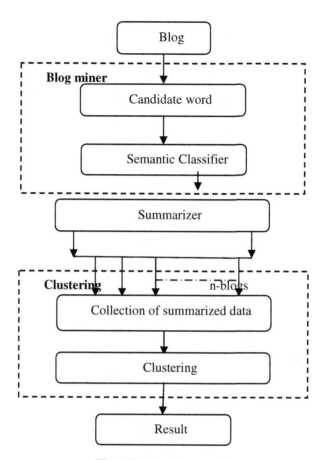

Fig. 1. Proposed Framework

After identifying the candidate words, a graph is constructed by considering each candidate word as a node of the graph [9, 11]. To complete the graph, each and every node is connected to other nodes. Next, we calculate the semantic distance between set of nodes (candidate words) in the graph using the measure of Jiang and conrath [13]. The difference between the information content of the individual concepts and that of their lowest common subsume will reveal how similar they are. If the sum of their individual information is close to that of their lowest subsume, then it suggests that the measure are located close together in the concept hierarchy. Thus they take the sum of the information content of the individual concepts and subtract from that the information content of their lowest common subsume. To find the overall distance between two nodes, when only the link strength is taken in the weighting scheme as a special case, the distance function can be given as follows.

$$\text{dist}_\text{j}\text{cn} \ (c_i 1, c_i 2) = \text{IC}(c_i 1) + \text{IC}(c_i 2) - 2 \text{''} \times \text{IC} \ (\text{lcs}(\text{''} \ c_i 1, c_i 2)) \quad (2)$$

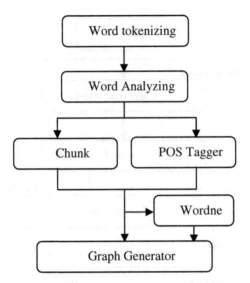

Fig. 2. Word processing in the Blog Miner

Where c1, c2 are the two concepts, IC, the information content of the concept, and lcs (c1, c2), the least common subsume of c1 and c2. Since this is a distance measure, concepts that are more similar have a lower score than less similar ones.

In order to maintain consistency among the measures, we convert this measure to semantic similarity by taking its inverse:

$$\text{sim}_{jcn}(c_1, c_2) = \frac{1}{\text{dist}_{jcn}(c_1, c_2)} \tag{3}$$

We will get a real number as result if both words have similarities. Otherwise 0(zero) will be assigned as the edge value. A part of a constructed graph is shown in Figure 3.

3.3   Summarizer

For summarizing the content, we first calculate the weight of each node in the graph. For this, the degree of the nodes, i.e., the edges present, of each node is counted. The weight of a node is calculated by summing up the weights of all the connecting edges in the graph to that node. With the following equation we calculate the weight of each node

$$W_n = \sum_{i=1}^{d} W_i \tag{4}$$

Where W_n is weight of the node, W_i is the weight of the graph and d is the degree of the node. The above stated procedure is repeated for all the nodes in the graph. Once the weights of all the candidate words are found, we calculate the score of each sentence. This is done by considering the weights of the candidate words present in that sentence and we add the weights so we can have the score of the sentence. Then we took the top 30% of the sentences based on the score for summary.

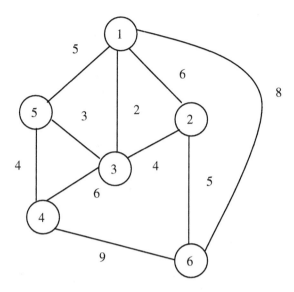

Fig. 3. The graph for calculating the distance between words

3.4   Clustering

For each blog in the collection as a result for a given query, we collected the summarized output. This is done for n blogs. This process is divided into two parts namely, collection of summarized from n number of blogs and, clustering the obtained summarized data. In the clustering process, we take all the summarized data from each blog and we cluster the documents using the Bisecting K-means clustering algorithm [15]. This is done by picking a cluster to split (split the largest). Then find 2 sub-clusters using the basic K-means algorithm. This step is repeated until the split that produces the clustering with the highest overall similarity. All the above steps in Bisecting K-means algorithm is repeated until the desired number of clusters is reached.

4   Experimental Results

We have taken search queries given by user to search a topic of their interest. We use the search result given by a blog search engine. The result blogs are taken as the input for our proposed approach. Finally we obtain summarized and clustered results from different blogs. In our experiment we used 200 different search keys used by different users of a search engine. Some of the keys are listed in the table 1 and we limited the obtained URL's to 10 for each dataset from the search engine. Table 1 lists the Query numbers for each query that was taken, and also the number of words and number of sentences each dataset has given when the framework is run.

4.1   Evaluation of the Summaries

It has been tested to find out the nearness of the constructed summaries to that of the queries given. Hence, we have tested the precision and recall for the summaries which are part of our results. Let NRS_{Doc} -the number of relevant sentences in the document, NRS_{Sum} -the number of relevant sentences in the summary, NS_{Sum} -the number of sentences in the summary. Then $Precision_{Sum}$ and $Recall_{Sum}$ can be calculated as follows:

$$Precision_{Sum} = \frac{NRS_{Sum}}{NS_{Sum}} \tag{5}$$

$$Recall_{Sum} = \frac{NRS_{Sum}}{NRS_{Doc}} \tag{6}$$

Table 1. Index of the input queries and the number of words obtained and the number of sentence it contained after the summarization

Query No	Query	Number of words	Number of sentences	$Precision_{Sum}$ (%)
1	Micheal Jackson	2508	74	81.08
2	Sachin Tendulkar	1249	36	83.33
3	Indian Politics	1783	59	62.33
4	Tamilnadu elections	2045	70	78.57
5	Anna hazare's lok pal bill	3089	90	74.41
6	Effects of global warming	2832	78	96.15
7	Western culture affecting Indian culture	3218	94	79.01
8	Science Fiction	1982	61	81.05
9	2G Scam in India	1046	51	90.04
10	Egypt crisis effect on India	`834	38	79.15

Finally, Table 2 gives the details about the identified clusters by the proposed approach. If a query is given as input, the result is the different number of clusters. For example, in query 1, there are two clusters. That is, <1, 2, 3> is one cluster, and <4> is another cluster. Here, 1, 2, 3, etc. are the result URLs suggested by search engine as the result of search key.

Table 2. Clusters of documents and their relevancy to the given query

Query No.	Clusters (Document numbers are given)			Relevant Clusters	Non-relevant Clusters
	C1	C2	C3		
1	1, 2, 3, 7	4, 6, 10	5, 8, 9	C1, C3	C2
2	1, 4, 5	2, 3, 7, 8	6, 9, 10	C3	C1, C2
3	1, 2	3, 4, 6, 8, 9	5, 7, 10	C1	C2, C3
4	1, 3, 6, 7	2, 4, 5	8, 9, 10	C3	C1, C2
5	1, 3, 4	2, 5, 6, 7	8, 9, 10	C1, C3	C2
6	1, 3, 4, 5	2, 6, 7	8, 9, 10	C1	C2, C3
7	1, 2, 3, 4	5, 6, 9	7, 8, 10	C1	C2, C3
8	1, 4, 5	2, 3	6, 7, 8, 9, 10	C2, C3	C1
9	1, 3	2, 4, 5, 6, 7	8, 9, 10	C1	C2, C3
10	1, 2, 4	3, 7, 10	5, 6, 8, 9	C3	C1, C2

5   Conclusion and Future Work

With the rapid growth of blogosphere, numerous blogs have come into existence. Reading the blog content from this huge information source becomes more and more difficult and staggering. Summarization and clustering the blog content, serves as a tool to facilitate users to read different summarized blogs of the same topic. The purpose of this research is to develop a hybrid approach for blog summarization tasks. Our proposed approach combines the text summarization term weighting scheme, which bases itself on a mathematical (probabilistic) ground, and the linguistic technique that explores term relationships by finding the connective strength of relationship between the words that signifies term and sentence semantics. Two experiments are conducted to verify our proposed approach. Results of Experiment I show the number of words and sentences obtained after the summarization Experiment II show percentage of relevance obtained in clustering the documents. The results obtained helps to reduce the fatigue in choosing the correct site through the summary we have given.

Even though the proposed method helps us to summarize a big content, it fails in clustering the summaries correctly. As we are not using the measure for calculating the semantic similarity, we ended with such incorrect results for some cases. We would like to improve the performance by improving the clustering of the documents as part of our future work, so that we could achieve more than 90 percent. When we incorporate semantic similarity between two documents, it could be possible to cluster them more clearly than proposed.

References

1. Chang, C.-H., Tsai, K.-C.: Aspect summarization from blogosphere for social study. In: Seventh IEEE International Conference on Data Mining Workshops, pp. 9–14 (2007)
2. Das, D., Martins, A.F.T.: A Survey on Automatic Text Summarization, Language Technologies, Institute Carnegie Mellon University (November 21, 2007)
3. Li, H., Ye, Y., Huang, J.Z.: Improved blog clustering through Automated Weighting of text Blocks. In: Proceedings of Eighth International Conference on Machine Learning and Cybernetics, Baoding, July 12-15, pp. 1586–1591 (2009)
4. Koren, Y., Bell, R., Volinksy, C.: Matrix factorization techniques for recommender systems, pp. 30–37. IEEE Computer Society (2009)
5. Michael Chau, L., Lam, P., Shiu, B., Xu, J., Cao, J.: A Blog Mining Framework. IEEE IT Pro., 36–41 (January/February 2009)
6. Lakshmanan, G.T., Oberhofer, M.A.: Knowledge Discovery in the Blogosphere Approaches and Challenges. IEEE Internet Computing, 24–32 (2010)
7. Lin, D., Cao, D., Li, S.: Mining Relation between the Blogger and Query in Blog Retrieval System. In: Proceedings of 2008 3rd International Conference on Intelligent System and Knowledge Engineering, pp. 267–272 (2008)
8. Chatterjee, N., Agarwal, N.: Ranking Products through Interpretation of Blogs Based on Users' Query. In: International Conference on Methods and Models in Computer Science, pp. 1–4 (2009)
9. Sornil, O., Greeut, K.: An Automatic Text Summarization Approach using content-Based and Graph-Based Characteristics. In: IEEE International Conference, pp. 1–6 (2006)

10. Alguliev, R.M., Alguliyev, R.M.: Effective Summarization Method of Text Documents. In: Proceedings of 2005 IEEE/WIC/ACM International Conference on Web Intelligence, pp. 264–271 (2005)
11. Thakkar, K.S., Dharaskar, R.V., Chandak, M.B.: Graph-Based Algorithms for Text Summarization. In: IEEE Third International Conference on Emerging Trends in Engineering and Technology, pp. 516–519 (2010)
12. Chang, T.-M., Hsiao, W.-F.: A hybrid approach to automatic text summarization. In: IEEE International Conference, pp. 65–70 (2008)
13. Jiang, J., Conrath, D.: Semantic similarity based on corpus statistics and lexical taxonomy. In: Proceedings on International Conference on Research in Computational Linguistics, Taiwan, pp. 19–33 (1997)
14. Li, B., Xu, S., Zhang, J.: Enhancing Clustering Blog Documents by Utilizing Author/Reader Comments. In: Proceedings of the 45th Annual Southeast Regional Conference, Winston-Salem, pp. 94–99 (March 2007)
15. Kashef, R., Kamel, M.S.: Enhanced bisecting k-means clustering using intermediate cooperation. Pattern Recognition 42, 2557–2569 (2009)

Performance Evaluation of IEEE 802.11e Based Wireless LAN in Multi Service Environments

M. Singaravelan

VIT University

Abstract. IEEE 802.11 based wireless local area network (WLAN) is widely used due to cheaper cost and easy installation features. Now-a-days voice over IP (VOIP) is becoming more popular because VOIP stream already has WLANS as access network to the internet. Current WLANS provide only best-effort services without QOS guarantees. Enhancement of QOS is the key challenge in WLAN. IEEE 802.11e is enhanced a MAC protocol for QoS. In this paper we analyze the performance of IEEE 802.11e based network in multi service environments such as real time VOIP and elastic data services in a single WLAN. We observe the QOS parameters using HCF enabled with EDCA. Our OPNET based simulation results show that traffic delay and throughput of one class of service are affected by the characteristics of other class of traffic. We observed that the throughput increase of around 80% over the existing standards and enormous decrease in end to end delay.

Keywords: We would like to encourage you to list your keywords in this section.

1   Introduction

Next generation communication looks forward to pervasive ubiquitous all IP-based networks. Many current generation networks are expected to converge in IP suite to multimedia and multi services support. Voice and video are require a certain minimum data rate and suffer significantly from high delay and jitter. WLAN is supporting a Voice-over-IP in corporate network and it is allowing the deployment of network services without disturbing the available infrastructure but 802.11 WLAN's could be provided a limited degree of QoS. The quality of service can be provided by introducing Hybrid Co-ordination function (HCF) in IEEE 802.11e. Two Schemes have introduced in the enhancement version that is The Enhanced Distributed Channel Access (EDCA) and the Hybrid Co-ordination Function (HCF) Controlled Channel Access (HCCA). In this paper we have addressed the QoS issue in an integrated network having HTTP and VoIP applications. Improvement of performance is demonstrated with the fine tuning of the QoS parameters. We observe the VoIP performance through WLAN under increasing HTTP traffic [3]. The results show that there the traffic must be limited in WLAN to provide threshold VoIP performance through WLAN [7].

P.V. Krishna, M.R. Babu, and E. Ariwa (Eds.): ObCom 2011, Part II, CCIS 270, pp. 701–708, 2012.
© Springer-Verlag Berlin Heidelberg 2012

2   IEEE 802.11 WLAN

Physical and Media Access Control (MAC) layer in OSI reference model covers the IEEE802.11 standard of WLAN model. Distributed Coordination Function (DCF) and Optional coordination function are operating on the MAC Layer for medium access control function [8](PCF).

A. Point Coordination Function (PCF)

PCF works on the principle of polling. Here the central coordinator (in our case, the access point) polls the stations present in LAN and provides them contention free access to the channel. PCF can not be used for prioritized traffic, which is necessary for VoIP applications. So, we will not use PCF in our performance analysis [8].

B. Distributed Coordination Function (DCF)

DCF is using carrier sense multiple access and collision avoidance CSMA/CA protocol [8] for shared medium access for both Adhoc and Infrastructure network. It is using an asynchronous transmission in 802.11 networks. Before attempting to transmit each station (STA) in the network need to check the medium whether it is idle. If it sensed as idle in the DIFS (Distributed Inter frame Space) period the STA starts transmitting the packet immediately. In the same time the other station adjusting their NAV and start the back off timer for getting the different transmission slot and Decrement the back off interval counter while the medium is idle. The STA's now computes a random time interval called backofftime selected from the Contention Window (CW).

BACK OFF TIME=RANDOM()X A SLOT TIME

Random () - is a number drawn from the interval [0,CW] of the uniform distribution The range of CW is;aCWmin<=CW<=CWmax.

3   IEEE 802.11e MAC QOS Enhancement

While comparing to the wired network WLAN has some unique features. In WLAN data rate could be varied based of the interference and error rate. The quality of real-time voice and video transmission [1] is based on the delay and jitters. These delays and jitters are caused by the high collision rate and frequent retransmission in wireless channel.

A. QOS Support in IEEE 80.11e

802.11e is having two types of QoS. Firstly, it is based on the priority wise effort service similar to Diffserv and secondly, it is providing parameterized QoS for the benefit of applications requiring QoS for different flows. DCF and PCF functionality is enhanced in IEEE 802.11e such as EDCF and EPCF and by providing a signaling mechanism for parameterized QoS. EDCF and EPCF are called as Hybrid Coordinated Functions (HCF)[2]. Differentiation in the priority is achieved by setting different probabilities for different categories for winning the channel contention. The probability can be changed by varying the values of Arbitration Inter Frame Space (AIFS), where AIFS is the listen interval for channel contention. AIFS determines the priority based on the traffic, with lower priority value, the listen interval required for channel contention is lower and hence the probability of winning the channel contention is higher.

B. QOS Support in IEEE 80.11e

QoS enhance Basic Service Set (QBSS) is used by a single coordination function called hybrid coordination function (HCF). The HCF is composed of two channel access mechanisms:

1) A contention based channel access referred to as the enhanced distributed channel access (EDCA); which provides distributed access method[2].
2) A controlled channel access referred to as the HCF controlled channel access (HCCA), which is controlled by the hybrid coordinator (HC). IEEE 802.11e defines other new features to give better QoS performance. A transmission opportunity (TXOP) is a bounded time interval reserved for a specific STA. If the frame length is shorter than the TXOP, the station is allowed to send as many frames as it can during its TXOPs. If the frame length is larger than the TXOP, the station must fragment the large frame into smaller blocks each of which can be sent in the length of TXOP[2].

4   Enhanced Distributed Channel Access (EDCA)

A. Prioritized Scheduling

EDCA is using in WLAN for QoS , and it supports DiffServ such as priority based best-effort service. Four access categories(ACs) has been introduced for providing the prioritized QoS. The differentiation in priority between ACs is achieved by setting different values for the AC parameters. These priority parameters are:

1) **Arbitrary Inter-Frame Space Number (AIFSn):** It is the minimum time interval between the wireless medium becoming idle and the start of transmission of a frame[2].
2) **Contention Window (CW):** A random number is drawn from this interval, or window, for the backoff mechanism. The medium access function in each station maintains a backoff . Min CW and Max CW has higher probability to draw a smaller random number, thus it is given higher priority.

Backoff=AIFS+random[CWmin:CWmax]

AIFS determines the priority with time as follows.

AIFS[AC] = AIFSN[AC] * aSlotTime + SIFS

Arbitration Interframe Space(AIFS) time period, the STA must sense the channel is idle before the message transmission. and then restrains itself from transmitting for a random length of time known as Back off (Bn). The value of AIFS and Bn depends on the AC of the traffic to be transmitted. Where the smallest AIFS is having the highest priority AC, and the largest AIFS is having the lowest priority traffic. This means that the highest priority traffic is more quickly accessing the channel. For each AC , EDCA uses the CW to assign priority. In most cases a high priority AC are assign a short CW ,high priority AC is able to transmit ahead of low priority one. For each AC the size of the CW also varies . The CW size determines for how long a node will backoff before attempting to gain access to the channel.

The equations below clearly shows the calculation of back-off times

802.11 : CWRANGE = [0 , 2 2+i − 1]
802.11e : newCW[AC] = [(oldCW[AC] + 1) * PF] − 1

B. EDCA Access Mechanism in IEEE 802.11e

IEEE 802.11e provides the enhancement of the quality of service to the 802.11 MAC by using distributed access mechanism called Enhanced Distributed Channel Access (EDCA).There are some situation where the real time data must be given higher priority for transmition where we have to provide different services such that faster access to the channel must be given to the real time data or the traffic classes with higher priorities [1]. This can be achieved by assigning different CSMA/CA access parameters for each traffic category [7]. This is show in the fig 1.

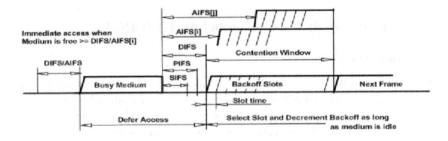

Fig. 1. EDCA Channel Access Timing Operation

Those include the parameters that regulate the contention window size like minimum contention window size (CWmin), maximum contention window size (CWmax) and persistent factor (PF) and the inter frame space called as Arbitrary Inter Frame Space (AIFS)[5]. Each backoff entity with in the stations contends for a TXOP independently. It starts down-counting the backoff counter after detecting the channel being idle for an Arbitration Inter Frame Space Duration (AIFSD [AC]). The AIFSD [AC] is at least PIFS, and can be enlarged per AC with the help of the parameter Arbitration Inter Frame Space (AIFS [AC]). The AIFS [AC] defines the duration of AIFSD [AC]

AIFSD [AC] = SIFS + AIFS [AC]* A Slot Time, where $1 \leq$ AIFS [AC] ≤ 10 The smaller AIFS [AC], the higher the channel access priority [7].

Another EDCF parameter is the minimum size of the contention window, CWmin [AC], and is dependent on the AC. The initial value for the backoff counter is a random number taken from an interval defined by the contention window (CW), similar to legacy DCF. The contention window may be the initial minimum size CWmin [AC], or higher values. In case packet transmission failures occurred, entity selects its counter as random number drawn from the interval [1, CW + 1].

After every unsuccessful attempt to transmit occurs the contention window size is increased that is new contention window size is set. The new CW size[7] is calculated by using scaling factor(PF).The following formula can be used to calculate the Contention window size

$$CWnew = (PF \times (CWold+1))-1$$

The table 1 shows the different ACs for the different AIFS.

In the EDCA architecture different queues are maintained according to the traffic categories that are each traffic category having its own queue. Figure. 2 shows the implementation model architecture of the mapping from higher layers into TC queues, each with their own channel access functions and virtual internal collision resolution [4].

STA can initiate a Transmission Opportunity (TXOP) once it has gained access to the medium. It is a bounded duration time interval in which the STA may perform frame bursting where a sequence of SIFS-separated data and ACK frames are exchanged [6].

In the fig, 2 four ACs are implemented within QSTA to support 8 priorities. Multiple ACs contends independently and the winning AC transmits the frame [1].

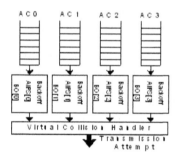

Fig. 2. EDCA Implementation Architecture

5   Network Model

A. Network Architecture

In fig:3 there are 9 Work stations running voice applications as voice data source and they are calling 5 workstations configured as voice destinations. The voice application is configured to generate G.711 encoded voice traffic at 64kbps. There are 4 workstations running HTTP web browsing application. All the voice source and destination nodes belong to the BSS and hence all the voice traffic has to flow through AP. similarly HTTP clients connect their server node through the Access point.

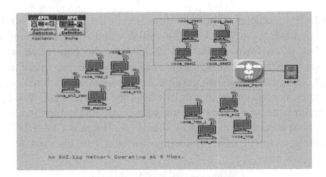

Fig. 3. WLAN Infrastructure Network

A. Network Architecture

Scenario 1: In the first scenario we have created the baseline infrastructure BSS (WLAN 11g) operating at 6Mbps with WLAN workstations running voice and HTTP application and measured the network performance observed at application layer. The setting is done as follows.

• The physical characteristics are given by Extended Rate PHY (802.11g).
• The data rate is 6Mbps and the HCF parameters are disabled.

Scenario 2: In the second scenario we have introduced 802.11e QoS functionality where HCF functionality is enabled for all WLAN nodes with Default EDCA (Enhanced Distributed Channel Access) parameters. The setting is done as follows.

• The second scenario 'WLAN_11e' for all the WLAN workstations we will enable HCF such that it is IEEE 802.11e capable and keep all the HCF parameters settings default.
• Then we have enabled QoS prioritization at the WLAN layer, Voice and HTTP traffic will be mapped to the WLAN voice and Best Effort access categories, respectively.

Scenario 3: In the third Performance tuning for 802.11e network is done. We have changed the EDCF parameters based on the network and traffic condition .Acknowledgement policies for the traffic categories corresponding to the application traffic are also changed to obtain better QoS. The setting is done as follows.

• AP is configured to use larger CWmax for voice service. CWmax is set to "15".
• Set service class of the voice traffic category to "No Acknowledgement" on AP' and make the same configuration to all Work stations.
• Promote the HTTP traffic from Best Effort to a Higher WLAN Access Category (Streaming Multimedia).

Scenario 4: In the Fourth Performance tuning for 802.11e network is done. We have changed the EDCF parameters based on the network and traffic condition .Acknowledgement policies for the traffic categories corresponding to the application traffic are also changed to obtain better QoS. Settings in fourth scenario:-

• AP is configured to use larger CWmax for voice access categories. Here the CWmin is set to "1" and CWmax is set to "255". • The other step to configure the scenario 4 is the same procedure that was followed for scenario 3.

time (sec)	voice_11e_better	voice_11e_default	voice_baseline	voice_baseline
1.2	891.4286	891.4286	891.4286	891.4286
3.4	780	780	780	780
6.6	693.3333	693.3333	693.3333	693.3333
10.8	624	624	624	624
12	567.2727	567.2727	567.2727	567.2727
13.2	520	520	520	520
14.4	480	480	480	480
15.6	445.7143	445.7143	445.7143	445.7143
16.8	416	416	416	416
18	390	390	390	390
19.2	367.0588	367.0588	367.0588	367.0588
20.4	346.6667	346.6667	346.6667	346.6667

6   Results

The following graphs were obtained after collecting statistics on OPNET. The graph shows a comparative picture of the four scenarios and provides an evident improvement in performance of the third and fourth scenario.

From fig. 4(a) and fig 4(b) we can observe that the delay for the third and fourth scenario is low when compared to the other scenarios. From the result, the scenario without HCF has the highest end to end delay.

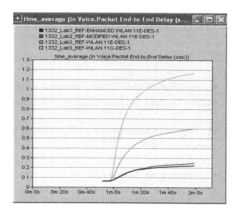

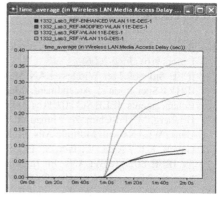

Fig. 4(a). Voice packet end to end delay

Fig. 4(b). Wireless LAN Media Access delay

From the above two statistics we can say that with the adjustment of the related WLAN 802.11e parameters, we increased the quality of the voice calls across our network by reducing end to end delay and media access delay variations.

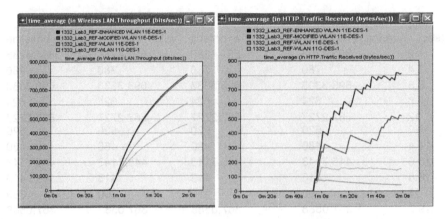

Fig. 5(a). Wireless LAN Throughput   **Fig. 5(b).** HTTP Traffic Received

From the fig.5(a) and 5(b) we can see that there is a considerable increase in global WLAN throughput and HTTP Traffic Received. It also confirms the positive outcome of our parameter adjustments. From the above results we can say that by deploying QoS functionality at the WLAN layer by adjusting traffic category parameters and EDCA parameters. Both the parameters are prioritized in medium access layer based on our network conditions and we configured the WLAN layer, so that now it performs at a level that provides acceptable quality for all applications running in our network.

References

[1] Banchs, A., Vollero, L.: A Delay Model for IEEE 802.11e EDCA. IEEE Communications Letters 9(6) (June 2006)
[2] IEEE Std 802.11e. Wireless LAN Medium Access Control (MAC) and Physical Layer (PHY) Speciation's; Amendment: Medium Access Control (MAC) Quality of Service Enhancements. IEEE Std 802.11e (2005)
[3] Drieberg, M., Fu-Chun, Z., Ahmad, R., Fitch, M.: Impact of Interference on Throughput in Dense WLANs with Multiple APs. In: IEEE Symposium 2009, pp. 752–756 (2009)
[4] Gavini, K.K., Apte, V., Iyer, S.: PLUS-DAC: A Distributed Admission Control Scheme for IEEE 802.11e WLANs. In: International Conference on Networking (ICON), Kuala Lumpur, Malaysia (November 2005)
[5] Ni, Q.: Performance Analysis and Enhancements for IEEE 802.11e Wireless Networks. IEEE Network (July/August 2005)
[6] Bruno, R., Conti, M., Gregori, E.: Design of an enhanced access point to optimize TCP performance in Wi-Fi hotspot networks. Wireless Networks (2006)
[7] Choi, S., Park, K., Kim, C.K.: On the Performance Characteristics of WLANs: Revisited. In: ACM Sigmetrics, Ban®, Alberta, Canada (June 2005)
[8] Bianchi, G.: Performance analysis of the IEEE 802.11 distributed coordination function. IEEE Journal on Selected Areas in Communications, 535–547 (March 2000)

Performance Analysis of Routing Metrics for MultiRadio MultiChannel WMN

Kavitha Athota[1,3], G. StalinBabu[2], and Atul Negi[3]

[1] Department of Computer Science and Engineering, JNTUH College of Engineering,
Hyderabad, Andhra Pradesh, India
[2] Department of Computer Science, AITAM,
Tekkali, Andhra Pradesh, India
[3] Department of Computer and Information Sciences, University of Hyderabad,
Andhra Pradesh, India
{athotakavitha,stalin1227}@gmail.com, atul.negi@ieee.org

Abstract. Wireless Mesh Networks(WMNs) with multiradio multichannel capability have received much attention from research community. Routing in WMNs has been active area of research for many years. Routing metrics that have been proposed for WMN provide better path selection in comparision with hop count which is popular in wired networks. Expected Transmission Time (ETT) was proposed as better metric as compared to ETX so as to give weighting to throughput. Weighted Cumulative ETT(WCETT) allows accounting for concatenated links that interfere when using the same channel. Adhoc on demand distance vector (AODV) is a popular routing protocol design for MANETs which is also considered applicable as a routing protocol for WMNs. Further, an extension of AODV may support Multiple Radios and Multiple channels. In this paper we integrate WCETT and AODV to realize better routing for WMNs. We attempt to study and investigate performance of above said routing metrics using simulations from NS2 simulator.

Keywords: WMN, AODV, WCETT, ETT, ETX routing metrics, NS2.

1 Introduction

Wireless mesh networks (WMNs)[1] are dynamically self-organized and self-configured, with the nodes in the network automatically establishing an adhoc network and maintaining the mesh connectivity. WMNs are comprised of three types of nodes Mesh router, Mesh Gateways and Mesh client. Mesh router (MR) relay packets to and from other mesh routers and clients. Mesh Gateway is a mesh router that connects other mesh router to internet through high speed wired link. Mesh clients connects to nearest mesh routers for access internet. Recently, a lot of research effort has been focused on multi Radio wireless mesh networks. Due to the relatively low cost of commodity wireless hardware such as Radio interfaces based on IEEE 802.11 standards, it is now feasible to include Multiple Radios on a single node. By operating these interfaces on orthogonal channels, the capacity of a Mesh Router

P.V. Krishna, M.R. Babu, and E. Ariwa (Eds.): ObCom 2011, Part II, CCIS 270, pp. 709–717, 2012.
© Springer-Verlag Berlin Heidelberg 2012

can be significantly increased, and overcomes the limitation of half duplex operation of single-Radio nodes. However, routing protocols must be designed to take advantage of the availability of multiple interfaces efficiently. Routing protocols are at the heart of Wireless Mesh Networks and control the formation, configuration and maintenance of the topology of the network. Routing metrics are a key element of any routing protocol since they determine the creation of network paths.

A metric is a measurement of performance in some product or system, such as a program or a network. A router use metrics to make routing decisions and metric is one of the fields in a typical routing table. The metric consists of any value used by routing algorithms to determine the best route among Multiple routes to a destination. Routing metrics are assigned to routes obtained by routing protocols to provide measurable values that can be used to judge how useful (how low cost) a route will be. Metrics provide a quantitative value to indicate the specific characteristics of the route. In this paper, we provide an extensive qualitative comparison of the most relevant routing metrics for multi-Radio wireless mesh networks.

1.1   Metric Components

Here we now state the key components that can be utilized to compose a routing metric for multi-Radio wireless mesh networks.

Number of Hops. Hop count can serve as a routing metric in itself, such as in most MANET routing protocols, but can also be a component in a more complex metric. Hop count as a routing metric for wireless mesh networks has significant limitations. It has been shown in [4] that a path with a higher number of high-quality links demonstrates significant performance improvements over a shorter path comprised of low-quality links. Additionally, it was found that hop count tends to route through a few centrally-located nodes, leading to congestion and hot spots[5].

Link Capacity. Measuring the link capacity gives the metric a view at the current throughput capability of a link. This can be done by actively probing the link and measuring transfer speeds, from the radio interface's current rate. Furthermore, as most Radio interfaces have the ability to automatically lower their transmission speeds in order to deal with lossy links, finding links with higher capacity will lower medium access time and increase the performance of the topology [6].

Link Quality. Finding high-quality links will greatly improve the overall performance of a path through higher transfer speeds and lower error rates. Link quality can be measured in a number of ways. The most common metrics are Signal to Noise Ratio (SNR) and Packet Loss Rate (PLR). This information is typically available from the device driver of a wireless interface. Alternatively, the PLR value can be determined through active probing [7].

Channel Diversity. Using the same channel on multiple consecutive hops of a path results in significant co-channel interference, and reduction of overall throughput. Ideally, all links of a path within interference range of each other should be operating on non-overlapping channels, resulting in significant performance gains [8]. The extent to which this can be achieved can be expressed as channel diversity. Obviously, channel diversity is only relevant for multi-Radio networks, since in single-Radio networks all interfaces are required to operate on the same channel to guarantee connectivity.

The rest of the paper organized as follows. Section 2 presents overview about routing metrics proposed for wireless mesh networks. Section 3 presents simulation results obtained using AODV on incorporating routing metrics. Section 3 is followed by conclusion section.

2   Routing Metrics

In this section, we discuss the major routing metrics for multi-Radio mesh networks. We begin by describing some metrics applicable to single-Radio mesh networks as much of the later metrics proposed based on these metrics.

2.1   Hop Count

This is the base metric used in most MANET protocols and is a simple measure of the number of hops between the source and destination of a path. However, hop count maintains a very limited view of links, ignoring issues such as link load and link quality. De Couto et al. [4] showed that a route with a higher number of short links can outperform a route with a smaller number of long distance and therefore lower quality links. This can lead the hop count metric to choose paths with low throughput and cause poor medium utilization, as slower links will take more time to send packets.

Hop count does not take into account link load, link capacity, link quality, channel diversity or other specific node characteristics. Neither does it consider any form of interference. While it has been shown that the hop count is not necessarily an optimal metric to establish high throughput paths [7], comparisons have demonstrated that under scenarios of high mobility, hop count can out-perform other load-dependent metrics [3]. Hop count is also a metric with high stability, and further has the isotonicity property, which allows minimum weight paths to be found efficiently.

2.2   ETX

Expected Transmission Count (ETX) [7] is a measure of link and path quality. It simply considers the number of times unicast packets need to be transmitted and re-transmitted at the MAC layer to successfully traverse a link. The ETX path metric is simply the sum of the ETX values of the individual links. ETX considers the number of transmission in both directions of a link, since the successful transmission of a unicast frame requires the transmission of the frame in one direction plus the successfully transmission of an acknowledgement in the reverse direction.

The ETX metric for a single link is defined in eq. (1) where d_f is the measured rate or probability that a packet will be successfully delivered in the forward direction and d_r denotes the probability that the corresponding acknowledgement packet is successfully received. Assuming these two probabilities are independent, we can say that the probability of a successful transmission, including Acknowledgement, is $d_f * d_r$. By utilizing the inverse of this value, the ETX calculation, defined below, provides a minimum-weight cost to higher quality links:

$$ETX = \frac{1}{df * dr}. \tag{1}$$

As many implementations of ETX [7] utilize small broadcast probe packets to detect losses there lies an issue where the measurements do not accurately reflect the loss rate of actual traffic due to the smaller size of the probe packets compared to the average packet size of network traffic. These effects could be mitigated by utilizing a cross-layer approach and directly obtaining the number of retransmissions from the link layer.

2.3   ETT

The Expected Transmission Time (ETT) metric [9] is designed to augment ETX [7] by considering the different link rates or capacities. This allows ETT to overcome the limitation of ETX that it cannot discriminate between links with similar loss rates but have a massive disparity in terms of bandwidth. This is particularly useful in multi-rate networks. ETT is simply the expected time to successfully transmit a packet at the MAC layer and is defined as follows for a single link:

$$ETT = ETX * \frac{S}{B}. \tag{2}$$

S denotes the average size of a packet and B the current link bandwidth. The ETT path metric is obtained by adding up all the ETT values of the individual links in the path. ETT retains many of the properties of ETX, but can increase the throughput of the path through the measurements of link capacities, and therefore increase the overall performance of the network. However, ETT still does not consider link load explicitly and therefore cannot avoid routing traffic through already heavily loaded nodes and links. ETT was not designed for multi-Radio networks and therefore does not attempt to minimize intra-flow interference by choosing channel diverse-paths. To resolve above issue a metric called Weighted Cumulative ETT (WCETT) is proposed for routing in multi-Radio, multi hop wireless networks.

2.4   WCETT

The goal of WCETT [9] metric is to choose a high-throughput path between a source and destination. Metric assigns weights to individual links based on the Expected Transmission Time (ETT) of a packet over the link. The individual link weights are combined into a path metric called Weighted Cumulative ETT (WCETT) explicitly consider interference among links that use the same channel, link quality and minimum hop-count. Let k be th total number of channels of a network and n be number of hops in path; the sum of transmission time over all hops on channel j is defined in eq.(3)

$$Xj = \sum_{i \ uses \ channel \ j} ETTi \quad 1 \leq j \leq k \tag{3}$$

As the total path throughput is dominated by the bottleneck channel, which has the largest X_j, WCETT propose to use a weighted average between the maximum value and the sum of all ETTs.This is shown in eq.(4)

$$WCETT = (1 - \beta) \sum_{i=1}^{n} W_i + \beta * \max_{1 \leq j \leq k} X_j \tag{4}$$

Where β is a tunable parameter subject to $0 \leq \beta \leq 1$. The first term can be considered as a measure of the latency of this path. The second term, since it represents the impact of bottleneck hops, can be viewed as a measure of path throughput. The weighted average is an attempt to balance between the two.

3   Simulation Results

For experimentation we implemented multi radio, multichannel support for an AODV then its WCETT routing metric is incorporated to improve quality of route selection[8]. The simulations are conducted in three different scenarios. First, basic simulations ran to understand performance gain of routing metrics by using single and multiple radios In the second scenario, the routing metrics are evaluated by varying numbers of nodes. The results are averaged among different topologies taken. In the second scenario, the routing metrics are evaluated 10-node topology varying network aggregate load.

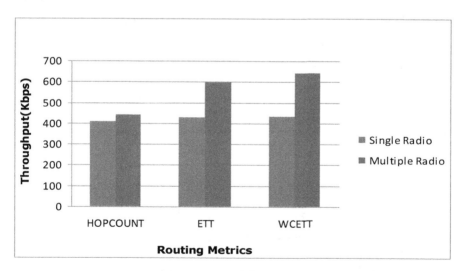

Fig. 3.1. Throughput Analysis of Routing Metrics using single radio and multiple radios

It is observed in Fig. 3.1 that WCETT utilizes multiple radios efficiently than ETT and Hop Count.

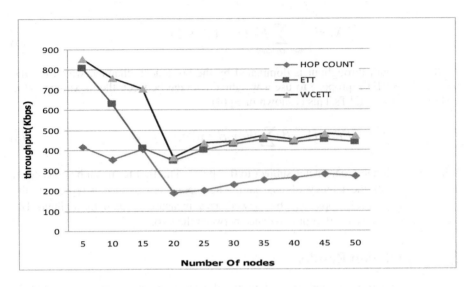

Fig. 3.2. Throughput Analysis of Routing Metrics increasing number of nodes

In Fig.3.2 it is observed that ETT, WCETT work better compared to Hop Count as the size of the network and path length increases.

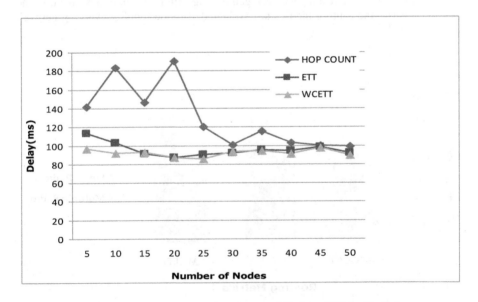

Fig. 3.3. Performance comparison between Number of Nodes Vs Delay

As shown in Fig.3.3 observed delay is minimum for ETT, WCETT compared to hopcount.

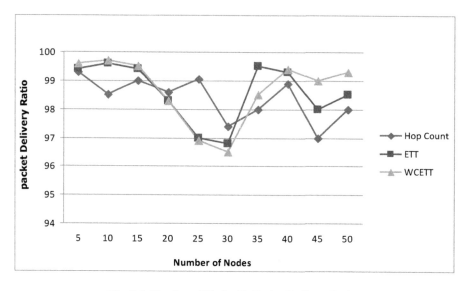

Fig. 3.4. Number of Nodes Vs Packet Delivery Ratio

As shown in Fig. 3.4 ETT and WCETT works better in overall compared hopcount interms of Packet Delivery Ratio.

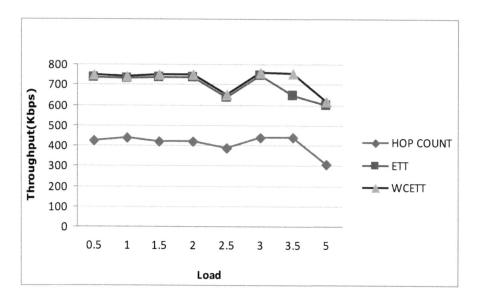

Fig. 3.5. Load Vs Throughput

In Fig. 3.5 it is observed that as the load is increasing for the 10 node topology ETT,WCETT continue to give better performance than hop count.

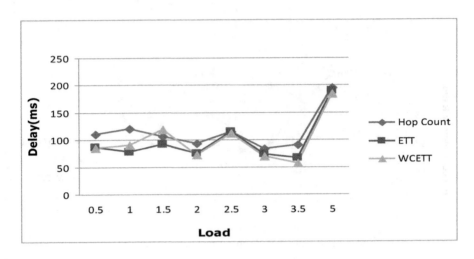

Fig. 3.6. Load Vs Delay

As shown in Fig.3.5, Fig. 3.6 also shows that ETT and WCETT work better than Hop Count in terms of delay.

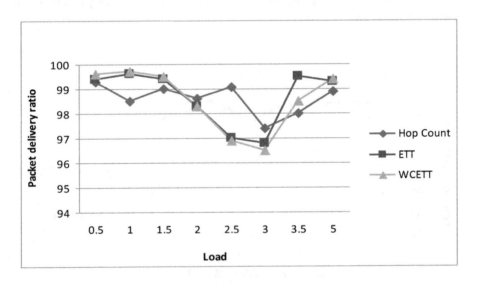

Fig. 3.7. Load Vs Packet Delivery Ratio

Fig. 3.7 shows that overall performance of ETT and WCETT work better than Hop Count.

4   Conclusion and Future Work

We present importance of channel diversity by addressing limitations of hop count and ETT through our study and simulations. It also shown that when nodes are equipped with Multiple Radios, it is important to select channel diverse paths in addition to accounting for the loss rate and bandwidth of individual links. We performed simulation for various scenarios in NS2 in order to show that performance of well known routing metrics hop count, ETT, WCETT. Performance analysis of hopcount, ETT, WCETT is carried in terms of throughput, delay and packet delivery ration.

WCETT does not consider the relative location of these links. It assumes all links of a path operating on same channel interfere with each other which can lead to selection of non-optimal paths. WCETT is not isotonic .i.e. it may not guarantee optimal and loop free path to destination. If a metric is not isotonic, then it is very difficult to use with link state routing protocols it can be implement further enhance of WCETT. A new routing metric can be proposed which addresses above said limitations.

Acknowledgment. This work is supported by AICTE-RPS project F.No.: 8023/BOR/RPS-90/2006-07

References

1. Akyildiz, I.F., Wang, X., Wang, W.: Wireless mesh networks: a survey. Computer Networks 47, 445–487 (2005)
2. Yang, Y., Wang, J., Kravets, R.: Designing Routing Metrics for Mesh Networks. In: Proceedings of the IEEE Workshop on Wireless Mesh Networks, WiMesh (June 2005)
3. Draves, R., Padhye, J., Zill, B.: Comparison of Routing Metrics for Static Multi-Hop Wireless Networks. ACM SIGCOMM Comput. Commun. Rev. 34, 133–144 (2004)
4. De Couto, S.J., Aguayo, D., Chambers, B.A., Morris, R.: Performance of Multihop Wireless Networks: Shortest Path is Not Enough. SIGCOMM Comput. Commun. Rev. 33, 83–88 (2003)
5. Hassanein, H., Zhou, A.: Routing with Load Balancing in Wireless Ad hoc Networks. In: MSWIM 2001: Proceedings of the 4th ACM International Workshop on Modeling, Analysis and Simulation of Wireless and Mobile Systems, pp. 89–96. ACM Press, Rome (2001)
6. Awerbuch, B., Holmer, D., Rubens, H.: High Throughput Route Selection in Multi-rate Ad Hoc Wireless Networks. In: Battiti, R., Conti, M., Cigno, R.L. (eds.) WONS 2004. LNCS, vol. 2928, pp. 253–270. Springer, Heidelberg (2004)
7. De Couto, S.J., Aguayo, D., Bicket, J., Morris, R.: A High- Throughput Path Metric for Multi-Hop Wireless Routing. In: 9th Annual International Conference on Mobile Computing, MobiCom 2003 (September 2003)
8. Ramon, A.C., Jesus, P.C.: Adding Multiple Interface support to NS2. Free Soft Ware Foundation (January 2007)
9. Couto, D.D., Aguayo, D., Bicket, J., Morris, R.: A high throughput path metric for multihop wireless routing. In: Mobicom (2003)

An Innovative Hybrid Hierarchical Model
for Automatic Image Annotation

T. Sumathi[1], and M. Hemalatha[2]

[1] Karpagam University, Coimbatore-21
[2] Department of Software Systems,
Karpagam University, Coimbatore
t_sumathi@yahoo.co.in, hema.bioinf@gmail.com

Abstract. This paper presents a novel image annotation framework for domains with large numbers of images. Automatic image annotation is such a domain, by which a computer system automatically assigns metadata in the form of captioning or keywords to a digital image. This application of computer vision method is used in image retrieval system to organize and locate images of interest from a database. Many techniques have been proposed for image annotation in the last decade that has given realistic performance on standard datasets. In this work, we introduce an innovative hybrid model for image annotation that treats annotation as a retrieval problem. The proposed technique utilizes low level image features and a simple combination of basic distances using JEC to find the nearest neighbors of a given image; the keywords are then assigned using SVM approach which aims to explore the combination of three different methods. First, the initial annotation of the data using flat wise and axis wise methods, and that takes the hierarchy into consideration by classifying consecutively its instances through position wise method. Finally, we make use of pair wise majority voting between methods by simply summing strings in order to make a final annotation. The result of the proposed technique shows that this technique outperforms the current state of art methods on the normal datasets.

Keywords: JEC, SVM, image annotation, image retrieval, Radial Basis Function.

1 Introduction

As high resolution digital cameras become more affordable and widespread the high quality digital image becomes ever more available and useful. With the exponential growth on high quality digital images, there is an urgent need to support more effective image retrieval over large scale archives. However content based image retrieval(CBIR) is still in its infancy and most existing CBIR systems can only support feature based image retrieval. Unfortunately, the naive users may not be well-known with low level visual features and it is very hard for them to specify their query concepts by using low level visual features directly. Thus there is a great need to develop automatic image annotation framework, so that the naive users can specify

P.V. Krishna, M.R. Babu, and E. Ariwa (Eds.): ObCom 2011, Part II, CCIS 270, pp. 718–726, 2012.
© Springer-Verlag Berlin Heidelberg 2012

their query concepts easily by using the relevant keywords. However the performance of image classifiers depends on two inter related issues: (1) suitable framework for image content representation and automatic feature extraction. (2) Effective algorithm for image classifier training and feature subset selection.

To address the first issue there are two broadly accepted approaches for image content representation and feature extraction. To address the second issue for automatic image annotation two approaches are widely used to train the image classifiers. (a) Model based approach by using Gaussian mixture model to approximate the underlying distribution of image classes in the high dimensional feature space (b) SVM-based approach by using support vector machine(SVM) to directly learn the maximum margins between the positive images and the negative images. In this work, SVM based approach is used to enable more effective classifier training with small generalization error rate in high dimensional feature space. So, for the annotation process we relied on SVM with a Radial basis function (RBF) kernel due to its outgoing performance. In this paper, we have proposed a hierarchical framework by incorporating the feature hierarchy and boosting to scale up SVM image classifier training. This framework is done in Mat lab using the popular label me web based annotation implementation.

2   Related Work

A large number of techniques have been proposed in the last decade. Most of these treat annotation as translation from image instances to keywords. The translation paradigm is typically based on some model of image and text co-occurrences. Latent Dirichlet Allocation (Corel LDA) considers association through a latent topic space in a generatively learned model [4], [18]. Mori et al. [4], [7] used a Co-occurrence Model in which they looked at the co-occurrence of words with image regions created using a regular grid. Monay and Gatica-Perez [4], [7] introduced latent variables to link image features with words as a way to capture co-occurrence information. The addition of a sounder probabilistic model to LSA resulted in the development of probabilistic latent semantic analysis (PLSA) [4], [6], [7]. Blei and Jordan [4], [18] viewed the problem of modeling annotated data as the problem of modeling data of different types where one type describes the other. Jeon et al. [4] improved on the result of Duygulu et al. by introducing a generative language model referred as Cross Media Relevance Model (CMRM) the same process used by Duygulu et al. was chosen to calculate the blob representation of images [12]. They assumed that this could be viewed as analogous to the cross-lingual retrieval problem to perform both image annotation and ranked retrieval. Lavrenko et al. [4],[14] argued that the process of quantization from continuous image features into discrete blobs, as the approach used by the machine translation model and the CMRM model, will cause the loss of useful information in image regions. While Feng et al. [4],[14] modified the above model such that the probability of observing labels given an image was modeled as a multiple-Bernoulli distribution. In addition, they simply divided images into rectangular tiles instead of applying automatic segmentation algorithms. Their

Multiple Bernoulli Relevance Model (MBRM) achieved further improvement on performance. Liu. et. al. [4], [18], they estimated the joint probability by the expectation over words in a pre-defined Lexicon. It involves two kinds of critical relations in image annotation. First is the word-to-image relation and the second is the word-to-word relation. Torralba and Oliva [4], [15] focused on modeling a global scene rather than image regions. This scene-oriented approach can be viewed as a generalization of the previous one where there is only one region or partition which coincides with the whole image. Yavlinsky et. al. [4], [16] followed an approach using global features together with robust non-parametric density estimation and the technique of kernel smoothing. Jin et.al [4], [10] proposes a new frame work for automated image annotation that estimated the probability for language model to be use for annotation an image.

3   Data Set Description

In this method we have utilized flicker dataset which contains 550 images of which 90% has been considered as training dataset and 10% as testing dataset.

4   Methodology

Annotation of images in this work undergoes several stages: first we extract information from the images and form a feature vector; hence we train several SVM's to create a model from the data for annotation accordingly to the mentioned approaches, flat and axis-wise, and position wise approaches herein tested. Finally we use majority voting, by summing strings, for a pair wise fusion between all three methods. We treat image annotation as a process of transferring keywords from nearest neighbors. The neighborhood structure is constructed using simple low-level image features resulting in a rudimentary model. A general flowchart of our procedure can be found in Fig. 1.

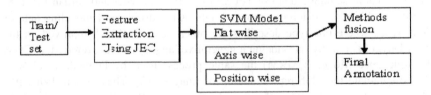

Fig. 1. A Frame work of our proposed system

4.1   Feature Extraction

To extract information from the images we used both global and a local image descriptor in a JEC approach. Feature selection was made accordingly to the desired image properties that we aimed to discriminate: color, texture and shape. All global descriptors were extracted using the Local and Web Image Retrieval Engine.

4.1.1 Color

RGB is the default color space for image capturing and display, both HSV and LAB isolate important appearance characteristics not captured by RGB. The RGB, HSV, and LAB features are 16-bin-per-channel histograms in their respective color spaces. To determine the corresponding L1 distance measures, as it performed the best for RGB and HSV, while KL-divergence was found suitable for LAB distances.

4.1.2 Combining Distances

Joint Equal Contribution (JEC). If labeled training data is unavailable, or the labels are extremely noisy, the simplest way to combine distances from different descriptors would be to allow each individual distance to contribute equally (after scaling the individual distances appropriately). Let Ii be the ith image, and say we have extracted N features $f_i^1, f_i^2, \ldots, f_i^N$. Let us define $d_{(i,j)}^k$ as the distance between f_i^k and f_j^k. We would like to combine the individual distances

$$d_{(i,j)}^k, \text{k} = 1 \ldots \text{N} \tag{1}$$

to provide a comprehensive distance between image I_i and I_j. Since, in JEC, each feature contributes equally towards the image distance, we first need to find the appropriate scaling terms for each feature. These scaling terms can be determined easily if the features are normalized in some way (e.g., features that have unit norm), but in practice this is not always the case. We can obtain estimates of the scaling terms by examining the lower and upper bounds on the feature distances computed on some training set. We scale the distances for each feature such that they are bounded by 0 and 1. If we denote the scaled distance as $d_{(i,j)}^k$ we can define the comprehensive image distance between images I_i and I_j as

$$\sum_{k=1}^{N} \frac{d_{(i,j)}^k}{N} \tag{2}$$

We refer to this distance as Joint Equal Contribution (JEC).

4.2 Annotation

For the annotation process we relied on SVM's with a Radial Basis Function (RBF) kernel due to their performance in the Image CLEF medical image annotation tasks. We have set up a framework in MATLAB using the popular label me web based implementation. We performed an extensive grid-search on the common approaches to this problem, flat and axis-wise strategies, to optimize the kernel parameters using

10-fold cross validation. Each image is classified one axis at the time but, unlike the axis-wise method, conceptualization of the image content does not take the full meaning of the axis into consideration. Instead, we first consider the highest hierarchical position of the axis, its root, and use the whole training set to perform an initial classification. Afterwards, we reduce the training set to those images which match the initial classification, a semantic reduction of the training set, and classify the hierarchically subsequent inferior position. We undergo this top-down process thorough the axis tree until it is completely classified. We undertake the same methodology for all axes and assemble the final annotation. After the annotation from the three methods separately we make pair wise fusions of these by summing strings. The chart given below shows the percentage of keywords being annotated in our flicker dataset.

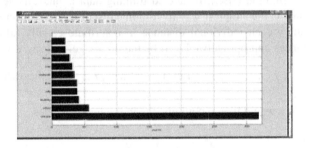

Fig. 2. Chart showing the annotation statistics

5   Evaluation and Discussion

5.1   Evaluation of Annotation

To evaluate annotation, we query images from the test dataset using 20 frequent keywords from the vocabulary. The image will be retrieved if the automatically established annotation contains the query keyword. We evaluate the result using P% and R% denotes the mean precision and the mean recall, respectively, over all keywords in percentage points. N+ denotes the number of recalled keywords. Note that the proposed simple baseline technique (JEC) outperforms state-of-the-art techniques in all datasets [2]. The precision, recall and common E measure which are defined as

$$P = NUM_{correct} / NUM_{retrieved} \qquad (3)$$

$$R = NUM_{correct} / NUM_{exists} \qquad (4)$$

$$E\,(p,r) = 1 - 2/([1/p] + [1/r]) \qquad (5)$$

5.2   Query Results

Label me tool is used to query the flicker dataset and label me dataset from different perspectives. This method has been implemented in mat lab by incorporating Label me tool. The figures below shows the query results of our proposed method.

5.2.1 Query 1

Query 1 is used to retrieve all the information for concept cars from the dataset.
>>LMdbshowobjects (LMquery (D, 'object. name', 'car'), HOMEIMAGES);

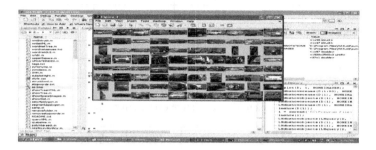

Fig. 3. Query and Output for all type of cars

5.2.2 Query 2

Fig. 4 shows output for query on "car side view, building, road and tree".
>>LMdbshowobjects (LMquery (D, 'object. name', 'car + side, building, road, tree'),
HOMEIMAGES);

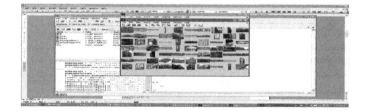

Fig. 4. Query and output for side view of car, building, road and tree

5.3   Discussion

We have evaluated our method based on various features like RGB, HSV and LAB.
The table 1 below shows their performance it can be stated that JEC when combined
with RGB feature performs well. Table 2 shows the results of comparison of our
method with other feature extraction methods like lasso, group lasso, least square, L2
regularization. From the results it is clear that JEC when combined with SVM gives
better results than other feature extraction methods. Table 3 shows the results of
comparison of our method with other two methods like new base line method which
makes use of greedy approach for annotation and hierarchical model which makes use
of bag of words for feature extraction. This comparative analysis of our method with
other methods has been clearly illustrated using the bar chart in figure 5. As per
results, our method has higher precision and recall rate compared with the other two
methods.

Table 1. Performance of JEC with various features

Methods	P%	R%	N+
RGB	18	22	110
RGB16	12	14	94
HSV	17	19	80
HSV16	14	16	108
LAB	12	13	102

Table 2. Comparison of other feature extraction methods with SVM

Methods	P%	R %	N+
JEC+SVM	19	22	110
Lasso + SVM	12	19	94
group lasso + SVM	10	18	87
Least Square + SVM	10	13	88
L2 –regularization + SVM	11	14	93

Table 3. Comparison with other methods

Methods	Overall Precision	Recall	E measure
Our Proposed method	0.77	0.35	0.513
New Baseline Method	0.20	0.23	0.786
Hierarchical Model	0.34	0.29	0.636

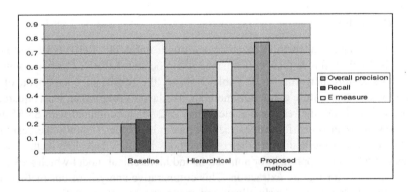

Fig. 5. Chart showing the results of comparison with other methods

6   Conclusion

To be able to solve the image annotation problem at the human level, perhaps one needs to first solve the problem of scene understanding. The goal of our work was to develop a new annotation method by combining the JEC distance measure with that of the hierarchical method for image annotation. It could be concluded from the results that our system with JEC feature is efficient for this image annotation purpose. Experiments on these dataset reaffirm the enormous importance of considering multiple sources of evidence to bridge the gap between the pixel representations of images and the semantic meanings. It is clear that a simple combination of basic distance measures defined over in extraction of image features has effectively served us to provide a better annotation results.

References

1. Makadia, A., Pavlovic, V., Kumar, S.: A New Baseline for Image Annotation. In: 2009 International Conference on Electrical Engineering and Informatics, August 5-7. IEEE (2009); ISSN: 978-1-4244-4913-2/09
2. Amaral, I.F., Coelho, F., da Costa, J.F.P., Cardoso, J.S.: Hierarchical Medical Image Annotation Using SVM-based Approaches. IEEE (2010); ISSN: 978-1-4244-6561-3/10
3. Sumathi, T., Hemalatha, M.: An Empirical Study on Performance Evaluation in Automatic Image Annotation and Retrieval. International Journal of Advanced Research in Computer Science 1(4) (November-December 2010)
4. Sumathi, T., et al.: An Overview of Automated Image Annotation Approaches. International Journal of Research and Reviews in Information Sciences 1(1) (March 2011)
5. Alham, N.K., Li, M., Hammoud, S., Qi, H.: Evaluating Machine Learning Techniques for Automatic Image annotations, pp. 53–58,
   http://ieeexplore.ieee.org/iel5/
6. Manal, S.A., Nordin, J.: Review on statistical approaches for automatic image annotation. In: International Conference on Electrical Engineering and Informatics. IEEE (2009); ISSN: 978-1-4244-4913-2
7. Alham, N.K., Li, M., Hammoud, S.: Evaluating Machine learning techniques for automatic image annotations. IEEE (2009); ISSN: 978-0-7695-3735-1/09
8. Gao, Y., et al.: Automatic image annotation by incorporating feature hierarchy and Boosting to scale up SVM classifiers. ACM Multimedia, October 22-28 (2006)
9. Herve Glotin, H., Zhao, Z.Q., Ayache, S.: Efficient image concept indexing by harmonic and arithmetic profiles entropy. In: 2009 IEEE International Conference on Image Processing, November 7-11 (2009)
10. Yang, C., Dong, M., Hua, J.: Region-based image annotation using asymmetrical support vector machine-based multiple-instance learning. In: Proceedings of the IEEE International Conference on Computer Vision and Pattern Recognition (2006)
11. Carneiro, G., Chan, A.B., Moreno, P.J., Vasconcelos, N.: Supervised learning of semantic classes for image annotation and retrieval. IEEE Transactions on Pattern Analysis and Machine Intelligence (2007)

12. Duygulu, P., Barnard, K., de Freitas, J.F.G., Forsyth, D.: Object Recognition as Machine Translation: Learning a Lexicon for a Fixed Image Vocabulary. In: Heyden, A., Sparr, G., Nielsen, M., Johansen, P. (eds.) ECCV 2002. LNCS, vol. 2353, pp. 97–112. Springer, Heidelberg (2002)
13. Lavrenko, V., Manmatha, R., Jeon, J.: A Model for Learning the Semantics of Pictures. In: Proceedings of Advance in Neutral Information Processing (2003)
14. Feng, S., Manmatha, R., Laverenko, V.: Multiple Bernoulli Relevance Models for Image and Video Annotation. In: IEEE Computer Society Conference on Computer Vision and Pattern Recognition, pp. 1002–1009 (2004)
15. Torralba, A., Oliva, A.: Statistics of natural image categories. Network: Computation in Neural Systems 14(3), 391–412 (2003)
16. Yavlinsky, A., Schofield, E., Riiger, S.: Automated image annotation, pp. 127–134. ACM Press (2003)
17. Pan, J., Yang, H., Faloutsos, C., Duygulu, P.: GCap: Graph based Automatic Image Captioning. In: Proceedings of the 4th International Workshop on Multimedia Data and Document Engineering (MDDE 2004), in Conjunction with Computer Vision Pattern Recognition Conference (CVPR 2004), Washington DC, July 2 (2004)
18. Blei, D.M., Jordan, M.I.: Latent Dirichlet Allocation. Journal of Machine Learning Research, 993–1022 (2003)

An Adaptive Subspace Clustering Dimension Reduction Framework for Time Series Indexing in Knime Workflows

T.M. Bhraguram, Shekha Chenthara, Geethu Gopan, and Anu R. Nair

Dept. of Computer Science,
Adi Shankara Institute of Engineering
and Technology, Kalady
bhruguram@gmail.com

Abstract. The performance of traditional index structures degrades with increasing dimensionality, concepts were developed to cope with curse of Data Dimensionality [2,5,6] for many domains. Most of the existing concepts exploit global correlations between dimensions to reduce the dimensionality of the feature space. In high dimensional data, however, correlations are often locally constrained to a subset of the data and every object can participate in several of these correlations. Here a novel framework for Knime (Data Analyzing Toolkit)[3] proposed. A subspace clustering is a method which is adopted for the dimension reduction framework. The system produces effective dimension reduction result for the Knime environment and is adaptive for the different data domains. Here each data representations can be plotted as a Tree structure and then can perform subspace extraction which is more helpful for the future pruning activity. The nodes are then transformed to the Knime workflows [3] and can act on different workflow nodes independently.

Keywords: Subspace, Clustering.

1 Introduction

This paper gives an efficient clustering scheme which is applicable for KNIME [3] workflow environment, a leading Data analyzing toolkit. The scheme which is presented in this paper is based on subspace clustering term which is most suitably consider for the domain systems based on Data Mining and Time series analysis. The incoming time series data(Time quantum generated data for a period of time) can be arranged with Time series databases and then perform a subspace clustering method for the dimension reduction on the data. Here Dimension reduction is an important function for the effective data handling. Normally all the data repositories handling dynamic data have huge dimension needed for holding up the incoming data. If the repository fails to handle such situation the system fails and the stored data can be thrown away. The dimension reduction frameworks can handle this problem and can monitor the features of the incoming data and according to the data the procedure can perform certain reduction mechanisms and process the data.

P.V. Krishna, M.R. Babu, and E. Ariwa (Eds.): ObCom 2011, Part II, CCIS 270, pp. 727–739, 2012.
© Springer-Verlag Berlin Heidelberg 2012

To follow the dimension reduction, similarity search in databases is an active research area with a wide range of application domains. In many of these domains, fast query times are crucial and long waiting periods are prohibited. For example, even minutes can be fatal in medical applications. Similarity search is typically realized in a content-based fashion, i.e. features like histograms are extracted from objects and the similarity between objects is modeled by a similarity function operating in the feature space. Usually distance functions are used for this purpose. The 'Lp-norm'[4,6,8] is a family of well suited distance functions:

$$d(q, p) = \sum_{i=1}^{d} \sqrt[p]{|q_i - p_i|^p} \quad \text{For } p=2.$$

It corresponds to the Euclidean Distance. An often used query type in similarity search is the k-Nearest-Neighbor (kNN) [4,5,8,10]query that calculates the k most similar objects to a query object. For efficient query processing on multidimensional feature spaces index structures were introduced and they are mostly based on hierarchically nested minimal bounding regions.

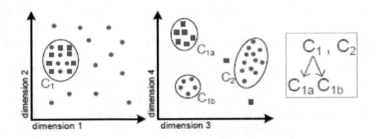

Fig. 1. Hierarchically nested local reductions

Filter and refine frameworks as well as revised and new index structures were introduced to weaken the effects of high dimensionality. In filter and refine a framework, an index is built on a dimensionality reduced representation of the database allowing for fast computation of possible candidates. The exact distances to these candidates are then computed in the subsequent refinement step. The dimensionality reduction is performed by exploiting correlations between the feature space dimensions corresponding to redundancy in the data. An example is the principal component analysis, which transforms the original feature space to a lower dimensional one containing most of the relevant information. Such filter and refine frameworks as well as the mentioned index structures weaken the curse of dimensionality, but the general problem is still not solved. The reason is the complex structure hidden in the data: specific correlations between the dimensions are often local, i.e. they are constrained to subsets of the data, and every object in the data can participate in several of these correlations. Reductions based on global correlations, however, cannot reflect the local correlations in an advantageous way for index construction; all objects in the data will be reduced to the same dimensions, and therefore many dimensions are discarded that are important for specific subsets of the data. In the remaining dimensions the values in these subsets have a high variance preventing compact minimal bound regions in the index and resulting in unnecessary large query times.

For complex data, indexing frameworks are needed whose corresponding filter steps are based on local reductions. One possible solution is to build an index for every local pattern in the data, i.e. every index corresponds to a different filter with another set of reduced dimensions [8]. These approaches, however, have a serious drawback: They do not consider that every object can participate in several local reductions, i.e. every object is only assigned to one of these reductions. The potential for several different filters for each data object and better pruning based on these filters is therefore wasted. In this paper, we introduce a novel index structure that is based on local reductions and that in particular regards the multiple local correlations of single data objects. This is achieved by building a hierarchy of local reductions that corresponds to the structure of the index tree; that is, a local reduction-based minimum bounding region can itself contain local reductions that enable compact bounding regions in lower levels of the index tree. As mentioned before, an index on dimensionality reduced data objects acts as a filter in filter-and-refine frameworks. Accordingly, our single index corresponds to a series of different filters for every data object; every query passes through an individual cascade of filters until it reaches a leaf node.

When clustering is used for index construction, there are issues: Clustering algorithms are often unstable, i.e. they are very parameter-sensitive and they deliver different results on every run; therefore we introduce a method that is motivated by train-and-test, a paradigm that is well established in the data mining and machine learning domain, e.g. for decision tree construction. In applications where the underlying distribution of incoming data objects changes, our index adapts its underlying clustering structure dynamically. Many existing index structures are designed for secondary storage, and thus technical constraints as block size must be adhered to. In many domains, however, these index structures are becoming obsolete: Main memory capacity of computers is constantly increasing and in many applications persistence of the index structure or even the data set has lost importance compared to the need for fast responses.

Summarized, our contributions are:

1   Our novel index structure is based on local reductions determined by subspace clustering.
2   The objects are multi-represented with different local reductions that are hierarchically nested. Queries have to pass through an individual series of filters allowing for faster pruning of candidates.
3   The index construction is enhanced by a train-and-test method providing more compact minimal bounding regions and the underlying structure of the index adapts to new data distributions by re-clustering sub trees.

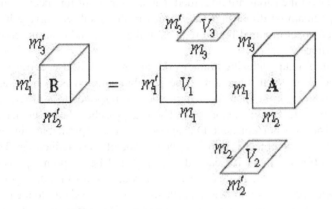

Fig. 2. Dimension view of sample TS Data

2   Related Work

In this section we give a short overview of relevant related work on indexing. Since our novel index structure is based on subspace clustering, we also give a short overview of this research area.

Indexing Techniques. Indexing techniques for fast similarity search can be categorized into approximate and correct solutions. Methods from the former category trade accuracy for speed, and one well-known example is Local Sensitive Hashing [10, 12]. Methods from the latter category produce exact results, i.e. there are no false dismissals or false positives in the result set. Since our proposed index is from this category, we focus on exact solutions in the following. The R-Tree [14] is one of the first multidimensional indexing structures. It is well suited for lower dimensions, but its performance rapidly degrades for higher dimensionalities due to the curse of dimensionality; therefore, dimensionality reduction techniques like PCA or cut-o_ reduction are used to reduce the dimensionality of indexed objects. Since dimensionality reduction induces information loss, false positives are produced that need to be rejected. This can be achieved by a filter-and-refine-framework (also called multistep query processing), e.g. GEMINI [10] or KNOP. The drawbacks of global dimensionality reduction techniques were discussed in Section 1. Several indexing structures for high dimensional feature spaces that are mostly based on the R-Tree were proposed. The R*-Tree [5] introduces new split and reinsertion strategies. The X-Tree [6] enhances the R*- Tree by introducing overlap-minimizing splits and the concept of super nodes; if no overlap-minimizing split is possible, super nodes of double size are generated, eventually degenerating to a sequential scan. The A-Tree[] uses quantization to increase the fan-out of tree nodes. The TV-Tree[] is based on a PCA-transformed feature space: Minimum bounding regions are restricted to a subset of active dimensions in this space. Active dimensions are the first few dimensions allowing for discrimination between sub trees. It has, however, the same drawbacks as the other global dimensionality reduction techniques. Distance based indexing is another type of transformation based indexing and is realized by iDistance: Data points are transformed into single dimensional values w.r.t their similarity to specific reference points. These values are indexed by a B+- tree and the search is performed by one-dimensional range queries in these trees. All of the described index structures are optimized for secondary storage, i.e. they have node size constraints. One of these index structures accounts for local correlations in the data. An approach that makes use of local correlations is LDR [8]. It uses subspace clustering to create a single clustering of the whole dataset. These clusters represent local correlations. Dimensionality reduction is performed individually on the clusters and an index is built for each of the reduced representations. LDR has several drawbacks: it applies subspace clustering only to the root of the constructed tree, while the sub trees are built the conventional way (one index for every sub tree). These indices are still prone to the curse of dimensionality. Another local-correlation based approach is MMDR. In difference to LDR, a single one-dimensional index is used. In both LDR and MMDR, there is no hierarchical nesting of subspace clusters, i.e. there is no multi-representation of objects according to different dimensions and there is no handling of local correlations in the used indices.

Subspace Clustering. Recent research in subspace clustering has introduced several models and algorithms. A summary can be found in and differences between the models are analyzed in. Subspace clustering aims at detecting groups of similar objects and a set of relevant dimension for each of these object groups. A general classification of the models can be done by considering the possible overlap of clusters. Partitioning approaches [2, 12] force the clusters to represent disjoint object sets while in non-partitioning approaches [4,] objects can belong to several clusters. Besides the huge amount of algorithms that keep the original dimensions, some algorithms [3] transform the data space on detected correlations. Initial work has also been done in detecting hierarchies of subspace clusters [1]. However, the complexity of the approaches avoids efficient application.

3   Subspace Clustering

The construction of subspace index based on subspace clustering is presented in this section. We consider the static case for a given database and the insertion and deletion of objects for dynamic usage.

The general idea of our index structure is to represent each object in multiple ways, such that different information can be used for pruning. To enable efficient query processing we partition the data in a hierarchical structure, allowing us to prune whole sub trees if they are not important for the current query. Each sub tree represents a subset of objects annotated with its local reductions avoiding the information loss attended by global reduction approaches. To determine these local reductions we use subspace clustering methods, since in high dimensional data we cannot find meaningful partitions with traditional approaches due to the curse of dimensionality [7].

A subspace cluster is a set of objects together with a set of locally relevant dimensions. The objects show high correlations and thus compactness within the relevant dimensions while in the irrelevant ones we cannot identify a good grouping for this set of objects. For different groups of objects different relevant dimensions are possible, thus we are not constrained to a global reduction of the data. A subspace clustering is a list of subspace clusters together with a list of outliers. The handling of outliers is important because not every object shows a good correlation to other objects. In Figure 3 the blue circles form a subspace cluster with the relevant dimensions 1 and 2 while the red squares depict a good grouping in the dimensions 3 and 4. We cannot identify clusters in the full-dimensional space. The green triangle is an outlier, because it shows no similarity to other objects in any of the subspaces.

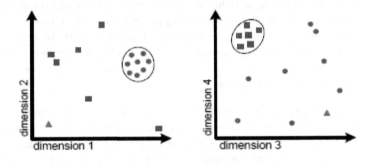

Fig. 3. Example of a Subspace Clustering

4   Tree Construction

For index construction, we distinguish two cases: First, the static construction, where we build the index for a database provided in whole. Second, the dynamic construction where we cope with insertion and deletion of objects.

4.1   Static Construction

Usually an initial set of data is available to construct our index via bulk-loading. To achieve the multi-representation of objects we need a subspace clustering for each inner node of the tree. A simple approach is to calculate only one clustering for the root node and recursively repeat this procedure for each subset to construct further nodes. However, this procedure can lead to instabilities during the index construction. Since there exist several clustering for a single dataset each clustering with different quality for grouping the objects it is unlikely to get a good result with a single run of a clustering algorithm. Since in our hierarchical structure the child nodes depend directly on the upper level clustering, we use the following approach to construct the index. We start with the root for which multiple clustering are calculated. Consequently, we get a set of partly constructed models -index structures. We select the best model from this set and we try to complete it. Therefore we select one cluster from the root node and we cluster this subset of objects again several times. Based on our first partly constructed model we get a new set of extended but still not complete index structures. The best index is selected and the approach is repeated until the complete index is obtained. Pruning potential of clustering to determine this best clustering we use an approach inspired by the train-and-test method used in other data mining applications. On the one hand, one can use train-and-test to evaluate the quality of an approach. On the other hand, train-and-test is used to construct better models itself, e.g. for decision trees [].

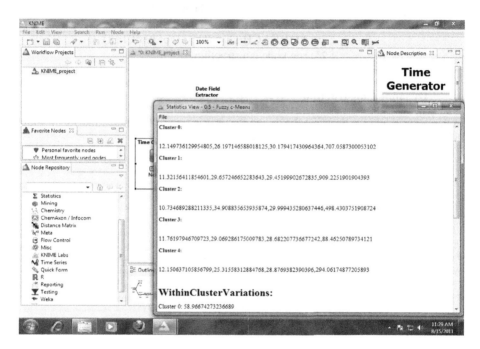

Fig. 4. Clustering Space in Knime Environment

The general idea is to build a set of models based on the training set and choose the best one w.r.t. the test set.

Algorithm 1: Node construction algorithm
1: input: set of objects O;
2: **IF**(jOj < minSize)
3:              constructLeafNode(); // based on O;
4:              return;
5:              Test = chooseT estSet();
6: // initial clustering
7: bestClust = performClusteringOn(O);
8: bestQuality = evaluateClust(bestClust; Test);

```
 9: stableCount = 0;
10: WHILE(stableCount < stableSteps)
11:     currClus = performClusteringOn(O);
12:     currQuality=evaluateClust(currClust;Test);
13:              IF(currQuality > bestQuality)
14                   bestClust = currClust;
15:                  bestQuality = currQuality;
16:                  stableCount = 0;
17:              ELSE
18:                  stableCount+ = 1;
19:     constructInnerNode();// based on bestClust;
20: FOREACH(Ci = (Oi; Si) of bestClust)
21: run node construction for Oi
```

4.2   Dynamic Construction

In the next section we describe the dynamic construction of the index, i.e. we consider
the insertion of new objects and the deletion of existent objects.

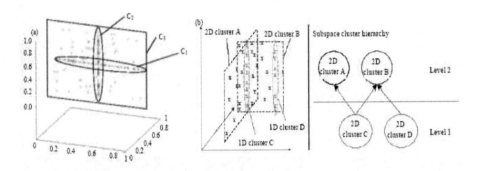

Fig. 5. Subspace Clustering Hierarchy (a) Clustering in a 3 Dimensional pane. (b) Subspace
Merging based on ID (c) Subspace Cluster Hierarchy.

Insertion. The insertion method makes use of an already existent subspace index.
First, we identify the leaf node whose enclosing rectangle (which is one layer above
the leaf) shows the smallest 'minDist'[3,6,11] w.r.t. the object we want to insert. The
objects in this leaf node are good candidates for clustering with the new object. To
assess if this leaf node is truly a good candidate for insertion we check whether the
volume of the enclosing rectangle does not increase too much. If it highly increases,
we recursively go one layer up in the tree and test the corresponding rectangle.
Instead of a leaf node we now analyze inner nodes, thus the object would be inserted
in the outlier list. Evidently, all enclosing rectangles including the novel object must
be updated to retain a correct approximation of the clusters.

Deletion. To delete an object we have to identify the path from the root to one leaf or inner node where the object is stored. Remember that the object could be an outlier and hence is stored in an inner node. The object is removed from the identified node and all enclosing rectangles up to the root are possibly downsized.

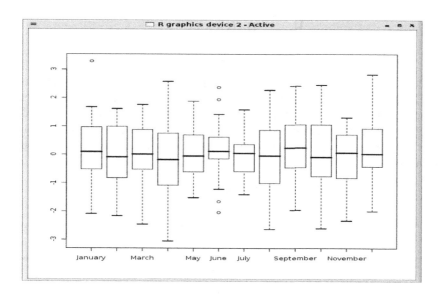

Fig. 6. Output Cluster Model from Knime Workflows

5   Query Processing

We focus on the k-Nearest-Neighbor processing with Euclidean Distance in subspace index but other types can be easily integrated. In Section IV we approximate the subspace clusters by subspace enclosing rectangles (SERs). To ensure completeness of our index, i.e. no false dismissals are allowed, we have to define a 'minDist' which has to be a lower bound for all objects within the underlying sub tree: The distance from the query object q to the aggregated information is smaller than the distance to each object in the sub tree.

Minimum distance to SERs

The 'minDist' between query $q \in R^{[Dim]}$ and the subspace
enclosing rectangle R=([i1; low1; up1],......., [id; lowd; upd])

$$minDist(q,R) = \sqrt{\sum_{j=1}^{d} \begin{bmatrix} (low_j - q|ij)^2 & ifq \ / \ ij < low_j \\ (low_j - q|ij)^2 & ifq \ / \ ij < low_j \\ 0 else \end{bmatrix}}$$

'kNN' Algorithm gives an overview of the query processing. Starting with the root node, a priority queue stores the currently active nodes. At each point in time we refine the node with the smallest 'minDist'. As mentioned before, in each node we are able to store full-dimensional objects. These objects are either outliers or objects from leaf nodes for which we perform a linear scan to update the temporary nearest neighbors.

Algorithm 2 : kNN queries in Subspace Indexing

```
1: input: query q, result set size k
2: queue = List of (dist; node) is ascending order by dist;
3: queue:insert(0:0; root);
4: resultArray = [(1; null); : : : ; (1; null)]; // k times
5: distmax = 1;
6: WHILE(queue 6= ; and queue:nextDist _ distmax)
7: n = queue:pollFirst;
8: // scan objects of leaf or possible outliers
9: IF(n is leaf node) toScan = n:O;
10: ELSE toScan = n:Out;
11: FOREACH(o in toScan)
12: IF(dist(q; o) _ distmax)
13: resultArray[k] = (dist(q; o); o);
14: resultArray:sort;
15: distmax = resultArray[k]:dist;
16: IF(n is inner node)
17: FOREACH(SER R in n)
18: IF(mindist(q;R) _ distmax)
19: queue:insert(mindist(q;R);R:child);
20: return resultArray;
```

We mentioned the use of transformation based approaches for cluster approximation. Thus, the 'minDist' calculation is also based on this transformation. However, due to our multi-representations we would use different transformations for each node/cluster and hence the query object has also to be transformed several times resulting in inefficient processing. Therefore we focus on the method of subspace enclosing rectangles.

6   Experimental Results

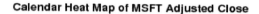

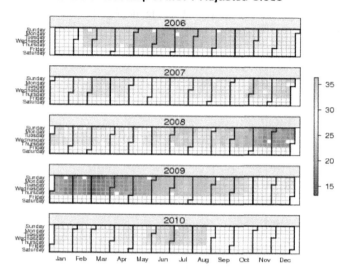

Fig. 7. Sample Time Series Data Plane in Knime

In the following experiment we change the information content by a different method: Instead of incrementally shifting the replicated databases by one dimension, we directly shift the databases by a factor of d.

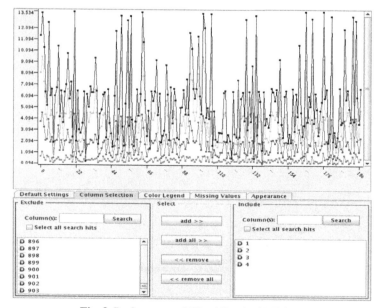

Fig. 8. Performance of 'K*nn*' Queries in Knime

This Subspace indexing can detect local correlations resulting in the highest efficiency. The global dimensionality reduction PCA exhibits a high number of calculations, even worse than the classical R*-Tree. With increasing number of subspace clusters global correlations become negligible and cannot be used for effective pruning.

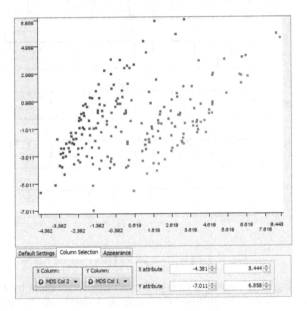

Fig. 9. Clustered Dimensions in knime

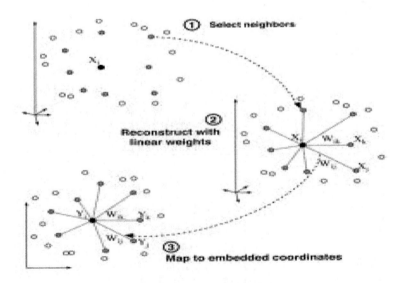

Fig. 10. Query performance against Clusters

This experiment displays how the query performance is influenced by the number of clusters to be found. The general tendency is that with a higher number of clusters the average number of distance calculations becomes more stable, i.e. the results for a low number of clusters are very fluctuant and show no good query performance.

7   Conclusion

Here we are giving a general depiction of Subspace clustering dimensionality reduction technique which is a novel approach for various Time series data. The overview of this framework has been modified with the help of Knime workflow environment. This is a novel indexing method which provides high level reduction result for various domains. By a hierarchical nesting of local reductions we generate a multi-representation of objects, so that queries have to traverse a cascade of different filters in the index. It achieves higher information content than global reductions. The data demonstrate that Subspace indexing enables fast query processing and reliably outperforms existing approaches.

References

1. Achtert, E., Böhm, C., Kriegel, H.-P., Kröger, P., Müller-Gorman, I., Zimek, A.: Finding Hierarchies of Subspace Clusters. In: Fürnkranz, J., Scheffer, T., Spiliopoulou, M. (eds.) PKDD 2006. LNCS (LNAI), vol. 4213, pp. 446–453. Springer, Heidelberg (2006)
2. Aggarwal, C., Wolf, J., Yu, P., Procopiuc, C., Park, J.: Fast algorithms for projected clustering. In: SIGMOD, pp. 61–72 (1999)
3. Aggarwal, C., Yu, P.: Finding generalized projected clusters in high dimensional spaces. In: SIGMOD, pp. 70–81 (2000)
4. Agrawal, R., Gehrke, J., Gunopulos, D., Raghavan, P.: Automatic subspace clustering of high dimensional data for data mining applications. In: SIGMOD, pp. 94–105 (1998)
5. Beckmann, N., Kriegel, H.-P., Schneider, R., Seeger, B.: The R*-tree: An efficient and robust access method for points and rectangles. In: SIGMOD, pp. 322–331 (1990)
6. Berchtold, S., Keim, D.A., Kriegel, H.-P.: The X-tree: An index structure for high-dimensional data. In: VLDB, pp. 28–39 (1996)
7. Beyer, K., Goldstein, J., Ramakrishnan, R., Shaft, U.: When is nearest neighbors meaningful? In: IDBT, pp. 217–235 (1999)
8. Chakrabarti, K., Mehrotra, S.: Local dimensionality reduction: A new approach to indexing high dimensional spaces. In: VLDB, pp. 89–100 (2000)
9. Faloutsos, C., Kamel, I.: Beyond uniformity and independence: Analysis of r-trees using the concept of fractal dimension. In: PODS, pp. 4–13 (1994)
10. Faloutsos, C., Ranganathan, M., Manolopoulos, Y.: Fast subsequence matching in time-series database. In: SIGMOD, pp. 419–429 (1994)
11. Frank, A., Asuncion, A.: UCI machine learning repository (2010), http://archive.ics.uci.edu/ml
12. Gionis, A., Indyk, P., Motwani, R.: Similarity search in high dimensions via hashing. In: VLDB, pp. 518–529 (1999)
13. Gunnemann, S., Muller, E., Farber, I., Seidl, T.: Detection of orthogonal concepts in subspaces of high dimensional data. In: CIKM, pp. 1317–1326 (2009)
14. Guttman, A.: R-trees: A dynamic index structure for spatial searching. In: SIGMOD, pp. 47–57 (1984)
15. Halkidi, M., Batistakis, Y., Vazirgiannis, M.: On clustering validation techniques. J. Intell. Inf. Syst. 17(2-3), 107–145 (2001)

Reliable Requirement Specification:
Defect Analysis Perspective

Sandeep Kumar Nayak[1,*], Raees Ahmad Khan[2], and Md. Rizwan Beg[3]

[1] Department of Computer Science and Application, Integral University,
Lucknow – 226 026, UP, India
[2] Department of Information Technology, Babasaheb Bhimrao Ambedkar University
(A Central University), Lucknow, India
[3] Department of Computer Science and Engineering, Integral University, Lucknow, India
nayak_sam@rediffmail.com, khanraees@yahoo.com,
rizwanbeg@gmail.com

Abstract. Reliability is a primary concern for the successful software development organizations. There is various threats point in the requirement phase that causes for requirement defects and so defect occurring in the further phases. A key aspect of delivering and improving the software reliability it is necessary to be confident that the requirement delivered to the further phases of SDLC must be reliable. A reliable requirement can be produce only after removing or resolving all types of requirement defects. In this paper we are proposing a Reliable Requirement Specification Procedure and concrete analysis process which will help out in producing the Reliable Requirement Specification for the designer.

Keywords: Reliable Requirement Specification, Reliability Assessment, Defect Analysis.

1   Introduction

Ineffectiveness of software Reliability Management in Software Life Cycle is the main cause of reliability faults in the completed software system. Stringent analysis, testing and managing of software reliability should be carried out at the initial stage of System Development Life Cycle (SDLC) [1]. According to Roger S. Pressman and Robert B. Grady the cost and effort incurred in finding and fixing the defects are 1% at requirement phase which is much more less than to fixing at test and deployment phase i.e. 15% and 80% respectively [2]. Both the authors surveyed various industries for elaborating defects they found that more than 50% defects are related to Requirement Phase that means

$$\text{Requirement Defects} = (> 0.5) * \text{Total No. of Defects [2]}$$

For proper defect identification the requirement Document must be written in either form:

  1) Textual Form 2) Matrix Form 3) Diagram Form 4) Models Form.

---

* Corresponding author.

P.V. Krishna, M.R. Babu, and E. Ariwa (Eds.): ObCom 2011, Part II, CCIS 270, pp. 740–751, 2012.

There are some specific characteristics which must be fulfilled at the earlier phase of the requirement gathering and preparation so that the defects may be identify at very starting point. The characteristics are as follows:

i.   Accurate: Accurate requirement data is free from error.
ii.   Complete: Complete requirement data contains all of the important facts.
iii.   Economical: Requirement data should be relatively inexpensive to produce.
iv.   Flexible: Flexible requirement data can be used for a variety of purposes, not for just one.
v.   Relevant: Relevant requirement data is important to the decision-maker.
vi.   Simple: Requirement data should be simple to find and understand.
vii.   Timely: Timely requirement data is readily available when needed.

Verifiable: Verifiable requirement data can be checked to make sure it is accurate.

2   Accessible Exertion

There are several studies conducted by different researchers for producing reliable software through error removal in code lines and software testing. But there are only few researchers who have given time in defect detection and removal in the requirement phase for delivering the reliable requirement specification. Few authors have given four ways to detect defects a) Checklist Based Detection b) Scenario Based Detection c) Perspective Based Detection d) Traceability Based Detection by [3], some authors depend upon "Defect Density" Model and Design Phase Analysis for defect detection [4], some emphasis on classify the defect similarities and their patterns[5], some researcher narrates to detect the defects phase wise as a) Elaboration b) Inception c) Construction d) Transition[6] and also detected defect through identification of risk item in the requirement document, establishing relationship between defects and their causes and by recording the requirement defects[7].

3   Proposed Approach

In this paper we are proposing a model (Fig.1) for proper analysis of requirement for producing Reliable Requirement document and also performing a review process for rechecking the analyzed document. In this paper we are stepping towards a concrete refinement process i.e. Requirement Analysis and Document Review for reaching maximum probable reliable requirement document. Through this approach designer will feel easiness to construct the most fitted and operable design for the further phases of the SDLC.

Generally Requirements are initiated by the customer or clients for the proposed project. Requirement analysts will be responsible for the preparation of proper methodology for gathering the requirements so that the requirement can be prepared. There are some tips for the requirement preparation:

i.   Examine the Project Need or Opportunity
ii.   Project Objectives Statement
iii.   Categorized the requirement into actual Needs and Wants.
iv.   Negotiate the Definition of Requirements in accordance with Customer

v.   Requirement validation
vi.   Requirement Gathering Techniques

Processed Requirements must be describe under some of the vital and specific heads such as: Budget, Risk, Project description, Data requirements, Functional process requirements, Security requirements, Recoverability requirements, System availability requirements, Performance requirements, Capacity requirements, Glossary/ Metadata, Overall product Functionality, Interface, Attributes, Barriers.

The proposed model for Requirement Analysis contains some of the essential steps through which gathered requirement will be passing and generates Reliable Requirement. Reliable Requirement will produce through assessing the reliability of the requirement which will be further delivered at the designer's end for proper structuring of the project. Actually, this model refers to a process of generating such defect less requirement specification (Reliable Requirement) prior to deliver for the design that:-

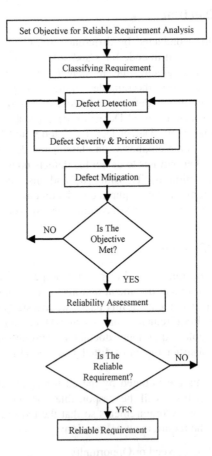

Fig. 1. Proposed Model for Reliable Requirement Analysis

i.   Satisfies the user's needs with respect to the proposed system
ii.   Provides sufficient information to construct the proposed system

Generally the results of requirement analysis are not directly presentable to a customer, who is usually an expert in his domain area but has little understanding of the completed documentation. Requirement analysis process is a concrete approach for analyzing the described and structured requirement properly.

3.1   Objective of Requirement Approach

Prior to start analyzing requirements there must be some objectives to be achieved by the Requirement Analysis Process are as:

i.   Improve Project planning for test Activities
ii.   Increase Defect Identification and Risk Assessment
iii. Increase Requirement Reliability
iv.   Decrease Requirement Defect Density
v.   Reduce Unconventional Requirement
vi.   Increase Requirement productivity
vii. Measurement of Reliability of Requirement
viii. Effective Defect Mitigation
ix.   Define and Refine all types of requirements in reference to reliability parameter
x.   Introduce absolute process to define functional parts of the software
xi.   Filter the top level architecture and requirements artifacts
xii. Produce practically analyzed structured documentation

Generate approval criterion to analyzed documentation

3.2   Requirement Classification

After setting the objective for the requirement analysis initiate the classification of requirement where requirements must be decomposed under some specific heads:

1) Requirement Scope, 2) Feasibility, 3) Verifiability, 4) Input Section 5) Problems/Issues, 6) Proper Solution, 7) Execution Plan, 8) Functional issue, 9) Human Resource/Team, 10) Output (Expected and Actual) and 11) Requirement Boundaries

Instead of these specific heads some sorts of tips for classifying the Requirements are given below:

i. Classify the progressed requirement at granularity level so that the team members may also infer of what is happening.
ii. Classify requirement data and their operations.

   iii. Structuring the relationship and dependency among the Requirement.
   iv. Designing and identification of metadata, data dictionary and data objects.
    v. Define Requirement Category, Relationship and Association Category
   vi. Transitions among the different Classified Requirement

3.3   Defect Detection

Requirement Defect should be identify under each of the classified requirements. There are some of the causes for unwanted emergence of defects:-

1) Loosely Explained Requirement 2) Erroneous user's Requirement 3) Improper Recording of Requirement 4) Improper Requirement Structuring 5) Lack of proper technique to requirement processing 6) Less involvement of organizational vision

There are some guidelines for narrating the defects.

    i. Defect Recognition in classified requirement
   ii. Defect Investigation Technique
- Prototyping
- Checklist Matching
- Inspection Technique

  iii. Defect Type
- Team oriented (Communication, Participation, Domain Knowledge, Process Execution)
- Process Oriented (Improper Methodology to achieve Objective, Mismanagement in selection of proper Process, Poor Elicitation)

  iv. Defect Location and Description
   v. Defect Severity

3.4   Defect Severity and Prioritization

Defect Prioritization can be defined in different ways:

    i. Defect Prioritization is associated with schedule to resolve the defects e.g. out of many issues to be tackled, which one should be addressed first by the order of its importance or urgency.
   ii. It is a pointer towards the importance of the Requirement Defect.
  iii. Priority refers to how soon the requirement defect should be fixed.
  iv. Priority to fix a requirement defect is decided in consultation with the client

In Table 1. the levels of defect priority, their impact and the possible measures are given. The below given chart (Table 2) mention the defect severity leveling and prioritization allotted to each and every severe defect and conclusion reflects all possible combinations and resultants of this phase in Requirement Analysis.

Table 1. Defect Priority with their Impacts and Measures

Defect Priority Level	Impact	Measures
Urgent(P1)	• Core functionality fails • Test execution is completely blocked.	• Fix the defect urgently
High(P2)	• Some of the functionality fails • Lower the execution process	• Fix the defect as soon as possible
Modest(P3)	• An important functionality fails but we don't need to test • it right away	• Fix the defect soon
Low(P4)	• Label missing, spelling or non-logical mistake	• Don't fix this defect before the high and medium defects are fixed. • Fix the defect any time

3.5   Defect Mitigation

Defect priority indicates the impact on the test team or test planning. If the defect blocks or greatly slows down test execution then these defects should have highest grade for the defect priority. Some of the key aspects must be considered before fixing the defects:-

i.   Software Product Type
ii. Associated Risk
iii. Defect Investigation Process
iv. Cost of Fixing the Defect
   • Number of Defect which are Fixed
   • Number of team members involved in fixing the Defect
   • Time taken by the Defect Fixing Process

Table 3 represents expected defects under some classified requirement which is labeled by severity and priority. On the basis of defect severity and priority defects may be fixing or not or action may be taken later depends on the Preventive Measures Guidelines for requirement defect mitigation are:-

i.   Complete and clear communicated data must be processed.
ii. Apparent dissemination of all functions and information flow with expected operational input and output.
iii. Feasible and obvious vision of expected system.

iv.   All types of text, images, graphics, quantitative operations and expected functional characteristics must be noticeable.

v.   The scope of specific operational input must be defined well.

vi.   A "Defect Sink" must be formed to contain all types of requirement defect so that it may not affect the rest of the requirement.

vii.   For defect mitigation there must be a proper checklist or prototype created by requirement analyst for identifying and resolving the defect.

viii.   Periodic scheduling must be there for preventing future defect.

ix.   Requirement changes must be traceable.

x.   Cross-functional requirement data must be identified separately.

xi.   Interdependent requirement defect must have the highest priority for mitigation.

xii.   Non-dependent requirement defect must have conditional priority among their domain.

xiii.   Requirement must be classify at granule level

3.6   Requirement Classification

Since in this paper we are discussing Requirement Defect Analysis Perspective so there will be some aspects on which the reliability of the Requirement may assess.

DD --   Number of Defects Detected
DM --   Number of Defects Mitigated
DR --   Number of Defects Unhealed
T1 --   Total time taken in defect detection
T2 --Total Time taken in Defect Mitigation/Rework

Failure rate = Total no of Defects Detected/Total time taken in defect detection (DD/T1)
Repair rate = Total no of Defects Mitigated/Total time in Defect Mitigation/Rework (DM/T2)
Mean Time to Failure (MTTF) = 1/ Failure rate
Mean Time to Repair (MTTR) = 1/ Repair rate

With the quantification of MTTF and MTTR we may identify at what extent the requirement defects have mitigated and number of defects as unhealed. Through this we may also assess the percentage of unhealed requirement and so the reliability of the requirement.

3.7   Reliable Requirement

This is the final outcome of the proposed model for Reliable Requirement Analysis. This phase will deliver a Reliable Requirement at the early stage of software development life cycle. Maximum of the Requirement defects which may create problems in structuring the operational parts of the design are removed or fixed for delivering the Reliable Requirement Specification.

4   Review

This is the second level of refinement process of the reliable requirement specification in terms of technical review (Fig 2). This review process is related with floating invigilation to detect deficiencies and risks such as:

4.1   Document Classification

The review process is executed by minimum of three to five requirement analysts or two or more group of minimum two experts. Whole document will be classified under different article for simplification of the review process by the experts. They will classify the reliability requirement specification document on the basis of their analytical and management skills.

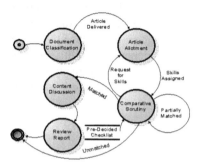

Fig. 2. Second Level Review Process

4.2   Article Allotment

Classified articles are allotted to each skilled member of the review committee to review the article. And also distribute the pre decided checklists along with the concerned article.

4.3   Comparative Scrutiny

Although some of reliable requirement specifications have been discussed in my earlier publication [8]. After receiving a copy of article along with the pre-decided checklists, reviewer starts scrutiny on the basis of the checklist. The reviewers individually inspect the objects (budget, risk and user requirements), classes and their features on the basis of the pre-decided checklist. They must write down their observations through considering the details that are needed for the review report. The allocation of articles and the pre-decided checklist must be included in the review report.

This comparative scrutiny based on Pre-Decided Checklist will be treated as surface review of overall reliable requirement document:-

    i. Suitable standard requirement documentation, fact & figures, tables, and diagrams labeled and referenced
   ii. Consistent, adequate and appropriate detailing of requirement
  iii. Reliability Characteristics of Requirement is mentioned
  iv. Confidence Level in terms of reliability
   v. Acceptable reference link and dependencies among the requirement and user characteristics description
  vi. All functional & non-functional requirement and their input, output, functions & features specified
 vii. Required hardware, software, environment and conditions for operation are specified
viii. Instructions for all phases of System Development Life Cycle specified
  ix. All types of requirement features included
   x. Is there any constraints or barriers in implementing the software defined as:-
     1) Regulatory policies 2) Hardware limitations 3) Interfaces to other applications 4) Parallel operation   5) Audit functions   6) Control functions 7) Higher-order language requirements 8) Criticality of the application
  xi. Quality attributes (efficiency, flexibility, interoperability, maintainability, portability, usability, availability) correctly specified
 xii. Time-critical functions and timing criteria identified for reliable requirement

4.4   Content Discussion

Whenever the Reliable Requirement Specification Document are reviewed with the help of provided checklist then this document must need to integrated at this stage where one to one or face to face discussion are needed to summarize the findings of scrutinized document which is studied by different reviewers. They also determine the contents which must be included in the review report.

4.5   Final Reliable Requirement Specification

The approved output of the review process in the form of review report must be delivering for finalizing the Reliable Requirement Document. This reviewed document may be treated as the final Reliable Requirement Specification Document which is further deliver to the design phase of the System Development Life Cycle. Now the designer may feel easiness in handling this document for constructing the actual design for developing the software.

    We would like to draw your attention to the fact that it is not possible to modify a paper in any way, once it has been published. This applies to both the printed book and the online version of the publication. Every detail, including the order of the names of the authors, should be checked before the paper is sent to the Volume Editors.

Table 2. Defect Severity & Priority with Conclusion

Defect Severity	Definition	Prioritization Based on Defect Severity	Conclusion
Critical (S_1)	This type of requirement defect is extremely severe and may capable to halt the entire system. If this requirement is implemented then the software application will refuse to execute or crooked of data.	• Urgent (P_1) • Low (P_4)	$S_1 + P_1$ If the requirement defect for short term application (Daily or weekly) and may halt the system then it should be fix urgently. $S_1 + P_4$ If the requirement defects for long term application (yearly or more) then fixation process may tolerate till the next release or enhancement.
Major (S_2)	This type of requirement defect is also a severe and may capable to halt some functions of the system with serious degradation in performance. Although this is also a failure, but some operations carry on at a lower rate of performance.	• High (P_2) • Urgent (P_1)	$S_2 + P_2$ If logical issue of requirement and lower rate performance defect but not halted the system defect may be fix in very second time (but not urgently) $S_2 + P_1$ If major severity of requirement and may halt the system then it should be fix urgently.
Minor (S_3)	This type of requirement defect is not so severe but caused a low-level disruption of the system or malfunctioning of some operations. This kind of disruption or non-availability of some functionality can be acceptable for a limited period. This type of disruption may cause for failure, but it continues to operate for short span of time at a lower rate of performance.	• Modest(P3)	$S_3 + P_3$ If some operational requirement disrupted which will not affect the core business logic then these defect may resolve in next release
Cosmetic (S_4)	This type of defect is one that mainly related to the appearance or the layout of the data which has no risk of corrupting the statistics and incorrect values. Since it converse about the headline, flag, marker and Colors so it has no actual effect on the operations and may carry on operating with system without any degradation in performance.	• Low (P4)	$S_4 + P_4$ There is no risk of corrupting the operational requirement (headline, labeling, tagging etc.) then the requirements are permissible with no degradation in performance, but need some improvement further.

Table 3. Defects under Classified Requirement with Severity & Priority and Preventive Action

Requirement Classification	Requirement Scope		Input Section		Output Section		Requirement Boundaries		Functional Issues	
Identified Defect	• Incorrect portrayal for Product • Business Case, behavior or Mission not defined • Unclear needs, goals, objectives • Operational Concepts lacks • Interface Description missing and others		• Input data repository missing • Inconsistency of data naming • Precondition detail missing • Input data dictionary not defined and others		• Output data sink missing • Precondition detail missing • Input data dictionary not defined • Missing detail of expected results and others		• Condition and environment detail missing • Limited cross functional data link • Improper partitioning of modules • Unclear Resource allocation/reallocations and others		• Actor and its role missing • Operational component missing • Component name & State missing • Casual defects of operations and others	
Defect Severity and Priority to Defect	(S1)	(P1)(P4)	(S1)	(P1)(P4)	(S1)	(P1)(P4)	(S1)	(P1)(P4)	(S1)	(P1)(P4)
	(S2)	(P2)(P1)	(S2)	(P2)(P1)	(S2)	(P2)(P1)	(S2)	(P2)(P1)	(S2)	(P2)(P1)
	(S3)	(P3)	(S3)	(P3)	(S3)	(P3)	(S3)	(P3)	(S3)	(P3)
	(S4)	(P4)	(S4)	(P4)	(S4)	(P4)	(S4)	(P4)	(S4)	(P4)
Preventive Action	o Fix Now o Fix later o No Action		o Fix Now o Fix later o No Action		o Fix Now o Fix later o No Action		o Fix Now o Fix later o No Action		o Fix Now o Fix later o No Action	

5   Conclusion

In this paper we proposed a concrete Requirement Analysis process for producing the Reliable Requirement software. The benefits of using this process are-

   i.   The main purpose of using this Analysis procedure is "To reduce rework", "Shortening the requirement document Length" and "Make Requirement reliable".

   ii. Defect Location and Description will shorten the search time for defect identification.

Projected preventive measure guidelines provides an approach for early detection of requirement defect and also assist for considering all perspective requirement corner.

The direction of further study is to be developing a framework to Reliable Requirement Life Cycle (A defect Perspective) for early identification and mitigation of requirement defects and a technique for mitigating requirement defect one by one as defect identified.

References

1. Chao, B., Zhu, X.D., Li, Q., Huang, A.C.: Reliability Management in Software Requirement Analysis. In: International Conference on Management of Innovation and Technology, pp. 1104–1107. IEEE Explore (2006)
2. Pressman, R.S.: Risk Mitigation, Monitoring and Management. In: Software Engineering – A Practitioner's Approach, 5th edn., p. 156. McGraw-Hill (2001)
3. Stefan, B., Michael, H.: Software Product Improvement With Inspection: A Large Scale Experiment On The Influence Of Inspection Process On Defect Detection In Software Requirement Documents. In: Proceedings of the 26th Euromicro Conference, vol. 2, pp. 262–269. IEEE Explore (2000)
4. Singh, L.K., Tripathi, A.K., Vinod, G.: Software Reliability Early prediction in Architectural Design Phase: Overview and Limitations. Journal on Software Engineering and Applications 4, 181–186 (2011)
5. Fuping, Z., Aizhen, C., Xin, T.: Study on Software Reliability Design Criteria Based On Defect Patterns. In: 8th International Conference on Reliability, Maintainability and Safety (ICRMS), pp. 723–727. IEEE Explore (2009)
6. Mohan, K.K., Verma, A.K., Srividya, A., Rao, G.V., Gedela, R.K.: Early Quantitative Software Reliability Prediction Using Petri-nets. In: Third International Conference on Industrial and Information Systems, pp. 1–6. IEEE Explore (2008)
7. Lee, E.S., Bae, J.M.: Design Opportunity Tree for Requirement Management and Software Process Improvement. In: International Conference on Multimedia and Ubiquitous Engineering, pp. 395–400. IEEE Explore (2007)
8. Nayak, S.K., Khan, R.A., Beg, R.: A Comparative Template for Reliable Requirement Specification. International Journal of Computer Applications 14(2), 27–30 (2011)

Comparative Analysis of IR Based Web Service Similarity Measures Using Vector Space Model

Vaneet Sharma[1] and Mukesh Kumar[2]

[1] Computer Science & Engineering Department, SLIET,
Longowal (Punjab), India
[2] UIET, Panjab University, Chandigarh, India
{Vaneet87,mukesh_rai9}@yahoo.com

Abstract. With the advent of Service Oriented Architecture (SOA), Web Services have gained tremendous popularity. Due to the availability of a large number of Web services, the task of finding relevant services becomes more and more difficult. Moreover, nowadays large enterprises increasingly rely on Web services as methodology for large-scale software development and sharing of services within an organization. . This warrants the need to establish an effective process of discovering similar services. Web service discovery involves three interrelated phases: 1- matching, 2-assessment, and 3- selection. Our work focuses on the phase 1, service discovery matching, in which we are using standard similarity measures i.e. Cosine Similarity and Euclidean distance to retrieve the most relevant services. As there is no predetermined formula or way to identify the parameters on which the similarity between two services can be identified, we develop a Regression Model to verify the significance of parameters used. In the end, we perform the comparative analysis of approaches we used.

Keywords: Semantic service discovery, Syntactic service discovery, WSDL (Web Service Discovery Language), Web services, Web service discovery, Information Retrieval.

1 Introduction

A Web service is a public interface of an application which can be invoked remotely to perform a business function or a set of functions. Web service has been defined as self contain ed, self-describing, modular application that can be published, located and invoked across the Web [1].

The wide spreading of Web Services is due to its simplicity and the data interoperability provided by its components namely XML (eXtended Markup Language), SOAP (Simple Object Access Protocol) and WSDL. These are open standards over an Internet Protocol backbone. WSDL is used for describing the services; SOAP is used to transfer the data; XML is used to describe the data in a structured way using custom defined tags. UDDI is used for listing what services are available. It is regarded as the de-facto standard registry for Web services. It not only

P.V. Krishna, M.R. Babu, and E. Ariwa (Eds.): ObCom 2011, Part II, CCIS 270, pp. 752–760, 2012.
© Springer-Verlag Berlin Heidelberg 2012

allows businesses to describe and register their services, but also allows them to disc-
-over services that fit their requirements. However, the discovery mechanism
provided by UDDI is keyword search on the names and the features of businesses and
service descriptions. Unfortunately, with the proliferation of Web services, keyword
search fails to satisfy the requirements of efficient discovery and semantic operability.
Discovery is the process of finding Web services Provider locations which satisfy
specific requirements. Web services are useless if they cannot be discovered. So,
discovery is the most important task in the Web service model (Fig.1). To efficiently
match similar services, it is important to get their underlying semantics. By
investigating the metadata from the WSDL structure, our approach tries to determine
the similarity between Web services. We use standard similarity measures that
retrieve the metadata present in the document tag of each WSDL from the collection
of Web services and discover likeness between them. Besides the similarity
measurement, we have also developed a model to test the significance of the
parameters used. Last but not the least; we have done a comparative analysis of the
classifiers we used.

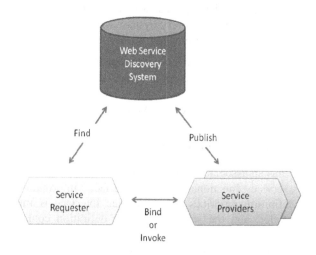

Fig. 1. Web Service Model

2   Web Service Model

The Web service model in Fig.1. shows the interaction between Service Requester,
Service Providers, and a Service Discovery System.

- The service providers offer Web services which provide functions or
  business operations. They are created by companies or organizations. In
  order to be invoked, the Web services must be described. This will facilitate
  discovery and composition. WSDL or service profile of semantic Web
  service is used to carry out this function.
- The Web service requester describes requirements in order to locate service
  providers. Service requesters usually contain a description of the Web

service, though it is not a Web service which can run on the Internet. The requirements are usually described by WSDL, service template or service profile

- The Web service discovery or service registry is a broker that provides registry and search functions. The service providers advertise their service information in the discovery system. This information will be stored in the registry and will be searched when there is a request from service requester. UDDI is used as a registry standard for non-semantic Web service. Semantic Web service discovery systems are developed for semantic Web services.

These components interact with each other via Publishing, Discovery, and Binding operations. These operations are elaborated upon as follows:

Publish: The Web service providers publish their Service information through the discovery system for requesters to discover. Through the publishing operation, the Web service provider stores the service description in the discovery system.

Discovery: The Web service requesters retrieve service providers from the service registry. Based on service descriptions, which describes the requirements of the Web service requesters, the discovery system will output a list of Web service providers which satisfy the requirements.

Bind: After discovering, the discovery system provides a number of Web service providers. The Web service requester invokes these Web service providers. The binding occurs at runtime. The Web service requesters and Web service providers will communicate via SOAP protocol for Web service exchange information.

3   The Structure of Web Services

Each Web service has an associated XML-based document called WSDL. WSDL file describes Web service functionality and interface information. The service implementation definition describes how a service interface is implemented by a given service provider, and the service interface definition contains the business category Information and interface specifications that are registered as UDDI tModels. A Web service is typically (though not necessarily) published by registering its WSDL file and a brief description in UDDI business registries. Each Web service consists of a set of operations. Regardless of the invocation information in WSDL that is useless for similarity matching, such as the binding and the port, we can identify three types of metadata from WSDL.

- **Name and text description:** A Web service is described by a name, a text description in the WSDL file, and a description that is put in the UDDI registry
- **Operation descriptions:** Each operation is described by a name and a text description in the WSDL file.
- **Input/output descriptions:** Each input and output of an operation contains a set of parameters. For each parameter, the WSDL file describes the name, data type and Parameters may be organized in a hierarchy by using complex types.

4   Approaches to Web Service Discovery

A lot of research has been conducted to fulfill the promises of Web services discovery [2]. [3] broadly classifies discovery system based two aspects: one stream of thought focuses on finding the WSs based on its *functional requirements*. For example, a Consumer could be looking for a Service Description (WSDL) that combines a set of related services for the travel domain giving an overall plan including airfare, hotel and car rental. As is evident, the Consumer wants the *functional or operational aspects* of the service. The second stream of thought is to discover WSs based its *non-functional requirements*. The predominant factor being *'Quality of Service' (QoS)*. A Consumer may want a Service that offers the fastest response time while for another reliability or constant availability could be the criteria and a third Consumer may treat security as his most important parameter. All these, namely, security, response time, reliability, availability come under the non-functional QoS requirements of a service.

Discovering services involves three interrelated phases [4][5]: 1- matching, 2- assessment, and 3- selection. In phase 1, the service description input by developer is matched to that of a set of available resources. In phase 2, the result of matching (typically the set of ranked web services) is assessed and filtered by a given set of criteria. In phase 3, services are actually selected for subsequent customizing and combining with others. This section focuses on the phase 1, service discovery matching, in which the whole set of matchmaking schemes can be divided into either Semantic or Syntactic based system to achieve the final goal of effective service discovery as summarized in Fig.2.

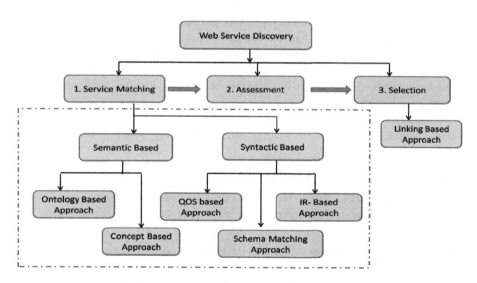

Fig. 2. Taxonomy of Web service discovery systems

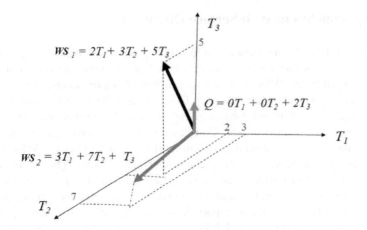

Fig. 3. Vector Space Model

Information Retrieval Based Approach

In IR community [6], document matching and classification is a long-standing topic and widely use in most search engines. Most of the solution to this problem is based on *Query–Sensitive Similarity Measures (QSSM)*. **QSSM** [18] aim to detect similarity by viewing the query terms as the silent features that define the context under which similarity is examined. This approach can be implemented through Vector space model.

Vector Space Model [6] [7]:- In Vector Space model a set of documents is represented as vectors in a common vector space is known as the vector space model. The VSM assumes that for each term there exists a vector and then the linear combination of these term vectors represents documents in the vector space. Vector space model can be used to find the similarity between two Web services by using various similarity measures such as cosine similarity and Euclidean Distance. The vector space model converts text-based information to numerical vectors that are then used for analysis. Fig.3. shows the example of how services are represented in the vector space model.

A collection of n services can be represented in vector space model by a term-service matrix. An entity in the matrix corresponds to the weight of the term in the service.

Important Terms for Calculating the Term Weights: -

Term Frequency (tf):- refers to the number of occurrences of the term t in a service. *Document Frequency (df):* - refers to the number of services in the collection that contains a term t.

Inverse Document Frequency (idf)(1): - refers to the idea of scaling down the term weights of terms with high frequency. It reduces the effect of terms that occur too often in the collection to be meaningful for relevance determination. The inverse document frequency of a rare term is high and of frequent term is low. Idf is calculated as:

$$Idf(t) = \log \frac{(N)}{Df} \tag{1}$$

Where

N :- number of services in the collection.

Df :- document frequency.

Tf-idf Weighting:- used to produce the composite score (3) for each service.

$$Tf - idf = Tf_{t,ws} \times idf_t \tag{2}$$

$$SCORE(q, ws) = \sum_{t \in q} Tf - idf_{t,ws} \tag{3}$$

Once the vectors for all the documents are achieved, the similarity is calculated using a similarity measure. A similarity measure is a function that computes degree of similarity between two vectors.

Cosine Similarity[7] [8] [9]:- it is a standard way of quantifying the similarity between two services ws_1 and ws_2 i.e. by computing the cosine similarity (4) of their vector representations $V(ws_1)$ and $V(ws2)$

$$Sim(ws_1, ws_2) = \frac{V(ws_1) \cdot V(ws_2)}{|V(ws_1)||V(ws_2)|} \tag{4}$$

where the numerator represents the dot product of vectors, while the denominator is the product of their Euclidean lengths. V(ws) denote the service vector for ws, with M components $V_1(ws)$.....$V_M(ws)$. The Euclidean length (5) of ws is defined to be

$$\sqrt{\sum_{i=1}^{M} V_i^2(ws)} \tag{5}$$

The problem is to find the services most similar to WS from the collection (suppose $WS_1...WS_N$) with the highest dot products. This can be resolved by computing the dot products between V (WS) and each of $V(WS_1)$......$V(WS_N)$, and then picking the highest resulting *sim* values. When the cosine is 1, the vectors are pointing in the same direction and when the cosine is 0, they are pointing in perpendicular directions. Typically, a the cosine is 0, they are pointing in perpendicular directions. Typically, a threshold value T is chosen such that if $|Cos\theta| \geq T$.

Euclidean Distance[10]: - The Euclidean distance or Euclidean metric is the "ordinary" distance between two points that one would measure with a ruler, and is given by the Pythagorean formula. Two services are said to be similar based using the Euclidean distance between the two points. Mathematically if the two points are:

$Q = (x_1, x_2, x_3, ..., x_n)$
And
$ws_j = (y_1, y_2, y_3, ..., y_n)$
Then, the Euclidean distance(6) Dis(Q, ws_i) is defined as

$$Dis(Q, ws_i) = \sqrt{\sum_{i=1}^{M}(x_i - y_i)^2} \tag{6}$$

Where

> Q: - query service.
> ws_j:- j^{th} web service in initial collection
> x_i: - i^{th} term of query service Q
> y_i: - i^{th} term of jth service from initial collection

5   Implementation

There is no publicly available Web Services dataset. So, we created an initial collection in which Web Services from 4 different domains (namely Weather, Address, Railways and Finance) are downloaded from different sources like xmethods, webServicex and strike iron in an CSV (Comma Separated) file. In order to explore the underlying semantics of this textual data, we first develop a tool that extracts the Document tag of each WSDL. Each description is preprocessed to obtain the valuable Keywords. Each web service is then represented in the form of vector and corresponding term weights are evaluated. Then we use the similarity classifiers (i.e. Euclidean distance and Cosine Similarity) to evaluate the similarity between the query and the service in the corpus.

We have used certain parameters like TF, IDF, TF-IDF, Cosine Similarity and Euclidean Distance in order to discover the similar Services. But there is no standard formula, preset notion or way to identify the parameters on which the similarity between two Web Services is dependent. So we need to develop a Regression Model in order to prove that the above said parameters are most significant in order to find similar Web Services. We use Linear Forward Regression Model that stepwise accept one parameter at a time and conduct tests for how much the Model is affected after each addition.

For this purpose, apart from the above used parameters, we use some more parameters as Number of operations, total number of Web Services in a corpus and Number of Input/ output parameters. Based on the data collected in past, we create a Dataset, which is fed as an input to SPSS Software.

Inference1: Based on Regression Model, it has been found that it two Models are generated as resultant. Both the Models exclude three parameters namely number_of_web_Services, number_of_operations and number_of_IO_parameters as their significant value is close to 1.

Inference2: based on F Test (which explains the variance between the rows and columns of the data matrix in question, it has been found that two variable has not passed the test as their value is close to 0. The value of r2 gives the measure of how good the data matrix value fit into the trend length and simply tells the goodness of

Inference3: Certain values of parameters in question of Data Matrix were highly outlier in nature therefore they were they were excluded. The missing values and rows were also discarded by the Model.

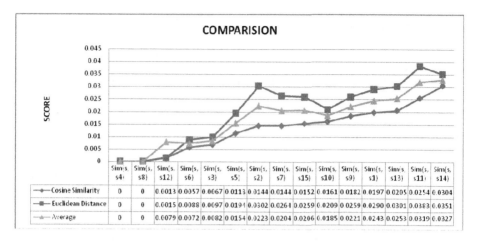

Fig. 4. Comparisons of Similarity Measures for Query US Zip Validator

Table 1. Similarity Scores for Query US Zip Validator

Similarity	Web Service Name(si)	Cosine Similarity	Euclidean Distance	Average
Sim(s,s4)	SeatStatus	0	0	0
Sim(s,s8)	StockQuote	0	0	0
Sim(s,s12)	NationalWeatherService	0.001393099	0.001580458	0.00790229
Sim(s,s6)	GetStationInfoByCity	0.005696549	0.008802274	0.007279412
Sim(s,s3)	USWeather	0.006783749	0.009783749	0.008283749
Sim(s,s5)	GlobalWeather	0.011393099	0.019431813	0.015412456
Sim(s,s2)	PlaceFinder	0.014411257	0.030271611	0.022341434
Sim(s,s7)	GeoMonsterZIPServe	0.014411257	0.026454525	0.020432891
Sim(s,s15)	PostalCodeWorldMexico	0.015285446	0.025970459	0.020627953
Sim(s,s10)	NorwegianPostalAddresses	0.016112275	0.020966692	0.018539484
Sim(s,s9)	ZipCodeWorld	0.018269602	0.02598602	0.022127811
Sim(s,s1)	StrikeIronGlobalAddress	0.019733426	0.029055131	0.024394279
Sim(s,s13)	ZipCodesLookup	0.020561374	0.030169129	0.025365252
Sim(s,s11)	GlobalSkiResortFinder	0.025475743	0.038331894	0.031903819
Sim(s,s14)	DOTSGeoCode	0.030449337	0.035095238	0.032772288

6   Results

We have analyzed 15 Web Services stored in the initial collection for result purpose. Fig.4. illustrates the comparison of the different similarity measures. The table 1 shows the values obtained through different similarity measures when the input query WS (i.e US Zip Validator) arranged in an increasing order of their score values.

7   Conclusions

In this paper we have tried to provide a glimpse of the huge spectrum of work investigated by researchers globally in the field of Discovering the Right Services either semantically or syntactically. Taxonomy of discovery systems was also introduced. Discovery system plays crucial role in Web service model for efficient service retrieval. In this paper, a comparative analysis of standard similarity Classifiers i.e. Cosine Similarity and Euclidean Distance in Vector Space Model is done. Also a strategy is developed to find similarity between Web Services based on underlying semantics within the document tag of each WSDL. A Regression Model is developed to identify the significance of the parameters used to identify similar Web Services. From the results obtained by comparing these similarity measures using vector space Model, it is analyzed that Cosine similarity outperforms Euclidean distance as the value of Euclidean Distance is large enough even though the distribution of terms in query and distribution of terms in Service are similar. Thus, it can be used to as an effective measure to determine similarity between Web Services. Many more similarity measures used for document matching can used to test their effectiveness for Service Similarity. We left it for future work.

References

1. Booth, D., Haas, H., McCabe, F.: Web Services Architecture. W3C Working Group Note (2004)
2. Christensen, E., Curbera, F., Meredith, G., Weerawarana, S.: Web Services Description Language(WSDL) 1.1. W3C Note (2001)
3. Nair, M.K., Gopalakrishna, V.: Look Before You Leap: A Survey of Web Service Discovery. The Proceedings of International Journal of Computer Applications 7(5) (September 2010)
4. Kokash, N., van den Heuvel, W., D'Andrea, V.: Leveraging Web Services Discovery with Customizable Hybrid Matching. University of Trento (2006)
5. Dutta, B.: Semantic Web Services: A Study of Existing Technologies, Tools and Projects. The Proceedings of Journal of Library & Information Technology 28(3) (2008)
6. Christopher, D.: Manning and Prabhakar Raghavan. An introduction to Information Retrieva. Preliminary draft© 2008 Cambridge UP (2008)
7. Tombros, A., Ali, Z.: Factors Affecting Web Page Similarity. In: Losada, D.E., Fernández-Luna, J.M. (eds.) ECIR 2005. LNCS, vol. 3408, pp. 487–501. Springer, Heidelberg (2005)
8. Srikant, R., Bayardo, R.J., Ma, Y.: Scaling Up All Pairs Similarity Search. In: The Proceedings of 16th International Conference on World Wide Web, Canada (2007)
9. Suebsing, A., Hranskolwong, N.: Feature Selection Using Euclidean Distance and Cosine Similarity for Intrusion Detection Model. In: The Proceedings of Intelligent Information and Database Systems, ACIIDS (2009)
10. Nargundkar, R.: Marketing Research: Test and Cases. Mc Graw Hill Edition (2008)

Comparative Study of Bit Loading Algorithms for OFDM Based Systems

Isha[1], Pankaj Rana[2], and Ravikant Saini[3]

[1] Shobhit University, Meerut(UP), India
[2] NITTTR,Chandigarh, India
[3] IIT Delhi, India
{isha0129,pankaj.rana2004}@gmail.com,
sravikantk2@rediffmail.com

Abstract. In OFDM-based systems, bit allocation techniques are used according to channel response, as noisy sub-channels should carry little or no data. In this paper, we compare three different types of bit loading algorithms and analyze bit allotment per sub channel and energy consumed at a fixed bit error rate and fixed target - total number of bits.

Keywords: adaptive bit allocation, Orthogonal Frequency Division Multiplexing (OFDM), multicarrier modulation, multipath channel, power line channel.

1 Introduction

Orthogonal frequency division multiplexing (OFDM) has developed into a popular scheme for wideband digital communication, whether wireless or over copper wires, used in applications such as digital video and audio broadcasting, wireless networking, broadband Internet access and Power line communication. Several broadband Power line communication standards [9],[10] employ OFDM. The OFDM systems can establish the coexistence with the existing shortwave wireless systems by masking appropriate subcarriers. and the cyclic prefix of OFDM could sufficiently mitigate the frequency selective channels caused by multipath effect[4].

OFDM is an effective technique to combat multipath fading in wireless communications and for high-bit-rate wireless applications. OFDM is a frequency-division multiplexing (FDM) scheme used as a digital multi-carrier modulation method. The primary advantage of OFDM over single-carrier schemes is its ability to cope with severe channel conditions without complex equalization filters. A large number of closely-spaced orthogonal sub-carriers are used to carry data. The data is divided into several parallel data streams or channels, one for each sub-carrier. The orthogonal sub-channels are spaced 1/T Hz apart and overlap in frequency. The use of a guard interval between OFDM symbols make it possible to eliminate intersymbol interference (ISI), so it can support efficient spectrum utilization. It is conveniently implemented using IFFT and FFT operations.[2]

P.V. Krishna, M.R. Babu, and E. Ariwa (Eds.): ObCom 2011, Part II, CCIS 270, pp. 761–767, 2012.
© Springer-Verlag Berlin Heidelberg 2012

Initially, OFDM-based systems employ conventional multi-carrier modulation that uses the same modulation scheme (such as quadrature amplitude modulation or phase-shift keying).Then, the overall bit-error rate (BER) performance of these systems is dominated by the sub-channels with the worst performance. Hence, in order to improve the system-wide BER performance, adaptive bit allocation is done to each sub-channel according to their channels states. More bits should be concentrated on the subchannels with a higher channel frequency response, and noisy sub-channels should carry little or no data[5].

In this paper, a comparison is made among different bit-loading algorithms for OFDM based on minimizing the bit error rate(BER) and total energy used with fixed target bits constraint. The second section explains channel model used for simulation, third section explains bit loading technique with different algorithms, then, in fourth section numerical results are shown and in the last conclusion is given.

2   Multipath Channel Model

We evaluate the bit loading algorithms on diverse multipath channels which are randomly generated according to Zimmermann's multipath power line channel model [3].The frequency responses of multipath power line channels can be approximated as,

$$H(f) = \sum_{l=0}^{L-1} g_l \, e^{-(a_0 + a_1 f^k)d_l} e^{-j2\pi f(\tau_l - \tau_0)}$$

where, the parameters are listed in Table 1.

Table 1. Parameters of multipath power line channels

L	Total number of dominant paths
g_l	Weighting factor for lth path
a_0	Attenuation constant for constant term(>0)
a_1	Attenuation constant for term of f^k(>0)
k	Exponent of the attenuation factor(between 0.2 and 1)
τ_l	Delay of lth path
d_l	Length of lth path(m)

OFDM-based systems divide the available bandwidth into a set of N orthogonal sub-channels. With a sufficiently long cyclic prefix playing the role of a guard interval, these N sub-channels can be treated as independent parallel locally flat channels corrupted by additive white gaussian noise (AWGN)[5]. We assume that the bandwidth of all sub-channels is narrower than the coherence bandwidth.

3   Bit Loading

The bit loading uses the channel estimates to determine an appropriate bit allocation across all the subcarriers. As a result, each subcarrier is allocated a different number of bits. Furthermore, constraints are applied to the algorithm to ensure that the allocation stays within a desired range of values. The objective of bit loading algorithms is to minimize the total energy used, while the constraint is a limit on the mean bit error rate (BER) and total number of bits allocated. Then, energy of each sub-channel is described in[1] as,

$$e_i = (2^{b_i} - 1).\frac{\Gamma}{CNR_i}$$

where, b_i is number of bits allocated on ith sub-channel, CNR_i is carrier to noise ratio on i-th sub-channel and Γ is the SNR gap that is obtained by the gap-approximation analysis based on the target bit error rate (BER), the applied coding scheme, and the system performance margin [5].

Where, $\Gamma = \ln (5* BER)/1.5$[7]

4   Different Types of Algorithms

In this paper, the comparison is done among different types of algorithms, used for bit loading in OFDM systems, on the basis of bit allocation and energy consumed on each sub-channel. Different algorithms are compared with No Bit Loading technique (where numbers of bits allocated evenly to each sub-channel) used as a reference for comparison.

The compared algorithms are,

1. No Bit Loading
2. Bit Loading algorithm
3. Fast Bit Loading algorithm
4. Simple Bit Loading algorithm

4.1   Bit Loading Algorithm

This algorithm assigns the in-phase and quadrature (IQ) mapping on each subcarrier for the given whole code rate and carrier to noise ratio (CNR) on each subcarrier, to maximize the throughput subject to a constraint that average BER is less than Pe, where Pe is bit error rate[4]. It optimizes the bits quantity on each subcarrier subject to constraints on the total BER and transmission power on each subcarrier. The incremental bit errors at every additional one bit on each subcarrier is used to maximize the bit rate and to make indicator matrix which tells about the number of bits allocated to each sub-carrier.

4.2   Fast Bit Loading Algorithm

This algorithm uses water filling solution to obtain the optimal solution of energy minimization problem with target bit rate and fixed energy constraints using the Lagrange multiplier method [5]. At the initial bit allocation step, most bits of the target rate are assigned to sub-channels according to channel states. The optimal solution is achieved by allocating b_i into sub-channel i:

$$b_i = \log_2(\frac{K.CNR_i}{\Gamma})$$

Where, $\quad K = 2^{\frac{Btarget - \Sigma_{i=0}^{N} \log_2 CNR_i}{number\ of\ sub\ channel}}$

At the final bit allocation step, multiple bits are assigned to sub-channels in order to guarantee the target rate. In order to converge to target bit, bits are allocated or removed accordingly.

4.3   Simple Bit Loading Algorithm

This algorithm converges to an optimal bit allocation without using a complex computation procedure to calculate k as in fast bit loading algorithm above. Most bits of the target rate are assigned to sub-channels at the initial bit allocation step, according to channel response and the computational steps are reduced efficiently.

Multiple bits are added to or removed from all sub-channels simultaneously in order to approach the optimum bit allocation with no more than 1 bit difference from the optimum bit allocation per sub-channel at the intermediate bit allocation step. At the final bit allocation step, algorithm uses a bit-filling or bit removal procedure in order to guarantee the target rate[5]. Energy required to add one more bit at sub-channel i that is carrying b_i,

$$\Delta e_i^+(b_i) = 2^{b_i} \cdot \frac{\Gamma}{CNR_i}, \qquad 1 \le i < N$$

And the power saved by removing 1 bit at sub-channel i that is carrying b_i is given by,

$$\Delta e_i^-(b_i) = 2^{(b_i - 1)} \cdot \frac{\Gamma}{CNR_i}, 1 \le i < N$$

5   Simulation and Results

In this section, numerical results are shown which indicates the comparison among different algorithms explained above with the help of graphs and tables. All the algorithms works on a particular channel having CNR values shown in figure 1 with noise spectral density is 10^-7.

- Figure 2 shows the comparison of number of bits allocated per sub channel, for different algorithms.
- Figure 3 shows comparison of energy used per sub channel, for different algorithms.
- Total energy consumed for different algorithms is shown in table 2.

The result is shown for 120 total target bits with 8 maximum bits allocated to each sub channel and bit error rate (ber) is 10^-3. Assume M-QAM modulation is applied.

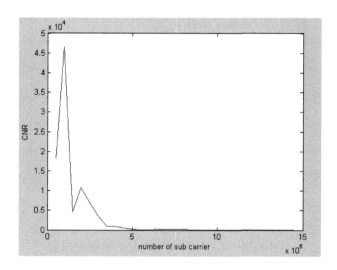

Fig. 1. CNR for different sub channel

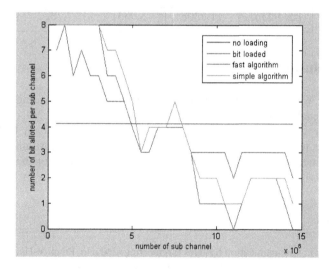

Fig. 2. Bit Allotment for target bits= 120

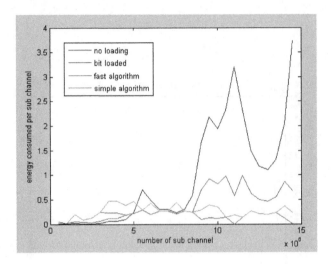

Fig. 3. Energy Consumed for target bit=120

Table 2. Total energy consumed for bit target=120

No Bit Loading	Bit Loading	Fast Bit Loading	Simple Bit Loading
[27.9236]	11.5308	5.0531	7.7822

6   Conclusion

In this paper, we compare three different algorithms with no loading technique for OFDM and analyze these techniques with bit allotment per sub carrier, energy consumed per sub carrier and total energy used with constraint on BER and total number of bits to be allocated. Finally, we conclude that fast algorithm has minimum energy consumed and simple algorithm has lowest complexity for the same optimal bit allotment.

References

1. Proakis, J.G.: Communication Systems Engineering, 2nd edn. Prentice-Hall (2002)
2. Litwin, L., Pugel, M.: RF signal processing. The principle of OFDM
3. Zimmermann, M., Dostert, K.: A multipath model for the power line channel. IEEE Trans. Commun. 50(4), 553–559 (2002)
4. Hayasaki, T., Umehara, D., Denno, S., Morikura, M.: A Bit-Loaded OFDMA for In-home Power Line Communications. In: IEEE International Symposium on Power Line Communications and Its Applications, ISPLC 2009, pp. 171–176 (2009)

5. Ko, H., Lee, K., Oh, S., Kim, C.: Fast Optimal Discrete Bit-Loading Algorithms for OFDM-based systems. In: Proceedings of 18th Internatonal Conference on Computer Communications and Networks, ICCCN 2009 (2009)
6. Chow, P.S., Cioffi, J.M., Bingham, J.A.C.: A Practical Discrete Multitone transceiver Loading Algorithm for Data Transmission over Spectrally Shaped channels. IEEE Transactions on Communications 43(234) (2002)
7. Jang, J., Lee, K.B.: Transmit Power Adaptation for Multiuser OFDM Systems. IEEE J. Select. Areas Commun. 21(2), 171–178 (2003)
8. HomePlug AV White Paper. HomePlug Powerline Alliance (HPA), http://www.homeplug.org/
9. Digital Home Specification White-paper. Universal Powerline Association (UPA), http://www.upaplc.org/

Comparison of PAPR of OFDM Systems Using CDF Plots for QAM and QPSK

T. Durga Prasad, K.V. Satya Kumar, P. Raju, R. Koteswara Rao Naik,
and V. Santosh Kumar

Department of Electronics and Communication Engineering,
GIT, GITAM University,
Visakhapatnam, India
{tumula.durgaprasad,k.v.satyakumar,dev241raju,
kotimail}@gmail.com,
santosh7732@yahoo.com

Abstract. Orthogonal frequency division multiplexing (OFDM) provides better spectral efficiency than frequency division multiplexing (FDM), while maintaining orthogonal relation between carriers hence traffic is better carried by OFDM than FDM within the same spectrum. This paper reveals a comparison of spectral efficiency, performance of communication system in context of bit error rate (BER) for the same information rate and peak to average power ratio (PAPR) of quadrature amplitude shift keying(QPSK)and16-quadratureamplitudemodulation(16-QAM)technique.

Keywords: OFDM, QPSK, 16-QAM, IFFT, frequency spectrum, PAPR, BER.

1   Introduction

In a basic communication system, the data are modulated onto a single carrier frequency. The available bandwidth is then totally occupied by each symbol. This kind of system can lead to inter-symbol-interference (ISI) in case of frequency selective channel. The basic idea of OFDM is to divide the available spectrum into several orthogonal sub channels so that each narrowband sub channels experiences almost flat fading. Orthogonal frequency division multiplexing (OFDM) is becoming the chosen modulation technique for wireless communications. OFDM can provide large data rates with sufficient robustness to radio channel impairments. Many research centers in the world have specialized teams working in the optimization of OFDM systems. In an OFDM scheme, a large number of orthogonal, overlapping, narrow band sub-carriers are transmitted in parallel. These carriers divide the available transmission bandwidth. The separation of the sub- carriers is such that there is a very compact spectral utilization. With OFDM, it is possible to have overlapping sub channels in the frequency domain, thus increasing the transmission rate. The attraction of OFDM is mainly because of its way of handling the multipath interference at the receiver. Multipath phenomenon generates two effects (a) Frequency selective fading and (b) Inter symbol interference (ISI).

P.V. Krishna, M.R. Babu, and E. Ariwa (Eds.): ObCom 2011, Part II, CCIS 270, pp. 768–779, 2012.
© Springer-Verlag Berlin Heidelberg 2012

2   Fourier Analysis of QAM

In the frequency domain, QAM has a similar spectral pattern to DSB-SC modulation. Using the properties of the Fourier transform, we find that

$$S(f) = \frac{1}{2}[M_I(f - f_0) + M_I(f + f_0)] + \frac{1}{2j}[M_Q(f - f_0) - M_Q(f + f_0)]$$

where S(f), MI(f) and MQ(f) are the Fourier transforms (frequency-domain representations) of s(t), I(t) and Q(t), respectively.

2.1   Quantized QAM Representation

In QAM, the constellation points are usually arranged in a square grid with equal vertical and horizontal spacing, although other configurations are possible (e.g. Cross-QAM). Since in digital telecommunications the data are usually binary, the number of points in the grid is usually a power of 2 (2, 4, 8 ...). Since QAM is usually square, some of these are rare—the most common As with many digital modulation schemes, the constellation diagram is a useful forms are 16-QAM, 64-QAM, 128-QAM and 256-QAM. By moving to a higher-order constellation, it is possible to transmit more bits per symbol. However, if the mean energy of the constellation is to remain the same (by way of making a fair comparison), the points must be closer together and are thus more susceptible to noise and other corruption; this results in a higher bit error rate and so higher-order QAM can deliver more data less reliably than lower-order QAM, for constant mean constellation energy. If data-rates beyond those offered by 8-PSK are required, it is more usual to move to QAM since it achieves a greater distance between adjacent points in the I-Q plane by distributing the points more evenly. The complicating factor is that the points are no longer all the same amplitude and so the demodulator must now correctly detect both phase and amplitude, rather than just phase.

2.2   Transmitter Structure

The following picture shows the ideal structure of a QAM transmitter, with a carrier frequency f0 and the frequency response of the transmitter's filter Ht:

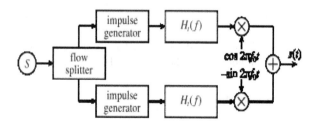

Fig. 2.1. QAM Transmitter structure

First the flow of bits to be transmitted is split into two equal parts: this process generates two independent signals to be transmitted. They are encoded separately just like they were in an amplitude-shift keying (ASK) modulator. Then one channel (the one "in phase") is multiplied by a cosine, while the other channel (in "quadrature") is multiplied by a sine. This way there is a phase of 90° between them. They are simply added one to the other and sent through the real channel.

The sent signal can be expressed in the form:

$$s(t) = \sum_{n=-\infty}^{\infty} \left[v_c[n] \cdot h_t(t - nT_s) \cos(2\pi f_0 t) - v_s[n] \cdot h_t(t - nT_s) \sin(2\pi f_0 t) \right],$$

Where $v_c[n]$ and $v_s[n]$ are the voltages applied in response to the nth symbol to the cosine and sine waves respectively.

2.3   Receiver Structure

The receiver simply performs the inverse process of the transmitter. It's ideal structure is shown in the picture below with H_r the receive filter's frequency response:

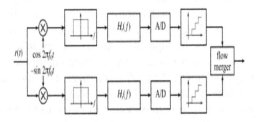

Fig. 2.2. QAM Receiver Structure

Multiplying by a cosine (or a sine) and by a low-pass filter it is possible to extract the component in phase (or in quadrature). Then there is only an ASK demodulator and the two flows of data are merged back. In practice, there is an unknown phase delay between the transmitter and receiver that must be compensated by synchronization of the receiver's local oscillator, i.e. the sine and cosine functions in the above figure. In mobile applications, there will often be an offset in the relative frequency as well, due to the possible presence of a Doppler shift proportional to the relative velocity of the transmitter and receiver. Both the phase and frequency variations introduced by the channel must be compensated by properly tuning the sine and cosine components, which requires a phase reference, and is typically accomplished using a Phase-Locked Loop (PLL). In any application, the low-pass filter will be within hr (t): here it was shown just to be clearer.

2.4   Quantized QAM Performance

$$Q(x) = \frac{1}{\sqrt{2\pi}} \int_x^{\infty} e^{-t^2/2} dt, \quad x \geq 0$$

$Q(x)$ is related to the complementary Gaussian error function by:

$$Q(x) = \frac{1}{2}\text{erfc}\left(\frac{x}{\sqrt{2}}\right)$$

which is the probability that x will be under the tail of the Gaussian PDF towards positive infinity.

The error rates quoted here are those in additive white Gaussian noise (AWGN).

Where coordinates for constellation points are given in this article, note that they represent a non-normalized constellation. That is, if a particular mean average energy were required (e.g. unit average energy), the constellation would need to be linearly scaled.

3   Introduction of OFDM

Orthogonal Frequency Division Multiplexing is a scheme used in the area of high-data-rate mobile wireless communications such as cellular phones, satellite communications and digital audio broadcasting. This technique is mainly utilized to combat inter-symbol interference, which will be described in the following document.

3.1   Orthogonality

In geometry, orthogonal means, "involving right angles" (from Greek *ortho*, meaning *right*, and *gon* meaning *angled*). The term has been extended to general use, meaning the characteristic of being independent (relative to something else). It also can mean: non-redundant, non-overlapping, or irrelevant.

Orthogonality is defined for both real and complex valued functions. The functions $\varphi_m(t)$ and $\varphi_n(t)$ are said to be orthogonal with respect to each other over the interval $a < t < b$ if they satisfy the condition:

$$\int_a^b \varphi_m(t)\, \varphi_m^*(t)\, dt = 0, \qquad \text{where} \, n \neq m$$

3.2   Introduction to OFDM Structures

All communication systems are, in its simplest form, composed of a transmitter, receiver and a channel of some sort for propagation. This is depicted in Fig. 3.1.

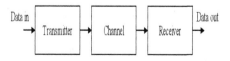

Fig. 3.1. Simplified communications system

However, an OFDM system is more complicated as seen in Fig. 3.2. Note that this block diagram will be used in this project and note that a typical OFDM system is a bit more involved than shown below.

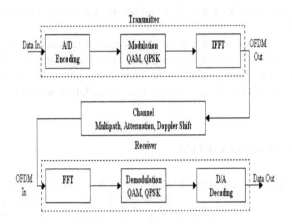

Fig. 3.2. OFDM block diagram

3.3   Transmitter and Receiver Structures

Again, the principle of any **F**requency **D**ivision **M**ultiplexing (FDM) system is to split the information to be transmitted into N parallel streams, each of which modulates a carrier using an arbitrary modulation technique. The total signal bandwidth is therefore, $N \cdot \Delta f$, where Δf is the frequency spacing between adjacent carriers.

Over a T-second interval, the complex envelope for the OFDM signal is

$$g(t) = A_c \sum_{n=0}^{N-1} w_n \varphi_n(t),$$

$0 > t > T$

Where A_c is the carrier amplitude, w_n is the element of the N-element parallel data vector

$\mathbf{w} = [w_0, w_1, \ldots, w_{N-1}]$, and the orthogonal carriers are:

$$\varphi_n(t) = e^{j2\pi f_n t} \tag{8}$$

$$\text{where } f_n(t) = \frac{1}{T}\left(n - \frac{N-1}{2}\right) \tag{9}$$

In order to implement an FDM system, N independent transmitter and receiver pairs have to be realized in the form of sinusoidal generators, making the system very complex and equally costly. However, the advent of the Discrete Fourier Transform (DFT) made this transmission scheme more plausible. The Fast Fourier Transform (FFT) and the Inverse Fast Fourier Transform (IFFT) are the more efficient implementations of the DFT, are utilized for the baseband OFDM modulation and demodulation process as indicated in Fig. 3.2

The associated harmonically related frequencies can be used as the set of sub channel carriers as required by an OFDM system. Now all sub channels are modulated and demodulated in one IFFT step. With respect to the block diagram of Fig. 3.2, the serial data stream is mapped to data symbols with a symbol rate of $1/T_s$, employing a general phase and modulation scheme. The resulting symbol stream is demultiplexed into a vector of N data symbols S_0 to S_{N-1}. The parallel symbol duration is N times longer than the serial symbol duration T_s. Hence the disperse channel (transmitted signal * CIR) becomes less damaging, affecting only a fraction of the extended signaling pulse duration.

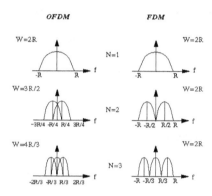

Fig. 3.3. PSD of OFDM and FDM

The IFFT of the data symbol vector is computed and its coefficients, s_0 to s_{N-1} constitute an OFDM symbol. The IFFT is used to realize the harmonically related and the modulated individual OFDM subcarriers, in order to transform the signal's spectrum to the time domain for transmission over the channel.

At the receiver, a spectral decomposition of the received time-domain samples r_n is computed employing an N-tap FFT, and the recovered data symbols R_n are restored in serial order and demuliplexed.

4   Peak to Average Power Ratio (PAPR)

The peak to average power ratio for a signal x(t) is defined as

$$papr = \frac{\max[x(t)x^*(t)]}{E[x(t)x^*(t)]}$$

Where x*(t) corresponds to conjugate operator expressing in decibels $papr_{dB} = 10\log_{10}(papr)$

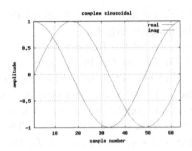

Fig. 4.1. Wave form of a complex sinusoidal

4.1   Maximum Expected PAPR from an OFDM Waveform

From the previous chapters, we have learned that an OFDM signal is the sum of multiple sinusoidal having frequency separation 1/T, where each sinusoidal gets modulated by independent information a_k . Mathematically, the transmit signal is,

$$x(t) = \sum_0^{K-1} a_k e^{\frac{j2\pi k i}{T}}$$

For simplicity, let us assume that for all the subcarriers $a_k=1$. In that scenario, the peak value of the signal is

$$\max[x(t)x^*(t)] = \max\left[\sum_0^{K-1} a_k e^{\frac{j2\pi k i}{T}} \sum_0^{K-1} a_k^* e^{\frac{-j2\pi k i}{T}}\right]$$

$$= \max\left[a_k a_k^* \sum_0^{K-1}\sum_0^{K-1} e^{\frac{j2\pi k i}{T}} e^{\frac{-j2\pi k i}{T}}\right]$$

$$= K^2$$

The mean square value of the signal is defined as

$$E[x(t)x^*(t)] = E\left[\sum_0^{K-1} a_k e^{\frac{j2\pi k i}{T}} \sum_0^{K-1} a_k^* e^{\frac{-j2\pi k i}{T}}\right]$$

$$= E\left[a_k a_k^* \sum_0^{K-1}\sum_0^{K-1} e^{\frac{j2\pi k i}{T}} e^{\frac{-j2\pi k i}{T}}\right]$$

$$= K$$

Given so, the peak to average power ratio for an OFDM system with subcarriers K and all subcarriers are given the same modulation is,

$$papr = \frac{K^2}{K} = K$$

If we have used 52 subcarriers. Given so, the maximum expected PAPR is 52 (around 17dB!!).

$$P(PAPR > z) = 1 - P(PAPR \leq z)$$
$$= 1 - F(z)^N$$
$$= 1 - (1 - \exp(-z))^N$$

5   PAPR Reduction Techniques

PAPR reduction techniques vary according to the needs of the system and are dependent on various factors. PAPR reduction capacity, increase in power in transmit signal, loss in data rate, complexity of computation and increase in the bit-error rate at the receiver end are various factors which are taken into account before adopting a PAPR reduction technique of the system. The various PAPR reduction techniques that follow are

- ✓ Amplitude Clipping and Filtering.
- ✓ Selected Mapping.
- ✓ Partial Transmit Sequence.

6   Results

6.1   Simulation-1

Performance Comparison of Different Digital Modulation Techniques
Let's take up some bandwidth-efficient linear digital modulation techniques (BPSK, QPSK and QAM) and compare its performance based on their theoretical BER over AWGN.

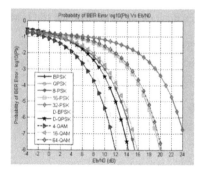

Fig. 6.1. Eb/N0 Vs BER over AWGN

6.2   Simulation-2

Constellation Vectors of QPSK and 16-QAM
Here we define two modulation schemes for OFDM transmission and obtain the constellation vectors and their respective constellation diagrams as shown below.

Let us consider a 16-QAM modulation scheme and obtain its constellation vector diagram.

For prescribed signal to noise ratio we obtain different simulated constellation diagrams.

SNR=50

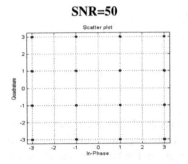

SNR=10

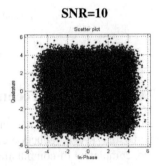

Fig. 6.2. Constellation diagram for SNR =50 for 16QAM modulation scheme

Fig. 6.3. Constellation diagram for SNR =50 for 16-QAM modulation scheme

SNR=200

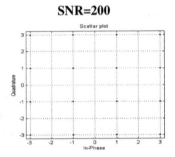

Fig. 6.4. Constellation diagram for SNR =200 for 16-QAM modulation scheme

Let us consider a QPSK modulation scheme and obtain its constellation vector diagram, where for prescribed signal to noise ratio values we obtain different simulated constellation diagrams

SNR=50

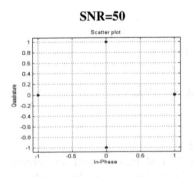

SNR=10

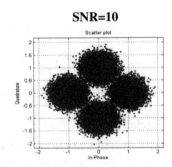

Fig. 6.5. Constellation diagram for SNR =50 for QPSK modulation scheme

Fig. 6.6. Constellation diagram for SNR =10 for QPSK modulation scheme

6.3   Simulation-3

Error Rate Performance of OFDM for QPSK and 16-QAM Modulation Schemes
This is the main evaluation regarding spectral efficiency of OFDM which determines
the best modulation scheme for OFDM transmission where Let us consider 16-QAM
modulation scheme where the number of constellation points are 16 and the fft size is
64. The number of data subcarriers specified are 52 with data symbol duration as
64μs and cyclic prefix duration of 16μs.The number of symbols transmitted are
10^4.here the value of energy per symbol to noise ratio is calculated as

$$Es/N0 = Eb/N0*(nDSC/nFFT)*(Td/(Td+Tcp)$$

we obtain the simulated bit error rate as shown below with comparison with
theoretical bit error rate whose value is calculated by

$$TheoryBer= (1/k)*3/2*erfc(sqrt(k*0.1*(10.^(Eb/N0dB/10))));$$

where k = log$_2$M where M is the number of constellation points varies from 16,64,
256. Erfc is the error function for bit error probability

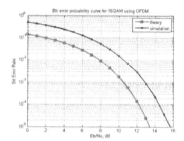

Fig. 6.7. Bit error probability curve for 16-QAM using OFDM

The table below specifies the values for bit error rate for different values of energy
per bit to noise ratio and also include the energy per symbol to noise ratio for 0 to 16
values

Let us consider QPSK modulation scheme where the number of constellation
points are 4 and the fft size is 64. The number of data subcarriers specified are 52
with data symbol duration as 64μs and cyclic prefix duration of 16μs.The number of
symbols transmitted are 10^4.here the value of energy per symbol to noise ratio is
calculated as

$$Es/N0 = Eb/N0*(nDSC/nFFT)*(Td/(Td+Tcp)$$
$$TheoryBer = 1/2*erfc(sqrt(Eb/N0dB*2)*sin(pi/4));$$

Where k = log$_2$M where M is the number of constellation points equal to 4Erfc is the
error function for bit error probability

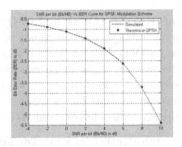

Fig. 6.8. Bit error probability curve for QPSK using OFDM

6.4   Simulation-4

Peak to Average Power Ratio Calculation for QPSK and 16-QAM Modulation Techniques

For determining the peak to average power ratio we have made the fast fourier transform size to be 128 point and the number of data carriers are assumed to be 114 with number of bits per symbol to be 52.

For modulated QPSK and 16-QAM inputs we have used the following expressions as shown below

ipMod = (1/sqrt(10))*qammod(ipBit,M)
ipQPSK = 1/sqrt(2)*(randsrc(1,nDSC*nSym,[-1 1]) + j*randsrc(1,nDSC*nSym, [-1 1]))

After obtaining the time domain signal from the modulated signals we have the signal expressions as shown below

xt = (nFFT/sqrt(nDSC))*ifft(fftshift(xF.')).'
xQPSK1t =FFT/sqrt(nDSC))*ifft(fftshift(xQPSK1F.')).'

Now as the time domain representation of OFDM signal is obtained for QPSK and 16-QAM modulation schemes we can now compute the peak to average power ratio by calculating the mean square value and the peak value as shown below

meanSquareValue = sum(xt.*conj(xt),2)/nFFT
peakValue = max(xt.*conj(xt),2)
paprSymbol = peakValue./meanSquareValue

The cumulative distribution plots for the respective modulation schemes for different values of the probabilities and their respective PAPR values in dB is shown below in both continuous as well as discrete form

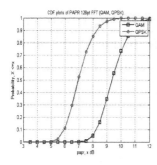

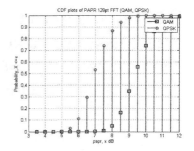

Fig. 6.9. CDF Curve in continuous form for QPSK and 16-QAM modulation

Fig. 6.10. CDF curve in discrete form for QPSK and 16-QAM modulation

7   Conclusion

The OFDM system seems to provide an ideal platform for transmitting data with the minimum error. The defects or disadvantages presented by OFDM systems can be effectively corrected by a simple change in the structure leading to MSE-OFDM systems. The MSE-OFDM system deals with every kind of situation that might arise in a communication channel. MSE-OFDM has proven to be very effective in fading channels in the presence of frequency offset also. Is the future, we can expect to see extensive use of MSE-OFDM for signal transmission in various communication channels.

8   Future Scope

Thus, MSE-OFDM study can lead us to easier and cheaper yet practically applicable ways of combating all communication channel problems. So, it will be useful in future to implement MSE-OFDM in communication channels.

References

[1] Guo, D.H., Hsu, C.-Y.: Systematic reducing the PARP of OFDM by cyclic coding. In: Asia-pacific Conf. Commun. APCC, Malaysia, pp. 133–137 (2003)
[2] Yusof, S.K., Fisal, N., Yin, T.S.: Reducing PAPR of OFDM signals using partial transmit sequences. In: Asia-Pacific Conf. Commun. APCC, Malaysia, pp. 411–414 (2003)
[3] Moose, P.H.: A technique for orthogonal frequency division multiplexing offset correction. IEEE Trans. Commun. 42(10), 2908–2914 (1994)
[4] Cai, X., Zhou, S., Giannakis, G.B.: Group-orthogonal multi- carrier CDMA. IEEE Trans. Commun. (2003) (to appear)
[5] Banelli, P., Cacopardi, S.: Theoretical analysis and performance of ODDM signal in nonlinear AWGN channels. IEEE Trans. Commun. 48(3), 430–441 (2000)
[6] Saeed, M.A., Ali, B.M., Habaebi, M.H.: Performance evaluation of OFDM scenes over multipath fading channel. In: Asia-Pacific Conf. Commun. APCC, Malaysia, pp. 415–419 (2003)

Green Technology and Assessment of the Environment and Challenges Faced by Regulatory Authorities in Uganda: A Case of the Electricity Regulatory Authority (ERA)

Ezendu Ariwa[1] and Isaac Wasswa Katono[2]

[1] London Metropolitan University, UK
[2] Faculty of Business and Administration,
Uganda Christian University, Mukono Uganda
e.ariwa@londonmet.ac.uk, ikatono@ucu.ac.ug

Abstract. Governments across Africa have established regulatory agencies for utilities but these have largely been modeled on those in developed countries and have had limited success. The Electricity Regulatory Authority in Uganda was set up to oversee this important sector but its success has so far been limited as evidenced by the quality, reliability and cost of the service. The Purpose of this study is to examine the factors that influence the performance of ERA, with a view to coming up with mitigation measures. In the first part of the study (presented in this paper), annual reports of the regulatory body, supplemented with press reports, academic papers, and conferences reports are examined. In the second part of the study, the Electricity Governance Toolkit (EGTK) will be used to collect data from relevant electricity laws, rules and regulations developed by the Government of Uganda as well as procedures developed by the regulatory body, and the decisions it has made overtime. In addition, the researchers will conduct interviews with regulatory members and staff, civil society and consumer groups that have filed cases before ERA, as well as a sample of domestic and industrial consumers within Kampala District. Both qualitative (arranging the findings in themes) and quantitative techniques (t tests, frequencies and means) will be utilized to analyze the data.

Keywords: green technology, corporate sustainability, assessment, environment, Uganda, electricity regulatory authority (ERA).

1   Introduction

The consistent failure of many African governments to provide services to their populations is well documented in the literature (Harris 2003) and cannot be easily rectified (Farlam 2005). Most of these governments lack the resources to maintain and expand infrastructure, and thus their response to this problem has been privatization and Public Private Partnership (PPPs). The benefits of both privatization and PPPs are also well documented in the literature, although critics (e.g. Dwyer 2004 in Farlam 2005) assert that separating privatization from PPPs is like creating a distinction

P.V. Krishna, M.R. Babu, and E. Ariwa (Eds.): ObCom 2011, Part II, CCIS 270, pp. 780–793, 2012.
© Springer-Verlag Berlin Heidelberg 2012

without a difference. However privatization and PPPs exist on a continuum defined by the extent of service obligations imposed, and the ultimate ownership of assets. PPPs can be successful under the right conditions and in the right sector, for example they have been successful in ports, telecommunications, transport, but not in water and power (Farlam 2005).

According to the South African National Treasury Manual (2004), a PPP is a "contract between a public sector institution and a private party, in which the private party assumes substantial financial, technical and operational risk in the design, financing, building and operation of a project"

The efficacy of PPPs cannot be taken for granted and hence they must be well thought out by goverments in order to reap benefits from them (Farlam 2005). They operate within a regulated environment that imposes detailed investment obligations and price ceilings. However many of the PPPs run into problems due to poor or inadequate regulation. Many studies e.g. Laffont (2005), Estache and Wrens-Lewis (2009) show that the regulation of PPPs has been problematic in many developing countries. For example, according to the official government daily the New Vision dated 7th December 2010, regulation of the PPPs in Uganda is currently facing a severe crisis, since the Chief Executive Officers four PPPs are either suspended or sacked, namely National Forestry Authority, The Uganda Communications Commission, and the Uganda Wildlife Authority and the Electricity Regulatory Authority. These agencies regulate key sectors in the economy of this country, hence any form of instability is detrimental to the development and welfare of her citizens. This study therefore specifically addresses itself to the factors that drive the performance of these regulation bodies, with a special focus on the electricity sector (ERA). The next section gives a background to the formation of the ERA, and the general performance of the electricity sector in this country.

2   The Power Sector in Uganda

In 1997, GOU through its ministry of Natural Resources drew up a strategic plan for the Uganda power sector, so that it is able to produce adequate and reliable energy, in order to ensure sustainable social and economic development, as well as maximize inter regional power exports. This effort gave way to the formation of The Electricity Regulatory Authority (ERA), following the enactment of the Electricity Act (1999). This act repealed the Electricity Act (1964) and its major aim is to transform the electricity sector into an independent industry, to enable it supply reliable power at reasonable prices and thus make a contribution to the economic and social development of Uganda.

The enactment of the Electricity Act (1999) provided the legal basis for the privatization of the Uganda Electricity Board (UEB), which was unbundled into three companies in March 2001 namely:

1.   The Uganda Electricity Generation Company Ltd. (UEGCL)
2.   The Uganda Electricity Transmission Company Ltd. (UETCL)
3.   The Uganda Electricity Distribution Company Ltd (UEDCL)

Under this arrangement, Uganda Electricity Distribution Company Ltd owns the electricity supply infrastructure operating at 33 kV and below. Its assets were finally leased to UMEME Ltd in 2005 under a 20 year concession. The Uganda Electricity Transmission Company Ltd owns and operates the grid connected electricity supply infrastructure operating above 33kV. It is the only company responsible for buying power in bulk from generators and selling it to distribution companies (Single model Buyer). The Uganda Electricity Generation Company Ltd owns the Kiira and Nalubale hydro-electric power stations. Its generation assets were leased to Eskom (U) Ltd in April 2003 under a 20 year concession agreement

According to the ESPR (2007), installed capacity of hydro generation is 314 MW of which 180 MW is from Nalubaale dam, 120 MW comes from Kiira dam, while the remaining 14MW comes from the combined installed capacity at Kilembe Mines Ltd and Kasese Cobalt Company Ltd. However, due to poor hydrology, as a result of the drought in 2005 that affected much of the East African region, there was deterioration in water levels which reduced the generation capacity of Nalubaale and Kiira to 120 MW, effective 2006. This forced government to diversify energy supply sources, hence the introduction of thermal power.   Electricity supply at peak stands at 250 MW, while maximum demand stands at 350 MW during the evening peak, thus the electricity deficit at peak is about 90MW resulting in serious load shedding. In order to cover the deficit 100MW are generated through diesel powered thermal generators (which is still below the 150 MW optimal diesel based thermal energy mix proposed by government). The country's GDP has as a consequence suffered due to insufficient power supply. The increased share of thermal electricity in the energy mix (now standing at 50%), coupled with rising oil prices necessitates the continued subsidization of the electricity tariff by government. For example in the first half of 2007, government spent 58,197 million Uganda shillings on electricity tariff subsidies. This money could have gone toward improvement of infrastructure in the sector. It is also important to note that electricity tariffs in Uganda are high compared to other countries in the East African Community, a fact works against the competitiveness of Ugandan products in this market.

The establishment of the ERA secretariat in 2001 was a step forward in the drive to instill confidence in this crucial sector in the national economy. According to ERA (2008), ERA has a statutory mandate of regulating the generation, transmission, sale, export, import and distribution of electrical energy in Uganda. It has the duty to ensure that the above PPPs earn a reasonable rate of return on their investment, while at the same time they provide quality electricity and service at affordable prices to all categories of consumers. Given the multiplicity of stakeholders that it serves, ERA tries as much as possible to get stakeholder on its operations and consults customers whenever there is a contentious issue in this sector through public hearings. Uganda has enjoyed a stable and predictable electricity sector regulatory environment. This is exemplified by the fact that the first Commissioners of the Electricity Regulatory Authority served two 5-year terms uninterrupted by politicians.

In a customer satisfaction survey commissioned by ERA and carried out by Makerere University Faculty of Social Sciences and Social Administration in 2006, a sizeable percentage of the respondents did not know what ERA was or how it was different from the utility companies. However what was alarming from this survey is that the overall rating of ERA's performance by commercial and domestic consumers was poor, since 51% said they were just fairly satisfied, 38% said they were not satisfied at all, while only 6% said they were satisfied (5% did not know).

Another important issue raised in this survey was that ERA was not assertive enough, while other respondents felt that ERA was an arm of government "dancing to the tune of government." Of major concern from this survey was the view held by the umbrella association of Ugandan manufactures (UMA), who expressed the view that ERA was there to defend the Utility companies and hence was not impartial (pg 35) stating "ERA is meant to be a regulator, but works too closely with the utility companies like UMEME, a relationship that makes other stake holders uncomfortable". Other stake holders like the National Environment Management Authority (NEMA) and the Uganda Electricity Transmission Company (UECTL) felt that ERA was faced with a challenge of adequate personnel and financial resources, and hence was not in position to monitor the utility companies.

In light of the above background, the purpose of this paper is to examine the factors that impact upon the performance of ERA. Specifically, the paper seeks to examine the extent to which ERA has been mandated to carry out its functions, and whether there are impediments if any that disrupt this mandate and suggest mitigation measures .This study report is presented in two parts. The first part which is presented in this paper is organized as follows. The next section outlines some of the regulation theory and models. Some of the problems and challenges with existing regulatory models are highlighted, including weak regulatory commitment, institutional fragility, lack of transparency and legitimacy, and lack of capacity and competence. This section is followed by the methodology used to carry out the study. A concluding discussion sums up the study.

3   Regulatory Theory

Definition and Importance of Regulation
In the attempt to increase investment and improve efficiency, many countries have opened their infrastructure industries to the private sector (Farlam 2005), and also increased the independence of regulation. Regulation is a great predictor of performance than the form of management used in a sector (Estache and Rossi 2005), and regulatory performance is influenced more by the institutional frame work than by the form of ownership or management. Estache and Wren-Lewis (2008) define institutions as the rules of the game that influence peoples' behavior, as well as the organisations that implement these rules. The literature on utility regulation points to a number of factors that influence the performance of regulatory authorities in developing countries and Laffont (2005) provides three important points that are notable in this regard.

First, regulatory authorities in developing countries face many challenges that are peculiar from those faced by similar bodies in developed nations. Second, policy makers are finding traditional regulatory theory as applied in the developed world to be of limited use in the developing countries. Hence the solutions to those problems are imperfect, contradictory, and may be different from those advocated in developed countries. Consequently, it is risky to advocate simply for a regulatory framework that is closer to some universal ideal. Third, while there has been significant improvement in the regulation theory (based on the tools of incentive theory and asymmetric information), there has been a persistent neglect of the specific characteristics of the developing countries, which undermines the reforms in these countries. Hence the literature on infrastructure reform in developing countries is replete with evidence that the original expectations of regulatory performance have not been met (Eberhard 2007). It was expected that regulatory agencies and contracts would depoliticize tariff setting and improve the climate for operational management and private investment through more transparent and predictable decision making. This has not been the case in many developing countries.   With this back ground in mind, the paper now discusses some of the factors that influence the performance of regulatory agencies in these countries.

Legal System

The legal system in which the regulatory authority functions greatly influences its performance (Eberhard 2007). Two legal systems are found to influence utility regulatory systems. In former Anglophone colonies, independent regulatory authorities have been established based on common law where the regulator acts in public interest and has sufficient though bounded and accountable discretion when setting tariffs and service standards. On the other hand, former Francophone countries rely on regulatory contracts e.g. concessions with pre specified tariff setting regimes administered within civil law backed by various provisions for contractual renegotiation and arbitration. Other countries like Uganda (a former British colony) prefer the hybrid model which combines independent regulation with regulatory contracts (for example long term concessions in electricity generation and distribution have been awarded in Uganda). In short, regulatory discretion and performance of the utility companies in a given country emanates from regulatory design followed in that country.

Autonomy

A contentious issue in the literature is the extent to which regulation authorities should be granted autonomy in decision making for effective regulation in developing states (Eberhard 2007). In this regard, a distinction is drawn between regulatory governance and regulatory substance (Brown *et.al* 2006). The former refers to the design of the regulatory system, institutional arrangements, and the process of regulatory decision making. The latter refers to the context and outcomes of regulation, e.g. tariff setting or service standards plus their impact on the customers or the utilities. Regulatory governance includes dimensions such as regulatory commitment, clarity of roles and functions between the regulator and policy makers, regulatory autonomy, organisation structure and resources of the regulator, transparency, participation, accountability, predictability, proportionality and discrimination.

There is little consensus on the role of regulatory design in the regulation of utilities, with some people arguing that the challenge for regulatory design is to come up with regulatory governance mechanisms that can balance regulatory discretion with issues such as tariff setting (Levy 1994), while others posit that a certain degree of regulatory discretion is inevitable (and even desirable) and thus the focus should be to find governance arrangements and procedures that permit this (Stern and Cubbin 2005).

Institutional Weaknesses
An examination of the institutional context and its implications is necessary when deciding upon regulatory policy. Laffont (2005) argues that regulation in developing countries suffers from a weak institutional environment which renders the regulatory contract between governments and firms incomplete. For instance, few countries enjoy the solid accounting data needed to set fair tariffs for regulated firms simply because the definition and/or the enforcement of accounting standards for monopolies responsible for public services tends to be weak. Tariffs end up being more negotiated than calculated in that kind of environment. Ideas from the literature on the economics of transaction costs, economic and legal contract theories are therefore being brought alongside the fundamental tools of incentive theory to lead to a theory of regulation more consistent with the LDC context (Estache and Wren-Lewis 2008).

Lack of Regulatory Commitment
In spite of the attempt to set up independent regulatory bodies in many developing countries, goverments in many cases resist the setting of tariffs in a transparent and objective manner for a number of reasons. At times, regulators are pressurized to overturn rational decisions. Tariff setting is a highly political issue, and goverments are sensitive to popular demands not to increase tariffs. In other words, political expediency undermines regulation. As Tremolet and Shah (2005) put it, there is a gap between law and practice. In short, a lack of regulatory commitment is characterized by resistance on the part of government or its officers to transfer regulatory decision-making powers to an independent regulator or a regulatory contract and by a reluctance to embrace cost-reflective or revenue sufficient tariffs. A low level of regulatory commitment is also evidenced in weak and slowly operating courts of law and ineffective appeal systems (Eberhard 2007).

The literature distinguishes between problems lack of commitment brings to regulation (see for example Maskin and Tirole 1999). First, commitment and negotiation is a situation where both parties are willing to negotiate after the contract has been signed (Laffont and Tirole 1993), while non commitment is a situation where government wants to renege on its commitments, often under the guise of expropriation (Perotti 1995). On the other hand, limited enforcement is a situation where the firm succeeds in renegotiating the contract in spite of government opposition (Laffont 2003), especially where the judiciary is weak or corruptible or because the firm is actually in a very powerful position. Lastly non commitment is a situation where neither side wishes to renegotiate the contract (Estache and Wren-Lewis 2008). Generally, an incomplete contract resulting from the inability of the parties to commit damages incentives and decreases efficiency. A possible solution around problems emanating from lack of commitment of both parties is to have an independent regulator (Estache and Wren-Lewis 2008).

Transparency and Accountability

Many regulators are not transparent in the way they arrive at their decisions, which breeds suspicion and mistrust. Lack of access to these contracts, makes the public assume the worst (that is, excessive profits or corruption), which leads to a lack of trust in the regulator and government in general. Transparency is often compromised in regulatory contracts, such as concession agreements or power purchase agreements. Transparency requires all stakeholders to understand and develop confidence in regulatory processes and decisions, which include the clarifying of objectives and functions of regulation; consulting various stakeholders in the process of developing new regulatory methodologies and standards; publishing final standards, regulatory contracts, and regulatory methodologies, including scheduled tariff review procedures and timetables; public hearings where stakeholders can make submissions and inputs into important regulatory decisions; written public explanations of regulatory decisions; prescheduled independent regulatory reviews and impact assessments; accountability through appeal mechanisms; and open access to information. Transparency measures provide a common understanding of the "rules of the game" and how they are applied (NERA 2005). Ease of complaining and taking action after a complaint has been lodged would add to transparency.

Transparency in utility regulation is most needed where institutions face grave governance and capacity challenges (as is the case in Uganda) but it is in precisely these situations that transparency is most difficult to achieve. Fostering transparency goes hand-in-hand with building institutions and capacity. Ultimately, transparency is critical for developing legitimacy. A common problem in developing states is that agents involved in the regulation process are not fully accountable to their principals (Maskin and Tirole 2004). This could be due to the fact that government may not be accountable to the citizenry or bureaucratic contact between the government and regulatory authority is incomplete (Estache and Wren-Lewis 2008). For example, an agent may collude with another party against the will of the principal, yet the principal may have limited capacity to control such corruption through contractual terms. In regulatory theory, the most commonly discussed form of collusion is that between the regulator and the firm, known as regulatory capture (Dal Bo 2006). This enables the firm to influence the decisions of the regulator in its favour, or bribe the regulator to hide information from government (Laffont and Tirole 1993), with the aim of increasing information asymmetry which increases the rents to the firm. Further, corruption in the enforcement process erodes the ability of government to enforce contracts (Guasch *et.al* 2003). All these problems are worsened in a situation where government is unaccountable to the people or where its officials collude with an interest group. An example is where policy is designed such that future generations are burdened with too great a share of costs (Aubert and Laffont 2005). Making the regulator directly accountable to the legislature is a possible solution to accountability problems, since the interests of the citizens may be more closely aligned with those of members of parliament.

Institutional Fragility

Many regulatory bodies in Africa are less than 10 years old (except Uganda where ERA is over 10 years), hence they are still fragile in terms of experience. They also face funding constraints particularly delays in approval of their budgets. African regulators have experienced high turnover of Board members and management (there are many corruption scandals and counter allegations in Uganda), thus institutional development and memory are disrupted (Tremolet and Shah 2005).

Lack of Regulatory Capacity and Confidence

Besides governance and institutional challenges, developing country regulators face huge issues around regulatory substance, that is, the quality, credibility, and impact of their regulatory decisions (Eberhard 2007). Regulatory substance is negatively affected by lack of well trained and experienced regulators. There is need to improve the professional capacity of new regulators and this is a huge challenge facing the infrastructure sector in Africa. A global study of regulators established that the most frequently reported constraint was the lack of specialized skills in utility regulation (Tremolet and Shah 2005). It is thus critical that core regulatory competencies are developed in order to strengthen regulatory substance. Capacity constraints may be mitigated by initially limiting regulatory discretion, minimizing regulatory complexity, building in mechanisms for outsourcing some utility functions, and adopting a gradual approach to modifying or expanding the scope of the regulator's responsibilities as capacity is built for a more fully fledged regulatory agency (Tremolet and Shah 2005). The greater the discretion enjoyed by the regulator, the more acute is the need for trained, experienced, and competent staff.

Theoretically the limited capacity of the regulator may be modeled as an increase in the asymmetry of information (Laffont and Tirole 1993). For example, staff inexperience and poor funding may erode regulator capacity to monitor effort (i.e. distinguish between controllable and uncontrollable costs) or even to observe the level of total costs. Further a poor resource envelope may limit the regulators efforts to pay the transaction costs involved in writing and enforcing the regulatory contract (Tirole 1999). This inability to pay transaction costs plus the bounded rationality of the regulator result in a suboptimal contract. There are two grave consequences of this scenario. First, it results into a lack of clarity on the regulatory frame work. Hence bargaining is bound to occur as soon as an event not covered in the contract occurs. Expectations of such an occurrence taking place in the future reduce the incentive of the firm to invest funds, or exert effort efficiently (Williamson 1975). Further, regulator bargaining power is weaker ex post, than ex ante since finding an alternative firm is problematic in mid contract (Williamson 1985), hence giving more concessions to the firm. Lobina (2005) adds that the regulator's position is likely to be even weaker in such a situation due to capacity constraints. Second, contractual incompleteness is likely to breed inefficiency in a number of ways. Lastly, in an incomplete contract environment, implementation will depend on where real authority rather than formal authority lies (Aghion and Tirole 1997). Real authority depends on information access, as well as the ability to process that information. Hence capacity constraints in developing states transfer authority from the regulator to the firm (resulting in an increase in the firm's rents and a decrease in efficiency) or to government (resulting in a loss of credibility and independence). In each of these cases the regulator is disempowered and rendered less efficient.

Limited Fiscal Efficiency

Inefficient tax administration is a major problem in many developing states. A major consequence of this problem is that redistribution of income is costly (Laffont 2005). Consequently many consumers that government wishes to join the networked infrastructural services are unable to afford the connection fee to these services, or once connected, they are unable to meet the regular bills that accompany their consumption. Hence many goverments resort to cross subsidies to pay for the network expansion instead of fiscal transfers. Given that it is crucial to distribute the gains from sector reforms for the development of effective institutions (Acemoglu *et.al* 2007), regulation in developing countries must be concerned with both distribution and efficiency. However, using regulation as tool for redistribution is not generally acceptable in these countries on the pretext that there are better ways of income redistribution (Vickers 1997:18). Laffont (2005) however insists that due to the limited fiscal space of these countries besides weaknesses in their tax regimes, separation of regulation and redistribution is not a viable strategy.

In summary, the core issue advanced by Laffont (2005) as well as else where in the literature on regulation is that caution should be exercised when applying recommendations from developing countries to developing countries. Most of the challenges that arise in regulation   and in regulatory contracts emanate from regulatory design, institutional weaknesses and governance issues, all of which are different in the developing countries compared to the first world.

4   Method

This study is an on going work in progress that utilizes a triangulation technique (Campbell and Fiske 1959) in that both qualitative and quantitative research designs are employed. The qualitative part of the study comes first, with a view to gaining a firm grasp of what is happening in this sector since the Makerere University survey in 2006, and in light of the current situation pertaining in this sector. The study commences with a review of the literature on regulation in developing countries, as well as a documentary review of various ERA reports, *supplemented with press reports, academic papers, and conferences reports and conversations with various stakeholder groups.* This ground work will enable the researchers to use the EGTK (Dixit *et.al* 2007), to rate the performance of ERA along a number of dimensions in the second part of the study.

5   Preliminary Findings

This section reports some of the initial findings of the study from documentary analysis and conversations with specific groups as explained above. The findings from the EGKT will be reported in the second phase of the paper. News paper reports especially the government owned New Vision, ERA reports and policy documents reveal six major happenings in the electricity sector in this country.

First, as highlighted in the introductory section of this paper, the top management of ERA (The CEO and Company Secretary) was suspended in October 2010 by the Minister of Energy who accuses them of insubordination and defiance when they refused to implement a policy directives on reviewing a policy directive on co-generated electricity in line with legal notices in the National Gazette (Kasiita 2010). The suspended officials have consequently filed an application in court for a judicial review of the matter, claiming that the minister's directive contravenes the Electricity Act (1999), and compromises the statutory duty and obligations of ERA as an independent body. They add that the policy direction on setting tariffs is illegal and against the law, and that refusing to obey the same is not insubordination or defiance but compliance with the law. Since the matter is before court and thus should not be discussed, it suffices to point out that what is happening in this case borders on issues of regulatory design and autonomy (Eberhard 2007) as well as arguments by Tremolet and Shah 2005 in concerning board member turn over.

Second, ERA itself has lost confidence in UMEME and suggests that the contract be reviewed (Ojwee 2010). ERA regards the operations of UMEME as incompetent and below expectation, arguing that UMEME lacks the incentive to expand Uganda's electricity network to the rural areas, disconnects customers before sending them bills, and generally offers poor service delivery. Further ERA asserts that it is only for the fear of costly litigation that the contact which has so far lasted five out of twenty years is not terminated. The article further posits that either the contact was poorly designed, or the technocrats are failing to interpret the provisions of the contract with UMEME correctly. This situation lends credence to capacity gap claims in regulatory bodies in developing countries as espoused by Laffont (2005). However the fact is that it is unfair for the consumers to bear the consequences of a flawed contract where they had no say in drafting it in the first place.

Third, there seems to be a general dissatisfaction with the services of Umeme country wide. This is evidenced by a quick scan through any Ugandan daily. Recent riots in Bugembe near the Kiira dam over a three day black out (Mugabi and Kiirya 2010) as well as complaints in Masaka in central region (Kalemera 2010), and Kampala city (Lule and Ninsiima 2010) to name a few areas bear out this fact. In all these cases, critical services like hospitals are off the grid, resulting in serious service delivery. What is more, many customers experience power surges that blow up their home appliances, besides load shedding in many parts of the country and poor or unfair billing. Consequently many customers have lost confidence in UMEME and have resorted to the courts for redress. In May 2010, about 50000 customers took UMEME to court for over charging them and using faulty meters (Nsambu 2010). They argue that the suspicious billing system and faulty meters cost them millions of shillings, adding that UMEME breached a contract and trust between it and the consumers for which court should compel UMEME to compensate them. Similarly, In September 2010, the African Institute for Energy Governance (AFIEGO) together with 1927 domestic consumers dragged UEDCL, UMEME, ERA and the Attorney

General to court, claiming that consumers are being exploited and that the electricity sector is in a serious crisis. The complainants want court to compel UMEME to recall meters, test them and have them certified by the National Bureau of Standards (UBOS) before installing them. They also want court to order a tariff reduction from the current Uganda shs385 per unit to shs 238 for all domestic users. Further, the complainants want court to terminate the 20 year concession that UMEME has with UEDCL, and compel UMEME to refund Uganda shs 452 billion which the company has received from government as subsidies since 2001 when the company entered the concession agreement.

Fourth, the utility companies have already taken steps to ensure that the tariff is raised (Kasiita 2010). UMEME first suggested a flat rate for all domestic users in June 2010 (Kasita and Kagoro 2010), such that those home using less than 50 units would pay a flat Uganda shs 12000 per month, those using 51-75 units would pay shs 26000, while those using over 75 units would pay shs 386 per unit. Consumers rejected this proposal as anti poor, and would discourage connections to the rural area. It was also described by opponents as a disincentive to energy saving, and it would also be punitive to good consumers. In October 2010, the power companies i.e. UEGC, UEDCL, UETCL and ESKOM applied to ERA for a 15% increase in the tariff in the first three months of 2011. They would like domestic consumers to pay Uganda shs 462 up from 385 commercial consumers to pay shs 455 up from shs 358, Small businesses to pay shs 457 up from shs 333, large businesses to pay shs 321 shs down from 330, while street lighting pays shs 461 up from shs 385. The business community reacted to this proposal as unfortunate and outrageously obscene. According to UMEME, the end user tariff is driven by the cost of the power generation, fuel and transport costs, non UMEME losses and the exchange rate, and most of these variables have been undergoing an upward trend. Hence for 2011, UMEME submitted a revenue requirement of shs 215 billion, translating into a distribution tariff of shs 191 per unit which is only part of the total end user tariff.

Fifth massive corruption, mistrust, arm-twisting, accusations and counter accusations have penetrated the electricity sector in this country. The former CEO of UMUME was relieved of his duties following allegations of abuse of office and is being investigated by police (Kasiita 2009). It is alleged that under his tenure in office, UMEME inflated power tariffs. The energy minister hence wants a forensic audit of UMEME (to be carried out by Deloitte and Touché), as well as accountability from this firm for US $11m advanced to it to invest in the power network. In July 2009, police on the orders of the minister raided the home of the accused CEO, took his photo graph, and downloaded personal files from his computer. He was also warned not to attempt to leave the country. The police also raided UMEME offices and the energy ministry. Investors did not take this matter lightly, branded the action irrational and wondered whether the country had not slipped back to the days of Idi Amin (Kasiita 2009). Investors further argued that the minister's action was ultra vires, since it is the mandate of ERA to investigate tariff charges whether or not a complaint has been made for any tariff adjustment.

6   Discussion

The above partial findings indicate that the electricity sector in Uganda is in a severe crisis, and something needs to be done to protect the end users who actually suffer in the long run.

Not only is ERA itself fragile (as admitted by the former CEO)(ERA 2008), but the consumers are up in arms against UMEME in many parts of the country. This paper will not discuss some of the matter of the sacked ERA officials because it is already before court, but it is important to note that whatever the out come, ERA will face a certain level of instability as the matter drags on. Hence the question of regulatory design and autonomy of ERA lingers on.

Another important question that comes to the mind is the issue of capacity in drafting and interpreting of the contracts. If ERA feels that UMEME is technically incompetent and lacks the incentive to build the power sector, then what should be done? Government, through the energy minister seems to have developed mistrust for this company and one wonders whether the 15 years left for the concession to expire are not too many. On the other hand this suspicious environment will make UMEME less efficient as it will not put in maximum effort since anything can happen any time.

The electricity tariffs in Uganda are the highest in East Africa, and are second highest in the world (after Sweden). Hence the raising of the tariff in the first three months of 2011 as proposed by the power companies will render Ugandan products less competitive in the East African Community, and reduce the welfare of many people especially the poor. For the time being however, government has stayed action over the tariff, by increasing the subsidy to the electricity sector. This is welcome news to many Ugandans, but it is important to know that 2011 is election year (Presidential and Parliamentary elections are scheduled for February). We hope that the winning government will not raise the tariff upwards after the elections.

Some of the cogeneration companies (e.g. the sugar companies) have complained about the slow decision making process by the regulator. They also think that the process of license application is too long, hence ERA needs to look critically at these issues in order to attract more investment in the electricity sector. Similarly, ERA needs to market itself so that people get to know what it is and what it does for more effective service delivery. Similarly, ERA needs to invest a significant part of budget into capacity building and research, since there are just too many issues that are going on this sector for which it has no proper answers.

7   Conclusion

This paper set out to establish the factors that impact upon the performance of regulatory bodies in Uganda, with special emphasis on the ERA. The study focused on the 10 years period since the formation of ERA. Preliminary findings are generally consistent with the literature as outlined in section two of this study. Consistent with Tremolet and Shah (2005) political interference in regulation bodies as well as capacity issues continue to take center stage in developing countries. While the PPP arrangement is a possible remedy to the problems of poor service delivery in LDCs, there is need to think through the contracts carefully before signing concessions, for the sake of the people in these countries. Corruption is an impediment that needs to be routed out of Africa, for us not to end with contacts that are a yoke around the necks of our people.

References

1. Acemoglu, D., Robinson, J.A.: Persistence of power, elites and institutions. Centre for Economic Policy Research, London (2006)
2. Aghion, P., Tirole, J.: Formal and Real Authority in Organizations. The Journal of Political Economy 105(1), 1–29 (1997)
3. Aubert, C., Laffont, J.-J.: Political renegotiation of regulatory contracts. In: EconWPA (2005)
4. Brown, A., Stern, J., Tannenbaum, B., Gencer, D.: A Handbook for Evaluating Infrastructure Regulatory Systems, World Bank, Washington, D.C (2006)
5. Campbell, D.T., Fiske, D.W.: Convergent and discriminant validation by the multitrait - multimethod matrix. Psychological Bulletin 56, 81–105 (1959)
6. Bó, D., Ernesto: Regulatory Capture: A Review. Oxford Review of Economic Policy 22(2), 203–225 (2006)
7. Dixit, S., Navroz, D., Crescencia, M., Sonita, N.: The Electricity Governance Tool kit 2007 NIPFP (2007)
8. Eberhard, A.: Infrastructure regulation in developing countries: An exploration of Transition models. Working Paper No.4, PPIAF (2007)
9. ERA: Electricity Sector Performance Report (2007)
10. ERA: Sector Update News Letter (2008)
11. ERA Stakeholder satisfaction survey, final report, Prepared by Makerere University Department of Social Work and Social Administration (2006)
12. Estache, A., Wrens-Lewis: Towards a theory of regulation for developing countries: Insights from Jean-Jacques Laffont's last book. ECORE Discussion Paper (2008/99) (2008)
13. Estache, A., Rossi, M.A.: Do regulation and ownership drive the efficiency of electricity distribution? Evidence from Latin America. Economics Letters 86(2), 253–257 (2005)
14. Farlam, P.: Working Together: Assessing Public-Private Partnerships in Africa. NEPAD Policy Focus Series, The South African Institute of International Affairs, SAIIA (2005)
15. Government of Uganda: The Electricity Act (1964)
16. Government of Uganda: The Electricity Act (1999)
17. Guasch, J.L., Laffont, J.-J., Straub, S.: Renegotiation of Concession Contracts in Latin America. World Bank (2003)
18. Harris, C.: Private Participation in Infrastructure in Developing Countries: Trends, Impacts and Policy Lessons. World Bank, Washington DC (2003)
19. Kabaale, K.: No Power for 12 days in Masaka. New Vision Printing and Publishing Company Ltd., Kampala (New Vision November 17, 2010)
20. Kasiita, I.: Power firms apply to raise tariffs. New Vision Printing and Publishing Company Ltd., Kampala (New Vision October 31, 2010)
21. Kasita, I.: Investors wary of Onek energy probe. New Vision Printing and Publishing Company Ltd., Kampala (New Vision July 7, 2009)

22. Kasita, I.: Police to continue Umeme Probe. New Vision Printing and Publishing Company Ltd., Kampala (New Vision July 8, 2009)
23. Kasita, I., Kagoro, F.: Umeme flat rate rejected. New Vision Printing and Publishing Company Ltd., Kampala (New Vision June 15, 2010)
24. Laffont, J.-J.: Enforcement, Regulation and Development. Journal of African Economies 12, 193–211 (2003)
25. Laffont, J.-J.: Regulation and Development. Cambridge University Press, Cambridge (2005)
26. Laffont, J.-J., Tirole, J.: A theory of incentives in procurement and regulation. MIT Press, Cambridge (1993)
27. Levy, B., Spiller, P.: The Institutional Foundations of Regulatory Commitment: A Comparative Analysis of Telecommunications Regulation. Journal of Law, Economics and Organization 10(2), 201–247 (1994)
28. Lobina, E.: Problems with Private Water Concessions: A Review of Experiences and Analysis of Dynamics. International Journal of Water Resources Development 21, 55–87 (2005)
29. Lule, J., Ninsiima, R.: Power shortage in Kampala. New Vision Printing and Publishing Company Ltd., Kampala (New Vision December 22, 2010)
30. Maskin, E., Tirole, J.: Unforeseen Contingencies and Incomplete Contracts. Review of Economic Studies 66(1), 83–114 (1999)
31. Maskin, E., Tirole, J.: The Politician and the Judge: Accountability in Government. The American Economic Review 94(4), 1034–1054 (2004)
32. Mugabi, F., Donald, K.: Riots in Bugembe protesting a three day black out. New Vision Printing and Publishing Company Ltd., Kampala (New Vision November 17, 2010)
33. Nera: Regulatory Transparency: International Assessment and Emerging Lessons. Report for the World Bank and NERA, London (2005)
34. Nsambu, H.: 50,000 to sue Umeme over power bills. New Vision Printing and Publishing Company Ltd., Kampala (New Vision May 2, 2010)
35. Ojwee, D.: Electricity Authority slams Umeme's work. New Vision Printing and Publishing Company Ltd., Kampala (New Vision May 31, 2010)
36. Perotti, E.C.: Credible Privatization. The American Economic Review 85(4), 847–859 (1995)
37. Public-Private Partnership Manual. Pretoria: South African National Treasury, Module 1, 4–5 (2004)
38. Stern, J., Cubbin, J.: Regulatory Effectiveness: The Impact of Regulation and Regulatory Governance Arrangements on Electricity Industry Outcomes. The World Bank (2005)
39. Tirole, J.: Incomplete Contracts: Where do We Stand? Econometrica 67(4), 741–781 (1999)
40. Tremolet, S., Shah, N.: Wanted! Good Regulators for Good Regulation: An evaluation of Human and Financial Resource Constraints for Utility Regulation. ERM and Tremolet Consulting report. World Bank, Washington, D.C (2005)
41. Vickers, J.: Regulation, competition, and the structure of prices. Oxford Review of Economic Policy 13(1), 15–26 (1997)
42. Williamson, O.E.: Markets and Hierarchies: Analysis and Antitrust Implications. Free Press, Collier Macmillan, New York, London (1975)
43. Williamson, O.E.: The economic institutions of capitalism: firms, markets, relational contracting. Free Press, New York (1985)

Spectral Expansion Method for QBD and QBD-M Processes in Performance Modeling of Computing and Communication Systems: A Review

Ram Chakka

Meerut Institute of Engineering & Technology,
Meerut
ramchakka@yahoo.com
http://www.miet.ac.in

Abstract. Spectral Expansion Method (SEM), forming the major part of the doctoral thesis of the author, was developed at the Newcastle University (United Kingdom) during the early nineties. Though it started as an alternative to the Matrix Geometric Method (MGM), evaluations by the author and independent evaluations by others have clearly shown the superiority of SEM over the MGM in a number of aspects. SEM computes the steady state probabilities of the QBD (Quasi-Birth-Death) and the QBD-M (Quasi-simultaneous-Multiple-Births-Deaths) processes which are continuous time Markov chains (CTMC) occuring rather abundantly in modeling advanced computing systems, emerging telecommunication systems, high speed networks, flexible manufacturing systems and many other discrete event systems. The method has been used for performability computations in very diverse areas of ICT (information and Communication Technologies) with tremendous success.

The applicability of this method is growing wider and becoming more crucial than before, with the advent of new paradigms such as computing clouds, server farms, IaaS (Infrastructure as a Service), broad band and high speed networks, mobile communications, Internet based service industry, the method is proven to be applicable and useful in all these. This paper would serve as a useful review of the SEM and as a tutorial for modelers and simulation technologists.

Keywords: performance evaluation, QoS, spectral expansion method, QBD, QBD-M, matrix geometric method.

1 Introduction

Performance evaluation of discrete event systems has been important with crucial applications in computing systems, communication networks, flexible manufacturing systems (FMS), transaction processing systems and many other discrete event systems. With the advent of new business models and paradigms of computing and communications, such as computing clouds, server farms, IaaS

P.V. Krishna, M.R. Babu, and E. Ariwa (Eds.): ObCom 2011, Part II, CCIS 270, pp. 794–810, 2012.
© Springer-Verlag Berlin Heidelberg 2012

(Infrastructure as a Service), SaaS (Software as a Service), PaaS (Platform as Service), high speed packet switched networks, broadband wireless networks, Next Generation Internet, etc., efficient performance evaluation methods and tools have become necessary for effective design, dimensioning and operation of ICT (Information and Communication Technologies) systems, and for effective resource utilization. The QoS requirements in the emerging Next Generation Networks (NGN) and Internet based services make performance evaluation and optimization very crucial indeed. Analytical modeling is a very important way of performance evaluation, characterized by much higher computational efficiency over stochastic discrete event simulation, the latter can become prohibitively expensive in a number of cases. As a general rule, performance computations from analytical models (exact or approximate) augmented and verified by simulation results can give rise to reliable performance studies which can be a strong basis for reliable design and dependable operation of these systems.

Spectral Expansion Method (SEM), developed at Newcastle University, forming the major part of the doctoral thesis of the author [1,2,3,4,5], has evolved to be a popular technique useful for the performance and dependability modeling of many discrete event systems. It solves Markov models of certain kind, called QBD (Quasi-Birth-and-Death) and QBD-M (Quasi-simulatneous-multiple-Births-and-Deaths) processes. Efficient solution algorithms for spectral expansion were developed in early nineties [1,2,4,5]. The earliest numerical results on this algorithm were reported in [2]. These algorithms seem to fare better than the matrix-goemetric methods in accuracy, speed and ease of use. This is shown by the author in [1,4] and also by several indepependent investigators [6,7,8]. QBD and QBD-M processes arise in a vast variety of practical system models in ICT and other areas. Some of the successful applications of the spectral expansion method include, performability modeling of several types of multiprocessors [2,9,1,5], computing clusters [10,11,12,13], multi-task execution models [14], webserver dimensioning and operation [15,16,17], non-product form networks of queues [18,19,20,21], queues with bursty traffic and bulk services [22,23,24,25,26], emerging telecommunication systems [27,28,29,30], generalised Markovian node models [22,23,25,26,27], evaluation of communication equipment [31,32], high speed networks [33,34], heavily loaded queuing systems [44], design of efficient protocols for ISP (Internet Service Provider) operations [35,36], FMS design and operations [9,10,37,38], retrial queues [39,40,41,42], computing clouds [43] and many other practical systems [37,45,46]. In this paper, we present the mathematics related to the development of the spectral expansion method and present the solution algorithms. The intended purpose of this paper is to serve modelers and simulation technologists as a useful review and for building useful tools.

2   The QBD Process X

The systems that are of interest are modeled by two-dimensional Markov processes on semi-infinite lattice strips. The state of the system at time t is denoted by two integer valued random variables (r.v), $I(t)$, $J(t)$; $I(t)$ taking a *finite* set of values and $J(t)$,an *infinite* set of values. Without loss of generality, we can assume the minimum value of $I(t)$ is 0 and N, the maximum. The minimum value of the random variable $J(t)$ is 0 and it can take non-negative integer values from 0 to ∞. The Markov process is denoted by $X = \{[I(t), J(t)]; t \geq 0\}$. We assume this is irreducible with a state space $\{0, 1, \ldots, N\} \times \{0, 1, \ldots\}$. For a convenient representation, it is assumed that $I(t)$ varies in the lateral or horizontal direction and $J(t)$ is represented in the vertical direction of the semi-infinite rectangular lattice strip. The possible transitions that underlie this Markov process are given by :

(a) A_j - purely lateral transition rate matrix - from state (i, j) to state (k, j), $(0 \leq i, k \leq N; i \neq k; j = 0, 1, \ldots)$;

(b) B_j - one-step upward transition rate matrix - from state (i, j) to state $(k, j + 1)$, $(0 \leq i, k \leq N; j = 0, 1, \ldots)$;

(c) C_j - one-step downward transition rate matrix - from state (i, j) to state $(k, j - 1)$,$(0 \leq i, k \leq N; j = 1, 2, \ldots)$;

As it is seen above, the possible change in J in any transition is either +1 or 0 or -1. Later in this paper, we shall also consider the Markov process Y in which multi-step jumps in J are possible, that is the QBD-M Process.

For the process X, let A_j , B_j and C_j be the transition rate matrices, square matrices each of size $(N+1) \times (N+1)$, associated with (a), (b) and (c) respectively. Thus, $A_j(i, k), (i \neq k)$ is the transition rate from state (i, j) to state (k, j), and $A_j(i, i) = 0$. $B_j(i, k)$ is the transition rate from (i, j) to $(k, j + 1)$. $C_j(i, k)$ is the transition rate from (i, j) to $(k, j - 1)$, and $C_0 = 0$, by definition.

We assume the process has a threshold, an integer $M, (M \geq 1)$ such that the instantaneous transition rates of (a), (b) and (c) do not depend on j when $j \geq M$ in the case of (a), $j \geq M - 1$ in the case of (b), and when $j \geq M$ for (c). In the references given for the application of spectral expansion, it can be seen that such a threshold does exist in a large variety of real world problems occuring in computing and communication systems. Thus, we have

$$A_j = A, j \geq M \; ; \; B_j = B, j \geq M - 1 \; ; \; C_j = C, j \geq M \; ; \qquad (1)$$

The states spanned by the finite r.v. $I(t)$ can be conveniently termed as the *operative states* of the system in consideration. The transitions in (a) are purely among the operative states, without any change in J, whereas the transitions in (b) and (c) are also among the operative states but with a fixed change in J by +1 and -1 respectively.

When the process is irredicible and the corresponding balance equations of the state probabilities have a unique normalizeable solution, we say the process is *ergodic* and there exists a steady state for that process. The objective of this analysis is to determine the steady state probability $p_{i,j}$ of the state (i, j) in terms of the known parameters of the system. $p_{i,j}$ is defined as:

$$p_{i,j} = \lim_{t \to \infty} P(I(t) = i, J(t) = j); \; i = 0, 1, \ldots, N; j = 0, 1, \ldots \qquad (2)$$

Let D_j^A , D_j^B and D_j^C be the diagonal matrices, of size $(N + 1) \times (N + 1)$ each, defined by their i^{th} diagonal element as,

$$D_j^A(i, i) = \sum_{k=0}^{N} A_j(i, k) \; ; \; D_j^B(i, i) = \sum_{k=0}^{N} B_j(i, k) \; ; \; D_j^C(i, i) = \sum_{k=0}^{N} C_j(i, k) \; ; \quad (3)$$

In other words, the ith diagonal element of each of these diagonal matrices is the ith row sum of the corresponding transition rate matrix. Then we also get similar diagonal matrices D^A, D^B and D^C for A, B and C respectively.

$$D^A(i, i) = \sum_{k=0}^{N} A(i, k); \; D^B(i, i) = \sum_{k=0}^{N} B(i, k); \; D^C(i, i) = \sum_{k=0}^{N} C(i, k); \quad (4)$$

3   Solution for Steady State Probabilities

All the states in a row of the lattice Markov process have the same value j for the unbounded r.v. $J(t)$. Similarly, any column consists of states with same i. Here, it is mathematically convenient to define the row vectors v_j as,

$$v_j = (p_{o,j}, p_{i,j}, \ldots, p_{N,j}); \; j = 0, 1, \ldots \quad (5)$$

Thus, the elements of v_j are the probabilities of all states in a row, where $J = j$. In order to solve for the probability distribution $\{p_{i,j}\}$, it is necessary to solve the balance equations. It is mathematically more elegant to work with vectors v_j compared to $p_{i,j}$. The steady state balance equations satisfied by the vectors v_j are:

$$v_j[D_j^A + D_j^B + D_j^C] = v_{j-1}B_{j-1} + v_jA_j + v_{j+1}C_{j+1}; \; j = 0, 1, \ldots, M - 1 \; ; \quad (6)$$

$v_{-1} = 0$ by definition. And, for $j \geq M$

$$v_j[D^A + D^B + D^C] = v_{j-1}B + v_jA + v_{j+1}C \; ; j = M, M + 1, \ldots \quad (7)$$

These equations (7) are infinite in number. In addition to them, we have another equation resulting from the fact that all the probabilities $p_{i,j}$ sum to 1.0:

$$\sum_{j=0}^{\infty} v_je = 1.0, \quad (8)$$

where e is the column vector of $N + 1$ elements each of which is equal to 1. This definition of e is valid throughout this paper.

It is the set of equations (7) that are infinite in number. Essentially, spectral expansion is a solution technique to solve these equations. The difference between the set (6) and the set (7) is that the former has coefficient matrices that are j-dependent whereas in the case of the latter the coefficient matrices are j-independent. The latter can be rewritten as

$$v_jQ_0 + v_{j+1}Q_1 + v_{j+2}Q_2 = 0 \; ; \; j = M - 1, M, \ldots \quad (9)$$

where $Q_0 = B$, $Q_1 = A - D^A - D^B - D^C$ and $Q_2 = C$. This is a homogeneous vector difference equation of order 2, with constant coefficients. $Q(\lambda)$ is the *characteristic matrix polynomial* associated with this difference equation.

$$Q(\lambda) = Q_0 + Q_1\lambda + Q_2\lambda^2. \tag{10}$$

We also refer to $Q(\lambda)$ as the characteristic matrix polynomial of the Markov process X. The solution of (9) is closely related to the eigenvalues and the left-eigenvectors of $Q(\lambda)$. Henceforth, throughout this paper, an eigenvalue means a finite eigenvalue and an eigenvector means a non-zero finite left-eigenvector. Let (λ, ψ) be an eigenvalue-eigenvector pair of $Q(\lambda)$, thus satisfying the equation:

$$\psi Q(\lambda) = 0 \; ; \; det[Q[\lambda]] = 0 \tag{11}$$

λ can be real or complex. If λ is real then ψ also is real, if λ is complex then ψ is complex. This is because the matrices Q_0, Q_1 and Q_2 are real. Also, if (λ, ψ) is a complex eigenvalue-eigenvector pair, then its conjugate pair (λ^*, ψ^*) also satisfies (11). $Q(\lambda)$ may also possess either a null eigenvalue or a multiplicity of null eigenvalues. Null eigenvalues are also refered as zero-eigenvalues throughout this paper. If Q_0 is non-singular then $Q(\lambda)$ will have no zero-eigenvalues. However, if Q_0 is singular with a rank $N + 1 - r_0$ ($1 \le r_0 \le N + 1$) then it will have zero-eigenvalues with a multiplicity of r_0 and corresponding non-zero independent eigenvectors, if the sum of all principal minors of order $N + 1 - r_0$ of Q_0 is non-zero. That condition is usually the case, hence, we assume the same. We also assume if Q_2 has a rank $N + 1 - r_2$, then the sum of all the principal minors of Q_2 of order $N + 1 - r_2$ is non-zero.

For a non-zero eigenvalue-eigenvector pair, (λ_k, ψ_k), by substituting $v_j = \psi_k \lambda_k^j$ ($j \ge M - 1$) in the equations (2,9), it can be easily seen that this set of infinite number of equations is satisfied. Hence, that is a particular solution. The expression may even be $\psi_k \lambda_k^{j+l_k}$ for any real l_k. These two expressions are equivalent since ψ_k can always be scaled without affecting its property of being an eigenvector. If zero-eigenvalues do exist, let them be r_0 in number denoted by $\lambda_{z,k}, (k = 0, 1, \ldots r_0 - 1)$ and the corresponding eigenvectors by $\psi_{z,k}, (k = 0, 1, \ldots r_0 - 1)$. Then clearly, for every $k\,(k = 0, 1, \ldots r_0 - 1)$, $v_j = \psi_{z,k}\lambda_{z,k}^{j-M+1}$ ($j \ge M - 1$) satisfies equations (7,9). It is assumed $0^0 = 1$. That expression can also be written as $v_j = 0$, if $j \ne M-1$ and $\psi_{z,k}$, if $j = M-1$. This also is a particular solution. Yet, what is necessary is the general solution of these equations that also satisfy equations (6,8).

Let us assume that $Q(\lambda)$ has d pairs of eigenvalue-eigenvectors. These can be real or in pairs of complex-conjugates. There can be simple or multiple eigenvalues. However, an assumption is made that when an eigenvalue is of multiplicity n, it does have n independent eigenvectors. In all our applications and experiments with several system models, this is what has been observed. Let (λ_k, ψ_k) be the kth eigenvalue-eigenvector pair, where k varies from 0 to $d - 1$. Then it is easy to see the general solution for v_j of the equations (7, 9) can be a linear sum of all the factors $(\psi_k\lambda_k^{j-M+1})$. In other words,

$$v_j = \sum_{k=0}^{d-1} a_k \psi_k \lambda_k^{j-M+1} \; ; \; j = M-1, M, \ldots \tag{12}$$

In the state-probability form:

$$p_{i,j} = \sum_{k=0}^{d-1} a_k \psi_k \lambda_k^{j-M+1} \; ; \; j = M-1, M, \ldots \tag{13}$$

where $a_k(k = 0, 1, \ldots, d-1)$ are arbitrary constants, some of them can be complex too. In order to get the relevant solution from the general solution, let us consider some of the known steady state properties of the probability distribution. We know the sum of the probabilities of all states in any column is less than 1 though these states are infinitely many. Now consider the probability sum,

$$\sum_{j=M-1}^{\infty} p_{i,j} = \sum_{j=M-1}^{\infty} \sum_{k=0}^{d-1} a_k \psi_k(i) \lambda_k^{j-M+1}.$$

The above is the sum of probabilities of all states in the ith column that are above $j \geq M-1$. It can be easily seen that the necessary condition that this sum is bounded is,

$$a_k = 0, if \, |\lambda_k| \geq 1$$

With this, by suitably numbering the eigenvalues, the general solution is modified as,

$$v_j = \sum_{k=0}^{c-1} a_k \psi_k \lambda_k^{j-M+1}; \; j = M-1, M, \ldots \tag{14}$$

This is equivalent to:

$$p_{i,j} = \sum_{k=0}^{c-1} a_k \psi_k \lambda_k^{j-M+1}; \; j = M-1, M, \ldots \tag{15}$$

where c is the number of eigenvalues that are present strictly within (also termed as within, strictly inside or inside) the unit circle. These eigenvalues appear some as real and others as complex-conjugate pairs as explained before, and so do the corresponding eigenvectors too. When the eigenvalues are complex-conjugate the corresponding constants also are complex-conjugate. This is so because, then only the right-hand side of equations (5,15) would be real. We also have another condition to be satisfied always. That condition is the right-hand sides of equations (5,15) are also positive. This can happen if the real parts of λ_k, ψ_k and a_k are positive. Indeed, this is what has been observed in all our experiments.

Now it remains to determine the constants a_k that are still unknown, to complete the solution. Their number c also is not known so far. Yet, we can now find $v_{M-1}, v_M, ...$ as linear expressions in the c unknowns, $a_k, (k = 0, 1, \ldots, c - 1)$. The other unknowns are, $v_0, v_1, ...v_{M-2}$. To get these unknowns, we have equations (6) for $j = 0, 1, ...M - 1$. This is a set of $M \times (N + 1)$ linear equations with $(M - 1) \text{x} (N + 1)$ unknown probabilities (all the probabilities in $v_j, (j = 0, 1, ...M - 2))$ plus the c unknown constants a_k. However $M \times (N + 1) - 1$ of these equations are linearly independent, since the generator matrix of the Markov process is singular. On the other hand, an additional independent equation is provided by (8). Hence, the number of independent linear equations is $M \times (N + 1)$.

Clearly, this set of $M \times (N + 1)$ independent linear equations with $(M - 1)$ x $(N + 1) + c$ unknowns has a unique solution if, and only if, $M \times (N + 1) = (M - 1) \times (N + 1) + c$. Or, that condition is $c = N + 1$. Here, we make the following hypothesis:

- If $c > N + 1$, there are more unknowns than the the number of equations to be satisfied. That means infinitely many different solutions of the balance equations are possible and hence many different steady states. Since, in reality, the process can have only a unique steady state if it is stable, it can be said that c cannot be greater than $N + 1$. On the other hand, if $c < N + 1$, a feasible solution does not exist for the balance equations and hence that corresponds to the instability of the process.

In fact, this is what has been found in all our examples. This analysis, together with the fact that an irreducible Markov process has a steady-state distribution if, and only if, its balance and normalisation equations have a unique solution, implies

Proposition 1. *The condition $c = N + 1$ (the number of eigenvalues of $Q(\lambda)$ strictly inside the unit disk is equal to the number of operative states of the Markov process), is necessary and sufficient for the ergodicity of the Markov process X.*

It is interesting to note, from proposition 1, as long as the process X is irreducible, the stability or ergodicity of this process is determined purely by the matrices A, B and C, and does not depend on the j-dependent matrices A_j , B_j and C_j. This is because the eigenvalues and eigenvectors depend purely on A, B and C.

4   Spectral Analysis

In this section the nature of the eigenvalues of $Q(\lambda)$ is examined. The eigenvalues and eigenvectors of $Q(\lambda)$ satisfy,

$$\psi[Q_0 + Q_1\lambda + Q_2\lambda^2] = 0. \tag{16}$$

We get the following results.

Theorem 1. *If Q_0 is non-singular, then $Q(\lambda)$ does not have zero-eigenvalues*

Proof. Let $\lambda = 0$, then we get, from (11) , $\det[Q(\lambda)] = \det[Q_0] \neq 0$. Hence, the result

Theorem 2. *If Q_0 is singular with a rank $N + 1 - r_0$, then (i) $Q(\lambda)$ has zero-eigenvalues of multiplicity r_0 if the sum of all principal minors of Q_0 of order $N + 1 - r_0$ is non-zero. (ii) it has r_0 corresponding independent eigenvectors.*

Proof. Let $\lambda = 0$ in (16), then we get $\psi Q_0 = 0$. Hence, the zero-eigenvalue of $Q(\lambda)$ and the zero-eigenvalue of Q_0 have the same multiplicity. Now, refer to Theorem 2.1.2, Lemma in pages 54-57 of [47] to complete the proof of part (i), and Definition (a) in page 21 of [47], Theorem 1.16.2 on page 45 of [47] for part (ii).

Theorem 3. *If Q_2 is non-singular, then $Q(\lambda)$ has $2N + 2$ eigenvalues.*

Proof. Multiply the equation (16) on right by Q_2^{-1}, then it becomes

$$\psi[T_0 + T_1\lambda + I\lambda^2] = 2$$

where $T_0 = Q_0 Q_2^{-1}, T_1 = Q_1 Q_2^{-1}$ and I is the Unit matrix. By introducing the auxiliary vector $\varphi = \lambda\psi$, this equation can be rewritten in the equivalent linear form as,

$$[\psi\ \varphi] \begin{bmatrix} 0 & -T_0 \\ I & -T_1 \end{bmatrix} = \lambda\,[\psi\ \varphi] \tag{17}$$

This linear eigenvalue problem has $2N+2$ finite solutions for λ [47]. Every (λ, ψ) that satisfies equation (17) does satisfy equation (16), and the converse also is true. Hence, $Q(\lambda)$ has $2N+2$ eigenvalues. Note that the square matrix involved in equation (17) is simple iff multiple eigenvalues would have independent multiple eigenvectors.

Theorem 4. *If Q_0 is non-singular and Q_2 is singular with rank $N + 1 - r_2$, then the number of eigenvalues of $Q(\lambda)$ is $2N + 2 - r_2$.*

Proof. Since Q_0 is non-singular, by Theorem 1, $\lambda = 0$ is not an eigenvalue of $Q(\lambda)$. Let us, then, introduce the auxiliary variable $\gamma = \frac{1}{\lambda}$ and, transform the variable to γ, by substitution. Then, we get,

$$\psi[Q_2 + Q_1\gamma + Q_0\gamma^2] = 0 \tag{18}$$

For every (λ, ψ) satisfying (16), there exists a $\gamma = 1/\lambda$, such that (γ, ψ) satisfies the new quadratic eigenvalue problem (18). And, for every $(\gamma \neq 0, \psi)$ satisfying (18), there exists a $\lambda = \frac{1}{\gamma}$, such that (λ, ψ) satisfies (16). Hence, the eigenvalues of (16) are the non-zero eigenvalues of (18). Applying Theorems 2, 3, in the case of (18), it can be said the non-zero eigenvalues of (18) are indeed, $2N + 2 - r_2$. Hence, the result.

Theorem 5. *If Q_0 is singular with a rank $N + 1 - r_0$ and Q_2 is singular with a rank $N + 1 - r_2$, then $Q(\lambda)$ has (i) r_0 zero-eigenvalues, and (ii) $2N + 2 - r_0 - r_2$ non-zero eigenvalues.*

Proof. Since Q_0 is singular, applying Theorem 2, part (i) is proved. In order to prove (ii), introduce an auxiliary variable $\gamma = \frac{(\theta+\lambda)}{(\theta-\lambda)}$, where θ is arbitrary θ can be so chosen that, for every λ from a finite set of values, the corresponding γ exists. λ can be expressed in terms of γ as,

$$\lambda = \frac{\theta(\gamma - 1)}{(\gamma + 1)} \tag{19}$$

substituting this in (16), we get

$$\psi[(Q_0 + \theta Q_1 + \theta^2 Q_2) + 2(Q_0 - \theta Q_2)\gamma + (Q_0 + \theta Q_1 + \theta^2 Q_2)\gamma^2] = 0 \tag{20}$$

The parameter θ is so chosen that $(Q_0 + \theta Q_1 + \theta^2 Q_2)$ is non-singular($\theta \neq 0, 1$). Applying Theorem 3, we can say that equation (20) has $2N + 2$ eigenvalues. Also, it can be seen by substitution, of those $2N + 2$ eigenvalues r_2 are multiple eigenvalues at $\gamma = -1$ and r_0 are multiple eigenvalues at $\gamma = 1$.

Now, for every (λ, ψ) satisfying (16), there exists a unique (γ, ψ) that satisfies (20). Also, for every $(\gamma \neq -1, \psi)$, there exists a corresponding unique (λ, ψ) satisfying (16). Hence, the λ's corresponding to the λ's that are not equal to -1, are all the eigenvalues of (16). When $\gamma = 1$, the corresponding $\lambda = 0$. Hence, the result.

5   The Dual Process $\overline{X}$

It is interesting, here, to examine a related irreducible process, $\overline{X}$, which we call the dual of the process X. The j-independent upward transition rates in X are the j-independent downward transition rates in $\overline{X}$, and the j-independent downward transition rates in X are the j-independent upward transition rates in $\overline{X}$. The j- independent lateral transitions are the same in both the processes. $\overline{X}$ is obtained by simply interchanging the matrices B and C in X. The j-dependent transition rate matrices of $\overline{X}$ can be quite arbitrary, but ensuring its irreducibility. The characteristic matrix polynomial of $\overline{X}$ is then given by

$$\overline{Q}(\beta) = Q_2 + Q_1\beta + Q_0\beta^2 \tag{21}$$

The eigenvalues and eigenvectors (β, ϕ) of $\overline{Q}(\beta)$ satisfy

$$\phi\overline{Q}(\beta) = 0 \ ; \ det[\overline{Q}(\beta)] = 0; \tag{22}$$

It can be shown as before that, $\overline{X}$ is ergodic if and only if $\overline{Q}(\beta)$ has $N + 1$ number of eigenvalues inside its unit circle, and it cannot have greater than $N + 1$ eigenvalues inside its unit circle.

It can now be conjectured that between X and $\overline{X}$, if one is stable, automatically the other is unstable (see [1]).

There is a close relationship between the eigenvalue-eigenvectors of $Q(\lambda)$ and those of $\overline{Q}(\beta)$. For every non-zero eigenvalue-eigenvector pair, (λ, ψ), of $Q(\lambda)$, there exist a unique $\beta = 1/\lambda$ and a $\phi = \psi$ that satisfy (22), hence that (β, ϕ) is an eigenvalue-eigenvector pair of $\overline{Q}(\beta)$. Thus, the number of non-zero eigenvalues of $Q(\lambda)$ is the same as those of $\overline{Q}(\beta)$.

The following three statements are proved earlier, and also numerically verified by limited examples:

(a) If Q_2 is non-singular then $Q(\lambda)$ has $2N + 2$ number of eigenvalues. If Q_0 is non-singular then $\overline{Q}(\beta)$ has $2N + 2$ number of eigenvalues.

(b) If Q_0 has a rank $N+1-r_0$ then $Q(\lambda)$ has r_0 number of zero-eigenvalues [47], that would also correspond to $\overline{Q}(\beta)$ having $2(N+1) - r_0$ number of eigenvalues. On the other hand, if Q_2 has a rank $N+1-r_2$ then $\overline{Q}(\beta)$ will have r_2 number of zero-eigenvalues which implies $Q(\lambda)$ will have $2(N+1)-r_2$ number of eigenvalues.

(c) Thus, if Q_0 has a rank $N + 1 - r_0$ and Q_2 has a rank $N + 1 - r_2$ then, $Q(\lambda)$ will have r_0 number of zero-eigenvalues and $2(N + 1) - r_0 - r_2$ number of non-zero eigenvalues, whereas $\overline{Q}(\beta)$ will have r_2 number of zero-eigenvalues and $2(N + 1) - r_0 - r_2$ number of non-zero eigenvalues.

In the following analysis, assume Q_0 has a rank $N + 1 - r_0$ and Q_2 has a rank $N + 1 - r_2$, where $0 \le r_0, r_2 \le N + 1$. Then, if X is stable, the number of eigenvalues within its unit circle is $N + 1$, exactly on the unit circle is one ($\lambda = 1.0$), and the remaining eigenvalues, $N - r_2$ in number, are outside the unit circle. The reciprocals of these last $N - r_2$ eigenvalues are the non-zero eigenvalues of $\overline{Q}(\beta)$ within its unit circle. $\overline{Q}(\beta)$ also has r_2 number of zero-eigenvalues. Thus, total number of eigenvalues of $\overline{Q}(\beta)$ that are strictly within its unit circle is $N - r_2 + r_2 = N$. Hence, $\overline{X}$ is unstable. It is also possible to prove, in similar lines, that if $\overline{X}$ is stable that implies X is unstable. Now, we have,

Proposition 2. *Between the irreducible processes X and $\overline{X}$, if one is ergodic that automatically implies that the other is unstable.*

In order to arrive at another result, let X have c number of eigenvalues inside its unit circle. There is one eigenvalue exactly on the unit circle. Thus, the number of eigenvalues strictly outside the unit circle is $2N + 2 - r_2 - 1 - c$. Hence, in the case of $\overline{X}$, the number of eigenvalues strictly within its unit circle is, r_2 zero-eigenvalues plus $2N + 2 - r_2 - 1 - c$ non-zero ones. That is a total of $2N + 2 - 1 - c$ eigenvalues strictly inside the unit circle of $\overline{Q}(\beta)$. We have already hypothesized that this number can not be greater than $N + 1$. That is possible only if c is not less than N. Hence, the following assertion is possible,

Proposition 3. *Given that X is irreducible and a unique non-negative solution exists, X is stable if and only if its characteristic polynomial $Q(\lambda)$ has exactly $N + 1$ eigenvalues strictly within the unit circle, and, X is unstable if and only if $Q(\lambda)$ has exactly N eigenvalues strictly within the unit circle.*

6   Multi-step Jumps in J: The QBD-M Process

Several generalisations and extensions of the model described above are possible. Work in [5] is related extending spectral expansion solution to Markov processes of finite state space. Many generalisations were reported in the literature, some examples are in [22,23,26,27]. A very important relavent generalisation is taken up in this section. This generalisation incorporates bounded multi-step jumps in J, in either direction. The resulting one is the QBD-M process.

This leads to a Markov process $Y = \{[I(t), J(t)]; t \geq 0\}$, on the state space $\{0, 1, \ldots, N\} \times \{0, 1, \ldots\}$, where the variable J(t) may jump by arbitrary, but bounded amounts in either direction. Y evolves due to the following possible transitions:

(a) A_j purely lateral transitions From state (i, j) to state $(k, j)(0 \leq i, k \leq N; i \neq k; j = 0, 1, \ldots)$;

(b) $B_{j,s}$ bounded s-step upward transitions From state (i, j) to state $(k, j+s)$ $(0 \leq i, k \leq N; 1 \leq s \leq y_1; y_1 \geq 1; j = 0, 1, \ldots)$;

(c) $C_{j,s}$ bounded s-step downward transitions From state (i, j) to state $(k, j - s)$ $(0 \leq i, k \leq N; s \leq j; 1 \leq s \leq y_2; y_2 \geq 1; j = 1, 2, \ldots)$.

A_j , $B_{j,s}$ $(s = 1, 2, \ldots, y_1)$ and $C_{j,s}$ $(s = 1, 2, \ldots, y_2)$ are the transition rate matrices associated with $(a), (b)$ and (c) respectively. $C_{j,s} = 0$ if $s > j$. We assume there is a threshold M, $M \geq y_1$, such that

$$A_j = A, j \geq M; \ B_{j,s} = B_s, j \geq M - y_1; \ C_{j,s} = C_s, j \geq M; \qquad (23)$$

for the possible values of s.

Defining again the diagonal matrices $D_j^A, D_{j,s}^B$ and $D_{j,s}^C$, whose i^{th} diagonal element is equal to the ith row sum of $A_j, B_{j,s}$ and $C_{j,s}$, respectively. Then the balance equations are,

$$v_j[D_j^A + \sum_{s=1}^{y_1} D_{j,s}^B + \sum_{s=1}^{y_2} D_{j,s}^C] = \sum_{s=1}^{y_1} v_{j-s}B_{j-s,s} + v_jA_j + \sum_{s=1}^{y_2} v_{j+s}C_{j+s,s};$$
$$j = 0, 1, \ldots, M - 1. \quad (24)$$

It is assumed $v_{j-s} = 0$ if $j < s$. The corresponding j-independent set is,

$$v_j[D^A + \sum_{s=1}^{y_1} D_s^B + \sum_{s=1}^{y_2} D_s^C] = \sum_{s=1}^{y_1} v_{j-s}B_s + v_jA + \sum_{s-1}^{y_2} v_{j+s}C_s, j \geq M \qquad (25)$$

where D^A, D_s^B and D_s^C are the j-independent versions of the diagonal matrices, $D_j^A, D_{j,s}^B$ and $D_{j,s}^C$ respectively.

In addition, we have for the sum of all probabilities,

$$\sum_{j=0}^{\infty} v_j e = 1.0 \qquad (26)$$

As before, (25) can be rewritten as a vector difference equation, of order $y = y_1 + y_2$, with constant cofficients:

$$\sum_{k=0}^{y} v_{j+k} Q_k = 0; \ j \geq M - y_1 \qquad (27)$$

Here , $Q_k = B_{y_1-k}$ for $k = 0, 1, \ldots, y_1-1$; $Q_{y_1} = A - D^A - \sum_{s=1}^{y_1} D_s^B - \sum_{s=1}^{y_2} D_s^C$
and $Q_k = C_{k-y_1}$ for $k = y_1 + 1, y_1 + 2, \ldots, y_1 + y_2$.

The corresponding matrix polynomial is

$$Q(\lambda) = \sum_{k=0}^{y} Q_k \lambda^k \tag{28}$$

The development, hence forth, is similar to that in section 3. The normalizeable solution of equation (25) is of the form,

$$v_j = \sum_{k=0}^{c-1} a_k \psi_k \lambda_k^{j-M+y_1}; \ j = M - y_1, M - y_1 + 1, \ldots \tag{29}$$

where λ_k are all the eigenvalues, c in number, of $Q(\lambda)$ strictly inside the unit disk, ψ_k are the corresponding independent eigenvectors, and a_k are the arbitrary constants $(k = 0, 1, \ldots, c-1)$. The latter constants are determined with the aid of the j-dependent balance equations, that is (24) for $j \leq M - 1$, and the normalisation equation. In this case, following the same line of thought as in sections 3, it is possible to find the value of c that is necessary and sufficient condition for the ergodicity of Y. This time, the number of linear simultaneous equations is $M(N + 1)$ from (24), and 1 from the (26) out of which $M(N + 1)$ are linearly independent. And, we have the unknowns $(M - y_1)(N + 1)$, the probabilities of states below $(j < M - y_1)$, and the c unknowns. These equations can have unique solution if and only if $(M - y_1)(N + 1) + c = M(N + 1)$, or, equivalently $c = y_1(N + 1)$. Thus,

Proposition 4. *The condition the number of eigenvalues of $Q(\lambda)$ strictly inside the unit disk, $c = y_1(N+1)$, is necessary and sufficient for the ergodicity of the irreducible Markov process Y.*

It is worth having another look at the stability properties of Y. Let us define an irreducible process $\overline{Y}$, the dual process of Y. In $\overline{Y}$, the $B_s(s = 1, 2, \ldots, y_1)$ are the downward transition rate matrices and the $C_s(s = 1, 2, \ldots, y_2)$ are the upward transition rate matrices. Since the stability condition depends only on the j-independent matrices A, B_s and C_s, and it does not depend on the j-dependent versions, we need not go at length to define the j-dependent matrices for $\overline{Y}$.

Define the row vector, $v = (q_0, q_1, \ldots, q_N)$. Following the same line of argument given in chapter-2 of [1], the necessary condition for the stability of $\overline{Y}$ is the existence of solution for the following equations,

$$v[A - D^A + \sum_{s=1}^{y_1}(B_s - D_s^B) + \sum_{s=1}^{y_2}(C_s - D_s^C)] = 0; \ ve = 0; \tag{30}$$

with the condition

$$q_i \geq 0 \ ; \ i = 0, 1 \ldots, N; \tag{31}$$

combined with the inequality condition,

$$v[\sum_{s=1}^{y_1} sB_s]e < v[\sum_{s=1}^{y_2} sC_s]e. \tag{32}$$

Similarly, the necessary condition for $\overline{Y}$ to be stable may be the existence of the solution for (10,31), and the opposite of (32) being valid. Hence, we have

Proposition 5. *Between the irreducible processes Y and $\overline{Y}$, if one is ergodic that automatically implies that the other is unstable.*

Also, it is possible to write the characteristic polynomial $\overline{Q}(\lambda)$ of $\overline{Y}$, as

$$\sum_{k=0}^{y} Q_{y-k}\lambda^k$$

and analyse the relationship between the eigenvalue-eigenvectors of $Q(\lambda)$ and $\overline{Q}(\lambda)$. We may workout in similar lines, as done for the case of X in the previous sections, and conclude,

Proposition 6. *Given Y is irreducible and a unique non-negative solution exists for (30), Y is stable if and only if its characteristic polynomial $Q(\lambda)$ has $y_1(N + 1)$ number of eigenvalues strictly within the unit circle, and, Y is unstable if and only if $Q(\lambda)$ has exactly $y_1(N + 1) - 1$ eigenvalues inside the unit circle.*

For computational purposes, the polynomial eigenvalue-eigenvector problem of degree y can be transformed into a linear one in much the same way as in [1]. For example, suppose that Q_y is non-singular and multiply on the right by Q_y^{-1}, then that leads to the problem,

$$\psi[\sum_{k=0}^{y-1} T_k\lambda^k + I\lambda^y] = 0 \tag{33}$$

where $T_k = Q_kQ_y^{-1}$. Introducing the vectors $\varphi_k = \lambda^k\psi, k = 1, 2, ..., y - 1$, we obtain the equivalent linear form

$$\left[\psi\varphi_1 \cdots \varphi_{y-1}\right]\begin{bmatrix} 0 & & & -T_0 \\ I & 0 & & -T_1 \\ & \ddots & \ddots & \\ & & I & -T_{y-1} \end{bmatrix} = \lambda\left[\psi\varphi_1 \cdots \varphi_{y-1}\right] \tag{34}$$

Other transformations to linear form, quite similar to those in [1], are pos- sible when Q_y is singular and Q_0 is not, or when both Q_0 and Q_y are singular.

7   Further Advances and Conclusions

We have presented an overview for the spectral expansion method to solve QBD and QBD-M processes, which can be used to evaluate the performance of various systems, services in information and communication technologies (ICT), and manufacturing [17,19,21,27,30,35,36,37,38,39,40,41,42,43,45,46]. As is evident, the method has given rise to tremendous successes in modeling a vast variety of ICT and other systems. Some other noteworthy works are in [50,52,51]. An effort for a classified bibliography on G-networks, that includes some papers on the spectral expansion was reported in [46].

The *HetSigma* queue in the Markovian framework has been proposed in order to model nodes in modern telecommunication networks [27]. An exact and computationally efficient solution of this new queue for steady state probabilities and performance measures is developed and presented. This queue with its variants has tremendous potential to evolve as a nodel model.

The *HetSigma* queue and its variants have been successfully applied to carry out the performance analysis of various problems in communication networks. SEM and the models based on SEM do provide a useful tool sfor the performance analysis of many problems of the emerging telecommunication systems and networks. The queuing model and its variants were successfully used to model Optical Burst/Packet (OBS) Switching networks [34] and another variant to successfully compute web server performance [17]. The *HetSigma* model has been successful to model the wireless networks [27].

References

1. Chakka, R.: Performance and Reliability Modelling of Computing Systems Using Spectral Expansion, Ph.D. Thesis, Newcastle University, Newcastle upon Tyne, United Kingdom (1995)
2. Chakka, R., Mitrani, I.: A Numerical Solution Method for Multiprocessor Systems with General Breakdowns and Repairs. In: 6th Int. Conf. on Performance Tools and Techniques, Edinburgh, pp. 289–304 (1992)
3. Chakka, R., Mitrani, I.: Fast Numerical Solution for a Class of Markov Models. In: Randell, B., et al. (eds.) Predictably Dependable Computing Systems, pp. 519–534. Springer, Heidelberg (1995); ISBN:3-540-59334-9
4. Mitrani, I., Chakka, R.: Spectral Expansion Solution for a Class of Markov Models: Application and Comparison with the Matrix-Geometric Method. Performance Evaluation 23(3), 241–260 (1995)
5. Chakka, R.: Spectral Expansion Solution for Some Finite Capacity Queues. Annals of Operations Research 79, 27–44 (1998); Special Issue on Queueing Networks with Blocking
6. Haverkort, B., Ost, A.: Steady State Analyses of Infinite Stochastic Petri Nets - A Comparison between the Spectral Expansion and the Matrix Geometric Methods. In: Proceedings of the 7th International Workshop on Petri Nets and Performance Models, Saint Malo, France, pp. 335–346 (1997)
7. Tran, H.T., Do, T.V.: Computational Aspects for Steady State Analysis of QBD Processes. Periodica Polytechnica, Ser. El. Eng., 179–200 (2000)
8. Tran, H.T., Do, T.V.: Comparison of some Numerical Methods for QBD-M Processes via Analysis of an ATM Concentrator. In: Proceedings of 20th IEEE International Performance, Computing and Communications Conference, IPCCC 2001, Pheonix, USA (2001)
9. Chakka, R., Mitrani, I.: Heterogeneous Multiprocessor Systems with Breakdowns: Performance and Optimal Repair Strategies. Theoretical Computer Science 125(1), 91–109 (1994)

10. Chakka, R., Gemikonakli, O., Basappa, P.: Multiserver Systems with Time or Operation Dependent Breakdowns, Alternate Repair Strategies, with Reconfiguration and Rebooting Delays. In: Proceedings of the 2002 International Symposium on Performance of Computer and Telecommunication Systems - Special Session on Modeling and Simulation based Multiprocessor Scheduling, San Diego, CA, USA, pp. 266–277 (2002); ISBN: 1-56555-252-0

11. Ever, E., Gemikonakli, O., Chakka, R.: A Stochastic Model for Highly Available Clusters with One Head Node and Several Identical Computing Nodes. In: Proceedings of The 9th International Conference on Computer Modelling and Simulation (UKSim 2006), pp. 32–373. Oxford University, Oxford (2006)

12. Ever, E., Gemikonakli, O., Chakka, R.: A Mathematical Model for Performability of Beowulf Clusters. In: Proceedings of the 39th Annual Simulation Symposium, Huntsville, Alabama, pp. 118–126 (2006)

13. Ever, E., Gemikonakli, O., Chakka, R.: Analytical Modelling and Simulation of Small Scale, Typical and Highly Available Beowulf Clusters with Breakdowns and Repairs. Simulation Modelling Practice and Theory (SIMPAT) 17(2), 327–347 (2009)

14. Ettl, M., Mitrani, I.: Applying Spectral Expansion in Evaluating the Performance of Multiprocessor Systems. In: Boxma, O.J., Koole, G.M. (eds.) 3rd QMIPS Workshop: Part 1, CWI TRACT, Amsterdam, pp. 45–58 (1994)

15. Do, T.V., Chakka, R., Nhat, T.L., Gemikonakli, O.: A New Performance Model for Web Servers. In: Proceedings of the 5th Eurosim Congress on Modelling and Simulation (EURISIM 2004), ESIEE Paris (2004)

16. Do, T.V., Chakka, R., Nhat, T.L., Krieger, U.: Performance Modeling of a Web Server with Dynamic Pool of Service Processes. In: Euro-NGI Network of Excellence Workshop on Stochastic Performance Models for Resource Allocation (STOPERA) in Communication Systems, Amsterdam (2006)

17. Do, T.V., Krieger, U., Chakka, R.: Performance Modeling of an Apache Web Server with a Dynamic Pool of Service Processes. Journal of Telecommunication Systems, Special Issue on Modelling and Performance Evaluation of Future Generation Internet Networks 39(2), 117–129 (2008)

18. Chakka, R., Mitrani, I.: Approximate Solutions for Open Networks with Breakdowns and Repairs. In: Kelly, F.P., Zachary, S., Ziedins, I. (eds.) Stochastic Networks: Theory and Applications. Royal Statistical Society Lecture Note Series, vol. 4, pp. 267–280. Oxford University Press, Oxford (1996); ISBN:0-19-852399-8

19. Chakka, R., Gemikonakli, O., Harrison, P.G.: Approaches to modelling open networks with bursty arrivals. In: Proceedings of the Eighth IFIP Workshop on ATM & IP Networks, Ilkley, pp. 13/1–13/13. Networks UK Publishers, U.K (2000)

20. Chakka, R., Ever, E., Gemikonakli, O.: An Approach to Modelling Open Networks with Unreliable Servers and Finite Buffers. WSEAS Transactions on Computers 5(11), 2536–2543 (2006) ISSN: 1109-2750

21. Chakka, R., Ever, E., Gemikonakli, O.: Joint-State Modelling for Open Queuing Networks with Breakdowns, Repairs and Finite Buffers. In: Proceedings of MASCOTS 2007 International Symposium on Modeling, Analysis, and Simulation of Computer and Telecommunication Systems, Turkey, pp. 260–266 (2007) ISBN: 978-1-4144-1854-1, ISSN: 1526-7537

22. Chakka, R., Harrison, P.G.: The MMCPP/GE/c Queue. Queueing Systems: Theory and Applications 38(3), 307–326 (2001)

23. Chakka, R., Harrison, P.G.: A Markov Modulated Multi-Server Queue with Negative Customers - The MM CPP/GE/c/L G-Queue. Acta Informatica 37(11-12), 881–919 (2001)

24. Harrison, P.G., Chakka, R.: The MM CPP/GE/c/L G-Queue at Equilibrium. In: Goto, K., et al. (eds.) Performance and QoS of Next Generation Networking. Springer, Heidelberg (2000)

25. Harrison, P.G.: The MM CPP/GE/c G-Queue: Sojourn Time Distribution. Queueing Systems: Theory and Applications 41(3), 271–298 (2002)

26. Chakka, R.: Towards a generalised Markovian node model: The MM $\sum_{k=1}^{K} CPP_k$/GE/c/L G-Queue. In: Artalejo, J.R., Krishnamoorthy, A. (eds.) Advances in Stochastic Modelling, pp. 313–344. Notable Publications Inc., New Jersy (2002)

27. Chakka, R., Do, T.V.: The MM $\sum_{k=1}^{K} CPP_k$/GE/c/L G-Queue with Heterogeneous Servers: Steady State Solution and an Application to Performance Evaluation. Performance Evaluation Journal 64(3), 191–209 (2007)

28. Do, T.V., Chakka, R., Nhat, T.L., Cigno, R.L.: A Generalised Queueing Model for the Performance Analysis of the GSM/GPRS System. Posts, Telecommunications and Information Technology Journal - Research, Development and Application on Electronics, Telecommunications and Information Technology, Vietnam (1), 18–23 (2007)

29. Van Do, T., Do, N.H., Chakka, R.: Performance Evaluation of the High Speed Downlink Packet Access in Communications Networks Based on High Altitude Platforms. In: Al-Begain, K., Heindl, A., Telek, M. (eds.) ASMTA 2008. LNCS, vol. 5055, pp. 310–322. Springer, Heidelberg (2008) ISSN: 0302-9743, ISBN-10: 3-540-68980-X

30. Do, T.V.: A New Computational Algorithm for Retrial Queues to Cellular Mobile Systems with Guard Channels. Compters & Industrial Engineering 59(4), 865–872 (2010)

31. Do, T.V., Chakka, R., Harrison, P.G.: Integrated Analytical Model for Computation and Comparison of the Throughputs of the UMTS/HSDPA User Equipment Categories. In: Proceedings of the Tenth ACM Symposium on Modeling, Analysis, and Simulation of Wireless and Mobile Systems (MSWiM 2007), Greece, pp. 45–51 (2007)

32. Do, T.V., Chakka, R., Do, N.M., Pap, L.: A Markovian Queue with Varying Number of Servers and Applications to the Performance Comparison of HSDPA User Equipment. Acta Informatica 48(4), 243–269 (2011)

33. Papp, D., Do, T.V., Chakka, R., Xuan, M.T.T.: Repair Strategies on the Operation of MPLS Routing. In: Nejat Ince, A., Bragg, A. (eds.) Recent Advances in Modeling and Simulation Tools for Communication Networks and Services, pp. 319–330. Springer Science+Business Media (2007) ISBN-13: 978-0-387-73907-6

34. Do, T.V., Chakka, R.: A New Performability Model for Queueing and FDL-related Burst Loss in Optical Switching Node. Computer Communications Journal 33(supplement 1), S146–S151 (2010)

35. Do, T.V., Chakka, R.: Simulation and Analytical Approaches for Estimating the Performability of a Multicast Address Dynamic Allocation Mechanism. Simulation Modelling Practice and Theory 18(7), 971–983 (2010)

36. Do, T.V., Chakka, R.: An Efficient Method to Compute the Rate Matrix for Retrial Queues with Large Number of Servers. Applied Mathematics Letters 23(5), 638–643 (2010)

37. Do, T.V., Krieger, U.R.: A Performance Model for Maintenance Tasks in an Environment of Virtualized Servers. In: IFIP/TC6 NETWORKING, Aachen, Germany, pp. 931–942 (2009)

38. Do, T.V.: A New Solution for a Queueing Model of a Manufacturing Cell with Negative Customers under a Rotation Rule. Performance Evaluation 68(4), 330–337 (2011)
39. Do, T.V.: An Efficient Solution to a Retrial Queue for the Performability Evaluation of DHCP. Computers & OR 37(7), 1191–1198 (2010)
40. Do, T.V.: M/M/1 Retrial Queue with Working Vacations. Acta Informatica 47(1), 67–75 (2010)
41. Do, T.V.: An efficient computation algorithm for a multiserver feedback retrial queue with a large queueing capacity. Applied Mathematical Modelling 34(8), 2272–2278 (2010)
42. Do, T.V.: Solution for a Retrial Queueing Problem in Cellular Networks with the Fractional Guarad Channel policy. Mathematical and Computer Modelling 53(1-2), 2059–2066 (2011)
43. Do, T.V.: Comparison of Allocation Schemes for Virtual Machines in Energy-aware Server Farms. Computer Journal (2011), doi:10.1093/comjnl/BXR007
44. Mitrani, I.: Approximate Solutions for Heavily Loaded Markov-Modulated Queues. Perform. Eval. 62(1-4), 117–131 (2005)
45. Do, T.V.: Modeling a Resource Contention in the Management of Virtual Organizations. Information Sciences 180(17), 3108–3116 (2010)
46. Do, T.V.: An Initiative for a Classified Bibliography on G-networks. Performance Evaluation 68(4), 385–394 (2011)
47. Lancaster, P.: Theory of Matrices. Academic Press, New York (1969)
48. Jennings, A.: Matrix Computations for Engineers and Scientists. John Wiely and Sons, New York (1977)
49. Neuts, M.F.: Matrix Geometric Solutions in Stochastic Models. John Hopkins University Press, Baltimore (1981)
50. Grassmann, W.K.: The Use of Eigenvalues for Finding Equilibrium Probabilities of Certain Markovian Two-Dimensional Queueing Problems. INFORMS Journal on Computing 15(4), 412–421 (2003)
51. Thornley, D.: On the Componentization of Queue Solution methods. In: UKPEW 2008, pp. 326–336 (2003)
52. Thornley, D., Zatschler, H.: Analysis and Enhancement of Network Solutions using Geometrically Batched Traffic. In: UKPEW 2003 (2003)

Eratum: Optimizing a Tone Curve for Backward-Compatible High Dynamic Range Image and Video Compression

S. Aravind Kumar

Anand Institute of Higher Technology, M.E- Computer Science and Engineering,
Kazhipattur, Chennai 601103
saravind123@gmail.com

P.V. Krishna, M.R. Babu, and E. Ariwa (Eds.): ObCom 2011, Part II, CCIS 270, pp. 596–605, 2012.
© Springer-Verlag Berlin Heidelberg 2012

DOI 10.1007/978-3-642-29216-3_86

The paper "Optimizing a Tone Curve for Backward-Compatible High Dynamic Range Image and Video Compression" by S. Aravind Kumar, appearing on pages 596-605 of this volume has been retracted due to a serious case of plagiarism. It is a plagiarized version of the paper by Zicong Mai; Mansour, H.; Mantiuk, R.; Nasiopoulos, P.; Ward, R.; Heidrich, W. "Optimizing a Tone Curve for Backward-Compatible High Dynamic Range Image and Video Compression," IEEE Transactions on Image Processing, vol. 20, no. 6, pp. 1558–1571, June 2011. doi: 10.1109/TIP.2010.2095866.

The original online version for this chapter can be found at
http://dx.doi.org/10.1007/978-3-642-29216-3_65

Erratum: Evaluation of Classifier Models Using Stratified Tenfold Cross Validation Techniques

Swarnalatha Purushotham and B.K. Tripathy

SCSE VIT University, Vellore – 632 014, Tamilnadu, India
{pswarnalatha,tripathybk}@vit.ac.in

P.V. Krishna, M.R. Babu, and E. Ariwa (Eds.): ObCom 2011, Part II, CCIS 270, pp. 680–690, 2012.
© Springer-Verlag Berlin Heidelberg 2012

DOI 10.1007/978-3-642-29216-3_87

In the paper starting on page 680 of this volume, the name of the second author was omitted. The three authors are:

    1. P. Swarnalatha   2. P. Praveen Babu   3. B.K. Tripathy

The original online version for this chapter can be found at
http://dx.doi.org/10.1007/978-3-642-29216-3_74

Author Index

Printed in the United States
By Bookmasters